D1253837

BECOMING VISIBLE

BECOMING VISIBLE

COUNSELING BISEXUALS ACROSS THE LIFESPAN

Beth A. Firestein

COLUMBIA UNIVERSITY PRESS   NEW YORK

Columbia University Press
Publishers Since 1893
New York   Chichester, West Sussex

Library of Congress Cataloging-in-Publication Data

Becoming visible : counseling bisexuals across the lifespan / edited by Beth A.
   Firestein.
      p.   cm.
   Includes bibliographical references and index.
   ISBN-13: 978-0-231-13724-9 (alk. paper)
   ISBN-10: 0-231-13724-9 (alk. paper)
   1.   Bisexuals—Mental health.   2. Bisexuals—Counseling of.   3. Gender
   identity.   I. Firestein, Beth A.   II. Title.

RC451.4.B57B43   2007
616.890086′63—dc22

                                                                    2006037805

Casebound editions of Columbia University Press books are printed on permanent
   and durable acid-free paper.

Printed in the United States of America

c 10 9 8 7 6 5 4 3 2 1

I dedicate this book to all of my lovers and friends, past and present, who have contributed to my understanding of bisexuality, the richness of my life, and the fullness of my being.

I especially dedicate this book to bisexuals everywhere who long to be loved and appreciated for who they are and to people of every sexual orientation and gender identity who have the courage to continue the journey of becoming through every season of their lives.

CONTENTS

PART 3 COUNSELING ETHNIC MINORITY AND GENDER-VARIANT BISEXUAL CLIENTS

PART 4 IDENTITY AND LIFESTYLE DIVERSITY AMONG BISEXUAL WOMEN AND MEN

FOREWORD

Beverly Greene

THIS VOLUME makes an important contribution to the scant psychological literature on bisexuality. Research on bisexual men and women usually falls between the cracks of the literature on lesbians and gay men, on the one hand, and heterosexual men and women on the other. At best it is often given a polite nod, but one rarely finds a detailed and critical analysis of this topic. A range of assumptions of questionable validity are commonly made about members of this group that tends to minimize their uniqueness as well as the special attention that is warranted in the delivery of clinical services to them. This volume represents a stark departure from that tendency in its comprehensive, accessible, and timely approach.

Bisexual men and women often find themselves between a social rock and a hard place. The lesbian and gay psychological literature has often viewed group members as people who are in denial about their "true" lesbian or gay orientation, taking advantage of heterosexual privilege while being honest about their lesbian or gay identity when it is convenient. From the heterosexual end of the spectrum they have been viewed similarly, as if they are confused about who they "really" are. In some ways they have been viewed as "defective" lesbians and gay men or "defective" heterosexuals. Neither of those deficit approaches serves to accurately inform us. If anything, they have been and continue to be instrumental in doing harm.

Unquestionably, society has needed to conceptually dichotomize sexual orientation just as gender is dichotomized, leaving those who do not neatly fit into either/or categories to explain themselves or be disparaged. This is true for biracial as well as transgendered individuals. Their inability to "fit" into socially constructed categories raises questions about the very nature of those categories and how we construct them, however, as all people who challenge the status quo, *they* have been viewed as the problem. There has been a longstanding need for more affirmative approaches to research and clinical work with members of this group, which Firestein ably addresses. This work compels us to consider new paradigms for explaining sexual behavior and desire across the spectrum of sexual orientation and in doing so challenges gender dichotomies as well. The complexity of these issues is a consistent thread running through this volume, always returning to the idea that there are elements of the "other" in all of us and that considering context in the shaping of experience is always important. Perhaps an even greater contribution is its attention to bisexuality as a category of many different types within it.

The contributors to this volume have been carefully chosen to address a wide range of concerns in logical and straightforward ways. The title reflects the diversity within this group as it examines dilemmas common to them at different stages of the lifespan as a continuous rather than stage process. Bisexual men and women are not discussed as if sexual orientation were isolated from other aspects of identity. It is always discussed in the context of gender, age, social class, cultural, and other distinctions that nuance the way bisexuality is shaped and experienced. The authors' approaches to the wide range of issues presented here are not in the least superficial. They ably grapple with the complexity that is inherent in the issues they address and do not offer simplistic and neat solutions to clinical and research quandaries. That said, they do provide rare and astute insights for clinical practitioners and research scientists about bisexual men and women that demand thinking about them as a diverse, particular group warranting distinct considerations and creativity on the part of the clinician.

Both novices as well as those with advanced knowledge about this population will find this book a rare find, useful in its coverage of a wide range of issues that are not commonly found in other texts. This volume moves us forward in our knowledge base and will serve as a major, foundational work in the field for some time to come.

THERE IS a revolution occurring in our consulting rooms. Our clients are no longer coming to us because they want to be "normal." They are coming to us because they want to be *whole*. They are requiring different things from us, and we are growing to meet the challenge. Our job is no longer to help those who seek our assistance to achieve the cultural ideal, the "mythical norm" of well-adjusted, middle class, heterosexual adulthood.[1] This mythical norm of a single trajectory of psychological health is an ideal that never really existed. The false gods of heteronormativity have been shattering at our feet for decades now, sometimes shattering the self-ideals and self-images of our clients in their fall. Our job is to help them pick up the pieces of their shattered selves and shattered dreams, to move beyond "normal" and help the person in our therapy rooms figure out what they are going to do instead.

There are many dimensions to the wholeness that bisexual, transgendered, gay, and lesbian individuals seek: sexual minority clients want to live lives free of depression, trauma, and pain. They seek to live authentic lives that feel congruent with their values and personalities, lives in which they are able to accept both their individual strengths and limitations. Individuals of both minority and majority identities (and those whose identities include a combination of these) really want the same things—to build lives from a basis of acceptance and to actualize the potential that is the focus of this book: discovering, creating, and expressing love and the erotic in life-affirming ways.

People come to me as a psychologist seeking many different kinds of wholeness with respect to gender and sexuality. Some come to therapy because their desires are at variance with the mythical norms of the culture and this tortures them emotionally, psychologically, and spiritually. They struggle with the belief that they cannot be "good people" in the eyes of their families of origin or "good members" of their religious denomination if they are lesbian, gay, or bisexual. They worry whether they will be accepted as members in good standing of their professional communities, respected as members of their civic communities, loved by their spouses or their children if they are members of a sexual or gender minority.

This is no less true for bisexual individuals than it is for others who seek internal and external acceptance for identities that are stigmatized in some way. Certainly, this is also true for lesbians and gay men, for transgendered, intersexed, and transsexual individuals, for sexual minority individuals who have disabilities and those who come from minority ethnic and religious backgrounds. It is equally true of those individuals, regardless of ethnic or racial identity, who are drawn to same-sex relationships, ambiguously gendered partners, and those who have specific sexual fantasies and fetishes that differ from those heterofetishes approved by mainstream society.

The majority of the people I work with in therapy are not and never really have been "normal." Normal is a statistical concept. Our clients are living, breathing human beings filled with complex and paradoxical characteristics and desires. They are better than normal—they are *alive*: as individual as their genetic blueprint, as unique as the circumstances of their birth, influenced by both culture and their family and shaped by the indescribable and unnameable stirrings of their individual souls and the collective unconscious.

So this is what we are actually doing when we sit with an individual, a dyad, or members of a family—we are encountering the mysteries of the universe in the form of the living, breathing, often suffering, individuals sitting before us. What is our response? Do we offer them the mythical norm and work to assist them in conforming to that standard? For some of our clients, there may be elements of the dominant culture that do, in fact, fit. But, for the majority of the people that I am seeing in my practice these days, offering *only* this would be an impoverished offering, a form of idolatry—worshipping false, cultural "man-made" gods at the expense of the Real.

What should our roles be with respect to providing services to our gender- and sexually diverse clients? What are our roles, in particular, with respect to our bisexual and transgender clients? That is the subject of the present book.

NOTE

1. The term *mythical norm* is used by African American lesbian poet Audre Lorde to refer to the ideals for individual, family, and cultural life put forth by the dominant, white, heterosexual culture as the standard to which all people should aspire. The dominant, majority culture maintains an ethnocentric perspective that assigns an "innate" and unquestioned superiority to the values, attitudes, and normative behavior of the majority. A corollary of this perspective is the absence of validity accorded to the lives and perspectives of those who are forced to live at the margins of dominant culture either because they are a minority with respect to the population demographics or distribution of political power within that culture.

ACKNOWLEDGMENTS

NO BOOK is ever actually written or edited by only one person. I wish to take this opportunity to thank the other people without whom this book could not have come into being. First, I wish to thank John Michel (now deceased), senior executive editor at Columbia University Press. He believed in this book from the beginning and gave me continuous encouragement throughout the process of proposing this book to the Press. I felt great sadness when I learned of his passing and I wish he could have been alive to celebrate the ripening of this fruit from the seed he originally nourished.

I also wish to thank his able assistant, Ann Young, who took over John Michel's duties when he became ill. I want to thank Shelly Reinhardt, senior executive editor, and her able assistant Christine Mortlock, for seeing this project through the next important steps and, finally, executive editor Lauren Dockett and senior manuscript editor Susan Pensak for seeing the project to completion. Many thanks also to Ron Fox and Emily Page, co-coordinators of APA Division 44's Task Force on Bisexual Issues in Psychology, for their excellent work promoting awareness of bisexual issues within APA and Division 44 and for their roles in organizing the Health Summit of the North American Conference on Bisexuality in San Diego in 2003. That conference and my exposure to the powerful work occurring in the arenas of research and practice with bisexual men and women served as the spark that ignited my desire to edit a second book—one focused on issues of bisexual mental health and counseling bisexual clients.

I also wish to thank each of the contributing authors; without them this book could not exist. Their combined expertise and willingness to write for very minimal compensation are truly a generous intellectual gift to the emerging fields of bisexual psychology and psychotherapy with bisexual and transgendered clients. I also feel a great deal of gratitude toward my long-time office manager, Vicki Frang, who has reliably supported the production of this book and virtually every other facet of my practice and professional work for a number of years. I have grown very fond of her. I also wish to express my sincere appreciation to Maryjo Faith Morgan, who provided extensive editing assistance on the manuscript, Stacey Coffman, who conscientiously edited portions of the manuscript, and Avery Fisher, who assisted with completion of the author questionnaire. Many thanks also to Jan Lund, Paul Ferris, Maryjo Faith Morgan, and Tania Israel for their helpful feedback on my introduction and to Marshall Browne for his very useful feedback on my preface. Of course, I alone am responsible for the final product.

On a more personal note, family and friends provided encouragement, support, and practical assistance through the two-plus years of my work on this volume. I wish to thank my life partner and husband, Marshall Browne, who provided immeasurable assistance by freeing me up from virtually all my domestic duties during the second half of my work on this book and never wavered in his belief in me and in this project. He is truly a blessing in my life! Fern Lawler has been a steadfast friend and companion to me on my journey these past several years, providing unconditional caring and immeasurably valuable assistance as I have navigated the complex waters of my own life's journey.

I also wish to thank my father, Louis Firestein, and my brother, David Firestein, for their continual support and encouragement as I edited this book, and Mark Schlichenmayer for making sure we never ran out of vanilla or coffee ice cream. I want to thank Cindy Kronauge for her companionship over hours spent in coffee shops working on our own respective projects. She and Dean Allison have been among my closest friends these past few years. My cat, Beau, and my horse, PJ Ferrari, provided me with much needed breaks for comfort and frequently restored my sanity while I was hard at work. Beau passed into that great kitty jungle in the sky at seventeen and a half years of age, shortly before the completion of this volume in manuscript. He will be missed.

I also wish to express my gratitude to the Association for Women in Psychology for serving as my "professional home" for over twenty years and to Division 44 of the American Psychological Association for their recognition of my contributions to the field of bisexual, lesbian, gay, and transgender issues in psychology. I am honored to have been selected as a Fellow of Division 44 and to now have the opportunity to serve on the executive committee of the division. Finally, I wish to thank my clients of the past twenty years for honoring me with their trust and their stories and for teaching me so much about courage, about healing, and about life.

Parts of chapter 4, "What's in a Name? Why Women Embrace or Resist Bisexual Identity," first appeared in *In the Family* and are used here with permission of the publisher, www. inthefamily.com. Chapter 7, "Cultural and Relational Contexts of Bisexual Women: Implications for Therapy," originally appeared in K. J. Bieschke, R. M. Perez, K. A. DeBord, *Handbook of Counseling and Psychotherapy for Lesbian, Gay, Bisexual and Transgender Clients,* 2d ed., copyright 2006 © American Psychological Association. Reprinted with permission. Parts of chapter 11, "Addressing Social Invalidaiton to Promote Well-being for Multiracial Bisexuals of African Descent," appeared in the *Journal of Bisexuality,* published by Haworth Press.

INTRODUCTION

BECOMING VISIBLE

VISIBILITY IS precious. It is an accident of destiny, a privilege, a hard-earned right. Visibility is not a given. Bisexual women and men have struggled for visibility for decades now, but it is difficult to maintain visibility in an either/or world that denies nondualistic realities such as those lived by individuals who are bisexual and transgendered. Our culture is in the midst of a revolution—multiple revolutions, actually—revolutions of science, revolutions of morality, revolutions of identity, sexuality, and gender expression. Bisexual women and men are at the forefront of some of these cultural revolutions. They make us think about difficult questions of identity stability and change over the life course, reconsider traditional relationship structures, and acknowledge the importance of love and the erotic in many people's lives.

My first book, *Bisexuality: The Psychology and Politics of an Invisible Minority* (Firestein 1996) focused on bisexual invisibility, seeking to highlight what was known and yet to be known about bisexual individuals, their identities, and their lives. Since that time, bisexuality has gained visibility, although progress is uneven and awareness of bisexuality is still minimal or absent in many of the more remote regions of our country and internationally. Transgendered and transsexual individuals have also gained a great deal of visibility in the past decade, sometimes increasing bisexual visibility and at other times almost eclipsing bisexual visibility as the powerful spotlight of awareness has begun to shine on their issues and concerns.

Visibility generates attention, both positive and, potentially, negative; but that which may be gained through visibility is so great, and the risks of invisibility so clear, that I believe it is worthwhile for bisexual women and men, transgender individuals, and other sexual minorities to take the risks associated with becoming visible. The intent of the present book, then, is to increase bisexual and transgender visibility, to educate, and to inform. This book is offered to empower bisexual women and men and transgendered individuals of every sexual orientation and to provide an open pathway to awareness and compassion for all lay and professional people who are interested in understanding and assisting bisexual and gender diverse people with the struggles they face in their lives.

ABOUT THIS BOOK

When I began this project, I set out to write a conventional academic book on an unconventional clinical topic: counseling bisexual clients. What has emerged is a book that, in its form and content, reflects the diversity of the clients we serve. I began with the notion that every author would contribute a chapter that looked pretty much like every other chapter—an introduction to the subject of the chapter, a literature review, some conceptual ideas, a few clinical examples, and ideas for therapeutic intervention. As is true in the lives of our clients, the components are there, but in variable and unpredictable configurations.

This is a professional book, combining the benefits of years of research, clinical practice, and the intuitive wisdom of authors from multiple disciplines for application to our educational and counseling endeavors with bisexual clients. This is a feminist book, integrating the personal and political into our perspectives on mental health and mental illness. This is also a book that embraces multiple perspectives, encompassing the empirical and the phenomenological, addressing scientific and practice-based approaches to the subject, and integrating the psychological, cultural—even spiritual dimensions of the issues confronting bisexual women and men.

BISEXUALITY: A DECADE OF RAPIDLY ACCELERATING KNOWLEDGE

It is important to understand that current human sexuality studies embrace multiple, sometimes conflicting definitions of what it means to be bisexual. Some authors view bisexuality as a third sexual orientation, one that includes attraction to both men and women rather than exclusive attraction to one sex or the other. Organizations, books, and workshops that previously referred to "gay and lesbian" now frequently contain the phrase "gay, lesbian, and bisexual," reinforcing the notion that there is now a third sexual orientation that needs to be acknowledged alongside gay and lesbian. This approach to understanding bisexuality is what Lisa Diamond terms a "conventional, gender-based conceptualization" of bisexuality, which she contrasts with "a more historically recent, 'radical' view of bisexuality that actually runs directly counter to conventional perspectives on sexual orientation" (L. Diamond, personal communication, March 18, 2006).

From this more recent perspective, bisexuality is more than a third sexual orientation: the term refers to the human capacity for loving, valuing, and sexually desiring other people in ways that are not limited by gender. A variety of researchers, writers, and clinicians have embraced this more expansive, less gender-anchored view of bisexuality, but both perspectives can be found in current research and writing on the topic. It is important that those reading the current literature understand the multiple perspectives and definitions of bisexuality that may underlie these research-based and clinical writings. With this awareness, readers can evaluate their own perspectives on current definitions of bisexuality and the assumptions that underlie various articles in the literature.

The present volume primarily reflects the more recent conceptualization of bisexuality as an orientation in which gender plays a fluid rather than a static role. In other words, this volume is premised on the ideas that gender is a pivotal consideration for some bisexual individuals and almost irrelevant to others. This second group of bisexual individuals, for whom gender is not the preeminent factor determining their attractions, may also be more likely to reject the term *bisexual* to describe their emotional and sexual attractions. Some of these individuals are in the forefront of pioneering new terminology to describe their experiences of romantic and sexual attraction. From the vantage point of the present volume, the term *bisexual* has come to embrace an even more comprehensive range of our capacity to love, including the ability to love individuals of multiple, indeterminate, or fluid genders and the ability of gender variant individuals to love others, both like and unlike themselves. This evolution in perspectives on definitions and bisexual identities has led to developments in a number of areas.

In the decade since the publication of *Bisexuality: The Psychology and Politics of an Invisible Minority*, there have been a number of significant developments in theory, research, and practice pertaining to bisexual, gay, lesbian, and transgendered lives. These include changes in language and terminology, an explosion of research-based knowledge about bisexual identities and lives, and developments in the politics surrounding sexual orientation, gender identity, and the relationship of these variables to the culture at large.

CHANGES IN LANGUAGE AND TERMINOLOGY

There have been two primary developments around language and terminology pertaining to bisexuality: the first is a broadened meaning associated with the term *bisexual* and the second is the development of alternative terminology to describe individuals whose attractions and romantic desires extend beyond exclusive interest in same- or opposite-gendered partners. As noted above, the term *bisexuality* originally referred to attractions and sexual behavior that included both men and women. This definition reflected our binary conceptions of gender and signaled attraction to, or romantic interest in, persons of the two recognized genders: women and men.

Transgender and transsexual individuals challenge our notion that human beings come in only two genders. These individuals frequently experience their inner sense of gender as being at variance with their externally assigned gender or physical appearance. Some transgender individuals experience a nondualistic sense of their personal gender identity—for example, their personal sense of gender may neither be strictly male nor strictly female but mixed, androgynous, or fluid (i.e., changing). With our growing awareness of the existence of transgendered and transsexual people, I have broadened my use of the term *bisexuality* to include an interest in *same-* and *other-gendered* partners, including individuals whose gender may defy classification in the existing male-female binary system.

Researcher Lisa Diamond points out that there are "clear links between radical conceptualizations of bisexuality and radical conceptualizations of gender." Bisexuality challenges the primacy of gender in sexual attraction while the transgender experience poses challenges to binary conceptions of gender itself and "just what it is that makes 'women women' and 'men men'" (L. Diamond, personal communication, March 18, 2006). Definitions of gender and gender differences have been the subject of psychological inquiry—particularly feminist inquiry—for several decades now. This expanded definition of bisexuality provides a stimulating new context for ongoing research into the meanings of gender within human psychological experience.

The second phenomenon related to language and terminology has two aspects: 1. the development of new, alternative, hyphenated, and multiple terms to describe one's sexual and affectional orientations and 2. the rejection of language altogether to label one's erotic and emotional desires. Some of the newer terms used to describe individuals formerly identified as bisexual include *ambisexual, queer, pansexual,* and hyphenated descriptors such as *bisexual-lesbian, bi-dyke,* and *gender-queer* (a term that refers to individuals acknowledging the fluidity of their gender identity). Other terms (discussed in Rust, chapter 1) may be unique to only one individual or adopted by only a few individuals. Several chapters in the book, such as those by Horner (chapter 15), Ochs (chapter 4), and Rust (chapter 1), also directly address some individuals' resistance to labeling their identities and the reasons for this resistance.

In this volume the material contained in the majority of the chapters will have relevance to a wide range of individuals with attractions to more than one gender, regardless of the language by which they identify—or their refusal of labels altogether. A new phrase, *lesbian, gay, bisexual, transgendered, intersexed, queer, and questioning* is used by some writers to refer to the ever widening expanse of identities encompassed by nonheterosexual and gender variant individuals. In this edited volume most of the authors use the terms *bisexual, queer, LGB, GLBT,* or *LesBiGay/Transgender* to refer to the population about whom they are writing.

EXPLOSION OF KNOWLEDGE

The second major development in the field of bisexual psychology has been the explosion of knowledge about bisexual identities and lives that has occurred in the last ten years. This great expansion of knowledge has included research-based knowledge, theoretical and conceptual formulations, and experiential accounts of sexual and gender diverse lives. Part of this "explosion of knowledge" from a research perspective has included researchers' discovery of some notable gender differences in the prevalence of bisexuality and in the ways men and women experience their bisexuality. The reasons for this are still largely undetermined. In aggregate this accumulation of new knowledge pertaining to bisexual peoples' lives has led to a proliferation of publications devoted to disseminating this new information. These publications have taken a variety of forms, including books, book chapters, journal articles, online resources, and articles in the popular press relating to bisexual, queer, and transgendered individuals as well as portrayals of bisexual and transgender themes in film and other forms of visual media.

In the past decade the Internet has become a primary vehicle for the dissemination of knowledge about sexual and gender diverse lives and identities, connecting individuals with similar concerns and interests across national and international geographic and cultural boundaries, and providing forums for the discussion of everything from Tantric sex practices to strategies of political activism. One limitation of this new medium is that access to the Internet requires a degree of economic privilege. There has also been a burgeoning of research conducted with Internet-based samples, ranging from simple surveys using specific bulletin boards and chat rooms to highly methodologically complex research designs delivered in cyberspace. These are trends that are likely to expand as we move into the future of research on sexual orientation and gender identity. With the expansion of these modes of inquiry, researchers need to remain cognizant of the socioeconomic demographics of their research participants and specify the limits of generalizability for results generated via such research approaches.

The last decade also witnessed the publication of several key volumes on gay, lesbian, and bisexual issues in psychology that have been bi-inclusive. These include the *Handbook of Counseling and Psychotherapy with Lesbian, Gay, and Bisexual Clients* (Perez, DeBord, and Bieschke 2000), now emerging in a second edition as the *Handbook of Counseling and Psychotherapy with Gay, Lesbian, Bisexual, and Transgender Clients* (Bieschke, Perez, and DeBord 2007) and *Handbook of Affirmative Psychotherapy with Lesbians and Gay Men* (Ritter and Terndrup 2002). Other publications focus specifically on bisexual and transgender lives. These include a recent special double issue of the *Journal of Bisexuality*, entitled *Affirmative Psychotherapy with Bisexual Women and Bi-*

sexual Men (Fox 2006) and *Transgender Emergence: Therapeutic Guidelines for Working with Gender-Variant People and Their Families* (Lev 2004). The *Journal of Bisexuality* also provides a rich, focal resource for information and publication of research on bisexuality. These developments attest to the great blossoming of knowledge in the field of bisexual psychology and bisexual studies over the past several years. There is a timely need for a volume providing guidance to clinicians working with a diverse range of bisexually oriented clients. The present volume is designed to meet this need.

CULTURAL AND POLITICAL DEVELOPMENTS

The third major development of the last decade consists of the wide-ranging changes that have occurred in the politics surrounding sexual orientation and gender identity and the forces at play in the culture at large with respect to these issues. A full treatment of these issues is beyond the scope of this introduction; yet these developments have affected the cultural climate in which knowledge is produced, the politics influencing the study of bisexuality, sexual orientation, and gender identity within the social sciences, and the application of this knowledge.

Without question, these developments are having a powerful effect on the U.S. population (as well as the populations of a number of other countries) and the emerging debates are entering into the public consciousness and our national political dialogue in ways that have never occurred before in the United States. Obvious examples include the issue of same-sex marriage, civil rights for LesBiGay and Transgender people, antidiscrimination legislation, domestic partnership policies of corporations, adoption laws, GLB individuals serving in the military, and hate crime legislation that includes sexual orientation and gender expression as recognized bases of hate crimes committed against individuals and groups of people.

Within the academy, queer theory, queer studies, and postmodern philosophical perspectives inform our ways of conceptualizing sexual and gender diversity and influence both how individual people self-identify and what those in academia choose to study. These forces also affect the approaches taken to research and clinical practice with nonheterosexual, queer, and gender-fluid clients. There is a great deal of new knowledge to embrace and there are a number of tensions (for example, between positivist and postmodern perspectives on research or between essentialist and social constructionist perspectives on sexual orientation and identity) that are unreconciled, perhaps even irreconcilable, and likely to exist for many years to come.

The present volume provides a clear window into some of these changes. Emerging trends in language and terminology, the production and dissemination of knowledge and research, developments in clinical practice, and several of the political issues internal and external to the LesBiGay and Transgender communities are all addressed within the scope of this volume. Without claiming to be comprehensive in its treatment of all these trends and issues, the authors contributing to this volume clearly provide a substantive discussion of these many trends and a valuable compilation of a considerable portion of the new knowledge being generated about bisexuality under the emerging LesBiGay/Transgender affirmative paradigm.

THEMES AND CHAPTER CONTENTS

Becoming Visible: Counseling Bisexuals Across the Lifespan is organized into five parts: 1. Critical Issues in Counseling Bisexual Clients, 2. Counseling Bisexual Women and Men Across the Lifespan, 3. Counseling Ethnic Minority and Gender Variant Bisexual Clients, 4. Identity and Lifestyle Diversity Among Bisexual Women and Men, and 5. Future Trends.

Part 1 consists of four chapters dealing with themes of bisexual identity, mental health research on bisexual clients, psychotherapy experiences of bisexual clients, and why women claim or resist the bisexual label to name their experiences and identities. Chapter 1, "The Construction and Reconstruction of Bisexuality: Inventing and Reinventing the Self," is written by sociologist and researcher Paula Rodríguez Rust. Rust discusses results from her international survey on bisexuality, highlighting the processes by which identity change and the revision of identity labels occur for her participants. In chapter 2, "A Review of Mental Health Research on Bisexual Individuals When Compared to Homosexual and Heterosexual Individuals," Brian Dodge and Theo Sandfort review research on mental health among behaviorally bisexual and self-identified bisexual participants. Their review identifies a pattern of results that indicates bisexual individuals frequently suffer from mental health difficulties at rates exceeding those of gay men, lesbians, and heterosexuals and posits preliminary theories to account for these findings. Chapter 3, "Bisexual Women's and Men's Experiences of Psychotherapy," authored by Emily Page, highlights findings from her research into the psychotherapy-related needs and experiences of her bisexual subjects. The final chapter in part 1, chapter 4, by Robyn Ochs, is entitled, "What's in a Name? Why Women Embrace or Resist Bisexual Identity." This chapter deals with the controversial nature of bisexual identity, how different women with similar histories of attraction choose to position themselves with respect to the issue of labeling, and the reasons for their choices.

Part 2 of the volume, "Counseling Bisexual Women and Men Across the Lifespan," includes six chapters. These chapters deal with issues spanning youth to old age and specific issues not previously dealt with in the published literature on bisexuality. These newer issues include domestic violence and the interactive effects of disability and sexual orientation on bisexual women. The first chapter in part 2 is chapter 5, "Developmental and Spiritual Issues of Young People and Bisexuals of the Next Generation," by Luke Entrup and Beth Firestein. This chapter discusses emerging trends among younger women and men who are exploring their sexuality (and their bisexuality) in the current cultural milieu. In chapter 6, "Counseling the Bisexual Married Man," Greg Carlsson addresses the issues and experiences of bisexual men in heterosexual marriages. He shares examples of clients' lives and provides practical suggestions for therapists working with married bisexual men. Chapter 7, "Cultural and Relational Contexts of Bisexual Women: Implications for Therapy," by Beth Firestein, addresses how interactions with the lesbian/gay community, bisexual communities, and heterosexual culture each affect bisexual women in different, but overlapping ways, and offers implications for conducting therapy with these women. Chapter 8, "Bisexuality and Broken Relationships: Working with Intimate Partner Violence" is coauthored by Sharon Horne and Shana Hamilton. This chapter discusses the occurrence of violence in same-sex relationships between women and what therapists need to know to assist bisexual women who find themselves in these situations in either the role of perpetrator or victim. Bobbi Keppel and Beth Firestein coauthor chapter 9, entitled "Bisexual Inclusion in Issues of GLBT Aging: Therapy with Older Bisexual Women and Men." While awareness of lesbian and gay elders is just now breaking the surface of consciousness in mainstream organizations concerned with aging, bisexuals remain largely invisible in these contexts. Keppel and Firestein highlight the need to attend to the needs of aging bisexuals when seeking to address the concerns of older lesbians and gay men. The final chapter in this section is chapter 10, by Stacey Coffman, entitled "Disability and Bisexuality: Confronting Ableism at the Intersection of Gender and Queer Desire." Individuals may find themselves dealing with issues of disability at any juncture in the life span, and the likely truth is that virtually all of us will be dealing with issues of disability at some point in our lives. Coffman's chapter provides a powerful discussion of the intersection of queer theory, disability theory, and feminist theory as these converge in the lives of our nonheterosexual, disability-challenged clients.

Part 3, "Counseling Ethnic Minority and Gender Variant Bisexual Clients," deals with multicultural issues in counseling bisexual clients and the issue of gender identity as a form of diversity. This part of the book consists of four chapters, three dealing with racial and ethnic diversity and bisexuality and the fourth addressing the intersection of gender identity and bisexuality. Chapter 11 takes as its focus "Addressing Social Invalidation to Promote Well-Being for Multiracial Bisexuals of African Descent," by Raymond Scott. Scott maps the intersections of race, sexuality, and a racist culture that invalidates the existence and legitimacy of nondominant, minority populations, particularly focusing on African American and bi- and multiracial bisexual men. In chapter 12, "Counseling at the Intersection of Identities: Asian/Pacific American Bisexuals," James Fuji Collins discusses issues involved in working with bisexuals of Asian and Pacific Island descent, particularly cultural and family issues. Next Luigi Ferrer and L. Angelo Jürgen Gómez present important concepts for therapists working with Latino/Latina bisexuals in chapter 13, "Counseling Bisexual Latinos: A Minority within a Minority." Part 3 concludes with chapter 14 by Dallas Denny, "Transgender Identities and Bisexual Expression: Implications for Counselors," which explores the emerging and evolving sexuality issues experienced by many transgender individuals as they move through their process of self-discovery and transition into their true gender expression.

"Identity and Lifestyle Diversity Among Bisexual Women and Men," part 4, consists of four chapters that highlight cutting-edge topics pertinent to clinicians working with a broad range of bisexual clients. The first chapter is 15, "Queer Identities and Bisexual Identities: What's the Difference?" by Evalie Horner. Horner deals with the rapid emergence of the concept of positive "queer identity" over the past decade, its historical path of emergence, and its impact on individuals, particularly youth, who, in previous generations, have frequently self-identified as bisexual. Chapter 16, "Gender Expression in Bisexual Women: Therapeutic Issues and Considerations," by Heidi Levitt and Sara Bridges, discusses how nontraditional gender expressions, such as butch and femme, add richness and challenge to the lives and relationships of some bisexual women. Chapter 17, "Counseling Bisexuals in Polyamorous Relationships," by Geri Weitzman, addresses the issue of ethical nonmonogamy or *polyamory*, a lifestyle that is increasingly visible among individuals of a variety of sexual orientations. Weitzman highlights research pertinent to polyamorous lifestyles and mental health and describes the preliminary results of a large-scale, Internet-based research study that included a large number of bisexual participants. In chapter 18, "Playing with Sacred Fire: Building Erotic Communities," Loraine Hutchins challenges readers to stretch their understanding of sexuality and to become knowledgeable about some of the new ways clients may be choosing to explore and express their sexuality. Hutchins discusses the development of sacred erotic communities in contemporary U.S. society, detailing important considerations for counselors working with individuals and couples seeking involvement in such groups and communities. Chapter 19 by William Henkin entitled, "Counseling Bisexuals on BDSM Lifestyle Issues" completes part 4. Henkin provides therapists with an in-depth understanding of the psychological and spiritual dimensions of this widely misunderstood set of sexual practices, offering clinicians the information they need to work knowledgeably and effectively with clients exploring these forms of sexual role-play and fantasy.

Part 5, the last of the volume, "Future Trends," deals with two different issues: training counselors to work with bisexual clients and counseling the heterosexual spouses of bisexual and transgender individuals. Chapter 20, "Training Counselors to Work Ethically and Effectively with Bisexual Clients," is by Tania Israel. She provides guidance to graduate program faculty and other educators who are training counselors to work with bisexual clients. Israel outlines deficits in existing training approaches and the knowledge, attitude, and skill components necessary for adequate counselor education in this area. Chapter 21, "Counseling Heterosexual Spouses of Bisexual or Transgender Partners," is written by Amity Pierce Buxton. Buxton deals with a neglected area of study—the importance of working with the non-GLBT family members of our Les-BiGay/Transgender clients and how to assist them through the necessary grief and healing processes that occur in the wake of a spouse or partner's decision to come out. All these topics have direct relevance to professional psychology, the practice of psychotherapy, and how we train clinicians to work with GLBT and other sexually alternative populations and their family members.

Becoming Visible: Counseling Bisexuals Across the Lifespan, is a diverse volume providing high-quality information on bisexuality, sexual diversity, and gender expression to readers interested in clinical practice, teaching, and research on sexual orientation and gender identity. In addition, *Becoming Visible* goes beyond the theoretical to provide a sampling of the worldviews and perspectives of the clients we hope to serve. The vision of this book extends beyond simply relieving the suffering of those who seek our assistance, though that is of critical importance. Its mission extends to the farthest reaches of our disciplines—to the very definitions of mental health and mental illness, dis-ease and well-being. *Becoming Visible: Counseling Bisexuals Across the Lifespan* opens new discussions about the optimal roles that diversity of sex and gender expression can play in our lives and in the lives of our clients.

No doubt the reader of this volume will be left with a great deal to think about, more questions than answers, and, just possibly, a profoundly deepened understanding of our roles as leaders and healers in a profession that is asked daily to respond to the suffering of bisexual men and women, and others who are different in these and similar ways. I hope that this book shall function as a truly valuable guide to professionals seeking to serve bisexual clients, students seeking to understand bisexuality and gender identity, the interested lay audience, and to educators of all kinds seeking to gather and impart knowledge relevant to human sexuality. I hope you enjoy reading *Becoming Visible: Counseling Bisexuals Across the Lifespan* as much as I have enjoyed editing it.

REFERENCES

Bieschke, K. J., Perez, R. M., and DeBord, K. A. (Eds.) (2007). *Handbook of counseling and psychotherapy with gay, lesbian, bisexual, and transgender clients* (2d ed.). Washington, DC: American Psychological Association.

Firestein, B. (Ed.) (1996). *Bisexuality: The psychology and politics of an invisible minority.* Thousand Oaks, CA: Sage.

Fox, R. C. (Ed.) (2006). *Affirmative psychotherapy with bisexual women and bisexual men.* Binghamton, NY: Haworth.

Lev, A. I. (2004). *Transgender emergence: Therapeutic guidelines for working with gender-variant people and their families.* Binghamton, NY: Haworth.

Perez, R. M., DeBord, K. A., and Bieschke, K. J. (Eds.) (2000). *Handbook of counseling and psychotherapy with lesbian, gay, and bisexual clients.* Washington, DC: American Psychological Association.

Ritter, K. Y., and Terndrup, A. I. (2002). *Handbook of affirmative psychotherapy with lesbians and gay men.* New York: Guilford.

PART 1

CRITICAL ISSUES IN COUNSELING
BISEXUAL CLIENTS

1

THE CONSTRUCTION AND RECONSTRUCTION OF BISEXUALITY

INVENTING AND REINVENTING THE SELF

Paula C. Rodríguez Rust

"Gay" and "Bisexual" are ... relative term(s). If I don't eat my dinner when it comes out of the oven, it will become "cold." My beer becomes "warm" though.
—SELF-IDENTIFIED "QUEER" RESPONDENT, AGE TWENTY-SIX, NO. 0073

CHANGE IS relative and depends on perception. Motion is a type of change. The fly on my right shoe as I walk thinks the earth is moving. I think my foot is moving. An astronomer will agree with the fly, but for different reasons. Identity is the location of the self in a social environment. Changes in identity reflect individuals' continuing efforts to locate their selves in their environments. Sometimes changes in identity reflect change in the self. Sometimes they reflect changes in the environment or changes from one environment to another. Often, changes in identity are reflected in the terms an individual uses to describe or label her or himself, as when an individual who previously self-labeled as heterosexual comes out as bisexual.

These self-labels are our "verbal surfaces," that is, the descriptions of ourselves we present to others in the hope they will understand our locations in the social environment. Sometimes, however, changes happen beneath the verbal surface; the self-label bisexual might mean one thing at age seventeen and quite another to the same person at age fifty-seven. If that person self-labeled as bisexual for forty years, others will perceive a remarkable consistency in that individual's sexual identity but the individual her or himself might recognize that considerable change has, in fact, occurred. Change is relative and depends on perception . . . and on our ability to describe it.

FROM "COMING OUT" TO A "MATURE STATE OF IDENTITY FLUX"

Considerable research on lesbian, gay, and bisexual populations indicates that sexual identity change is normative. Early research on sexual identity cast identity change as a process of "coming out," and considerable contemporary research maintains this construction of identity change processes. "Coming out" refers to a goal-oriented, stage-sequential developmental process whereby individuals who are sexually attracted to others of their own sex first question their culturally prescribed heterosexual identity and then gradually come to adopt—and accept—a nonheterosexual identity.

In the 1960s through the 1980s, the culmination of the coming out process as described by psychologists and social scientists was the adoption of lesbian or gay identity. Bisexual identity, when considered at all, was usually given a cameo role as a transitional identity (e.g., Chapman and Brannock 1987). Many researchers acknowledged that individuals often do not follow the stages of coming out in a predictable order, that some people stall and never complete the process, and that interaction with the social environment plays an important role in shaping the coming out process (e.g., Cass 1979, 1990; McDonald 1982). Despite these deviations from a strictly linear developmental process however, coming out is generally described as a process of self-discovery, which necessarily ends when one accepts an identity that accurately reflects one's true, or "essential," sexuality (Diamond 1998; Esterberg 1997; Rust 1996a, 2002; Savin-Williams 2001).

Beginning in the 1980s, some researchers argued that bisexual identity could also be a valid end-stage identity (Fox 1996; Levine and Evans 1991; Rust 1993; see also Coleman and Remafedi 1989; cf. Cass 1990; Rosario et al. 2001), and some researchers argued that individuals could "come out" twice, for example, a first time as lesbian or gay and a second time as bisexual as they reacknowledged submerged heterosexual feelings (e.g., Schwartz and Blumstein 1998; Rust 1993). Nevertheless, within this theoretical framework there is no reason for further change once the coming out process is completed; psychosexual maturity is characterized by a stable sexual identity as part of an integrated self-concept.

In a study of eighty-nine women, Diamond (1998) found that the self-reported sexual histories of most women did not conform to a traditional stage-sequential model of coming out. She found that only 26 percent of self-identified bisexual women and 29 percent of self-identified lesbian women fit the traditional pattern consisting of childhood indicators of sexual orientation, followed by awareness of same-sex attraction, and then the questioning of heterosexual identity with reported stability of feelings of sexual attraction over time (see also Rust 1993). In other words, the traditional model of coming out that was originally based on research on lesbians and gay men not only fails to describe the identity change processes of many self-identified bisexuals, it also fails to describe the experiences of many lesbians and gay men. A model of bisexual identity set forth by Weinberg, Williams, and Pryor (1994, 2001), which is based on research on bisexuals, consists of a very different series of stages: initial confusion, discovery and adoption of bisexual identity, followed by continued uncertainty—not by a stable "true" identity—due to lack of social support for bisexual identity (see also Colker 1996, Collins 2000, Thompson 1999). In traditional coming out models, the end stage of identity stability implicitly characterizes continued identity change as an indication of psychosexual immaturity. However, in Weinberg's model, identity confusion is to be expected of psychosexually mature bisexual individuals living in a sexual culture that fails to acknowledge their sexualities. As a stage-sequential model, the Weinberg model retains the developmental focus of earlier coming out models.

Other theorists have suggested nondevelopmental ways of understanding identity change. First and foremost, these theorists argue that identity change must itself be seen as normative rather than as a normative process toward a goal of identity stability. Most of these theorists also characterize identity change as the continual product of ongoing interaction between the individual and the social environment, rather than as a process of essential sexual self-discovery that might be influenced by interaction with the social environment. For example, Eliason (1996) described bisexuals as "subject positions from which to speak" rather than as autonomous individuals with static essences reflected by stable identities. Adam (2000) discussed the "deployment of sexual identity categories" to invoke "a world of possibilities" among men who have sex with men (pp. 326, 336). Rust (1993, 1996b) argued for a concept of "identity maintenance" in which a psychologically mature individual maintains a socially viable sense of sexual identity by changing her or his nominal self-label as her/his social context changes over time and place.

Once identity change is recognized as normative, the question becomes one of studying the identity change process as way of understanding identity itself. If we understand what motivates individuals to change the ways in which they label their sexual selves—or resist labeling—we can map the ground underneath these verbal surfaces. Numerous studies have shown that bisexual individuals experience identity change more frequently than other individuals (Rust 1993). The fact that bisexuals experience more identity change is not surprising; living in a cultural world in which sexuality is still predominantly constructed as either heterosexual or lesbian/gay, bisexual individuals struggle to maintain their identities within a social environment in which their very existence is questioned. This constant challenge is an exaggeration of the challenge facing all sexually identified individuals, that is, the challenge of locating oneself in a social environment. Understanding identity change and identity stability among bisexuals is, therefore, crucial to any understanding of sexual identity in general.

The focus of this chapter is on the process of sexual identity change with an emphasis on bisexual identity and upon the ways therapists can help individuals who are undergoing processes of identity change or sexual self-exploration. To some extent, an understanding of the ways in which self-identified bisexuals conceptualize and define bisexuality is important to understanding the process of sexual identity change among these individuals. An extensive exploration of the meanings of bisexual identity is, however, outside the scope of this chapter. For a detailed discussion of the meanings of bisexual identity, see Rust (2000, 2001). The current chapter describes the various ways in which individuals who identify as bisexual perceive their own past and current processes of identity change and the factors they feel motivated them to change their sexual identities or influenced the processes by which they did so.

THE STUDY

METHODS

The International Bisexual Identities, Communities, Ideologies, and Politics (IBICIP) study is the first large-scale study to focus on bisexuality and involve systematic data collection from an international sample. For the purpose of this study, bisexuality is defined broadly. The study includes individuals who identified as bisexual at the time of the study or at any previous time during their lives, who were questioning their sexuality or preferred not to label themselves, or who ever, even if at different times in their lives, felt attracted to or had sex with at least one man and at least one woman. One focus of the study as a whole is on the ways in which these individuals, any of whom could claim a bisexual identity, construct sexual identities for themselves. What determines which individuals do, in fact, choose to identify themselves as bisexual, and what influences the changes that occurred prior to, and will probably occur subsequent to, the choice to identify as bisexual?

Data were collected via a self-administered IBICIP questionnaire. The questionnaire was distributed at conferences on sexuality, during meetings of bisexual and LesBiGay social and political organizations, and through social networks, the Internet, and advertisements in bisexual newsletters and "alternative" newspapers. Efforts were made to reach individuals who were isolated from bisexual or lesbigay social networks and to maximize the age, gender, sexual, geographic, and racial/ethnic diversity of the respondents.

In the questionnaire, respondents were asked a series of questions about their current and past sexual identities.

FIGURE 1.1 SURVEY QUESTION

1. When you think about your sexual orientation today, what term do you use most often to describe yourself? Do you think of yourself as bisexual, lesbian, gay, or heterosexual, or do you prefer another term? (If you use more than one term, you may circle all that apply, but indicate which one you use most often when you think about yourself.)

A. Bisexual

B. Lesbian

C. Gay

D. Homosexual

E. Heterosexual

F. Straight

G. Bisexual lesbian

H. Lesbian-identified bisexual

J. Gay bisexual

K. Lesbian who has sex with men

L. Bisexual-identified gay man

M. Heterosexual-identified bisexual

N. Queer

P. Dyke

Q. Bi

R. Pansexual

S. Pansensual

T. Polyfide or Polyfidelitous

U. Ambisexual

V. Polysexual

W. Bisexual Queer

X. Other: _____

Y. I am not sure what my orientation is

Z. I prefer not to label myself

Current sexual self-identity was assessed with the question "When you think about your sexual orientation today, what term do you use most often to describe yourself?" followed by twenty-one identity terms and "other," "I am not sure," and "I prefer not to label myself" response options. Figure 1.1 provides a complete list of these identity terms, which included traditional identities such as *lesbian, gay, bisexual*, and *heterosexual*; compound identities such as *lesbian-identified bisexual* and *gay bisexual*; and alternative identities such as *queer, pansexual*, and *polyfidelitous*. Respondents were instructed that they could choose more than one response option, but asked to indicate which one they used most often. Respondents who chose the "other" response were asked to write in their personalized identity, and for the purpose of analyses these respondents are classified as having *alternative* identities. Respondents who chose "I am not sure" or "I prefer not to label myself," and who did not also choose identity terms in accordance with instructions permitting more than one response choice, were asked appropriate contingency questions; they were not asked to reconsider choosing an identity term.

All respondents who chose identity terms were then asked a series of open-ended questions about the meanings their self-labels held for them, about the events or circumstances that led to their adoption of these self-labels and that had caused any change in the meanings of these self-labels over the years, and about the event or circumstance that initially caused them to question their heterosexuality. Those who indicated a current lesbian, gay, or homosexual identity were asked if they had ever identified as bisexual and, if so, about the events or circumstances that caused them to begin, and then to stop, identifying themselves as bisexual. All respondents were also asked similar questions about their first non-heterosexual identities. Except where otherwise noted, all respondents quoted in this paper were currently identified as "bi" or "bisexual"—although this was not necessarily their only or primary identity—at the time of the study.

RESULTS: DESCRIPTION OF SAMPLE

This chapter is based on information from 703 respondents who lived in the United States of America at the time they participated in the study. Almost two thirds of the USA sample (62.2 percent, n = 436) is nontransgendered women and one third (33.4 percent, n = 234) is nontransgendered men. Nine percent (8.6 percent, n = 22) of male-born respondents, compared to only 2 percent (1.8 percent, n = 8) of female-born respondents, report being transgendered, including transsexuals, cross-dressers, and male women. Hereafter, *women* will refer to nontransgendered female-born women and *men* will refer to nontransgendered male-born men. Respondents ranged in age from eighteen to eighty-six at the time they completed the questionnaire, with the majority of respondents in their twenties (36 percent), thirties (34 percent), or forties (19.6 percent). On average, women were four years younger than men (34.8 v. 38.8, p < .0001), with 40.1 percent of women compared to 28.7 percent of men in their twenties, and men more likely to be aged fifty or above (15.9 percent v. 7.3 percent). Two thirds were employed full-or part-time, including 8.9 percent who were employed students, and an additional 18.5 percent were unemployed students. Seven percent were unemployed nonstudents. Among employed nonstudents, the median income was in the range $20–29,999, and 11.5 percent earned less than $10,000 annually. Respondents are very highly educated and predominantly white; one quarter are college graduates, 46 percent had had some advanced education beyond college, and 88.8 percent identified themselves as having Anglo/white/European ancestry. For further demographic details regarding this sample, see Rust (2001).

SELF-LABELS: MULTIPLE IDENTITIES
AND PERSONALIZED IDENTITIES

Most respondents chose more than one current self-label. Only 36.6 percent of all women and 39.9 percent of all men chose only one self-label. Among respondents who chose at least one self-label, on average women chose 2.7 self-labels and men chose 2.4. Approximately 1 out of 7 respondents indicated that they were not sure of their orientation or preferred not to label themselves. However, because respondents were permitted more than one response choice, most of these respondents did also choose a self-label; only 1 in 20 did not self-label at all.

Among the often multiple self-labels chosen by respondents, two thirds of both women (69.2 percent) and men (64.8 percent) chose bisexual or bi self-labels. Half of all bisexual- and bi-identified respondents also chose alternative self-labels such as queer, pansexual, pansensual, polyfidelitous, ambisexual, polysexual, or personalized identities such as "byke" or "biphillic." One quarter of bisexual- and bi-identified respondents also chose lesbian or gay self-labels, and one quarter also chose compound self-labels. Despite these multiple self-labels, three quarters of all bisexual- or bi-identified women (n = 226, 75.1 percent) and men (n = 114, 75.5 percent) indicated that their bisexual or bi self-labels were their primary identities.

Among the 117 women and 77 men who did not currently identify as bisexual and answered the question regarding whether they had ever identified as bisexual, 91.5 percent of women and 75.3 percent of men indicated that they had identified as bisexual in the past. Additionally, in response to a question regarding the first nonheterosexual identity they had adopted after realizing that they might not be heterosexual, 56.5 percent of women (n = 235) and 50.7 percent of men (n = 111) responded that they had initially identified as bisexual.

Thus, the sample of 703 respondents includes—with overlap—346 individuals who came out initially as bisexual, 165 who had identified as bisexual at some-time in the past but not at the time of the survey, and 452 individuals who identified as bisexual at the time of the survey. The accounts provided by these respondents regarding the events or circumstances surrounding their various identity changes and the meanings of their bisexual identities paint a picture of the construction and reconstruction of bisexual identity across the life course.

ACCOUNTS OF IDENTITY CHANGE TO OR FROM BISEXUAL IDENTITY

Respondents described their identity changes in many different ways. Some described them as the result of deepening or changing sexual self-awareness; some described them as a response to changes in their sexualities; some described discovering a new identity term that fit their experiences of them-selves better than their existing identity or discovering a new meaning for an identity term that permitted them to adopt it as a self-label. Some respondents described a change in social circumstances, which required a change in the way they presented themselves to themselves or to others, or explained that they adopted their bisexual identities to make social or political statements in a given social context. Although self-awareness and social context undoubtedly play interacting roles in all identity change processes, some respondents focused more on the internal processes of self-discovering and self-labeling, whereas others focused more on the social contexts that had facilitated their identity changes.

IDENTITY CHANGE AS A PERSONAL PROCESS

I noticed I began looking at women in a sexual manner though I have always been with male lovers. I am very confused about why I feel this way. I am still not fully comfortable with the fact that I am attracted to women.   —NO. 0302

SOME DO "COME OUT": IDENTITY CHANGE AS A DISCOVERY OF ONE'S SEXUALITY Identity change as a result of deepening or changing self-awareness is similar to the traditional understanding of identity change as "coming out." Some respondents did see their adoption of bisexual identities as a process of coming out in which they discovered, came to understand more clearly, or accepted an internal truth about their sexuality—a truth that had existed prior to their recognition of it—and then adopted a bisexual identity that reflected that internal truth. Many of these individuals had previously identified as heterosexual or assumed that they were heterosexual and, upon discovering an attraction to members of their own sex, came out as bisexual. For example, this twenty-four-year-old woman's account of her identity change is a textbook description of the traditional lesbian/gay coming out process except that her coming out ended in bisexual, rather than lesbian or gay, identity:

> I fell in love/lust with my then best friend. After . . . realizing that it wasn't just in reaction to a bad het relationship six months earlier and that I was still attracted to men, I began to tentatively call myself bi. I didn't think about it much for the next year or so. I just let it percolate till I was comfortable with the idea before I came out. (no. 0007)

However, the process of bisexual identity formation cannot simply be understood by substituting bisexual identity for lesbian or gay identity as the outcome in traditional coming out models. There are a few important ways in which coming out as bisexual sometimes differs from coming out as lesbian or gay. First, in the traditional model, an individual who is coming out as lesbian or gay first questions her/his socially prescribed heterosexual identity when s/he recognizes or acknowledges a sexual attraction to members of her/his own sex. Any previous heterosexual behaviors—and even attractions—are then explained or reconstructed as responses to social pressure or a lack of awareness of one's true sexuality, that is, as ego-dystonic or false reflections of one's sexuality. When an individual comes out as bisexual, however, past heterosexual behaviors and attractions need not be reconstructed or otherwise denied, a fact illustrated poignantly by a woman who initially tried to disavow her attractions to men in an effort to come out as a lesbian:

> For a long time I acknowledged that I was attracted to women. When I finally accepted that this was part of me, I tried to think of myself as a lesbian, for 3 days. But on the street, when I noticed attractive men, I tried to look away because I was now a "lesbian." I quickly noticed that this would not work, I can't ignore half the population. I may never meet a person, who is a man, that I want to date, but I will always find them attractive and sexy. (no. 0154)

A second way in which coming out as bisexual differs from coming out as lesbian or gay is that individuals who come out as bisexual often come out not from a presumed heterosexual identity, but from an already adopted lesbian or gay identity. In other words, coming out as bisexual is often a second coming out. A previously gay-identified man wrote,

> I was in a monogamous relationship with a man and was happily identified as gay. I had been attracted to a woman co-worker and one day to (all) our mutual surprise the woman and I had sex together. After much introspection and chaos I realized this (hetero sex) was not just a fling but something I didn't want to give up. (no. 0119)

As a result of coming out first as lesbian or gay, many such individuals had previously reconstructed their earlier heterosexual experiences as false. These individuals experienced their second coming out as a *re-recognition* of heterosexual feelings, that is, a reacknowledgement of a truth about the self that had been temporarily submerged during their period of lesbian or gay identification. As one individual wrote, "My thinking I was exclusively gay, like a period of thinking I was actually exclusively heterosexual a few years earlier, lasted only a few months. Basically, I recovered my senses in both cases."

In a third variation on the traditional coming out process, some respondents did not describe ever having identified as heterosexual. When asked "before you began to question your sexuality, did you think of yourself as heterosexual?" 44 percent of bisexual- and bi-identified respondents chose the response "Yes, I went through a 'period' of heterosexual identity before I realized I was not heterosexual," but 29.7 percent responded either "No, as soon as I became aware of myself sexually as a child or teenager I knew that I was not heterosexual" or "No, I never really thought about my sexual orientation before I started questioning the assumption that I was heterosexual." For these respondents, the realization that they are attracted to both men and women, or some similar experience, led directly—although not necessarily immediately—to a bisexual identity rather than a coming out from a heterosexual identity:

> I met a woman at a club when I was sixteen. We became friends then ultimately lovers. This wasn't my first sexual experience—but my first sexual experience with a woman. I never considered myself to be anything other than bisexual. I knew I liked girls—I knew I liked boys. (no. 0184)

AN IDENTITY FOR ALL SEASONS Changes in sexuality need not require changes in identity. Some respondents, after having struggled to figure out if they were gay or straight or after having changed back and forth between gay and straight identities, seized on bisexual identity as a self-description that could weather a certain amount of change in their underlying sexualities:

> I didn't seem to fit with the terms *straight* or *gay* even though I felt more attract- ed to men (sometimes) and other times more attracted to women. So now I call myself bisexual to include all my feelings that I am capable of feeling (whatever they are predominantly at any time in my life). (no. 0306)

For such individuals, bisexual identity can be a way of avoiding the need to construct and reconstruct one's sexual identity. If change is relative and a matter of perception, then change can not only be constructed and reconstructed—it can also be deconstructed.

IDENTITY CHANGE OCCURS IN A SOCIAL CONTEXT

[Identifying as bisexual is] as much a way of relating to the world as who I'm at- tracted to.　　　　　　　　　　　　　　　　　　　　　　　　　　—NO. 0022

"THERE ARE OTHERS LIKE ME": THE DISCOVERY OF A SOCIAL CONTEXT FOR ONE'S SEXUAL SELF Ghosts have no reflection in a mirror. If individual identity is the location of the self in a social context, individual identity can- not exist without a social context. For individuals who recognize that they are somehow different from others, their first encounter with others who are also different is a moment of self-discovery because it is the moment they first see themselves reflected in the social mirror. This is the moment they discover that there is a context for their sexual selves; i.e., the moment they cease to be social ghosts. In these cases the discovery is not of one's own feelings but of the fact that one's feelings—previously uninterpretable and unnameable—can in fact exist and be named. For example, one individual who took a human sexuality class in college wrote, "I began to feel different about myself when my feelings were given names. . . . Our class assignment was to attend a GLB Awareness Week event and I felt at home there" (no. 0256).

THE "A-HA! THAT'S ME" EXPERIENCE: DISCOVERING A NEW IDENTITY POSSIBILITY Although a few respondents were already familiar with the concept of bisexuality when they recognized their own attractions to both sexes and were able to label their feelings bisexual upon recognition, most were not. These individuals described a period of trying to figure out if they were heterosexual, lesbian, or gay or of feeling unsatisfied with their lesbian, gay, or heterosexual identity because it didn't seem to fit their experiences of their sexualities. When asked to describe the experience, event, or circumstance that caused them to adopt a bisexual identity, they recounted the moment they discovered the possibility of bisexual identity. For example, "I was having a lot of trouble figuring out if I was gay or straight until friends . . . suggested bi. . . . It felt right and I began to feel much better about myself" (no. 0049).

THE "A-HA, IT COULD BE ME!" EXPERIENCE: DISCOVERING A NEW MEANING FOR BISEXUAL IDENTITY Some respondents were aware of the existence of bisexual identity before adopting the identity themselves, but attributed a meaning to the identity that did not apply to them. Then they discovered a new meaning for the identity and realized that bisexual identity could describe their sexual selves. Often, this was the discovery that bisexual identity could be a valid identity, not just a temporary identity used as a phase in coming out as gay or lesbian or a "fence-sitter's" identity used to avoid choosing between gay and straight identities:

> I attended a Bisexual Forum and learned that there were people who had experienced male-to-male sex but didn't feel they were just in denial about being homosexual. I learned that "bisexuality" could mean many things to many people and encompassed attitude as well as actions and fluctuated with time and circumstances. (no. 0220)

A few respondents described other changes in the meaning of bisexual identity that allowed them to apply the label to themselves. One woman, for example, explained that the "first time I identified as bisexual was the first time I heard the word applied to a woman. Somehow I didn't put things together when I had previously heard it applied to men" (no. 0333). Others were able to call themselves bisexual when they discovered the bisexual political movement; because of their previous experiences in lesbian or gay politics, they had not been able to identify with a term they saw as devoid of political meaning.

SOCIAL CONTEXTS AS A SOURCE OF SOCIAL VALUATION AND PERSONAL EVALUATION

Social contexts provide not only the conceptual structures individuals use to interpret and label their sexual feelings; they also provide the moral and other evaluative meanings attributed to these feelings. Historically, in many Western cultures, homosexual attractions are devalued. Traditional coming out models recognize the influence of social prejudice against homosexuality in many ways. For example, these models include stages in which individuals learn to revalue homosexual feelings so that they can acknowledge their own same-sex attractions and frequently define the coming out process as complete only when shame regarding one's homosexuality is replaced with self-acceptance and then pride (e.g., Cass 1979; Coleman 1982).

Coming out as bisexual, like coming out as lesbian or gay, involves rejecting social disapproval of same-sex attractions and sexual activity. Often this occurs because one finds oneself in a new social context in which same-sex attractions are less socially disapproved or even celebrated. This new social context might be a bisexual, lesbian, or gay organizational meeting or event, a college course, a welcoming religion, a diverse neighborhood, or even a relationship with one person: "My boyfriend had told me that he thought he may be 'bisexual' and that opened my mind. I finally let my feelings out and admitted to myself that I like women too" (no. 0189).

In traditional coming out stories, bisexual identity is sometimes presented as a "transitional identity" or stepping stone toward gay or lesbian identity because, conceptualized as a hybrid combination of heterosexuality and homosexuality, it is perceived to be only half as unacceptable as full homosexuality. Many bisexual identified individuals, however, find that bisexual identity is *less* socially acceptable than lesbian or gay identity because, in addition to the disapproval of homosexuality they encounter in heterosexual society, they also experience disapproval of bisexuality from lesbians and gay men. In the lesbian community, for example, bisexuals are sometimes not accepted because they are seen as fence-sitters, traitors, or political "cop-outs" (Ault 1994; Esterberg 1997; Ochs 1996; Rust 1995; Weise 1992).

Women in the lesbian community who are also attracted to men sometimes feel guilty or inadequate because these attractions make them "less" lesbian. Those who see themselves privately as bisexual often, therefore, hide this personal identity and present a lesbian identity within the lesbian community. In counterpoint to the construction of bisexual identity as a transitional identity, when these women eventually "come out" publicly as bisexual, their lesbian identity can be seen, retrospectively, as a transitional identity used while they became comfortable enough with their bisexuality to proclaim it in opposition to social disapproval:

> I was living with a man I loved but very strongly attracted to being a part of the women's community. I wanted to be a lesbian, but my boyfriend's existence made it impossible. I finally came to the point that I stopped feeling guilty for not being purely lesbian—no one incident sparked it, just a slow process. (no. 0208)

IDENTITY POLITICS: IDENTITY CHANGE AS A POLITICAL STATEMENT

Several respondents mentioned that they chose their identities, at least in part, as a way of making a social or political statement within a particular social context. Most often, these individuals explained that their identities accurately reflected their sexualities. The political statement was in the act of being honest about their sexualities in the way they presented themselves to others, usually heterosexual or gay/lesbian others who might otherwise perceive bisexuality as a transitional phase or political cop-out. The assertion implied by bisexual identity is "I exist!" or "Bisexuality exists!"

> I joined a new social/religious group. Many members needed to label others. I felt that I needed to claim a label that was most honest for me. Most members identify as gay or lesbian and negate/omit bisexuals; therefore, there was also a compelling urge to be counted and increase the visibility of bisexuals amidst the larger group. (no. 0318)

ALTERNATIVE IDENTITIES: CREATIVE SELF-CONSTRUCTION

If sexual self-identity is the description of the location of the self in a social environment, then it is the social environment that provides the possible locations for the self. Most people search their environments for a location they feel fits them and use the available identity term to describe themselves in that location. But over time, as the social landscape changes, old locations disappear or shift position and new locations appear. Identity terms change in cultural meaning, old terms pass out of favor, and new terms arise. The term *homosexual*, for example, has a clinical flavor and a history in scientific accounts of psychopathology that make the term unpalatable to many contemporary lesbians and gay men. The term *lesbian* grew in popularity during the 1970s as feminism encouraged *gay women* to stop making coffee for gay men and form their own lesbian feminist political movement. *Queer, dyke,* and *faggot* began as pejorative terms; more recently, *dyke* and *faggot* have been reclaimed as proud self-identities, and new efforts to bring people of varying sexualities together into a unified and diverse political movement have popularized *queer* identity. As the bisexual political movement has grown, the concept of bisexuality has become more culturally familiar and bisexual identity more popular.

The social landscape changes because the people who populate it are creative. Instead of finding an existing location and adopting the identity term available to describe that location, some people actively work to reconstruct the social landscape to create a location that feels comfortable for them. Often these efforts involve taking existing bits and pieces of identities and recombining them into new identities. Some of these identities resonate with other individuals, who have also been searching the existing landscape without complete success; these individuals adopt the new identities, and as these identities become increasing popular they become increasingly available. The landscape is reconstructed and a new location—a new identity—is created.

QUEER IDENTITY

At the March on Washington I didn't want to identify and march with any one contingent. I wanted all us queers to march together, but I marched with the bisexual contingent anyway because everyone separated. —NO. 0483

Popularized in the wake of Queer Nation and other political activist groups, "queer" identity—although perhaps unfamiliar to many heterosexuals—is a well-developed, nuanced identity within the sexual minority community. It represents a challenge to traditional dichotomous notions of sex (female, male), gender (woman, man), and sexuality (homo-, heterosexual). It reconstructs bisexuality, commonly conceptualized as a hybrid combination of homo- and heterosexuality, by calling into question the distinction between these two forms of gendered sexuality. "Queer" is about crossing, blurring, and erasing boundaries, both conceptual and political.

A number of respondents in the current study identified themselves as queer. For example, one woman changed from a bi to a queer identity when she "decided that I wanted to be defiant, in my everyday life, of . . . mainstream ways and attitudes" (no. 0077) and another woman changed from a lesbian to a queer identity because "the word queer was presented to me as an identity which both fags and dykes could reclaim and work under together" (no. 0307). Many individuals use both queer and bisexual, lesbian, or gay identities; they use queer identity to represent their political or social attitudes, and bisexual, lesbian or gay identity to reflect their sexualities.

COMPOUND IDENTITIES: RECONSTRUCTING THE PIECES

Many individuals who can't find a single identity with which they feel comfortable use multiple identity terms to describe themselves. As noted above, less than two fifths of respondents in this study chose a single self-label when asked about their current sexual identities. Some individuals, instead of or in addition to using multiple sexual identities, create their own self identities by combining two or more identity terms into a single identity. Some of these combinations have become popular enough that, within the sexual minority community, they function as distinct, singular identities. Many of these identities were identified during a pilot study and included as response options in the question about sexual identity in the IBICIP questionnaire. For example, 13.7 percent of male respondents self-identify as "heterosexual-identified bisexual" and 12.6 percent of women self-identify as "lesbian-identified bisexual." In all, 26.0 percent of women and 24.5 percent of men indicated that they used a self-identity that combined bisexual identity with either a lesbian/gay or heterosexual identity, including "bisexual lesbian," "gay bisexual," or "bisexual-identified gay." Other compound identities that were "written in" by respondents included "bi-dyke" and "byke."

NOVEL IDENTITIES: WHEN EVEN THE PIECES DON'T FIT

I realized that the labels for alternative sexualities with which society grudgingly furnished me were inadequate to describe my sexual interactions with the real world. The experience of defining my own sexual category and coming out made me feel much more honest and in touch with myself than any other previous epiphanies.

—SELF-IDENTIFIED POLYSEXUAL, NO. 0463

Some individuals find that even compound identities fail to describe them. These individuals sometimes invent their own identities. Often different individuals invent the same identity independently of each other. These new sexual identities might, over time, become more popular just as *queer* has become more popular, thus reconstructing the sexual landscape. As these terms become more socially available, other individuals will be able to discover them in the landscape and no longer have to reinvent them independently; of course, even these new identities will not suffice for everyone, and newer identities will continue to be invented. At the time of this study, some of the newer identities used by respondents, many of whom reported that they had invented them and were the only person they knew who identified as such, were bi-lovable, lesbodyke, Qweirdo, and BiNinfo. A bi-lovable woman explained that she:

> married a heterosexual man and I realized it wasn't the "sex" I missed, not having a female—it was the emotion—the love I missed. Both male and female relationships fulfill only half of the emotional spectrum, neither can fulfill all of the emotional needs—forget the sex part—sex with a man was just as fulfilling—it was the emotion side of the relationship that was lacking. (no. 0086)

TRIGGERING EVENTS, CIRCUMSTANCES, AND EXPERIENCES

When asked to describe the "experience, event, or circumstance" that caused them to adopt their bisexual identities, most respondents were able to clearly describe a specific experience, event, or circumstance to which they attributed their change to or from their bisexual identity. Two types of events were most commonly mentioned. One type consists of first sexual experiences, including the first experience of feeling attracted to, or of having sexual contact with, someone of a particular sex. The second common event is a conversation, usually with a sex partner, friend, family member, or therapist. Also commonly mentioned were new social environments, including college, Internet communities, or bisexual organizations.

SEXUAL EXPERIENCES

Sexual experiences that motivate identity changes are sometimes unexpected and impromptu; other times they are long sought after and finally realized. These experiences might consist simply of feelings of attraction for another individual, whether that individual is a friend, an acquaintance, or someone more distant such as a television character. For some people, it is a feeling of love or romantic attraction and sometimes it is a feeling of sexual attraction. One respondent wrote, "A woman friend and I (who were both married at the time) realized that we had sexual feelings for each other" (no. 0188). For other people, it might be an actual sexual experience, as one woman who "had been thinking about women for almost two years" explained, she "could not feel 'justified' in calling myself 'Bi' until I actually had S-E-X with a woman."

SOCIAL INTERACTION PRODUCES SOCIAL SELVES: THE ROLE OF CONVERSATIONS IN MOTIVATING IDENTITY CHANGES

Conversations with friends, relatives, or therapists take many forms. Sometimes, a friend or relative points out something about one's sexuality that one had not previously recognized. Perhaps the most dramatic such conversations occur between sex partners—sometimes during sexual activity. One man wrote, "While I explored and read and taught about sexual identity, it was when I was in bed with a woman and she directly asked me if I was bisexual that I said 'yes' and began to be clear about that identity" (no. 0030). But more socially distant individuals can also spark self-reflection and identity change, including friends, relatives, acquaintances, strangers, and employers. One woman recalled that "the 'event' that pushed me over the edge from denying my Bisexual identity . . . was my straight female boss's comment that she thought I had difficulty relating to men . . . she sensed my duplicity—sensed that I was passing."

Sometimes, one is encouraged to examine one's own sexuality when someone else reveals their own bisexual or gay/lesbian identity. A close same-sex friend who comes out might call one's own sexuality into question because it calls into question the construction of the relationship as a friendship. A family member who comes out might bring up one's own sexual issues, especially if one believes that there might be a biological basis for homosexuality. For example, a mother in the IBICIP study who identified herself as a "heterosexual-identified bisexual" explained, "My daughter came out as bisexual, and I realized that I had to sharpen up my own fuzzy feeling about my own bisexuality" (no. 0006).

LARGER SOCIAL CONTEXTS:
REAL-TIME AND ELECTRONIC COMMUNITIES

The most frequently mentioned large social context to which respondents attributed their adoption of bisexual identity was college. Some mentioned the presence of lesbian and gay communities on their college campuses, some mentioned the more permissive or experimental college atmosphere, some encountered lesbian, gay, and/or bisexual student organizations or events, and some took college courses on sexuality:

> I had thought "we are all bisexual" since I was sixteen, but I didn't consider myself "really" bisexual, or *different*, until I was nineteen. I became increasingly attracted to women and now had a social setting, my friends in my first-year college dorm, who seemed friendly to my feelings. (no. 0135)

Both in and outside of college, some respondents recalled that their exploration of their sexuality was, at least in part, facilitated by political activism. Some women, for example, recalled that feminism had motivated them to explore their sexual feelings for other women:

> My feminist consciousness-raising, I looked around me and wondered why I had so few female friends, I decided to cultivate more, then realized there was a general sexual attraction as well. So I decided I must be bisexual and almost immediately came out as such. (no. 0094)

The existence of a bisexual political movement has enabled many people to find other bisexuals and to validate bisexual identity: "Although I've always 'known' I was Bi, it was meeting Lani Ka'ahumanu in 1987, hearing her talk about bisexuality as a 'valid' identity and movement, which made me choose this identity wholeheartedly" (no. 0019). Encounters with conducive social contexts, including communities and political movements, need not be "in person." The Internet has enabled individuals who might never find each other in real time to locate each other electronically. It has allowed many types of communities—especially those whose members are scattered and hidden throughout the general population and/or whose members find safety in the faceless privacy of electronic communication—to grow with a speed not possible before the Internet age. Similarly, books and other written material can provide a quasi-community within which one can safely explore one's sexuality without revealing oneself to flesh-and-blood others until one is ready to do so.

DISCUSSION

THE PROCESSES OF CONSTRUCTION AND RECONSTRUCTION

Changes in sexual identity involve construction and reconstruction at several different levels. First, the adoption of a new self-identity is, in and of itself, a reconstruction of the self. Adopting a new identity involves a reconceptualization of the self, including recognition of aspects of the self previously not codified by identity, and a reorganization of the possibilities for one's feelings, sexual behaviors, and future relationships. This reconstruction of the self might also require the reconstruction of previous feelings and behaviors, as when heterosexual experiences are attributed to social pressure to support a lesbian or gay identity and then later reacknowledged to support a bisexual identity. Second, the discovery of new identity terms—such as the discovery of the concept of bisexuality—involves a reconstruction of one's sexual world to allow the introduction of the new sexual concept. Similarly, the discovery of a new meaning—whether objective or evaluative—for an identity term such as *bisexual* involves reconstructing one's sexual world as other concepts are adjusted in accommodation. Third, the use of bisexual identity to make a political statement such as "Bisexuality exists!" is an effort to reconstruct others' sexual worlds to include the concept of bisexuality.

RECONSTRUCTION OF THE SELF

The traditional process of coming out, in which one "discovers" one's true sexuality, is, in effect, a process of reconstruction of the self and of one's current and previous feelings and behaviors. The self is reconstructed as having a heretofore unrecognized capacity for certain types of sexual attractions, and the past is reconstructed to support this new understanding of the self. For example, reconstructing childhood or adolescent feelings toward members of one's own sex as sexual attractions provides evidence that these same-sex attractions have always existed, thereby validating a new nonheterosexual identity as a reflection of one's "true sexuality." For some people, the process of self reconstruction is immediate:

> I was unemployed, alone a great deal, became hooked on General Hospital during episodes with Emma Samms. One day she was trying to seduce Luke . . . and I realized I was totally attracted to and excited by *her*—not him. Sudden flash of realization—had been attracted to and in love with a number of women through my life—going back to grade school—but could never admit it. (no. 0118)

For other people, the reinterpretation of feelings takes place gradually. For example, one woman came out after she "came to the awareness one warm April day while riding the NYC subway, that the affection I was feeling for a female friend was in fact a crush—sexual and somewhat romantic" (no. 0010). She not only reconstructed her attraction to her friend as a sexual attraction, she also reconstructed it as an experience that was relevant to her sexual identity. Whether reconstruction is immediate or gradual, it is codified as an aspect of the sexual self by the adoption of a bisexual, lesbian, or gay identity.

RECONSTRUCTION OF ONE'S OWN PSYCHOSEXUAL WORLD

One's sexual world is reconstructed when new concepts are introduced or existing concepts acquire new meanings, for example, when bisexuality becomes a "viable option and not just a place from which one eventually moved to straightness or gayness" (no. 0036), when it acquires a political meaning, or when it becomes applicable to women as well as men. Sometimes, before the reconstruction of their psychosexual worlds, individuals might feel frustrated and unsatisfied because they cannot make sense of their experiences or find appropriate sexual identities. After reading about the "histories, emotions and experiences of others who identify as bisexual" in an electronic discussion group, one woman "realized this was an appropriate concept under which to organize what had previously been my confused and fragmented identity" (no. 0215). Her comment conveys the relief she felt when she was able to reconstruct her sexual world into a place in which there was a location for her.

In other cases individuals already have satisfying identities, but find cause to change their identities when their sexual worlds are reconstructed. For example, a fifty-year-old man was entirely satisfied with his heterosexual identity when "a young male partner asked if I considered myself gay, and I said no because I *prefer* my wife as a sexual partner" because in his sexual world, sexual orientation was defined in terms of a preference for one gender or the other. Despite his same-sex activities, he felt his heterosexual identity was appropriate because it reflected his preference for his wife. He went on to write, "He then suggested that I was bisexual and I agreed, despite never having heard the word used with respect to sexual orientation" (no. 0024). His sexual world, which had not previously included a concept of bisexuality, was reconstructed to include bisexuality; in this new sexual world he realized that the appropriate identity for him would be bisexual—and he adopted it.

RECONSTRUCTION OF SOCIOCULTURAL SEXUAL WORLDS

From the point of view of the individual who "discovers" a new identity or a new meaning for bisexual identity, the experience is a reconstruction of one's own psychosexual world. However, the moment that individual adopts the identity and then presents the new identity to another person who was not already familiar with it, the process becomes one of reconstructing the other person's sexual world. As more individuals become aware of bisexual identity—both those who adopt the identity and those who do not—the concept of bisexual identity acquires an increasing cultural presence. Like tributaries flowing into a river, the individual process of psychological reconstruction of the self becomes a social process of cultural reconstruction of the sexual world.

The process of cultural reconstruction is, in part, a process of natural cultural evolution, but it can be facilitated by the intentional efforts of individuals. For example, individuals whose bisexual identity is a statement to others that "bisexuality exists" and bisexual political activists who work to educate others about the existence of bisexuality are engaged in an intentional process of sociocultural reconstruction. As evidenced by the number of respondents who began identifying as bisexual when they went to a workshop about bisexuality, read a book about bisexuality, or met someone who identified as bisexual, these efforts are effective; our sexual world is changing. Bisexual identity is becoming part of our sexual culture.

So far, these changes have occurred primarily within the sexual minority community; bisexual—like queer—identities have only begun to reach beyond the community's borders. The word *bisexual* has been used in mainstream magazines in cover stories announcing the "new bisexual movement," although current mainstream discourse about same-sex rights continues to center on "lesbians and gay men." The process of cultural reconstruction is an ongoing one; even as bisexual identity becomes an established aspect of sexual minority culture and begins to reach mainstream society, newer identities are already emerging and beginning to acquire a cultural presence within the sexual minority community. In the year 2020, will we see support groups for "bykes," a "trisexual political movement," or photos of "qweirdos" on the cover of *Newsweek?*

THE ROLE OF THERAPISTS IN THE PROCESS OF CONSTRUCTING AND RECONSTRUCTING THE SELF

Psychotherapists played a role in the identity change processes of several of the individuals who participated in this study. Most important, therapists can provide a safe environment where individuals can explore their thoughts and feelings. A therapist can also be an audience for a client who wants to "try an identity on for size" before committing to it by presenting it to others outside the protective walls of the therapist's office or support a client who chooses not to identify her or himself sexually.

Many of the men and women in this study mentioned that their therapists had provided them with options or possibilities, allowing them to explore those possibilities that held promise for them and reject those that did not work for them. The recommendations for therapists that emerge from the identity change processes described by individuals in this study are as follows.

Therapists can:

■ *Offer possibilities for the interpretation of feelings toward others.* Clients in the process of exploring their attractions toward others can be presented with possibilities for understanding these attractions. Attractions to others can be interpreted as platonic affection, admiration, sexual attraction, friendship, or any number of other possibilities. "Interpreting" such feelings is, to a large extent, a process of classifying feelings according to available social categories of emotion, no less than the process of developing a sexual identity is the process of placing oneself into a socially available sexual category. When appropriate to facilitate self-exploration, "sexual" feelings need not be sharply distinguished from other sensual feelings; sexual feelings can be viewed as part of the range of human emotional attractions rather than as a separate and clearly distinct form of human attraction.

If a client's feelings for another individual are ultimately constructed as sexual, then the question arises as to whether these feelings are toward this particular individual only, or whether these feelings generalize to all individuals of that sex or gender. When appropriate, the therapist can call into question the gender-based cultural construction of sexuality, pointing out that although our culture defines sexual attraction in terms of the gender of the "attractee," the client need not construct her or himself along these lines. Disentangle the "sexual" aspect of the attraction from the "sex/gender" of the person to whom the client is attracted. What is it that attracts the client to this person? Is the person's sex/gender relevant and, if so, is it the only characteristic that is relevant?

The client need not assume that feelings of attraction to one person of their own (other) sex means that they are attracted to their own (other) sex; maybe they are attracted to individuals with green eyes or to individuals with athletic bodies or generous personalities, some of whom might be men and some of whom might be women. It is important to be affirmative of same-sex attractions. However, it is also important not to overcompensate for social or internalized homophobia by assuming that the first glimmer of attraction toward someone of the same sex is an indication that the client is "really lesbian or gay" or even "bisexual."

■ *Offer possibilities for the implications of one's feelings and sexual behaviors.* If one's feelings for another individual are constructed as sexual, the therapist can explore with the client whether or not these feelings and behaviors should be codified into an identity. Feeling does not necessarily have to implicate being. For some clients, the shift from feelings to identity might feel necessary or comfortable. Others might feel quite comfortable enjoying their feelings and activities without adopting a sexual identity. Some might feel social pressure to adopt an identity, e.g., if they have friends who know of their same-sex attractions and are waiting for them to "come out." Both internal (psychological) and external (social) motivations for codifying feelings and sexual behaviors into an identity should be explored, and both should be validated.

Resistance to social pressure can be explored; is it fear of acknowledging one's sexual feelings, or is it resistance to being defined by others in a way that is not ego-syntonic? A client can be given permission not to identify and supported in the face of social pressure to choose an identity. Alternatively, if a client chooses to identify because s/he feels social pressure to identify, even if s/he does not feel s/he has found an identity that feels completely comfortable psychologically, that choice should also be supported. Explain to such a client the difference between self-identity and presented identity and give the client permission to use an identity in social situations to facilitate social interaction, while still keeping one's private mind open to further self exploration or to "freedom from identity."

■ *Assure clients that attractions to men and attractions to women are not mutually exclusive or contrary types of attraction.* Although men and women are commonly referred to as "opposite sexes," in fact, men and women are not opposites. Although there are differences, there is considerable overlap between the characteristics of men and the characteristics of women culturally, socially, psychologically, and physically, and there are other differences between people besides sex/gender that are also important. Recognizing attractions for one's own sex need not invalidate attractions for the other sex, and vice versa. Give a client permission not to choose.

■ *Give clients permission to see their sexuality as changing over the life course.* Validate previous, as well as current, sexual identities. Clients who perceive their sexuality as potentially flexible or changing over time rather than essential and stable need not reconstruct previous self-understandings to support a new current sexual identity. For example, if a woman saw herself as a lesbian for ten years and then fell in love with a man, she need not reconstruct her entire history as bisexual. She can keep her lesbian history—which undoubtedly has great social and psychological significance to her—and perceive her sexuality as having changed; she was lesbian and now she is bisexual rather than "Oops; I thought I was a lesbian but then I found out I was bisexual." Or, she can understand herself as a "lesbian-identified bisexual" to recognize both her long-term ties to lesbian culture, lifestyle, and community as well as her current sexual feelings.

- *Give clients permission to embrace identities within their own unique narrative.* Notwithstanding the previous point, although the current preference among the psychological and sociological professions is for social constructionist understandings of identity, individuals who are seeking ways of understanding themselves might or might not find such an approach useful. Some might feel freed to explore their feelings more honestly by the suggestion that identities are social constructions and that they need not fit themselves into one of the socially available sexual identity categories. Others might feel reassured by the thought that their sexuality is something essential, waiting to be discovered. One respondent gratefully recalled that "I was terrified of being gay. In my early twenties, I saw a therapist, who explained to me that it was not something I could influence, that instead I could 'discover' what was true about me" (no. 0232).

- *Provide outside resources.* Suggest books on sexuality and make referrals to local support groups for bisexuals, lesbians, gays, and people exploring their sexualities. Put clients in touch with online communities of sexual minority individuals. Encourage clients to explore as much as possible others' thoughts and feelings about their sexualities, and the ways in which others use identity to reflect their sexualities. This process helps break down the simplistic "you are heterosexual unless proven otherwise, but if you're attracted to your own sex, you're gay or lesbian" construction of sexuality found in mainstream cultural sources.

To be able to provide clients with these resources, the therapist must be familiar with them. Don't wait to collect these resources "until I need it for someone." Check local telephone book listings; call your local LesBiGay community center. Participate in the nearest gay pride celebration and read the banners to find more local groups. Call local religious establishments to ask if they have support groups or social action groups for LesBiGay or supportive members and call local universities and colleges to see if there are campus political or social groups for sexual minority students; such religious and collegiate organizations are not usually listed in the phone book. Have the information ready for the clients who need it.

REFERENCES

Adam, B. D. (2000). Love and sex in constructing identity among men who have sex with men. *International Journal of Sexuality and Gender Studies, 5*(4), 325–339.

Ault, A. (1994). Hegemonic discourse in an oppositional community: Lesbian feminists and bisexuality. *Critical Sociology, 20*(3), 107–122.

Cass, V. C. (1979). Homosexual identity formation: A theoretical model. *Journal of Homosexuality, 4*(3), 219–35.

Cass, V.C. (1990). The implications of homosexual identity formation for the Kinsey model and scale of sexual preference. In D.P. McWhirter, S.A. Sanders, and J.M. Reinisch (Eds.), *Homosexuality/heterosexuality: Concepts of sexual orientation* (pp. 239–266). New York: Oxford University Press.

Chapman, B.E., and Brannock, J.C. (1987). Proposed model of lesbian identity development: An empirical examination. *Journal of Homosexuality*, 14(3/4), 69–80.

Coleman, E. (1982). Developmental stages of the coming out process. *Journal of Homosexuality*, 7(2/3), 31–43.

Coleman, E., and Remafedi, G. (1989). Gay, lesbian, and bisexual adolescents: A critical challenge to counselors. *Journal of Counseling and Development*, 68, 36–40.

Colker, R. (1996). *Hybrid: Bisexuals, multiracials, and other misfits under American law.* New York: New York University Press.

Collins, J.F. (2000). Biracial-bisexual individuals: Identity coming of age. *International Journal of Sexuality and Gender Studies*, 5(3), 221–253.

Diamond, L.M. (1998). Development of sexual orientation among adolescent and young adult women. *Developmental Psychology*, 34, 1085–1095.

Eliason, M.J. (1996). Identity formation for lesbian, bisexual, and gay persons: Beyond a "minoritizing" view. *Journal of Homosexuality*, 30(3), 31–58.

Esterberg, K.G. (1997). *Lesbian and bisexual identities: Constructing communities, constructing selves.* Philadelphia: Temple University Press.

Fox, R.C. (1996). Bisexuality in perspective: A review of theory and research. In B.A. Firestein (Ed.), *Bisexuality: The psychology and politics of an invisible minority* (pp. 3–50). Thousand Oaks, CA: Sage.

Levine, H., and Evans, N.J. (1991). The development of gay, lesbian, and bisexual identities. In N.J. Evans and V.A. Wall, *Beyond tolerance: Gays, lesbians and bisexuals on campus* (pp. 1–24). Alexandria, VA: American College Personnel Association.

McDonald, G.J. (1982). Individual differences in the coming out process for gay men: Implications for theoretical models. *Journal of Homosexuality*, 8, 47–60.

Ochs, R. (1996). Biphobia: It goes more than two ways. In B.A. Firestein (Ed.) *Bisexuality: The psychology and politics of an invisible minority* (pp. 217–239). Thousand Oaks, CA: Sage.

Rosario, M., Hunter, J., Maguen, S., Gwadz, M., and Smith, R. (2001). The coming-out process and its adaptational and health-related associations among gay, lesbian, and bisexual youths: Stipulation and exploration of a model. *American Journal of Community Psychology*, 29(1), 133–160.

Rust, P.C. (1993). "Coming out" in the age of social constructionism: Sexual identity formation among lesbian and bisexual women. *Gender and Society*, 7(1), 50–77.

Rust, P.C. (1995). *Bisexuality and the challenge to lesbian politics: Sex, loyalty, and revolution.* New York: New York University Press.

Rust, P.C. (1996a). Managing multiple identities: Diversity among bisexual women and men. In B.A. Firestein (Ed.), *Bisexuality: The psychology and politics of an invisible minority* (pp. 53–83). Thousand Oaks, CA: Sage.

Rust, P.C. (1996b). Finding a sexual identity and community: Therapeutic implications and cultural assumptions in scientific models of coming out. In E.D. Rothblum and L.A. Bond (Eds.), *Preventing heterosexism and homophobia* (pp. 87–123). Thousand Oaks, CA: Sage.

Rust, P.C. (2000). *Bisexuality in the United States: A social science reader.* New York: Columbia University Press.

Rust, P. C. ((2001). Two many and not enough: The meanings of bisexual identities. *Journal of Bisexuality*, 1(1): 33–68.

Rust, P. C. (2002). Bisexuality: The state of the union. *Annual Review of Sex Research*, 13, 180–240.

Savin-Williams, R. C. (2001). A critique of research on sexual-minority youths. *Journal of Adolescence*, 24(1), 5–13.

Schwartz, P., and Blumstein, P. (1998). The acquisition of sexual identity: Bisexuality. In E. J. Haeberle and R. Gindorf (Eds.), *Bisexualities: The ideology and practice of sexual contact with both men and women* (pp. 182–212). New York: Continuum.

Thompson, B. Y. (1999). *The politics of bisexual/biracial identity: A study of bisexual and mixed race women of Asian/Pacific Islander descent.* Reno: That Damn Book! And Money to Authors Ink.

Weinberg, M. S., Williams, C. J., and Pryor, D. W. (1994). *Dual attraction: Understanding bisexuality.* New York: Oxford University Press.

Weinberg, M. S., Williams, C. J., and Pryor, D. W. (2001). Bisexuals at midlife: Commitment, salience, and identity. *Journal of Contemporary Ethnography*, 30(2), 180–208.

Weise, E. R. (1992). *Closer to home: Bisexuality and feminism.* Seattle: Seal.

2

A REVIEW OF MENTAL HEALTH RESEARCH ON BISEXUAL INDIVIDUALS WHEN COMPARED TO HOMOSEXUAL AND HETEROSEXUAL INDIVIDUALS

Brian Dodge and Theo G. M. Sandfort

RESEARCH ON mental health among behavioral and self-identified bisexual individuals has been largely absent from previous scientific literature, including studies that examine relationships of sexual orientation and identity with mental health. Most previous research on mental health among "lesbian, gay, and bisexual" and "same-sex" populations has not distinguished bisexual individuals from lesbians and gay men. The aim of this chapter is to provide an overview of findings from studies that have examined bisexual women and men separately from and compared with homosexual and heterosexual individuals with regard to depression, anxiety, suicidality, and substance use and abuse. These papers seem to indicate a pattern whereby bisexuals have reported higher rates of mental health problems when compared with both homosexuals and heterosexuals. Based on our review, we suggest some preliminary hypotheses that may assist in explaining these findings. Last, we offer new directions for research and clinical practice specifically with bisexual individuals in order to better understand and address their mental health needs.

BISEXUAL BEHAVIORS AND IDENTITIES

Pioneering sexuality research has shown that, in addition to exclusively heterosexual and exclusively homosexual individuals, substantial numbers of men and women in North American samples report sexual attractions and involvement with both men and women (Kinsey, Pomeroy, and Martin 1948; Kinsey et al. 1953). In addition, *bisexual* has also emerged as a contemporary sexual orientation and identity label over recent decades (Hutchins and Ka'ahumanu 1991), although as of yet its development and meaning have received notably less scientific attention than homosexual identity (Angelides 2001).

Bisexuality is certainly not rare. However, interpretation of data on the general prevalence of bisexuality is complex (Messiah et al. 1996). Differences exist across studies in terms of the time frame in which the bisexual behavior was measured. In large empirical studies, behavioral bisexuality among men has been found to be between 0.7 percent and 5.8 percent (respectively in the previous year and since puberty) in the general United States population (Laumann et al. 1994) and between 0.6 percent and 8.6 percent (respectively in the preceding year and lifetime) in ten European nations (Sandfort 1998). Among women, behavioral bisexuality has been estimated to be between 0.3 percent and 3.7 percent in the general United States population (Laumann et al. 1994) and between 0.1 percent and 3.9 percent in Europe (Sandfort 1998), depending on the time period in which the behavior took place (i.e., past six months, past twelve months, past five years, or lifetime). In terms of bisexual identity, Laumann and colleagues (1994) estimated that the percentage of individuals who self-identify as "bisexual" in the general population of the United States is around 0.8 percent for men and 0.5 percent for women. Although these percentages may seem relatively small, they reflect a large number of individuals when the total size of the population is considered.

Within more specialized samples, such as "gay and bisexual men" and "men who have sex with men" (MSM), the prevalence of bisexuality has varied widely depending on the recruitment venue and the demographics of the participants, particularly in terms of ethnicity. Reported rates of behavioral and self-identified bisexuality have been consistently found to be higher among African American and Latino men than among white men (Chu et al. 1992; Doll et al. 1992; Goodenow, Netherland, and Szalacha 2002; Heckman et al. 1995; Kalichman et al. 1998; Thomas and Hodges 1991).

The relationship between sexual behavior and identity is complex and fluctuations in self-identity have been found to occur often (Diamond 2003). However, longitudinal studies of bisexuals show that bisexual identity remains stable for many self-identified bisexual men and women (Weinberg, Williams, and Pryor 1994, 2001). Self-identified bisexual individuals also report high rates of bisexual behaviors. For example, in one sample of currently sexually active MSM, Carballo-Dieguez and Dolezal (1994) found that 80 percent of Latino self-identified bisexual MSM had engaged in sexual activity with women in addition to their sexual involvement with men in the past year. These men reported greater levels of sexual involvement with women than did the MSM who identified as heterosexual (63 percent).

BISEXUAL DIVERSITY

Numerous patterns of bisexual behaviors and identities have been documented across cultures and societies demonstrating that bisexual individuals are diverse in their experiences and expressions of their sexualities (Aggleton 1996; Blumstein and Schwartz 1976a, 1976b; Fox 1995; Firestein 1996; Garber 2000; Hemmings 2002; Herdt 1990, 2001; Klein 1978; Lever et al. 1992; Rust 2000; Tielman, Carballo, and Hendriks 1991; Weinberg, Williams, and Pryor 1994). The cultural and social context in which bisexuality occurs has proven to be an important factor in understanding bisexual behaviors, identities, and related factors (Firestein, chapter 7; Stokes, Miller, and Mundhenk 1998). For example, a substantial body of ethnographic research has shown that Latin American and Caribbean bisexual men are unique in the ways they construct, express, and experience their sexualities (Carrier 1985; De Moya and Garcia 1996; Parker 1991, 1996, 1999; Taylor 1978). Such research reminds us that familiar Anglo-American conceptualizations of sexual orientation are culturally specific and that their imposition on Latinos and other groups may be problematic (Ferrer and Gómez, chapter 13; Muñoz-Laboy 2004; Muñoz-Laboy and Dodge 2005; Rust 1996).

While research on diverse expressions of bisexuality is critically important, this review focuses only on research findings within the North American, British, and Australian contexts since studies on mental health among bisexual individuals in other contexts have not been published. Even within the studies we review, both behavioral and self-identified bisexuals are an exceedingly diverse population. Caution must be used in interpreting the results of the studies we review based on the demographics of the samples (including gender, race/ethnicity, age, national culture, sexual identity, etc.) and the methods used to recruit them (including convenience sampling, community-based sampling, probability sampling, etc.).

BISEXUALITY AND MENTAL HEALTH

Mental health can be conceptualized as "(a) state of well-being in which the individual realizes his or her own abilities, can cope with the normal stresses of life, can work productively and fruitfully, and is able to make a contribution to his or her community" (World Health Organization 2001:1). It is determined by socioeconomic and environmental factors, is linked to behavior (including sexual risk behavior), and may be positively influenced by effective public health interventions (World Health Organization 2003). While mental health is "more than the absence of mental illness" (World Health Organization 2003), we have chosen to focus our review specifically on mental health problems, given the higher rates of mental health problems among sexual minority populations previously reported.

With the emergence of gay and lesbian identity theory in the early 1960s and 1970s, a relatively polarized debate arose among North American mental health professionals who held "antigay" and "gay-affirmative" perspectives on sexual orientation. While homosexuality was ultimately declassified as a mental disorder by the American Psychiatric Association in the *Diagnostic and Statistical Manual of Mental Disorders* in 1973 (Bayer 1981; Meyer 2003), bisexuality, per se, has never been officially classified or declassified as a mental disorder. The concept of bisexuality has been either implicitly subsumed under the label of *homosexuality* (Fox 1996) or altogether left out of the debate between those who sought to affirm the lives and lifestyles of "homosexual" individuals and those who sought to pathologize them (Angelides 2001). While a debate still continues as to the pathology of nonheterosexual orientations in some mental health and religious circles (Nicolosi 1991), in this review we assume current best clinical practice that characterizes bisexual, homosexual, and heterosexual orientations and identities as healthy and valid (American Psychological Association 2004).

A substantial amount of recent literature has explored relationships between sexual orientation and identity to mental health. In discussing the limitations of one of the most comprehensive reviews of mental health among "LGB" populations to date, Meyer (2003:690) acknowledges "the review, and the studies I cite, fails to distinguish bisexual individuals from lesbian and gay individuals. Recent evidence suggests that this distinction is important and that bisexuals may be exposed to more stressors and may have greater mental health problems than lesbians or gay men (Jorm et al. 2002)." Indeed, the personal and social circumstances of bisexual women and men may be markedly different from lesbians and gay men, including both mental health stressors and supports (Friedman 1999; Ochs 1996). The inability to distinguish bisexual individuals from homosexual individuals has been cited as a significant limitation of previous research if the intention of such inquiry is to understand relationships between sexual orientation and identity to mental health (Jorm et al. 2002).

METHOD

Similar to other research reviews on mental health among sexual minority populations (Meyer 2003), we sought studies pertaining to bisexuality and mental health from the previous ten years (1994–2004) using a psychologically based electronic database, PSYCHINFO. In relation to depression, anxiety, suicidality, and substance use, we identified studies that were published in peer-reviewed journals that presented information on these issues specifically among "bisexual" individuals when compared to "homosexual" and/or "heterosexual" individuals. We did not include, or indeed find, "case studies" or studies that looked only at bisexual individuals without a comparison group (heterosexual and/or homosexual individuals). Table 2.1 presents an overview of the studies that we included in our review, including samples, methodology, and basic findings.

TABLE 2.1 Summary of Previous Studies on Mental Health Among Bisexual Individuals When Examined Separately from Homosexual and Heterosexual Individuals

AUTHORS/YEAR	DEFINITION OF BISEXUAL	METHOD	SAMPLE	FINDINGS
Jorm et al. 2002	Self-identified sexual orientation	Community-based survey	4,824 adults (71 bisexual, 78 homosexual) in Australia	Bisexuals scored highest on measures of anxiety, depression, negative affect, and suicidality; bisexuals report more current adverse life events, greater childhood adversity, less positive support from family, more negative support from friends, higher frequency of financial problems
Paul et al. 2002	Self-identified sexual orientation	Telephone probability sampling of MSM (9% bisexual, 84% homosexual, 3% heterosexual, 4% other)	2,881 MSM in urban USA (9% bisexual)	Highest prevalence of suicide attempts was found among bisexual and nonidentified respondents ("other," i.e., neither homosexual/gay, heterosexual, nor bisexual), as well as Native Americans
Robin et al. 2002	Behavioral sexuality	Four large, representative population-based high school surveys	14,623 Vermont students and 8,141 Massachusetts students (USA)	Prevalence of suicide attempts was highest among bisexual participants; bisexual participants were also more likely to report serious harassment, engaging in violence, alcohol and other drug use, and unhealthy weight control practices
Udry and Chantala 2002	Behavioral sexuality	Home interviews from comprehensive national study of adolescents, grades 7–12 (National Longitudinal Study of Adolescent Health)	20,745 students (USA)	Males: 3,123 no sexual partners, 5,951 opposite-sex only partners, 57 same-sex only partners, 87 both-sex partners Females: 3,167 no sexual partners, 6,191 opposite-sex only partners, 100 same-sex only partners, 123 both-sex partners
Warner et al. 2004	Self-identified sexual orientation	Cross-sectional survey using "snowball sampling"	1,285 gay, lesbian, and bisexual individuals in England and Wales (85 bisexual men and 114 bisexual women)	Bisexual men scored significantly higher than gay men on presence and severity of low mood, depression, nonhealth-related worry, general anxiety, phobic anxiety, panic attacks, compulsive behaviors, and obsessions; no significant differences between bisexual women and lesbians

Additionally, we found several previously published papers that had highlighted themes specifically relevant to sexual risk and substance abuse among bisexual individuals. We also summarized the major findings from these papers for our review.

DEFINITIONS

We anticipated and found that definitions of "heterosexual," "homosexual," and "bisexual" would vary across studies. Bearing this in mind, several basic conceptual definitions framed our exploration of mental health among bisexual individuals.

1. *Bisexuality*: Sexual attraction and involvement with both men and women (and sometimes transgender individuals), as distinct from exclusive sexual attraction and involvement with members of the other sex (*heterosexuality*) or of the same sex (*homosexuality*).
2. *Self-Identified Bisexual*: Individuals who use the word *bisexual* with regard to their own sexual orientation, preference, and/or identity.
3. *Behavioral Bisexual*: Individuals who engage in sexual activity with male and female (and sometimes transgender) partners, usually within a specific period of time.

CONCERNS AND LIMITATIONS

A problem in reviewing evidence on mental health problems among bisexual individuals is the very small number of available studies that have specifically examined bisexuals in comparison to homosexuals and heterosexuals. Meyer (2003) detailed other potential problems that can occur while conducting such a review which were also relevant to our investigation. Most notably, publication bias may exist whereby material that shows significant differences is more likely to be published in peer-reviewed journals than material that does not show significant differences.

Given the dearth of summarized information on mental health among bisexuals at the present time, this review represents a starting point for future larger-scale empirical research into mental health among bisexual men and women. It is also noteworthy that we were not able to locate research on mental health among bisexual transgender individuals for this review.

RESULTS

RESEARCH COMBINING BISEXUAL INDIVIDUALS
WITH HOMOSEXUAL INDIVIDUALS

One of the most significant findings of our review is that although a substantial literature exists on mental health among "LGB" and "same-sex" (including bisexual) individuals, the vast majority of studies have not examined bisexual individuals separately. Some of these studies have shown the existence of a generally high prevalence of mental health problems among "lesbian, gay, and bisexual (LGB)" populations when compared to "heterosexual" populations (Meyer 2003), including higher rates of depression, anxiety, suicidality, and substance use disorders (Bagley and Tremblay 1997; D'Augelli, Hershberger, and Pilkington, 2001; Fergusson, Horwood, and Beautrais 1999; Gilman et al. 200l; Gruskin et al. 2001; Herrell et al. 1999; Hershberger et al. 1997; McDaniel et al. 2001; Remafedi et al. 1998; Russell and Joyner 2001; Safren and Heimberg 1999). Higher rates of such problems have often been found in samples that report engaging in "same-sex" behavior (including behaviorally bisexual individuals) as opposed to those who report exclusively engaging in "other sex" behavior (Cochran and Mays 2000a, b; DuRant, Krowebuk, Sinal 1998; Garofolo et al. 1998, 1999; Gilman et al. 1999, 200l; Sandfort, de Graaf, R., and Bijl 2001; Sandfort et al. 2001).

The rationales for combining bisexual with homosexual individuals seem to vary across studies. One obvious reason is that the proportion of bisexual individuals is sometimes too small to examine separately from a statistical perspective. The small number of bisexual participants may be the consequence of several factors including the choice of participant recruitment venues (including "gay-oriented" venues), the stringent classification of participants' sexuality based only on recent bisexual behavior (e.g., past six months, past year, etc.), and the relatively smaller numbers of individuals who self-report bisexual behavior and/or identity in the general population. Given the already small number of homosexual individuals in the general population, combining them with bisexual individuals allows for increased statistical power when comparing LGB groups to heterosexual groups.

For example, Peterson, Folkman, and Bakeman (1996) examined associations between stress, physical health, psychosocial resources, coping, and depressive mood in a community sample of 139 African American gay (66), bisexual (19), and heterosexual (54) men who were solicited through print advertisements in gay and community newspapers in the San Francisco Bay area. Although they initially found that bisexual participants reported more negative life events than gay men, the groups were combined as "gay/bisexual men" in subsequent analyses due to the lack of statistical power.

Even when bisexuals are present in sufficient numbers to analyze them separately from homosexuals, some researchers have combined bisexual and homosexual participants without an explicit rationale (Warner et al. 2004). Some studies have combined "gay, lesbian, and bisexual" participants without reporting any results for bisexual participants, not even the number of bisexuals in the samples (Cochran, Sullivan, and Mays 2003; Johnson, Mercer, and Erens 2001). Indeed, some studies have more "bisexual" participants than "gay" participants but still collapse them into one "gay and bisexual" category. For example, French and colleagues (1998:119) hypothesized that "homosexual orientation would be associated with higher rates of body dissatisfaction, dieting, and eating disordered behaviors in males, but lower in females, relative to those of hetero-sexual orientation." While the hypothesis was described in strictly dichotomous (homosexual-heterosexual) terms, the sample actually included substantially more self-identified bisexual participants (131 males and 144 females) than homosexual participants (81 males and 38 females). In the analyses and inter-pretation of the results, the authors collapsed bisexual and homosexual partici-pants together as "homosexual" and reported that "homosexual males" were more likely to report a poor body image, frequent dieting, and binge/purge behaviors compared with "heterosexual males." As a result, the role of eating disorders in the lives of bisexual, as well as homosexual, individuals remains completely unclear.

RESEARCH SEPARATING BISEXUAL INDIVIDUALS FROM HOMOSEXUAL INDIVIDUALS

In reviewing the literature, we were able to locate a small number of studies (N = 5) that examined mental health concerns among bisexual individuals sep-arately from homosexual and heterosexual individuals. In this section we briefly detail the main findings from each paper.

JORM AND COLLEAGUES (2002) Jorm and colleagues (2002) recruited par-ticipants for a large-scale twenty-year longitudinal study of mental health using sampling frames established through electoral rolls in several Australian cities. They compared mean scores of several standard mental health measures, adjust-ed for age and gender, among bisexual, homosexual, and heterosexual partici-pants. The authors found significant differences between the sexual orientation groups such that the bisexual group was highest on all measures of depression, anxiety, alcohol misuse, and negative affect. The homosexual group tended to fall between the bisexual and heterosexual groups on these measures.

Furthermore, the authors developed regression models to assess risk factors for "worse mental health." In comparisons to heterosexuals, the bisexual group reported "more childhood adversity, more current adverse life events, less posi-tive support from family, more negative support from friends, more years of education (forty to forty-four year olds), and more often (had) financial difficul-ties" (Jorm et al. 2002:424). In comparisons to homosexuals, the bisexual group reported more adverse life events and more financial difficulties. When these risk factors were entered into regression equations to determine whether they could explain disparities in mental health, differences between the homosexual and heterosexual groups disappeared while differences between the bisexual and other groups remained significant. Thus, bisexuality remained the significant negative predictor of most severe mental health indicators.

Based on these findings, Jorm and colleagues (2002) stated that bisexual orientation is associated with more psychological distress and higher rates of mental health problems in comparison to homosexual and heterosexual orientations. The authors hypothesized "it is possible that having neither a clear heterosexual nor homosexual orientation is an important stressor, in addition to the social pressures of having a different sexual orientation to the majority" (2002:425) However, the authors acknowledged that a limitation of the study was that it was not specifically designed to explore issues related to sexual orientation such as stigma and discrimination.

PAUL AND COLLEAGUES (2002) Paul and colleagues (2002) examined the lifetime prevalence of suicide attempts and psychosocial correlates in a large population-based sample of men who have sex with men (MSM). In terms of sexual identity, 84 percent self-identified as homosexual or gay, 9 percent as bisexual, 4 percent as other, and 3 percent as heterosexual. The authors found that 21 percent of the total sample had ever made a suicide plan and 12 percent had attempted suicide; of these, almost half were multiple attempters. The highest prevalence of suicide attempts was found among bisexual participants, nonidentified participants ("other," i.e., neither homosexual/gay, heterosexual, nor bisexual), and Native American participants. Specifically, 30 percent of self-identified bisexual participants reported having had a suicide plan, compared to 25 percent of "other" MSM, 20 percent of homosexual/gay MSM, and 17 percent of heterosexual MSM. Twenty-one percent of self-identified "other" participants had previously attempted suicide as had 16 percent of bisexual MSM, compared to 12 percent of heterosexual MSM and 11 percent of homosexual/gay MSM.

The major finding that suicide attempts were highest among bisexual- and "other"-identified individuals was not further explored or discussed. While race/ethnicity was included as an antecedent to suicide attempts in the logistic regression, sexual identity was not. Paul and colleagues (2002:1343) suggested that "the emergence of a visible, vital gay, lesbian and bisexual community has apparently provided a broader array of possibilities for roles and life careers among those who self-define as 'gay'"; however, the implications for individuals who self-identify as bisexual or "other" were not discussed.

ROBIN AND COLLEAGUES (2002) Robin and colleagues (2002) found a similarly elevated risk for suicidal intent among behaviorally bisexual adolescents in the Northeastern United States as well as high risk for other health behaviors. The authors analyzed cross-sectional data collected in Massachusetts and

Vermont with four large, population-based high school surveys from 1995 and 1997. Using multiple logistic regressions, they reported various significant differences in mental health problems among young people who reported experience with "both-sex" (or behaviorally bisexual) as compared to those with exclusively "same-sex" (or homosexual) and exclusively "other-sex" (or heterosexual).

In both states from which the data were collected, bisexual participants were significantly more likely to report health risk behaviors than were other participants. For example, bisexual participants were three to six times more likely than heterosexual students of being threatened or injured with a weapon at school, making a suicide attempt requiring medical attention, using cocaine, or vomiting or using laxatives to control their weight. Homosexual participants were equally as likely as heterosexual participants to report these health risk behaviors. Robin and colleagues (2002) concluded that, relative to heterosexual and homosexual high school students, bisexual individuals may be at significantly higher risk of injury, disease, and death by experiencing serious harassment and engaging in violence, suicidal behavior, alcohol and other drug use, and unhealthy weight control practices.

UDRY AND CHANTALA (2002) Udry and Chantala (2002) also found several major differences in substance use, and overall health risks, among adolescent students (grades 7–12) with "same-sex," "other-sex," "both-sex," and "no-sex" experiences. The authors examined male and female participants separately and differences between groups were dependent on gender. Bisexual males were found to be at significantly higher risk for substance use and overall delinquent behavior than all other male participants. Specifically, they were significantly more likely to report cigarette smoking, alcohol consumption, and any illegal drug use (including marijuana, cocaine, inhalants, injecting drugs, or "any illegal drug"). Additionally, bisexual males were more likely to report selling sex for drugs or money. In this study exclusively homosexual males were found to be at higher risk than bisexual and exclusively heterosexual males for depression. Interestingly, the authors also noted that, of all the males in the sample, "those with no sex partners show the healthiest behavior all around" (Udry and Chantala 2002:89).

Among female participants Udry and Chantala (2002:84) found that exclusively homosexual females were "never a high-risk group" while bisexual females were "the high-risk category in every case." Bisexual females were significantly more likely to report cigarette smoking, alcohol consumption, any illegal drug use, and selling sex for drugs or money. In addition, bisexual females reported higher rates of suicidality, depression, victimization (including being attacked or involved in a physical fight), and general delinquency. With regard to their findings, the authors themselves noted that "the results of our analysis are surprising to us . . . in the literature we reviewed . . . all studies pooled same-sex and bisexual respondents. What is surprising is that no study separated them. Therefore our findings have not been anticipated in previous studies" (Udry and Chantala 2002:91). Bisexual females, a particularly neglected group in previous literature, emerged as the highest-risk group in their study. In comparison to bisexual males, overall health risks among bisexual females were amplified since their generally delinquent behaviors were also accompanied by signs of extreme emotional distress. The authors concluded that bisexual adolescents are a group requiring serious and special attention; however, they cautioned that "we do not know what kind of public health effort would be appropriate on their behalf, and what the political acceptability of such an effort might be" (Udry and Chantala 2002:91).

WARNER AND COLLEAGUES (2004) Warner and colleagues (2004) recruited a sample of self-identified gay men, lesbians, and bisexual men and women through "snowball sampling" techniques and advertisements in local and national "gay venues" in England and Wales. Of all those who took part, 43 percent of the sample met the criteria for mental disorder and 31 percent had attempted suicide. In comparative analyses bisexual men scored significantly higher on the measure of mental disorder than did gay men. Overall, bisexual men reported more frequent and severe low mood, depression, nonhealth related worry, general anxiety, phobic anxiety, panic attacks, compulsive behaviors, and obsessions. The authors hypothesized that poorer social integration may be a causal factor for higher rates of psychological distress reported by bisexual men. No significant differences were found on these measures, however, between bisexual women and lesbians.

Warner and colleagues (2004) noted that they had succeeded in sampling large numbers of self-identified gay and lesbian respondents but had less success in recruiting bisexual individuals. The authors hypothesized that one possible explanatory factor is that "the distribution of sexuality is bimodal and bisexuality is uncommon" (Warner et al. 2004:484). They also noted that the participants in their sample may have been less willing to identify themselves as bisexual as data showed that "bisexual respondents were less open about their sexuality with family and friends and felt less comfortable about their sexuality" (Warner et al. 2004:484). Interestingly, the authors did not cite that recruitment from exclusively "gay-oriented" venues may have been associated with smaller numbers of bisexual participants. In closing, Warner and colleagues (2004:484) concluded that "our findings suggest that bisexual people should be treated as a separate group for the purposes of health-related research."

SEXUAL RISK AND SUBSTANCE ABUSE AMONG BISEXUAL INDIVIDUALS It is significant that bisexual and homosexual participants have been combined together in the majority of behavioral science research studies on HIV/AIDS despite the emergence of a voluminous body of literature that has explicitly identified bisexual behavior and identity as significant psychosocial risk factors for HIV infection, particularly among men (Aggleton 1996; Chu et al. 1992; Doll et al. 1992, 1997; Goodenow, Netherland, and Szalacha 2002; Heckman et al. 1995; Kalichman et al. 1998; Kennedy and Doll 2001; McKirnan et al. 1995; Morse et al. 1991; Solorio, Swendeman, and Rotheram-Borus 2003; Stokes, McKirnan, and Burzette 1993; Stokes, Vanable, and McKirnan 1997; Tielman et al. 1991; Wood et al. 1993). For example, Doll and Beeker (1996) found that bisexual men report higher rates of sex work, injecting drug use, and sexual identity exploration with both genders than exclusively homosexual men. Additionally, an alarming increased risk was recently reported among bisexually active African American and Latino men in the United States, who were found to be fifteen to thirty times more likely to be HIV positive than both their exclusively homosexual and exclusively heterosexual counterparts (Brooks et al. 2003). This is of great concern considering that relatively few intervention efforts have been designed considering the patterns, meanings, and implications of bisexual men's sexual behavior with both male and female partners (Brooks et al. 2003; Muñoz-Laboy and Dodge 2005).

Research on "substance abuse" and its relationship with "sexual risk" also experienced a rapid increase with the emergence of HIV/AIDS as a public health issue. As such, a number of studies have illuminated that "MSM" drug users are often behaviorally and self-identified bisexual, including those who report using marijuana, cocaine, crack cocaine, methamphetamine, alcohol, and injecting drugs (Gorman, Morgan, and Lambrey 1995; Lewis and Watters 1994; Myers et al. 1992; Rhodes et al. 1999; Seidman, Sterk-Elifson, and Aral 1994). A small body of literature examining injecting drug using (IDU) women who have sex with women (WSW) has also emerged, suggesting that WSW IDUs report higher rates of HIV and other risk behaviors than non-WSW IDUs (Young et al. 2000). However, little or no distinction has been made between these women by sexual orientation and identity since researchers have collapsed participants together as "WSW" or "lesbian/bisexual women."

Lewis and Watters (1994) were among the first to point out that bisexual men, in particular, had been largely ignored in early and influential studies on injecting drug use even though they comprised a sizable subset of individuals in IDU samples. While self-identified and behaviorally bisexual men had been present in these samples of IDUs, they, too, were lumped together with homosexual men in analyses of risk and subsequent HIV/AIDS surveillance data (Lewis and Watters 1994). This trend was particularly disturbing given that reports of significant differences between bisexual and homosexual men had already been published, including data that showed bisexual men with AIDS were twice as likely as homosexual men to be IDUs and that bisexual men represented nearly 30 percent of those men who acquired HIV through injecting drug use and same-sex behavior at that time (Chu et al. 1992). Lewis and Watters (1994) also noted that many sexual interactions among bisexual substance-abusing men take place within the context of sex work. Despite these well-documented differences between bisexual and homosexual substance abusers, most studies on the relationship between sexual orientation and substance abuse still collapse bisexual and homosexual individuals together during analyses and discussions (Halkitis and Parsons 2002; Klitzman et al. 2000; McCabe et al. 2003).

EMERGING RESEARCH TRENDS

It is important to note that some researchers have recognized the problems involved with atheoretically combining bisexual participants with homosexual participants and have begun to discontinue this practice. For example, in a recent study of health risk factors for "gay American Indian and Alaska Native adolescent males," Barney (2003:142) affirmed that

> bisexual adolescents were excluded from the present analysis, as bisexuality is believed by some authors to be a different sexual orientation from either homosexuality or heterosexuality. . . . In many research studies, bisexual males have been combined with gay males into a homosexual orientation category in a belief that the two identities are sufficiently similar, or to increase sample size for statistical power. . . . However, this practice may be of questionable value, as recent studies have determined that the bisexual male subpopulation is substantially different from gay males. (Broido 2000)

As in the case of this study, however, this brings with it the possibility that bisexual individuals may be "excluded" altogether from scientific research unless studies are designed to focus specifically on their needs.

Innovative research is emerging which examines mental health among bisexual individuals as separate from homosexual and heterosexual individuals. For example, Mathy, Lehmann, and Kerr (2004) specifically examined suicidal intent, behavioral difficulties, and rates of mental health treatment among a sample of self-identified bisexual men, women, and transgender individuals recruited from the Internet. The authors found that bisexual women and transgender individuals reported higher frequencies of these mental health problems compared to bisexual men, which the researchers attributed to the combined effects of sexism and heterosexism. Studies such as these illuminate important "within group" differences between bisexual individuals that can further improve sexuality research and clinical practice. Indeed, these results also imply that combining "gay male" and "lesbian" individuals may also be questionable if it causes researchers to overlook important gender differences in how sexual orientation relates to mental health.

DISCUSSION

LIMITATIONS OF PREVIOUS RESEARCH ON MENTAL HEALTH AMONG BISEXUAL INDIVIDUALS

In summary, there is an absence of scholarly attention previously given to mental health among bisexual individuals when compared to homosexual and heterosexual individuals. The number of articles we could locate that present relevant information specific to bisexuals in terms of mental health is a minuscule proportion of the published literature on sexual orientation and mental health. This body of research is already problematic given that definitions of LGB and same-sex sexuality vary widely among studies. Indeed, only one of the articles we were able to locate (Jorm et al. 2002) aims to focus directly on bisexuals in comparison to homosexuals and heterosexuals.

Additionally, while substantial numbers of men and women in individual studies of mental health in "gay, lesbian, and bisexual" populations identify as bisexual or report sex with both men and women, the patterns we have identified may not be readily distinguishable given the traditionally dichotomized (homosexual-heterosexual) framework operating within mental health research. Most previous studies on depression, anxiety, suicidality, substance use, and other health problems in sexual minority populations have included self-identified and/or behaviorally bisexual individuals. However, Meyer (2003:674) and others have interpreted and presented the findings from these samples such that "compared with their heterosexual counterparts, *gay men and lesbians* suffer from more mental health problems including substance use disorders, affective disorders, and suicide" (italics ours). Hence, in previous research, "bisexual" individuals have most often simply been subsumed under the label of *gay men and lesbians.* The relative invisibility and social denial of bisexuality in contemporary society, including academia, may contribute to the lack of scholarly research on bisexuality and mental health (Rust 2000:5).

If similar previous, influential studies on mental health concerns combine LGB findings and report them as pertaining only to lesbian and gay individuals, the significance of bisexuality in relation to suicidality risk and other mental health problems may have been erased. Indeed, Jorm and colleagues (2002) cautioned that previous research demonstrating high rates of adverse mental health concerns among LGB populations may have "overstated" the risk of problems for lesbians and gay men by including bisexual women and men in that group.

EXPLAINING DIFFERENCES AMONG BISEXUALS, HOMOSEXUALS, AND HETEROSEXUALS

Attempting to interpret differences in mental health problems among bisexual, homosexual, and heterosexual individuals is complex. Given the diversity of bisexual individuals, and the ways in which they experience and express their sexuality, it is difficult to isolate global factors that may be related to increased risk of mental health problems observed in previous studies. For example, bisexuality in high school students may be markedly different from bisexuality in urban adults. However, we believe that bisexual individuals in numerous contexts may exhibit higher rates of mental health problems for several reasons specifically related to their sexual orientation and/or identity.

First, it has been established that bisexuals share with lesbians and gay men similar burdens on the basis of their sexual orientation and identity, particularly with regard to their same-sex practices and desires. Herek (2002) has suggested that, similar to lesbians and gay men, bisexual individuals face hostility, discrimination, and violence on the basis of their sexual orientation. The psychological and social effects of stigma, discrimination, and "minority stress" have been repeatedly documented in LGB samples (Meyer 2003; Meyer 1995). However, for methodological reasons indicated above, Herek (2002) has pointed out that the prevalence of such experiences specifically among bisexuals is difficult to estimate.

Another potential explanation for elevated rates of mental health problems among bisexuals is that, along with the burdens shared with lesbians and gay men, bisexual individuals may also face additional stressors specifically on the basis of their *bisexual* behaviors and/or identity. Rust (2000:434) has affirmed that "bisexuals face many issues . . . some similar to those faced by lesbians and gay men and others unique to bisexuals." These unique factors might also explain the higher rates of mental health problems among bisexual individuals when compared to homosexual and heterosexual individuals in previous mental health research. The existence of biphobia, or the stigma and discrimination experienced by bisexual individuals from both heterosexual and homosexual individuals on the basis of their bisexual orientation and/or identity, has been extensively illuminated in activist and, more recently, scientific literature (Herek 2002; Hutchins and Ka'ahumanu 1991; Mulick and Wright 2002; Ochs 1996). For example, Herek (2002) found that heterosexual individuals expressed more negative feelings toward bisexual men and women than all other religious, racial, ethnic, and political minority groups assessed except injecting drug users (including lesbians and gay men). Rust (1992) also proposed that many individuals, particularly lesbians and gay men, stereotype bisexual individuals as "confused" and in transition to eventual homosexual or heterosexual lives.

Consequently, bisexual individuals may be at risk of social isolation since they may often lack social support from any ongoing and visible community, including the "gay" community. Indeed, Weiss (2004) has recently argued that, even with the emergence of nominally inclusive LGBT services and organizations intended to assist and provide support to lesbian, gay, bisexual, and transgender individuals, in practice some gay men and lesbians continue to reject and ostracize bisexuals and transgendered individuals, seeking to disavow these more "radical" forms of sexuality in an attempt to accommodate to the larger hetero-normative society. Researchers have just begun to investigate how bisexual individuals may experience such "double discrimination" from both heterosexuals and homosexuals and how biphobia may impact the lives and, in particular, mental health of bisexuals (Eliason 1997; Herek 2002; Mohr and Rochlen 1999; Spaulding and Peplau 1997).

IMPLICATIONS AND SUGGESTIONS FOR FUTURE RESEARCH AND CLINICAL PRACTICE

The few studies we were able to locate suggest higher rates of depression, anxiety, suicidality, substance use, and other health problems among bisexual individuals when compared to homosexual and heterosexual individuals. These findings have major implications for mental health practitioners and others who deal with sexuality-related issues and bisexual individuals in their work

Based on our review, we offer several suggestions for more relevant and effective work with bisexual individuals and, indeed, all sexual minority populations. First and foremost, we feel researchers and practitioners must explicitly distinguish between bisexual and homosexual individuals in their practices in order to more effectively deal with them in research and clinical settings. Clearly, collapsing bisexual and homosexual individuals under the common auspices of lesbian, gay, and bisexual mental health concerns has proven to be problematic. Although examining mental health problems among combined LGB and same-sex populations may, indeed, be useful for some purposes, such as exploring stigma and discrimination shared by nonheterosexual individuals, research is also needed to explore mental health specifically among self-identified and behaviorally bisexual individuals (Meezan and Martin 2003). Indeed, Udry and Chantala (2002:91) have contended that, when examined separately from homosexuals and heterosexuals, bisexual individuals' "across-the-board problem profile" urgently highlights them as "a priority group for both research and clinical attention, because we obviously have failed in the past to recognize them as a high-risk group."

Empirical research is needed that more appropriately reflects the diverse and complex forms of sexual and gender expressions that flourish in North America and around the world (Alexander and Yescavage 2004). However, studies with this aim, and the funding and resources to carry them out, are currently few and far between. Such research will require sincere, accessible, and ongoing financial and resource support from academic and research institutions. In addition, researchers and academics must be committed to moving beyond the repeatedly disproven beliefs that sexual orientation and gender are fixed, binary, and categorical concepts—worldviews that are still deeply entrenched in academia and popular culture (Garber 2000).

Overall, it is critical that future research on mental health among sexual minority populations be based on more diverse populations of bisexual, homosexual, and transgender individuals. Sullivan and Losberg (2003) have suggested that generalizing to all nonheterosexual individuals from previous samples of primarily white, well-educated, upper middle-class self-identified lesbians and gay men is dangerous, as results may be misleading and simplistic. For example, research has suggested that many bisexual individuals have little or no interaction in "gay" social spaces, including gay bars, clubs, parades, and community centers (Doll and Beeker 1996; Stokes, Miller, and Mundhenk 1998). Few researchers have made attempts to specifically recruit bisexual individuals outside "gay" spaces from which LGB samples are often drawn (Rust 2001). Future research may benefit from the development of innovative strategies to locate, recruit, and examine bisexual individuals who may not frequent gay-identified venues. Furthermore, additional research on bisexual women is particularly necessitated, since the majority of previous behavioral science research studies have focused on bisexual men. More research on bisexual women, men, and transgendered individuals is also required outside the context of HIV/AIDS risk and drug use. While these are certainly important topics, in their current form these research studies reveal only a limited amount of information about a very small segment of the bisexual population. As such, research is needed that explores the lived experiences of bisexual individuals beyond HIV/AIDS risk and drug use in more representative cross sections of bisexual women, men, and transgendered people.

Finally, mental health practitioners should also be aware of the possibility that their bisexual participants and clients may face unique stressors that put them at elevated risk for certain mental health problems and be equipped to assist them accordingly. If practitioners are not comfortable with or confident in their ability to work pragmatically and nonjudgmentally with bisexual individuals, as separate and distinct from heterosexual and homosexual individuals, they should have the resources to refer bisexual participants or clients to places where they can receive appropriate evaluation, treatment, and care.

NOTE

During the production of this manuscript, the authors acknowledges support in the form of center grant P30 MH43520 from the National Institute of Mental Health to the HIV Center for Clinical and Behavioral Studies, Anke A. Ehrhardt, Ph.D., principal investigator, and NRSA T32 MH19139, Behavioral Sciences Research in HIV Infection, Anke A. Ehrhardt, Ph.D., program director. The authors would also like to express their sincere appreciation to Robert Kertzner, M.D., for the original inspiration to conduct this review and to Beth Firestein, Ph.D., for her invaluable feedback on earlier drafts of this paper and for her vision to complete this project.

REFERENCES

Aggleton, P. (Ed.) (1996). *Bisexualities and AIDS: International perspectives.* Bristol, PA: Taylor and Francis.

Alexander, J., and Yescavage, K. (Eds.) (2004). *Bisexuality and transgenderism: InterSEXions of the others.* Binghamton, NY: Harrington Park.

American Psychological Association. (2004). *Guidelines for psychotherapy with lesbian, gay, and bisexual clients.* Washington, DC: American Psychological Association. Retrieved online at http://www.apa.org/pi/lgbc/publications/guidelines.html.

Angelides, S. (2001). *A history of bisexuality.* Chicago: University of Chicago Press.

Bagley, C., and Tremblay. P. (1997). Suicidal behaviors in homosexual and bisexual males. *Crisis, 18,* 24–34.

Barney, D. D. (2003). Health risk-factors for gay American Indian and Alaska Native adolescent males. *Journal of Homosexuality, 46*(1/2), 137–157.

Bayer, R. (1981). *Homosexuality and American psychiatry: The politics of diagnosis.* New York: Basic.

Blumstein, P. W., and Schwartz, P. (1976a). Bisexuality in women. *Archives of Sexual Behavior, 5*(2), 171–181.

Blumstein, P. W., and Schwartz, P. (1976b). Bisexuality in men. *Urban Life, 5*(3), 339–358.

Broido, E. M. (2000). Constructing identity: The nature and meaning of lesbian, gay, and bisexual identities. In R. M. Perez, K. A. DeBord, and K. A. Bies (Eds.), *Handbook of counseling and psychotherapy with lesbian, gay, and bisexual clients* (pp. 13–33). Washington, DC: American Psychological Association.

Brooks, R., Rotheram-Borus, M. J., Bing, E. C., Ayala, G., and Henry, C. I. (2003). HIV and AIDS among men of color who have sex with men and men of color who have sex with men and women: An epidemiological profile. *AIDS Education and Prevention, 15*(1), 1–6.

Carballo-Dieguez, A. and Dolezal, C. (1994). Contrasting types of Puerto Rican men who have sex with men (MSM). *Journal of Psychology and Human Sexuality, 6*(4), 41–67.

Carrier, J. M. (1985). Mexican male bisexuality. *Journal of Homosexuality, 11*(1/2), 75–85.

Cochran, S. D. and Mays, V. M. (2000a) Lifetime prevalence of suicide symptoms and affective disorders among men reporting same-sex sexual partners: Results from NHANES III. *American Journal of Public Health, 90,* 573–578.

Cochran, S. D. and Mays, V. M. (2000b) Relation between psychiatric syndromes and behaviorally defined sexual orientation in a sample of the US population. *American Journal of Epidemiology, 151,* 516–523.

Cochran, S. D., Sullivan, J. G., and Mays, V. M. (2003). Prevalence of mental disorders, psychological distress, and mental health services use among lesbian, gay, and bisexual adults in the United States. *Journal of Consulting and Clinical Psychology, 71,* 53–61.

Chu, S. Y., Peterman, T. A., Doll, L. S., Buehler, J. W., and Curran, J. W. (1992). AIDS in bisexual men in the United States: Epidemiology and transmission to women. *American Journal of Public Health,* 82(2), 220–224.

D'Augelli, A. R., Hershberger, S. L., and Pilkington, N. W. (2001). Suicidality patterns and sexual orientation-related factors among lesbian, gay, and bisexual youth. *Suicide Life Threatening Behavior, 31,* 250–264.

De Moya, A., and Garcia, A. (1996). AIDS and the enigma of bisexuality in the Dominican Republic. In P. Aggleton (Ed.), *Bisexualities and AIDS: International perspectives* (pp. 121–135). London: Taylor and Francis.

Diamond, L. M. (2003). Was it a phase? Young women's relinquishment of lesbian/ bisexual identities over a five-year period. *Journal of Personality and Social Psychology,* 84(2), 352–364.

Doll, L. S., and Beeker, C. (1996). Male bisexual behavior and HIV risk in the United States: Synthesis of research and implications for interventions. *AIDS Education and Prevention,* 8(3), 205–225.

Doll, L. S., Myers, T., Kennedy, M., and Allman, D. (1997). Bisexuality and HIV risk: Experiences in Canada and the United States. *Annual Review of Sex Research,* 8, 102–147.

Doll, L. S., Peterson, L. R., White, C. R., Johnson, E. S., Ward, J. W., and the Blood Donor Study Group. (1992). Homosexually and nonhomosexually identified men who have sex with men: A behavioral comparison. *Journal of Sex Research,* 29(1), 1–14.

DuRant, R. H., Krowebuk, D. P. and Sinal, S. H. (1998). Victimization, use of violence, and drug use at school among male adolescents who engage in same-sex sexual behavior. *Journal of Pediatrics, 132,* 13–18.

Eliason, M. J. (1997). The prevalence and nature of biphobia in heterosexual undergraduate students. *Archives of Sexual Behavior, 26,* 217–326.

Fergusson, D. M., Horwood, J. and Beautrais, A. L. (1999). Is sexual orientation related to mental health problems and suicidality in young people? *Archives of General Psychiatry, 56,* 876–880.

Firestein, B. A., Ed. (1996). *Bisexuality: The psychology and politics of an invisible minority.* Thousand Oaks, CA: Sage.

Fox, R. C. (1995). Bisexual identities. In A. R. D'Augelli and C. J. Patterson (Eds.), *Lesbian, gay, and bisexual identities over the lifespan: Psychological perspectives* (pp. 48–86). New York: Oxford University Press.

Fox, R. C. (1996). Bisexuality in perspective: A review of theory and research. In B. A. Firestein (Ed.) *Bisexuality: The psychology and politics of an invisible minority* (pp. 3–50). Thousand Oaks, CA: Sage Publications.

French, S. A., Story, M., Remafedi, G., Resnick, M. D., and Blum, R. W. (1998). Sexual orientation and prevalence of body dissatisfaction and eating disordered behaviors: A population-based study of adolescents. *International Journal of Eating Disorders,* 19(2), 119–126

Friedman, R.C. (1999) Homosexuality, psychopathology, and suicidality. *Archives of General Psychiatry, 56*, 887–888.

Garber, M. (2000). *Bisexuality and the eroticism of everyday life.* New York: Routledge.

Garofalo, R., Wolf, C., Kessel, S., Palfrey, S.J., and DuRant, R.H. (1998). The association between health risk behaviors and sexual orientation among a school-based sample of adolescents. *Pediatrics, 101*, 895–902.

Garofalo, R., Wolf, C., Kessel, S., Woods, E.R., and Goodman, E. (1999). Sexual orientation and risk of suicide attempts among a representative sample of youth. *Archives of Pediatric and Adolescent Medicine, 153*, 487–493.

Gilman, S.E., Cochran, S.D., Mays, V.M., Hughes, M., Ostrow, D., and Kessler, R.C. (2001). Risk of psychiatric disorders among individuals reporting same-sex sexual partners in the National Comorbidity Survey. *American Journal of Public Health, 91*, 933–939.

Goodenow, C., Netherland, J., and Szalacha, L. (2002). AIDS-related risk among adolescent males who have sex with males, females, or both: Evidence from a statewide study. *American Journal of Public Health, 92*(2), 203–210.

Gorman, E.M., Morgan, P., and Lambrey, E. (1995). Qualitative research considerations and other issues in the study of methamphetamine use among men who have sex with men. In E.Y. Lambert, R.S. Ashery, and R.H. Needle. (Eds.) *Qualitative methods in drug abuse and HIV research* (NIDA Research Monograph, 157, NIH Publication 95–4025) (pp. 156–181). Rockville, MD: National Institute on Drug Abuse.

Gruskin, E.P., Hart, S., Gordon, N., and Ackerson, L. (2001). Patterns of cigarette smoking and alcohol use among lesbians and bisexual women enrolled in a large health maintenance organization. *American Journal of Public Health, 91*, 976–979.

Halkitis, P.N., and Parsons, J.T. (2002). Recreational drug use and HIV-risk sexual behavior among men frequenting gay social venues. *Journal of Gay and Lesbian Social Services: Issues in Practice, Policy and Research, 14*(4), 19–38.

Heckman, T.G., Kelly, J.A., Sikkema, K.J., Roffman, R.R., Solomon, L.J., Winett, R.A., Stevenson, L.Y., Perry, M.J., Norman, A.D., and Desiderato, L.J. (1995). Differences in HIV risk between bisexual and exclusively gay men. *AIDS Education and Prevention, 7*(6), 504–512.

Hemmings, C. (2002). *Bisexual spaces: A geography of sexuality and gender.* London: Routledge.

Herdt, G. (1990). Developmental discontinuities and sexual orientation across cultures. In D. McWhirter, S. Sanders, and J: Reinisch (Eds.), *Homosexuality/heterosexuality: Concepts of sexual orientation* (Kinsey Institute Series, 2) (pp. 208–36). Bloomington, IN: Indiana University Press.

Herdt, G. (2001). Social change, sexual diversity, and tolerance for bisexuality in the United States. In A.R. D'Augelli and C.J. Patterson (Eds.), *Lesbian, gay, and bisexual identities and youth: Psychological perspectives* (pp. 267–283). London: Oxford University Press.

Herek, G.M. (2002). Heterosexuals' attitudes toward bisexual men and women in the United States. *Journal of Sex Research, 39*(4), 264–274.

Herrell, R., Goldberg, J., True, W.R., Ramakrishnan, V., Lyons, M., Eisen, S., and Tsuang, M.T. (1999). Sexual orientation and suicidality: a co-twin control study in adult men. *Archives of General Psychiatry, 56*, 867–874.

Hershberger, S.L., Pilkington, N.W., and D'Augelli, A.R. (1997). Predictors of suicide attempts among gay, lesbian, and bisexual youth. *Journal of Adolescent Research, 12*. 477–497.

Hutchins, L., and Ka'ahumanu, L. (Eds.) (1991). *Bi any other name: Bisexual people speak out*. Boston: Alyson.

Johnson, A. M., Mercer, C. H., and Erens, B. (2001). Sexual behavior in Britain: Partnerships, practices, and HIV risk behaviours. *Lancet, 358,* 1835–1842.

Jorm, A. F., Korten, A. E., Rodgers, B., Jacomb, P. A., and Christensen, H. (2002). Sexual orientation and mental health: Results from a community survey of young and middle-aged results. *British Journal of Psychiatry, 188,* 423–427.

Kalichman, S. C., Roffman, R. A., Picciano, J. F., and Bolan, M. (1998). Risk for HIV infection among bisexual men seeking HIV-prevention services and risks posed to their female partners. *Health Psychology, 17*(4), 320–327.

Kennedy, M., and Doll, L. S. (2001). Male bisexuality and HIV risk. *Journal of Bisexuality, 1*(2/3), 109–135.

Kinsey, A. C., Pomeroy, W., and Martin, C. (1948). *Sexual behavior in the human male.* Philadelphia: Saunders.

Kinsey, A. C., Pomeroy, W., Martin, C., and Gebhard, P. (1953). *Sexual behavior in the human female.* Philadelphia: Saunders.

Klein, F. (1978). *The bisexual option: A concept of one hundred percent intimacy.* New York: Arbor House.

Klitzman, R., Greenbert, J., Dolezal, C., and Pollack, L. (2002). MDMA ("Ecstasy") use and its association with high risk behaviors, mental health and other factors among gay/bisexual men in New York City. *Drug and Alcohol Abuse, 66,* 115–125.

Laumann, E. O., Gagnon, J. H., Michael, R. T., and Michaels, S. (1994). *The social organization of sexuality: Sexual practices in the United States.* Chicago: University of Chicago Press.

Lever, J., Kanhouse, D. E., Rogers, W. H., Carson, S., and Hertz, R. (1992). Behavior patterns and sexual identity of bisexual males. *Journal of Sex Research, 29*(2), 141–167.

Lewis, D. K., and Watters, J. K. (1994). Sexual behavior and sexual identity in male injection drug users. *Journal of Acquired Immune Deficiency Syndromes, 7,* 190–198.

McCabe, S. E., Boyd, C., Hughes, T. L., and d'Arcy, H. (2003). Sexual identity and substance use among undergraduate students. *Substance Abuse, 24*(2), 77–91.

McCombs, S., McCray, E., Wendell, D., Sweeney, P. A., and Onorato, I. M. (1992). Epidemiology of HIV-1 infection in bisexual women. *Journal of Acquired Immune Deficiency Syndromes, 5,* 850–852.

McDaniel, J. S., Purcell, D., and D'Augelli, A. R. (2001). The relationship between sexual orientation and risk for suicide: Research findings and future directions for research and prevention. *Suicide and Life Threatening Behavior, 31,* 84–105.

McKirnan, D. J., Stokes, J. P., Doll, L. S., and Burzette, R. G. (1995). Bisexually active men: Social characteristics and sexual behaviors. *Journal of Sex Research, 32*(1), 66–76.

Mathy, R. M., Lehmann, B. A., and Kerr, D. L. (2004). Bisexual and transgender identities in a nonclinical sample of North Americans: Suicidal intent, behavioral difficulties, and mental health treatment. *Journal of Bisexuality, 3*(3/4), 93–109.

Meezan, W., and Martin, J. I. (2003). Exploring current themes in research on gay, lesbian, bisexual, and transgender populations. *Journal of Gay and Lesbian Social Services, 15*(1/2), 1–14.

Messiah, A., and the ACSF Group. (1996). Bisexuality and AIDS: Results from French quantitative studies. In P. Aggleton (Ed.), *Bisexualities and AIDS: International perspectives* (pp. 61–75). Bristol, PA: Taylor and Francis.

Meyer, I. H. (1995). Minority stress and mental health in gay men. *Journal of Health and Social Behavior*, 36(March), 38–56.

Meyer, I. H. (2003). Prejudice, social stress, and mental health in lesbian, gay, and bisexual populations: Conceptual issues and research evidence. *Psychological Bulletin*, 129(5), 674–697.

Mohr, J. J., and Rochlen, A. B. (1999). Measuring attitudes regarding bisexuality in lesbian, gay male, and heterosexual populations. *Journal of Counseling Psychology*, 46, 353–369.

Morse, V., Simon, P. M., Osofsky, H. J., Balson, P. M., and Gaumier, H. R. (1991). The male street prostitute: A vector for transmission of HIV infection into the heterosexual world. *Social Science and Medicine*, 32, 535–539.

Mulick, P. S., and Wright, L. W. (2002). Examining the existence of biphobia in the heterosexual and homosexual populations. *Journal of Bisexuality*, 2(4), 47–64.

Muñoz-Laboy, M. (2004). Beyond MSM: Sexual desire among bisexually active Latino men in New York City. *Sexualities*, 7(1), 55–80.

Muñoz-Laboy, M. A. and Dodge, B. (2005). Bisexual practices: Patterns, meanings, and implications for HIV/STI prevention among bisexually active Latino men and their partners. *Journal of Bisexuality*, 5(1), 81–100.

Myers, T., Tudiver, F. G., Kurtz, R. G., Jackson, E. A., Orr, K. W., Rowe, C. W., and Bullock, S. L. (1992). The talking sex project: Descriptions of the study population and correlates of sexual practices at baseline. *Canadian Journal of Public Health*, 83, 47–52.

Nicolosi, J. (1991). *Reparative therapy of male homosexuality*. Northvale, NJ: Aronson.

Ochs, R. (1996). Biphobia: It goes more than two ways. In B. A. Firestein (Ed.), *Bisexuality: The psychology and politics of an invisible minority* (pp. 217–239). Thousand Oaks, CA: Sage.

Parker, R. (1991). *Bodies, pleasures and passions: Sexual culture in contemporary Brazil*. Boston: Beacon.

Parker, R. (1996). Bisexuality and HIV/AIDS in Brazil. In P. Aggleton (Ed.), *Bisexualities and AIDS: International perspectives* (pp. 148–160). London: Taylor and Francis.

Parker, R. (1999). *Beneath the equator: Cultures of desire, male homosexuality, and emerging gay communities in Brazil*. New York: Routledge.

Paul, J. P., Catania, J., Pollack, L., Moskowitz, J., Canchola, J., Mills, T., Binson, D., and Stall, R. (2002). Suicide attempts among gay and bisexual men: Lifetime prevalence and antecedents. *American Journal of Public Health*, 92(8), 1338–1345.

Peterson, J. L., Folkman, S., and Bakeman, R. (1996). Stress, coping, HIV status, psychosocial resources, and depressive mood among African American gay, bisexual, and heterosexual men. *American Journal of Community Psychology*, 24(4), 461–487.

Remafedi, G., French, S., Story, M., Resnick, M. D., and Blum, R. (1998). The relationship between suicide risk and sexual orientation: results of a population-based study. *American Journal of Public Health*, 88, 57–60.

Rhodes, F., Deren, S., Wood, M. M, Shedlin, M. G., Carlson, R. G., Lambert, E. Y., Kochems, L. M., Stark, M. J., Falck, R. S., Wright-DeAguero, L., Weir, B., Cottler, L., Rourke, K. M., and Trotter, R. T. (1999). Understanding HIV risks of chronic drug-using men who have sex with men. *AIDS Care*, 11(6), 629–648.

Robin, L., Brener, N. D., Donahue, S. F., Hack, T., Hale, K., and Goodenow, C. (2002). Associations between health risk behaviors and opposite-, same-, and both-sex sexual partners in representative samples of Vermont and Massachusetts high school students. *Archives of Pediatrics and Adolescent Medicine, 156*, 349–355.

Russell, S. T., and Joyner, K. (2001). Adolescent sexual orientation and suicide risk: Evidence from a national study. *American Journal of Public Health, 91*, 573–578.

Rust, P. C. (1992). The politics of sexual identity: Sexual attraction and behavior among lesbian and bisexual women. *Social Problems, 39*, 366–386.

Rust, P. C. (1996). Managing multiple identities: Diversity among bisexual women and men. In B. A. Firestein (Ed.) *Bisexuality: The psychology and politics of an invisible minority* (pp. 52–83). Thousand Oaks, CA: Sage.

Rust, P. C. (2000). *Bisexuality in the United States: A social science reader.* New York: Columbia University Press.

Rust, P. C. (2001). Make me a map: Bisexual men's images of a bisexual community. *Journal of Bisexuality, 1*(1), 31–68.

Safren, S. A., and Heimberg, R. G. (1999). Depression, hopelessness, suicidality, and related factors in sexual minority and heterosexual adolescents. *Journal of Consulting and Clinical Psychology, 67*(6), 859–66.

Sandfort, T. G. M. (1998). Homosexual and bisexual behaviour in European countries. In M. C. Hubert, N. Bajos, and T. G. M. Sandfort (Eds.), *Sexual behaviour and HIV/AIDS in Europe* (pp. 68–105). London: UCL.

Sandfort, T. G. M., de Graaf, R., and Bijl, R. V. (2001). Same-sex sexuality and quality of life. *Archives of Sexual Behavior, 32*(1), 15–22.

Sandfort, T. G. M., de Graaf, R., Bijl, R. V., and Schnabel, P. (2001). Same-sex sexual behavior and psychiatric disorders: Findings from the Netherlands Mental Health Survey and Incidence Study (NEMESIS). *Archives of General Psychiatry, 58*, 85–91.

Seidman, S. N., Sterk-Elifson, C., and Aral, S. O. (1994). High-risk sexual behavior among drug-using men. *Sexually Transmitted Diseases, 21*, 73–80.

Solorio, R., Swendeman, D., and Rotheram-Borus, M. J. (2003). Risk among young gay and bisexual men living with HIV. *AIDS Education and Prevention, 15* (Supplement A), 80–89.

Spaulding L. R., and Peplau, L. A. (1997). The unfaithful lover: Heterosexuals' perceptions of bisexuals and their relationships. *Psychology of Women Quarterly, 21*, 611–625.

Stokes, J. P., McKirnan, D. J., and Burzette, R. G. (1993). Sexual behavior, condom use, disclosure of sexuality, and stability of sexual orientation in bisexual men. *Journal of Sex Research 30*, 201–213.

Stokes, J. P., Vanable, P., and McKirnan, D. J. (1997). Comparing gay and bisexual men on sexual behavior, condom use, and psychosocial variables related to HIV/AIDS. *Archives of Sexual Behavior, 26*(4), 383–397.

Stokes, J. P., Miller, R. L., and Mundhenk, R. (1998). Toward an understanding of behaviorally bisexual men: The influence of context and culture. *Canadian Journal of Human Sexuality, 7*(2), 101–113.

Sullivan, G., and Losberg, W. (2003). A study of sampling in research in the field of lesbian and gay studies. *Journal of Gay and Lesbian Social Services, 15*(1/2), 147–162.

Taylor, C. (1978). El Ambiente: Male homosexual social life in Mexico City. Doctoral dissertation. University of California at Berkeley.

Thomas, S. G., and Hodges, B. (1991). Assessing AIDS knowledge, attributes, and risk behaviors among black and Hispanic homosexual and bisexual men: Results of a feasibility study. *Journal of Sex Education and Therapy, 17*(2), 116–124.

Tielman, R. A. P., Carballo, M., and Hendriks, A. C. (Eds.) (1991). *Bisexuality and HIV/ AIDS: A global perspective*. Buffalo, NY: Prometheus.

Udry, J. R., and Chantala, K. (2002). Risk assessment of adolescents with same-sex relationships. *Journal of Adolescent Health, 31,* 84–92.

Warner, J., McKeown, E., Griffin, M., Johnson, K., Ramsay, A., Cort, C., and King, M. (2004). Rates and predictors of mental illness in gay men, lesbians, and bisexual men and women: Results from a survey based in England and Wales. *British Journal of Psychiatry, 185,* 479–485.

Weinberg, M. S., Williams, C. J., and Pryor, D. W. (1994). *Dual attraction: Understanding bisexuality*. New York: Oxford University Press.

Weinberg, M. S., Williams, C. J., and Pryor, D. W. (2001). Bisexuals at midlife: Commitment, salience, and identity. *Journal of Contemporary Ethnography, 30(2),* 180–208.

Weiss, J. T. (2004). GL vs. BT: The archaeology of biphobia and transphobia within the U.S. gay and lesbian community. In J. Alexander and K. Yescavage (Eds.), *Bisexuality and transgenderism: InterSEXions of the others* (pp. 25–55). Binghamton, NY: Harrington Park.

Wood, R. W., Krueger, L. E., Pearlman, T., and Goldbaum, G. (1993). HIV transmission: Women's risk from bisexual men. *American Journal of Public Health, 83(12),* 1757–1759.

World Health Organization. (2001). Strengthening mental health promotion. Geneva, Switzerland: World Health Organization. Retrieved August 1, 2003, from http://www .who.int/mental_health/evidence/en/promoting_mhh.pdf.

World Health Organization. (2003). Promoting mental health: Concepts, emerging evidence, practice. Geneva, Switzerland: World Health Organization. Retrieved August 1, 2003, from http://www.who.int/mental_health/evidence/en/promoting_mhh.pdf.

Young, R. M., Friedman, S. R., Case, P., Asencio, M. W., and Clatts, M. (2000). Women injecting drug users who have sex with women exhibit increased HIV infection and risk behaviors. *Journal of Drug Issues, 30(3),* 499–523.

3

BISEXUAL WOMEN'S AND MEN'S EXPERIENCES
OF PSYCHOTHERAPY

Emily Page

UNTIL THE 1970s, mental health providers considered same-sex attractions to be pathological. Clients who told clinicians about same sex attractions were offered mental health services designed to change their attractions and behavior to a heterosexual orientation. (Drescher 1998). In 1973 the American Psychiatric Association voted to remove homosexuality from the *Diagnostic and Statistical Manual of Mental Disorders* that is the standard for mental health services in the United States (American Psychiatric Association 1974). Since then, virtually all major professional organizations devoted to mental health have affirmed the view that there is nothing innately unhealthy about same-sex attractions. These professions advise their members to take an affirmative approach to minority sexual orientations and identities as well as to assist homosexual and bisexual clients to overcome the effects of societal prejudice directed against them (American Counseling Association 1996; American Psychiatric Association 1974; Conger 1975; National Association of Social Workers 1996).

Since this time, research has focused on developing theory and establishing an empirical basis for affirmative clinical approaches to working with lesbian, gay, and bisexual clients and exploring the therapy experiences of these sexual minority clients (D'Augelli and Patterson 1995; Greene and Croom 2000; Perez, DeBord, and Bieschke 2000; Ritter and Terndrup 2002). Several recent studies have found that comparatively more lesbians and gay men use psychotherapy and other mental health services than do heterosexual women and men (Cochran, Sullivan, and Mays 2003). In addition, lesbian and gay clients tend to participate in more numerous and longer courses of mental health services and to value those services more highly than their heterosexual counterparts (Bieschke et al. 2000). However, lesbian and gay clients have given variable assessments of providers' knowledgability, skill, and helpfulness in addressing lesbian and gay issues (Bieschke et al. 2000; Jones and Gabriel 1999; Lebolt 1999; Nystrom 1997).

Most of these studies are presumed to include bisexual women and men in their sample populations (Chung and Katayama 1996). Therefore, it could be presumed that their findings apply to bisexual as well as gay and lesbian clients. However, few studies have specified what portion of their samples consisted of bisexual women and men and almost none of these studies reported their findings specifically distinguishing between lesbian, gay and bisexual participants. In the two studies that specified findings by sexual orientation, the bisexual women and men in their samples experienced more heterosexual bias from their providers than did lesbian and gay participants (Lucksted 1996; Moss 1994).

More recently, some comparative studies of mental health indicators have found bisexual individuals to have greater anxiety, depression, suicidality, and negative affect than lesbian, gay, and heterosexual respondents. Researchers have suggested that these differences may stem from the effect of prejudice against bisexuality as well as prejudice against homosexuality (Balsam and Rothblum 2002; Jorm et al. 2002; Dodge and Sandfort, chapter 2). The effect of these dual prejudices has also been discussed in research on bisexual identity (Fox 1996; Rust 2001), professional discussions of bisexuality (Firestein 1996), and anecdotal accounts of the bisexual experience (Bisexual Anthology Collective 1995; Hutchins and Ka'ahumanu 1991; Orndorff 1999). In light of these findings, it is important that the specific experiences and needs of bisexual mental health clients be empirically explored.

To this end, the author distributed a forty-nine-item questionnaire, asking self-identified bisexual women and men about their experiences in mental health services and their suggestions for mental health providers. This article will present an overview of the findings from that study and then discuss some of the themes emerging from the study in more detail, using comments from participants for illustration.

THE STUDY

THE INSTRUMENT AND DISTRIBUTION

Two hundred seventeen self-identified U.S. bisexual women (71 percent) and men (29 percent) responded to the questionnaire, which was distributed via an Internet Web site (42 percent), email (22 percent), and paper (36 percent) circulated at conferences on bisexuality, and snowball distribution via the researcher's network of personal and professional connections. The questionnaire was composed mainly of multiple-choice items. In addition, respondents were encouraged to write comments about their multiple-choice responses as well as to provide open-ended answers to three questions:

1. Respondents' most difficult problem being a bisexual mental health client
2. A description of exemplary services the respondent had experienced, if any
3. Three prioritized suggestions to clinicians

DATA ANALYSIS

Frequencies of multiple-choice responses were computed. Qualitative methods were used to identify six themes drawn from open-ended statements (Miles and Huberman 1994; Smith, Feld, and Franz 1992). Comparisons were made between demographic variables and content responses and statistical tests were conducted, as appropriate. Details of the statistical analyses conducted may be found in a description of the study methodology found in an article published in the *Journal of Bisexuality* (Page 2004).

THE SAMPLE

DEMOGRAPHIC CHARACTERISTICS

On the whole, the sample was similar to other lesbian and gay samples that have been surveyed about their psychotherapy experiences (Bieschke et al. 2000) and to samples of bisexual women and men in studies on bisexual identity (Firestein 1996; Fox 1996). For example, this study contained more female (71 percent) than male (29 percent) subjects and respondents were primarily of European American descent (84 percent) with small numbers of all racial and ethnic minorities represented (16 percent). There were more urban (49 percent) and suburban-based (36 percent) than rural subjects (15 percent), and participants had higher levels of education and lower incomes than overall national norms for the general population (Bieschke et al. 2000).

MENTAL HEALTH CHARACTERISTICS

PRIMARY REASONS FOR SEEKING MENTAL HEALTH SERVICES AND CLINICIAN'S DIAGNOSIS Respondents reported a variety of reasons for seeking mental health services and a variety of diagnoses offered by clinicians to explain their psychological difficulties. Participants sought assistance with *depression* (40 percent), *family or relationship problems* (19 percent), *post-traumatic stress disorder* (10 percent), *anxiety* (7 percent), *issues connected to participants' sexual identity* (6 percent), *an addiction* (4 percent), *issues connected to participant's gender identity* (3 percent), *a suicide attempt* (2 percent), or other reasons (10 percent). Their providers' primary diagnoses included *depression* (38 percent), *generalized anxiety disorder* (10 percent), *post-traumatic stress disorder* (7 percent), and *bipolar disorder* (7 percent), as well as *adjustment disorder, bereavement, sexual* or *gender dysphoria*, and *borderline personality disorder* (< 3 percent each), or *schizophrenia, schizoaffective disorder*, or *dissociative identity disorder* (< 2 percent each).

SERIOUSNESS OF MENTAL HEALTH ISSUES A smaller proportion of respondents had *more serious* (18 percent), as opposed to *more moderate* (82 percent) *mental health issues* than in the overall U.S. population of mental health clients. Large-scale epidemiological studies on the population of the United States have typically found that mental health issues are about equally distributed between more moderate and more serious intensity (U.S. Department of Health and Human Services 1999). A respondent was classified as having more serious clinical issues if they had had one or more of the following experiences: a suicide attempt, participation in residential services, rehabilitation, or day services, or a psychiatric hospitalization. Bisexual women's mental health issues were comparatively more serious than those of bisexual men responding to the survey (33 percent vs. 17 percent). (χ^2 = 5.370, DF = 1, *Fisher's Exact Test, p* = .021). On the other hand, male respondents reported that they experienced issues connected to their sexual orientation as more stressful than did female respondents (χ^2 = 8.775, DF = 4, *Fisher's Exact Test, p* = .0092). In addition, male respondents had sought mental health services for help with sexual orientation issues in greater proportion than had female respondents (χ^2 = 13.5164, DF = 4, *Fisher's Exact Test, p* = .0096).

SEXUAL ORIENTATION CHARACTERISTICS

SELF-IDENTIFICATION AS BISEXUAL Participants self-identified as bisexual: *before fifteen years of age* (18 percent), *between fifteen and nineteen years* (39 percent), *between twenty and thirty years* (30 percent), or *at thirty years or older* (15 percent). Paths of self-identification included *heterosexual and then bisexual* (55 percent), *heterosexual, then lesbian or gay and then bisexual* (13 percent), *lesbian or gay, then bisexual* (10 percent), *bisexual throughout life* (11 percent), and various multiple self-identification sequences (11 percent). These milestones were similar to and slightly younger than those in some previous studies of bisexual identity (Fox 1996) and research on lesbian and gay mental health experiences (Bieschke et al. 2000). This may be attributable to the large portion of this data set that was gathered via electronic means and/or recent reports that bisexual women and men are coming out at earlier ages in recent years (Rust 2001).

IDEAL AND ACTUAL RELATIONSHIP PATTERNS These participants were also similar to those in prior bisexual identity research with respect to their current and ideal relationship arrangements and preferences: nonmonogamous relationships (54 percent) were the preferred ideal over monogamous ones (33 percent), although actual relationship patterns were fairly evenly spread between monogamous (33 percent) and nonmonogamous (33 percent) forms, with a substantial minority of individuals reporting that they were in no relationship at the time of participating in the study (25 percent). The remainder of the sample (8 percent) declined to report their relationship status.

In the next section of the chapter I review the results of the present study with regard to several variables: timing of self-identification as bisexual in relation to an individual's participation in psychotherapy, stress related to bisexuality, disclosure to clinicians, and clients' perceptions of therapist helpfulness with bisexual issues in counseling. Next I review the six themes that emerged from the qualitative data of the study and provide examples of these themes. I also discuss several of these themes based on bisexual clients' reports of their experiences in counseling.

RESULTS

TIMING OF SELF-IDENTIFICATION AS BISEXUAL

Participants first self-identified as bisexual *before* (56 percent), *during* (19 percent), or *after* (16 percent) entering mental health services. A small portion (8 percent) did not recall this information. Only one fifth of participants sought out mental health services for help with an issue having to do with bisexuality (20.3 percent). This may suggest that bisexual clients do not see mental health services as a resource for assistance with sexual orientation issues to the same degree found in prior surveys of lesbian, gay, and bisexual clients (Liddle 1996). Approximately one third of participants had not sought help for concerns having to do with their sexual orientation but found that bisexual issues came up during the course of their counseling (33.6 percent).

STRESS RELATED TO BISEXUALITY

Participants indicated the degree of stress they experienced in relation to bisexuality as *no stress at all* (5.1 percent), *only minor stress* (22.3), *some stress* (39.5 percent) *quite difficult* (27.9 percent), or *the hardest thing in life* (5.1 percent). Men experienced proportionately more stress than women (χ^2 = 8.775, DF = 4, *Fisher's Exact Test*, p = .0092).

DISCLOSURE OF BISEXUALITY TO CLINICIAN AND RATINGS OF CLINICIAN'S ACCEPTANCE

Almost half the participants (47 percent) reported that they *always* let their provider know that they were bisexual, while less than a fifth either *never* (11 percent) or *rarely* (6 percent) disclosed their sexual orientation to their mental health provider. Of those who disclosed their bisexuality to their clinician, most respondents experienced their providers as either *extremely* (27 percent) or *moderately accepting* (62 percent). Participants with more serious mental health issues were significantly less likely than those with more moderate mental health issues to be open about their bisexuality (M = 4.1871, SD = 1.2421 versus M = 3.6774, SD = 1.2251) (*Independent means t-test, t* = 2.758, *p* = .009) and fewer participants with serious mental health problems perceived acceptance for their bisexuality from their providers when they did choose to disclose (M = 4.2190, SD = .8464 versus M = 3.7554, SD = .9502) (*Independent means t-test, t* = −3.201, *p* = .002).

HELPFULNESS WITH BISEXUAL ISSUES

Mean ratings for helpfulness with bisexual issues in participants' most recent course of mental health services were halfway between *neither helpful nor unhelpful* and *somewhat helpful* (N = 212; M = 3.5; SD = 1.11). This is a lower helpfulness rating than indicated by comparable prior research on lesbian, gay, and bisexual clients' psychotherapy experiences (Bieschke et al. 2000; Jones and Gabriel 1999; Page 2002).

THEMES EMPHASIZED IN OPEN-ENDED RESPONSES

Six general themes were identified in participants' open-ended responses:

1. Whether a participant experienced their practitioner as providing validation of their sexual orientation or helping them to achieve greater internal validation of their bisexuality
2. Whether the participant perceived the provider as seeing bisexuality as healthy or unhealthy per se
3. Whether the provider had adequate knowledge of bisexual issues
4. The degree of skill a provider exhibited in assisting their clients with bisexual issues
5. What general therapeutic skills respondents experienced as helpful with their progress in establishing a positive bisexual identity and lifestyle

6. The value and importance of providers intervening proactively in support of bisexual issues

This chapter will discuss several of these themes, using participants' comments to illustrate what bisexual clients perceive as helpful and unhelpful in interacting with their mental health service providers.

THE IMPACT OF A CLINICIAN'S VALIDATION OF BISEXUALITY

There is a strong emphasis in anecdotal reports of bisexual experience of the importance of recognizing bisexuality as a valid, psychologically healthy orientation in its own right, equal in legitimacy with lesbian, gay, and heterosexual orientations (Bisexual Anthology Collective 1995; Hutchins and Ka'ahumanu 1991; Orndorff 1999). This theme has also been emphasized in discourse about affirmative mental health services for bisexual clients (Dworkin 2001; Matteson 1996) and in the *Guidelines for Psychotherapy with Lesbian, Gay, and Bisexual Clients* (American Psychological Association 2003).

The polarization of sexual orientation into a heterosexual/homosexual dichotomy places unique stressors on bisexual youth and adults. Such polarization invalidates bisexuality, and as noted in the report of the APA's Task Force on psychotherapy guidelines, "This view has influenced psychological theory and practice as well as societal institutions." (Division 44/Committee on Lesbian, Gay, and Bisexual Concerns Joint Task Force on Guidelines for Psychotherapy with Lesbian, Gay, and Bisexual Clients 2000:1445).

Participants in this study emphasized the importance of having clinicians validate their bisexuality as real and healthy per se, over any other theme mentioned in the study. They highlighted this in a variety of ways. Respondents were asked to check any of *six biased interventions* they had experienced in their interactions with mental health providers. This list was generated based on prior studies of lesbian and gay psychotherapy clients and expanded to include situations specific to bisexuality (Garnets et al. 1991; Lucksted 1996). The two most frequent examples of biased interventions were 1. erroneously assuming that sexual orientation was connected to a client's clinical goals and 2. confounding bisexuality and pathology in a way that can be seen as invalidating bisexuality (see table 3.1).

Invalidation of bisexuality was also the most emphasized theme in open-ended descriptions provided by participants of *most difficult problem they had faced as bisexual mental health clients*. Furthermore, the importance of validating bisexual identities was the most frequently mentioned *suggestion to clinicians* (see table 3.2).

TABLE 3.1 Examples of Biased Provider Interventions

BIASED INTERVENTIONS	N	%
1. Assumption that sexual orientation is connected to clinical goals, when client does not agree	55	25.3
2. You aren't really bisexual. It's part of your illness	34	15.7
3. To get better: limit interest in the same sex	17	7.8
4. Attempted conversion to heterosexual	16	7.4
5. To get better: limit interest in the other sex	10	4.6
6. Attempted conversion to lesbian or gay	8	3.7

TABLE 3.2 Greatest Problem in Services and Top Suggestion to Clinicians

THEMES	GREATEST PROBLEM IN SERVICES		TOP SUGGESTION TO CLINICIANS	
	N	%	N	%
Validation/Invalidation of Bisexuality	92	42.4	121	55.8
Knowledge/Lack of Knowledge of Bisexual Issues	57	26.3	38	17.5
Views/Doesn't View Bisexuality as Healthy Per Se	42	19.4	44	20.3
Proactive Intervention/Lack of Proactive Intervention	14	6.4	7	3.2
Skill/Lack of Skill with Bisexual Issues	3	1.4	7	3.2
General Clinical Skills	0	0.0	0	0.0
Not Indicated	9	4.0	0	0.0
Total	217	100.0	217	100.0

HOW PARTICIPANTS EXPERIENCED CLINICIANS' INVALIDATION OF THEIR BISEXUALITY

Study participants contributed many examples of clinicians who maintained attitudes of invalidation toward bisexual orientations, including the idea that bisexuality is "nonexistent" or that it is part of a client's pathology. For example, one participant related, "I was almost always told that there was no such sexual orientation as bisexual." Some found that announcing a bisexual identity closed the door to assistance with it: "The counselor in effect told me that my sexual orientation didn't exist and [he] wouldn't help until I'd decided if I was hetero- or homo-sexual."

COUNTERTHERAPEUTIC EFFECTS OF COUNSELOR INVALIDATION

If clinicians do not think of a bisexual orientation or identity as real, they are likely to seek a clinical explanation for why a client experiences both-sex attractions or solicits help with establishing a bisexual lifestyle. Numerous participants' comments in the present study revealed that many practitioners maintain attitudes that are aligned with common negative stereotypes about bisexuality. For instance, one provider associated her client's insecurity about her sexual attractions with other issues about which she was conflicted and saw her client as indecisive: "I've had a therapist tell me that my bisexuality was just one more way that I was trying to avoid making clear choices in my life."

Clinicians may see the client's current relationship as the marker of the client's *true* homo- or hetero-sexual orientation. "[My psychotherapist] ignored my words and thoughts concerning my female friends because I had a boyfriend at the time. It was passed off as a phase." A gay or lesbian clinician may assume the client reporting bisexual feelings as being in transition to a lesbian or gay identity. One respondent wrote: "My first [therapist, a lesbian,] was very accepting as long as it was on her terms (meaning as long as I was gay and not bisexual)."

An assumption that both-sex attraction is not a valid sexual orientation may also lead to errors in diagnosis and treatment planning. For example, a practitioner may erroneously confound other issues being addressed in the therapy with the client's bisexual orientation: "[I was told] that my dysfunctional sexual orientation was simply ambiguous feelings related to my dysfunctional family upbringing" or, in the words of another participant, "[My biggest problem was] being told that my sexuality is a manifestation of problems with men." If a client is uncomfortable with his or her newly acknowledged attractions to more than one sex, a well-meaning but misinformed clinician may reinforce his or her hesitancy under the guise of empathetic support: "[The clinician said] 'one experience doesn't make you bi' and what I felt was the counselor's need to reassure me vs. my need to be told I was straight."

A provider who interprets same-sex and other-sex attractions as a manifestation of pathology and/or immaturity would be quite likely to have a negative impact on that client's self- esteem and self-confidence, possibly compounding, rather than alleviating, mental health symptoms like depression and anxiety. Furthermore, when mental health providers reinforce the same prejudices a bisexual individual encounters in society, the bisexual individual is likely to avoid seeking help in the future from mental health service providers. In addition, those seeking help with other issues would be less likely to be open with their provider about a bisexual orientation if they perceive or fear the provider will react negatively to it. This can lead to the omission of information that may be crucial to positive therapeutic outcomes.

In this study, a woman wrote: "I thought I might want to talk to this therapist about bisexual issues when I first went for therapy. She made a comment that one could be 'either straight or gay' . . . meant to convey her openness about orientation but [this was] uncomfortable to me to hear." This woman indicated that she was currently in A *primary sexual partner/relationship while secretly sexual with one or more others*. She also indicated that her ideal relationship would be to be "in a primary relationship with her sexual partner and *openly* sexual with one or more others," i.e., in an honest, consensual polyamorous relationship. She may have wanted assistance with issues such as coming out, negotiating open relationships, choosing relationship partners, and enhancing a positive bisexual identity. When the clinician voiced an invalidating viewpoint about bisexuality, she denied her client the safety to ask for help with these issues.

THE POSITIVE IMPACT OF VALIDATION

Numerous research participants also talked about the beneficial effects of a clinician's validating stance toward bisexuality. One put it very simply: "The [counselors] I have stayed with were accepting." A more detailed example illustrates the subtleties, complexities, and impact that acceptance and validation can have on a bisexual client. The respondent said she was "married and bisexual" and that her "spouse does not know—only a very few friends know." She reported, "Initially, my only reason for seeking help was to address issues regarding my bisexuality; however, through several sessions I realized that I needed to deal with other issues (abusive mother), in order to understand my bisexuality." Her ideal relationship was *having a committed relationship with my husband and a long-term relationship with a woman that my husband "approves of."* She was currently in a committed relationship with her husband and "secretly sexual" with one or more other people. She wrote:

[My counselor] has in no way "judged" me regarding my relationship(s)—she is very sincere, and committed to helping me find myself. . . . She accepts me for who I am and is trying to help me accept me for myself. She has helped me find ways of communicating with my husband and of experiencing my bisexuality without leaving my marriage. Being met with nonjudgment and openness has been a very healing experience.

Another participant, who rated her services highly, had been in a relationship with another woman for six years and had considered herself a lesbian. She wrote:

> Emotionally I FELT bisexual, but felt forced to make a choice. For a long time I considered myself as solely lesbian despite my continued attraction to men. . . . Initially, my sexuality was not my primary preoccupation in therapy. However, it came up in terms of my attachment to certain people in my life in terms of what was or wasn't "permissible" as well as in terms of recognizing, admitting, and handling desire.

She reports that her clinician's supportive and nonjudgmental stance made it easier for her to accept her desire for men and thereby increase her overall level of self-acceptance. The validating stance of these clinicians enabled them to access crucial experiences and details of the client's process, enhancing the client's self-esteem and self-confidence, and simultaneously creating a safe environment for helping the client solve sexual-orientation-related challenges that otherwise might never have been addressed in the therapy.

THE NEED FOR ACCURATE KNOWLEDGE OF BISEXUAL ISSUES

Validation of a client's bisexuality is a necessary but not sufficient condition for therapists who wish to address the many challenges specific to establishing and living a positive bisexual identity. Accurate knowledge about bisexual identity is another prerequisite for such detailed assistance. This includes knowledge of the variability and fluidity of sexual attractions (Fox 1996; Rust 1996) as well as the variability of relationship patterns preferred and engaged in by bisexual individuals (Rust 1996). It also includes sensitivity to the impact of cultural bias, not only from the society at large but also experienced on occasion from the lesbian and gay community who sometimes interpret a bisexual orientation as a threat (Rust 1993; Esterberg 1997).

IMPACT OF CLINICIANS' LACK OF KNOWLEDGE

The frustration of not being able to find knowledgeable clinicians came across in numerous participant comments. One wrote: "I screened many therapists over the phone and found many to be clueless or openly uncomfortable with bisexuality. Of course, I didn't go to them." The suggestion made by another betrays her frustration (via sarcasm) when she tells providers to "not flinch; have enough exposure in their own personal friendships to be relaxed about the topic. And, geeze, get online and pretend to learn the scene if you have to."

Some participants spoke about providers who extrapolated from personal experience rather than seeking out accurate information about bisexual identity. One respondent commented:

> I think that I wanted to deal with this issue more than I had realized when entering therapy. My [heterosexual] therapist had . . . one experience of an attraction to a woman and assumed experiences based on this. Her guidance was sometimes clearly related to her own personal experiences and is very different from my own. She called me a "swinger."

Others contributed examples of therapist misconceptions due to incomplete information about bisexuality. A man who rated a course of services as *mostly unhelpful* with his bisexuality commented: "I was having issues with my then partner, a bisexual woman, who had had an affair with another woman, and my therapist couldn't understand that bisexuality meant different things to different people and wasn't simply 'it doesn't matter what gender someone is.'"

BENEFITS OF ACCURATE INFORMATION AND SKILL WITH BISEXUAL ISSUES

With accurate information about bisexuality, a clinician can help a client transform negative misconceptions related to her/his orientation that affect self-esteem. One respondent described how a clinician helped him let go of the stereotype that all bisexuals are equally attracted to both sexes. He rated this psychotherapist as *extremely helpful,* commenting: "She made me realize that a person could be truly bisexual with leanings more toward one than the other. That's when I really started dealing with what I was." A clinician who is informed about bisexual issues can understand the subtle impact of bias: "I sometimes fear that people are interested in me because of the 'oddness' of my bisexuality and their fantasies thereof [*sic*]. It affects my self esteem. My therapist understands that it affects my trust in the motivation of others in sexual situations."

Knowledge of the variations in bisexual relational styles can enable clinicians to assist bisexual clients with solving the challenges that monogamous and nonmonogamous (polyamorous) relationships present for bisexual individuals. For example, one participant wrote: "The therapist didn't seem to think that it would be impossible to be in multiple relationships at the same time." Another wrote: "I was involved in a triad and pretty defensive about it. My therapist [got] across that 3 people = 7 relationships, i.e., many more than a couple . . . more chances for problems." A third participant shared, "I experienced the breakup of a polyamorous relationship this fall. My depressed mood and problems in my primary relationship were why I started seeing a counselor. . . . [My counselor] realized I was grieving the breakup of the poly relationship . . . it was a 'real relationship' to him."

Many bisexual women and men see themselves as monogamous. Some of these individuals seek help exploring issues connected to the choice of a partner: "[Wanting to have] a counselor help me find a way to be in a relationship of any kind without preconception of who (what gender) my partner would be. I wanted a close relationship but am exploring what that would be like with a woman versus with a man." Others are partnered and seeking help with how their bisexual identity can fit into their relationship in a way that feels authentic. There are a myriad of challenges that both-sex attracted individuals face in claiming and living their unique version of bisexuality. Regardless of whether bisexual clients seek help with monogamous or nonmonogamous relationships, coming out at work, or support for coming out to members of their family of origin, knowledge and skill are essential prerequisites for optimal mental health services outcomes.

GENERAL THERAPEUTIC QUALITIES EXPERIENCED AS HELPFUL BY BISEXUAL CLIENTS

The second most frequent type of exemplary service mentioned by participants was a therapist with strong general therapeutic skills. Acceptance, understanding, supportiveness, and confidence in the trajectory of the client's unfolding process as healthy and moving in a positive direction are paramount to successful therapeutic work with bisexual clients (see table 3.2). Clinicians with well-developed therapeutic skills can assist bisexual clients to gain self confidence, resiliency, and an ability to negotiate the complex layers of interface between their sexual identity, their personal networks, and the culture at large. A bisexual woman wrote: "She refers to me as a person—an individual—rather than a sexual 'sample.' Her attitude makes me feel less fearful and abnormal and [able] to recognize when other people also don't consider my bisexuality an 'issue.'" Another wrote:

> My therapist is very supportive of my sexuality. She has manifested it in her acceptance of my "emotional rollercoasting" between my lover (female) and my best friend (male and gay) and tries to help me work THROUGH my emotional doubts rather than around it. It is more her attitude than any specific action she has undertaken that make[s] me feel comfortable and safe.

A third respondent wrote: "She is nonjudgmental, supportive and positive. She encourages me to celebrate all that is me."

THE NEED FOR PROACTIVE INTERVENTIONS

Of the sixty (28 percent) respondents who provided examples of exemplary interventions, the most frequent examples given were of service providers *intervening proactively in affirmation of bisexuality* (n = 18). Theories about affirmative psychotherapy for lesbian and gay clients suggest that active interventions are needed with minority sexual orientation clients to counteract the external and internalized impact of social stigma (Browning, Reynolds, and Dworkin 1991; Fassinger 2000). Participants in this study contributed the full spectrum of suggestions noted in that literature, ranging from challenging a client's internalized homophobic or biphobic thinking, to providing empirically-based information and community resources, to engaging in social activism at the level of advocating for bisexual issues with professional colleagues and within society as a whole.

THE IMPACT OF AN OVERLY PASSIVE APPROACH

Given the pervasiveness of antigay and antibisexual bias, a therapist's silence or lack of seriousness about sexual orientation issues may be perceived as hostile or uncaring to the client. One woman wrote:

> My therapist's lack of conversation at times I talked about coming out difficulties left me feeling vulnerable and unsupported. She was a lesbian and it was hard not to interpret her silence as disapproval and . . . [sic] the invisibility of the issue. I was in treatment to get help with things I felt vulnerable about, so it would have been particularly helpful to have someone be more proactive about this issue.

By failing to create a safe space to discuss bisexual issues, a practitioner may miss information crucial to accurate diagnosis and goal-setting. One participant seemed to feel that her depression stemmed from barriers she faced to fully realizing a personally-congruent bisexual identity, but did not feel that she had the clinician's support to address this within her therapy. This respondent noted, "The therapist told my husband (in his session alone) that a long term affair I had was probably due to the depression . . . but nothing has ever been said (by me) regarding my bisexuality."

THE POSITIVE IMPACT OF PROACTIVE INTERVENTIONS

In order to be helpful, a clinician needs to embrace a frame of reference that clearly recognizes the stigmatizing societal attitudes that may be influencing her bisexual and questioning clients. The proactive therapist respectfully offers inquiries, comments, and suggestions using that frame, while honoring her client's expressed priorities and pacing. One participant summed it up in the following way: "[What I really need from a counselor is] serious good questions helping me explore issues of my sexuality and what it means to me." Another participant made comments that illustrate the positive effect of having a therapist who did not shy away from discussing bisexual issues when they were raised in the session: "I didn't feel it was 'important enough' to discuss in therapy (especially compared to things like abuse), but it came up and was helpful to discuss. Since then, I have been more active in bringing up issues related to bisexuality in therapy and I now view it as one of the reasons that I am in therapy."

For a client who comes to therapy to deal with traumatic experiences, or other serious issues, a bisexual identity about which he/she feels positive may seem like an area of relative contentment that doesn't need to be examined in therapy. However, given that society as a whole still either ignores or criticizes bisexuality, it is likely that most individuals having same- and other-sex attractions are still affected negatively in some ways. Thus, for bisexual clients, it is particularly important for clinicians to proactively demonstrate interest, curiosity, appreciation, and support toward clients who may be exploring any areas having to do with fluidity or difference of sexual attraction, behavior or relationship patterns. One participant described an intervention in which her therapist raised the issue using a proactive approach that signaled affirmation and support.

I wasn't even planning to talk to my therapist about my bisexuality because, in twenty-odd years of therapy with . . . I don't know HOW many therapists I have barely found any who didn't get weird if they heard about me being attracted to women, much less . . . well I didn't risk trying them out on the Bi Thing. This woman just dropped these little remarks like . . . "If you could have the perfect relationship would he . . . or she . . . or maybe there'd be a he and a she . . . " It was like she just talked like any version of attractions [was] the most normal thing going!! And before I knew it, I found myself talking about my bisexuality as though it was normal too. What a relief!

In summary, when participants in the present study were asked to describe barriers they had experienced to effective mental health care, they tended to emphasize the concerns found in both clinical theory and anecdotal reports: a lack of validation for bisexuality as authentic and healthy. However, when asked to describe their best mental health experiences, their writing emphasized situations in which clinicians took action to make them feel safe to discuss their bisexual issues and, through these discussions, helped them gain greater skill and confidence in constructing and living their own unique bisexual lives.

SUGGESTIONS FOR CLINICIANS

A growing body of research and literature exists about how to conduct affirmative therapy with lesbian and gay clients (D'Augelli and Patterson 1995; Greene and Croom 2000; Perez, DeBord, and Bieschke 2000; Ritter and Terndrup 2002). In the present study clients provided descriptions of harmful and exemplary interventions as well as guidance for therapists working with bisexual women and men in the context of delivering mental health services. Foremost among these suggestions are the importance of validating bisexual identity and viewing bisexuality within an affirmative framework that emphasizes bisexuality as one among several healthy sexual orientation identities.

Participants also made other suggestions relevant to clinicians. First, clinicians need to apply the basic tools used in all good clinical practice, including respect, empathy, positive inquisitiveness, and a "bias" in favor of the client's uniquely unfolding development. Second, therapists and counselors need to challenge themselves and their clients by taking an active stance toward bisexual issues, inquiring about possible sexual orientation issues more actively than they might typically inquire with heterosexually oriented clients. Third, therapists need to remain alert to ways that bisexual clients may have internalized cultural bias deeply into their sense of self and their sense of well-being. Fourth, it is valuable for counselors to use creative approaches to strengthen the client's positive self-identity.

Finally, participants emphasized the necessity of reaching out to offer information and resources to clients and to professional colleagues who may not even realize yet that they need this information. In order to perform these latter tasks, of course, clinicians need take the time to become accurately informed about local community resources, using tools such as the Bisexual Resources Guide (Ochs 2001), and to become well-acquainted with the expanding base of information that is already available about many aspects of the bisexual experience (Fox 2004).

SUGGESTIONS FOR FURTHER RESEARCH

The present study provides a preliminary understanding of the issues and mental health service needs of bisexual women and men. As the responses of a convenience sample of 217 same-and-other-sex-attracted women and men at a particular point in time, it cannot be assumed to represent the experiences or suggestions of all bisexual clients. Many more studies addressing numerous aspects of this topic are needed before anything approaching *empirically sound* suggestions to clinicians can be established.

The following are some of the questions that future studies might address. How can students in counseling, clinical graduate programs, and practicing clinicians learn about the bisexual experience in the most efficient and practical way? What aspects of establishing a positive sexual identity are unique to the bisexual experience? What interventions are most effective in assisting bisexual women and men with this process? What barriers do bisexual women and men confront in creating relationships that work for them? What do clinicians need to know to help bisexual clients with relationship and family issues?

Do bisexual clients with more serious mental health issues have different needs from those with more moderate clinical issues? How can practitioners go about the complex task of teasing out what mental health challenges stem from the impact of cultural bias toward bisexuality and difficulties a client may experience with her bisexual orientation due to depression, for example, or the effects of psychological trauma? And last, but by no means least, what stances are optimal for clinicians to take with regard to their colleagues and society as a whole to benefit their bisexual clients?

There is a great deal that knowledgeable and skilled mental health providers can do to assist bisexual clients to identify, claim, and flourish in their lives as well as to gain the self-esteem and well-being these services are intended to provide to them. There is also much providers can do to assist everyone to understand bisexual women and men in all the personal and professional venues that make up our twenty-first-century world. It is time to get busy building the solid empirical base from which providers can make that contribution.

REFERENCES

American Counseling Association. (1996). ACA code of ethics and standards of practice. In B. Herlihy and G. Corey (Eds.), ACA ethical standards casebook (5th ed.) (pp. 26–59). Alexandria, VA: American Counseling Association.

American Psychiatric Association. (1974). Position statement on homosexuality and civil rights. American Journal of Psychiatry, 131, 497.

American Psychological Association. (2003). Guidelines for psychotherapy with lesbian, gay, and bisexual clients. In L. D. Garnets and D. C. Kimmel (Eds.), Psychological perspectives on lesbian, gay, and bisexual experiences (2d ed.) (pp. 756–785). New York: Columbia.

American Psychological Association. (1998). Appropriate therapeutic responses to sexual orientation in the proceedings of the American Psychological Association, Incorporated, for the legislative year 1997. American Psychologist, 53(8), 882–939.

American Psychological Association Division 44/Committee on Lesbian, Gay, and Bisexual Concerns Joint Task Force on Guidelines for Psychotherapy with Lesbian, Gay, and Bisexual Clients. (2000). Guidelines for psychotherapy with lesbian, gay, and bisexual clients. American Psychologist, 55(12), 1440–1451.

Balsam, K. F., and Rothblum, E. D. (2002). Sexual orientation and mental health: A comparison of adult siblings. Paper presented at the 110th Annual Convention of the American Psychological Association, Chicago.

Bieschke, K. J., McClanahan, M., Tozer, E., Grzegorek, J. L., and Park, J. (2000). Programmatic research on the treatment of lesbian, gay, and bisexual clients: The past, the present, and the course for the future. In R. M. Perez, K. A. DeBord and K. J. Bieschke (Eds.), *Handbook of counseling and psychotherapy with lesbian, gay and bisexual clients* (pp. 309–336). Washington, DC: American Psychological Association.

Bisexual Anthology Collective. (1995). *Plural desires: Writing bisexual women's realities.* Toronto: Sister Vision Black Women and Women of Colour.

Browning, C., Reynolds, S. L., and Dworkin, S. H. (1991). Affirmative psychotherapy for lesbian women. *Counseling Psychologist 19,* 177–196.

Chung, Y. B., and Katayama, M. (1996). Assessment of sexual orientation in lesbian/gay/ bisexual studies. *Journal of Homosexuality, 30*(4) 49–64.

Cochran, S. D., Sullivan, J. G., and Mays, V. M. (2003). Prevalence of mental disorders, psychological distress, and mental services use among lesbian, gay, and bisexual adults in the United States. *Journal of Consulting and Clinical Psychology, 71*(1) 53–61.

Conger, J. (1975). Proceedings of the American Psychological Association, Incorporated, for the year 1974: Minutes of the annual meeting of the Council of Representatives. *American Psychologist, 30,* 620–651.

D'Augelli, A. R., and Patterson, C. J. (Eds.) (1995). *Lesbian, gay, and bisexual identities over the lifespan: Psychological perspectives.* New York: Oxford University Press.

Drescher, J. (1998). I'm your handyman: A history of reparative therapies. *Journal of Homosexuality, 36*(1), 19–42.

Dworkin, S. (2001). Treating the bisexual client. *Journal of Clinical Psychology, 57*(5), 671–680.

Esterberg, K. G. (1997). Gay cultures, gay communities: The social organization of lesbians, gay men, and bisexuals. In R. C. Savin-Williams and K. M. Cohen (Eds.), *The lives of lesbians, gays, and bisexuals: Children to adults* (pp. 377–392). Fort Worth: Texas: Harcourt Brace.

Fassinger, R. E. (2000). Applying counseling theories to lesbian, gay and bisexual clients: Pitfalls and possibilities. In R. M. Perez, K. A. DeBord and K. J. Bieschke (Eds.), *Handbook of counseling and psychotherapy with lesbian, gay and bisexual clients* (pp. 107–132). Washington, DC: American Psychological Association.

Firestein, B. A. (Ed.) (1996). *Bisexuality: The psychology and politics of an invisible minority.* Thousand Oaks, CA: Sage.

Fox, R. C. (1996). Bisexuality in perspective: A review of theory and research. In B. A. Firestein (Ed.), *Bisexuality: The psychology and politics of an invisible minority* (pp. 3–50). Newbury Park, CA: Sage.

Fox, R. C. (2004). Bisexuality: A reader's guide to the socials science literature. *Journal of Bisexuality, 3*(3/4) 161–254.

Garnets, L., Hancock, K. A., Cochran, S. E., Goodchilds, J., and Peplau, L. A. (1991). Issues in psychotherapy with lesbians and gay men: A survey of psychologists. *American Psychologist, 46,* 964–972.

Greene, B., and Croom, G. L. (Eds.) (2000). *Education, research, and practice in lesbian, gay, bisexual, and transgendered psychology: A resource manual.* Thousand Oaks: Sage.

Heid, R. J. (2000). The relationship between sexual orientation, psychologist attitudes, and perception of psychotherapeutic prognosis. Doctoral Dissertation: Temple University, UMI: Sep Vol. 61(3-B) 1637.

Hutchins, L., and Ka'ahumanu, L. (Eds.) (1991). *Bi any other name: Bisexual people speak out*. Boston: Alyson.

Jones, M.A., and Gabriel, M.A. (1999). Utilization of psychotherapy by lesbians, gay men, and bisexuals: Findings from a nationwide survey. *American Journal of Orthopsychiatry*, 69(2), 209–219.

Jorm, A.F., Korten, A.E., Rodgers, B., Jacomb, P.A., and Christensen, H. (2002). Sexual orientation and mental health: Results from a community survey of young and middle-aged adults. *British Journal of Psychiatry*, 180, 423–427.

Lebolt, J. (1999). Gay affirmative psychotherapy: A phenomenological study. *Clinical Social Work Journal*, 27, 355–370.

Liddle, B.J. (1996). Therapist sexual orientation, gender and counseling practices as they relate to ratings of helpfulness by gay and lesbian clients. *Journal of Counseling Psychology*, 43, 394–401.

Lucksted, A. (1996). *Lesbian and bisexual women who are mental health care consumers: Experiences in the mental health system*. Paper presented at the Annual Conference of the Association of Women in Psychology, March, Portland.

Matteson, D.R. (1996). Counseling and psychotherapy with bisexual and exploring clients. In B.A. Firestein (Ed.), *Bisexuality: The psychology and politics of an invisible minority* (pp. 185–213). Thousand Oaks, CA: Sage.

Miles, M.B., and Huberman, A. M. (1994). *Qualitative data analysis: An expanded sourcebook* (2d ed.). Thousand Oaks, CA: Sage.

Moss, J.F. (1994). The heterosexual bias inventory (HBI): Gay, lesbian and bisexual clients' perceptions of heterosexual bias in psychotherapy. (Doctoral dissertation, Michigan State University, Lansing, MI). *Dissertation Abstracts International*, 55(12), 5571-B.

National Association of Social Workers. (1996). Code of ethics of the National Association of Social Workers Retrieved online on April 19, 1997, at http://www.socialworkers.org/pubs/code/default.arp.

Nystrom, N.M. (1997). Oppression by mental health providers: A report by gay men and lesbians about their treatment. *Dissertation Abstracts International*, 58(6), 2394A.

Ochs, R. (Ed.) (2001). *Bisexual resource guide* (4th ed.). Cambridge: Bisexual Resource Center.

Orndorff, K. (Ed.) (1999). *Bi lives: Bisexual women tell their stories*. Tucson: See Sharp.

Page, E.H. (2002). Mental health treatment experiences of self-identified bisexual women and bisexual men (pp. 102–105). (Doctoral dissertation, Antioch New England Graduate School, Keene, NH). *Dissertation Abstracts International*, 63(9), 4382B.

Page, E.H., (2004). Mental health services experiences of bisexual women and bisexual men: An empirical study. *Journal of Bisexuality*. 3(3/4), 137–160.

Perez, R.M., DeBord, K.A., and Bieschke, K.J. (Eds.) (2000). *Handbook of counseling and psychotherapy with lesbian, gay and bisexual clients*. Washington, DC: American Psychological Association.

Ritter, K.Y., and Terndrup, A.I. (2002). *Handbook of affirmative psychotherapy with lesbians and gay men*. New York: Guilford.

Rust, P.C., (1993). "Coming out" in the age of social constructionism: Sexual identity formation among lesbian and bisexual women. *Gender and Society*, 7(1) 57–77.

Rust, P.C. (1996). Monogamy and polyamory: Relationship issues for bisexuals. In B.A. Firestein (Ed.), *Bisexuality: The psychology and politics of an invisible minority*. (pp. 127–148). Newbury Park, CA: Sage.

Rust, P. C. (2001). Two many and not enough: The meanings of bisexual identities. *Journal of Bisexuality*, 1(1), 31–68.

Smith, C. P., Feld, S. C., and Franz, C. E. (1992). Methodological considerations: Steps in research employing content analysis systems. In C. P. Smith and J. W. Atkinson (Eds.), *Motivation and personality: Handbook of thematic core analysis* (pp. 515–536). New York: Cambridge University.

U.S. Department of Health and Human Services. (1999). *Mental health: A report of the Surgeon General*. Rockville, MD: U.S. Department of Health and Human Services.

4

WHAT'S IN A NAME?

WHY WOMEN EMBRACE OR RESIST BISEXUAL IDENTITY

Robyn Ochs

SOME WOMEN have relatively simple stories. They may meet their romantic partner in their youth, bond strongly, and mate for life. At least in terms of sexual orientation, this can result in a relatively simple narrative. Others have had multiple sexual and/or romantic attractions, but toward people of only one sex. These individuals too face a relatively simple task when describing their sexual orientation.

But many women's stories are less straightforward (pun intended). They may have experienced attraction toward or had sexual or romantic experiences with people of more than one sex. They may be attracted to the qualities of androgyny, masculinity, or femininity in an individual, regardless of the person's biological sex (Levitt and Bridges, chapter 16). Or they may find themselves attracted to gender-queer, intersex, or transgendered individuals who simply do not fit into binary categories (see Horner, chapter 15; Denny, chapter 14).

Why do some women with attractions toward people of more than one sex embrace a bisexual identity, and others resist it? How do we label or describe our sexual orientation? Is it even necessary or desirable to self-label? Lives are complex narratives, existing over time and on various levels. Is there any one word that can adequately describe a person's sexual orientation? For some, the answer is "yes," for others, "no," and for yet others, the answer is "to some extent."

In the present chapter I outline the experiences of bisexual women, focusing on the realities of oppression as it manifests in the forms of external homophobia, heterosexism, external biphobia, and internalized biphobia that compromise our ability to freely and comfortably self-identify. I explore the reasons that some women resist or decline a bisexual label, reasons that may or may not stem from internalized biphobia: some women simply prefer a different label or see the bisexual label as inadequate or problematic. I will explore why other women choose a bisexual identity despite these myriad difficulties. Finally, I suggest ways to foster mutual respect between those who choose a bisexual identity and those who resist or decline one as well as to arrive at a nuanced and mature understanding of bisexual—and other—identities.

THE ROLES OF HOMOPHOBIA AND BIPHOBIA

THE BIG PICTURE

Identity development involves a complex process of interaction with our environment. Every woman inhabits a different body and occupies a specific geographic, temporal, and interpersonal environment. We have our own experiences, our own thoughts, our own desires. Furthermore, we exist over time, and our experiences may be dramatically different at different points in our lives. To this constellation we assign meaning. We interpret and name ourselves.

We do not choose our identities in a vacuum. We are given, based upon our individual context, a menu of options, and a system of feedback, punishment, and reinforcement. How we interpret ourselves is in part dependent upon the tools available (Bower, Gurevich, and Mathieson 2002). Our imagination is limited by our environment, by our culture, by our vocabulary, and by our experience (Fox 1991). Furthermore, we not only interpret and name ourselves (self-identity); we are constantly interpreted and named by others (ascribed identity), resulting in a complex negotiation between an individual and those around her. Even the most independent individual cannot help but be affected by external feedback. And sexual orientation—like sex, gender identification, and race—is what Allport (1954) calls a "label of primary potency," a label that is seen to be of such significance that it overshadows other labels applied to the same individual and is thus assigned disproportional importance. Thus, our sexual orientation identities *matter*.

Individuals in society are punished and rewarded based upon our perceived majority or minority group status (Greene 2003; Ochs and Deihl 1992). We are either given preferential treatment or denied our fair share. Furthermore, dominant identities are universalized: they are seen as natural, normal, and unproblematic. When we assert a nondominant identity, we often encounter surprise and disbelief, and our assertions can be perceived as threatening—an aggressive challenge to the status quo. Furthermore, the visibility or invisibility of a particular minority population directly affects its members' experience of oppression (Greene 2003; Ochs 1996). Members of a visually identifiable group can easily identify each other and can be easily targeted by others. Those with visible and invisible identities have qualitatively different experiences of prejudice and oppression, though none escapes the effects of stereotyping (Greene 2003).

Members of groups with invisible identities, such as bisexuals or lesbians, have the advantage of not being easily identifiable, which may in certain contexts protect us from discrimination (Ochs 1996). However, we have the disadvantage of not being able to readily identify other members of our own group. Both minority and majority people are likely to assume that everyone else—until proven otherwise—is in the majority, resulting in a gross underestimation of the size of these minority groups. One bisexual college sophomore I was introduced to in 2001 exclaimed, "You are the first grown-up bisexual I've ever met!" As she grew up in a medium-sized town and attended a large university, this was surely not the case, but she had been unable to "see" any of the others.

In addition, the "privilege" of passing also carries as its counterweight the onus of having to actively announce our identity to avoid incorrect assumptions as well as feelings of guilt or discomfort that may arise when we are silent. If we are silent, we are subject to misinterpretation, invisibility, and even the perception that we do not exist. We carry the weight of constantly having to make the decision of how and when to come out—and at what cost. It is also important to remember we are each members of numerous identity groups. We simultaneously have racial, ethnic, religious, political, gender, sex, sexual orientation identities and other identities (Firestein 2007; Rust 1996). To further complicate reality, many of us have complex identities within a given category. For example, someone may have Mexican and Chinese ancestry; and the identity lesbian can be both a description of one's sexual orientation and a social and political category (Rust 2000). Our identities in one category affect our construction or experience of other categories, resulting in identities that are a complex, multi-dimensional tapestry (Rust 1996).

BIPHOBIA, HOMOPHOBIA AND HETEROSEXISM

Biphobia is fear of the other and fear of the space between our categories.

—OCHS AND DEIHL 1992:69

Biphobia shares many characteristics with other forms of oppression, especially homophobia and heterosexism,[1] and women who are attracted to people of more than one sex, regardless of how we identify, generally experience our share of all three (Ochs 1996; Ochs and Deihl 1992). This oppression may take a number of forms, ranging from social prejudices to name-calling and antigay violence, to discrimination in housing, employment or public accommodations, to the devaluation of our same-sex relationships, to legislation resulting in second-class citizenship (Blumenfeld 1992).

How does oppression affect sexual minorities? Allport (1954) lays out multiple ways in which individuals respond negatively to stigmatization that he calls "traits due to victimization" (p. 142). Of special importance to the discussion of biphobia are two of these characteristics: aggression and blame directed at our own group and prejudice and discrimination directed against other minorities. This may assist us in understanding theoretically two phenomena frequently observed in sexual minority populations: 1. internalized homophobia and biphobia and 2. hostility directed at bisexuals and transgender people by some lesbians and gay men. Individuals may act out feelings of victimization through anger toward and rejection of those within or outside our group who are perceived as even less acceptable than ourselves (Blasingame 1992). One reason for this is the fear that these people who are even more marginal will give lesbians and gay men an even worse image than that which they already hold in the eyes of the dominant culture, further impeding the struggle for acceptance and legal equality. Paradoxically, hostility may also be directed at individuals perceived as *less* marginalized: they may be called to task for not having suffered as much as their peers (Herek 2002). Bisexuals may be considered too queer or not queer enough (Esterberg 1997).

There is debate within LGBT communities over where biphobia and homophobia/heterosexism overlap and where they differ. I contend that there is both considerable overlap between homophobia/heterosexism and biphobia as well as specific ways in which each is unique. Furthermore, homophobia/ heterosexism and biphobia affect men and women differently, both as subject and as object (Ochs 1996).

How do biphobia and homophobia/heterosexism overlap? It is obvious that a homophobic school board will fire a bisexual teacher, not place her on half-time status because she identifies publicly as bisexual rather than lesbian. Visible bisexual women, like visible lesbians, may be targeted for discrimination. The key factor is not whether we are bisexual or lesbian but whether our minority status is known (Ochs 1996; Ochs and Deihl 1992).

Another area of congruence between the experience of biphobia and the experience of homophobia may be with respect to "coming out" issues. A bisexual woman coming to terms with her same-sex attraction is likely to experience shame, ambivalence, and discomfort similar to that experienced by lesbians (Fox 1991). Both homosexuality and bisexuality are denied and distorted. Furthermore, people in the general population, as well as professionals, lack accurate information about both homosexuality and bisexuality (Dworkin 2000; Firestein 1996). In fact, these two identity groups are actually rather fluid and tend to have considerable overlap (Bower, Gurevich, and Mathieson 2002). Many bisexually-identified women have in the past considered themselves to be lesbian, and many lesbians have in the past considered themselves to be bisexual, and individuals may use different words to describe similar narratives (Esterberg 1997; Rust 1995, Rust, chapter 1). Fox (1995) found in his study of 835 bisexually identified people that 38.3 percent of women had previously identified as lesbian or gay. Rust (1992, 1995) maintains that the line between lesbians and bisexual women is blurry and that the two identities in fact overlap.

In summary, invisibility, isolation, and oppression are experiences shared by bisexual women and lesbians in the United States. Any visible sexual minority may be a target of oppression, and each suffers internally when forced to remain silent.

EXTERNAL BIPHOBIA

A primary manifestation of biphobia is denial of the very existence of bisexual people. We live in a culture that thinks in binary categories, with each category having its mutually exclusive opposite. Thus, those of us whose sexual orientation, sex, or gender defies simple labeling create profound discomfort simply by making our existence known. This is a major root of the hostility directed toward bisexual and transgender persons (Alexander and Yescavage 2004).

Bisexuals are pressured to remain silent about our existence because a great deal is at stake. Our silence allows the dominant culture to exaggerate the differences between heterosexual and homosexual and to ignore the fact that human sexuality exists on a continuum (Ochs and Deihl 1992). There is considerable anxiety in being forced to acknowledge that the "other" may not be quite as different from you as you might wish.

Binary thinking renders bisexuals invisible and contributes to biphobia (Ochs and Deihl 1992). A quiet bisexual will be assumed to be either heterosexual or homosexual. To avoid being mislabeled, a bisexual woman must declare her bisexuality and risk being seen as aggressively and inappropriately flaunting her orientation, an experience shared by other sexual minorities. Otherwise, bisexuality only becomes visible as a point of conflict. Bisexuality becomes visible *as bisexuality* only in the context of complicated, uncomfortable situations: a woman leaves her husband for another woman; a woman leaves a lesbian relationship for a male lover. Often, when bisexuality is given attention, it is portrayed as a transitional category, an interim stage in an original or subsequent coming out process, usually from heterosexual to homosexual (Bower, Gurevich, and Mathieson 2002; Fox 1996). This has the effect of associating bisexuality in many people's minds with conflict and impermanence. Bisexuals whose lives are noncontroversial are the least visible.

And the word *bisexual* itself can be problematic. Many people struggling to understand bisexuality can only imagine the concept of bisexuality as a fifty-fifty identity. In their minds, if a third category exists, it must fall midway between the other two. They struggle to fix bisexuals in the middle of the scale, further assuming that if bisexuality is a fifty-fifty identity there are very few "true" bisexuals.

Lesbians sometimes see an insistence on a bisexual identity as a holding back, a failure to declare full allegiance to the "community" (Bower, Gurevich, and Mathieson 2002; Esterberg 1997; Rust 1995). This is similar to the response by some people who identify as African American to those who identify as bi- and multiracial (Blasingame 1992; Funderburg 1994). Instead of being understood as an insistence on claiming one's full self, it may be viewed as an attempt to opt out of the more oppressed group (see Scott, chapter 11). Like so many stereotypes, this may be true of some individuals but certainly is not true of all. In fact, for many, coming out and declaring a bisexual or biracial identity requires a great deal of courage.

INTERNALIZED BIPHOBIA

Biphobia does not only come from the outside. Internalized biphobia can be powerful, sometimes overpowering, and the experience of isolation, illegitimacy, shame, and confusion felt by many bisexuals can be disempowering, even disabling (Fox 1991; Ochs 1996; Page 2004). What contributes to internalized biphobia and how does it manifest?

Even today, with modest improvements in this area, bisexual individuals have few role models (Firestein 2007). Though there has been some improvement, bisexuals are rarely mentioned or represented in mainstream or in the lesbian and gay media and when we are mentioned, it is often in a negative context (Ochs and Deihl 1992). In most parts of the United States, there are no organized groups for bisexual people (Fox 1991; Firestein 2007). Except in the largest cities, we cannot walk into a neighborhood bookstore and find resources on bisexuality, and even there the best we can hope for is to find a book or two in the "Lesbian and Gay" section. Due to bisexual invisibility and the paucity of bisexual role models or bisexual community, most bisexuals develop and maintain our bisexual identities in isolation (Bradford 1994; Ochs 1996; Page 2004)

Most bisexuals spend a majority of their time in the community that corresponds with the sex of our romantic partner (Bradford 2004; Ochs 1996). Partner changes—especially when our new partner is of a different sex than the previous one—can result in a sense of social discontinuity (Esterberg 1997; Ochs and Deihl 1992). Other bisexual women have a strong social affiliation with either a heterosexual, lesbian, or queer community. This can result in a different challenge: a feeling that if our partner is not of the "correct" sex we are hurting or betraying our community (Ochs and Deihl 1992; Firestein 2007).

Contributing to bisexual invisibility, many women privately identify as bisexual but, to avoid conflict and preserve ties to a treasured family or community, allow others to assume that they are lesbian or straight (Ochs and Deihl 1992).

Those in this position are likely to feel like imposters, outsiders, or second-class citizens in their community of choice.

Therefore, it is not surprising that some bisexual women experience bisexual desire as more a burden than a gift (Bower, Gurevich, and Mathieson 2002). To avoid internal and external conflict, they may feel a pressure or a wish to choose heterosexuality or homosexuality. Many desire the ease they imagine would come with having one clear, fixed, socially acceptable identity.

Ironically, bisexual individuals in "permanent" relationships may experience a feeling that insistence on a bisexual identity constitutes a double betrayal of both our community of primary identification (whether heterosexual or homosexual) and of our partner. Alternatively, the partner may believe that a bisexual person continuing to identify as bisexual is not committing fully to the relationship. This sentiment overlooks the fact that identity is, in actuality, distinct from current behavior. By contrast, heterosexuals' ability to establish and maintain committed relationships with one person is not assumed to falter even though they, while in a relationship, may retain their heterosexual identity and acknowledge feeling attractions to other people. These pressures can come not only from lovers but also from parents or other interested parties who want the bisexual woman to stop "holding out" or feel that she is making much ado about nothing by holding onto her bisexual identity. The road to a positive, affirming bisexual identity is a long and arduous journey (Bradford 2004). Our conditioning, invisibility, and the negative images that surround us make it extremely difficult to feel an unqualified sense of pride in our bisexuality.

RESISTING A BISEXUAL LABEL

Many women avoid a bisexual label (Bower, Gurevich, and Mathieson 2002). Some don't like any label. Some privately identify as bisexual but do not want to deal with other people's fear and stereotyping. Others are not sure whether they are "bisexual enough" to call themselves bisexual. Some feel that their attraction toward a person of a different-from-usual sex is an isolated incident, as such insufficient to motivate them to change their identity. Some women decline the bisexual label because they feel that a different label better meets their current needs. And, finally, some reject the bisexual label because they believe that the *bi* in *bisexual* reifies the binary sex/gender system. I will discuss each of these in turn.

To recruit respondents for the present study, I posted the following message to three email lists:

This is a question for women who are attracted to both men and women but don't like to use the word *bisexual* to define themselves.

Can you send me an email to explain WHY? Your answers will be confidential. I am on deadline, so please respond immediately!

Within thirty-six hours, I had heard back from thirty-six women. Their responses are summarized below.

DON'T PUT ME IN A BOX

One third of the respondents shared a distaste for labels. Some women said that they resist all labels. "I decided that my sexuality was too complicated and ever changing to pinpoint on a line, so I came up with the undefined thing (it's NOT the same as undecided). I won't limit my love to words or put it in a box (even if the box has pretty ribbons)." Another woman wrote: "The very accurate term *bisexual* has the unfortunate side effect of sounding important, or like it should be capitalized, or worn emblazoned on a purple baseball hat."

Some women feel that their attractions are not defined by sex/gender. "I just like people, and the best thing to really label myself as is 'sexual,' I suppose. Sexuality, for me, does not involve gender." One teenager wrote:

I used to use the term *bisexual* to describe myself but now I no longer do. It is a stereotype like any other. I'm not straight, I'm not gay, I'm not bi, I'm just me. . . . I don't stereotype and label myself because I have the ability to love anyone regardless of gender, race, religion, age, etc., because I have an open mind and that is all one needs. No labels, just openness and the ability to potentially love anyone regardless.

BI IS TOO BINARY!

This response would have been rare ten or twenty years ago, but one third of the respondents objected to the binary implicit in the word bisexual. One wrote, "I don't like the word *bisexual* because I don't want to reinforce the gender binary—I'm attracted to people of more than two genders." In the words of another respondent:

I date people who identify as men, women, trans, boi, boy, grrrl, intersexed, hermaphrodite, and a whole slew of other gender-related terms. Their genitalia ranges, their hormones range, their chromosomes range. . . . How can I possibly classify myself as bisexual given this? Doing so would do a disjustice [sic] to both my political and social beliefs as well as to the identities of my partners.

Another wrote: "I'm not bisexual. I'm sexual. . . . I don't limit myself by outdated systems of categorization like genitalia or gender."

BUT ISN'T BI FIFTY-FIFTY?

Some women have difficulty identifying as bi because they have not yet been in a relationship with a woman (or with a man, or with either). There are many women who have a history of relationships with people of one sex but who have fallen in love (or in lust) at some point with someone of the unexpected sex. Often this is perceived as an isolated event unlikely to be repeated. In the words of one respondent: "As for sex, well, I'm certainly attracted to male people a lot more often than female people, which is one reason not to call myself bisexual—it seems misleading. . . . I don't feel right calling myself 'bisexual' when I haven't *had sex* with someone female." Another wrote: "I'm not sure I have a right to call myself bisexual. Most of my attractions are toward women."

BI IDENTITY HAS TOO MANY NEGATIVE CONNOTATIONS

Several women said that the plethora of negative stereotypes about bisexuality make identifying as bisexual "too hard." A stereotype commonly cited was the idea that bisexuals are just horny, sexually active/promiscuous people. One woman felt that the word itself was part of the problem:

> I wish that someone would come up with a word that didn't have "sex" right in it. Self-identified bisexuals are sometimes seen as traitors, or as being in a state of transition (sliding down the slippery slope from straight to gay). Maybe a gay friend will say, "Traitor," or a straight friend will say, "Oh it was just a phase," and either way it makes me want to cry, so I try not to talk about it anymore and just answer people's questions honestly with as few labels as possible.

Bi identity can be seen as having too many disadvantages and too few perks:

> I have to deal with "bi-phobia" (I got enough phobias to battle) and "gee—can i watch" from the boys at the bar, and frankly, bi folks don't get all the cool perks that "gay" folks and straight folk do in terms of community and resources. Ofttimes

bisexuals get ostracized, or told that they can't be a part of things because they aren't "hardcore" enough to be lesbians or gay men (or whatever).

Another stated, "I'm afraid that if I say I'm bisexual people are more likely to make assumptions about me that are really wrong." Another said:

> There's a lot of suspicion in the queer community toward bisexuals. If you declare yourself as one, people don't see you as queer, at best, and they see you as a trend follower. It's annoying not to be thought of as a "real" homosexual, and my fear of being mocked discourages me from openly calling myself a bisexual.

According to one woman, "The problem with the word *bisexual* is that it implies, at least in today's day and age, that you are attracted to everyone. Or at least to more people than, say, a straight person is. I don't believe this is true at all."

LESBIAN TRUMPS BISEXUAL

One fourth of the women who responded identify simultaneously as lesbian and bisexual but choose to identify publicly as lesbian, citing a number of reasons. Some stress the political power of the word *lesbian* or their desire to ally themselves with lesbians. Others are now in what they expect will be life partnerships with someone of their own sex and thus feel that their lesbian identity overshadows their bisexual identity. Others said that their home is centered in the lesbian community, where it would be very uncomfortable to maintain a bisexual identity. "I see being out as lesbian as the best political statement you can make, and I've always felt more ties to the lesbian community, so I choose to make my political statement for lesbians, rather than bisexuals."

> I came out as lesbian fifteen years ago, and I am so connected to my identity as a lesbian that it feels just plain wrong, and not who I am, to change it in any way (even though I'm now attracted to men too); I'm afraid of giving up/losing some of my community that is strongly lesbian identified due to their judgment (real or perceived).Though I have used that word to describe myself in the past, it feels like after ten years in a relationship with my partner . . . the term *bisexual* doesn't really seem to fit, except technically. What's that about? Why such passion? And what's so bad about identifying as bisexual, anyway?

EMBRACING A BISEXUAL LABEL

To locate women who embrace a bisexual identity, I sent the following message to several email lists:

I'm writing an article and need your help.

WHY DO YOU CHOOSE TO USE THE WORD *BISEXUAL* TO DESCRIBE YOURSELF?

If you self-identify as a woman, and if you identify as bisexual, please help me out by answering this question. I'll need to hear back from you within the next few days, and please do reply, even if your responses are short.

Coincidentally, thirty-six women responded to this inquiry as well, although their responses arrived over a seven-day period. A summary of their responses follows:

IF THE SHOE FITS . . .

Almost all who responded said that they use the word *bisexual* because it is the best available word to describe them. For example, "The bisexual label describes my present, living, daily reality: I am sexually attracted to both men and women. My life partner is a man, but like anyone who is 'married,' I am still attracted to other people, and those people are of both sexes."

Women used different criteria—sexual experience, attraction, relationship history, potential, or a combination of these factors—to explain why they consider themselves bisexual. Some appeared to accept the idea that there are two sexes; others challenged it; some said that they were attracted to both men and women; others said that their attraction was irregardless of sex or gender. "I've been able to be in meaningful relationships with people of both sexes." "It's the only word (so far) that fits how I feel—attracted to and capable of being in relationships with people regardless of gender." "I have a history of forming lasting partnerships with people of both genders, as well as those who are transgender. While I appreciate certain experiences that I consider to be unique to being with a man or a woman, gender is not something that is a determining factor for me when it comes to attraction." "I'm emotionally and sexually attracted to men, women, and people who don't exactly meet either description. There isn't any other single word that works quite as well to describe me."

Some described their attractions as fifty-fifty and felt that bisexuality was therefore a perfect fit for them; others embraced a bisexual identity although their attractions or relationship history is skewed toward one people of one sex. "I call myself bisexual because it fits so perfectly. I would put myself smack dab in the middle of any scale that measures attractions as I really do find both males and females attractive. Or perhaps I should say that the sex of the person is not material. I find specific people attractive." "I call myself bisexual not simply because I've had sex with both men and women, but because I have been in love with both sexes. My attraction is about 70 percent toward men, but I have been in a loving relationship with a woman as well." "I have never had a sexual encounter with a woman, but I still am bisexual because the attraction is there."

Four women made specific reference to ascribed identity, saying that one reason they identify as bisexual is that it is "the word that best describes my sexual identity in a way that others would understand" or "because that is what others would identify me as."

Others said that bisexual identity was broad enough to encompass all of their experience: One woman wrote, "Bisexual identity is flexible enough to encompass variations in my past, present and future, without pretending that some relationships were authentic and others weren't." Another wrote, "rather than seeing myself as half-lesbian and half-straight, I feel like all of me is attracted to women, and all of me is attracted to men. There is no lesbian half and no straight half. I am a third category that contains the first two but is wholly different, and that is bisexual."

OR AT LEAST FITS BETTER THAN ANY OTHER

Several women made reference to the limitations of the bisexual label but felt that it was nonetheless the best choice available to them: "I know that the binary view of gender is a chimera, and that my attractions to people involve other aspects than sexual, but the alternatives to the word *bisexual* have their own drawbacks and require so much more explanation." "I call myself bisexual because it is the least inaccurate of all the labels available." "I hate the word *bisexual* because of the fact that sex is right there in the name. . . . I wish we had a word similar to *lesbian* or *gay* that envelopes ideas of sex, relationships, and culture rather than just sex. But until then I guess I will be stuck with *bisexual*."

STRATEGICALLY BI: POLITICS AND VISIBILITY

Seven women said that they identify as bisexual for political or educational reasons, seeing themselves as role models for others. "Using the term *bisexual* as much as possible will help to get more people to understand that there are more than just the options of *heterosexual* or *homosexual* for describing one's sexuality." "Being out as bi challenges the myth that there's a vast difference between straight and gay and that people can easily distinguish one from the other." "I think I'm continuing to call myself bi simply because so many people are afraid of the label. Maybe I'm a lesbian-leaning bisexual, but I would hate to give someone ammunition to the prejudices that bis are undecided, going through a phase, or disloyal to the gay community. We're legitimate, we're queer, and we all identify as bi for different reasons." "Bisexual people are often invisible and assumed to be either straight or gay, so I feel it is valuable to claim a bisexual identity proudly and publicly to counter that invisibility." "I use the word *bisexual* often, loudly, clearly, proudly, because who I am, unfortunately, is not written on my face, and I use it in the hopes that, as much as humanly possible, I will not find myself hiding behind either heterosexual privilege or lesbian appearances."

MOVING TOGETHER TOWARD THE FUTURE: SUGGESTIONS FOR COUNSELORS

Labels are problematic. Human languages are inadequate to the task of describing the complexities of human experience. Even women who embrace a given label may find it only partially succeeds in serving its descriptive function. And those who reject a label may still recognize its merits. The responses above are clear evidence that choosing how to identify is a complex issue with a myriad of possible opinions and strategies and no simple solution or correct answer. Each individual must find her own way.

My own experience of identity has been an ongoing process and may serve as one example. The bisexual label works for me and has greatly enhanced my life. It has also, at times, cost me dearly.

I call myself bisexual because I acknowledge in myself the capacity to be attracted to and sexual with people of more than one sex, not necessarily at the same time, not necessarily in the same way, and not necessarily to the same degree. It is clear to me that I was bisexual long before I ever "acted on it," just as a person who has never had sex can be lesbian or straight. After all, identity is not only about behavior. It is also about what we feel inside. A woman can be bisexual even if she never ends up acting on it, or even if—like me—she is in a monogamous relationship that she expects will last the rest of her life.

On the negative side, by calling myself bisexual I exposed myself to anger, hostility, stereotyping, and lowered my status in the "gay and lesbian" community.

On the positive side, my bisexual identity was a route to community. By responding in September 1982 to an announcement in the paper about a discussion about bisexuality, I found my way into a room of women who also identified as bisexual, who understood my experience. This led to membership in a support group, to friendships, and subsequently to advocacy and activism, all of which have greatly enhanced my life.

I have become, over time, less a believer that there is some sort of essential difference between people who use various words to describe ourselves. Lesbian, bisexual, queer, even "choose-not-to-label"—these are tags that we place on ourselves to give others information about how we understand ourselves. These words mean different things to different women.

I have been committed to a woman (for life, we hope) for eight years, and we have been legally married since the first day it was legal in Massachusetts to do so: May 17, 2004. I haven't slept with a man since 1992. Many other women whose stories are similar to mine would by now have adopted a lesbian label. I haven't. I am happy to be grouped with lesbians. Queers too. But it is important to me that I be seen in full: past, present, and potential future, internal and external, and that no part of me be obscured or erased.

We use words to describe ourselves, but these words are at best tools to help us explain—to ourselves and to others—who we are and how we see ourselves. They have value insofar as they can be used to make us visible, and to help us find others with similar experiences, but in reality each of us has our own path and unique experience. And while this may not feel like a very stable foundation upon which to hang one's hat, it is in fact facing up to reality.

It can be very frustrating for those of us who identify as bisexual when others reject the label we have worked so long and hard to create a space for. I am left with the question: is my bisexual activism about making it safe for these women to identify as bisexual? Or is it about making it safe for all of us to identify, or not identify, however we choose and to be respected as we are?

My answer, clearly, is the latter. However, we still live in a world in which people think in either/or binaries; most people are uncomfortable with notions of fluidity. How can we make it safe for women who identify as bisexual? Or not? How can "not bi" women be visibly "not straight" and "not gay" either so that they can help dispel binary notions? This is the challenge that I put forth to all of us: let us respect one another, speak our truths, listen to each other's stories, refrain from imposing our own assumptions and understanding on others, and figure out ways that we can increase the space available for all of us.

NOTE

1. Homophobia: Fear or hatred of homosexuals and homosexuality; heterosexism: prejudice and antagonism shown by heterosexual persons towards homosexuals; discrimination against homosexuals; the belief in the superiority of heterosexuality. *Oxford English Dictionary Online*. Biphobia is not in this dictionary. I use it to mean prejudice and antagonism toward bisexuals and bisexuality.

REFERENCES

Alexander, J., and Yescavage, J. (Eds.) (2004). *InterSEXions of the others: Bisexuality and Transgenderism*. Binghamton, NY: Haworth.

Allport, G. (1954). *The nature of prejudice*. Cambridge: Addison-Wesley.

Blasingame, B. M. (1992). The roots of biphobia; Racism and internalized homophobia. In E. R. Weise (Ed.), *Closer to home: Bisexuality and feminism* (pp. 47–53). Seattle: Seal.

Blumenfeld, W. J. (Ed.) (1992). *Homophobia: How we all pay the price*. Boston: Beacon.

Bower, J., Gurevich, M. and Mathieson, C. (2002). (Con)Tested identities: Bisexual women reorient sexuality. In D. Atkins (Ed.), *Bisexual women in the twenty-first century* (pp. 23–52). Binghamton, NY: Harrington Park.

Bradford, M. (2004). The bisexual experience: Living in a dichotomous culture. *Journal of Bisexuality*, 4(1/2), 7–23.

Dworkin, S. H. (2000). Individual therapy with lesbian, gay, and bisexual clients. In R. M. Perez, K. A. DeBord, and K. J. Bieschke (Eds.), *Handbook of counseling and psychotherapy with lesbian, gay, and bisexual clients* (pp. 157–182). Washington, DC: American Psychological Association.

Esterberg, K. G. (1997). *Lesbian and bisexual identities: Constructing communities, constructing selves*. Philadelphia: Temple University Press.

Firestein, B. A. (Ed.) (1996). *Bisexuality: The psychology and politics of an invisible minority*. Thousand Oaks, CA: Sage.

Firestein, B. A. (2007). Cultural and relational contexts of bisexual women: Implications for therapy. In K. J. Bieschke, R. M. Perez, and K. A. DeBord (Eds.), *Handbook of counseling and psychotherapy with lesbian, gay, bisexual, and transgender clients*. Washington, DC: American Psychological Association.

Fox, A. (Firestein, B. A.) (1991). Development of a bisexual identity: Understanding the process. In L. Hutchins and L. Ka'ahumanu (Eds.), *Bi any other name: Bisexual people speak out* (pp. 29–36). Boston: Alyson.

Fox, R. C. (1995). Coming out bisexual: Identity, behavior, and sexual orientation self-disclosure. (Doctoral dissertation, California Institute of Integral Studies 1993). *Dissertation Abstracts International*, 55(12), 5565B.

Fox, R. C. (1996). Bisexuality in perspective: A review of theory and research. In B. A. Firestein (Ed.), *Bisexuality: The psychology and politics of an invisible minority* (pp. 3–50). Thousand Oaks, CA: Sage.

Funderburg, Lisa. (1994). *Black, White, Other: Biracial Americans talk about race and identity*. New York: Quill/William Morrow.

Greene, B. (2003). Beyond heterosexism and across the cultural divide: Developing an inclusive lesbian, gay, and bisexual psychology: A look to the future. In L. D. Garnets and D. C. Kimmel (Eds.), *Psychological perspectives on lesbian, gay and bisexual experiences* (2d ed.) (pp. 357–400). New York: Columbia University Press.

Ochs, R. (1996). Biphobia: It goes more than two ways. In B. A. Firestein (Ed.), *Bisexuality: The psychology and politics of an invisible minority* (pp. 217–239). Thousand Oaks, CA: Sage.

Ochs, R., and Deihl, M. (1992). Moving beyond binary thinking. In W. J. Blumenfeld (Ed.), *Homophobia: How we all pay the price*. Boston: Beacon.

Ochs, R., and Rowley, S. E. (Eds.) (2005). *Getting bi: Voices of bisexuals around the world*. Boston: Bisexual Resource Center.

Page, E. (2004). Mental health services experiences of bisexual women and bisexual men: An empirical study. *Journal of Bisexuality*, 4(1/2) 137–160.

Rust, P. C. (1992). The politics of sexual identity: Sexual attraction and behavior among lesbian and bisexual women. *Social Problems*, 39(4), 366–386.

Rust, P. C. (1995). *Bisexuality and the challenge to lesbian politics: Sex, loyalty, and revolution*. New York: New York University Press.

Rust, P. C. (1996). Managing multiple identities: Diversity among bisexual women and men. In B. A. Firestein (Ed.), *Bisexuality: The psychology and politics of an invisible minority* (pp. 53–83). Thousand Oaks, CA: Sage.

Rust, P. C. (2000). Heterosexual gays, homosexual straights. In P. Rodríguez Rust (Ed.), *Bisexuality in the United States: A social science reader* (pp. 279–306). New York: Columbia University Press.

PART 2

COUNSELING BISEXUAL WOMEN AND MEN
ACROSS THE LIFESPAN

5

DEVELOPMENTAL AND SPIRITUAL ISSUES OF YOUNG PEOPLE AND
BISEXUALS OF THE NEXT GENERATION

Luke Entrup and Beth A. Firestein

IT IS impossible to speak accurately about the relational and sexual experiences of an entire generation, but it *is* possible to look at trends and tendencies of a specific culturally and historically situated generation and to characterize some of the subcultures within that general population. Sexuality, like personality, bears the overlapping imprints of genetics, culture, and individual differences. A generation's sexuality takes shape within the complexities of these multiple contexts, and there are some very interesting trends and subcultures emerging in The Next Generation.

This chapter will discuss emerging trends among youth, ages fifteen to thirty-five, now coming to be known as TNG—The Next Generation. The Next Generation has a sexuality that is characterized by fluidity, ambisexuality, a reluctance to label their sexuality, and an interest in the sacred. Through efforts such as Beyond the Machine, an experiential learning process directed at helping youth understand and expand themselves and connect with "elders," we are developing tools and approaches helpful in facilitating youth in their process of sexual self-exploration and self-identification. Subself dialogue and intergenerational dialogues are two techniques that can be used to help youth connect with and explore nontraditional sexual and gender identities. Counselors will be introduced to these techniques and their application to work with bisexual, ambisexual, and gender-fluid individuals, ages fifteen to thirty-five.

DEVELOPMENTAL ISSUES OF LESBIAN, GAY, AND BISEXUAL ADOLESCENTS

In the past several decades considerable work has been done to investigate and theorize the developmental and adjustment issues of lesbian, gay, and bisexual youth, particularly adolescents (Anhalt and Morris 2003; Coleman and Remafedi 1989; Hershberger and D'Augelli 2000; Martell, Safren, and Prince 2004;

Savin-Williams 2003). Bisexual youth, like gay and lesbian youth, face a major challenge—the challenge of developing a positive sense of identity while coming of age in a culture that devalues same-gender erotic and affectional feelings. This creates another developmental task unique to nonheterosexual youth. "The primary task involves the transformation of a negative, stigmatized identity into a positive one" (Garnets and Kimmel 2003:217). Ethnic sexual minority youth face additional challenges when coming out to their parents, other family members, and ethnic or racial communities (Fukuyama and Ferguson 2000; Greene 1994, 2003; Morales 1989; Savin-Williams 2003).

Membership in a socially disadvantaged and marginalized sexual identity group has been noted to contribute to both psychological vulnerability and psychological resilience among members of such groups (Greene 2003). Adopting a bisexual, gay, lesbian, queer, transgender, or "questioning" identity inevitably alters a person's sense of self in relation to the world. Sociologist and researcher Paula Rust (2003) notes that "because identity is the link connecting the individual to the social world, this change in sexual identity usually leads to changes in the individual's relationship with others and with society as a whole" (p. 227).

Bisexual, lesbian, and gay youth are members of such a marginalized population, and their psychological, emotional, and spiritual development is clearly shaped by this important facet of their identity. To the extent that one expresses romantic feelings or desire directed toward same-sex or transgender potential partners, one is subject to the homonegative, antigay attitudes and homophobic treatment of some members of the dominant, largely homophobic culture. Bisexual youth may simultaneously or alternately occupy both positions of privilege and positions of oppression in relation to this dynamic of homonegativity, depending on their community of affiliation and choice of dating partner (or partners) at a given time. These factors create sometimes complex difficulties for members of The Next Generation (ages eighteen to thirty-five) in forging a bisexual, fluid or ambisexual identity, in embracing their life experiences while resisting identity labels, and in locating communities of support.

Overall, less is known about the issues of concern to bisexual, queer, and questioning youth than is presently known about the needs and concerns of lesbian- and gay-identified youth (Russell and Seif 2002). Material pertaining to gay and lesbian youth is still relatively scarce, and, in a positive movement, some of the newer writing attempts to address issues of bisexual and questioning youth as well as the concerns young lesbians and gay males. While a review of the theoretical and empirical literature on the mental health of gay and lesbian youth is beyond the scope of the present chapter, a number of authors have noted the similarities of issues confronting bisexual and lesbian/gay young people (Anhalt and Morris 2003; Garnets and Kimmel 2003; Savin-Williams 2003). The interested reader is referred to several recent chapters reviewing the issues and empirical literature pertaining to LGB youth (Anhalt and Morris 2003;

Hershberger and D'Augelli 2000; Garnets and Kimmel 2003; Russell and Seif 2002).

A search on the Internet of resources for "bisexual youth" uncovered very few sites specifically addressing the needs of bisexual young people apart from those of gay or lesbian youth, though resources relevant to the needs of bisexual youth have recently begun to appear on the World Wide Web (see, for example, Advocates for Youth's Web site, http://www.youthresource.com/living/bi.htm). Other valuable resources for Generation X and Millennial-age bisexual youth include Robyn Ochs's *International Directory of Bisexual Groups* (Ochs 2001), the Bisexual Resource Center Web site (www.biresource.org), and other Internet resources, including the bisexual activist organization, BiNet USA (www.binetusa.org), Bisexual Options (www.bisexual.org), a bisexual resource site based in the United Kingdom (www.bi.org), and BiCafe (www.bicafe.com). We turn now to look at some of the relationship trends evident in The Next Generation.

GENERAL RELATIONSHIP TRENDS OF THE NEXT GENERATION

The Next Generation includes the people born in the latter years of Generation X (or Gen X, as it is commonly called) and most of Generation Y (also known as the Millennial Generation). Generation X consists of individuals born between the years 1964 to 1982 (ages twenty-three to thirty-nine), and Generation Y is typically considered to include individuals born between the years 1983 to 2000 (ages five to twenty-two). In the year 2005, the Next Generation included approximately eighty-two million people between fifteen and thirty-five years of age. This is about 29 percent of the U.S. population (US Census Bureau 2002).

Every generation manifests qualities associated with the historical and cultural period during which it comes of age. Referring to the characteristics of Generation X and the Millennials, Hain (2004) states that

> both groups were formed in the postmodern world. Both groups are extremely diverse—ethnically and culturally. And both are weary of our current labeling processes, which continue to be based on our modernistic understandings. While postmodern folks believe in multiple and simultaneous realities, modernity adheres to the notion of universals. While postmodernity allows for multiple self-identities and journeys, the modern model appears to follow the assumption that all people follow along singular, predictable stages of development. (p. 1)

The cultural and relational experiences of this generation have been shaped by events as diverse as the Stonewall riots that took place in New York City in 1969, the removal of homosexuality as a category of mental illness from the *Diagnos-*

tic and Statistical Manual of Mental Disorders by the American Psychiatric Association in 1973 (Conger 1975), and the legalization of gay marriage in San Francisco and Boston in 2003. Furthermore, TNG experiences have been shaped by technologies as diverse as the popularization of Internet dating and cellular phones, the availability of a wide range of sexual information and education through the print and electronic media, and the advent of organizations as diverse as Gay/Straight Student Alliances in high schools and BDSM educational and support organizations in large urban areas. The evolution of the culture has spurred some interesting trends with respect to relationship and sexuality in The Next Generation.

These trends include experimentation with "open" and polyamorous relationship styles including the redefinition (and reprioritization) of commitment within interpersonal relationships, an openness to more fluid ways of expressing gender and sexuality and new ways of defining that expression (e.g., "ambisexuality"), a rejection of sexual identity labels, and an exploration of "sacred" forms of masculinity and femininity in the spirit of traditions such as Jungian psychology and Buddhist spirituality. The next section will explore each of these trends briefly and discuss the sociocultural factors that seem to be influencing the development of these trends.

THE NEXT GENERATION AND THE DIVORCE WOUND

The divorce rate for first marriages between women and men in the United States remains around 40 percent to 50 percent according to the National Center for Health and Human Services (NCHS) and the Census Bureau (Marks 2004). A large number of young people have parents who are divorced. The effects of divorce on an individual's relationships and patterns of adult intimacy can be devastating. That is not to say that the effects would be lessened if their parents remained together in an unhappy or spiritually divorced relationship. Rather, we would assert that young people with divorced parents have felt the effects and are patterning lives in relation to their *divorce wound*. The *divorce wound* is common among young people. Some indications that young adults are suffering from the effects of the divorce wound are fear of intimacy, fear of commitment, distrust of marriage, and the struggle between competing needs for independence and companionship.

Erin, a twenty-four-year-old white American from the South, addressed this issue:

> My parents divorced when I was four months old. They fought for much of my childhood. Neither remarried until I was in my teens. I'm sure if all of that would have been different I would be a different person. The longest relationship I've

ever had with a man is four months. Right now I'm celibate. I sometimes wonder why, but it just seems easier. Relationships are too much work. Every time I make friends with a guy it is hard because he eventually always wants more. I'm sure a lot of this has to do with my parents being divorced.

The divorce wound, coupled with growing disillusionment with organized religion and other complex factors, have led to a basic mistrust of the institution of marriage. Marriage is seen by some TNG subcultures as a religious-political institution meant to stifle the freedom of the individual. To some, marriage represents something much different than the interpersonal connection of a relationship. The interpersonal connection itself is seen as more important than entering into the legal agreement of marriage, even for increasing numbers of heterosexual youth. The number of heterosexual and opposite-sex involved younger people "living together" without the legal arrangement of marriage continues to rise (Janus and Janus 1993). A number of other trends are also evident in the youth culture, some of which pertain to sexual behavior and identity among younger people fifteen to thirty-five.

OPEN RELATIONSHIPS, POLYAMORY, AND COHABITATION

One major trend among TNGs is the growing number of young people that are experimenting with *open relationships*. Open relationship and the term *open marriage* originated in the 1970s with publication of the book *Open Marriage* by O'Neill and O'Neill (1972). The new term for such alternative relationship structures is *polyamory*, a word that refers to "loving more than one" (Anapol 1997; Easton and Liszt, 1997; see Weitzman, chapter 17, for a fuller description of polyamory). This trend toward the inclusion of more than just the "couple" as the unit of social and family relation is not just limited to singles. Young heterosexually married people and committed same-sex partners are making open agreements as well (Anapol 1997; Easton and Liszt, 1997; Munson and Stelboum 1999; West 1995; Weitzman, chapter 17).

The AIDS epidemic and other sexually transmitted infections (STIs) have spurred a necessary increase in consciousness around the safety issues involved with polyamorous sexualoving arrangements, and have led to some catch phrases defining safe sex outside a monogamous relationship that are often heard in polyamorous youth subcultures. Terms such as *fluid agreement, fluid covenant,* or *body-fluid monogamous* describe negotiated, consensual decisions on the part of primary partners to limit unprotected sexual practices to the individual or individuals who are core members of an open relationship arrangement. Within this type of agreement, all sexual contact with others must be protected or safer sex.

SEXUAL IDENTITY EXPLORATION AND BISEXUALITY AMONG THE NEXT GENERATION

Often young people feel a push by parents, peers, elders, and the greater community to define their sexual identity based on how many and what type of sexual activities the person has participated in. With this pressure the mark of identity is not internally generated, but externally tied to the quantity of experiences a person has had with partners of various genders. This often creates a split between the core identity and the sexual identity. One is not allowed to sexually identify without having to have actual behavioral experience, although, in fact, many gay and lesbian-identified youth name their orientation and core identity before ever having had a physical same-sex experience. Yet bisexually identified youth are frequently doubted and challenged regarding their ability to know their own bisexual orientation until the point at which they can lay claim to having had sexual partners of more than one gender.

There are many complex patterns of thought and emotion occurring in the inner psychic realms of TNG young people around sexual identity. It is important in the development of the individual youth or young adult to be able to really ask the questions "Who am I?" and "What do I like sexually?" The erotophobia and sex-negativity of the culture work against individuals of any age knowing and expressing their sexual desires, regardless of the form these desires may take (Queen 1996; Hutchins, chapter 18). Many young people report feeling an internal sense of certainty about aspects of their sexual desires and possibly even a certain sense about their identity, yet feel pressure from some peers and the culture at large to not try on the label without the experiences. It is important that educators and counselors empower a young person to explore different behaviors and identities until they find one that feels right. The identities are then intrinsically motivated rather than assigned from exterior sources. In spite of the barriers that still exist to identifying as bisexual or "updating" sexual identity maps through the life cycle, it is also accurate to reflect that more choices, communities, and sources of validation are available to gender- and orientation-fluid youth than has actually been available in prior generations.

BI AND BI-CURIOUS BEHAVIOR AS A PHASE

Many bisexual youth that Entrup has worked with in the workshop or coaching context report being told by someone in their life they will soon move through their phase of sexual exploration. This challenge comes both from heterosexual society and also from the gay and lesbian community. Many gays and lesbians who are members of older generational cohorts look back through their lives and see their periods of bisexual expression as very confusing. Therefore, an assumption is made that the same experience is happening for all bisexuals, particularly young bisexuals. This perspective presents TNG youth with the message that bisexuality is a phase and that they need to "push through" their confusion in order to realize that they are actually gay or straight.

These messages can be very disempowering to the present experience of a person's bisexual feelings and relationships, regardless of whether or not the individual does eventually shift to some other identity. This undermines the core challenge of youth's sexual development, which is about being with *what is present* in this time. Telling a young person that it is "just a phase" that everyone goes through and that they will either discover that they are gay or straight increases the complexity and strain of this process of exploration and perpetuates the culture's dichotomous models of sexual identity.

IDENTITY AND LABELING

There is a clear difference between sexual identity, sexual activity, and an individual's core identity. *Sexual identity* refers to how an individual distinguishes their sexual label to others. *Sexual activity* refers to the actual experiences that the individual has sexually with one or more partners. *Core identity* refers to how the individual identifies sexually to themselves. One's core identity is formed through both fantasy and reality (D'Augelli and Patterson 1995).

Many young people are reluctant to identify with any sexual label (Bower, Gurevich, and Mathieson 2002; Hain 2004). By identifying with a specific sexual identity label, an individual fears being put into a "box" and endorsing boundaries that unnecessarily limit his or her sense of self (See Ochs, chapter 4). Melissa, a twenty-year-old Italian American from New York, put it this way:

> I have been with women and men. I have relationships with women and sometimes sleep with men. I really like to be with gay men. I'm not just a lesbian. I'm not just attracted to men. I'm not just bisexual because sometimes I only want to be with women. So if you are going to make me pick an identity, I guess it would be queer or fluid, but I'd prefer to not have to wear a label. It is too restricting.

We do not yet have the language to encompass the different identities that are arising. The identifications of fluid and queer are becoming more prevalent. *Queer* is an umbrella term that refers to an individual who has any sexual orientation, identity, or attraction that is not heterosexual (see Horner, chapter 15). *Fluid* refers to the the that fact that for some TNG youth sexual orientation, identity, and attractions may change and frequently depend on the mood, setting, and people in the individual's life. An individual who perceives their sexual orientation, gender expression, or sexual identity as fluid recognizes that their attractions may change in response to a host of variables and are at least somewhat comfortable with their recognition that these things change.

Diamond (2000) comments that Western culture expects sexuality to come in one neat package, but this is usually not the case. In Diamond's (2000) study, fully one half of the eighty lesbian, bisexual, and unlabeled women had changed sexual identities more than once in a two-year period. Other researchers, such as Fox (1995) and Rust (1996) have noted similar patterns in research involving bisexual participants. Reviewing the empirical literature pertaining to patterns of sexual identity change and stability, sociologist Paula Rust (2000, 2003) discusses the apparent permeability of the categories of sexual orientation constructed by social scientists. The studies reviewed include both her research and studies conducted by other researchers over the past thirty years. Summarizing findings across multiple studies, Rust (2003) notes that 43 to 91 percent of lesbian-identified women in these studies have had romantic or sexual heterosexual relationships *since* coming out as lesbians.

AMBISEXUALITY AND FLUIDITY OF SEXUAL EXPRESSION

With the lack of appropriate language and a growing realization of the fluidity of individual sexuality, the identity of ambisexual has become popular in some TNG subcultures. *Ambisexuality* is a term that overlaps in meaning with the term *bisexuality* but refers to a more clearly defined iteration of bisexuality in which there is usually a tendency toward opposite-sex sexual attraction coexisting alongside occasional sexual attractions and encounters with the same sex. Jake is a twenty-five-year-old European American from the West who identifies as ambisexual:

> I love women. I love the softness of a women's body. I enjoy the emotional connection I feel with women. I want to spend my life with a woman. But every once and a while if the music is right, the light is right, and he's sexy enough, I love to be with a man. This probably happens only 5 percent of the time. It is a very important and special aspect of who I am.

Ambisexuality differs from bisexuality in some significant ways. There tends to be a somewhat greater congruence between core sexual identity and sexual identity label and the relative frequency or "balance" of gender of partner choice such that individuals in the fifteen-to-thirty-five-year-old age group identifying as bisexual tend to have more balanced distributions of attractions across genders then individuals identifying as ambisexual. Individuals identifying as ambisexual often have a preponderance of opposite-sex partners, greater frequency of sexual experience in cross-gender pairings, and a core sexual identity that is more likely to be different from the sexual identity label they choose. This identity label may also be adopted by an individual that has same-sex tendencies and enjoys occasional opposite-sex sexual encounters. Clearly, youth culture reflects some new trends in self-identification and labeling.

INTEGRATION OF SEXUALITY AND SPIRITUALITY

Another trend among The Next Generation relates to the integration of sexuality and spirituality. A review of the history of sexual/spiritual traditions is beyond the scope of the present chapter (see Hutchins, chapter 18, for further information). However, it is clear that some TNG youth place a substantial value on exploring the personal and traditional links between sexuality and spirituality. Some TNG subcultures have taken an interest in Tantric and Taoist sexuality practices, neo-pagan sacred sexuality, and celibacy as ways of integrating sexuality with greater meaning both personally and relationally. Young people have found the concepts of the *sacred masculine* and the *sacred feminine* especially relevant for self-understanding and deepening intimate relationships.

In our time, some of the qualities of both sacred masculinity and sacred femininity are what C. G. Jung described as "in the Shadow." The sacred masculine refers to qualities of potency, directness, assertiveness, generativity, and the purpose-driven life that can be embodied by people of any gender. The sacred feminine refers to qualities of receptivity, nurturance, yielding, and openness. The feminine is perceived as Soul and considered to be descending, of the Earth, and in the body. The masculine is conceptualized as Spirit, relating to the notion of ascension as well as to ideas, abstraction, and the quality of spaciousness. The Shadow refers to the unacknowledged part of us. It also refers to the parts of our selves that we repress, deny, and hide (Mattoon 1981). Shadow functions at both the individual and collective level.

Working with these symbolic aspects of the human psyche in relationship can expand one's sense of self and facilitate the evolution of individual consciousness. These are ways of filling out and expanding one's ways of relating to the world and to intimate partners. Because the sacred feminine is suppressed in this patriarchal culture, the sacred masculine is also repressed. Men are unable to surrender into the feminine; they also do not know the possibilities of true sacred masculinity. Paradoxically, men can only be as potent as they are capable of being receptive. This plays out in both the sexual and emotional arenas of intimate relating.

Our present-day culture lacks meaningful rites of initiation for men and because of this men are constantly trying to prove their manhood in unconscious ways. Examples include fraternity hazing practices, drive-by shootings, sexual risk taking, and extreme and self-destructive orientation toward work. The present-day culture also lacks meaningful rites of passage for women. Femininity is trivialized and ridiculed, resulting in oppression and devaluation of the sacred feminine. When the sacred feminine is devalued and distorted, the individual becomes vulnerable to abuse and may fail to develop a healthy, protected sense of self.

Men's bisexual and homosexual experiences are frequently seen as existing in opposition to manhood and masculinity. We do not have healthy role models of masculinity. Bisexuality in women is often appropriated by the male gaze rather than acknowledged as a potent erotic force between women. When appropriate and updated rituals of male and female initiation are reintroduced into individual lives and the culture at large, they not only restore the role of the sacred masculine and feminine within the individual but may also empower the culture to flourish in a way that balances masculine and feminine energies. These initiation rites can be especially rewarding and empowering for nonheterosexual people and allow every individual more freedom to live his or her truth. These rites can function as a doorway for reexamining the meaning and nature of the Self.

THE NATURE OF THE SELF AND SEXUALITY

On a more philosophical level, to be clearly defined is in many ways to see the self as "solid," but Zen Buddhism and other Eastern traditions teach us that the Self is not solid. Ed Podvoll, an American Buddhist psychiatrist, writes the following in *Recovering Sanity:*

> Selves come and go. They are utterly real, new visions of oneself, at times a processional of them. . . . There may be many of them, new personalities, momentary, short-lived. They may be lives of nobility or of infamy. One may experience them like a tearing apart, a tearing down, or stripping away. While that is happening there might be flashes of insight: "There is no one self. There are no ten selves. There is no self. SELF is only a position of equilibrium. One among a thousand others continually possible and always ready." (1990:160–161)

The nature of the human psyche is fluid, not concrete and solid. It is the "ego mind" with which we identify that is the part of the human psyche that defines "I am this and I am not that." The ego either pushes away what the individual believes she is not or brings in what he believes he is. The ego wants to clearly define our sense of self in concrete terms. Once the individual sees through this, she realizes that life is fluid and in motion, one's sense of self also in a process of evolution and lifelong change. Bisexual youth who are aware of their ability to love people of more than one gender may be acutely aware of this sense of internal fluidity with respect to their attractions, fantasies, and emotional attachments.

Given the rapidity and constancy of the process of change, it is helpful to offer individual clients the opportunity to participate in experiential exercises that heighten their self-awareness and their awareness of the complexity of their position in relation to others of differing generations. Subself dialogue and intergenerational dialogue are two experiential techniques for facilitating this process of individual growth and self-exploration.

TECHNIQUES AND APPLICATIONS

DIALOGUE OF SUBSELVES OF THE SEXUAL SELF

A component of the human condition is our complexity. Subpersonalities, or subselves, develop through an individual's relationship to the environment and through natural growth. A subpersonality is a facet of the self that evolves over time and represents an aspect of an individual's personality. Subpersonalities are dynamic; they change over time and interrelate with other subpersonalities, other "baskets of the self." Upon closer examination and dialogue with an individual's subselves, it is possible to understand oneself at a deeper level, make clearer decisions, and move toward health.

Bisexual young people in my workshops and coaching practice report being caught in the teeth of the dichotomous sexual identity enculturation. The present climate of the culture requires youth to make a decision between heterosexual and homosexual identities. Making such a choice can lead to the disowning of the fullness of the individual. Subself dialogue allows bisexual youth of The Next Generation both to explore parts of themselves and to understand their own identity more fully. By intentionally separating aspects of one's self, the central, or aware, ego can explore itself more fully. By separating and giving voice to various aspects of oneself, one can perceive the self with a fresh perspective.

This subself dialogue technique is based on a technique known as Voice Dialogue, developed in the 1980s by Hal and Sidra Stone. It also draws heavily on Shadow Work developed in the 1990s by Clifford Barry and Mary Ellen Blandford, and the work of C. G. Jung, R. Assagioli, and J. L. Moreno. The subself dialogue technique serves multiple purposes: It assists the client to relax their internalized dichotomous enculturation and to heal the wound that many bisexual young people carry around, but perhaps the most significant purpose of this exercise is to know one's self in a deeper way by examining unexplored realities and aspects of self.

SUBSELF DIALOGUE EXERCISE

It is important to create an environment in which all aspects of a person can emerge. During exploration of subselves people often will say and do things that they would not normally say or do. Perhaps this will be the first time a person acknowledges a particular aspect of themselves. This is why it is important for those working with bisexuals in this context to be very present and empty of personal agenda, i.e., the facilitator should be open to what arises for the individual without preconceived notions about that individual's sexual identity process or what the outcome is likely to be. This emptiness can be brought forth through quieting the thoughts (some do this by focusing on the breath or on a mantra) and by bringing awareness to the sensations in the body. Disciplined practices such as one-pointed meditation and mindfulness training can be very helpful in grounding both client and counselor.

Subself Dialogue is a technique that is most effective in a group setting where others may role-play the various subselves. It is important to ensure a clean therapeutic container before beginning the process.

The first step of the exercise is to ask the person who is working what they would like to have happen during the subself work. The answer the person gives can be used to guide the process, and if the process becomes stagnant or tangential, the facilitator redirects it toward the client's stated questions. When the individual becomes clear as to the nature of the issue that he or she wishes to explore, that person is invited to fully identify and speak out of one of the subpersonalities connected to that issue.

When the facilitator invites the participant to become fully identified with one part of him- or herself, it is best to allow a few moments for the person to make this internal shift. This allows them to settle into the part. It is helpful to invite them to breathe deeply into this part and take on the body posture and stance of the part. Once the client has moved into the subpersonality, it is very important that the facilitator and the group welcome the part. It is important to facilitate each subpersonality without imposing judgment and criticism; otherwise, the subpersonality will retreat much as a criticized person might (Stone and Stone 1989). The facilitator should ask for a name by which the individual may choose to identify this subself aspect. The key is to gain understanding of how the part is operating in the client's life.

Next invite the client to fully become this part of themselves. The facilitator may suggest stepping into one end of the emotional polarity pertaining to their issue. Take, for example, a twenty-one year old named Mark. Mark is bisexual and felt that his attraction to men was keeping him from deeply exploring his attraction to women. He was invited to fully step into the part of him that is gay. After fully becoming his "gayness," he realized that both his gayness and straightness wanted the same thing for him—love. He was then able to move more fully into what he wanted in his relationships with women, with the understanding that his attraction to men was a part of him, too.

Each voice carries motivations, impulses, thoughts, and dialogue that are both helpful and unhelpful to the client's ideals. Even the most destructive and seemingly detrimental parts have some way in which they are serving the client. The skillfulness of this technique is in helping the client find the wisdom of each voice. There is a temptation for the client to disown a part once they bring it out of the unconscious and see its effects on behavior, but if the newly recognized part is denied and disowned, it will only return to the unconscious and perhaps be "acted out" in less constructive ways in the person's life.

Depth of understanding gained through subself exploration often relies upon the facilitator's ability to ask skillful questions and evoke a genuine dialogue among the parts. Each part is given a "name" or identity, and this part is then addressed directly. Examples of direct questions include "How do you feel about (name)? What do you like sexually? How has the world responded to you and your sexual desires? Does (name) listen to you? What is it you have always wanted to say but never could? What is the message you are bringing?"

It is important to explore at least two parts. This allows the client to see things from a third perspective and step out of dichotomy and paradox. It is also important to allow the parts to dialogue with one another. This can be done by rotating the participant through the various parts using empty chairs to represent them or having people role-play the other parts. The role players repeat the dialogue vocalized by the original participant as she moves through various role positions.

If several parts are pulled out, it is helpful to have them speak to each other. It is also helpful to rotate the client back into the ego role frequently so that they can see the voices from the detached ego role or perspective. This is one way that an *inner witness* is cultivated. Dass and Gorman (1985) explained this inner witness aspect of psyche as "that stance behind experience in which we merely acknowledge *what is*, without judgment of ourselves or of others" (p. 187). The inner witness allows the individual to see to inner forces at work within her personality, thereby preventing alienated or disowned aspects of the self from unconsciously persuading one's behavior. The ego is less reactive and "automatic" when the whole person has access to an acknowledged and exercised inner witness. With a developed and exercised inner witness, bisexual youth can gently resist and press through the exterior pressures of dichotomous models of sexuality and gender (Firestein 1996). They can also relax the internalized messages of dichotomy.

LISTENING TO THE VOICE OF THE PRIMITIVE SELF

An important voice that often will arise in this experience is the *primitive self.* This "primitive" subself has often been repressed and disowned through development in the sex-negative and sexually repressed dominant culture. This is an aspect of self that is not allowed to have a voice in the present culture. It carries an important message about how to live on and with the earth as a sexual being. As this voice is hidden, so are the messages of sexual spiritual harmony. Hal Stone and Sidra Stone (1989) write the following about the repressed primitive self:

> When these natural energies, such as survival, sexuality and aggression, are disowned over time, they cycle back into the unconscious and go through a significant change. Since we cannot destroy energy, they do not disappear. Instead, these disowned instincts begin to operate unconsciously and attract additional energy to themselves. They become engorged. (p. 32)

The voice of the primitive self often holds a great deal of wisdom about how to live a more passionate and creative life. If this voice is in shadow, its power can be destructive to the individual's relationships and environment. When the primitive self is in shadow, an individual's sexual behavior may take a form that violates her integrity, may cause physical dis-ease and/or trigger the denial or repression of the individual's healthy sexuality. Disavowal of the primitive self can lead to passive-aggressive sexual behavior and unconscious choices, including compulsive sexual behavior and unregulated or unhealthy sexual behavior. If the goal is to create wholeness and integrated sexuality through individual transformation, this can be the most crucial subself to offer a space to be heard. It has much to say.

It is also helpful to use subself dialogue to explore internalized introjects around sexuality. When the participant sees the messages that he has internalized in an unquestioning way from a detached observer position, he may then consciously choose which aspect of these introjects presently serve him and release the rest. The process involves making the unconscious conscious and empowering it with voice and choice. In his work with groups, Entrup has noticed that the subself dialogue technique has proven useful for many different situations of wounding in which identity defies dichotomization, for example, biracial, transgender, transsexual individuals or those having multiracial or multicultural identities. It is important to allow genuine dialogue to occur between parts having differing, even opposing, perspectives. Through this dialogue, clarity and understanding are gained at an individual level and this frequently translates into increased levels of group understanding as well.

The natural next steps following personal healing is community recognition of the self followed by cultural action. The larger process set in motion by subpersonality dialogue eventually leads to social action and cultural evolution. In summary, this exercise generates progressive movement through stages of awareness, dialogue, synthesis, personal healing, formation of community, and social action, and can ultimately result in cultural evolution. It is useful for the counselor or group facilitator to have these tools when assisting bisexual, transgendered, ambisexual, bi-curious, and sexually exploring clients to move through the stages of their own process of self-discovery.

Intergenerational dialogue is another transformative exercise that supports goals of integration and transformation of consciousness.

INTERGENERATIONAL DIALOGUE: RECONNECTING YOUTH AND ELDERS

Another helpful approach for assisting young bisexuals live lives of health and spiritual seeing is mentoring. Mentoring is the transfer of wisdom that comes with life experience. One of the shadow aspects of capitalism in industrial and postindustrial society is an unbridled push for productivity. With this push, those that are either no longer able to produce or not yet ready to produce are seen as expendable. In previous eras young people spent much of their time with their elders. The evolution of industrialized society and even the postindustrial information age has led to increasing physical and psychological separation of the generations. In such a culture the wisdom of elder's life experience is much less available to young people and the hope for the future represented by youth is often kept from elders.

The repression of nonheterosexual lifestyles in recent centuries has led to an utter lack of healthy role models for young bisexual women and men. The AIDS epidemic has further reduced the number of role models in non-heterosexual communities. On the impact of AIDS on relationships between lesbian, gay, and bisexual youth and elders, Garnets and Kimmel (2003) comment,

> Today it appears that the younger generation is beginning also to think of themselves as survivors and is looking to the older generation for clues to survivorship and a greater sense of historical continuity. Thus the potential exists for forming new bonds across the generations. The older generation is, of course, benefiting from the changes, and the benefits for them are in many ways as profound as for younger people. (p. 222)

Intergenerational dialogue is crucial to the survival of the next generation and the gifts that bisexuals and other queer-identified, nonheterosexual people bring to the world. Intergenerational dialogue is also a format in which mentoring may occur. It is an exchange of thoughts and perceptions between members of different generations and, as such, it is a critical process of the continuation of healthy human lives and healthy expression of sexuality.

CREATING CONDITIONS FOR HEALTHY INTERGENERATIONAL DIALOGUE

In order for there to be a genuine dialogue between generations, young people must first be willing to listen. If a TNG individual asks for help from an elder, she is more likely to receive help. When young people are encouraged to seek mentoring, mentoring is more likely to be successful. Ideally, the intention of mentors in an intergenerational dialogue is to pass down the wisdom of their life experience, using the combined energies of loving wisdom and honesty. The intention of the dialogue is to cultivate learning, broaden perspective, and promote receptive listening on the part of both elder and youth participants.

INTERGENERATIONAL DIALOGUE EXERCISE

There are many ways to facilitate an intergenerational dialogue. The following exercise is one form that has proven quite effective in empowering young people to seek advice.

Prepare a council or panel of mentors and elders. Begin by requesting that the most elder person in the group bestow a blessing upon the individuals in the group and upon the group itself. Allow young people to ask any and all questions. This is done by having a moderator call on young people one at a time to ask questions. Once the young person verbalizes his question, any mentor that has an answer raises her or his hand. The young person then calls on as many mentors with raised hands as she or he wishes until a satisfactory understanding of the question is reached. This empowers the young person to take the initiative in asking for help from mentors. It is not necessary for the young person to call upon all mentors with raised hands. It is important to instruct all the mentors to answer only the questions the young person asks and not to use the forum as an opportunity to express personal agendas. This will further empower the young person. Toward the end of the exercise, it can be interesting to reverse roles and allow the mentors to ask questions of the young people using the same format.

There are a number of themes that counselors and educators need to keep in mind when working with Generation X and Millennial youth. Life cycle themes of young people are about defining and affirming a unique sense of self; therefore, it is important to allow young people the opportunity to explore and "try on" different sexual labels and experiences. This is a process that may take months, years, or may even be a lifelong process for some people. With mentoring and support from those with more life experience, the process of identity exploration can be safer both physically and psychologically. Mentoring facilitates the depth of understanding and the fullness of the individual's experiential process.

It is important to keep in mind those cultural factors (e.g., religious background, family of origin, ethnic and racial identities, disability status) that affect sexuality and identity development. Furthermore, youth are in a historically unique cultural position; they have more exposure to sexually and gender diverse populations and access to more resources than prior generations. Bisexual and queer youth have even more specific positioning within the culture and face specific challenges.

There are strong cultural trends, postmodern in nature, that move youth in the direction of resistance to identity boxes and labels. How then does a counselor or educator work with identity and relationship issues with a population that prefers not to label themselves? Perhaps counselors and therapists can assist youth with permission to adopt provisional labels, to identify temporarily with a community, or, perhaps, to identify with multiple communities.

Therapists can assist bisexual, queer, and questioning youth to decrease shame and increase pride and self-esteem, even when this goes against the cultural grain. This might include providing Generation X and millennial youth with information and options regarding a variety of relationship "styles": marital, nonmarital, cohabiting, polyamorous, sexually experimental. Certain youth subcultures find particular meaning in the integration of sexuality and spirituality. Counselors can use experiential techniques to enhance self-awareness and a sense of group belonging among youth whose explorations potentially place them in marginalized positions relative to the dominant culture. Weaving new, healthier intergenerational connections becomes a real potential outcome of this process—a process with great transformative potential. The Next Generation has the power to touch all our lives with hope for the future and a desire to reach out to one another.

REFERENCES

Anapol, D. (1997). *Polyamory: The new love without limits*. San Rafael, CA: IntiNet Resource Center.

Anhalt, K., and Morris, T. L. (2003). Developmental and adjustment issues of gay, lesbian, and bisexual adolescents: A review of the empirical literature. In L. D. Garnets and D. C. Kimmel (Eds.), *Psychological perspectives on lesbian, gay and bisexual experiences* (2d ed., pp. 571–601). New York: Columbia University Press.

Bower, J., Gurevich, M., and Mathieson, C. (2002). (Con)Tested identities: Bisexual women reorient sexuality. In D. Atkins (Ed.), *Bisexual women in the twenty-first century* (pp. 23–52). Binghamton, NY: Harrington Park.

Coleman, E., and Remafedi, G. (1989). Gay, lesbian, and bisexual adolescents: A critical challenge to counselors. *Journal of Counseling and Development, 68*, 36–40.

Conger, J. (1975). Proceedings of the American Psychological Association, Incorporated, for the year 1974: Minutes of the annual meeting of the Council of Representatives. *American Psychologist, 30*, 620–651.

D'Augelli, A., and Patterson, C. J. (1995). *Lesbian, gay, and bisexual identities over the lifespan*. New York: Oxford University Press.

Dass, R., and Gorman, P. (1985). *How can I help?* New York: Knopf.

Diamond, L. (2000). Sexual identity, attractions, and behavior among young sexual-minority women over a two-year period. *Developmental Psychology, 36*(2), 241–250.

Easton, D., and Liszt C. A. (1997). *The ethical slut: A guide to infinite sexual possibilities*. San Francisco: Greenery.

Firestein, B. A. (1996). *Bisexuality: The psychology and politics of an invisible minority*. Thousand Oaks, CA: Sage.

Fukuyama, M. A., and Ferguson, A. D. (2000). Lesbian, gay, and bisexual people of color: Understanding cultural complexity and managing multiple oppressions. In R. M. Perez, K. A. DeBord, and K. J. Bieschke (Eds.), *Handbook of counseling and psychotherapy with lesbian, gay, and bisexual clients* (pp. 81–105). Washington, DC: American Psychological Association.

Garnets, L. D., and Kimmel, D. C. (2003). Identity development and stigma management. In L. D. Garnets and D. C. Kimmel (Eds.), *Psychological perspectives on lesbian, gay and bisexual experiences* (2d ed., pp. 217–225). New York: Columbia University Press.

Greene, B. (1994). Ethnic minority lesbians and gay men: Mental health and treatment issues. *Journal of Consulting and Clinical Psychology, 62,* 243–251.

Greene, B. (2003). Beyond heterosexism and across the cultural divide: Developing an inclusive lesbian, gay, and bisexual psychology—a look to the future. In L. D. Garnets and D. C. Kimmel (Eds.), *Psychological perspectives on lesbian, gay and bisexual experiences* (2d ed., pp. 357–400). New York: Columbia University Press.

Hain, D. W. (2004). Drop the labels! The new generation's plea. *the e. word, 3*(2), 1–3. http://www.ucc.org/evangelism/Package 32/7DropTheLabels.pdf.

Hershberger, S. L., and D'Augelli, A. R. (2000). Issues in counseling lesbian, gay, and bisexual adolescents. In R. M. Perez, K. A. DeBord, and K. J. Bieschke (Eds.), *Handbook of counseling and psychotherapy with lesbian, gay, and bisexual clients* (pp. 225–248). Washington, D.C.: American Psychological Association.

Janus, S. S., and Janus, C. L. (1993). *The Janus report on sexual behavior.* New York: Wiley.

Marks, L. (2004). Healing the war between the genders. Newton, MA: HeartPower.

Martell, C. R., Safren, S. A., and Prince, S. E. (2004). *Cognitive behavioral therapies with lesbian, gay, and bisexual clients.* New York: Guilford.

Mattoon, M. A. (1981). *Jungian psychology in perspective.* New York: Free.

Morales, E. S. (1989). Ethnic minority families and minority gays and lesbians. *Marriage and Family Review, 14,* 217–239.

Munson, M., and Stelboum, J. P., Eds. (1999). *The lesbian polyamory reader: Open relationships, non-monogamy, and casual sex.* Binghamton, NY: Harrington Park.

Ochs, R., Ed. (2001). *The international directory of bisexual groups.* Cambridge: Bisexual Resource Center.

O'Neill, N., and O'Neill, G. (1972). *Open marriage: A new life style for couples.* New York: Evans.

Podvoll, E. (1990). *Recovering sanity.* New York: Harper Collins.

Rust, P. R. (Ed.) (2000). *Bisexuality in the United States: A social science reader.* New York: Columbia University Press.

Rust, P. R. (2003). Finding a sexual identity and community: Therapeutic implications and cultural assumptions in scientific models of coming out. In L. D. Garnets and D. C. Kimmel (Eds.), *Psychological perspectives on lesbian, gay, and bisexual experiences* (pp. 227–269). New York: Columbia University Press.

Queen, C. (1996). Sexual diversity, bisexuality and the sex positive perspective. In B. A. Firestein (Ed.), *Bisexuality: The psychology and politics of an invisible minority* (pp. 103–124). Thousand Oaks, CA: Sage.

Russell, S. T., and Seif, H. (2002). Bisexual female adolescents: A critical analysis of past research and results from a national survey. In D. Atkins (Ed.), *Bisexual women in the twenty-first century* (pp. 73–94). Binghamton, NY: Harrington Park.

Savin-Williams, R. C. (2003). Lesbian, gay, and bisexual youths' relationships with their parents. In L. D. Garnets and D. C. Kimmel (Eds.), *Psychological perspectives on lesbian, gay, and bisexual experiences* (pp. 299–326). New York: Columbia University Press.

Stone, H. and Stone, S. (1989). *Embracing ourselves*. San Francisco: Nataraj.

U.S. Census Bureau. (2002). Projections of the Resident Population by Age, Sex, Race, and Hispanic Origin: 1999 to 2100 (NP-D1-A). Population Projections Program, Population Division, U.S. Census Bureau, Department of Commerce, Washington, D.C. www.census.gov

West, C. (1995). *Lesbian Polyfidelity*. San Francisco: Booklegger.

6

COUNSELING THE BISEXUAL MARRIED MAN

Greg Carlsson

MARRIED BISEXUAL men and women are among the most invisible segments of the bisexual population. While some bisexuals come out to their spouses prior to marrying, others are not even aware of their same-sex sexual and emotional desires until well into their family life. Virtually all bisexual men struggle with some degree of conflict between their bisexual identity and their marriage. Isolation, depression, judgment, guilt, and grief are common emotions these men experience. While many married bisexual men choose to remain closeted, others reveal their identities to their spouses and choose to work on their relationships. This chapter will explore the journey of bisexual married men by examining the lives of three men. To work effectively with these men, therapists will need to address issues of heterosexual privilege, "external" (i.e., socially perceived) sexual expression, grief, identity, as well as shifts required in the marital dyad for the marriage to continue. Therapists may also be challenged to address the countertransference issues that arise for them during the therapeutic process.

UNDERSTANDING BISEXUAL MEN IN CONTEXT

Many of society's negative responses to minority groups in general and bisexual men in particular are steeped in fear. We can see this fear operating as we study the history of race relations, gender bias, and discrimination against people based on sexual orientation. It has taken years for gay men, lesbians, women, ethnic, and cultural minorities to penetrate the perceptions and framework from which our heterosexual, Caucasian, male-dominated society operates. We are slowly moving through a metamorphosis from a societal framework that pathologizes and devalues gay and bisexual experience to a society that is more inclusive and accepting of the sexual minority community. As our society presses forward, this metamorphosis of its "sociological framework" has given birth to a more robust comprehension of the dynamics of our fears. Unfortunately, negative cultural narratives and our lack of empirical knowledge leave us apprehensive about accepting new affirmative information about sexual minorities.

As has been the case with many other struggles for liberty, sexual minorities' battles for acceptance and equality have not been without casualties. The rape and brutal murder of Brandon Teena, a transgender youth in Nebraska, in 1993 and the kidnapping and heinous murder of Matthew Shepard, a political science student at the University of Wyoming, in 1996 are just two examples of the risks and costs associated with choosing to be out and proud as a sexual or gender minority person (Roussel 1996; Savin-Williams 2003).

Death by depression-related suicide or by hate-motivated violence remains at record levels. Thirty percent of gay and bisexual adolescent males attempt suicide at least once (Remafedi, Farrow, and Deisher 1991) and gay and lesbian youth represent 30 percent of all completed teen suicides (Gibson 1989). By extrapolation, this means a "successful" suicide attempt by a gay or bisexual teen occurs every five hours and forty-eight minutes (Gibson 1989).

As we take a closer look at bisexual married men, it is important to keep these societal forces in mind. Every man who becomes aware of his same-sex attractions must cope with a variety of influences. His ego development and personal sense of sexual identity may be either cultivated or arrested based on the information he digests and the attitudes he internalizes from society and from his family of origin.

The goal of the present chapter is to provide counselors and educators with an understanding of the struggles involved when married bisexual men make the courageous decision to seek assistance by reaching out to individual counselors or support groups. For many bisexual men, particularly those living in traditional monogamous male/female marital relationships, the societal, religious, and political stigma attached to bisexuality weighs heavily upon their shoulders. These men struggle to reconcile their attraction to both sexes and their marital commitments to their partner.

SOCIETAL VIEWS OF BISEXUALITY

Our society perpetuates the idea that individuals must settle on one of two dichotomous sexual orientations: a person is considered to be either heterosexual or homosexual. Individuals who find themselves in the middle may find hostility and support lacking from both the heterosexual and homosexual communities (Blumstein and Schwartz 1977). Despite the fact that the American Psychiatric Association removed homosexuality as a diagnostic category of mental illness from the *Diagnostic and Statistical Manual of Mental Disorders* in 1973, the dichotomization of sexual orientation into heterosexuality and homosexuality has remained largely undisturbed. This dichotomous construction of sexual orientation has perpetuated the belief that bisexuals are psychologically maladjusted (Fox 1995a, b).

For every additional "minority category" that a person adds to his own core sense of identity, an additional sense of alienation can arise. Bisexual married men in monogamous mixed-orientation marriages are "a minority within a minority;" part of the sexual minority community, but involved in a marriage that is perceived as heterosexual.

EMOTIONAL AND PSYCHOLOGICAL ISSUES FOR BISEXUAL MARRIED MEN

In our predominantly Judeo-Christian culture, most men feel the pressure to marry heterosexually and have children, and the majority of men continue to do so. As mentioned earlier, bisexual married men find themselves with the added dilemma of being attracted to both men and women. Outwardly, the married man who is secretly struggling with his bisexuality is perceived as the "ideal" product of society. Men are supposed to marry women, produce children, and continue the family lineage. We are born into a society that still elevates the two-parent, heterosexual, and married-with-children family as ideal. Knowing this, many bisexual men feel lonely and alienated in their heterosexual roles as husbands and/or fathers because their fulfillment of that role is, in part, a pretense.

Heterosexual individuals who marry in this culture experience a lifestyle that is congruent with their sexual orientation. Their friends, the majority of their neighbors, their community of religious affiliation, and most of their relatives are assumed to be heterosexual. For the bisexual man, there is incongruence between his presumed heterosexuality and actual bisexual feelings and desires. The incongruence between his orientation and his lifestyle can cause severe intrapsychic discord as well as strife within his primary relationships.

Bisexual married men face the additional challenge of biphobia within the gay community. Often these men are told that bisexuality is just a transitional identity, a "way station" in the journey to accepting their true identity as completely homosexual (Firestein 1996). For some men and women, bisexuality does serve as a temporary identity, but this is only true for a minority of these individuals (Matteson 1985; Stokes, McKirnan, and Burzette 1993). Bisexual married men may experience resentment from both the heterosexual and homosexual communities.

The bisexual man's relationship to the heterosexual and gay communities can be likened to that of a child from a divorced family who looks like one of the parents. If there is unresolved hurt and pain resulting from the divorce experience, the parent who sees their ex-partner in the eyes of their child may lash out at that child because they are reminded of the pain and hurt that is unresolved. In this case the child (bisexuality) is the constant reminder that the two sides (gay and heterosexual) will always be connected through the life of the child.

EMERGENCE OF BISEXUAL IDENTITY WITHIN HETEROSEXUAL MARRIAGE

Most bisexual men that enter into mixed-orientation marriages do not disclose their same gender feelings to their spouse before they marry (Buxton 2001). The nature of this population makes it very difficult to assess how many men are bisexual, how many bisexual men are married, and at what point a man realizes his bisexual attractions, though Buxton estimates that approximately two million marriages contain a gay or bisexual spouse (Buxton 2001). Unfortunately, very few mixed-orientation marriages survive following a gay or bisexual partner's disclosure of her or his same gender attractions (Gochros 1989; Buxton 1991). In addition, some men who are clearly bisexual in their attractions or behavior become aware of this much later in life or embrace their attractions without choosing to identify as bisexual.

A plethora of issues arise for bisexual men depending on when they become aware of their bisexuality. Many young men may be confused about their identity, believing that they are heterosexual at the time of marriage (Gochros 1989; Buxton 1994). At the point of self-identification as bisexual, many men struggle with whether, how, and under what circumstances to express their sexuality. Of men who are aware of their bisexuality prior to marriage, some are incredibly open and comfortable about talking with their spouses about their sexuality, while others keep it well hidden.

The dynamics of the therapeutic process will vary tremendously depending on the timing of the bisexual man's own awareness of his sexuality and the timing of his disclosure to his spouse. Some bisexual married men in mixed-orientation marriages may choose never to disclose their bisexual attractions to their wife. If disclosure occurs, his spouse's feelings and reactions may also vary considerably based on several factors, including her own ego strength, her religious background and affiliations, and her values and ethical convictions. Furthermore, her prior understanding of bisexuality will also have an impact on how she processes her partner's bisexual identity (Gochros 1989).

JOURNEYS OF THREE BISEXUAL MEN

The variety of paths that married men take toward a bisexual identification are most clearly illustrated in the lives of the bisexual men I have counseled over the past seven years who have participated in my weekly bisexual men's group. These weekly support groups began in 1997 in Pasadena, California to help bisexual men share and process their feelings and experiences. The group is open to all men who identify as bisexual or pansexual men who are attracted to more than one gender. Some of the participants prefer not to label their sexuality.

An intake and assessment is conducted prior to their first session to make sure the candidate is appropriate for the group. Some candidates are interested in joining a group for dating. Others may want casual sex. During the intake the candidate's needs and wants are explored. I explain that the purpose of this group is to provide a confidential and encouraging place to share thoughts and feelings about his bisexuality and learn from other members, but that it is not designed to be a group for casual sex.

When appropriate, I refer the candidate to a place more suitable for his needs. On other occasions, I have worked individually with a client until he was emotionally strong enough to join the group. As the facilitator, I provide a safe, encouraging arena for the men to share details of their personal and sexual lives and identities. I may have specific questions I intend for the group to address, but the true therapy and individual ego building comes from the interaction and accountability that the group as a whole provides to its members.

CARLOS: A MARRIED LATINO BISEXUAL MAN

Carlos is a thirty-eight-year-old, first-generation Mexican American living in the San Gabriel Valley in California. He has been married for eighteen years and has three children; he is very involved in their lives. Carlos was raised Catholic and is financially stable. Although he has had sexual fantasies about men, he has not acted on these urges during his marriage. He states that the fear and shame steeped in him through his religion and culture have kept him from acting sexually outside his marriage. Even though he knew he had an attraction toward men, he identified as heterosexual.

Although Carlos remembers being fascinated by the male figure as a young boy of six or seven, he wonders if his bisexuality is related (in a complex way) to his history of prior sexual victimization by a male uncle. When Carlos was ten, he was with his oldest brother and uncle, both seventeen years of age. On this day the three boys were playing on the beach in a secluded area. As the boys ran along the beach, Carlos remembered his uncle tackling him to the ground and trying to remove his swim trunks. Carlos's brother continued running away. Immediately Carlos began to panic, realizing that his uncle was not playing around but was going to do something sexual to him. He managed to break free of his uncle's hold and run back home. Although Carlos had experimented sexually with his peers on a consensual basis, this event was not consensual and was thus devastating. Afterward, Carlos questioned himself. He struggled with his experience of the event, how it happened, his (and his uncle's) sexual identity and his brother's abandonment. Carlos never addressed these issues with either his brother or his uncle. It was a deeply buried secret until he shared his story at the bisexual men's support group.

Carlos continues to wonder what effect this experience had on his attractions toward men and women. Did the incident somehow foster his attraction toward men? During one of the group discussions, Carlos shared the following comments about his process.

> As a Latino, I know I am more "macho" than "femme." In my country, married guys do have gay sex, but nobody talks about it. Gay guys are always portrayed in movies as being effeminate and weak. I don't fit that stereotype, and I am married, so it is easier to pass as straight and think of myself as straight. But now, at this time in my life, I have decided that I can't live this way anymore. I have to figure out who I am and if I am going to continue to be married. I have never told my wife about being attracted to men. I feel that if she found out she would kick me out of my house and try and keep my kids away from me. I couldn't bear that.

Carlos's past sexual abuse, the resulting ambiguity of his sexual identity, and the uncertainty of his marriage had left him depressed and anxious. As he started attending the support group and weekly individual sessions, he began coming to terms with the sexual abuse and how this experience could be separated from, yet related to, his attraction to men. Carlos was also evaluated for his depression and began taking antidepressants. He successfully resolved the depression and began to deal more proactively with his issues. He also realized that he had become emotionally distant from his wife and had targeted her with his frustrations. He never told her about his bisexual attractions; however, by processing and understanding his feelings and through his involvement in the support group and individual therapy, he was able to build a healthier sense of self and communicate better with his wife.

RON: MARRIAGE BETWEEN TWO OPENLY SELF-IDENTIFIED BISEXUAL PARTNERS

Ron is a forty-nine-year-old Caucasian living with his wife of twenty-five years. Ron was five years old when his parents divorced. He has two younger sisters. Ron said, "In my own mind, I became the 'man of the house,' making sure my sisters were safe and feeling like it was my responsibility to make sure everything was under control." Ron remembers being twelve or thirteen years old and going to sleepovers at friends' house.

> It was at this time that I started noticing other guys. I wasn't thinking about having sex with them, it was more . . . boys seeing who was "bigger." We would skinny-

dip, get a hard-on, masturbate, and joke about the experience, but I didn't feel sexually attracted to the other guys. We were also going out with the neighborhood girls and making out.

Ron didn't realize consciously that he was attracted to men until he was twenty-nine years old. Ron had dated women during college and into his twenties. During his late twenties he began feeling more emotionally attracted to men. In contrast, he felt men wanted more of a physical interaction with him. Around that time, Ron began attending co-gender bisexual support groups. He met his wife through one of the groups. He shared his experience of their relationship in the bi men's support group.

We have always been very open with each other. Because we are both bisexual, we can comment on men and women that we find attractive and not feel like we have to keep it a secret; I can share my "bi" thoughts with my partner. There have been times when we have asked another person or couple to join us in sex. As a couple we talk about it first and decide if it is something we want to bring into our relationship. Anonymous sex has never been part of the equation. Both of us have said that we will not engage in sex with strangers. I think because we have open communication with each other and are secure in the relationship, we are able to add a "poly" element to enhance our marriage.

Through the group process, Ron realized that the open communication he fostered with his wife was a primary factor in keeping their marriage intact. Through their openness they were able to share in each other's ongoing sexual development.

ROBERT: A BISEXUAL JEWISH MARRIED MAN AND "LATE BLOOMER"

Robert is fifty-eight years old. He is Jewish and lives on the west side of Los Angeles, California. He has been married for thirty-eight years and has two grown children. For most of his married life, his social circle has centered on his family, their synagogue, and his professional relationships. Robert is a family practice physician winding down a successful career in medicine. Robert has previously identified as heterosexual. In high school he played football and was part of a fraternity in college before entering medical school. Looking back, Robert states that he can't remember ever being attracted sexually to men. He states that he has always felt comfortable in social settings around men and women and that his wife is his best friend. Robert has two sisters and one brother who also live in the area. Robert remembers his childhood as being a positive experience. His mother was a homemaker and his father was a banker.

Four years ago, while at his local gym, Robert began noticing guys sexually. He remembers thinking that his perception of men was starting to change. He began fantasizing about having sex with them. At the same time, he felt very uneasy and puzzled about the feelings. He wanted to share the dilemma with his wife, but was fearful about what she would say. She had always been his confidant. Could he tell her this? He began thinking back over his life, wondering if he had somehow masked his gay feelings.

As he thought about his past, he wasn't sure whether or not he had suppressed his feelings in order to protect himself from admitting he was gay. Robert felt very alone and isolated. Reluctantly he confided in a gay colleague. Robert began by saying, "Something odd is beginning to happen to me. I am starting to find men sexually attractive. I don't know what to do with these feelings and I am afraid my situation might break up my marriage." Robert could tell by the timbre of his listener's voice that he was annoyed with Robert's dilemma. His colleague responded, saying, "Come on, you can't tell me that you have not had these feelings before. Whenever I hear about guys like you, I think to myself, 'Yeah, they just want what straight people have and won't admit that they are really gay.'" Robert felt even more isolated.

In desperation, hoping to find men in similar situations, Robert joined a gay father's group. Unfortunately, he also found judgment there. Many of the men were involved in bitter custody battles with their ex-wives and were not supportive of Robert, who was looking to continue his marriage. Eventually, the loneliness became overwhelming. One evening, three months later, with his heart pounding and through many tears, Robert broke down and shared his story with his wife. He also shared with her that he had acted on his feelings via mutual masturbation in the steam room at the gym. Although she was overwhelmed and held some doubt about their future, she realized that Robert was still her best friend and the man she loved. She chose to redefine their marriage and progress down an unfamiliar path.

Working through a number of mixed feelings, Robert and his wife eventually told the children about their father's sexuality. Currently, Robert defines himself as gay with bisexual tendencies. He grew up in an era in which there was a prevailing belief that the normal orientation was heterosexual and the other one, homosexual, was pathologized. For Robert, a bisexual orientation felt too foreign to embrace. Although she was tolerant, Robert's wife did not want to hear about her husband's behavior. Robert bought her Amity Pierce Buxton's book, *The Other Side of the Closet: The Coming Out Crisis for Straight Spouses*, and tried to be supportive, as she too had to reassess herself and her marriage.

As a sign of support, on occasion, Robert's wife would accompany him to Pasadena, window-shop while the group was in session, and then meet him for dinner to discuss the group or other aspects of their marriage. For Robert, the Bisexual Men's Support Group gave him a nonjudgmental place to share his frustrations and fears. The group also held him accountable as he continued in his exploration, asking him if he was considering his wife's needs as well as his own. Because the group was truly supportive, Robert did not feel judged by their loving confrontation. Robert is a living example that for some people sexual orientation is fluid and can change over a lifetime.

Each of these men struggled with their bisexuality in unique ways. The following sections will explore the psychological issues that bisexual married men present in therapy as well as therapeutic strategies that are useful when working with these men.

PSYCHOLOGICAL ISSUES BISEXUAL MARRIED MEN PRESENT IN THERAPY

Bisexual behavior has always been a part of society, but only recently have we begun to regard bisexuals' experiences as having worth and validity. Bisexual men become involved in mixed orientation marriages for many reasons: societal and family pressures, true love for the woman they are choosing to marry, the desire to raise a family, and sometimes in response to the internalization of negative feelings about gay life (Rust 2000; Beemyn and Steinman 2001). They may also believe that their same sex feelings will diminish once they become a husband and/or father.

As mentioned earlier, negative perceptions from the heterosexual and homosexual communities also make it difficult for bisexual married men to receive the support needed to talk through some of their ongoing issues. In a study by Gregory Herek (2002), heterosexual women felt less favorably toward bisexuals than toward homosexuals, regardless of gender. In contrast, heterosexual men held less favorable attitudes toward sexual minority men (whether bisexual or homosexual) than they did toward sexual minority women (whether bisexual or lesbian). This is one of the first studies to demonstrate the empirical basis of some of the negative perceptions bisexual men report experiencing from their heterosexual and gay peers and acquaintances (Herek 2002).

Without the means to talk about their bisexual feelings, bisexual men may experience levels of emotional pain that may push them into extreme feelings of depression and isolation. Many men in my groups have been on psychotropic medication for depression and anxiety. The prevalence of depression and anxiety among bisexual men may be due to their inability to reconcile their bisexual orientation with themselves and their marriages or might occur as a side-effect of society's harsh judgments of bisexual married men and their subsequent decisions to remain closeted. We live in a society that is strict regarding behavior that is considered appropriate within the marital dyad. Because of the heightened probability of depression or despair among men in this population, it is always important to assess such men for current or recent suicidal ideation, as some men report feeling that there is no other way out of their situation. The next section explores the implications of these intrapsychic, interpersonal, and societal factors for working clinically with the bisexual married man in therapy.

SUGGESTIONS FOR THERAPISTS AND COUNSELORS

Counselors need to be aware that their client may have long-standing feelings of attraction toward both men and women or may only recently have begun noticing genders other than his partner's in a more sexual manner. Either way, the discord in his life has brought him into therapy to start to address this complex issue. Your bisexual male client may be coming to you with a primary concern about internally accepting his bisexuality. Establishing trust and a solid therapeutic relationship are essential to building a foundation for successful therapeutic work with your client. As a bisexual married man, your client may already feel judged by most people outside the therapy room. If you are to help him with his bisexual development, you must be able to provide him with a different experience than that which he is likely encountering in mainstream society.

Some sexual minority men may come to your office hoping that you can help them change their sexual orientation (McConaghy 1987). These men may have heard about changing their sexual orientation through "reparative" or "conversion" therapies. Although this type of approach is still being practiced, in 1998 the American Psychiatric Association declared that reparative or conversion therapy to change a person's sexual orientation is potentially dangerous (American Psychiatric Association 1998). Current professional associations, such as the American Psychological Association and the National Association of Social Workers, endorse affirmative approaches to counseling bisexual, gay, and lesbian clients (American Psychological Association 2003).

There are a number of issues that are specifically of importance when counseling married bisexual male clients. In the following remarks I draw extensively from my clinical experience with bisexual men in individual therapy and support groups. Some of the issues that bisexual men bring to therapy include issues of heterosexual privilege, decisions about "external" sexual expression, identity and systems congruency, marital and dyadic relationship issues, and grief.

HETEROSEXUAL PRIVILEGE Heterosexual privilege consists of the spoken and unspoken rules, rights, and privileges given to the dominant heterosexual community. Both the heterosexual and homosexual communities have accused bisexuals of wanting "heterosexual privilege." Gay men sometimes refer to bisexual men's interactions with heterosexuals and these men's investment in maintaining close ties with the straight community as evidence of their attachment to heterosexual privilege.

In truth, all minority people want to have the same privileges shared by the majority community. Most members of sexual minority populations work within a heterosexual environment, a "straight" dominant culture, and may alter their behavior and/or mannerisms depending on the level of acceptance or tolerance of same-sex orientations within that subculture. This behavior is not limited to the bisexual community. Unfortunately, for the bisexual married man, the fear of losing heterosexual privilege may increase his anxiety as he attempts to begin acting upon his same sex desires.

EXTERNAL SEXUAL EXPRESSION Most bisexual married men have the added difficulty of needing to make choices about whether to stay monogamous within their marriages or to act on their homosexual desires. This sometimes results in the decision to engage in covert same-sex behaviors and may include decisions to engage in anonymous sex, frequent gay bathhouses, or seek same-sex sexual encounters in public places. A bisexual married father's greatest fear is usually that his behavior will be discovered or found out, his relationship will crumble, and the legal issues that ensue will result in the loss of his parental rights, e.g., that his children may be kept from him (Money 1988).

For many bisexual married men, fear continues to permeate their psychological reality, leading them to keep their two worlds compartmentalized and dividing their sense of self in the process. Some bisexual men rationalize their same gender sexual behavior as being "OK" because it is not with a woman. They have been taught that sex with women is more sacred than having sex with a man. Often, these men do not become involved with women outside their marriages and may not even consider themselves to be gay or bisexual. Black men engaging in sex with other men may use the phrase on the *down low* or DL. They do not want to be associated with white gay culture so they have come up with the term *down low* (King 2004). In addition, some bisexual Latinos engage in same-sex sexual relationships without ever identifying as gay or bisexual (Manalansan 1996; Dube and Savin-Williams 1999; Ferrer and Gómez, chapter 13). When engaging in same-sex behavior, bisexual men may have their own set of rules such as "no kissing" or "keeping their clothes on." Men who meet at known cruising places for anonymous sex know why they are there, so protocol is reduced to a minimum (Money 1988).

It is easy to make the claim that many bisexual married men are involved in HIV-related behaviors and thus are responsible for transmitting the virus to their partners. Society must remember that an orientation cannot transmit HIV. Unprotected sex and the sharing of needles while engaging in intravenous drug use spread the HIV virus. Both men and women who have multiple sexual partners or who are not 100 percent sure they are in a monogamous relationship need to behave responsibly by keeping themselves safe and protected.

Few studies have been conducted to track men's bisexual behaviors, but in recent studies researchers have suggesting three trends. First, bisexual men do engage in relatively high rates of unprotected sex with male partners (McKirnan et al. 1995). Second, there are also indications in the research literature that bisexual men may engage in less reciprocal anal sex (Stokes et al. 1996). And third, bisexual men appear to be having less sex with male partners than do homosexual men; thus the risk of sexual transmission from a bisexual male partner may be less than previously thought (Doll et al. 1992; Lever et al. 1992; Stokes, Burzette, and McKirnan 1991). Nonetheless, due to the very secretive nature of some of this external sexual behavior, these men may face little accountability within their marriages.

Many of the bisexual married men I have worked with will not wear a condom while engaging in sex with their wives. They justify this choice by saying that their same-sex sexual interaction is low risk and not reciprocal in nature (meaning, they give rather than receive oral sex with anonymous male partners) so consequently they believe that there is little need to wear a condom. In addition, these men worry that if they suddenly began wearing a condom, their wives would realize that they are being unfaithful. Dealing with guilt over past and current behavioral choices that may have put their marital partner at risk is one significant element of therapeutic work with this population that may need to be addressed in session. The bisexual men's support group has been a safe environment for the men to talk about their behavior and discuss the ramifications of each other's conduct.

COMING OUT BISEXUAL Research on the sexual identities of lesbian, gay, and bisexual youth have indicated that gay and bisexual male respondents first became aware of their same-sex attractions at an average age of 10.8 years, and that 58 percent of those men who reported other-sex attractions first became aware of them at an average age of 10.6 years. Ninety-five percent had first same-sex sexual contact at an average age of 13.3 years and 56 percent had first other-sex contacts at an average age of 11.9 years (Rosario et al. 1996). In studies conducted in 1983, Weinberg, Williams, and Pryor found that the average age of men identifying as bisexual was 27.2 years. Earlier studies, such as the study by Klein (1978), found the average age for men self-identifying as bisexual was 24.1 years, though a study by Ron Fox (1995a, b) indicated bisexual men coming out at somewhat earlier ages, though at ages older than their gay and lesbian counterparts. Due to external and internal pressures, many bisexual married men who experienced same gender feelings during their preteen years may have suppressed their feelings to conform to societal pressures, only to have these desires and attractions reemerge later in their adult lives.

SEXUAL IDENTITY CONGRUENCY As same gender feelings begin to emerge or start to intrude upon their current identity, these men's understanding of "who they are" and "how they fit" into their current lifestyle may begin to deteriorate. The first step for the therapist may be to help the client understand his own thoughts and feelings; perhaps he is having bisexual fantasies or has only recently realized that he is attracted to a gender outside the guidelines of his current orientation. Sharing this information with the therapist may be the first time the client has verbalized his internal sexuality struggle. During this first stage of therapy, acceptance and empathy is paramount to the therapeutic process. If a client does not embrace his sexual identity, and instead attempts to stifle it, there is a high probability that he will fail to find congruency and may continue to feel lonely and isolated in his ongoing internal conflict.

For instance, I have seen this struggle for congruency occur with married fundamentalist Christian and Jewish men who do not work through the sexual identity process but choose to "pray" or "white knuckle" their same-sex attractions away. Most of them have been taught through fundamentalist religious institutions and/or their families of origin that they cannot be attracted to the same sex and be accepted fully by God. This lack of acceptance and shame has forced many of these men away from their families and places of worship, producing additional angst within their marriages as well as fostering depression and suicidal tendencies. Currently, many mainstream denominations are struggling with accepting qualified "out" clergy. As some religious denominations begin to embrace these clergy, the sexual minority community will have another affirming arena in which to address their ongoing concerns about their sexuality.

SYSTEMS CONGRUENCY   If bisexual men can begin to make an internal shift and embrace their bisexual identity, they can then begin to address how their bisexuality is going to impact their marriage and other components of their current external life system. The process may be ongoing as the paradigm shift begins to evolve. At this time, to gain "internal systems congruency" within the self, the therapist will want to help the client address any internalized biphobia.

RELATIONSHIP CONCERNS AND THE MARITAL DYAD

Although this chapter deals primarily with the bisexual married man as an individual, this section will look at your client's orientation as it affects the marital dyad. A major paradigm shift may need to occur in the relationship if the couple decides to continue their marriage. One of the main gender differences in our society involves the typically gendered nature of attitudes toward recreational sex. Heterosexual men tend to be far more accepting of casual sex than are women (Firestein 1996) due primarily, I believe, to their socialization around issues of sex. Some men have recreational sex without viewing it as "love." The gay community frequently echoes this acceptance of sex without love or commitment via advertisements in gay media, the existence of gay bathhouses, and the frequency with which many out and closeted gay men utilize other venues for anonymous sexual encounters. Some recent research indicates that women in our society are better trained in the skills that sustain intimacy and that both men and women tend to fall in love with women more than men (Weinberg, Williams, and Pryor 1994). In addition, both bisexual men and women report longer lasting relationships with women than with men (Weinberg, Williams, and Pryor 1994).

In working with mixed-orientation couples where one partner is heterosexual and the other is bisexual, there are several areas of major conflict that are almost certain to surface. In most cases, the partner who is not bisexual feels betrayed and deeply hurt by the emergence of the bisexual partner's feelings and desires. This partner's present knowledge of their relationship has changed. The reality may be overwhelming for the marital dyad, especially if the marriage is already weathering some storms. Unfortunately, even when communication skills are superior, it is rare that a mixed sexual orientation couple can shift from a traditional marriage commitment to an open relationship unless clear agreements are made that the marriage relationship is to remain primary (Brownfain 1985). Once spouses come out as gay, lesbian, or bisexual, divorce results in the majority of cases (Buxton 2001).

If the couple decides to stay together, a new base of communication needs to be developed and fostered. The couple must find ways to satisfy the moral values and sexual, emotional, and social needs of each spouse (Buxton 2001, Buxton, chapter 21). As the transition begins to occur, new ground rules, new understandings, and a new agreement around accountability (different for each couple) need to be negotiated.

In the context of a committed gay or lesbian relationship, the honest acknowledgment of bisexuality will also usually warrant some change in the relationship. If the relationship has a solid foundation, there may be a period of adjustment, with the couple figuring out new contracts and agreements so the relationship can continue to grow (Latham and White 1978; Matteson 1985).

Regardless of whether one is working with a same-sex or other-sex couple, the therapist can help the couple devise tools that will assist them to strengthen their relationship. If the bisexual partner wants to act on his bisexual feelings, this will need to be discussed. During each step of the counseling process, the couple must expand their conceptual matrix of what "commitment" means to them. They may decide that the primary relationship will stay paramount while secondary relationships are purely reserved for sexual expression. The therapist must let the couple decide what is appropriate for them and their needs, while supporting them with feedback, facilitation, information, and resources relevant to their specific goals as a couple.

In looking at some of the factors associated with marital success when bisexual men are married to heterosexual women, honesty, communication, peer support, talk therapy, and taking time were said to be positive contributing factors in helping the marriage stay together (Buxton 2001). In a study by Stuart J. Edser and

John D. Shea (2002), twenty bisexual married men in monogamous, heterosexual marriages were interviewed to address the stability of their marriages. The study set out to determine if the marriages were successful and, if so, to what degree. The study also aimed to identify the primary factors associated with these men that made their marriages successful. The study concluded that the men in this sample seemed to be psychologically stable, not under inordinate stress, and the majority of their marriages appeared to be in relatively good condition. Thus, for bisexual men with characteristics and attitudes similar to the men of this sample, monogamous marriage is a viable life option (Edser and Shea 2002).

GRIEF Grief frequently accompanies the coming out process, and both grief and coming out are major issues for individuals in the sexual minority community. For the bisexual male, grieving may involve the loss of hopes and dreams approved of by heterosexual society and the losses associated with having to make necessary adjustments to adapt to a more complicated emotional and relational reality. For many of these men, their marriage and, therefore, their sense of a personal future may feel unstable in the wake of coming out as bisexual to their loved ones. For example, Carlos had never acted upon his same gender feelings but was grieving over the reality of his bisexual orientation. Cultural and conservative religious values had forced him to keep his secret to himself to the point that he had seriously thought of ending his life three times.

Bisexuals coming out from a prior gay or lesbian orientation or identity have already faced the losses associated with coming out once and must now mourn a new loss—loss of full membership in their gay community (Matteson 1996). This can be very difficult for some bisexual men, though the difficulty is likely to vary depending on the particular man's internal strength, his support system, and the attitude of his same-sex partner. Grieving is an ongoing process that the bisexual married man experiences as he works therapeutically to understand how bisexuality is or is not going to fit into his current and future life.

THERAPEUTIC STRATEGIES IN WORKING WITH BISEXUAL MARRIED MEN

There are several therapeutic strategies that I have found useful in helping my married bisexual male clients embrace their bisexuality. In order to foster a man's development of his positive bisexual identity, it may be beneficial to help him articulate what bisexuality means to him. Second, you can address his same gender feelings by exploring how bisexuality is currently manifesting in his life. Third, if he is currently in a heterosexual or same-sex relationship, investigate whether he wants to continue to be in it. When coming out to others is a primary issue of concern to the client, I use the tool of writing "sample letters," addressing how he would share information about his sexual identity with close friends and family members.

It is helpful to educate your client that for some people sexual orientation can be fluid and that an individual's orientation may change over a period of time. The Klein Sexual Orientation Grid (KSOG) (Klein, Sepekoff, and Wolf 1993) is a visual and conceptual tool for assisting clients to look at seven different areas of sexuality: sexual attraction, sexual behavior, sexual fantasies, emotional preference, social preference, self-identification, and degree of involvement in a heterosexual or homosexual lifestyle. The KSOG can help clients chart past, present, and ideal ways of addressing these seven areas. In the past seven years I have administered the KSOG to over three hundred people. For many individuals it is profound to be able to visualize and chart the fluidity of their male/female interaction in these seven areas of sexuality. The therapist may assist bisexual married men to address these areas by using the KSOG to look at their past, current, and ideal thoughts about their sexuality. This can aid them in embracing who they are and how bisexuality affects their lives and marriages.

Finally, I also conduct a three-hour workshop on bisexuality in which I educate participants on bisexuality and assist them in exploring their own sexual orientation, feelings, and desires. At the end of my three-hour workshop, I utilize a role-playing experience and have the participants come out as bisexual to a significant person in their lives. This variation of "empty chair" Gestalt work is one tool you can utilize with your client to address the internal and external fears of bringing the various compartmentalized areas or "systems" in their lives into greater congruency.

One of the best ways to help individuals feel less isolated is to suggest that they become involved in a support group. For some bisexual married men who are only recently coming to grips with their orientation, this suggestion may be too overwhelming. But, for others, gender- and sexuality-specific groups can help them learn to talk about their fears and life situations in a safe, caring environment. The Internet, GLBT resource centers, bisexual social groups, books, newspapers, and magazines can all be useful resources for individuals new to the bisexual community. Many of the co-gender support and discussion groups encourage friends, partners, and spouses to attend as well so that they can learn more about bisexuality and meet other families who are in similar situations.

When working with bisexual married men, it is imperative that the therapist's countertransference is kept in check. Clients have frequently shared with me that they either never told their therapist about their bisexuality or, conversely, that their therapist constantly asked them about their bisexuality even though it was not part of the presenting problem.

As the therapist, notice your own internal dialogue as your client talks about his bisexual feelings and experiences. Pay attention to what may be difficult for you about working with your married bisexual clients. If clients sense disapproval from you, and depending on how invested your client is in pleasing you, they may alter their responses to conform to a sense of what you value or may seek another therapist who is more congruent with their process. If you find that you are exceptionally uncomfortable assisting an individual with bisexual concerns, it is best to refer to another qualified therapist.

FUTURE TRENDS

Increasingly, bisexual men are also living in nontraditional, same gender, or transgender relationships. Between February 12, 2004, and March 12, 2004, San Francisco held civil marriages; licenses were issued to 4,161 same-sex couples. Some people believe that these civil marriages shake the very foundation of the institution of marriage. Is the sexual minority community destroying the fabric of marriage or is it straightening and redefining the very fibers that keep the marital fabric woven? The conservative heterosexual community does not have a patent on "family values." Many individuals in the sexual minority community want to embrace positive ethical values for their families as well. It is startling to realize that in some states sexual minority couples can adopt children, but these same individuals are not given the right to marry their same-sex partners. Given that some states deem bisexual men and women, gay men, and lesbians fit to parent, permitting same-sex marriage would only seem to strengthen their roles as parents and spouses and enhance "family values." As we push forward for equal rights, our country is being forced to address the inequalities that impact the sexual minority community. In turn, bisexuality continues to gain acknowledgment and understanding through the personal growth efforts of bisexual individuals, positive media attention, and increasing community awareness of the existence of bisexuals in gay and heterosexual communities.

Therapists can aid bisexual married men to become internally congruent as these men learn to address and integrate their bisexuality within themselves and in their current living situations. Ron, Robert, and Carlos all found support by joining a bisexual married men's support group. Some group members shared similar struggles while others learned from these three men. The therapeutic group or individual setting is a powerful venue where bisexual married men can begin to unpack the many years of isolation and internal pain they have held within.

REFERENCES

American Psychiatric Association. (1998). Position Statement on therapies focused on attempting to change sexual orientation ("Reparative" or "Conversion" therapies).

American Psychological Association (2003). Guidelines for psychotherapy with lesbian, gay, and bisexual clients. In L. D. Garnets and D. C. Kimmel (Eds.), *Psychological perspectives on lesbian, gay, and bisexual experiences* (2d ed., pp. 756–785). New York: Columbia University Press.

Beemyn, B. and Steinman, E. (2001). *Bisexuality in the lives of men: Facts and fictions.* Copublished as *Journal of Bisexuality,* 1(2/3). Binghamton, NY: Harrington Park.

Blumstein, P. W., and Schwartz, P. (1977) Bisexuality: Some social psychological issues. *Journal of Social Issues,* 33(2), 30–45.

Brownfain, J. J. (1985). A study of the married bisexual male, paradox and resolution. *Journal of Homosexuality,* 11(1/2), 173–188.

Buxton, A. P. (1991). *The other side of the closet: The coming-out crisis for straight spouses.* Santa Monica: IBS.

Buxton, A. P. (1994). *The Other Side of the closet: The coming out crisis for straight spouses and families.* New York: Wiley.

Buxton, A. P. (2001). Writing our own script: How bisexual men and their heterosexual wives maintain their marriages after disclosure. In B. Beemyn and E. Steinman (Eds.), *Bisexuality in the Lives of Men: Facts and fictions* (pp. 155–189) Binghamton, NY: Harrington Park.

Doll, L. S., Peterson. L. R., White, C. R., Johnson, E, Ward. J. W., and the Blood Donor Study Group (1992). Homosexually and nonhomosexually identified men who have sex with men: A behavioral comparison. *Journal of Sex Research,* 29, 1–4.

Dube, E. M., and Savin-Williams, R. C. (1999). Sexual identity development among ethnic sexual-minority male youths. *Developmental Psychology,* 35(6), 1389–1398.

Edser, S. J., and Shea, J. D. (2002). An exploratory investigation of bisexual men in monogamous, heterosexual marriages. *Journal of Bisexuality,* 2(4), 7–43.

Firestein, B. A. (Ed.) (1996). *Bisexuality: The psychology and politics of an invisible minority.* Thousand Oaks, CA: Sage.

Fox, R. C. (1995a). Bisexual identities. In A. R. D'Augelli and C. J. Patterson (Eds.), *Lesbian, Gay and bisexual identities over the life span: Psychological perspectives* (pp. 48–86). New York: Oxford University Press.

Fox. R. C. (1995b). Coming out bisexual: Identity, behavior, and sexual orientation self-disclosure (Doctoral dissertation, California Institute of Integral Studies, 1993). *Dissertation Abstracts International,* 55(12), 556b.

Gibson, P. (1989). Gay male and lesbian youth suicide. In M Feinleib (Ed.), *Prevention and Intervention in Youth Suicide* (pp. 110–142). Report to the Secretary's Task Force on Youth Suicide, vol. 3. Washington, DC: U.S. Department of Health and Human Services.

Gochros, J. S. (1989). *When husbands come out of the closet.* Binghamton, NY: Harrington Park.

Herek, G. (2002) Heterosexuals' attitudes toward bisexual men and women in the United States. *Journal of Sex Research,* 39(4), pp. 264–274.

King, J. L. (2004). *On the down low: A journey into the lives of "straight" black men who sleep with men.* New York: Broadway.

Klein, F. (1978). *The bisexual option* (2d ed.) Binghamton, NY: Harrington Park.

Klein, F., Sepekoff, B., and Wolf, T. J. (1985). Sexual orientation: A multi-variable dynamic process. *Journal of Homosexuality*, 11(1/2), 35–50.

Latham, J.D., and White, G.D. (1978). Coping with homosexual expression within heterosexual marriages. Five case studies. *Journal of Sex and Marital Therapy*, 4, 198–212.

Lever, J., Kanouse, D.E., Rogers, W.H., Carson, S., and Hertz, R. (1992). Behavior patterns and sexual identity of bisexual males. *Journal of Sex Research*, 29, 141–167.

McConaghy, N. (1987). Heterosexuality/homosexuality: Dichotomy or continuum. *Archives of Sexual Behavior*, 16(5), 411–424.

McKirnan, D.J., Stokes, J., Doll L., and Burzette, R. (1995). Bisexually active men: Social characteristics and sexual behavior. *Journal of Sex Research*, 32(1), 65–76.

Manalansan, IV., M.F. (1996). Double minorities: Latino, Black, and Asian men who have sex with men. In R.C. Savin-Williams and K.M. Cohen, (Eds.), *The Lives of lesbian, gay and bisexual: Children to adults* (pp 393–415). New York, Harcourt Brace.

Matteson, D.R. (1985). Bisexual men in marriage: Is a possible homosexual identity and stable marriage possible? *Journal of Homosexuality*, 11(1/2), 149–172. Newbury Park, CA: Sage.

Matteson, D.R. (1996). Counseling and psychotherapy with bisexual and exploring clients. In B.A. Firestein (Ed.), *Bisexuality: The Psychology and Politics of an Invisible Minority* (pp.185–213). Thousand Oaks, CA: Sage.

Money, J. (1988). *Gay, straight, and in-between: The sexology of erotic orientation*. Oxford University Press.

Remafedi, G., Farrow, J.A., and Deisher, R.W. (1991). Risk factors for attempted suicide in gay and bisexual youth. *Pediatrics* 87(6), 869–875.

Rosario, M., Heino, F.L., Meyer-Bahlburg, Hunter, J., Exner, T.M., Gwadz, M., and Keller, A. M. (1996). The psychosexual development of urban lesbian, gay, and bisexual youth. *Journal of Sex Research*, 33(2), 133–126.

Roussel, B. (1996). *The Callan*. Laramie: University of Wyoming.

Rust, P.C. (2000). *Bisexuality in the United States: A social sciences reader*. New York: Columbia University Press.

Savin-Williams, R.C. (2003). Matthew Shepard's death: A professional awakening. In L.D. Garnets and D. C. Kimmel (Eds.), *Psychological perspectives on lesbian, gay and bisexual experiences* (2d ed., pp. 207–216). New York: Columbia University Press.

Stokes, J.P., Burzette, R., and McKirnan D.J. (1991). Bisexual men: Social characteristics and predictors of AIDS-risk behavior. Poster presented at Seventh International Conference on AIDS, June, Florence, Italy.

Stokes, J. P., McKirnan, D.J., and Burzette, R. G. (1993). Sexual behavior, condom use, disclosure of sexuality, and stability of sexual orientation in bisexual men. *Journal of Sex Research*, 30(3), 203–213.

Stokes, J.P., Taywaditep, K., Vanable, P.A., and McKirnan, D.J. (1996). Bisexual men, sexual behavior, and HIV/AIDS. In Beth A. Firestein, ed., *Bisexuality: The Psychology and Politics of an Invisible Minority* (pp. 149–168). Thousand Oaks: Sage.

Weinberg, M.S., Williams, C.J., Pryor D.W. (1994). *Dual attraction: Understanding bisexuality*. New York: Oxford University Press.

7

CULTURAL AND RELATIONAL CONTEXTS OF BISEXUAL WOMEN

IMPLICATIONS FOR THERAPY

Beth A. Firestein

WOMEN WHO are bisexual in their behavior, emotional bonding, attractions, and self-identification frequently seek therapy yet are underrepresented in the professional literature on counseling (Israel 2003a; Martin and Meezan 2003; Pachankis and Goldfried 2004). The cultural, relational, and community contexts of bisexual women shape these women, their identities, and their life experiences (Bradford 1997; Hutchins 1996; Rust 1996a, 1996b). Bisexual women live as both "insiders" and "outsiders" within mainstream heterosexual and lesbian communities (Bradford 1997; Ochs 1996). It is therefore critical to understand bisexual women in context in order to offer effective psychotherapy to this population (Firestein 1996a). This chapter highlights several areas of theoretical, empirical, and clinical importance related to counseling bisexual women.

The cultural contexts of bisexual women overlap significantly with those of heterosexual women and lesbians, yet embody certain complexities unique to their sexual identity and orientation (Falco 1996; Israel 2003a). The relational contexts of bisexual women also vary tremendously (Rust 1996b). Bisexual women may maintain relationship involvements with lesbians, heterosexual men, bisexual men, bisexual women, and with people who are diverse with respect to gender identity (transgendered or transsexual) or gender expression (butch/femme) (Alexander and Yescavage 2004). Clinicians and counselors need to be prepared to assist bisexual women within a variety of life contexts, including bisexual women in monogamous relationships; women maintaining honest, consensual relationships with more than one person; and women who may affiliate with alternative sexual communities (Hutchins 2001, 2002; Lenius 2001; Rust 1996b, Queen 1996a, 1996b). Bisexual women are frequently invisible when embedded in heterosexual relationships and stigmatized or rendered invisible when living within same-sex relationships and queer communities (Bradford 1997; Hutchins 1996). Relational issues and issues of community affiliation frequently overlap in complicated ways for bisexual women; for example, these women face a variety of difficulties when attempting to form relationships within lesbian social and political communities (Esterberg 1997; Ochs 1996; Rust 1995).

There is presently a small but growing body of professional literature addressing issues of bisexuality and mental health, including both qualitative and quantitative empirical research. This research is beginning to explore several of the mental health and lifestyle concerns of bisexual women and men (Firestein 1996a, 1996b; Jorm et al. 2002; Ketz and Israel 2002; Mathy, Lehmann, and Kerr 2004; Page 2004) and bisexual adolescents (Robin et al. 2002; Russell and Joyner 2001; Russell and Seif 2002).

I begin this chapter by discussing the challenges and positive aspects of identifying as bisexual and exploring the gender, racial, and community contexts that effect bisexual women. Next I discuss the community contexts embracing bisexual women as they interface with lesbian culture and with heterosexual society and discuss the question of whether a bisexual women's community really exists. The following section explores bisexual women's experiences in several different relational contexts. Bisexual women's relationships with lesbians, relationships with men, and relationships with bisexual women and bisexual men are discussed in some detail.

In the last section of the chapter, I turn to the empirical research on bisexual women, including mental health and service utilization, empirical research addressing other areas of importance to bisexual women, and implications of the research literature for counseling bisexual women. Finally, I turn to a discussion of affirmative approaches to conducting therapy with bisexual women and propose that counseling bisexual women is, in fact, a multicultural competency requiring significant shifts in the attitudes and skills sets of counselors seeking to work in effective and culturally sensitive ways with this population. I conclude by discussing the larger shift occurring in the field of psychology— toward a LesBiGay/Transgender affirmative paradigm for understanding sexual behavior and working with sexual minorities across a variety of disciplines.

CHALLENGES AND POSITIVE ASPECTS OF BISEXUAL IDENTIFICATION

Falco (1996) notes that women who love women experience several common identifiable stressors, such as the continual nature of choices to disclose or "pass" with respect to one's sexual minority identification, absence of social support for loving another woman, internalized homophobia/biphobia, and the absence of visible role models and cultural history. Bisexual women often face stressors that are unique to them as a group, including pressure to adopt a non-bisexual identity based on the gender of one's partner and bisexual women's own resistance to self-identifying or adopting the label *bisexual* (Bower, Gurevich, and Mathieson 2002). These stressors frequently compel many bisexual women to confront their own intellectual and emotional confusion because of the conflicts inherent within many of society's demands.

For example, there is considerable pressure on women who are in a current relationship with a woman to identify as lesbian, for women in current relationships with men to pass as heterosexual, and for women involved with more than one gender to "make a choice" (Rust 2003). Rust's (1995) careful analysis of lesbians' relationship to bisexuality and bisexual women revealed that lesbians consider bisexuality "politically irrelevant or nonexistent, placing bisexually identified women in continual positions of invalidation and political exclusion relative to a significant portion of other women-loving-women" (p. 200).

Bisexual individuals also face the challenge of self-acceptance (Fox 1991), the challenge of choosing relational forms and structures that fit with their identity (Rust 1996b), and the challenge of finding a sense of community to which one's "whole self" can belong (Esterberg 1997; Hutchins 1996; Ochs 1996). Bisexual identity has been conceptualized as multidimensional, involving elements of attraction, fantasy, behavior, social preference, emotional preference, sexual identity, and lifestyle (community affiliation) (Klein 1990; Klein, Sepekoff, and Wolf 1985). Incongruence among these dimensions and the experience of confusion are natural sequelae for bisexuals living in a culture that "permits" only gay and heterosexual identities.

There are both negative consequences and psychological benefits to embracing a bisexual identity. A disproportionate amount of attention has been given to the negative consequences of embracing a bisexual identity, but there are a number of psychological benefits to identifying as bisexual as well. The positive aspects of identifying as bisexual include the sense of freedom to define oneself, the satisfaction of having the ability to function as a bridge between straight and gay worlds, and the richness of being able to develop intimate relationships with either sex (Oxley and Lucius 2000).

Empirical evidence supports the notion that adopting a bisexual identity can accompany positive psychological outcomes. For example, it has been shown that bisexual individuals may be more flexible in their relationship roles (Matteson 1996), more resilient (Zinik 1984), and have life satisfaction and self-esteem equivalent to that found in their gay, lesbian, and heterosexual counterparts (Fox 1995; Jorm et al. 2002). Bradford's (1997) research participants reported that their bisexuality affected their self-concepts in three major ways: increased self-reliance, openness to others who are "different," and personal and/or spiritual enrichment (p. 167). The benefits of acknowledging one's bisexuality and embracing a bisexual identity exist in a delicate and dynamic balance with the difficulties of doing so. I encourage counselors working with bisexual women to attend carefully to the balance of supportive and challenging influences in their client's life and to actively assist the client to focus on the positive aspects of their identity to counteract the damaging effects of the culture's negative messages about being bisexual.

Clearly, there are factors unique to bisexual women's struggle to establish a positive identity, and these challenges pose unique and sometimes ongoing trials for women living these identities and experiences. But bisexual women's identity development, mental health, and emotional well-being are also strongly influenced by sexism, heterosexism, homophobia, racism, and other cultural factors (Greene 2003).

GENDER, RACIAL, AND COMMUNITY CONTEXTS OF BISEXUAL WOMEN

SEXISM AND HETEROSEXISM

Bisexual women, like all women, live in a culture pervaded by sexism, racism, classism, heterosexism, and homophobia (Balsam 2003; Pharr 1988; Rothblum and Bond 1996). In particular, bisexual women face issues of discrimination that include many of those faced by women with exclusive same-sex orientations, with the addition of elements unique to the bisexual experience (Nichols 1994; Ochs 1996). For example, lesbians, heterosexual women, and bisexual women are all vulnerable to the effects of institutionalized sexist and heterosexist bias and may have similar histories with respect to violence and traumatic victimization (Balsam 2003; Nichols 1994).

The sexism that pervades heterosexual society operates in powerful and unquestioned ways. Blackwood and Wieringa (2003) note that "because sexualities are informed by and embedded in gender hierarchies and gender ideologies that impose different constraints on women and men, sexual roles, behaviors, meanings and desires are different for women and men" (p. 419). Bisexual women and lesbians may experience a layering of the negative effects of oppression because of their dual status as women and as sexual minorities (Balsam 2003). Race, culture of origin, religion, and immigrant status also have dramatic influences on the sexual identity development of these women (Greene 1994, 1997).

RACE AND ETHNIC MINORITY STATUS AS CULTURAL FACTORS AFFECTING BISEXUALS

The past twenty-five years have witnessed substantial growth in published writing in the areas of understanding the experiences of ethnic and racial minority LGB individuals living in European American and North American cultures (Comas-

Diaz and Greene 1994; Chan 1992; Greene 1994, 2003; Morales 1989). Within the past ten to fifteen years, such writing has begun to take seriously the issues of bisexual people of color (Diamond and Savin-Williams 2003; Hutchins and Ka'ahumanu 1991; Rust 1996a, 2000, 2003). Critiques of sexual identity development models have begun to address both the white Eurocentric focus of such models as well as the limitations of such models predicated on dichotomous conceptions of sexual identity (Fox 1996; Rust 2000) and teleological, linear notions of sexual identity development (Diamond and Savin-Williams 2003; Rust 2003).

While a complete review of this literature is beyond the scope of the present chapter, it is valuable to highlight some of the recurring themes emerging out of the more recently published literature. First, LGB ethnic minority individuals are likely to encounter multiple marginalizations (Rust 2000) where they face both the dominant culture's racism and their own ethnic or racial group's heterocentrism and homophobia/biphobia (Greene 1994, 2003; Pachankis and Goldfried 2004; Rust 2000). Second, models of coming out and sexual identity development tend to be Eurocentric, with little or no acknowledgment as to the extent and the ways that expressions of sexuality vary culturally (Rust 1996a, 2000, 2003). Counselors need to be mindful of the ways that sexual identity labels and sexual terms differ across cultural, racial, and ethnic groups (Rust 1996a). Finally, although within-group variations are notable, the differences that exist among racial, ethnic, and cultural groups with regard to LGB affirmation and acceptance have important implications for counseling LGB clients (Rust 2000, 2003). This is especially significant for counselors who are assisting LGB clients contemplating coming out to their families and social support networks. For example, counselors must be prepared to intervene in varied ways with clients depending on the recency of their immigration to the U.S., their degree of acculturation to U.S. sexual norms, and whether or not they are currently living with other members of their families. It is sometimes unwise to strongly urge unacculturated clients or those who are financial dependent upon their families to come out to their families without carefully exploring the client's options of economic and emotional independence first.

Recently, research and theoretical work have begun to explore the challenging and positive elements associated with biracial identities. Further, this work has examined the potential value of comparing models of biracial identity development and models of bisexual identity development (Collins 2000; Gillem and Thompson 2004; Israel 2004; Rust 2000; Stanley 2004). Both biracial and bisexual individuals (and particularly women who are both biracial and bisexual) must learn to balance living in multiple, simultaneous cultural contexts. Many bisexual women, for example, must learn to live successfully in both lesbian culture and heterosexual society. Biracial and multiracial women must balance loyalties to multiple heritages, families, and communities. This is complicated by the fact that both the heterosexual and the predominantly Euro-American LGB cultures are not immune to the effects of racial and ethnic discrimination, stereotyping, and prejudice (Greene 1994; Rust 2000, 2003).

On a positive note, achieving a personal sense of empowerment with respect to racial or multiracial heritage may allow ethnic minority sexual minority women to develop many of the coping skills needed to successfully negotiate their sexual minority identity within a predominantly heterosexual culture (Matteson 1996; Rust 1996a, 2000). Skills developed to cope with racial or ethnic marginalization may assist bisexual women in handling their sexual marginalization (Rust 1996a, 2000). Biracial sexual minority women face challenges that reflect significant similarity to the challenges bisexual women of all racial and ethnic backgrounds face when intimately involved in predominantly lesbian women's communities. It is to the issue of bisexual women and lesbian culture that we now turn.

BISEXUAL WOMEN AND LESBIAN CULTURE

Several authors have written about the cultural issues and challenges that arise when bisexual women affiliate within lesbian communities (Bower, Gurevich, and Mathieson 2002; Ochs 1996; Rust 1992, 1993a, 1993b, 1995). Rust (2000) notes, "Bisexuality is particularly controversial in lesbian communities" (p. 413). In support of her assertion, Rust (2000) provides an excellent overview of the research on relations among bisexual women and lesbians. Counselors need to understand the complicated histories of feminism, lesbianism, and bisexual women and how these histories have influenced one another (Rust 1995) in order to serve their female bisexual (and lesbian) clients in optimal ways. An extensive explanation of this history is beyond the scope of the present chapter, but here I highlight the primary themes discussed in Rust's review.

The literature in this area has focused on three primary topics: the content of the negative attitudes lesbians hold with respect to bisexual women, the sociopolitical and historical roots of this antipathy, and the social, political, and psychological explanations for the tension between lesbians and bisexual women. In her sample of 346 lesbian participants, Rust (1993b) found that that a majority of her participants endorsed the belief that bisexual women were "in transition" or in denial of a "true" lesbian identity, that bisexual women are "not as committed to other women as lesbians are" (p. 485), and that bisexuals want to pass as heterosexual more than lesbians want to pass as heterosexual. Obviously, Rust's work provides evidence for the existence of some lesbians' negative beliefs about bisexual women.

The sociopolitical and historical roots of the antipathy between some lesbians and bisexual women are complex, but most authors have discussed this tension as having some basis in the emergence of identity-based politics in the

1970s and 1980s and the subsequent development of lesbian feminist political perspectives that assigned lesbians a "higher moral status" than bisexual women (Rust 1992, 1995, 2000, 2003). Although many lesbians are supportive of bisexual women and bisexuality, some lesbian communities have historically reduced the "threat" posed by inclusion of bisexual women in the larger lesbian/queer community by dismissing bisexuals as "confused individuals" (Rust 1993b). By depoliticizing bisexual identity, these groups have effectively denied bisexual women's unique perspectives and political concerns (Rust 1993b). These issues differ significantly for women who are coming out as bisexual after identifying as heterosexual than for women who are coming out as bisexual after identifying as lesbian (Esterberg 1997; Matteson 1996).

Women who are in the initial stages of exploring their attractions toward other women and who are emerging from heterosexual identities and cultural contexts often find that lesbian and/or queer communities provide gathering places and cultural events where they are likely to meet other same-sex loving women, most of whom identify as lesbian. Many women with established bisexual identities and some women who are in relationships or marriages with men also find that participating in women's communities, whether feminist, lesbian, or queer, meets important social and emotional needs (Weise 1992; Hutchins and Ka'ahumanu 1991). Many bisexual women find that only a part of their identity can be reflected and supported within the lesbian community, yet being a part of this community is extremely important to them (Esterberg 1997). Counselors will need to assist bisexual women in realistically evaluating the potential for support or hostility in their local lesbian communities and in making decisions that take this into account. Bisexual women experience different issues when interacting primarily with the dominant heterosexual culture.

BISEXUAL WOMEN AND HETEROSEXUAL SOCIETY

Whether monoracial, biracial, Caucasian, or minority in ethnic identification, all sexual minorities in the United States exist within the structures of Western, American culture that declare heterosexuality to be normative and all other sexual identities aberrant or otherwise suspect. This has led several writers to talk about the heterosexism and heteronormative culture as major factors influencing the identity development and lived experiences of all sexual minority individuals, regardless of their gender (Blumenfeld and Raymond 1988; Herek 2003).

Heterosexism refers to the "system by which heterosexuality is assumed to be the only acceptable and viable life option" (Blumfeld and Raymond 1988:226). The term *heteronormative culture* refers to the fact that society is structured to reflect the unquestioned and largely unconscious assumption that everyone living in the culture is heterosexual—or should be heterosexual (Pharr 1988; Rothblum and Bond 1996). Any person who is not heterosexual is perceived as abnormal, unnatural, and, in some cases, sinful and morally corrupt (Herek 2003; Pharr 1988). Society's laws and structures, such as the institution of marriage and the definition of family reflect these assumptions (Herek 2003; Rothblum and Bond 1996).

Within heteronormative society, LGBT people are considered undeserving of equal access to heteronormative structures, such as marriage, family, inheritance laws, or adoption privileges. These are the unquestioned rights and privileges of the heterosexual majority. The effects of heterosexism are pervasive. As Greene (2003) notes, "Heterosexism is not a singular or isolated experience or event. As such, heterosexism cannot be disconnected from the broader context of an individual's development or existence any more than sexism, for example, can be understood apart from the context of a woman's ethnicity, socioeconomic class, religion, or other significant aspects of her life" (p. 358)

Recently, gay marriage has become a major issue for the culture at large and is currently being actively contested in legislatures and courts across the United States. Bisexuals are in a unique position with respect to the institution of marriage. Bisexual men and women are allowed to marry complementary sex partners but not same-sex partners (Solot and Miller 2001). Therefore, bisexuals have the right to marry, to the extent that they are heterosexually involved and choose to remain invisible with respect to their bisexuality, but face barriers similar to those confronted by gays and lesbians when involved in committed same-sex partnerships. Therefore, the issue of concern to society is actually same-sex marriage rather than gay marriage, since gay men, lesbians, and bisexual people routinely marry other-gender partners.

The privileging of heterosexual desire and lifestyle choices are perceived by some lesbians as influencing bisexual women to choose heterosexual relationships over relationships with women (Ochs 1996; Rust 1995). However, Adrienne Rich (1980) asserts that even heterosexual women are without meaningful "choice" due to the heterosexual imperatives that pervade the culture. Providing some evidence for this, Bradford (1997) noted that eleven out of the twenty bisexual women and men she interviewed indicated first thinking that they were heterosexual before coming to a realization of their bisexuality. Many of her participants cited societal reinforcement of heterosexuality as a factor in their assumption that they were straight, in spite of the fact that these men and women had same-sex attractions and experiences. Interestingly, approximately 30 percent of Bradford's (1997) interviewees reported coming out as lesbian or gay prior to identifying as bisexual, which might be taken to provide evidence of the power of same-sex attraction in the face of pervasive heterosexism and the pressure to conform.

Counselors must be careful not to underestimate the complexity of certain decisions, such as the decision to marry a man, in a heterosexist, biphobic, and homophobic culture. Some bisexual women find the decision to marry one involving a great deal of ambivalence and concern, particularly insofar as they may see such a decision as having a potentially negative impact upon their standing vis-à-vis the lesbian and queer women's communities. We turn now to the question of the existence of bisexual women's community.

IS THERE A BISEXUAL WOMEN'S COMMUNITY?

Community is a major issue in the lives of bisexual women. Bisexual women face the difficult reality that there are few heterosexual or gay and lesbian communities in which they can feel a sense of full belonging and acceptance, although this is an important need for women who are seeking to develop positive bisexual identities (Fox 1991). These difficulties exist regardless of whether bisexual women choose to affiliate primarily within the dominant heterosexual culture (a necessity for all sexual minority individuals) or to affiliate primarily within lesbian and gay communities (Ochs 1996), though the challenges within these cultural contexts differ.

So, are there bisexual communities, and what do these communities have to offer? Bisexual women seek and sometimes find a sense of community with other bisexual women and with bisexual men (Bradford 1997, 2004). Much of this community occurs via the Internet, at local, regional, national, and international bisexual gatherings, or in the few large urban centers that have some sort of organized bisexual community. Therefore the organized bisexual community, insofar as it exists at all, has two components: physical communities and virtual communities.

Physical bisexual communities exist in some larger, urban areas, such as Boston, San Francisco, Chicago, Seattle, New York City, and Los Angeles. These bi communities are often fluid in structure and participation levels and may be difficult to locate relative to gay and lesbian resources in a given community (Bradford 1997). Physical bisexual communities generally consist of some combination of the following: support groups: the proactive inclusion of bisexuals in PFLAG (Parents and Friends of Lesbians and Gays) and other lesbian, gay, and queer organizations, bisexual events and conferences, and bisexual political organizations (such as BiNet chapters). Some urban centers also contain communities (such as polyamory, kink, and BDSM communities) whose membership may be pansexual or include substantial numbers of openly bisexual individuals. To my knowledge, there are no bisexual bookstores, coffeehouses, theaters, or other gathering places specifically catering to bisexuals, though the Twin Cities of Minneapolis–St. Paul have a local television program, *Bi Cities*, that is produced by and for the bisexual community. Some bisexual women may choose to establish their own support groups or special interest groups within women's centers, gay and lesbian community centers, or queer youth groups (Bradford 1997).

These physical community resources are supplemented by a large number of virtual community resources for bisexuals. If one is able to weed through the enormous number of sex-specific ads and services that cater to people of all sexual orientations who are titillated by notions of bisexual women, there are a number of excellent online resources to be found. These include bisexual-specific educational sites (e.g., www.bisexual.org), online discussion groups or forums, and social and sexual networks for meeting same- and other-gender partners (e.g., www.lovemore.com). Any attempt to comprehensively list such virtual resources is likely to be outdated quickly, given the ever changing nature of online resources and communities. Suffice it to say that such resources perform vital functions, particularly for LGB and gender-variant individuals in more rural geographic locations. Robyn Ochs's (2001) *International Directory of Bisexual Groups* provides the most comprehensive list of active bisexual organizations and support groups world wide. Fortunately, it is updated every few years (Ochs and Rowley 2005).

In summary, bisexual communities have several dimensions. Such communities have both a physical component and a virtual component that perform differing but equally vital functions for bisexual women in search of community. In actuality, bisexual communities consist of a fluctuating, dynamic, loosely connected network of distinct organizations, groups, and events. Physical communities tend to be event oriented, time limited, and located in larger urban areas. This limits bisexual women's access to bisexual communities to those women who are aware, electronically "connected," socioeconomically advantaged (able to attend events), or located in the few urban areas housing substantial populations of bisexually identified activists willing and able to organize activities for the bi community. Counselors need to understand these various dimensions and limitations of bisexual communities and be familiar with how to assist clients in locating and becoming involved with such communities. While it is critical to understand the cultural contexts permeating the lives and experiences of bisexual women, it is equally vital to understand the variety of relational contexts of bisexual women.

RELATIONAL CONTEXTS OF BISEXUAL WOMEN

BISEXUAL WOMEN IN LESBIAN RELATIONSHIPS

Many bisexual women find themselves in relationships with women who self-identify as lesbian. Some of these lesbian partners have had past heterosexual involvement or marriages and others have had only female lovers. Women with histories of past sexual involvement with men and who currently identify as lesbi-an may have identified as bisexual or heterosexual in the past (Abbott and Farmer 1995; Dixon 1984, 1985; Strock 1998) and may have a variety of positive and/or negative feelings about their past identities and relational involvements. Some lesbian women believe bisexual women are really lesbians who have simply failed to complete the coming-out process (Fox 1996; Esterberg 1997). Many lesbians express reluctance to become involved with bisexual women (Rust 1995).

A bisexual woman in a committed relationship with a woman may adopt a lesbian identity for the duration of her primary involvement with a woman (Esterberg 1997). Other bisexual women in same-sex relationships choose to retain a bisexual identity, while still others reject identity labels altogether. Counselors are frequently asked to assist bisexual women in deciding when and how to come out to their lesbian-identified partners or to women they are just beginning to date. A bisexual woman whose attractions to women are substan-tially stronger than her attractions to men may be willing to let go of her bisex-ual identity to accommodate her partner's need to perceive her as lesbian (Ochs, chapter 4). If these women choose to maintain a monogamous relationship, this may make the bisexual partner's identity less problematic for her lesbian part-ner, even when the bisexual partner maintains her private awareness of her bisexual identity.

It is clear that bisexual women in same-sex relationships face a variety of issues, including unique pressures around self-identification, social affiliation, and negotiation of intimacy issues within their woman-to-woman relationships. As is the case with bisexual women involved with men, bisexual women may choose to be monogamous or may negotiate agreements that allow for the expression of attractions and feelings for opposite or other gendered people within the context of their primary relationship with a woman (Rust 1996b). Bisexual women who identify as polyamorous are likely to conduct these nego-tiations openly with their partner, while women who are unfamiliar with ethical nonmonogamy may not feel comfortable doing so.

BISEXUAL WOMEN IN RELATIONSHIPS WITH MEN

Many women have long histories of heterosexual involvement, including mar-riage and children, before discovering or accepting their lesbian or bisexual ori-entations (Abbott and Farmer 1995; Dixon 1984, 1985; Strock 1998). There is no single trajectory characterizing the life paths of bisexual women. Bisexual women who are presently involved in relationships with men frequently strug-gle with issues of invisibility, lack of validation of their women-loving feelings, and an absence of community and opportunities for self-expression. In addition, bisexual women are frequently fetishized and hypereroticized by mainstream heterosexual culture and sometimes by their male partners. This can create conflict and confusion for a bisexual woman, especially for one whose first introduction to bisexuality may occur in the context of her heterosexual partner's attraction to lesbian sexuality.

Bisexual women have used a variety of approaches to living in relationships with men once they have discovered their bisexual orientation. Some women make a continued commitment to monogamous sexual involvement with their male partner. Other bisexual women negotiate exceptions to monogamy for the expression of her bisexuality, with clear, well-thought-out guidelines for protecting the primary relationship (see Anapol 1997; Easton and Liszt 1997, and Nearing 1992 for practical manuals on negotiating these agreements in a respectful and consensual manner).

Counselors need to be prepared to assist these women in finding creative, workable strategies that support both the individual woman and her primary relationship partner or partners. Therapists need to let women and couples know that these options exist, that there are people living them successfully, and refer their clients to appropriate resources and community supports (Weitzman, chapter 17). Finally, it is important that the counselor or psychotherapist listen nonjudgmentally to the needs of all partners in the relationship to ascertain areas of acceptable expression and issues of common concern within the framework of that couple's or expanded family's ethics, values, and aspirations, which may be nontraditional relative to the conventional structures governing most committed, heterosexual relationships.

BISEXUAL WOMEN INVOLVED WITH BISEXUAL WOMEN AND MEN

Unless a woman lives in a fairly large, urban center in the United States, she is unlikely to have access to an organized bisexual community. This diminishes the likelihood that she will have the experience of being involved with another self-identified bisexual woman or man or an individual who is transgendered. I believe that there are special joys and challenges associated with being involved in a same-orientation relationship and a number of writers have noted that the gender of one's partner influences the specific "flavor" of that relational involvement (see Hutchins and Ka'ahumanu 1991).

For example, it seems apparent that a bisexual woman's involvement with a bisexual woman who is predominantly lesbian in orientation will be quite different from her involvement with a bisexual man who is predominantly heterosexual. Her involvement with a male who cross-dresses will bring up different issues for her than her relationship with a pre-operative transgender person. These issues will differ yet again from those posed by an involvement with a queer-identified femme bisexual woman. When these issues are considered along with the diversity of demographic factors (e.g., race, age, social class, education) that can influence one's identity and perspective on relationships, it is clear why counselors must be exceptionally open to the variety of relationship styles they are likely to encounter when working with bisexual women.

Consider an example of a same-sex relationship between two bisexual women. The two women may share similarities in the balance of their attractions and their relationship preferences around issues of monogamy and polyamory, yet one woman may be extremely "out" to her family while another woman may be entirely closeted. This would likely set up dynamics of tension that would need to be addressed, possibly in couple therapy.

In relationships with other self-identified bisexuals, women may feel an increased sense of permission to name and express all elements of her attractions and desires and to discuss her full history without the fear of homophobic or heterophobic responses that may be more likely to occur in relationships with a monosexual partner. Counselors may wish to support their bisexual female clients in actively thinking about the possibility of romantic involvement with another bisexually identified partner, as many clients may never have considered this to be a viable option. The client's responses to such a discussion may provide the clinician with a useful understanding of the projected meanings and internalized dimensions of biphobia yet to be addressed within the individual client. In bringing forward the individual's projections about what it would be like to be involved with other bisexual people, internalized myths, fears, and stereotypes can be effectively explored in the emotional safety of the consulting room.

Let us turn now to an examination of what empirical research tells us about bisexual mental health, particularly the mental and psychological health issues affecting bisexual women.

EMPIRICAL RESEARCH ON BISEXUAL WOMEN

MENTAL HEALTH RESEARCH AND SERVICE UTILIZATION

Research on sexual minority women (SMW) and mental health includes research on lesbians, bisexual women, and women who have past or current female sexual partners. It may also include some women who are diverse with respect to gender identity or presentation. Silverschanz (2004) describes SMW as "women who have had (or wish to have) conscious and meaningful sexual contact with other women, regardless of how they name that desire" (p. 38). Most studies on SMW focus on lesbians or fail to differentiate between lesbian and bisexual women (Horowitz, Weis, and Laflin 2003), collapsing data on all women who have sex with women, thereby obscuring differences between these groups of women. Until recently, there has been relatively little empirical research specifically targeting bisexual mental health or the therapy experiences of bisexual women and men (Martin and Meezan 2003).

Research differentiating between lesbian and bisexual women or gay and bisexual men or comparing lesbian, gay, bisexual, and heterosexual participants across a variety of dimensions of lifestyle and psychological functioning has increased greatly in the past five to ten years, giving us a much richer understanding of between-group differences and similarities. The past five years witnessed the emergence of a refereed journal on bisexual issues. The *Journal of Bisexuality*, established by Dr. Fritz Klein and Haworth Press and edited by Dr. Klein (until his untimely death in 2006), publishes a wide variety of articles, including many on bisexual health and mental health. This refereed professional publication provides a much-needed focal point for gathering and disseminating high-quality, up-to-date research on bisexuality and the psychological and physical health of bisexual people.

To date, studies examining bisexuality and mental health have produced results that have been somewhat inconsistent (Horowitz, Weis, and Laflin 2003). I briefly review several key studies in this area.

Utilizing data from the National Opinion Research Center (NORC), a longitudinal, large-scale population study covering an eight-year period (1988–1996) (Davis and Smith 1996), Horowitz, Weis, and Laflin (2003) examined quality of life, lifestyle, and health indicators from 11,563 interviews with LGB and heterosexual individuals. These authors reported "no significant differences among [sexual orientation] groups for happiness, job satisfaction, perceived health, drinks too much, used illegal drugs, tried to quit smoking, or hours of TV watched" (p. 24). Echoing these results, one recent study (Ketz and Israel 2002) also discovered no differences in perceived wellness between women who have sex with both women and men, regardless of whether they identify as bisexual or lesbian. Similarly, Bronn (2001) found that bisexual participants did not have substantially lower scores than other participants on self-reflective quality of life scales. Finally, on an optimistic note, Bradford (2004) found that forming and maintaining a bisexual identity had positive effects on her participants' self-concept, including enhanced self-reliance, openness to others who are also "different," and life enrichment (such as a deepened ability to love and increased opportunities for personal growth).

In contrast, Silverschanz's (2004) review of the literature found that bisexual participants, when they could be distinctly identified within the study populations, frequently manifested higher levels of psychological distress and greater mental health difficulties relative to gay, lesbian, and heterosexual respondents (Jorm et al. 2002; Rothblum and Factor 2001; Saphira and Glover 2000). More specifically, Jorm and colleagues (2002) found significant differences between Australian bisexual, homosexual, and heterosexual survey respondents, with bisexual participants reporting higher levels on all measures of anxiety, depression, alcohol misuse, and negative affect. Mathy, Lehmann, and Kerr (2004) found that bisexual females and transgendered individuals reported significantly higher rates of suicidal intent, mental health difficulties, and psychological service utilization than bisexual males. Unfortunately, bisexual females also appear to be at higher risk for physical assault than are their female heterosexual counterparts (Horowitz, Weis, and Laflin 2003).

An even more recent review by Dodge and Sandfort (chapter 2) reaches similar conclusions about the health and mental health risks associated with a bisexual orientation. To make matters more confusing, one of the studies mentioned previously that found no differences among sexual orientation groups in measures of overall quality of life (Bronn 2001) did find that female and male bisexual respondents reported slightly lower scores on measures of self-esteem and general well-being.

Cultural factors, such as contemporary economic and political conditions within the United States and abroad, characteristics of urban, suburban, and rural environments, and the specific racial, ethnic and cultural communities within which bisexual individuals are living also likely have an impact on findings related to the psychological adjustment and mental health of the bisexual individuals studied (Bradford 2004). Mathy, Lehmann, and Kerr (2004) interpret their finding of substantial psychological risk factors among their bisexual participants as suggestive of the fact that sexism and heterosexism (particularly affecting both bisexual females and transgendered individuals) have an interactive effect that "compounds the social weight of oppression and increases risks for overwhelming sexual minorities' adaptive functioning" (p. 104).

Given the data described above, perhaps one of the most important areas of recent research on bisexual women is on their use of mental health services. Silverschanz (2004) found that SMW utilize psychological services at rates considerably higher than utilization rates reported in general population studies, although some studies indicate that the reasons bisexual people seek therapy are often for clinical issues unrelated to their sexual orientation per se (Page 2004). Rogers, Emanuel, and Bradford (2003) found considerable support for previous findings indicating high levels of utilization by bisexual and lesbian women relative to their heterosexual counterparts. Page (2004) found that approximately three fourths of the participants in her sample were utilizing mental health services at the time of her survey.

One recent review reported on two studies that found mental health providers directed greater degrees of heterosexual bias toward bisexual participants than they directed at lesbian and gay participants (Lucksted 1996; Moss 1994; cited in Page 2004). Page (2004) also completed an investigation that constituted a major step in defining what constitutes deficient practice and exemplary practice in conducting psychotherapy with bisexual women and men. Based on her participants' substantive responses, Page (2004) found that the key ingredients to affirmative therapy with a bisexual woman included the counselor's validation of her bisexuality, support for her bisexual identity and its expression, thoughtful and discerning feedback for her around issues of relationship and community, and, finally, a proactive and celebratory stance toward her capacity to love people of more than one gender.

To summarize, the state of empirical research on bisexual women is still in a very early stage of development. Research differentiating between lesbian and bisexual women, gay and bisexual men, or comparing participants of varying sexual orientations across a variety of dimensions psychological functioning has increased greatly in the past five to ten years, giving us a much richer understanding of between-group differences and similarities. There has not been enough replication of studies using reliable and valid instrumentation to conclusively determine the risk factors and individual or cultural benefits associated with bisexual identification.

Clearly, however, cultural factors and the specific racial and ethnic communities within which bisexual individuals are living have an impact on the psychological adjustment and mental health of the bisexual individuals studied (Bradford 2004). Recent research suggests that mental health providers direct greater degrees of heterosexual bias toward bisexual individuals than they direct at lesbian and gay participants (Lucksted 1996; Moss 1994). This finding needs further study and clarification. Future research needs to further refine our understanding of what constitutes deficient and exemplary practice in conducting psychotherapy with bisexual women and men. Fortunately, research on bisexual women is beginning to branch out in new directions.

EMPIRICAL EVIDENCE IN ADDITIONAL AREAS CRITICAL TO BISEXUAL WOMEN

A number of recent studies have explored areas that are of paramount importance to the provision of mental health services to bisexual women. These studies have addressed such topics as the psychological adjustment of bisexual women in marriages with heterosexual and bisexual male partners (Buxton 2004; Pallotta-Chiarolli and Lubowitz 2003), factors in the success of mixed-orientation marriages after husbands or wives come out as bisexual or lesbian (Buxton 2004; Edser and Shea 2002), and the impact of heterosexism and biphobia on bisexual mental health (Israel and Mohr 2004; Mulick and Wright 2002).

There has also been recent empirical research on the interacting effects of biracial identity, bicultural identification, religious identity, and politics on bisexual women's identity development (Dworkin 2002); the impact of feminism and women's communities on the physical appearance and attire that bisexual women choose when interfacing with various (lesbian and straight) communities (Taub 2003); and unique factors impacting bisexual women's friendships with heterosexual women (Galupo, Sailer, and St. John 2004). Every new study increases our understanding of the intrapsychic, social, and cultural-community dimensions of bisexual women's lives. All these studies are essential for charting directions for effective and ethical counseling and psychotherapy with this population of women. I strongly encourage counselors seeking to serve this population to familiarize themselves with the recent published literature. The *Journal of Bisexuality* provides one excellent resource in this regard, and a number of other professional journals are also publishing work in this area.

IMPLICATIONS OF EMPIRICAL RESEARCH FOR COUNSELING BISEXUAL WOMEN

Bisexual female clients may seek counseling for a variety of presenting concerns. These include confusion about their sexuality, awareness of bisexuality but discomfort with accepting it, internalized biphobia, working through others' reactions to their bisexuality, feelings of rejection or isolation related to being bisexual, the desire to expand an existing stable relationship to include another partner or partners, an internal pressure to express other important aspects of their sexual identity, and previous unsatisfying experiences with therapists who were unable to embrace or affirm a bisexual identity (Oxley and Lucius 2000).

Recent empirical research suggests that bisexual individuals may suffer from the effects of oppression or "double discrimination" by heterosexuals and some members of the lesbian and gay community (Ochs 1996; Rust 2000) and may manifest psychological difficulties at rates exceeding those of lesbian, gay, and heterosexual people (Jorm et al. 2002). Therefore it is crucial that counselors be attentive to the presence of psychological manifestations of distress (e.g., depression, anxiety, panic, substance abuse, suicidality) and be prepared to identify and assist clients with these profound sources of personal suffering. This remains important regardless whether the origins of these difficulties are external (e.g., societal oppression, biphobia, sexism, racism or homophobia) or internal (e.g., internalization of these forces of oppression within the individual, predispositions to suffering grounded in the genetic heritage of the client, or early developmental trauma). Working with clients that have multiply layered and internally complex identities "raises the bar" with respect to counseling standards for practitioners working with these individuals and families.

When bisexuality is a primary therapeutic issue, counselors play crucial roles in validating women in their bisexuality (Page 2004) and assisting them in exploring their own personal feelings for other women, apart from influences of partner(s) or culture (Bradford 2004). Clients benefit from working with counselors who are knowledgeable about negotiating nonmonogamy in intimate relationships (McLean 2004) and about successful paradigms for maintaining mixed-orientation marriages when one or both partners are bisexual (Buxton 2004; Edser and Shea 2002; Pallotta-Chiarolli and Lubowitz 2003). Additionally, therapists can assist bisexual women in confronting myths and shame-based conceptions of bisexuality, providing these women with the support and information necessary to enhance well-being and assisting them in placing their experiences in a larger cultural perspective.

Empirical research on bisexuality and mental health is still relatively young, but the past ten years have witnessed a substantial increase in the number of quantitative and qualitative studies conducted that pertain to bisexual women. Early research on sexual identity formation and the existence of bisexual behavior among populations who self-identify with a variety of labels is now being enhanced by studies on numerous topics related to bisexuality. Research focusing on the individual is being expanded to include the cultural, relational, ethnic, and community contexts of bisexual women and their psychological, sociological, and political implications. In the next section I explore what I believe to be the essential elements for developing an affirmative approach to counseling women dealing with bisexuality.

AFFIRMATIVE COUNSELING AND PSYCHOTHERAPY WITH BISEXUAL WOMEN

Diversity and complexity characterize the lives of women whose hearts and souls embody bisexuality in any of its multiple expressions. Women who experience themselves as capable of multiply gendered forms of love and attraction come in every shape, size, color, socioeconomic status, and religious or spiritual orientation. The unique and varied cultural, relational, and community contexts of bisexual women raise a number of important considerations for therapists working with these women. In this section I create a frame for providing therapeutic assistance to bisexual women, explore LGB counseling as a form of multicultural competence, and discuss the necessary shifts in perspective that lead us toward effective, culturally sensitive clinical practice with bisexual women.

CREATING THE FRAME

Bisexuality disrupts our most fundamental assumptions about gender and the nature of sexual attraction, and in so doing challenges some of our most deeply held convictions about the nature of love, intimacy, and committed partnership. As noted in my earlier writing, bisexuality functions as a lens through which a more fluid, continuous understanding of sexual and gender identity and expression become visible (Firestein 1996c). But that which becomes visible can also be profoundly disturbing. The acknowledgment of bisexual reality shines a light on the frequency with which inconsistencies occur between behavior, attraction, and self-identity, ultimately challenging some of our most cherished concepts with regard to sexual orientation. Bisexuality challenges essentialist notions of sexual identity—the "achievement" of sexual identity stability as a marker of psychological health and the use of biological, ethnic, and assimiliationist approaches to achieve social acceptance and civil rights for gay, lesbian, bisexual, and transgendered people within the dominant culture.

Counselors and psychotherapists need to acknowledge the reality and existence of identity fluidity and change, just as we have acknowledged change and fluidity in clients' choice of career, relationships, and identity in other areas of life functioning. Understanding the cultural, relational, and community contexts of women who embody bisexual feelings and desire is an important step toward ethical, effective, and affirmative practice with bisexual, lesbian, transgender, and gay clients, their partners, and families.

THERAPY WITH BISEXUAL CLIENTS: A MULTICULTURAL COMPETENCY

Effective psychotherapy and counseling with bisexual women is not an uncomplicated extension of affirmative counseling for gays and lesbians. Counseling bisexual women overlaps considerably with the multicultural counseling competency necessary to effectively work with ethnic and racial minority clients and biracial clients. In an innovative contribution to the training and psychotherapy literature, Tania Israel and Mary Selvidge (2003) have brought the two together by outlining the contributions of multicultural counseling to three areas of counselor competence with LGB clients: conceptualization of competence, counselor education and training, and assessment of counselor competence.

Israel and Selvidge (2003) note the similarities in the identity development process, shared experiences of stereotyping by the culture, and histories of stigmatization within the field of psychology common to these two groups, while acknowledging that the cultural and social realities of LGB individuals differ in significant ways from those of ethnic minorities. They apply models of counselor competence that address knowledge, attitudes, and skills needed for multicultural counseling and extend application of these concepts to work with LGB clients. Israel (2003b) recommends using guidelines for counseling women and LGB individuals as adjuncts to existing multicultural counseling competencies. Encouraging our counseling-related disciplines to move in this direction would be of particular benefit to ensuring effective training in counseling bisexual clients, especially bisexual women of color and biracial/multiracial bisexual women. These considerations add up to a rather complex challenge for practitioners: the challenge to continually expand and integrate more facets of identity and culture into our understanding and work with our individual clients and their families.

IMPLICATIONS FOR THERAPISTS AND DIRECTIONS FOR FURTHER EXPLORATION

Interactions with bisexual women bring into relief the uncomfortable truth of difference—difference not simply of degree but of "kind." For many of our clients it is profoundly challenging to embrace an identity that so powerfully undermines their own unconscious assumptions about identity and intimacy. It can be uncomfortable simply *being* a bisexual person in this society, much less trying to discover ways to live out this identity while achieving a sense of belonging within one's family and community. Furthermore, I believe that many therapists are made uncomfortable by their bisexual clients, particularly those who are exploring polyamory. In addition, few identities are as politicized as bisexual identities across both lesbian and heterosexual cultures. What does all this mean for practitioners?

It is clear that clinicians cannot afford to ignore the sociological and political dimensions of bisexual identity or dismiss the strength of their own internalized, frequently unconscious investment in dichotomous models of sexual orientation or gender. Practitioners who wish to effectively serve clients of all sexual orientations and gender identities must be willing to reexamine a number of traditional notions about psychological health and maturity, love and committed partnership, monogamy and marriage.

Specifically, counselors and therapists need to explore their own monosexual assumptions, acknowledge the possibility that committed relationships may involve the simultaneous expression of love and intimacy with more than one partner of more than one gender, embrace the possibility that these forms of loving can occur in psychologically and emotionally healthy ways, and cultivate the skills and perspectives necessary to distinguish individual differences from pathology in psychologically meaningful ways. This ultimately requires the development of new models of sexual identity development that take into account experiences of sexual fluidity and identity change across the lifespan.

I am intrigued with several questions at the present time. For example: what constitutes a healthy developmental trajectory for a bisexual woman, man, or transgendered person growing up in a culture that is still largely dichotomous with respect to gender identity and sexual orientation? How might a bisexual young person be encouraged to constructively explore their authentic interests in bisexual expression, polyamory, or alternative sexuality? What constitutes optimal psychological and social functioning for a polyamorous bisexual woman? For single bisexual women? For older, African American bisexual

women in a racist society? For a bisexual women coming out in a biphobic lesbian community? Or for a transgendered individual who is recently discovering
her or his bisexual desires? This is an exciting time to be studying and serving
bisexual people. There are far more questions than there are answers. But at
least we are now able to begin framing the questions.

Affirmative practice is ethical practice; enough is now known about bisexuality to allow counselors that wish to work with this population to become adequately informed. Specific psychotherapy training in working effectively with
bisexual clients is seldom, if ever, formally available through current graduate
training programs for therapists. However, the APA/Division 44 *Guidelines for
Psychotherapy with Lesbian, Gay, and Bisexual Clients* (2000) and the ethical
standards of several counseling associations pertaining to the provision of services to LGBT individuals and families provide valuable guidance to counselors
seeking support in this area of practice.

There is considerable evidence of the emergence of the LGBT-affirmative paradigm I first discuss in the paradigm shift chapter of my first book, *Bisexuality:
The Psychology and Politics of an Invisible Minority* (Firestein 1996c). LGBT-
affirmative psychotherapy goes beyond tolerance—even beyond acceptance—
to the level of affirmation and celebration of our incredibly rich and diverse
sexualities. As we transform our paradigms of research, our paradigms of practice must change to reflect this transformation.

Providing cultural and therapeutic space for women to explore, express, and
validate their bisexuality also provides more psychological, social, and cultural
space for the expression of lesbian, gay, and transgender identities (Firestein
1996c). This context of permission and validation also provides support for individuals who may move through and among a variety of sexual or gender identity
categories over their lifespan.

Embracing this new understanding of the ethnic, cultural, and relational
contexts of bisexual women, we move powerfully to create truly affirmative
LGBT approaches to counseling and psychotherapy that embrace diversity and,
in so doing, give bisexual women a place of belonging, acceptance, and inclusion—a place to call home.

REFERENCES

Abbott, D., and Farmer, E. (Eds.) (1995). *From wedded wife to lesbian life: Stories of
   transformation.* Freedom, CA: Crossing.
Alexander, J., and Yescavage, J. (Eds.) (2004). *InterSEXions of the others: Bisexuality and
   transgenderism.* Binghamton, NY: Haworth.

American Psychological Association Division 44/Committee on Lesbian, Gay, and Bisexual Concerns Task Force on Psychotherapy with Lesbian, Gay, and Bisexual Clients (2000). Guidelines for psychotherapy with lesbian, gay, and bisexual clients. *American Psychologist*, 55(12), 1440–1451. Reprinted in L. D. Garnets and D.C. Kimmel (Eds.) (2003), *Psychological perspectives on lesbian, gay, and bisexual experiences* (pp. 756–785). New York: Columbia University Press.

Anapol, D. (1997). Polyamory: The new love without limits. San Rafael, CA: IntiNet Resource Center.

Balsam, K. (2003). Traumatic victimization in the lives of lesbian and bisexual women: A contextual approach. *Journal of Lesbian Studies*, 7(1), 1–14.

Blackwood, E., and Wieringa, S. E. (2003). Sapphic shadows: Challenging the silence in the study of sexuality. In L. D. Garnets and D. C. Kimmel (Eds.), *Psychological perspectives on lesbian, gay and bisexual experiences* (2d ed., pp. 410–434). New York: Columbia University Press.

Blumenfeld, W., and Raymond, D. (1988). Looking at gay and lesbian life. New York: Philosophical Library.

Bower, J., Gurevich, M., and Mathieson, C. (2002). (Con)Tested identities: Bisexual women reorient sexuality. In D. Atkins (Ed.), *Bisexual women in the twenty-first century* (pp. 23–52). Binghamton, NY: Harrington Park.

Bradford, M. (1997). The bisexual experience: Living in a dichotomous culture. Unpublished doctoral dissertation. Fielding Institute, Santa Barbara.

Bradford, M. (2004). The bisexual experience: Living in a dichotomous culture. *Journal of Bisexuality*, 4(1/2), 7–23.

Bronn, C. D. (2001). Attitudes and self-images of male and female bisexuals. *Journal of Bisexuality* 1(4), 5–29.

Buxton, A. P. (2004). Works in progress: How mixed-orientation couples maintain their marriages after the wives come out. *Journal of Bisexuality*, 4(1/2), 57–82.

Chan, C. S. (1992). Cultural considerations in counseling Asian-American lesbians and gay men. In S. Dworkin and F. Gutierrez (Eds.), *Counseling gay men and lesbians: Journey to the end of the rainbow* (pp. 115–124). Alexandria, VA: American Association for Counseling and Development.

Collins, J. F. (2000). Biracial-bisexual individuals: Identity coming of age. *International Journal of Sexuality and Gender Studies*, 5(3), 221–253.

Comas-Diaz, L., and Green, B. (Eds.). (1994). Women of color: Integrating ethnic and gender identities in psychotherapy. New York: Guilford.

Davis, J. A., and Smith, T. W. (1996). *General social surveys, 1972–1996: Cumulative Codebook*. Chicago: National Opinion Research Center.

Diamond, L., and Savin-Williams, R. C. (2003). Explaining diversity in the development of same-sex sexuality among young women. In L. D. Garnets and D.C. Kimmel (Eds.), *Psychological perspectives on lesbian, gay, and bisexual experiences* (2d ed., pp. 130–148). New York: Columbia University Press.

Dixon, J. K. (1984). The commencement of bisexual activity in swinging married women over age thirty. *Journal of Sex Research*, 20(1), 71–90. Reprinted in P. Rodriguez Rust (Ed.) (2000), *Bisexuality in the United States: A social science reader* (pp. 203–216). New York: Columbia University Press.

Dixon, J. K. (1985). Sexuality and relationship changes in married females following the commencement of bisexual activity. *Journal of Homosexuality*, 11(1/2). Reprinted in F. Klein and T. J. Wolf (Eds.) (1985), *Two lives to lead: Bisexuality in men and women* (pp. 115–133). Binghamton, NY: Harrington Park.

Dworkin, S. H. (2002). Biracial, bicultural, bisexual: Bisexuality and multiple identities. *Journal of Bisexuality*, 2(4), 93–107.

Easton, D., and Liszt C. A. (1997). *The ethical slut: A guide to infinite sexual possibilities*. San Francisco: Greenery.

Edser, S. J., and Shea, J. D. (2002). An exploratory investigation of bisexual men in monogamous heterosexual marriages. *Journal of Bisexuality*, 2(4), 5–43.

Esterberg, K. G. (1997). *Lesbian and bisexual identities: Constructing communities, constructing selves*. Philadelphia: Temple University Press.

Falco, K. (1996). Psychotherapy with women who love women. In R. P. Cabaj and T. S. Stein (Eds.), *Textbook of Homosexuality and Mental Health* (pp. 397–412). Washington, DC: American Psychiatric.

Firestein, B. A. (1996a). Introduction. In B. A. Firestein (Ed.), *Bisexuality: The psychology and politics of an invisible minority* (pp. xix–xxvii). Thousand Oaks, CA: Sage.

Firestein, B. A. (1996b). Bisexuality as paradigm shift: Transforming our disciplines. In B. A. Firestein (Ed.), *Bisexuality: The psychology and politics of an invisible minority* (pp. 263–291). Thousand Oaks, CA: Sage.

Firestein, B. A. (1996c). *Bisexuality: The psychology and politics of an invisible minority*. Thousand Oaks, CA: Sage.

Fox, A. (Firestein, B. A.) (1991). Development of a bisexual identity: Understanding the process. In L. Hutchins and L. Ka'ahumanu (Eds.), *Bi any other name: Bisexual people speak out*. Boston: Alyson.

Fox, R. C. (1995). Bisexual identities. In A. R. D'Augelli and C. J. Patterson (Eds.), *Lesbian, gay, and bisexual identities over the lifespan* (pp. 48–86). New York: Oxford University Press.

Fox, R. C. (1996). Bisexuality in perspective: A review of theory and research. In B. A. Firestein (Ed.), *Bisexuality: The psychology and politics of an invisible minority* (pp. 3–50). Thousand Oaks, CA: Sage.

Galupo, M. P., Sailer, C. A., and St. John, S. C. (2004). Friendship across sexual orientations: Experiences of bisexual women in early adulthood. *Journal of Bisexuality*, 4(1/2), 37–53.

Gillem, A. R., and Thompson, C. A. (2004). Biracial women in therapy: Between the rock of gender and the hard place of race. Binghamton, NY: Haworth.

Greene, B. (1994). Ethnic-minority lesbians and gay men: Mental health and treatment issues. *Journal of Consulting and Clinical Psychology*, 62, 243–251.

Greene, B. (1997). *Ethnic and cultural diversity among lesbians and gay men*. Thousand Oaks, CA: Sage.

Greene, B. (2003). Beyond heterosexism and across the cultural divide: Developing an inclusive lesbian, gay, and bisexual psychology: A look to the future. In L. D. Garnets and D. C. Kimmel (Eds.), *Psychological perspectives on lesbian, gay, and bisexual experiences* (2d ed., pp. 357–400). New York: Columbia University Press.

Herek, G. M. (2003). Why tell if you're not asked? Self-disclosure, intergroup contact, and heterosexuals' attitudes toward lesbians and gay men. In L. D. Garnets and D. C. Kimmel (Eds.), *Psychological perspectives on lesbian, gay and bisexual experiences* (2d ed., pp. 270–298). New York: Columbia University Press.

Horowitz, S. M., Weis, D. L., Laflin, M. T. (2003). Bisexuality, quality of lifestyle and health indicators. *Journal of Bisexuality*, 3(2), 5–28.

Hutchins, L. (1996). Bisexuality: Politics and community. In B. Firestein (Ed.), *Bisexuality: The psychology and politics of an invisible minority* (pp. 242–259). Thousand Oaks: Sage.

Hutchins, L. (2001). Erotic rites: A cultural analysis of contemporary U.S. sacred sexuality traditions and trends. Unpublished doctoral dissertation. Union Institute Graduate College.

Hutchins, L. (2002). Bisexual women as emblematic sexual healers and the problematics of the embodied sacred whore. In D. Atkins (Ed.), *Bisexual women in the twenty-first century* (pp. 205–226). Binghamton, NY: Harrington Park.

Hutchins, L. and Ka'ahumanu, L. (Eds.) (1991). *Bi any other name: Bisexual people speak out.* Boston: Alyson.

Israel, T. (2003a). What counselors need to know about working with sexual minority clients. In D.R. Atkinson and G. Hackett (Eds.), *Counseling diverse populations* (pp. 347–364). Boston: McGraw Hill.

Israel, T. (2003b). Integrating gender and sexual orientation into multicultural counseling competencies. In G. Roysircar, P. Arredondo, J.N. Fuertes, J.G. Ponterotto, and R.L. Toporek (Eds.), *Multicultural counseling competencies 2003: Association for Multicultural Counseling and Development* (pp. 69–77). Alexandria, VA: AMCD.

Israel, T. (2004). Conversations, not categories: The intersection of biracial and bisexual identities. In A.R. Gillem and C.A. Thompson (Eds.), Biracial women in therapy: Between the rock of gender and the hard place of race (pp. 173–184). Binghamton, NY: Haworth.

Israel, T., and Mohr, J.J. (2004). Attitudes toward bisexual women and men: Current research, future directions. *Journal of Bisexuality,* 4(1/2), 117–134.

Israel, T., and Selvidge, M. M. D. (2003). Contributions of multicultural counseling to counselor competence with lesbian, gay, and bisexual clients. *Journal of Multicultural Counseling and Development,* 31, 84–97.

Jorm, A.F., Korten, A.E., Rodgers, B., Jacomb, P.A., and Christensen, H. (2002). Sexual orientation and mental health: Results from a community survey of young and middle-aged. *British Journal of Psychiatry,* 188, 423–427.

Ketz, K., and Israel, T. (2002). The relationship between women's sexual identity and perceived wellness. In D. Atkins (Ed.), *Bisexual women in the twenty-first century* (pp. 227–242). Binghamton, NY: Harrington Park.

Klein, F. (1990). The need to view sexual orientation as a multi-variable dynamic process: A theoretical perspective. In D.P. McWhirter, S.A. Sanders, and J.M. Reinisch (Eds.), *Homosexuality/heterosexuality: Concepts of sexual orientation* (pp. 277–282). New York: Oxford University Press.

Klein, F., Sepekoff, B., and Wolf, T.J. (1985). Sexual orientation: A multi-variable dynamic process. In F.K. Klein and T.J. Wolf (Eds.), *Two lives to lead: Bisexuality in men and women* (pp. 35–49). Binghamton, NY: Harrington Park.

Lenius, S. (2001). Bisexuals and BDSM: Bisexual people in a pansexual community. *Journal of Bisexuality,* 1(4), 71–78.

Lucksted, A. (1996). Lesbian and bisexual women who are mental health care consumers: Experiences in the mental health system. Paper presented at the Annual Conference of the Association for Women in Psychology, March, Portland.

McLean, K. (2004). Negotiating (non)monogamy: Bisexuality and intimate relationships. *Journal of Bisexuality,* 4(1/2), 83–97.

Martin, J. and Meezan, W. (2003). Applying ethical standards to research and evaluations involving lesbian, gay, bisexual, and transgender populations. *Journal of Gay and Lesbian Social Services,* 15(1/2), 181–201.

Mathy, R.M., Lehmann, B.A., and Kerr, D. (2004). Bisexual and transgender identities in a nonclinical sample of North Americans: Suicidal intent, behavioral difficulties, and mental health treatment. In J. Alexander and J. Yescavage (Eds.), *InterSEXions of the others: Bisexuality and Transgenderism* (pp. 93–109). Binghamton, NY: Haworth.

Matteson, D. (1996). Counseling and psychotherapy with bisexual and exploring clients. In B. A. Firestein (Ed.), *Bisexuality: The psychology and politics of an invisible minority* (pp. 185–213). Thousand Oaks: Sage.

Morales, E. S. (1989). Ethnic minority families and minority gays and lesbians. *Marriage and Family Review*, 14, 217–239.

Moss, J. F. (1994). The heterosexual bias inventory (HBI): Gay, lesbian and bisexual clients' perceptions of heterosexual bias in psychotherapy. (Doctoral dissertation. Michigan State University, Lansing.) *Dissertation Abstracts International*, 55(12), 5571-B.

Mulick, P. S. and Wright, L. W., Jr. (2002). Examining the existence of biphobia in the heterosexual and homosexual populations. *Journal of Bisexuality*, 2(4), 45–64.

Nearing, R. (1992). *The polyfidelity primer* (3d ed.). Captain Cook, HI: PEP.

Nichols, M. (1994). Bisexuality in women: Myths, realities, and implications for therapy. In E. Cole and E. Rothblum (Eds.), *Women and sex therapy: Closing the circle of sexual knowledge* (pp. 235–252). Binghamton, NY: Harrington Park.

Ochs, R. (1996). Biphobia: It goes more than two ways. In B. Firestein (Ed.), *Bisexuality: The psychology and politics of an invisible minority* (pp. 217–239). Thousand Oaks, CA: Sage.

Ochs, R. (Ed.). (2001). *The international directory of bisexual groups*. Cambridge: Bisexual Resource Center.

Ochs, R., and Rowley, S. E. (Eds.) (2005). *Getting bi: Voices of bisexuals around the world*. Boston: Bisexual Resource Center.

Oxley, E., and Lucius, C. A. (2000). Looking both ways: Bisexuality and therapy. In C. Neal and D. Davies (Eds.), *Issues in therapy with lesbian, gay, bisexual and transgender clients*. Buckingham: Open University Press.

Pachankis, J. E., and Goldfried, M. R. (2004). Clinical issues in working with lesbian, gay, and bisexual clients. *Psychotherapy: Theory, research, practice, training*, 41(3), 227–246.

Page, E. (2004). Mental health services experiences of bisexual women and bisexual men: An empirical study. *Journal of Bisexuality*, 4(1/2) 137–160.

Pallotta-Chiarolli, M., and Lubowitz, S. (2003). "Outside Belonging": Multi-sexual relationships as border existence. *Journal of Bisexuality*, 3(1), 53–85.

Pharr, S. (1988). *Homophobia: A weapon of sexism*. Inverness, CA: Chardon.

Queen, C. (1996a). Sexual diversity, bisexuality and the sex positive perspective. In B. A. Firestein (Ed.), *Bisexuality: The psychology and politics of an invisible minority* (pp. 103–124). Thousand Oaks, CA: Sage.

Queen. C. (1996b). Women, S/M, and therapy. *Women and Therapy*, 19(4), 65–73.

Rich, A. (1980). Compulsory heterosexuality and lesbian existence. In *Signs: Journal of Women in Culture and Society*, 5(4): 631–660.

Robin, L., Brener, N. D., Donahue, S. F., Hack, T., Hale, K., and Goodenow, C. (2002). Associations between health risk behaviors and opposite-, same-, and both-sex sexual partners in representative samples of Vermont and Massachusetts high school students. *Archives of Pediatrics and Adolescent Medicine*, 156, 349–355.

Rogers, T. L., Emanuel, K., and Bradford, J. (2003). Sexual minorities seeking services: A retrospective study of mental health concerns of lesbian and bisexual women. In T. L. Hughes, C. Smith, and A. Dan (Eds.), *Mental health issues for sexual minority women: Redefining women's mental health* (pp. 127–146). Binghamton, NY: Harrington Park.

Rothblum, E. D. and Bond, L. (Eds.) (1996). *Preventing heterosexism and homophobia* (pp. 36–58). Thousand Oaks, CA: Sage.

Rothblum, E. D., and Factor, R. (2001). Lesbians and their sisters as a control group: Demographic and mental health factors. *Psychological Science*, 12(1), 63–69.

Russell, S. T., and Joyner, K. (2001). Adolescent sexual orientation and suicide risk: Evidence from a national study. *American Journal of Public Health*, 91, 573–578.

Russell, S. T., and Seif, H. (2002). Bisexual female adolescents: A critical analysis of past research and results from a national survey. In D. Atkins (Ed.), *Bisexual women in the twenty-first century* (pp. 73–94). Binghamton, NY: Harrington Park.

Rust, P. C. (1992). The politics of sexual identity: Sexual attraction and behavior among lesbian and bisexual women. *Social Problems*, 39(4), 366–386.

Rust, P. C. (1993a). "Coming out" in the age of social constructionism: Sexual identity formation among lesbian and bisexual women. *Gender and Society*, 7(1), 50–77.

Rust, P. C. (1993b). Neutralizing the political threat of the marginal woman: Lesbians' beliefs about bisexual women. *Journal of Sex Research*, 30, 214–228.

Rust, P. C. (1995). *Bisexuality and the challenge to lesbian politics: Sex, loyalty, and revolution.* New York: New York University Press.

Rust, P. (1996a). Managing multiple identities: Diversity among bisexual women and men. In B. A. Firestein (Ed.), *Bisexuality: The psychology and politics of an invisible minority* (pp. 53–83). Thousand Oaks, CA: Sage.

Rust, P. C. (1996b). Monogamy and polyamory: Relationship issues for bisexuals. In B. A. Firestein (Ed.), *Bisexuality: The psychology and politics of an invisible minority* (pp. 127–148). Thousand Oaks, CA: Sage.

Rust, P. C. (2000). Heterosexual gays, homosexual straights. In P. Rodríguez Rust (Ed.), *Bisexuality in the United States: A social science reader* (pp. 279–306). New York: Columbia University Press.

Rust, P. C. (2003). Finding a sexual identity and community: Therapeutic implications and cultural assumptions in scientific models of coming out. In L. D. Garnets and D. C. Kimmel (Eds.), *Psychological perspectives on lesbian, gay and bisexual experiences* (2d ed., pp. 227–269). New York: Columbia University Press.

Saphira, M., and Glover, M. (2000). New Zealand national lesbian health survey. *Journal of the Gay and Lesbian Medical Association*, 4(2), 49–56.

Silverschanz, P. (2004). *Sexual minority women and mental health: A review of the research, 1992–2002.* Lesbian Unpublished Manuscript Award, Association for Women in Psychology. Philadelphia.

Solot, D., and Miller, M. (2001). Unmarried bisexuals: Distinct voices on marriage and family. *Journal of Bisexuality*, 1(4), 81–90.

Stanley, J. L. (2004). Biracial lesbian and bisexual women: Understanding the unique aspects and interactional processes of multiple minority identities. In A. R. Gillem and C. A. Thompson (Eds.), *Biracial women in therapy: Between the rock of gender and the hard place of race* (pp. 159–172). Binghamton, NY: Haworth.

Strock, C. (1998). *Married women who love women.* New York: Doubleday.

Taub, J. (2003). What should I wear? A qualitative look at the impact of feminism and women's communities on bisexual women's appearance. *Journal of Bisexuality*, 3(1), 9–22.

Weise, E. R. (1992). *Closer to home: Bisexuality and feminism.* Seattle: Seal.

Zinik, G. A. (1984). The relationship between sexual orientation and eroticism, cognitive flexibility, and negative affect. (Doctoral dissertation, University of California, Santa Barbara, 1983.) *Dissertation Abstracts International*, 45(8), 2707B.

8

BISEXUALITY AND BROKEN RELATIONSHIPS

WORKING WITH INTIMATE PARTNER VIOLENCE

Sharon G. Horne and Shana V. Hamilton

HOW IS it possible that people can beat the ones they claim to love? It seems contrary to human nature, yet partner abuse is far more common than generally realized. Because it is seen infrequently and seldom a topic of conversation, it is assumed to occur rarely. However, decades of research on relationship violence in heterosexual relationships has suggested that between 12 percent and 33 percent of couples experience physical violence at some point during the relationship, and, for many, physical abuse is frequent (Koss 1990; Straus 1993; Tjaden and Thoennes 2000). Although a body of research on gay and lesbian relationship violence has just begun to emerge, it is thought that the rates of violence for these groups are equivalent to those of heterosexual relationship violence (Burke, Jordan, and Owen 2002; Coleman 1996; Lockhart et al. 1994; Renzetti 1998; Turrell 2000). Other researchers claim that rates of violence in gay and lesbian relationships are significantly higher than in heterosexual relationships, although these studies have largely been conducted with convenience samples (Bernhard 2000; Greenwood et al. 2002; Lie et al. 1991). The majority of studies on same-sex domestic violence, however, have found lower or comparable rates to heterosexual couples (e.g., Morris and Balsam 2003; Burke and Follingstad 1999; Descamps et al. 2000; Matthews, Tartaro, and Hughes 2003).

Just how much do we know about relationship violence among bisexual individuals? The answer to that question is "not very much." Unfortunately, studies that have investigated partner violence among gay, lesbian, and heterosexual populations have typically failed to include bisexuality as a category, rendering the experiences of bisexuals who perpetuate partner abuse, or who are victimized by their partners, invisible. Similarly, many studies with couples assumed to be heterosexual have not asked participants to disclose their sexual identity; therefore we do not know how many individuals who identify as bisexual, gay, or lesbian may have remained undetectable in these studies.

Same-sex domestic violence appears to be increasing, at least in the degree of reporting, according to the National Coalition of Anti-Violence Programs (2001;

NCAVP). The NCAVP is a coalition of twenty-five GLBT victim advocacy and documentation programs located in large urban areas; the coalition collects agency and police reports of same-sex domestic violence. The NCAVP recorded violence reports accounting for 4,048 incidents in the year 2000, increasing from 3,120 in 1999. After removing all individuals who did not report their sexual identity in this study, 9 percent of the participants remained, and it can be speculated that at least some portion of these participants may have been bisexual. The authors believe that many of their participants may have identified as gay or lesbian rather than bisexual due to biphobia and monosexist assumptions made by most reporting agencies (i.e., the belief that everyone is either homosexual or heterosexual and that people attracted to more than one gender are, in actuality, either straight or gay). Unfortunately this report, like most others, did not perform independent analyses of their bisexual respondents.

A few studies have included bisexual participants as a separate category of individuals within a larger study on lesbian and gay individuals. These studies may shed light on the phenomenon of domestic violence within this population. In Turrell's study (2000), 27 (5 percent) of the individuals identified as bisexual. Bisexual individuals reported less abuse than the gay and lesbian individuals in the study; however, there were so few bisexual individuals that the validity of this outcome should be considered with caution. Within the sample as a whole, Turrell (2000) found that 32 percent of her subjects had experienced physical violence. In contrast, a study of 521 youths, ages thirteen to twenty-two, found that, among male participants, bisexual males reported more dating violence (57.1 percent) than gay males (44.6 percent), and both bisexual and gay males experienced significantly more violence than heterosexual males (28.6 percent; Freedner et al. 2002). The rates for dating violence among females were similar for lesbian and bisexual women as compared to their heterosexual female counterparts (lesbians, 43.4 percent; bisexual, 38.3 percent; heterosexual, 32.4 percent). In addition, bisexual youth experienced higher levels of threats about disclosure of their sexual orientation by peers and dating partners to family of origin and significant others than their gay cohorts. These findings indicate that young bisexual males may be most at risk for intimate partner victimization.

In the largest sample of bisexual participants collected in a domestic violence study, the present authors found an 11.7 percent victimization rate of physical violence among 116 bisexual women in same-sex relationships; these bisexual women did not differ from the lesbian participants in reported victimization (Hamilton and Horne 2005). This rate of occurrence is much lower than that reported in much of the research on interpersonal violence; for example, using the same scale, Straus and colleagues (1996) found that 35 percent of male partners reported having been physically abusive toward a female partner at least once. In the present study of bisexual women in same-sex relationships, physical assault was defined as any one incident on the physical abuse subscale of the Conflict Tactics Scale within the last year (e.g., grabbing partner). Six percent reported having pushed or shoved her partner, 5.1 percent reported having twisted her partner's arm or hair, 3.4 percent reported having thrown something at her partner, and 1.7 percent reported punching her partner with something that could hurt. No participant reported having used a gun or knife on her partner, having burned or scalded her partner, or having beaten her partner up. Two participants reported having slammed their partners against the wall and one participant reported having choked her partner.

In examining the history of abuse among the bisexual participants, it was revealed that the rate of victimization in a former female relationship was significantly lower than being a victim in a past relationship with a male. With respect to data on the perpetration of violence, more participants reported physical and psychological perpetration against male partners than against female partners. There are a couple of reasons why this greater frequency of abuse against male partners might exist. Perhaps the perpetration of mild violence (e.g., slapping) against men is more socially acceptable, bisexual women who were in violent relationships may have engaged in self-defense, or the bisexual women in the study may have had more past relationships with men, thereby increasing the likelihood of perpetrating abuse simply by virtue of the number of relationships they had with persons of each gender.

What factors contribute to the occurrence of BLGT relationship violence? For the most part, it appears that many of the same factors involved in other-sex intimate partner violence appear in same-sex relationship violence as well. For example, although it is not a cause of intimate partner abuse, a history of childhood exposure to interparental violence is commonly correlated with abuse of a partner (Whitfield et al. 2003). This correlation was also found for bisexual and lesbian women in same-sex relationships (Hamilton and Horne 2005). Similarly, anxious emotional attachment appears to be associated with increased intimate partner violence. Individuals with anxious attachment styles are defined as "individuals who are emotionally dependent on others, yet fearful and angry, with their feelings easily triggered by situational factors such as perceived abandonment" (Barnett, Miller-Perrin, and Perrin 1997:282). Male batterers tend to have higher anxious attachment needs than their victims (Babcock, Jacobson, Gottman, and Yerington 2000; Kesner, Julian, and McKenry 1997; Rankin, Saunders, and Williams 2000). Anxious attachment has been found to play a significant role in perpetration of violence against same-sex female partners as well (Hamilton and Horne 2005). Although substance abuse has a strong relationship with male perpetrated violence against female partners, research on lesbian partner violence has not been conclusive in this regard. Some studies have found substance abuse to be present among both victims and perpetrators (e.g., Coleman 1991), while other studies found no relationship (Renzetti 1998; Waldner-Haugrud, Gratch, and Magruder 1997).

Finally, other factors contribute to heightened relational stress, such as lower socioeconomic status, unemployment, and younger age.

GLBT individuals in same-sex relationships may contend with additional stressors that may increase the likelihood of partner violence. Minority stress theory (Brooks 1981) may be somewhat helpful in explaining the connection between same-sex relationships, bisexual identity, and intimate partner violence. Minority stress is thought to occur when stigmatized minorities have no control over the dominant culture, which perceives them as subordinate to other groups of individuals (Balsam 2001). Bisexual men and women are at risk for this stress due to their invisibility within both heterosexual and gay and lesbian communities. This stress may result from either internal or external factors. An example of one type of stress for bisexual individuals is internalized biphobia or the internalization of negative attitudes and assumptions about bisexuality that exist in society. Internalized biphobia/homophobia has been found to be positively associated with both perpetration of and victimization in lesbian and bisexual relationships (Balsam, Szymanski, and Nilsen 2002; Hamilton and Horne 2005). A related stressor is the degree of an individual's self-disclosure of bisexuality. Depending on how "out" a partner is about his or her bisexuality, this disclosure can impact the relationship, causing additional stress in their lives. If other factors are present that typically correlate with intimate partner violence (e.g., witnessing violence as a child, anxious attachment style), then a partner's internalized biphobia and sexual orientation nondisclosure could add stress to the relationship, possibly resulting in the perpetration of relationship violence. As Balsam (2003) suggested, it is possible that self-disclosure of bisexual orientation may either increase the risk of domestic violence or serve as a protective factor from same-sex partner violence. For example, a bisexual man who is out to family and friends may have a support system should he disclose that his partner is physically abusing him; however, it may put him at greater risk due to greater visibility, placing stress on the relationship, particularly if the partner is closeted and resistant to disclosure of the relationship. With respect to domestic violence, self-disclosure has been explored only as it relates to degree of outness or closetedness, which appears to positively relate to healthy relationship dynamics. Indeed, Hamilton and Horne (2005) found sexual orientation variables, such as internalized biphobia and less disclosure of bisexuality to significant others, extended family, and those in the workplace, to play a role in the occurrence and frequency of perpetration of physical and psychological violence.

Although the research on bisexuality in relationship to intimate partner violence is limited, it is encouraging that so many studies have been initiated within the past five years. In spite of the limited number of studies available, it is useful, nevertheless, to examine the clinical implications of these findings within the context of what is already known about treatment of intimate partner violence in general. The remainder of this chapter focuses upon the unique issues that a bisexual individual experiencing intimate partner violence might encounter. The purpose of this section is to sensitize clinicians to work effectively with these issues.

CONCERNS OF BISEXUAL CLIENTS IN SAME-SEX RELATIONSHIPS

Bisexual individuals who are in same-sex relationships are often assumed to be gay or lesbian by helping professionals (Firestein 1996). Such invisibility can impact a bisexual victim seeking services for treatment of partner abuse in a number of ways. For example, they may experience similar kinds of discrimination and lack of support as frequently reported by gay, lesbian, and transgendered individuals who seek services in traditional family violence resource centers. The vast majority of domestic violence services are not prepared to serve clients who don't fit the typology of the stereotypical victim of intimate partner violence (female victim, male perpetrator). Most support groups, resource materials, and shelters are geared toward serving heterosexual women victims. Consequently, many bisexual individuals in same-sex relationships may choose not to seek services or may hide their orientation, thereby limiting their access to quality treatment. They may be exposed to hostility or even endangerment in shelters or resource centers that usually serve only heterosexual clients (Merrill and Wolfe 2000). When services are developed to serve nonheterosexual women, they are typically designed to meet the needs of lesbian women (Crane et al. 1999). Many of these services may exclude bisexual individuals, either explicitly or inadvertently, by not addressing the specific needs of this population. Bisexual men and women who are victims of other-sex perpetrators may be subjected to biphobia from helping professionals who assume heterosexuality, while bisexual men and women victims of same-sex perpetrators may be ostracized or fail to receive support because they are highlighting a problem that many BLGT community members do not want to acknowledge. Likewise, bisexual men and women of color often experience racism in BGLT communities and may be more likely to be perceived as violent by police and helping professionals even when they have not initiated the violence.

Other institutional barriers exist that marginalize same-sex relationship violence. Resource centers for intimate violence prevention and treatment are often affiliated with religious organizations, many of which are not accepting of bisexuality, even as acceptance of gay and lesbian individuals is increasing in some denominations. Same-sex relationships are not granted equivalent legal protection in the U.S., and this lack of protection extends to same-sex relationship partners who may be involved in domestic violence; therefore bisexual victims in same-sex relationships may be unlikely to initiate an official report to seek justice (Burke, Jordan, and Owen 2002). For example, in more than seven states domestic violence protection orders exclude gay and lesbian individuals; other states have left civil protections up to the discretion of the court. A refreshing alternative is the National Coalition of Anti-Violence Programs (2001), which exists to protect and serve gay, lesbian, bisexual and transgendered persons. Located in twenty urban areas, they are available as a helping resource for BGLT victims and can make interventions with police and courts on behalf of bisexual individuals.

Bisexual individuals in same-sex relationships are also faced with the burden of representing a minority group that encounters a societal lack of acceptance. Bearing such a burden of ostracism and rejection may cause members of minority groups to overlook negative issues in their communities, due to the fear that acknowledging such stigmatized behavior will reflect poorly on the group as a whole. Because intimate partner violence brings such shame to both perpetrators and victims when it is revealed, there is a tendency for members of minority groups to dismiss or minimize violent behavior. For example, intimate partner violence is sometimes treated as a "fair fight" by members of the GLBT community as well as law enforcement officers. When bisexual women engage in partner violence with female partners, there is a tendency to overlook this violence due to the myth that women in general are not violent. When bisexual men perpetrate violence against male partners, it is sometimes treated as if it were sexual play. These attitudes and behaviors inhibit mental health treatment for both perpetrators and victims of domestic violence.

CONCERNS OF BISEXUAL PARTNERS IN OTHER-SEX RELATIONSHIPS

Bisexual individuals in other-sex relationships who are dealing with violence in the relationship may encounter additional issues when seeking help for intimate partner violence because they are often assumed to be heterosexual. Assumptions of heterosexuality can impact treatment and serve to silence individuals who may already be suffering from psychological distress and low self-esteem. In addition, bisexual victims of violence may fear being outed by other-sex partners if they are not out to others. Being outed as bisexual can jeopardize child custody, divorce settlements, and support from family and friends. If the victim was active in the BGLT community prior to the other-sex relationship, she may be reluctant to seek support from this community if the other-sex partner is using sexual orientation to threaten, withhold, or sue for property or custody of children.

BISEXUAL PARTNERS IN POLYAMOROUS RELATIONSHIPS

Research has not explored the presence of domestic violence in polyamorous relationships, however, given the rates of relationship violence in general, it may be expected that violence can exist in all types of relationships. On the one hand, polyamory may provide some support for victims of domestic violence; they may have other intimates to turn to for help. On the other hand, a perpetrator may use polyamory against a victim by threatening exposure of sexual orientation and polyamorous sexual behavior. Similarly, when a victim seeks help, he may experience rejection and/or discrimination should he also come out about polyamory. In addition, other partners who are not abusive may be perceived to be violent or may be treated with disrespect by helping professionals due to the nature of the relationship.

HELPING INTERVENTIONS

Helping professionals working with couples should always screen for relationship violence.

This is no less true for bisexual individuals in other-sex, same-sex, or polyamorous relationships. Therapists are rarely trained to work with abuse issues, much less BGLT concerns. Given that lifetime prevalence rates of victimization are reported to be between 12 percent and 33 percent, therapists should expect that, at a minimum, one out of every five couples has had some experience with relationship violence. Given the severity of relationship violence, it is vital that therapists treat domestic violence as seriously as other couple concerns.

Effective assessment includes exploration of client disclosure of repeated fights, how conflict is resolved, and any past history of domestic violence either in family of origin or prior relationships. Typically, asking direct questions about abuse and violence is not very effective; rather, clinicians can explore the presence of fears of one's partner or intimidation by the partner, power and control dynamics, and social support. All exploration should be conducted within the conceptual context of bisexual lives, including the role of internalized biphobia and other, possibly multiple, dimensions of oppression, such as racism, sexism, ableism, and ageism.

Therapists should be cautioned not to provide couple counseling for people who are in actively abusive relationships. Working with a violent couple can reinforce violent dynamics and render the victim more vulnerable and isolated. Ideally, screening for abuse should occur before initiating couple therapy; if the presence of ongoing abuse is indicated, individual therapy is recommended, and couple therapy should be initiated only after the perpetrator has benefited from treatment and the violence has stopped. Even when violence in a relationship has ceased, specific, patterned dynamics of power and control between partners have been reinforced through repeated interactions over lengthy periods of time; therefore therapists should explore the meanings associated with behaviors that are connected with prior abuse (e.g., what does the raising of the voice indicate in the couple relationship currently and previously, when there was active abuse).

Although bisexual identity can increase risk for experiencing multiple stressors, including biphobia, ostracization from both LGB and heterosexual communities, and stereotyping, there may be some aspects of resilience associated with being bisexual (e.g., Balsam 2003). It may be that sexual minority identity may offer some resources and protective measures for offsetting the impact of negative experiences, including domestic violence. For example, feminist identity and endorsement of feminist values appears to be common among bisexual and lesbian women; therefore, they may be more likely to acknowledge, name abuse, and initiate measures to end it within their relationships. Likewise, the positive use of psychotherapy within the BGLT community may allow bisexual individuals to seek treatment for victimization and perpetration through individual practitioners, despite the lack of services for BGLT individuals in community-based service centers. Finally, the endorsement of equality of roles within relationships appears to be very important for BLG couples (Kurdek 1995; Biss and Horne 2005); such values draw attention to the existence of inequalities and allow for closer scrutiny of the relationship's dynamics by partners and other BLG community members.

As in approaching all victims of domestic violence, focusing on strengths, identifying coping strategies, and offering support in place of blaming or scapegoating is the most effective approach to working with bisexual victims of violence. All too often, therapists focus on the powerlessness of the victim; contrary to the perceptions of victims of violence as helpless and weak, research has shown that victims typically engage in many help-seeking behaviors when preparing to leave a violent relationship (Gondolf 1998; Nabi and Horner 2001). Therapists are more effective when they focus on ending the abuse, rather than ending the relationship. Despite the heterosexism within domestic violence treatment and prevention, clients can still find value in many of the materials that are directed at heterosexual relationship violence, since so many of the variables (e.g., family of origin violence, anxious attachment, drug and alcohol abuse) are shared in common. However, therapists must address additional factors that bisexual individuals face including internalized biphobia, issues of social support, and self-disclosure of sexual orientation. To do this effectively, counselors should have a strong, working knowledge of domestic violence issues, awareness of BLGT identity development and concerns, and an understanding of the impact of minority stress of bisexual clients. Effective treatment often requires therapists to be knowledgeable about childhood victimization and trauma treatment as well as conflict resolution, health communication, and stress management.

With appropriate training, counselors and therapists can work effectively with domestic violence issues as they relate to bisexual individuals. The good news is that resources are currently being expanded to meet the needs of bisexual individuals dealing with abuse issues. However, as helping professionals we must continue to advocate for the inclusion of bisexual individuals in *all* support systems in order to end domestic violence in every relationship where it occurs.

REFERENCES

Babcock, J. C., Jacobson, N. S., Gottman, J. M., and Yerington, T. P. (2000). Attachment, emotional regulation, and the function of marital violence: Differences between secure, preoccupied, and dismissing violent and nonviolent husbands. *Journal of Family Violence*, 15, 391–409.

Balsam, K. F. (2001). Nowhere to hide: Lesbian battering, homophobia, and minority stress. In E. Kaschak (Ed.), *Intimate betrayal: Domestic violence in lesbian relationships* (pp. 25–37). Binghamton, NY: Haworth.

Balsam, K. F. (2003). Traumatic victimization in the lives of lesbian and bisexual women: A contextual approach. *Journal of Lesbian Studies*, 7, 1–14.

Balsam, K. F., Szymanski, D. M., and Nilsen, C. (2002). Lesbian internalized homophobia, relationship quality, and domestic violence. Poster session presented at the annual meeting of the American Psychological Association, Chicago.

Barnett, O. W., Miller-Perrin, C. L. and Perrin, R. D. (1997). *Family violence across the lifespan: An introduction*. Thousand Oaks, CA: Sage.

Bernhard, L. A. (2000). Physical and sexual violence experienced by lesbian and heterosexual women. *Violence Against Women*, 6, 68–79.

Biss, W. J., and Horne, S. G. (2005). Equality within lesbian couples: The role of internalized homophobia, self-disclosure, and social support. Manuscript.

Brooks, V. R. (1981). *Minority stress and lesbian women*. Lexington, MA: Lexington.

Burke, L. K., and Follingstad, D. R. (1999). Violence in lesbian and gay relationships: Theory, prevalence, and correlational factors. *Clinical Psychology Review*, 19, 487–512.

Burke, T. W., Jordan, M. L., and Owen, S. S. (2002). A cross-national comparison of gay and lesbian domestic violence. *Journal of Contemporary Criminal Justice*, 18, 231–257.

Coleman, V. E. (1991). Violence in lesbian couples: A between groups comparison. (Doctoral dissertation, California School of Professional Psychology, Los Angeles, 1991). *Dissertation Abstracts International*, 51, 5634.

Coleman, V. E. (1996). Lesbian battering: The relationship between personality and the perpetration of violence. In K. Hamberger and C. Renzetti (Eds.), *Domestic partner abuse* (pp. 77–102). New York: Springer.

Crane, B., LaFrance, J., Leichtling, G., Nelson, B., and Silver, E. (1999). Lesbians and bisexual women working cooperatively to end domestic violence. In B. Leventhal and S. E. Lundy (Eds.), *Same-sex domestic violence: Strategies for change* (pp. 125–134). Thousand Oaks, CA: Sage.

Descamps, M. J., Rothblum, E., Bradford, J., and Ryan, C. (2000). Mental health impact of child sexual abuse, rape, intimate partner violence, and hate crimes in the National Lesbian Health Care Survey. *Journal of Gay and Lesbian Social Services,* 11, 27–55.

Firestein, B. A. (1996). *Bisexuality: The psychology and politics of an invisible minority.* Thousand Oaks, CA: Sage.

Freedner, N., Freed, L. H., Yang, Y. W., and Austin, S. B. (2002). Dating violence among gay, lesbian, and bisexual adolescents. Results from a community survey. *Journal of Adolescent Health, 31,* 469–474.

Gondolf, E. W. (1998). The victims of court-ordered batterers. *Violence Against Women, 4,* 659–676.

Greenwood, G. L., Relf, M. V., Huang, B., Pollack, L.M., Canchola, J.A., and Catania, J.A. (2002). Battering victimization among a probability-based sample of men who have sex with men. *American Journal of Public Health, 92,* 1964–1969.

Hamilton, S. V., and Horne, S. G. (2005). Female same-sex relationship violence. Manuscript.

Kesner, J. E., Julian, T., and McKenry, P. C. (1997). Application of attachment theory to male violence toward female intimates. *Journal of Family Violence, 12,* 211–228.

Koss, M. P. (1990). The women's mental health research agenda: Violence against women. *American Psychologist, 45,* 374–380.

Kurdek, L. A. (1995). Developmental changes in relationship quality in gay and lesbian cohabiting couples. *Developmental Psychology, 31,* 86–94.

Lie, G., Schilit, R., Bush, J., Montagne, M., and Reyes, L. (1991). Lesbians in currently aggressive relationships: How frequently do they report aggressive past relationships? *Violence and Victims, 6,* 121–135.

Lockhart, L. L., White, B. W., Causby, V., and Isaac, A. (1994). Letting out the secret: Violence in lesbian relationships. *Journal of Interpersonal Violence, 9,* 469–492.

Matthews, A. K., Tartaro, J., and Hughes, T. L. (2003). A comparative study of lesbian and heterosexual women in committed relationships. *Journal of Lesbian Studies, 7,* 101–114.

Merrill, G. S., and Wolfe, V. A. (2000). Battered gay men: An exploration of abuse, help seeking, and why they stay. *Journal of Homosexuality, 39,* 1–30.

Morris, J. F., and Balsam, K. F. (2003). Lesbian and bisexual women's experiences of victimization: Mental health, revictimization, and sexual identity development. *Journal of Lesbian Studies, 7,* 67–85.

Nabi, R. L., and Horner, J. R. (2001). Victims with voices: How abused women conceptualize the problem of spousal abuse and implications for intervention and prevention. *Family Violence, 16,* 237–253.

National Coalition of Anti-Violence Programs. (2001). *Lesbian, gay, bisexual, and transgender domestic violence in 2000.* New York: New York City Gay and Lesbian Anti-Violence Project.

Rankin, L. B., Saunders, D. G., and Williams, R. A. (2000). Mediators of attachment style, social support, and sense of belonging in predicting woman abuse in African American men. *Journal of Interpersonal Violence, 15,* 1060–1080

Renzetti, C. M. (1998). Violence and abuse in lesbian relationships: Theoretical and empirical issues. In R. K. Bergen (Ed.), *Issues in intimate violence* (pp. 117–127). Thousand Oaks, CA: Sage.

Straus, M. A. (1993). Physical assaults by wives: A major social problem. In R. J. Gelles and D. R. Loseke (Eds.), *Current controversies on family violence* (pp. 67–87). Newbury Park, CA: Sage.

Straus, M. A., Hamby, S. L., Boney-McCoy, S., and Sugarman, D. B. (1996). The revised Conflict Tactics Scale (CTS2). *Journal of Family Issues*, 17, 283–316.

Tjaden, P., and Thoennes, N. (2000). *Extent, nature, and consequences of intimate partner violence* (NCJ Publication No. 181867). Washington, DC: U.S. Department of Justice.

Turrell, S. C. (2000). A descriptive analysis of same-sex relationship violence for a diverse sample. *Journal of Family Violence*, 15, 281–293.

Waldner-Haugrud, L. K., Gratch, L. V., and Magruder, B. (1997). Victimization and perpetration rates of violence in gay and lesbian relationships: Gender issues explored. *Violence and Victims*, 12, 173–184.

Whitfield, C. L., Anda, R. F., Dube, S. R., and Feletti, V. J. (2003). Violent childhood experiences and the risk of intimate partner violence in adults: Assessment in a large health maintenance organization. *Journal of Interpersonal Violence*, 18, 166–185.

9

BISEXUAL INCLUSION IN ISSUES OF GLBT AGING

THERAPY WITH OLDER BISEXUALS

Bobbi Keppel and Beth A. Firestein

ONE OF the last remaining acceptable prejudices in this society stigmatizes elderly people and the process of aging. Perhaps one of the most potent myths related to aging has to do with aging and sexuality. Older people are presumed to lose both sexual interest and sexual function as they age and are perceived as inappropriate, dirty, and disgusting when they express their sexuality. They frequently become the object of ridicule. Differences in sexual orientation are ignored entirely, and bisexual, gay, or lesbian elders may be driven underground and silenced. This chapter sensitizes counselors to the needs of bisexual (and other nonheterosexual) clients who continue to have sexual needs, questions, and concerns as they move through the later decades of their life cycle. Issues covered will include myths about aging and sex, fostering positive sexual self-esteem in older people, sexual problems that arise as a consequence of aging and health-related changes, and the ongoing importance of providing safer sex information and education to individuals as they get older. The inclusion/exclusion of bisexuals in current GLBT aging initiatives will also be addressed.

GLBT AGING CONCERNS: AN EMERGING ISSUE

The earliest organized efforts to offer support to lesbians and gay men around issues of aging began formally in the mid- to late-1970s with the emergence of two gay- and lesbian-specific organizations. SAGE (Senior Action in a Gay Environment) was the first U.S. community agency to specifically serve lesbian and gay male elders. The organization was first established in Manhattan in 1977. Initially SAGE met in members' homes; later the group established a significant organizational presence in the arena of gay and lesbian aging. As an organized social service agency, SAGE began by offering services to homebound and mobility-impaired elderly gay men and lesbians, such as "friendly visiting," shopping assistance, and assistance for seniors needing to get places

(Kling 2004). Since then, SAGE has expanded its services considerably: conducting national needs assessments, working to improve social services nationwide, and lobbying to influence legislation. Even the name has changed to reflect the times. SAGE now stands for "Services and Advocacy for GLBT Elders," although GLBT inclusion has yet to fully reflect any real prioritization of the needs of its bisexual constituents.

Another organization, the National Association for Lesbian and Gay Gerontology (NALGG), was founded in 1978. NALGG sponsored the first National Conference of Lesbian and Gay Aging in 1981. The organization was formed to dispel myths about older lesbians and gay men, advance research, establish programs and services for lesbian and gay elders, and encourage and provide support for lesbian and gay gerontologists (Raphael and Meyer 2004). NALGG also published a Senior Resource Guide (authored by Will Hubbard) and was the first organization to produce an annotated bibliography on gay and lesbian aging (Raphael and Meyer 2004). The organization dissolved in the mid-1990s. The Lesbian and Gay Aging Issues Network (LGAIN) of the American Society for Aging, was formed around the same time. It was formally recognized as a constituency group of the American Society for Aging in 1994. This organization has become a leading force in increasing awareness and services to LGBT elders across the United States. Other important organizations include the nonprofit Gay and Lesbian Association of Retiring Persons (GLARP) and Project Rainbow: Society for Senior Gay and Lesbian Citizens (SSGLC) in Los Angeles (Ritter and Terndrup 2002). More recent initiatives are beginning to address the needs of African American GLBT elders and other special populations (Hoctel 2003).

The 2005 ASA-NCOA (American Society on Aging–National Council on the Aging) Joint Conference on Aging, held in Philadelphia, demonstrates just how far the movement has come. The Joint Conference offered an impressive array of events and sessions on topics of interest to lesbian, gay, bisexual, and transgender attendees and professionals working in the field of aging. Session titles were inclusive and sessions were offered on a wide variety of topics including legal issues affecting LGBT aging communities, sensitivity training for frontline workers, stigma and discrimination in mental health and aging, and gay men and lesbians as overlooked family caregivers. However, bisexual- and transgender-specific programming was still extremely sparse, pointing to the ongoing need for greater awareness and efforts at bisexual and transgender inclusion in LGAIN and similar organizations. So what are the needs of bisexual and LGBT elders?

NEEDS OF THE AGING LGBT POPULATION

Historically, LGBT elders have been underrepresented in the psychological literature (Greene 2001, 2003). More recent literature in the area has begun to highlight the unique and varied concerns of GLBT elders (Greene 2001). For example, LGAIN's newsletter *OutWord* has published articles on topics as diverse as gay and lesbian invisibility in nursing homes (Klein 2003), the scarcity of images of transgender elders in film and print media (Hilbert 2003), and providing spiritual care for LBGT older adults (Marshall 2003). Issues of identity and difference are quite salient to BLGT seniors (Greene 2001, 2003). Keppel (1995) notes that "even when LBGs do not identify themselves by using a particular label, internally, they distinguish themselves from heterosexuals" (p. 1).

Some of the unique needs of BLGT elderly reflect the circumstances associated with gay and lesbian lifestyles of past decades (Barón and Cramer 2000; Greene 2001). Amber Hollibaugh (2005) notes that GLBT elders coming from the pre-Stonewall generation have much smaller support networks than the general older adult population. In addition, they are five times less likely than the general older adult population to use senior services. She interprets this reluctance to utilize necessary services as strongly related to these individuals' histories of encountering discrimination, homophobia, biphobia, and mainstream service providers who are ignorant of their needs (Hollibaugh 2005). Post-Stonewall generation LGBT older adults have acquired skills and attitudes that empower them to advocate for their needs in more vocal and openly assertive ways.

Other issues confronting BLTG elders include a lack of family support comparable to that available to most aging heterosexuals, feelings of isolation (especially for unpartnered BLTG elders), legal options that fail to take into account the needs of LBGs and/or their partners, and the potential for increased use or abuse of substances as individuals resort to potentially dysfunctional coping strategies in response to anxieties association with isolation and aging (Keppel 1995). "Lack of family support" includes the fact that some BGLT elders are alienated or emotionally distant from their families of origin as a result of coming out BGLT as well as the fact that few individuals with a significant history of same-sex involvements have had children within the context of their same-sex relationships. This results in "diminished support networks" relative to the support networks of LBGT elders' straight counterparts, a much greater likelihood of entering old age as a single person, and decreased likelihood of having children to call upon in times of need (Greene 2003; Hollibaugh 2005; Ritter and Terndrup 2002). Greene (2003) discusses work by Ehrenberg (1996), who notes that finding a partner is an issue of concern for many older gay men and lesbians. On a slightly different note, Williams (1998) makes a compelling case for the need to develop creative intergenerational bonds between LGB elders and young people so that nonreproductive elders are offered appropriate care in their later years even when they do not have children.

Developmental theories of adulthood have generally been formed based on the presumption of participants' heterosexuality (Kimmel 1978; Ritter and Terndrup 2002) with few exceptions (e.g., Vaillant 1977). Developmental theories accounting for mid-life transitions, such as those developed by Levinson (1978) and Erikson (1963) need to be modified to be applied meaningfully to bisexual, gay, and lesbian lives (Ritter and Terndrup 2002). For example, Kimmel (1978) has identified six adult social-sexual life patterns for gay men and lesbians that also have considerable relevance to bisexual individual's lives. Ritter and Terndrup (2002) review the empirical research and provide an excellent overview of the developmental challenges, psychosocial stressors, and adaptive strengths of LBG elders. Let us turn now to a consideration of available material speaking specifically to the needs of bisexual elders.

SEARCH FOR THE MISSING BISEXUAL ELDER

A search for articles dealing specifically with bisexuality on the ASA members' Web site under "publications" (using ArticleSearch) listed 116 recent articles including the word *bisexual* in the title. Strikingly, only 4 of 116 articles found in the ASA publications database actually dealt with the specific issues of bisexual elders (Edwards 2002; Keppel 2002; Kingston 2002; Smith 2002). All four appeared in a single issue of *OutWord* devoted specifically to understanding the needs of bisexual elders and increasing awareness of bisexuality among professionals serving LGBT clients (Yoakam 2002). Articles in this issue dealt with debunking the stereotypes about bisexuals held by professionals in aging (Smith 2002), arguments about the definitions of lesbian and bisexual and how these terms are applied over the life course (Edwards 2002), the experience of being an out bisexual elder (Keppel 2002), and a panel discussion of concerns related to bisexuality and aging and potential responses to those concerns (Kingston 2002).

Although this spring 2002 issue of *OutWord* was devoted to bisexual elders' issues, there is a remarkable absence of any other articles on bisexuality or the needs of bisexual elders over the eight-year span (1997–2005) covered by this database. Bisexual individuals are mentioned in more recent chapters on LGB aging (e.g., Martell, Safren, and Prince 2004; Perez, DeBord, and Bieschke 2000; Ritter and Terndrup 2002), but the issues specific to bisexual individuals are, for the most part, merged into discussions of gay and lesbian aging. Yet bisexual women and men constitute a substantial portion of the larger population of same-sex loving individuals (Firestein 1996), and it is not uncommon for men and women to come out as lesbian, bisexual, or gay at older ages (Ritter and Terndrup 2002; Edwards 2002; Kingston 2002).

Issues confronting older lesbians and gay men do overlap with the experiences of older people who are bisexual, but only partially. Fox's (1996) review of the empirical research, which included a review of several large-scale epidemiological studies on sexual orientation, found that a significant number of individuals report both same-sex and other-sex relationships and experiences. Fortunately, there is a large and rapidly expanding knowledge base pertaining to bisexuality in psychology and the social sciences (see Firestein 1996 and Fox 2004 for a rather comprehensive listing of these materials). In light of these realities, it is startling to realize how little attention is being directed toward older bisexual men and women by organizations focused on LGBT aging that nominally include *bisexuals* in the titles of their organizations and in their mission statements.

The present chapter focuses on the needs of bisexual elders. Smith (2002) states, "All professionals who provide services to people ages 50-plus deal with bisexual elders—even if they don't realize it" (p. 2). Bisexual men, women, and transgendered individuals face both similar and differing challenges to those faced by gay men and lesbians as they age. This chapter reviews some of the key issues involved in bisexual aging. Bisexuals exist both as elders and as caregivers for elderly parents; they also function as spouses, partners, and as parents, as siblings and as daughters and sons in their families of origin.

ISSUES CONFRONTING BISEXUAL ELDERS

If, as many older Americans say, "Old age is not for sissies!" then old age for bisexuals is for the truly brave. Reid (1995) notes that "examination of the lives of older bisexuals, lesbians, and gay men illustrates how age, personal characteristics, and social context continually interact to shape identity" (p. 217). Bisexual elders face society's ageism, society's homophobia/homonegativity, and the biphobia and binegativity of both heterosexuals and homosexuals (Morrow 2000). Any and all these oppressions are probably affecting bisexuals who come into your practice.

CONCEPTS AND TERMINOLOGY (AND EXAMPLES)

In order to understand and effectively serve this population, it is important to know the meaning of a few important terms.

AGEISM   U.S. society is generally ageist (Atkinson and Hackett 1988). Here are some examples: older people are used as comic media figures. Their contributions are often devalued while their needs are neglected and/or resented. Barriers prevent appropriate and adequate health and mental health care even though declines in physical and mental functioning are expected (Atkinson and Hackett 1988). Elders have inadequate housing and transportation alternatives. Elders have the fastest-rising rate of HIV infection of any U.S. population group and show increasing incidences of other sexually transmitted infections (STIs). Lack of safer sex education is partly due to ageist views of elders as asexual.

HETEROSEXISM AND HOMOPHOBIA/HOMONEGATIVITY Heterosexism refers to the unearned privileges of the heterosexual majority. Homophobia or homonegativity refers to judgment, stigma, and discrimination directed at nonheterosexual people. Nonheterosexuals, including bisexuals, face heterosexism and homophobia in U.S. society. Morrow (2000) notes,

> The sociopolitical dimensions of LGB client concerns must be addressed regardless of the therapeutic method used by the therapist, because most LGB people live in environments that continually assault their sense of self and create distress that may not be recognized by clients as a consequent to living in a homonegative culture. (p. 147)

There is a pervasive shortage of professionals trained and experienced in dealing with sexual minority issues, especially with elderly nonheterosexuals.

BIPHOBIA, BINEGATIVITY, AND BISEXUAL INVISIBILITY Biphobia refers to judgment, stigma, and discrimination directed at bisexual people. People often experience discomfort about bisexuality and bisexual people (Bohan 1996). Binegativity refers to negative and stereotyped attitudes commonly held about bisexual people. Greene (2003) writes that "group membership is often defined as a function of the dichotomous poles of sexual orientation, reserving a special brand of cynicism, and hostility, for bisexual, transsexual, and transgendered people" (p. 371). Bisexuals are largely omitted in both common and professional discussions of issues related to sexual orientation (Dworkin 2000; Firestein 1996; Yoakam 2002). Older bisexuals share the issues and the experience of binegativity and invisibility of bisexuals of other ages. Furthermore, older bisexual women and men probably never heard the word *bisexual* until they were adults and the gay pride movement was underway. Then and now, bisexuals have been largely invisible in both the straight and G/L (gay and lesbian) communities (Bradford 2004; Keppel 2002; Smith 2002). Lesbian and gay people tend to believe that bisexuals are hiding in the heterosexual community while heterosexuals assume bisexual men and women are part of the homosexual world (Ochs 1996; Smith 2002).

QUEER Queer is a nonpejorative umbrella term for people who don't consider themselves to be heterosexual. In this chapter *queer* is used interchangeably with the acronym *BLTGIQ* (bisexual, lesbian, transgender, gay, intersexed, and queer/questioning); the term *queer* is also used by people who don't identify in any of these ways, yet perceive themselves outside the heterosexual mainstream. Older people tend to be sensitive to this word because it was used as an insult in earlier times (Barón and Cramer 2000; Ritter and Terndrup 2002). However, *queer* is now being reclaimed as a term of unity and pride among sexual minorities and frequently used as a term of sexual identification, particularly by younger people (see Horner, chapter 15; Ritter and Terndrup 2002).

At any age, bisexual visibility requires dealing with many myths and stereotypes about bisexuals (Kingston 2002; Smith 2002). Both young and old bisexual people experience invisibility and binegativity (Kingston 2002). These experiences contribute to isolation and loneliness and to the low self-esteem and mental health issues experienced by bisexuals of all ages (Bradford 2004; Dworkin 2000; Jorm et al. 2002; Page 2004; Smith 2002).

ET TU, THERAPIST?

Bisexuals are invisible in most professional education: undergraduate, graduate, and continuing education programs, as well as within professional associations. Even when health, mental health, and other professionals are informed about gay and lesbian issues, they are unlikely to know about bisexual women and men (Dworkin 2000; Greene 2003; Keppel 2002). In fact, if they have any views at all, they are often binegative (Greene 2003).

The find feature of word processing programs make it as easy to insert "BGLT" into a document as "GL," satisfying requirements for academic and editorial correctness. However, a careful reading of these materials often reveals that bisexuals have been subsumed under discussions of gay men and/or lesbians with no understanding of the differences between these groups. Keppel notes that most of the professional aging and queer therapy workshops she has attended group bisexuals with lesbians and gay men as well. Bisexuals are included in the workshop descriptions, but presenters and authors seem surprised when asked to describe the ways in which bisexuals are different from gays and lesbians in the presented material. They don't seem to know the differences, but that doesn't keep them from claiming inclusivity.

BISEXUAL MENTAL HEALTH

Since we have no studies of mental health among older U.S. bisexuals, we need to make inferences from the research and writing that is available. Sources include studies of mental health among bisexuals in other countries (Jorm et al. 2002), mental health of younger bisexuals (Bradford 2004; Page 2004; Russell and Seif 2002), studies of nonbisexual U.S. elders (Atkinson and Hackett 1989), studies of gay and lesbian elders (Adelman 1991), and anecdotal material from clinical experiences with bisexual elders (Keppel 2002). A recent study by Emily Page (2004) focused on the psychotherapy experiences of bisexual clients and the quality of these mental health services (see also Page, chapter 3). All these studies have something important to contribute to our understanding of bisexual elders.

Should we be worried about older bisexuals' mental health? Dworkin (2006) refers to the aging bisexual as "the invisible of the invisible." In perhaps the first comprehensive chapter devoted to the aging bisexual, Dworkin (2006) outlines some of the issues around relationships, community support, and gender differences that pose challenges to the bisexual elder. According to an Australian mental health study (Jorm et al. 2002), bisexuals had poorer mental health than either heterosexuals or homosexuals and are a "high-risk group for mental health problems and suicidal ideas and actions." This study reported that bisexuals had higher levels of anxiety and depression than either heterosexuals or homosexuals, as well as "more current adverse life events, greater childhood adversity, less positive support from family, more negative support from friends and a higher frequency of financial problems" (Jorm et al. 2002). For several excellent overviews of the literature concerning mental health issues of bisexual people, see Fox (1996), Dodge and Sandfort (chapter 2), Firestein (1996), and Page (chapter 3).

If we could guarantee the same anonymity to other survey respondents given to survey respondents by the Research Group in Australia, Keppel believes the findings on bisexual mental health would be similar for most Western countries. An international group of bisexuals attending the eighth International Bisexual Conference in Sydney, Australia in 2000 offered feedback to the study's principal author, Anthony Jorm (2002). This discussion revealed remarkable similarities between the mental health experiences and outcomes of bisexual respondents in the Australian study and those of the bisexual conference attendees. In a position paper by the Ontario (Canada) Public Health Association, Cheryl Dobinson and colleagues (2005) confirm the existence of mental health problems among bisexuals, especially older bisexuals, as they struggle with isolation, stereotyping, and inadequately trained health and mental health professionals. Yet these issues may differ significantly for bisexuals who come from differing age cohorts within the population of the United States (Hollibaugh 2005).

SIMILARITIES AND DIFFERENCES AMONG AGE COHORTS

Only "seniors" are viewed by society as a homogenous population, even though their age group spans over fifty years. Within that fifty-year span, these women and men are actually in many different stages of adult development (Barón and Cramer 2000). Whether old is defined as over fifty, over fifty-five, over sixty-two, over sixty-five, or even over seventy, there is no other segment of the population for which the rest of society assumes that ten years in age makes no difference. One useful way to understand older bisexual clients and their lives is to place them in their age cohorts according to when they reached adolescence, when they came out, and their current ages (Reid 1995; Ritter and Terndrup 2002).

In each decade there have been enough changes to profoundly influence our society and those within it. Each era imposed particular hardships on all sexual minorities and, in special ways, on bisexuals. It is easy to miss the effect on client lives of having grown up and/or been adults during these eras and through events of life-changing importance (Barón and Cramer 2000; Kimmel and Sang 1995; Reid 1995). These events are very important to the people whose lives were changed by them, yet these eras may seem historical and irrelevant to therapists and counselors who came of age during a different period of history. If the professional grew up after the gay rights movement began, she or he may have particular difficulty understanding what older bisexuals have been through.

Here are some examples of how membership in different age cohorts may affect older bisexuals' experiences:

Everyone now over fifty became an adult when the American Psychiatric Association still listed homosexuality as a diagnosable mental illness (until 1973). Homosexuality was equated with being sick and crazy. Although not widely known among heterosexuals, many in the "queer" population knew about some of the frightening consequences of the mental illness diagnosis. Parents sometimes committed their children to mental institutions. Electroshock, hospitalization, and other measures were used to "cure" adult and child "patients." Threats of these "treatments" provided valid reasons for staying closeted or keeping a low profile if out as lesbian or gay. In 1973 the American Psychiatric Association (APA) reversed their official position and proclaimed that homosexuality was not, in and of itself, a diagnosable mental illness (Conger 1975). The APA removed the diagnosis from the *Diagnostic and Statistical Manual of Mental Disorders* (DSM), but outdated concepts of homosexuality as mental illness linger.

The American Psychiatric Association never officially classified or declassified *bisexuality*; in fact, the DSM never mentioned it at all. The word was not in professionals' usage until much later. But bisexual women and men knew they were included in professional thinking about homosexuality and would likely be treated in a similar fashion to gay men and lesbians. When it was an option, many bisexuals, like many gay men and lesbians, married and had families and passed as "normal" heterosexuals (Edwards 2002).

You are unlikely to have clients who were adults in the Roaring Twenties, but there are plenty of us still around who grew up and came of age in the Great Depression of the 1930s. People were desperate for jobs, and those who appeared "different" were less likely to compete successfully for what was available. Scrabbling for a living wasn't conducive to coming out or to developing sexual minority communities.

The wartime 1940s changed society profoundly. Many of the bisexual elders Keppel reports having met were eighteen years of age and over during that period. They report meeting and mingling with people from other places and of different classes, races, ethnic origins, religions, and sexual attractions. Whether civilian or military, many people were moving inside and outside the U.S. Along the way, lots of them learned about same-sex attractions, even if those attractions were not their own.

Keppel has talked with several older bisexual veterans who were in uniform with the other 150,000-plus women of the WACs (Women's Army Corp). They learned about love between women from other WACs. Women in the work force, military or not, learned they could support themselves and didn't need to marry for financial security. Some of these women set up households and lived together, even though their relationships were not generally recognized and they could not marry each other.

During World War II, transience and the stress of combat allowed some men to risk same-sex experiences they would not have risked in their earlier, settled environments. Official antigay policies were only selectively enforced. With luck and skill, some men escaped policy enforcement. In big ports some veterans tell of military personnel and local gay and bisexual men who crossed barriers to be together for community and mentoring—and for sex. Some started relationships far from home and stayed on to continue those relationships at war's end. Colleagues who have worked with elderly male veterans report their clients do not usually talk either about combat or about sex. Male veterans have different rules. For the most part, older male veterans deal with combat and sex as equally taboo topics. Both these topics might put them in touch with their emotions, and these emotionally charged subjects tend to be avoided.

If the World War II era opened Pandora's box in terms of change, mobility, and opportunities for sexual encounters, the cold war and McCarthyism of the 1950s slammed the lid back on. Although we know now that Senator Joseph McCarthy had gay men as his associates and FBI director J. Edgar Hoover was in a same-sex relationship, at that time Hoover, McCarthy, and their associates smeared many reputations by alleging connections between sympathy for communism and same-sex behavior. "Tendencies toward subversion," "alleged tendencies toward subversion," and "homosexuals" were all included in the same federal order used to dismiss or suspend federal workers. When asked for job references, government policy was to give all three categories and refuse to identify which of the three was the cause of suspension or dismissal. The witch-hunt was on, and alleged homosexuality was considered as heinous a crime as alleged communist leanings.

Although the 1948 and 1952 Kinsey reports detailed a high incidence of same-sex sexual experiences among American men and women, same-sex behaviors still carried the stigma of both mental illness and disloyalty to the U.S. throughout this historical period (Kinsey, Pomeroy, and Martin 1948; Kinsey et al. 1952). These connections are clearly illustrated in the film *Kinsey* (Mutrux and Condon 2004).

The 1960s encompassed a series of social and cultural revolutions that affected many of the marginalized and disenfranchised segments of the U.S. population. African Americans, gay men and lesbians, and youth were among the constituency groups empowered by the societal changes of the period. Youth included both Vietnam War military service personnel and "flower children" involved in protesting the Vietnam War. These were just a few of the radical social changes rocking American society during this period. Sexuality was radically affected by both technological developments (e.g., invention and dissemination of the birth control pill) and social developments, such as the "free love" component of the hippie and peace movements, that brought new (but incomplete) freedom to younger women and men coming of age during this generation.

These social changes included a broad, diffusely defined increase in tolerance for "gay people." In the later years of the decade, gay and lesbian communities emerged with some prominence in larger urban areas, culminating in one of the pivotal events in "gay history": the Stonewall rebellion of 1969, about which a great deal has been written. This was an exciting time for bisexual people as well because definitions of gay liberation promoted by Clark (1987) and others in the late 1960s and early 1970s were inclusive of bisexuals, who were also considered to be included under the umbrella term *gay*.

The 1970s witnessed a continuation of this cultural revolution in new forms. Sexual freedom was a component of the "sex, drugs, and rock and roll" lifestyle embraced by a number of youth; though, in retrospect, some of this liberation served male youth to a greater degree than it served female youth. Women's liberation brought feminism out of the closet and gave women (albeit mostly white and middle-class women) a voice and a significant presence on national and international political stages for the first time in the history of this country since the suffragette movement of the early 1900s. Bisexuality emerged for the first time as a distinct entity. Bisexuals and their stories began to appear in print and in other media. The 1970s witnessed the true beginning point for the identity politics that would come to shape subsequent decades of lesbian, gay, bisexual, and transgender efforts at visibility and inclusion. Individual women and men of the 1970s were probably the first to claim a bisexual identity.

Identity politics continued to gain force and momentum in the 1980s. The 1980s saw a proliferation of bisexual political organizing and the establishment of networks and social institutions addressing the particular needs of bisexual women and men (Hutchins 1996). However, as the decade progressed, the HIV/AIDS epidemic profoundly influenced all nonheterosexual people (Kimmel and Sang 1995; Martell, Safren, and Prince 2004), including bisexuals who were coming out as part of the gay pride movement and attempting to form bisexual communities. Many in the bisexual movement's leadership were either killed by AIDS and/or exhausted by caring for dying partners and friends (Kingston 2002). The hubs of bisexual activism—San Francisco, New York, and Boston—were decimated. Mentors and potential mentors disappeared; there were no replacements. Bisexuals became hate targets when falsely accused of spreading HIV from the gay community to heterosexuals. The San Francisco Bisexual Center closed. The lost energy and momentum were never fully recovered.

If you are working with clients who were out or thinking about coming out as bisexual during these pivotal eras, you will want to find out how they were affected. You will need to know what memories and fears they still carry with them.

ISSUES OF BISEXUAL ELDER CLIENTS

What are the most common issues older bisexual men and women bring to counseling and therapy? You may be surprised by how many older people are coming out as bisexual! People who chose marriage and family during the bi-oppressive times of their younger years may be reconsidering their options, especially if they have lost a life partner through death, separation, or divorce. Or they may have identified as heterosexual in those younger years, but, as they—and society—have changed, new options may have opened up. As one man put it, "I finally opened the door to the other part of myself—and I didn't shut it behind me." He wanted to explore new possibilities while retaining the old ones.

Other people have lived as lesbians or gay men and want to explore other-sex attractions they never lost or have rediscovered. A woman who wants to explore relationships with men may be very apprehensive about losing her current community if she is part of a lesbian community that is binegative. Many lesbians have a reputation for cutting off women who "consort with the enemy," i.e., have affectional relationships with men. These women may look for a bisexual community that will include them. Unfortunately, they probably will not find one because none exists—at least not near them—particularly one that embraces older bisexual women.

With the loss of life partnerships, some people start "dating" again—or think about dating—and are scared by the prospect. They may already have had some unsettling or frightening experiences as they rejoin the dating game. Keppel has heard many say "I just don't know how to date as a (fifty-, sixty-, seventy-plus) year old. The rules have changed. What about sex?" (See below for some special sexual issues to be addressed.) If they are exploring dating a different sex/gender from the sex/gender of a previous partner, then they are likely to be even more uncertain about the process and the rules. For example, if the community they are entering is different than the community they have been living in, these women and men are likely to find that each community has its own norms. Their bisexual, gay male, lesbian, and heterosexual communities may all have different models for dating and socializing.

DISSONANCE OF STAGES OF DEVELOPMENT (DOSD) FOR OLDER BISEXUALS "COMING OUT"

When adults come out later than the usual years for initial identity formation, they experience a particular kind of dissonance because they are in more than one developmental stage simultaneously (Ritter and Terndrup 2002). For example, a person goes through adolescence in her teens, negotiating developmental, social, and sexual tasks focused on other-sex relationships (the heterosexual model). If she comes out later in life, she has a "second adolescence"; that is, she has to negotiate a new and different identity with sexual and social tasks focused on same-sex relationships. At the same time, she has the social and sexual tasks of her chronological age, which are different from those of adolescence. If one subscribes to the concept of generativity for older adults, this individual may simultaneously be a generative adult in relationships with younger persons while needing the generative guidance of older adults (actually, her peers) for that part of her currently negotiating her own "adolescence." These factors may produce a DoSD (dissonance of stages of development) that makes the individual feel crazy, especially if she does not understand what is happening. The therapist's job is to identify the DoSD and explain it to the client. Expect to explain it several times.

When people come out after adolescence and young adulthood, they are out of sequence with their bisexual, lesbian, and gay age cohorts. This phenomenon has also been noted by other authors writing about LGB aging (Barón and Cramer 2000). Not surprisingly, age cohorts who have been out for decades often have little sympathy for the enthusiasms and fears of late bloomers. Since older people grew up with severe restrictions on talking about sex, they are often repelled by people their own age, newly out, who want to talk about sex and do so with the enthusiasm of youth!

In Keppel's experience, the most acute DoSD often shows up in older bisexuals. The pervasive invisibility of bisexuality has given these individuals little or no identity model—not even a label for who they are. They may not have *bisexual* in their vocabularies. Looking back at coming out bisexual in his fifties, a friend of Keppel's observed, "We have no reflection. There's no one we can see who is like the self we have discovered. We have nothing to go on."

The degree of dissonance of stage development that an individual is likely to experience increases with age for several reasons. For example, the individual has lived longer as heterosexual and/or in a heterosexual society absorbing those norms, his/her current age cohorts have also lived longer in a heterosexual society regardless of their sexual self-identity, and, if the person reached adulthood before World War II, she or he is less likely to have ever used language to talk about sex or her or his own sexuality.

Some people have been out to themselves and others for a long time but are facing life changes that require them to evaluate risks associated with being out to a new group of others. They may have come to you for help with risk assessment.

Here are some common scenarios:

- Giving up driving necessitates moving to a new facility, maybe even a new city or state, or the person may be able to stay in the same home but is cut off from previous social contacts.
- Financial loss due to loss of partner may force a move to less expensive living quarters.
- Failing health necessitates a move to congregate housing, assisted living, or a nursing home.
- The person may be connected with other family members, like his or her adult children; he may not be out to them but is considering moving closer to them for assistance and companionship.

Similar to many people who come for counseling, the client may present with problem(s) of depression or anxiety or in other ways that keep identity issues hidden until the client feels safe in coming out. Let us turn briefly to the issues of bisexual, gay, and lesbian adult giving care to elderly parents.

BISEXUAL, GAY, AND LESBIAN ADULTS GIVING CARE TO ELDERLY PARENTS

There are unique issues affecting bisexual, gay, and lesbian adult children within families as parents become older and require care. Within some cultures, bisexual, gay, or lesbian family members may function as the center of an extended family (Williams 1998) or take a primary role in caring for aging parents (Martell, Safren, and Prince 2004). Gollance (2003) notes that approximately 26.6 percent of the adult U.S. population has been involved in giving care to an older adult within the past twelve months, and 17.1 percent of these adult child caregivers for elderly parents are "never married" adults. It is quite likely that a substantial percentage of these individuals are not heterosexual.

Gollance (2003) speaks eloquently of the intrapsychic conflicts that may occur for nonheterosexual daughters and sons who feel pressure to take on a primary caregiving role with aging parents. Gollance (2003) notes, "Like their heterosexual counterparts, most gay men and lesbians share a desire for love, loyalty and support from their families of origin" (Gollance 2003:4). Some of these sons and daughters may experience internal conflict between their feelings of resentment over past parental failure to acknowledge their sexual minority identity and their feelings of compassion and the desire to help their aging parents. Others BLG adult children were closeted but experience similar emotional ambivalence. He provides guidance to therapists seeking to help adult children come to terms with these conflicts.

Gollance (2003) suggests that therapists assist these adult children to clarify their conscious and unconscious motives for wanting to assist their aging parents and the potential outcomes of utilizing the opportunity to give care. For some BLG adults, the opportunity is seen as a "last-ditch effort" to win parental acceptance that did not occur earlier in life. He notes that "when parents become old and need help, the resulting dilemmas often expose the inner dynamics—and the fault lines—underlying the family system. And that is the time when the family most needs to be healed" (Gollance 2003:4). That healing may or may not be possible for any given family under their unique circumstances.

SUGGESTIONS FOR THERAPISTS WORKING WITH BISEXUAL ELDERS

How can therapists, counselors, medical practitioners, and other professionals be most helpful to older bisexual clients?

First, create an environment where clients feel safe and supported in coming out or talking about same- and other-sex attractions and about aging. This is absolutely vital to good treatment. Look beyond appearances of conformity. Maybe the word *bisexual* will never be spoken, but the issues will be revealed if you are informed, open, and supportive. The word *old* may not come up right away either, but it will be there. Clients will be checking your language and attitudes carefully. They have probably heard some particularly derisive expressions about older lesbians, gay men, and bisexual people used by younger members of those communities. Some of them fear that they will hear those kinds of comments from professionals as well.

Make your office/practice/work site bi-positive and bisexual inclusive. You've taken a step by reading this book. Continue educating yourself about bisexual women and men and bisexuality in general. Explore some of the resources recommended for you and your clients. Download the Bisexual Resource Center's pamphlets, read them, and keep them visible in your professional space along with other bi-friendly materials. You may also download the Sexual and Affectional Orientation and Identity Scales (Keppel and Hamilton 2000) and try filling them out for yourself (www.biresource.org).

Use language and ask questions in ways that are bisexual inclusive. What myths and stereotypes do you have about bisexuals? About older people? Check yourself for symptoms of ageism. You won't find much information about older bisexuals in print, especially in the professional literature, a fact that has also been noted by other authors who have reviewed (or looked for) existing litera- ture on bisexual elders (Barón and Cramer 2000; Reid 1995). Bisexuals may be virtually invisible in the print literature on sexual orientation and aging or may be assumed to have the same experiences as lesbians and gay men. Fortunately, this is beginning to change (Dworkin 2006). What you see and hear in profes- sional meetings may be biphobic or binegative. Keep looking. Inclusive and explicit materials, such as the *Journal of Bisexuality*, and books and articles on counseling and therapy with bisexual clients are beginning to appear (Firestein 1996; Fox 2006; Page 2004).

Warning: although part of your work may involve helping clients join social networks, many of the strategies you use to connect clients with supportive com- munity resources are not available, especially for older bisexuals. Even major cities have few bisexual and bisexual-inclusive organizations. Rural areas usual- ly have none. Rural areas are often at least a decade behind urban areas in sup- ports for gay men and lesbians—even more with respect to bisexual and trans- gender issues.

Find out about bisexual conferences and workshops and support your clients in attending these events. Isolated bisexuals have been very heartened by spend- ing even one day in the presence of other bisexual people. They carry home the experience of even a short time in any bisexual community. A client from rural Maine, viewing the other one thousand bisexual and bisexual-friendly attendees at the Fifth International Bisexual Conference, said, "It's the first time in my adult life I've just opened my mouth and said what I'm thinking without censor- ing myself first."

If community and area resources do not exist in the client's area, what else can the helping professional do? This is where the Internet comes in. Clients and therapists alike can learn a great deal if they google the terms *bisexual, bisexuali- ty, bisexual aging*, and related terms. You can encourage your client to learn to surf the net. Steer her to one of the Internet access resources: public libraries, local adult education and community college programs, and CyberSeniors are good choices. Many programs are free or charge lower fees for seniors. AARP's website has instructions for getting online and using the Web. There are multi- ple, excellent resources on the Internet devoted to bisexuality. The usual cau- tions apply. Clients need to be safe online. They must learn to protect themselves from online identity theft, unwelcome intrusions, and spam. Many will want accounts that can screen out pornography. Some may want porn left in.

There is an online bisexual community. One of the best places to access that community is the Web site of the international Bisexual Resource Center in Boston (www.biresource.org). The BRC Web site has multiple links: everything from local social groups to bisexual chat groups on many subjects. By the time you read this, there may well be a bisexual elders' chat group. The BRC also maintains an international online directory of thousands of bisexual and bi-inclusive groups, replacing the print directory published previously. An excellent new printed BRC resource is the book, *Getting Bi: Voices of Bisexuals Around the World*, an international compilation of more than 180 personal essays, some of them by older bisexuals (Ochs and Rowley 2005).

WHAT ABOUT SEX?

Wait, wait, don't tell me. We've all heard that older people aren't sexual—despite survey after survey reporting older folks are still sexual or are sexual again. (Remember Viagra?) But what about those other myths? Bisexuals are oversexed, can't be monogamous, have to have at least one male and one female partner, play the field, can't be faithful . . . (*Myths About Bisexuality*, a pamphlet on the Bisexual Resource Center's Web site, has a more complete list. See also Sumpter 1991.)

In case you missed it near the beginning of this chapter, Americans over fifty have the fastest rising *rate* of HIV infection of any U.S. population group. This group also has an increasing incidence of other sexually transmitted infections (STIs), including syphilis, which is also life threatening (Ginty 2004). Lack of safer sex education for seniors is partly due to ageist views of elders as asexual and partly due to professionals' ignorance and discomfort in addressing both bisexuality and sex (Keppel 2002).

If you don't know whether or not your client is sexually active—or if your client is coming out and exploring a new social scene and new relationships, you will need to get comfortable with conversations about sex. Most therapists, counselors, and medical practitioners aren't comfortable talking about sex. They are even more uncomfortable when the client is substantially older than the professional or is viewed as elderly. There's something about "talking sex" with clients the ages of one's parents or grandparents that shuts down even the most talkative practitioners. "Don't talk" rules fill the air. Remind yourself that people's lives may depend on these conversations.

Books that can help you and your clients talk about sensuality and sex include Joani Blank's *Still Doing It: Men and Women Over Sixty Write About Their Sexuality* and the Hen Co-op's *Growing Old Disgracefully* and *Disgracefully Yours*. Excellent resources are also available online: the San Francisco Department of Public Health (www.sfdph.org) and HIV>50 (www.hivoverfifty .org) are two such resources.

Don't expect your elderly clients to know how to talk about sex (although a few may surprise you). When we older folks were growing up, most of us didn't have the words. Instead, we had strict orders *not* to talk about sex. We weren't

supposed to know those words. Parents and others often equated a child knowing "the words" with them having done really bad things. However, to be safe
now, we need to talk specifically with partners about routes of transmission, use
of barriers, wetness of kissing, and other necessary precautions—all new topics
for elders with, perhaps, the exception of condoms and diaphragms used for
pregnancy prevention.

We also need to learn to negotiate well about sex. Most of us did not learn to
negotiate about sex with our partners when we were younger. We didn't have
the language. If we were in traditional sex roles and/or had been in long-term
relationships, we probably have not learned negotiation skills yet—and may
need to have you teach us. Older adults usually don't know about STIs (sexually
transmitted infections). Most of the current common STIs were not known
when we elders were young adults. Like Rip Van Winkles, older people emerging from long-term relationships have missed most of the current list of STIs:
herpes, cervical cancer, anal cancer, HIV/AIDS, Chlamydia, LGV (Lympho-
granuloma Venereum), genital warts, hepatitis B, hepatitis C, parasites, and
shigella. We heard of syphilis and gonorrhea because testing for them was man-
datory for marriage licenses and because extensive prevention and treatment
programs were developed for service men and women during and immediately
after World War II. Unfortunately, because syphilis and gonorrhea responded to
the earliest antibiotics, older people may think these diseases have been eradi-
cated and might be astonished to find out that syphilis was epidemic in most
large U.S. cities in 2004 (Centers for Disease Control and Prevention 2004).

STI information changes quickly. The following resources stay current and
give accurate information that will help you and your clients assess actual risks
and identify preventive measures: Columbia University's health website (www.
goaskalice.columbia.edu), San Francisco Department of Public Health, Fen-
way Community Health (www.fenwayhealth.org), National Association on HIV
over fifty (NAHOF) (www.hivover50.com), and Planned Parenthood (www
.plannedparenthood.com).

Don't assume you know who is doing what with whom. Assume all possibilities. Give safer sex information. Keep safer sex supplies, printed safer sex handouts, and lists of community and online resources ready for show and tell. You
may be the only person between your client and a life-threatening STI like HIV
or syphilis.

SYSTEMS INTERVENTIONS ON BEHALF OF OLDER BISEXUALS

How else can you help your older clients? On a systems level, you can work at
decreasing the pervasive binegativity among professionals in the field of aging.
The current level of biphobia is probably at the level that homophobia was ten

or more years ago. Be an advocate wherever you are working: hospitals, nursing homes, assisted living facilities, and within your local, regional, and national professional groups.

Does your professional organization have a sexual minorities committee or network with *lesbian* and *gay* in its title but not *bisexual?* Can you use your professional code of ethics to show your colleagues how this omission actually contributes to bisexual invisibility and, therefore, directly affects bisexual women's and men's mental health? You could work to change the name to *equality* or *sexual minority equality* network/committee or another more inclusive title with a mission statement to match. If you are a gay or lesbian professional, consider advocating for bisexual inclusion within your group. In the spring 2002 issue of *Out-Word* devoted to the issues of bisexual elders, Laurie Toby Edison commented,

> In the queer world, you have limited resources. If we divide ourselves into gay, lesbian, bisexual and trans people and we don't try to take care of our own collectively . . . then we are not going to be able to take care of our people. Our resources will continue to be fragmented. So developing inclusiveness is profoundly important. (Kingston 2002:5)

We cannot leave bisexual people behind without abandoning a vital part of our community of queer elders.

So much to do; so little time.

REFERENCES

Adelman, M. (1991). Stigma, gay lifestyles, and adjustment to aging: A study of later-life gay men and lesbians. *Journal of Homosexuality, 20*(3/4), 7–32.

Atkinson, D.R., and Hackett, G. (1988). Treatment of non-ethnic minorities: A historical overview. In D.R. Atkinson and G. Hackett, *Counseling non-ethnic American minorities.* Springfield, IL: Thomas.

Barón, A., and Cramer, D.W. (2000). Potential counseling concerns of aging lesbian, gay, and bisexual clients. In R.M. Perez, K.A. DeBord, and K.J. Bieschke (Eds.), *Handbook of counseling and psychotherapy with lesbian, gay and bisexual clients* (pp. 207–223). Washington, DC: American Psychological Association.

Bohan, J. (1996). *Psychology and sexual orientation.* New York: Routledge.

Bradford, M. (2004). The bisexual experience: Living in a dichotomous culture. *Journal of Bisexuality, 4*(1/2), 7–23.

Centers for Disease Control and Prevention. (2004). *Sexually transmitted disease surveillance 2003 supplement, syphilis surveillance report.* Atlanta: U.S. Department of Health and Human Services, Centers for Disease Control and Prevention.

Clark, D. (1987). *Loving someone gay.* Berkeley: Celestial Arts.

Conger, J. (1975). Proceedings of the American Psychological Association, Incorporated, for the year 1974: Minutes of the annual meeting of the Council of Representatives. *American Psychologist, 30,* 620–651.

Dobinson, C., MacDonnell, J. Hampson, E., Clipsham, J., and Chow, K. (2005). Improving the quality and access of public health services for bisexuals. *Journal of Bisexuality*, 5(1), 39–78.

Dworkin, S. (2000). Individual therapy with lesbian, gay, and bisexual clients. In R. M. Perez, K. A. DeBord, and K. J. Bieschke (Eds.), *Handbook of counseling and psychotherapy with lesbian, gay and bisexual clients* (pp. 157–182). Washington, DC: American Psychological Association.

Dworkin, S. (2006). Aging bisexual: The invisible of the invisible minority. In D. Kimmel, T. Rose, and S. David (Eds.), *Lesbian, gay, bisexual, and transgender aging: Research and clinical perspectives.* New York: Columbia University Press.

Edwards, N. (2002). Bisexuals, "real" lesbians, "political" lesbians: Sexual orientation across the lifecourse. *OutWord*, 8(4), 3, 7.

Ehrenberg, M. (1996). Aging and mental health: Issues in the gay and lesbian community. In C. Alexander (Ed.), *Gay and lesbian mental health: A sourcebook for practitioners* (pp. 189–209). Binghamton, NY: Harrington Park.

Firestein, B. A. (Ed.) (1996). *Bisexuality: The psychology and politics of an invisible minority.* Thousand Oaks, CA: Sage.

Fox, R. C. (1996). Bisexuality in perspective: A review of theory and research. In B. A. Firestein (Ed.), *Bisexuality: The psychology and politics of an invisible minority* (pp. 3–50). Thousand Oaks, CA: Sage.

Fox, R. C. (2004). Bisexuality: A reader's guide to the social science literature. *Journal of Bisexuality*, 4(1/2), 162–255.

Fox, R. C. (Ed.) (2006). *Affirmative psychotherapy with bisexual women and bisexual men.* Binghamton, NY: Harrington Park.

Ginty, Molly M. (2004). HIV/AIDS cases still rising among older women. *Call* (Internet ed.), March 26, Kansas City, retrieved March 29, 2005, from http://www.kccall.com/News/2004/0326/Community/082.html.

Gollance, R. (2003). Groups support gay men and lesbians facing the challenges of caring for aging parents. *Healthcare and Aging*, 10(4), 4.

Greene, B. (2001). Older lesbians' concerns and psychotherapy: Beyond a footnote to the footnote. In F. K. Trotman and C. M. Brody (Eds.), *Psychotherapy and counseling with older women* (pp. 161–174). New York: Springer.

Greene, B. (2003). Beyond heterosexism and across the cultural divide: Developing an inclusive lesbian, gay, and bisexual psychology: A look to the future. In L. D. Garnets and D. C. Kimmel (Eds.), *Psychological perspectives on lesbian, gay and bisexual experiences* (2d ed., pp. 357–400). New York: Columbia University Press.

Herdt, G., and Beeler, J. (1998). Older gay men and lesbians in families. In C. J. Patterson and A. R. D'Augelli (Eds.), *Lesbian, gay, and bisexual identities in families* (pp. 177–196). New York: Oxford University Press.

Hilbert, G. (2003). Looking for images of transgender older adults on film, in print and on the web: Do they exist? *OutWord*, 10(2), 7.

Hoctel, P. (2003). Former NVL partner's program teaches about service needs of African American LGBT elders. *Diversity Currents*, 4(3), 3, 6.

Hollibaugh, A. (2005). The aging of the post-Stonewall generation requires new priorities for LGBT communities. *OutWord*, 11(3), 4–5.

Hutchins, L. (1996). Bisexuality: Politics and community. In B. A. Firestein (Ed.), *Bisexuality: The psychology and politics of an invisible minority* (pp. 240–259). Thousand Oaks, CA: Sage.

Jorm, A. F., Korten, A. E., Rodgers, B., Jacomb, P. A., and Christensen, H. (2002). Sexual orientation and mental health: Results from a community survey of young and middle aged. *British Journal of Psychiatry, 188,* 423–427.

Keppel, B. (1995). Aging and sexual minority cultural issues in Maine. Manuscript.

Keppel, B. (2002). The challenges and rewards of life as an outspoken bisexual elder. *OutWord,* 8(4), 1, 6.

Keppel, B., and Hamilton, A. (2000). Your sexual orientation: Using the Sexual and Affectional Orientation and Identity Scale to teach about sexual orientation. In R. S. Kimball (Ed.), *Our whole lives: Sexuality education for adults* (pp. 157–161). Boston: Unitarian Universalist Association and United Church Board of Homeland Ministries. (An older version of these scales is available as a downloadable pamphlet at www.biresource.org).

Kimmel, D. C. (1978). Adult development and aging: A gay perspective. *Journal of Social Issues,* 34(3), 113–130.

Kimmel, D. C., and Sang, B. E. (1995). Lesbians and gay men in midlife. In A. R. D'Augelli and C. J. Patterson (Eds.), *Lesbian, gay, and bisexual identities over the lifespan* (pp. 190–214). New York: Oxford University Press.

Kingston, T. (2002). Roundtable: "You have to speak up all the time," bisexual elders address issues, concerns of aging. *OutWord,* 8(4), 4–5.

Kinsey, A. C., Pomeroy, W. B., and Martin, C. E. (1948). *Sexual behavior in the human male.* Philadelphia: Saunders.

Kinsey, A. C., Pomeroy, W. B., Martin, C. E., and Gebhard, P. H. (1952). *Sexual behavior in the human female.* Philadelphia: Saunders.

Klein, M. (2003). Lesbian and gay invisibility in a nursing home. *OutWord,* 10(1), 2–3, 7.

Kling, E. (2004). SAGE New York: A pioneer in serving LGBT older adults. *OutWord,* 10(3), 3.

Marshall, F. (2003). Spiritual care for LGBT older adults: The role of chaplains. *OutWord,* 10(1), 7.

Martell, C. R., Safren, S. A., and Prince, S. E. (2004). *Cognitive behavioral therapies with lesbian, gay, and bisexual clients.* New York: Guilford.

Morrow, S. (2000). First do no harm: Therapist issues in psychotherapy with lesbian, gay, and bisexual clients. In R. M. Perez, K. A. DeBord and K. J. Bieschke (Eds.), *Handbook of counseling and psychotherapy with lesbian, gay, and bisexual clients* (pp. 137–156). Washington, DC: American Psychological Association.

Mutrux, G. (producer), and Condon, B. (writer/director). (2004). *Kinsey: Let's talk about sex.* (Motion picture.) United States: Fox Searchlight.

Ochs, R. (1996). Biphobia: It goes more than two ways. In B. A. Firestein (Ed.), *Bisexuality: The psychology and politics of an invisible minority* (pp. 217–239). Thousand Oaks, CA: Sage.

Ochs, R., and Rowley, S. E. (2005). *Getting Bi: Voices of bisexuals around the world.* Boston: Bisexual Resource Center.

Perez, R. M., DeBord, K. A., and Bieschke, K. J. (Eds.). (2000). *Handbook of counseling and psychotherapy with lesbian, gay and bisexual clients.* Washington, DC: American Psychological Association.

Raphael, S., and Meyer, M. (2004). The first national association for professionals addressing the issues of lesbian and gay aging. *OutWord,* 10(3), 2–3, 8.

Reid, J. D. (1995). Development in later life: Older lesbian and gay lives. In A. R. D'Augelli and C. J. Patterson (Eds.), *Lesbian, gay, and bisexual identities over the lifespan* (pp. 215–240). New York: Oxford University Press.

Ritter, K.Y., and Terndrup, A.I. (2002). Midlife and later-life issues for sexual minority adults. *Handbook of affirmative psychotherapy with lesbians and gay men* (pp. 130–145). New York: Guilford.

Russell, S.T., and Seif, H. (2002). Bisexual female adolescents: A critical analysis of past research and results from a national survey. In D. Atkins (Ed.), *Bisexual women in the twenty-first century* (pp. 73–94). Binghamton, NY: Harrington Park.

Smith, P.R. (2002). Bisexuality: Reviewing the basics, debunking the stereotypes for professionals in aging. *OutWord*, 8(4), 2, 8.

Sumpter, S.F. (1991). Myths/realities of bisexuality. In L. Hutchins and L. Ka'ahumanu (Eds.), *Bi any other name: Bisexual people speak out* (pp. 12–13). Boston: Alyson.

Vaillant, G. (1977). *Adaptation to life*. Boston: Little, Brown.

Williams, W.L. (1998). Social acceptance of same-sex relationships in families: Models from other cultures. In C.J. Patterson and A.R. D'Augelli (Eds.), *Lesbian, gay, and bisexual identities in families: Psychological perspective* (pp. 53–71). New York: Oxford University Press.

Yoakam, J.R. (2002). Network News. *OutWord*, 8(4), 1, 7.

10

DISABILITY AND BISEXUALITY

CONFRONTING ABLEISM AT THE INTERSECTION OF GENDER AND QUEER DESIRE

Stacey L. Coffman

According to the doctors, I was supposed to enter this world on May 20, 1978. I would arrive with much anticipation, but little surprise. My name would be Stacey and I would have ten tiny fingers, ten tiny toes, and a clean bill of health. I would stay in the hospital for a day or two, and would then be brought home by beaming, proud parents. According to fate (or the moral model), I would enter the world on February 28, 1978. I would be connected to a respirator and call an incubator home for eleven weeks. I would also be disabled.

PEOPLE ALWAYS talk about similarities because they are afraid of difference. I want to *claim* difference. We have to look at the ways oppressed and marginalized people are *constructed* as different. Sometimes, stereotypes get filled in certain ways. I may be shunned for saying that, but my life is dramatically different than others through the course of my daily activities and the ways I am approached. Rather than existing as the Other in this story, my possession of my own disability puts me in a dominant position for the first time.

Reactions to disability range from pity, to admiration, to fear, and to separation. I do not like any of these reactions, even the admiration, but only because of the place it comes from. It is a form of pity manifesting itself in another way. Mostly, admiration means, "Congratulations! You chose to get out of bed today even though you have a disability." To me admiration and being a hero means standing in the middle of oppression and understanding it for what it is. I use my "condition" to better understand how humans have held one another down for so long and to be a *witness* in order to break the cycle. I know the most amazing people who are heroes because they choose to be who they are in the midst of hatred, discrimination, and prejudice.

THE EXPERIENCE OF DISABILITY

As Rhoda Olkin (1999b) asserts, the experience of disability places individuals in a unique cultural and social position. A forced dual-occupation in the world labels the able-bodied as *normal* and the physically challenged or disabled as *abnormal*. She terms the bridge of her experience between the worlds of the disabled and nondisabled as a bicultural experience. Disability, while not possessing its own unique heritage, language (excluding American Sign Language), and other specific markers of ethnicity, binds its occupants through the collective experience of devaluing those with mobility impairments, who speak differently, and who walk differently. Olkin distinguishes between the mobility impaired and others by referring to people without disabilities as "able-bodied" or "temporarily able-bodied."

Tatum (2000) argues that we are who others say we are; she refers to Cooley's concept of the "looking glass self" and how we see ourselves through the mirror in which others see us. This mirror often becomes distorted because of factors relating to diversity and the multiple identities we occupy. Tatum states, "The parts of our identity that *do* capture our attention are those that other people notice, and that reflect back to us." (p. 11). Because of this tendency, people are commonly defined in terms of ethnicity, gender, ability, socioeconomic status, sexual orientation, and religion, among a variety of other factors.

Tatum (2000) refers to Audre Lorde's concept of the *mythical norm*, the idea that each person fits into the dominant groups of traditional society. Lorde's mythical norm in America is "white, thin, young, heterosexual, Christian, and financially secure" (as cited in Tatum 2000:11). Those who fit within this mold hold the majority of power and privilege within our society. The effects of this mythical norm extend in two ways: first, individuals receive intellectual reminders that they do not fit within the mold and, second, systematic privilege and power reach those who fit the norms of "American" society. Adrienne Rich (1986) refers to the process of being unable to see oneself reflected in the larger culture as if you "looked in the mirror and saw nothing" (p. 199). In this respect, a sense of psychic dissonance develops when certain groups face devaluation by society. This occurs when women, sexual minorities, religious minorities, ethnic minorities, old people, and people with disabilities do not receive positive messages from dominant culture.

In "The Cycle of Socialization" Harro (2000) discusses the role multiple social identities play in our access to power and privilege in society. Harro states, "Instead we are each born into a specific set of *social identities*, related to categories of difference mentioned above, and these social identities predispose us to unequal *roles* in the dynamic system of oppression" (p. 15). These roles vary from person to person, based on the unique categories she possesses. Each person is likely to belong to several oppressed and several dominant groups. In regard to dominant groups, Harro states that these groups define what is considered normal in society and categorize less privileged groups. Because people with disabilities do not hold dominant status, people without disabilities often create ideas and assumptions about their lives and abilities. Davis (2002) argues that as "traditional" categories of identity become less distinctive in their ability to shape our identity, the concept of disability becomes even more complex.

In terms of identity politics, disability remains the youngest and thus most developmental category of identity. In terms of oppositional consciousness, disability is the last to emerge, trailing behind the gay rights movement. "Oppositional consciousness" refers to the efforts of marginalized groups to protest negative ideas generated about them by dominant culture (Morris and Braine 2001). Specific acts of consciousness and dissent challenge the claim that marginalized groups possess less value and worth. This trend is apparent in the academic departments of many colleges and universities. Disability studies still trails behind and slowly emerges after gender/women's studies and queer/gay and lesbian studies.

LANGUAGE AND RECOGNITION

In our hierarchical society it is the social meanings of words that have power. Why do we choose "disabled?" It has negative connotations; the dictionary definition is "unfit" or "useless." But being disabled/impaired is not a negative, not something to be ashamed of; rather it is a shared identity among those who have the experience of being disabled in a world dominated by non-disabled people.

—RUSSELL 1998:14

Embracing the term *disabled* reflects the pride of a movement that identifies the capability and the inherent rights of its members. People with disabilities face common experiences of oppression, discrimination, and prejudice. We exist in a world that wishes to deny our existence, that refuses to remove physical and psychic barriers standing in our way, and that historically (in the Nazi era) referred to people with varying abilities as "unworthy of life."

Within the disabled community, language is a topic of great dissonance and debate. Arguments occur over the terminology used to describe people with disabilities. Some terms are embraced by nearly all members of the community, while others are seen as derogatory or empowering depending on the individual person. Morris (2001) states, "To pay attention to the words we use is not to be 'politically correct' but to struggle for a language which describes the denial of our human rights" (p. 2). According to Morris, conscious use of language helps people with disabilities in their struggle to obtain equal rights and to give voice to a unique physical experience.

One of the most hurtful and pervasive forms of ableism manifests itself in the way language creates and perpetuates ideas surrounding ability. The discussion of language usually cannot occur without some sort of reference to political correctness. However, framing disability in terms acceptable to people with disabilities expands beyond the typical notions of political correctness; it allows choice over what you wish to be called. Certain terms are "triggering" for the disabled community and a great deal of divergence exists in the terms people do or do not find acceptable. For Mairs (1997), reclaiming the word *crippled* serves as a source of personal power and triumph while its casual use by the nondisabled makes people with disabilities cringe with disgust. The slang term *lame* falls easily from the mouths of kids and teenagers who use it to mean stupid or worthless now that *gay* is rightfully socially unacceptable.

Groch (2001) mentions the evolution of terms referring to the disabled community in the same manner as the evolution of "acceptable" terms for African Americans. Groch states, "They [disability rights activists] reject the language of rehabilitation medicine and special education. Activists replace 'architectural barriers' with 'segregation,' 'mainstreaming' with 'integration,' and 'attitudinal barriers' with 'prejudice'" (pp. 85–86). The pain associated with inappropriate language comes from devaluation. "Tiny" words reflect larger attitudes, and many of the phrases uttered so carelessly hint at the structural barriers impeding my own life and the lives of many others. Educators and therapists can use experiential exercises, such as guided imagery, to assist the able-bodied to understand more fully the experiences of people with disabilities (see appendix).

A BRIEF OVERVIEW OF MODELS OF DISABILITY

Life seems so complex at times, and so many things are impossible to understand. It is so difficult to imagine why pain and suffering exist, why children go hungry, why there is war, or why someone can walk down the street one day and suddenly be in a wheelchair the next. Yet, all of these things are part of the human experience. I believe that these are tools in hiding—they exist in our lives so that we can hold compassion toward others, strive to make a difference, and celebrate our simplicity.

Disability scholars use three basic theoretical models to explain societal construction of disability: the moral model, the medical model, and the social model. Olkin (1999b) provides extended definitions to work from and expand upon. Many scholars base their theoretical foundations on Olkin's definitions and propose new ideas working from her position. Olkin defines the moral and medical model as the most harmful to people with disabilities, while equating the social model to the struggles of other minority groups. According to the moral model, disability stems from bad deeds or immorality. Disability is something to be defeated; the person with a disability accepts the shame and stigma of the condition.

The moral model plays quite nicely into society's assumptions of disability: that people with disabilities are evil and bitter (think Shakespeare's *Richard III* or Disney's villainous Captain Hook) or that disability is ordered by God as a form of divine will. Many parents of children with disabilities are told that disabling conditions are "God's will." The moral model, although outdated, still exerts its influence in a society founded on Judeo-Christian tradition and anxious to place the blame on someone or something. Even the view of people with disabilities as "chosen by God" creates unreal expectations and feeds into the idea of the "supercrip" or someone who ultimately rises above disability and meets or exceeds society's expectations. Smiling poster children fit into the framework of the moral model and the idea of the supercrip.

The medical model picks up where the moral model leaves off and places the treatment of disability into the "capable" hands of medical professionals who view disability as a problem to be fixed. According to Olkin (1999b), the medical model defines disability as a form of pathology that must be corrected.

The most recent and least problematic model is the minority or social model. This model avoids the pitfalls of the previous two models by citing the "problem" of disability as society's negative interpretation of disability. This model treats people with disabilities as a minority group working to access equal rights in a discriminatory and inequitable society. Olkin (1999b) states that the social model refers to disability as a "social construction" and that the "problems" of disability stem from a society that fails to accommodate the needs of a minority group. People with disabilities, like other minority populations, are subject to prejudice, discrimination, and the denial of basic human rights. The problem stems from the physical barriers of an able-bodied world, not the physical difference itself.

Disability scholars embrace the social model because it forces people to change their interpretation of disability and analyze the way individual attitudes shape the behavior of the society as a whole. For instance, a belief in accessibility as an individual problem or a medical problem diminishes the need for universal accessibility to all public places. Clare (2001) refers to the far-reaching consequences of ableism including inaccessible buildings and oppression. This oppression includes "high unemployment rates, lack of access, gawking, substandard education, being forced to live in nursing homes and back rooms, [and] being seen as childlike and asexual" (p. 360). Clare addresses the core issues of disability politics in a brief summation of the many forms of ableism.

Unfortunately, most people with disabilities do not discover the minority model until later in life.

This model, although clearly important in its ability to reframe ideas of the self and ability, does not match the ideas perpetuated by the authority figures in disabled people's lives. Doctors, teachers, and caregivers still hold on to many of the erroneous ideas surrounding the moral and medical models. My own awareness of the social model came over time—and with resistance—because it forced me to realize how hurtful society is toward those with different abilities.

GENDER, SEXUALITY, AND DISABILITY STATUS

In addition to having a disability, I am also female. My identity as a woman can never be separated from my identity as a person with a disability, placing me in a unique series of circumstances with regard to oppression. Disability oppression theory is the most recently developed theory now being applied to understand the structural and systemic devaluation of people with disabilities in society (Castaneda and Peters 2000). Andrew Potok (2003) refers to the disabled as the "most marginalized sector of society" (p. 163). Our oppression as a group both mirrors and illuminates the oppression of other marginalized groups. Because disability cuts across all sectors of society, people with disabilities are likely to be members of *multiple* groups facing oppression. Multiple identities within groups create further complications.

Gender, sexuality, and disability create a series of issues in terms of identity, leading to a contrast in the amount of support and rejection received from different communities. O'Toole and Brown (2003) argue that other oppressed groups may offer support, but access, such as disabled women's ties to the lesbian community, may be hard to come by, resulting in further isolation. They state that membership in these groups "provides valuable support and resources" (p. 38). Embracing another stigmatized identity may ease the burden of constantly identifying as disabled. One identity can be placed "on hold" while another identity is explored.

Despite the initial difficulty managing multiple identities, the literature (see, e.g., Clare 1999, 2001; Panzarino 1994) emphasizes the need to integrate multiple aspects of self. The challenge individuals' face in managing and embracing multiple identities has interesting implications for the development of multicultural theory and for doing therapy with people who have disabilities. Multicultural theorists propose that single identities do not occur for anyone and that most individuals' identities emanate from a variety of political and cultural factors.

Multiculturalism, when addressing both women's needs and the needs of people with disabilities, recognizes the multiplicity of identity in multiple cultural contexts. Wolf (1994) reflects the complexity of addressing women's needs within multiculturalism. Rather than existing solely as gendered individuals, women retain strong ties to their cultural backgrounds. In order to adequately meet their needs, they cannot be viewed only as women. Wolf states that identity often stems from women's recognition as "nothing but women," with problems arising because women are rarely defined beyond their status as females.

MULTICULTURALISM, DISABILITY STATUS, AND SELF-CONCEPT

The only experience I have ever known is my disability. I will never know what it is like to walk without effort or to have a body that automatically responds to commands without a second thought. I will never be able to break into a run and arrive at a destination in the nick of time or to skate on a frozen pond with blade-marked ice. I will always know what it is like to struggle to get my body to respond to my impatient commands and how much effort it has taken to get where I am today. But I will know the simple victory of taking a step and writing my name on a piece of paper, the feel of the numbers being pressed as I dial the telephone, and the wonder of being able to speak clearly to the person on the line. I will always know what it is like to witness the joy and compassion of other people with disabilities.

The ways in which recognition does and does not occur in society holds tremendous power over the self-concept and identity of members of marginalized groups. One of the aims of multiculturalism, from the vantage point of Taylor (1994), is to restore a positive self-concept to groups who face derogatory messages about their worth and value. Taylor states, "a person or a group of people can suffer real damage, real distortion, if the people or the society around them mirror back to them a confining or demeaning or contemptible picture of themselves" (p. 25). Over time, more diverse portrayals of people with disabilities appear throughout mainstream culture. The film *Frida* received critical acclaim. Share a Smile Becky became the first of Barbie's friends to sport a wheelchair (and, incidentally, could not fit into the doorways or elevator of Barbie's Dream House). The American Girl doll line, also by Mattel, sells wheelchairs as an accessory for girls who "need their own wheels." Aimee Mullins, an amputee, was one of *People Magazine*'s Fifty Most Beautiful People in 1999. In her work as a model, Mullins's prosthetic legs are incorporated into fashion shows, turning a visible aspect of disability into couture. Despite flaws, these "pictures," as Taylor would call them, demonstrate a greater willingness to include people with disabilities as a "normal" part of the American cultural landscape.

Frida, a biographical film, is notable for its strong portrayal of a feminist, Chicana woman with a disability and serves as an example of a well-rounded life shaped by disability (Taymor 2002a). The film possessed some minor faults and even faced criticism for its *lack* of emphasis on disability. Taymor (2002b), commenting on her choices, affirms, "I didn't want to do another painter-angst movie. Pain is there but pleasure is equally there" (p. 14). Kahlo herself places emphasis on her zest for life. In her journal, she states, "In spite of my long illness, I feel an immense joy in LIVING" (Kahlo 1994).

Frida illustrates several key principles of disability studies: disability can be acquired at any stage in life (Kahlo had polio as a child followed by a bus accident in her early teens); disability cuts across lines of gender, ethnicity, sexuality, and socioeconomic status; people with disabilities possess sexuality (her affairs with men and women were notorious); and people with disabilities experience a full range of human emotions while rarely indulging in excessive sorrow over their condition. Frida's life, at least as portrayed on film, contains little contact with other people with disabilities. Despite this, she develops a positive sense of self and leads a full life through contact with many sectors of the world.

IMPLICATIONS FOR THERAPISTS WORKING WITH CLIENTS WITH DISABILITIES

While each person experiences a wide array of strengths and weaknesses, not everyone experiences the structural and internalized oppression of disability (Wisdom and Coffman 2005). Olkin (1999a) addresses the tendency for therapists and the general public to minimize the experience of disability by stating that "each person has some kind of disability" or "everyone is different." While we each live a unique experience, disability oppression binds people with disabilities together through similar experiences of prejudice, discrimination, and sociopolitical strife.

Childhood, according to disability scholars, poses significant emotional and physical risks because of abuse, substance abuse, higher drop-out rates, and higher rates of unemployment (Olkin 1997; Shakespeare, Gillespie-Sells, and Davies 1997). Olkin outlines thirteen human rights of children with disabilities to ensure quality of life. These include awareness and autonomy of disability, control over medical procedures, freedom from abuse, and treatment as a human being rather than a medical anomaly. Rights related to identity include the reflection of positive role models with disabilities across the lifespan, positive acceptance of disability as a form or part of identity, and the right of people with disabilities to exist in the world. Olkin also asserts that individuals with disabilities have the right to a full emotional life and to receive a sensible interpretation of the implications of their disability. Children with disabilities have the right to the expectation of a "normal" romantic life including sexuality and parenthood. They can also expect interactions with the disabled and nondisabled population, accurate and proper assessment of their needs, an accessible and accepting environment, and the right "to be a child." These rights, delineated by Olkin, describe the key issues faced by people with disabilities.

So who are people with disabilities and what do they want? People with disabilities are sexual beings who want it all: romance, marriage or domestic partnership, and children. Silence surrounds the sexuality of people with disabilities due to false assumptions of a nonsexual existence. Dominant ideology rejects the notion of people with disabilities as suitable partners or parents. Similar resistance surrounds people with disabilities and the queer community in terms of beliefs of who it is or is not appropriate to love and who is best suited to raising children. As the gay marriage debate edges on, a slogan exists that applies to the disabled, to gays, and to the world at large: "love makes a family."

A second portion of gaining a realistic view of disability, according to Olkin (1997), rests in gaining a realistic view of the future. Questions regarding the future cause a great deal of anxiety for people with disabilities and their loved ones. The future is never really certain for anyone, but, for people with disabilities, expectations compound with the diagnoses provided by doctors, the climate of the society, and a variety of other factors.

For example, my fate as proposed by the doctors bears no resemblance to the life I am living today. However, Olkin (1997) demonstrates the need to provide a solid support system that enables realistic goals and dreams while cushioning the disappointment of those that cannot or will not be met. From my own experiences, I know what people with disabilities want: we want everything. We want the same rights and opportunities as people without disabilities. We want lives filled with passion, creativity, and meaning.

THE INTERSECTION OF WOMEN, DISABILITY AND SEXUAL ORIENTATION

Disability and sexuality do not coexist; at least, they do not coexist in the minds of able-bodied society (Shakespeare, Gillespie-Sells, and Davies 1997). The dominant culture believes that people with disabilities must not possess sexuality; reflecting the same invisibilizing norms denying and curtailing sexual expression among consenting same-sex couples, the elderly, teenagers, and children. If people with disabilities do possess sexuality (and indeed they do), it must not be recognized, expressed, or glorified in the same manner as heterosexual sex. Shakespeare, Gillespie-Sells, and Davies state, "Just as public displays of same-sex love are strongly discouraged, so two disabled people being intimate in public will experience social disapproval" (1997:10).

This also bridges the worlds of disability and queer representation in terms of what is deemed acceptable on mainstream television. Although the tide is beginning to turn, these puritanical norms forced *Ellen* off the air, kept many gay characters in the televised closet, and kept Will (of *Will and Grace* fame) from engaging in an onscreen long-term, meaningful relationship until the show's final season. As soon as Ellen's sitcom character pursued a relationship and began to acknowledge a lesbian identity, viewers and advertisers responded in horror to the pervasive, blatant references to homosexuality and the flaunting of love between two women. In episodes that were exceedingly chaste and pastoral compared to the raunchy and explicit love scenes between heterosexual couples on daytime television, characters explored the subtleties of beginning a new relationship and venturing outside the closet as a couple. These same moments of hand-holding, kissing, and embracing go unquestioned in heterosexual contexts.

Saxton (1987) echoes the sentiments of many scholars who write on women, disability, and sexuality. For women with disabilities, or "women of difference," according to Saxton, the desire for romance and passion extends to partners of one or both sexes. Making this desire a reality proves difficult when women with disabilities are considered asexual or not thought of as female at all. She states, "Other myths affecting the perception of disability and sexuality include the idea that disability may be contagious and that sex is somehow a rare and precious commodity that should be reserved for highly-valued people, that is, the attractive and able-bodied" (p. 48). The use of the phrase *women of difference* hints at the construction of asexuality or deviant sexuality around women with any type of difference. In addition to disability, enormously hurtful stereotypes surround women of color, older women, lesbians, and women who do not fit into the stereotypes of the perfect woman: the airbrushed aesthetic ideal impossible for any woman to achieve without the aid of plastic surgeons, stylists, and others involved in the business of conformity and complacency.

Back in 1997, I think Ellen's coming out scared people because it forced them to realize the normality (on a subconscious level) of same-sex relationships and their similarity in comparison to opposite-sex relationships. At the end of the day, we all want the same things. We want a partner who inspires us, who believes in us, who offers unconditional love and support, and someone we cannot imagine living without. In 2005 the issue resides in whether or not same-sex couples are entitled to the same rights and privileges as heterosexual couples. For me and many others, activist or not, the issue comes down to basic civil rights. Nothing should impede the basic civil liberties of two consenting adults. However, the possibility of gay marriage, according to conservatives, undermines the foundation of family and married life. Because of this ultraconservative viewpoint and its exclusionary nature, I understand the queer community's resistance to "traditional" marriage and its trappings.

The argument usually stems from the idea that marriage, as North American society defines it, defies the ideals embraced by queers: the fluidity of gender and gender norms, the acknowledgment of loving outside boundaries, and the adoption of progressive social structures and policies. From this standpoint, many of us would rather not have anything to do with marriage. On the opposite pole, the option needs to exist. Out of basic respect for our common humanity, love, and ability to make responsible choices, we must possess the option to marry the partner of our choosing even though we may not buy into the staunch ideology of the stereotypical American dream with its 2.5 children, white picket fence, family car, and its pervasive legacy of intolerance, segregation, and bigotry.

DISABILITY AND BISEXUAL IDENTITY

Sexual orientation creates multiple challenges for those who identify as both a sexual minority and a person with a disability. Homophobia creates great difficulties for those who "violate" gender norms and who feel attraction to the same or both sexes. In addition to the constraints of disability, people who fall into sexually diverse categories face additional identity issues. Shakespeare, Gillespie-Sells, and Davies (1997) refer to the absence of acceptance and community for bisexual disabled people. In fact, bisexual people with disabilities have existed throughout history. Such figures span centuries and include Alexander the Great, Julius Caesar, Cole Porter, Frida Kahlo, and Sarah Bernhardt.

In addition to a lack of role models, people with disabilities also face a lack of acceptance by the gay community, in a manner unfortunately similar to the ways heterosexuals treat homosexuals. According to Shakespeare, Gillespie-Sells, and Davies (1997) the gay and lesbian community treats people with disabilities with similar disdain and intolerance, much like the treatment the queer community receives from heterosexuals who deem their lifestyles inferior. Also, the venues favored by the gay community such as bars, nightclubs, and sports complexes offer restricted access in terms of physical accessibility. The combination of physical and social inaccessibility severely limits the opportunities available for sexual minority women with disabilities.

WOMEN WITH DISABILITIES AND SEXUAL VIOLENCE

Along with the discussion of sex and sexuality must occur the discussion of sexual violence toward people with disabilities. Sexual violence remains a major concern among feminists due to the gendered nature of the majority of sex crimes: most victims of sexual crimes are female while most perpetrators are male.

College campuses and community-based women's centers both work to educate all members of the community about sexual violence, but feminist perspectives reveal that we live in a culture that consistently disrespects women in many ways and condones multiple forms of sexual violence. The same stigma surrounding the sexuality of people with disabilities surrounds them when they face sexual abuse and sexual violence. Because of the myth of asexuality, many believe that people with disabilities are not subjected to acts of sexual violence.

Unfortunately, a disproportionate number of women endure these atrocities. The analysis provided by Crawford and Ostrove (2003) documents that many women with developmental disabilities face some form of sexual assault, often before they reach their early twenties. Many of these women never receive the appropriate medical, psychological, or legal support to recover from the experience. According to the authors, a variety of factors help explain this phenomenon, including reduced socialization, reduced opportunities for romantic encounters, and a physical inability to fight back. Despite social constructions of women with disabilities as asexual and shielded by society, they often face victimization by the people who should protect them. Crawford and Ostrove state, "There is a great irony to being depicted as asexual while simultaneously enduring extreme sexual violence and brutality" (2003:183).

ORGANIZING RESISTANCE: THE TROUBLE WITH ORGANIZING DISABILITY "CULTURE"

There is no universally acceptable term to describe the disabled population as a whole. This helps, in part, to explain the adoption of the social model of disability because of the specific "location" it provides for its members. According to Crow (1999), the social model provides a model for social change and transformation. Olkin (2002) refers to a variety of benefits derived from the social model: it examines oppression from a societal standpoint, taking away individual blame, it allows individuals a way to come to terms with their "disabled" identity, and it calls for greater social organization. However, Olkin also points out the drawbacks involved in recognizing the societal constraints of disability, including feelings of "powerlessness" and frustration in making larger structural changes (2002:133).

Psychotherapists may translate the social model into action through a variety of methods. Psychotherapists accomplish this by transforming their own thinking about disability from viewing disability as a medical issue to understanding it as a social issue. Therapists and their clients can examine problems and difficulties from a social stance: How is the client's access to resources, relationships, and opportunities limited by an ableist society? Which resources can be acquired to change these limitations? Does the client have an interest in connecting with other people with disabilities through books, media, the Internet, or real life?

In addition to forming a therapeutic relationship that stems from a place of mutual trust, respect, and advocacy, therapists can help clients to examine and reframe their own stories. My "adoption" of the social model resulted from reading the stories of other women with disabilities facing multiple identity issues, writing about my own experiences, and educating others about the impact of disability. Interventions may be as simple as storytelling or as complex as the creation of autobiographical art in the form of creative writing or the visual arts. Clients may take action through advocacy groups outside the therapy room: grassroots efforts and periodicals, such as the *Disability Rag*, arose out of the search for common ground within the disability rights movement.

The organization of the disability rights movement suffers because of the diverse range of disabling conditions. Structural inequality occurs across public and private lines, trapping women, people with disabilities and other minorities in limiting cultural scripts. A universal symbol of disability fails to exist, and there is no consistent set of circumstances that frames each individual's experience of "disability." As such, we must look to particular stories and anecdotes that fit within our particular frames of reference: for example, the nontraditional political ties of Helen Keller and Frida Kahlo, the activism and feminist/lesbian viewpoint of Connie Panzarino, and the multicultural teachings of psychologist Rhoda Olkin.

Clare (1999) argues that we must be wary of supercrip stories that treat "successful" people with disabilities as the true representation of disability while glossing over the presence of structural inequities. According to Clare, a focus on exceptional people with disabilities downplays dominant problems such as dating, finding a job, having adequate personal care, and other vital issues.

Russell (1998) emphasizes the dominant role that disability plays in the lives of people with disabilities, despite their membership in other subordinate groups. Russell refers to disabled people as an "unexpected minority" and states, "We are the 'unexpected' minority having undeniable similar socio/political experiences that make disability our primary identity" (p. 16). For many people with disabilities, including disabilities not obviously visible, identifying as disabled is a difficult but empowering decision.

Perhaps, as members of the disabled community, we can use the visual evidence of our disabilities to create space for dialogue regarding difference, physical diversity, and the assumptions and stereotypes surrounding those with disabilities. Rather than fearing dialogue or questions, we can bridge our understanding to connect with the experiences of other marginalized and underrepresented groups. By examining and fighting the oppression of other groups of people, in addition to our own, we assist in the assertion of equality and dignity for all people.

PERSONALIZING THE EXPERIENCE OF DISABILITY

Throughout childhood, I faced the fact that people would see my disability first and me second. I developed a second skin to preserve myself from the cuts that teasing and misunderstanding made in my soul. I struggle with the fact that I address something through my existence that many do not want to see: I am the "what if." I am the statistic, the invisible minority, with a condition that many would say graced my life by chance. "She's so unlucky, what a shame." "Thank God that never happened to me." "That will never be my problem."

Disability is such a complex issue in the eyes of other people because it is something they cannot imagine surviving. It is so far from their version of life experience, yet it is not. It is something they cannot imagine living through, yet they find themselves unable to react with compassion and, even more important, unable to deal with the reality that each person is only a step or two away from disability. Unlike personal attributes such as ethnicity and race, which will never change, disability is something that can happen to anyone at any time.

I could choose to be bitter and convince myself that I have been dealt a bad hand, that fate interceded and gave me a less than normal shot at life. But I choose not to—I was given a challenge, and it is up to me to take the conquest and find the reward. There are so many things beyond our comprehension. As Hamlet stated, "There are more things in heaven and earth . . . than are dreamt of in your philosophy." The same is true of life with a disability. Life is not simply the experience of becoming someone and taking a place in the world. I believe it involves exploring the strength of the human spirit, the compassion that people feel for one another, and the appreciation of all the things usually taken for granted. That is the gift cerebral palsy offered me and the one I chose to accept.

ANOTHER VISION: VOICES FROM THE MARGINS

Circumstance has a strange way of weaving in and out of our lives, bringing smiles, tears, and lessons that will shape our life experience and determine what we offer to the world. I would not choose to disown my experiences. I am disabled. That simple fact will not change. Despite that, I received a gift that teaches me the wonder and mystery of life. I also learned that in my imperfection I am closer to perfect. According to me, I am Stacey. With my disability, I am complete.

Perhaps one of the most important parts of the identity politics movement arises from the attention paid to voices pushed to the margins. In courses specific to identity, students receive encouragement to express their insight and experiences within the constructed academic framework. Without hearing the voices of those who survive their experiences, identity politics fails to transcend the trappings of paperwork and policy. As Crow (1999) reminds us, if we fail to speak for ourselves, those without our experiences feel free to do it for us in ways that are demeaning, objectifying, or false.

This power to reclaim our lives and the possession of our stories demonstrates the incredible alchemy of the personal and the academic. Each thought, pattern, and path that we take is distinctly ours, based on the unique series of events we live through. My life dances around disability; my differences make me who I am in this world. By growing up in a world quick to label and judge, I learned about the statute of limitations placed on each person. This does not stop me. As a phoenix with strength, I rise from the ashes of limitation, inequality, and discrimination.

REFERENCES

Castaneda, R., and Peters, M. (2000). Ableism: Introduction. In M. Adams, W. J. Blumenfeld, R. Castaneda, H. W. Hackman, M. L. Peters, and X. Zuniga (Eds.), *Readings for diversity and social justice* (pp. 319–323). New York: Routledge.

Clare, E. (1999). *Exile and pride: Disability, queerness, and liberation.* Cambridge: South End.

Clare, E. (2001). Stolen bodies, reclaimed bodies: Disability and queerness. *Public Culture,* 13(3), 359–365.

Crawford, D., and Ostrove, J. M. (2003). Representations of disability and the interpersonal relationships of women with disabilities. In M. E. Banks and E. Kaschak (Eds.), *Women with visible and invisible disabilities: Multiple intersections, multiple issues, multiple therapies* (pp. 179–194). New York: Haworth.

Crow, L. (1999). Including all of our lives: Renewing the social model of disability. In J. Morris (Ed.), *Encounters with strangers.* London: Women's Press.

Davis, L. J. (2002). *Bending over backwards: Disability, dismodernism, and other difficult positions.* New York: New York University Press.

Groch, S. (2001). Free spaces: Creating oppositional consciousness in the disability rights movement. In J. Mansbridge, and A. Morris (Eds.), *Oppositional consciousness: The subjective roots of social protest* (pp. 65–98). Chicago: University of Chicago Press.

Harro, B. (2000). The cycle of socialization. In M. Adams et al. (Eds.), *Readings for diversity and social justice* (pp. 15–21). New York: Routledge.

Kahlo, F. (1995). In C. Fuentes (Ed.), *The diary of Frida Kahlo: An intimate self-portrait.* New York: Abradale.

Mairs, N. (1997). *Waist high in the world: A life among the nondisabled.* Boston: Beacon.

Morris, J. (2001). Impairment and disability: Constructing an ethics of care that promotes human rights (electronic version). *Hypatia,* 16(4), 1–16.

Morris, A., and Braine, N. (2001). Social movements and oppositional consciousness. In J. Mansbridge and A. Morris (Eds.), *Oppositional consciousness: The subjective roots of social protest* (pp. 20–37). Chicago: University of Chicago Press.

Olkin, R. (1997). The human rights of children with disabilities. *Women and Therapy*, 20(2), 29–43.

Olkin, R. (1999a). The personal, professional, and political when clients have disabilities. *Women and Therapy*, 22(2), 87–103.

Olkin, R. (1999b). *What psychotherapists should know about disability*. New York: Guilford.

Olkin, R. (2002). Could you hold the door for me? Including disability in diversity. *Cultural Diversity and Ethnic Minority Psychology*, 8(2), 130–137.

O'Toole, C. J., and Brown, A. A. (2003). No reflection in the mirror: Challenges for disabled lesbians accessing mental health services. In T. L. Hughes, C. Smith, and A. Dan (Eds.), *Mental health issues for sexual minority women: Redefining women's mental health* (pp. 35–49). Binghamton, NY: Harrington Park.

Panzarino, C. (1994). *The me in the mirror*. Seattle: Seal.

Potok, A. (2003). *A matter of dignity: Changing the world of the disabled*. New York: Bantam.

Rich, A. (1986). *Blood, bread, and poetry: Selected prose*. New York: Norton.

Russell, M. (1998). *Beyond ramps: Disability at the end of the social contract*. Maine: Common Courage.

Saxton, M. (Ed.). (1987). *With wings: An anthology of literature by and about women with disabilities*. New York: Feminist Press at the City University of New York.

Shakespeare, T., Gillespie-Sells, K., and Davies, D. (1997). *The sexual politics of disability: Untold desires*. London: Cassell.

Tatum, B. D. (2000). The complexity of identity: "Who am I?" In M. Adams et al. (Eds.), *Readings for diversity and social justice* (pp. 9–14). New York: Routledge.

Taylor, C. (Ed.). (1994). *Multiculturalism*. Princeton: Princeton University Press.

Taymor, J. (director). (2002a). *Frida* (motion picture). United States: Miramax.

Taymor, J. (2002b). Introduction: Director's notes. In L. Sunshine (Ed.), *Frida: Bringing Frida Kahlo's life and art to film* (pp. 9–15). New York: Newmarket.

Wisdom, J. P., and Coffman, S. L. (2005). Review of the book *Women with visible and invisible disabilities: Multiple intersections, multiple issues, multiple therapies. Sex Roles*, 52, 5/6, 413–414.

Wolf, S. (1994). Comment. In C. Taylor (Ed.), *Multiculturalism* (pp. 75–85). Princeton: Princeton University Press..

APPENDIX: GUIDED IMAGERY

You wake up in a body one day and it is unlike anything you have ever known. You know that something is wrong, something is out of balance, yet you cannot quite put your finger on what it is.

Everything in your mind still seems the same; you feel the same emotions, and when you look up the sky is still velvety black, sprinkled with white stars. But then you notice that you are in a chair and you are unable to move. You send a thought to your limp leg just hanging there. "Move, I command you to move," and you know that you thought it and you know that you said it, but nothing happens.

The struggle begins. It is you, but it is more your body against your mind as you try to make it follow commands that it fails to recognize. This frustrates you because all you want to do is to get up, to change the situation. While the situation cannot be changed, you can.

So you journey out into the world, attached to your chair, armed with multiple thoughts. Your perception has changed and you hold onto the black velvet sky sprinkled with stars with all of your might. It is your one constant. It reminds you that there is a great mystery beyond your immobile legs, that there are secrets you will discover and hopes you will fulfill.

All of this becomes your experience: you try to hang onto it, to conjure it up to the forefront of your mind when people stare as you try to walk, when they ask what is wrong with you, when they tease you, ignore you, call you crippled, when you feel like no one understands, and when you feel enwrapped in the isolation but somehow find the courage and the stamina to continue on.

Sometimes you think of it in terms of my world versus their world. They use different terminology and they do not think the same way. They also think of it as their world versus yours. In their world disabilities are something to be feared, segregated, and ignored. The disabled are another category, on another continent, in another classroom because it is too difficult to share the perspective and make the worlds begin to mirror each other.

Somehow you manage to forget all this because in your dreams you fly. Your mind holds no bounds and you find insight within your own experience. Within the separation, there is peacefulness and an appreciation. The mundane becomes beautiful, and sometimes what is beautiful becomes mundane to you.

You learn to look for hope where there is none, and you marvel at this fabulous opportunity called life. Even though people tell you that you cannot, you should not, and you will not, you will. That is your only option.

Sometimes people tell you that you are brave and strong, but you do not consider this true. You are simply taking the given circumstances. You get angry sometimes, at the world, at the Universe, at whatever, because sometimes it seems like too much to handle. You are so tired, tired of the limitations of your own body, tired of no one understanding, tired of the stares, the feelings of worthlessness, and the people around you who do not recognize everything they have in their own lives.

You are walking one day, with the same legs that refuse to do what you command, and the woman in front of you breaks into a swift run. You are overcome with jealousy for a moment because you know that she did not think about it; she just did it. You wish you could be her, that it was your legs pumping beneath you, with the wind in your hair. But it is not. You keep taking one calculated step after another, but you remain so caught up in the moment you start to think.

You recognize that life is such a gift, despite your own limitations. Everything seems more alive to you, and this is your chance to share what lies within. The outside world may laugh and may not understand, but you have a mission to live up to yourself, to stand up to the world, not to let anything stop you.

It is so complex, all the images flashing before your eyes. You remember the rage and self-hatred you felt when your physical education teacher imitated the way you ran in front of the entire class. You remember the shame that you felt every time you walked past a full-length mirror and saw how the world views your legs. You were filled with sorrow and terror when you found out that people with disabilities were the first to be murdered in concentration camps.

Finally, you wonder where you are within this mosaic of images. Most of the reflections of disabilities, of yourself, are smiling poster children or actors in movies who have never spent a minute in your mind. They are heroes or they are bitter, but they are not on the same level as everyone else. Despite this, you know you can change people's perceptions and teach them to recognize the light that shines within you.

You wake up in a body and it is unlike anything you have ever known before. You know that something is right and your limbs will follow your every command with ease. But, this time, you will think about it with compassion and understanding because you recognize how lucky you are to occupy this location. At the same time, you also recognize that in the stigma, in the way that ableism permeates your society, something is lost. But that does not stop you. There are secrets you will discover and hopes you will fulfill.

PART 3

COUNSELING ETHNIC MINORITY AND
GENDER-VARIANT BISEXUAL CLIENTS

11

ADDRESSING SOCIAL INVALIDATION TO PROMOTE WELL-BEING FOR MULTIRACIAL BISEXUALS OF AFRICAN DESCENT

Raymond L. Scott

IN 2000 approximately seven million people indicated that they belonged to more than one race in their responses to the U.S. census (Sondik et al. 2000). That is, approximately 3 percent (2.4 percent) of the country's 281.4 million individuals endorsed a "multiracial" identity. Of these, 93 percent endorsed a "biracial" identity and 7 percent endorsed membership in three or more racial backgrounds. According to Root (2001), these numbers suggest that the United States is moving in the direction of becoming an intimately interracial and multiracial country (Tashiro 2002). With the number of interracial couples and multiracial individuals of African descent continuing to increase, it is highly probable that most psychotherapists will deliver services to this population. To provide effective and competent services to bisexuals within this population, psychotherapists have to become aware and knowledgeable about the history as well as the issues, concerns, and strengths of this subpopulation.

From a narrative perspective, multiracial bisexuals of African descent take form as readers and writers within the multiple texts of the U.S. culture. They are read and understood through dominant narratives that circulate in the larger society and their local communities. Here multiracial bisexuals of African descent "actively" construct their identities and experience often in opposition to the moral, political, and ideological concerns of their families of origin and communities (Esterberg 1997; Firestein 1996; Harris 2002; Nobles 1985). Reading bisexuality in this manner redirects the therapeutic focus toward intersecting narratives of cultural histories, invalidation, and class dynamics that shape bisexuality and homoerotic desire. At times the story line reflects a critical reflexive movement away from the individual's psyche toward a socially and historically informed focus on the particulars in that client's experiences of oppression, ostracism, or liberation (Prilleltensky and Nelson 2002).

Invalidation or the failure of many black subcultures to affirm the lived experiences of multiracial bisexuals of African descent is expressed through linguistic constructs such as hegemony, positionality, and identity politics (Eggerling-

Boeck 2002; Harrison and Harrison 2002). Hegemony means "predominant influence," especially when it involves defining heterosexual performances of gender as desirable and natural (Mellstrom 2002; Wood 2000). In consequence, therapists may assist multiracial bisexuals of African descent to continually deconstruct hegemonic forms of femininity and masculinity, demoralized public media representations of their being, and the stigma and shame attached to homoerotic expressions of sexuality (Adeleke 1998; Butler 1993; Constantine-Simms 2000; Greene and Croom 2000; Norton 2002; Williams 1997).

Deconstructions of hegemonic femininities and masculinities are often accompanied by a need to resist the nature of a particular self, constructed by indigenous Africentric patriarchal psychologies. Indigenous Africentric patriarchal psychologies, for the purposes of this chapter, refer to a set of ideas put forth by theorists including Atwell and Azibo (1991), Azibo (1989, 2003), Baldwin (1989), and Nobles (1985, 1986) that equate African American bisexual identities with a pathological personality disorder, misorientation, in which the consequence is a "loss of self." The main tenets of these theories hold that misorientation is diseaselike; that it is constituted of particular behaviors; that it is a self-diagnosed but widespread condition; and that its cure hinges on a therapeutic recovery process (reparative therapy).

Through the propagation of concepts such as an "African self-consciousness," "African's psychological blackness," and "psychological misorientation" (Atwell and Azibo 1991; Baldwin, Brown, and Rackley 1990; Dennard 1998), these ideologies perpetuate hegemonic discourses on identity development. These theorists conceptualize African American bisexual identities within a disease model and posit that these identities have an onset, a definable course, and, if left untreated, a predictable outcome (see the diagnostic nosology of American Psychiatric Association 2000). Despite disagreement on its ontological basis-whether or not it is a disease, these theorists agree that it is a painful and ultimately self-destructive "physical, mental, emotional, and spiritual condition" (Atwell and Azibo 1991).

This chapter focuses on the intersections between social invalidation and two aspects of the self: self-identification as a bisexual and as one of African descent, particularly in addressing these issues therapeutically toward the promotion of well-being. My exploration draws from critical and multiracial scholar activists (Prilleltensky and Nelson 2002; Root 2001), feminism (Garnets 2002; Moraga and Anzaldúa 2002; West 2001), and ecological and political theorists (Foucault 1972, 1978; Mezey 2003; Renn 2003). I move beyond situating bisexuality solely within love relationships. Rather, my focus is twofold. First, attention is directed to the complexity of multiracial bisexuals of African descent's identities and their relationships to each other and to heteronormative-hegemonic structures (Hunter and Alexander 1996; Loiacano 1989; Nero 2004; Peplau and

Spalding 2003; Reid-Pharr 2002; Weinberg, Williams, and Pryor 2004). Second, attention is directed to the therapeutic aspects of assisting these clients to achieve a sense of self and well-being by reauthoring the dominant narratives of their lives.

Although biological science does not furnish empirical support for the existence of distinct races, these constructs are endowed with differential social capital for individuals depending on group membership (Sundstrom 2001; Wilson 1999). Using the terms *race* and *multiracial* rather than ethnicity in this chapter signifies that race, albeit a social construction, profoundly affects the lives of multiracial bisexuals of African descent (Pfeiffer 1996). As such, the content addresses the following themes to assist therapists working with this population. These themes include:

1. Discussion of the sociocultural and political dimensions that shape identity development for multiracial bisexuals of African descent;
2. Their experience of invalidation, marginality, and oppression related to heterosexist and patriarchal gender and sexual ideologies that are often prevalent in African American communities; and
3. An exploration of the benefits to amassing sufficient social capital toward the promotion of mental health and well-being in their lives.
4. The use of narrative therapies to reauthor their disparaged sense of self and life experiences.

WELL-BEING AND SOCIAL CAPITAL

Physical, psychological, and political well-being are hierarchical and multidimensional concepts. The presence or absence of health-promoting factors at all ecological levels can have positive or negative synergistic effects on well-being (Henderson and Whiteford 2003; Pilkington 2002). Collective action promoting social justice and access to valued resources improve the likelihood that physical, psychological, and political well-being will ensue as well as social capital. Social capital is broadly defined by important predictors of mental health, both directly and mediated through the role of informal networks as well as formal associational ties, and draws attention to the accrued and compounding value of wide connections between and among individuals (Lin 2000). Conceptually, it directs the practitioners' attention to the quantity and/or quality of resources that a client can access or use through her or his location in one or more social networks.

This dual emphasis on the resources embedded in social relations or social resources and network or network characteristics has been demonstrated empirically to bolster well-being. That is, social capital has been demonstrated to enhance the likelihood of instrumental returns, such as better jobs, earlier promotions, higher earnings or bonuses, and expressive returns, such as better mental health (Lin 2000). The concept of social capital accounts for the role of social networks and social activities in preventing disease and facilitating recovery from illness or adaptation to chronic illness. Good mental health derives from participation and membership in family groups, social networks, or other social structures that enhance self-acceptance, personal growth, trust, safety, and reciprocity (Frumkin 2003).

Conversely, mental health may be threatened by the absence of most of the factors discussed above, which lead to declines in social capital. Injustice, racism, invalidation, and exploitation may be associated with decreases in social capital and with the emergence of ill health, suffering, and oppression (Prilleltensky and Nelson 2002). While personal beliefs and perceptions are important, a state of well-being rests on a balanced satisfaction of personal, relational, and collective needs. Therapists working with this population are advised to be cognizant of how social and political forms of invalidation languaged as psychopathology are used to silence the voices of multiracial bisexuals of African descent. Thus, one aspect of promoting well-being for these clients may involve incorporating an overt acknowledgment of social and political issues that decrease social capital into the therapeutic content and process, as appropriate (de Certeau 1984; Dennard 1998).

IDENTITY AND CRITICAL RACE THEORY

For clarity, the constructs of identity, self-concept, self-awareness, and self-consciousness are used interchangeably in this chapter, as are black and African American. In the current postmodern era, therapists and scholars are increasingly problematizing the notion of unitary fixed identities, particularly in addressing the subjectivity of hybrid individuals. Collectively, multiracial individuals represent examples of hybrid individuals who often occupy borderland or marginalized spaces between various cultures and racial groups (Hise 2004; Luke and Luke 1999). The discourse of the borderlands signifies the fluidity and potentially subversive qualities of hybrid identities. It is a discourse about people who often live in the margins where binary, oversimplified, and essentialistic construction of identity are contested (Elenes 1997). As such, this discourse provides therapists with an additional understanding of how the absence of social capital and social, political, and historical influences on the lives on these clients are signified through concepts related to difference, displacement, and oppression.

A fundamental premise underpinning critical and feminist theories is the understanding that identities like race are social constructions (Abreu et al. 2000) coconstructed by the subject, the demands of the context, and the larger society, particularly when the subject is marked as "inferior," "deviant," or "despised" (Disch 1999; Elenes 1997). Conceptualizing multiracial individuals of African descent as an inferior Other harks back to the antebellum South and the invalidation of African identities. This invalidation stemmed from a rigid monoracial ideology prevalent within U.S. society where race was constructed as a black-white dichotomy that does not allow for any variation between. Such ideology is traceable to the legacy of the one-drop rule that determines assignment to "only" one of these categories, and where validation "inhered" to the latter (McClain 2004; Smith 2002). That is, social capital, "social status, privileges, and burdens are parsed out according to a racial hierarchy that places whiteness at the top and darkness at the bottom" (Sundstrom 2001:292).

The one-drop rule "applies" to any individual perceived to have a drop of "black blood" or any African ancestry. Within the discourse of the borderlands, the one-drop rule operates as a metaphor for the social, historical, and political contexts from which stigma, invalidation, oppression, and discrimination arise (Christian 2003; McPherson and Shelby 2004; Myrdal 1996; Spickard 1999). Public policy derived from nineteenth-century slave-owning patriarchy serves as the foundation of the "one-drop rule" for black and white racial inheritance. Jim Crow laws and the racial classification as reflected in the United States census since 1920 are other examples of public policies (Zack 1995).

ASCRIBED VERSUS RACIAL SELF-IDENTIFICATION

For therapists working with multiracial bisexuals of African descent, it is important to understand how forms of invalidation continue to shape their self-identification and lived experiences (Rockquemore and Laszloffy 2003). In particular, it is crucial for therapists to understand how experiences with social invalidation contribute to psychological distress. Until recently, many multiracial bisexuals of African descent were situated in historical contexts where they lacked the power to define or represent themselves as anything other than an African American. Definitional power belonged to others who often viewed these individuals as inferior and who had the means to promote the image of their inferiority broadly throughout the society. As a result, many of these individuals were given an "ascribed Negro or black identity" by the larger society and others within their communities based on racial categories established by the U.S. census (Mezey 2003).

Concomitant to the larger civil rights movement within black communities, social and political processes prompted many within the larger population of persons of African descent to move from an ascribed Negro or black identity to adopt an African American racial identity. Moving away from an ascribed identity was widely recognized as a form of resistance aimed at reclaiming lost land, language, culture, and identity for many in the African Diaspora. Cornell and Hartmann (1998), for example, explain that

> while the racial identity "Black" is predominantly an assigned identity, African Americans "also have become an ethnic group, a self-conscious population that defines itself in part in terms of common descent (Africa as homeland), a distinctive history (slavery in particular), and a broad set of cultural symbols (from language to expressive culture) that are held to capture much of the essence of their peoplehood". (p. 33)

In consequence, many clinicians and researchers assumed that a black identity was the only "healthy" option (Cross 1996). Because research assumed that an exclusively black identity was healthy and that negative mental health outcomes could be associated with internalizing negative views about blackness (Williams and Williams-Morris 2000), therapeutic models were oriented to assist multiracial individuals of African descent to develop an understanding of their racial identity as black. The socialization processes in many African American communities also created standards of authenticity around a black identification (Thomas 1997). These socialization processes were often grounded in Africentric ideologies that propagated concepts such as an "African self-consciousness," "African's psychological blackness," and "psychological misorientation" and compulsory heterosexuality (Azibo 2003). This propagation of an "authentic" black/African American identity and compulsory heterosexuality did not allow for hybrid or borderland, multiracial identities. Ironically, as a large number of African Americans were embracing a new sociopolitical identity, they were concomitantly "ascribing" this same racial identification on the multiracial individuals within its communities.

To repeat, many of the attitudes, norms, mores, and symbols within many black communities are informed by Africentric ideologies (Baldwin 1989; Baldwin, Brown, and Rackley 1990). Africentric theorists direct attention "to ideology lived and articulated in everyday understandings of the world and one's place in it" (Lubiano 1998a:232; Prilleltensky and Nelson 2002). Africentric ideologies assume an authentic "black" self and equate African American identity with the concept of African self-consciousness (Atwell and Azibo 1991; Baldwin, Brown, and Rackley 1990; Dennard 1998) as embodied within a macro-level narrative referred to as the "jargon of authenticity" (Bush 1999; Thomas 1997). At meso- and micro-levels this narrative manifests in demoralized public media representations that attach shame and stigma to bisexual desires, identities, and behavior (see Flannigan-Saint-Aubin 1993; Hunter and Alexander 1996; Lubiano 1998a, 1998b; May and Strikwerda 1992; Stokes and Peterson 1998), and in the conflation of femininity, masculinity, and sexual behavior with compulsory heterosexuality (see Constantine-Simms 2000 and Hemphill 1991 for excellent reviews of relevant literatures).

The "jargon of authenticity" marks boundaries that establish compulsory heterosexuality as the *norm* within many black subcultures and, thereby, polices emotional and sexual bonding between multiracial bisexuals of African descent (Bruce 2001; Cole and Guy-Sheftall 2003; Westover 2002). Such policing has been effective through the languaging of all forms of homoeroticism as deviant or pathological (e.g., Atwell and Azibo 1991; Azibo 1989; Baldwin 1989; Baldwin, Brown, and Rackley 1990; Jackson 1970, 1990; Nobles 1985, 1986) and through the use of politically charged linguistic constructs such as hegemony, marginalization, and identity politics (Eggerling-Boeck 2002; Harrison and Harrison 2002; Tate 1988). These constructs continue to function as forms of oppression that effectively dislodge and excommunicate multiracial bisexuals of African descent from African American communities and ethnicities by framing them as inauthentic or not *truly* "black" (Adeleke 1998).

Therapists may assist these clients to understand that this narrative is predicated on the notion that homoerotic desire (Tolman and Diamond 2001) or homosexuality did not exist in precolonial Africa (Black 1997; Jackson 1970, 1990). Patton (1992) and more recent scholar-activists (Cohen 1999; Epprecht 2002; Eskridge 1993; Mkhize 2001; Murray and Roscoe 1998; Summers 2002) refute this heteronormative hegemonic revisioning of collective memory by proponents of Africentricism. In rebuttal, they demonstrate that homoerotism and homosexual emotional bonding and cohabitation were not unusual in precolonial African cultures. While increasing a client's understanding of this hegemonic myth may lead to more adaptive behavior, it may also be necessary to assist the client to find heterosexual and homosexual allies and alternate spaces and communities for support, validation, emotional bonding, and liberation.

RACIAL SELF-IDENTIFICATION

In accord with African American traditions of subversion and identity politics (Baldwin 1989; Conerly 1996; Firestein 1996; Harris 2002; Harrison and Harrison 2002; Icard 1985; Munoz 1999; Ongiri 1997; Reid-Pharr 2002; Somerville 2000; Tate 1988), African American bisexual identities may represent subversive discourses that undermine two binaries common to the dominant U.S. culture and patriarchal Africentric worldviews. These dichotomous systems include the male-female gender/sex system and the homosexual-heterosexual binary (Butler 1993; Gambs 2003). An understanding of these subversive features of gender and sexual identities will permit clinicians to reconceptualize identities, desire, and the expression of sexual behavior as located along intracultural and intraethnic continuums. Conceptualized in these ways, bisexuality emerges as a more inclusive category than sexual activity alone. Depending on the client's goals, a therapeutic focus on the subversive qualities of the client's identities may assist the client to achieve psychic and social liberation. For some clients, this therapeutic focus may germinate the seeds of an emancipatory cultural politics (Smith 2003). It becomes emancipatory through the deconstruction of the oppressive, homosexual-heterosexual binary and the male-female gender/sex system in contemporary U.S. society (Butler 1993; Cowie and Rivers 2000; Davies and Neal 1996, 2000; D'Augelli and Patterson 1995; Degges-White, Rice, and Myers 2000; de la Huerta 1999; Palma and Stanley 2002; Rubinstein 2003).

PROMOTING WELL-BEING AND AMASSING SOCIAL CAPITAL

COUNTERING HEGEMONIC REPRESENTATIONS OF THE BISEXUAL AS "OTHER"

Other hegemonic structures that many multiracial bisexuals of African descent encounter are demoralized and stereotypical social representations of themselves. Derogatory labels such as Creole, half-breed, happa, high yellow, Mestizo, metis, mixed, mixed blood, mongrel, Moreno, mulatto, mutt, and red bone (Alcoff 1995) frequently refer to multiracial bisexuals of African descent. Their lived experiences are clearly distinct from the racial experiences of mono-raced individuals. They are often viewed as individuals who lack of an "authentic" identity. "They are turned away from as if from an unpleasant sight, the sight and mark of an unclean copulation, the product of a taboo, the sign of racial impurity, cultural dilution, colonial aggression, or even emasculation" (Sundstrom 2001:302).

I use the concept of positionality to denote to the social position of the knower (here, it is the multiracial bisexual client) as shaped by variables such as class, race, gender, and sexual orientation. Questions of positionality are epistemological in nature in that they relate to how knowledge is produced and how the knower obtains knowledge of her- or himself. Given that many multiracial bisexuals of African descent are not members of the privileged classes, they may benefit from a therapeutic focus on how the limited perspective and ignorance of members of the privileged class shape their identities and their personal, social, and sexual development.

Epistemology involves theorizing about knowledge and the exploration of the nature, scope, and legitimacy of knowledge claims. As Foucault (1972, 1978) points out throughout much of his work, that which is determined to be true is largely the product of who has the power to assert and insert a specific discourse into the public's or a specific sector's awareness. Richardson (1981) adds that "wherever truth is claimed, so is power; the claim to truth is a claim to power" (p. 173). Research on homosexuality, for example, has frequently been framed within a social deviance paradigm that *produced knowledge* by situating lesbian, gay, and bisexual people within certain theoretical assumptions that in turn contributed to negative conceptions of their lives and their identities (Tierney 1993). Clearly, the stance these theorists brought to their studies shaped what were purported to be objective findings. Foucault's work (i.e., 1978) has consistently illustrated the role of power expressed through language and discourse in situating sexual identities. It is difficult to refute Foucault's contention that a variety of social practices have served to situate heterosexuality in a hegemonic relationship to homosexuality that marginalizes the latter. The power of the *norm* is central to Foucault and his explanation of how homosexuality has come to occupy the margins of social life. As Foucault argues, the emergence of homosexual as a category of people has brought about the possibility of large-scale oppression of homosexual people.

Other critical postmodern and feminist theorists also call attention to the idea that knowledge is relational (e.g., Agger 1991, Benhabib 1986; Butler 1993; Flannigan-Saint-Aubin 1993; Fox 2003; Garnets 2002; Hall 1990; Harrison and Harrison 2002; Kellner 1988, 1990; Maroda 2000; May and Strikwerda 1992; Munoz 1999; Prilleltensky and Nelson 2002; Said 1993; Somerville 2000; Tolman and Diamond 2001; Wyatt 1997). Truth claims do not exist on their own (Lyotard 1984). Instead, they must be grounded in specific assumptions (i.e., the jargon of authenticity) that first must be accepted within a particular community of individuals. Like notions of truth, identities are also framed by discourses contingent to a large degree on power relations. Power is evident through the ability to control the discourse or language of identity. Hall (1990) elaborates on this idea when he points out that identities are essentially unstable, because they are shaped within historical and cultural discourses. The contentious nature of history and culture situates identities within a contested field resulting in ongoing struggle, which is often played out within identity politics.

Issues of identity and hegemonic representational practices are particularly germane to many multiracial bisexuals of African descent who are at a crucial point in their identity development. Therapeutically, identity negotiation may become highly salient given the risks associated with coming out, as discussed below. Clients may find it beneficial to explore how hegemonic representational practices owe their existence to the creation narratives that defame nonheterosexual identities/subjectivities (Felski 1997). In these instances the exploration of the *Other* (Said 1993) often involves assisting clients to understand how and why stereotypical, disparaging, and demoralized public media representations of multiracial bisexuals of African descent are created and circulated and how they maintain power imbalances and oppression.

COUNTERING HEGEMONIC GENDER/IDENTITY/SEX SYSTEMS

Gender identity represents a social construction linked to anatomical sex and one's performance of masculinity and/or femininity (Felluga 2003). Kimmel and Messner (1992), for example, conceptualize gender as hierarchical relationships where "doing hetero-sexuality" is equivalent to "doing masculinity" and, by extrapolation, to doing femininity. They use the term *doing* to connote performance and situate heterosexual performances of femininity and masculinity as hegemonic in relation to nonheterosexual performances of gender (Ferree, Lorber, and Hess 1998). To repeat, hegemony means predominant influence, especially when it involves defining heterosexual performances of gender as desirable and natural (Mellstrom 2002; Wood 2000). This in turn makes the meanings chosen by the dominant heterosexual groups appear to be universal by conceptualizing women and men as two distinct homogenous groups. This practice of elevating group specific behavior to a universal etic serves to communicate to American females and males expectancies for conformity to the dichotomized construction of gender as female or male.

Emancipatory cultural politics for change (Smith 2003), in contrast, encompass the lived experiences of African American bisexual performances of femininity and masculinity that subvert both dominant cultural hegemonic and Africentric patriarchal constructions of sex/gender systems. The recognition, for example, that bisexuality involves emotional bonding with another regardless of his or her perceived gender is the antithesis of the doctrine that gendered behavior can only be interpreted within one of two categories, female or male, and that sexual and romantic bonds are only possible between rather than within these categories. As such, bisexuality is in a sense a rejection of a particular construction of gender and the traditional meanings of masculinity and femininity. As a result, multiracial bisexuals of African descent go through a process of reinterpreting their social worlds. An important aspect of this reinterpretation involves confronting masculine and feminine prescriptions for gendered and sexual behavior. Therapists may assist their bisexual clients to assess the degree to which the power struggles couched within the homosexual-heterosexual binary and the male-female gender/sex system in contemporary U.S. society have relevance for their lives.

DISCUSSION

In contrast to numerous psychotherapeutic stances that pathologize bisexuality, affirmative views of bisexuality, particularly those grounded in theoretical approaches, are emerging (e.g., Cowie and Rivers 2000; Lipkin 2000; Milton and Coyle 1999; Rubinstein 2003). Given that we are in the infancy of understanding the "normative" processes of development for multiracial bisexuals of African descent, I can only suggest ways in which practitioners can provide culturally competent therapy to assist these clients in the promotion of well-being and amassing social capital based on the current clinical literature (D'Augelli and Patterson 1995; Esterberg 1997; Perez, DeBord, and Bieschke 2000; Ritter and Terndrup 2002). To avoid generating additional stereotypes, this chapter draws from existent literature to provide examples of good and harmful practices (e.g., Fukuyama and Ferguson 2000; Greene 1994; Greene and Croom 2000).

THERAPIST VARIABLES

Providing culturally competent therapy represents the adoption of particular stances that include a degree of advocacy in promoting an explicit agenda of raising experiences of oppression into consciousness, deprogramming, undoing negative conditioning associated with negative stereotypes of multiracial bisexuals of African descent, and minimizing the effects of direct violence and oppression (Milton and Coyle 1999; Palma and Stanley 2002). Therapeutic work with this population requires an understanding of the literature on the social construction of meaning as ascribed to identities, gender, and various expressions of sexuality (Butler 1993; Felluga 2003; Garnets 2002; Norton 2002; Schueller 1999). Clinical work with this population also requires an understanding of how general psychological constructs within the rubrics of cognition, perception, and emotional bonds are often conflated with sexual behaviors. This level of understanding permits clinicians to distinguish emotional and cognitive bonding from manifestations of bisexuality based solely on sexual object choice (McKirnan et al. 1995; Peplau and Spalding 2003; Peterson 1991; Stokes, sMcKirnan, and Burzette 1993; Stokes et al. 1996; Stokes and Peterson 1998; Stokes, Vanable, and McKirnan 1996). Belief and praxis are not always consistent.

More specifically, providing culturally competent therapy to multiracial bisexuals of African descent requires that the clinician has worked through her or his own sexual identity formation and has reached a point where he or she is comfortable with this identity (or identities). This comfort level may permit the clinician to formulate case conceptualizations that transcend the hetero-homo and male-female binaries that constrain behaviors associated with these categories. An understanding of how social and political practices have and continue to police the sexuality of African Americans is also essential to assisting multiracial bisexuals of African descent within these subcultures find meaning and validation of their experiences (Carbado, McBride, and Weise 2002; Carby 1992; Constantine-Simms 2000; Herdt 1998; Morton 1996; Munoz 1999; Reid-Pharr 2001; Somerville 2000).

The emphasis here on the social construction of meaning and experience requires a departure from positivist approaches and the etic formulations produced within these paradigms. Similarly, it requires a departure from overemphasizing the role of bisexual identities in the content and process of the therapeutic encounter. This phenomenon often manifests when clinicians situate "all or most" of the clients' concerns within or arising from their bisexual identities. Overemphasizing the role of bisexual identities represents an indirect form of pathologizing these identities (Milton and Coyle 1999).

COMING OUT

To date, no models of identity development for multiracial bisexuals of African descent have been formulated. Current stage models of bisexual identity development are premised on an assumption that "coming out" is fundamental to establishing psychological health and well-being. That is, coming out to others serves as an indication of "positive" identity progression or achievement. Therapists must recognize that environmental constraints may prohibit public disclosure despite a successfully achieved bisexual identity (Labriola 2003; Reynolds and Hanjorgiris 2000; Weinberg, Williams, and Pryor 2004). Unlike many other types of minority status, a person's sexual identity may be hidden. Such camouflage has distinct advantages for multiracial bisexuals of African descent (e.g., avoidance of discrimination) and disadvantages (e.g., isolation and lack of family support). Maintaining this camouflage may also serve as a survival mechanism given that public disclosure of sexual orientation by multiracial bisexuals of African descent may lead to their social fragmentation and marginalization as this disclosure may sever connections to important relationships within black subcultures (Icard 1985). These relationships provide a network of social and psychological supports that facilitate the development of appropriate skills to cope with institutionalized racism and the development of positive ethnic identities (Conerly 1996; hooks 1989; Loiacano 1989; Stokes and Peterson 1998).

At the micro-level of experience, multiracial bisexuals of African descent must continually negotiate and manage "multiple identities" that provide ties to African American subcultures in the maintenance of healthy ethnic identities (Eggerling-Boeck 2002; Harrison and Harrison 2002) and ties to gay, lesbian, bisexual, transgender, and intersexed (GLBTI) communities in the maintenance of healthy sexual identities (Garnets 2002; Kraft et al. 2000; MacQueen et al. 2001). Given the often overt hostility and homophobia emanating from Africentric and Eurocentric ideologies, African American and gay subcultures may be more harmful than supportive of a positive sense of self for multiracial bisexuals of African descent (Icard 1985:84). On the other hand, historical and cultural marginalization and invisibility of sexual minorities is decreasing (Degges-White, Rice, and Myers 2000). The current culture may allow newly identifying multiracial bisexuals of African descent the opportunity to come to self-acceptance of their sexual identities before feeling a need to seek out other multiracial bisexuals of African descent. In past decades, the primary method for learning what it meant to be bisexual was through direct interaction with gays and lesbians. Today men and women who are wrestling with their sexual orientation have a plethora of resources (e.g., books, magazines, support groups, and Internet) available that do not require them to seek out the mainstream homosexual subculture for information or validation.

To provide effective and culturally competent services to bisexuals within this population, clinicians must become aware and knowledgeable about the history as well as the issues of frequent concern to this group. Similarly, an understanding of how social and political practices have and continue to police the sexuality of African Americans is also essential to assisting multiracial bisexuals of African descent find meaning in and validate their diverse experiences. In accord with African American traditions of subversion and identity politics, African American bisexual identities may represent subversive discourses that undermine two binaries common to the dominant U.S. culture and patriarchal Africentric worldviews. These dichotomous systems include the male-female gender/sex system and the homosexual-heterosexual binary.

An understanding of these subversive features of gender and sexual identities will permit clinicians to reconceptualize identities, desire, and the expression of sexual behavior as points along intracultural and intraethnic continuums. Conceptualized in these ways, bisexuality emerges as a more inclusive category than sexual activity alone. The recognition, for example, that bisexuality involves emotional and cognitive bonding with another regardless of his or her perceived gender is the antithesis of the doctrine that gendered behavior can only be interpreted within one of two categories, female or male, and that sexual and romantic bonds are only possible between rather than within these categories. Therapeutically, such recognition allows the clinician to move beyond situating bisexuality solely within love relationships. Rather, each case conceptualization addresses the complexity of identity for multiracial bisexuals of African descent and their relationship to each other and to heteronormative-hegemonic structures. Reading bisexuality in this manner redirects the therapeutic focus toward intersecting narratives of cultural histories, invalidation, and class dynamics that shape bisexuality and homoerotic desire.

Theoretically, it is recommended that clinicians ground each case conceptualization in a strategic eclectic model, where narrative therapy serves as a metatheory that emphasizes the important role of language and a collaborative approach to working with clients. This collaboration allows each client to construct her or his problems as stories that have been reinforced by dominant narratives circulating within his or her cultural histories and that are often internalized as a habitual pattern for construing reality. Here multiracial bisexuals of African descent "actively" construct (and are actively constructed by) the moral, political, and ideological concerns of their families of origin and communities.

Clinicians can use theories and techniques from a variety of models in a compatible way to facilitate the change processes of narrative therapy. Such change typically involves assisting the client in achieving desired outcomes through creating more preferred stories about problems and their lives. Developing alternate narratives becomes liberating because they enable these clients to reauthor their lives and resist impoverishing, subjugating and, disenfranchising dominant narratives such as the one-drop rule and the jargon of authenticity.

One technique that helps clients to create more functional stories about their problems and lives involves assisting them to understand their hybrid identities and the borderland or marginalized spaces they often occupy between their various cultures and racial groups. Framing their identities as borderland stories may allow these individuals to understand the fluid nature of their self-concepts and the importance of occupying marginal spaces where binary, over-simplified, and essentialistic construction of identity are contested. Framing their sense of self within borderland stories allows these individuals to become mindful how their racial identities are also social constructions that contest the one-drop rule of the dominant society.

Occupation of the borderlands becomes empowering and assists these clients to resist the nature of a particular self premised on the jargon of authenticity. This dominant narrative is used to effectively dislodge and excommunicate multiracial bisexuals of African descent from African American communities and ethnicities by framing them as inauthentic or not *truly* "black." It is crucial for therapists to assist clients in understanding how this form of social invalidation may signify an absence of social capital that contributes to their psychological distress. Thus garnering access to valued resources may become a therapeutic goal aimed at improving the likelihood that physical, psychological, and political well-being will ensue as well as social capital.

Depending on the client's goals, a therapeutic focus on the subversive qualities of the client's identities may assist the client to achieve psychic and social liberation. For some clients, this therapeutic focus may germinate the seeds of emancipatory cultural politics that have the power to deconstruct the oppressive, homosexual-heterosexual binary and the male-female gender/sex system in contemporary U.S. society. An emancipatory cultural politics for change encompassses performances of femininity and masculinity that subvert both dominant cultural hegemonic and Africentric constructions of sexual and gender systems. Bisexuality is, in a sense, a rejection of patriarchal constructions of gender and the traditional meanings of masculinity and femininity. As a result, multiracial bisexuals of African descent go through a process of reinterpreting their social worlds by overwriting heteronormative prescriptions for masculine and feminine behavior.

Therapists may assist their multiracial bisexual clients to challenge cultural productions (e.g., cinema, photography, literature), social practices (e.g., identity politics, gender roles), and public health discourses (e.g., HIV prevention and treatment) premised on the oppositional homosexual-heterosexual binary and the male-female gender/sex system in contemporary U.S. society. Ultimately, some multiracial bisexuals of African descent achieve emancipation and demonstrate their emancipation through their ability to reveal truth about their multiple identities and experiences. In the powerful words of Richardson, "Wherever truth is claimed, so is power; the claim to truth is a claim to power" (1981:173).

REFERENCES

Abreu, J.M., Goodyear, R.K., Campos, A., and Newcomb, M.D. (2000). Ethnic belonging and traditional masculinity ideology among African Americans, European Americans, and Latinos. *Psychology of Men and Masculinity*, 1, 75–86.

Adeleke, T. (1998). *Unafrican Americans: Nineteenth-century black nationalists and the civilizing mission*. Lexington: University Kentucky Press.

Agger, B. (1991). Critical theory, poststructuralism, postmodernism: Their sociological relevance. *Annual Review of Sociology*, 17, 105–131.

Alcoff, L. (1995). Mestizo identity. In N. Zack (Ed.), *American mixed race: The culture of microdiversity* (pp. 257–278). Lanham, MD: Rowman and Littlefield.

American Psychiatric Association (2000). *Diagnostic and statistical manual of mental disorders* (4th ed.). Washington, DC: American Psychiatric Association.

Atwell, I., and Azibo, D.A. (1991). Diagnosing personality disorders in Africans (blacks) using the Azibo nosology: Two case studies. *Journal of Black Psychology*, 17, 1–22.

Azibo, D.A. (1989). African-centered theses on mental health and a nosology of black/African personality disorder. *Journal of Black Psychology*, 15, 173–214.

Azibo, D.A. (Ed.) (2003). African-centered psychology: Culture-focusing for multicultural competence. Durham, NC: Carolina Academic.

Baldwin, J.A. (1989). The role of black psychologists in black liberation. *Journal of Black Psychology*, 16, 67–76.

Baldwin, J.A., Brown, R., and Rackley, R. (1990). Some socio-behavioral correlates of African self-consciousness in African-American college students. *Journal of Black Psychology*, 17, 1–17.

Benhabib, S. (1986). *Critique, norm, and utopia*. New York: Columbia University Press.

Black, D.P. (1997). Dismantling *black manhood: An historical and literary analysis of the legacy of slavery*. New York: Garland.

Book, H.E. (1995). The "erotic transference": Some technical and countertechnical difficulties. *American Journal of Psychotherapy*, 49, 504.

Brandt, S. (2000). American Culture X: Identity, homosexuality, and the search for a new American hero. In R. West and F. Lay, (Eds.) *Subverting masculinity: Hegemonic and alternative versions of masculinity in contemporary culture* (pp. 67–93). Atlanta: Rodopi.

Bruce, D. D. (2001). The *origins of African American literature, 1680–1865*. Charlottesville: University Press of Virginia.

Bush, L. (1999). Am I a man? A literature review engaging the sociohistorical dynamics of black manhood in the United States. *Western Journal of Black Studies, 23*, 49–58.

Butler, J. (1993). *Bodies that matter: On the discursive limits of "sex."* New York: Routledge.

Carbado, D. W., McBride, D. A., and Weise, D. (2002). *Black like us: A century of lesbian, gay, and bisexual African American fiction*. San Francisco: Cleis.

Carby, H. V. (1992). Policing the black woman's body in an urban context. *Critical Inquiry, 18*, 738–755.

Christian, M. (2003). More than black? Multiracial identity and the new racial order. *Western Journal of Black Studies, 27*, 279–281.

Cohen, C. J. (1999). The boundaries of blackness: AIDS and the breakdown of black politics. Chicago: University of Chicago Press.

Cole, J. B., and Guy-Sheftall, B. (2003). *Gender talk: The struggle for women's equality in African American communities*. New York: One World/Ballantine.

Conerly, G. (1996). The politics of black lesbian, gay, and bisexual identity. In B. Beemyn and M. Eliason (Eds.), *Queer studies: A lesbian, gay, bisexual and transgendered anthology* (pp. 133–145). New York: New York University Press.

Constantine, M. G, Lewis, E. L., Conner, L. C., and Sanchez, D. (2000). Addressing spiritual and religious issues in counseling African Americans: Implications for counselor training and practice. *Counseling and Values, 45*, 28–39.

Constantine-Simms, D. (2000). The *greatest taboo: Homosexuality in black communities*. Los Angeles: Alyson.

Cornell, S., and Hartmann, D. (1998). *Ethnicity and race: Making identities in a changing world*. Thousand Oaks, CA: Pine Forge.

Cowie, H., and Rivers, I. (2000). Going against the grain: Supporting lesbian, gay and bisexual clients as they "come out." *British Journal of Guidance and Counseling, 28*, 503–514.

Cross, W. E., and Fhagen-Smith, P. (1996). Nigrescence and ego identity development: Accounting for differential black identity patterns. In P. B. Pedersen, J. G. Draguns, W. J. Lonner, and J. E. Trimble (Eds.), *Counseling across cultures* (pp. 108–123). Thousand Oaks, CA: Sage.

Davies, D. and Neal, C. (Eds.) (1996). *Pink therapy: A guide for counselors and therapists working with lesbian, gay and bisexual clients*. Buckingham: Open University Press.

Davies, D. and Neal, C. (Eds.) (2000). *Therapeutic perspectives on working with lesbian, gay and bisexual clients*. Buckingham: Open University Press.

D'Augelli, A. R., and Patterson, C. J. (Eds.) (1995). *Lesbian, gay, and bisexual identities over the lifespan: Psychological approaches*. New York: Oxford University Press.

de Certeau, M. (1984). *The practice of everyday life*. Trans. S. Rendall. Berkeley: University of California Press.

Degges-White, S., Rice, B., and Myers, J. E. (2000). Revisiting Cass' theory of sexual identity formulation: A study of lesbian development. *Journal of Mental Health Counseling, 22*, 318–334.

de la Huerta, C. (1999). Coming out spiritually: The next step. New York: Penguin Putnam.

Dennard, D. (1998). Application of the Azibo nosology in clinical practice with black clients: A case study. *Journal of Black Psychology, 24*, 182–195.

Disch, L. (1999). Judith Butler and the politics of the performative. *Political Theory*, 27, 545–559

Eggerling-Boeck, J. (2002). Issues of black identity: A review of the literature. *African American Research Perspectives*, 8, 17–26.

Elenes, C.A. (1997). Reclaiming the borderlands: Chicana/o identity, difference, and critical pedagogy. *Educational Theory*, 47, 359–366.

Emig, R. (2000). Queering the straights, straightening queers: Commodified sexualities and hegemonic masculinity. In R. West and F. Lay, *Subverting masculinity: Hegemonic and alternative versions of masculinity in contemporary culture* (pp. 207–226). Atlanta: Rodopi.

Epprecht, M. (2002). Male-male sexuality in Lesotho: Two conversations. *Journal of Men's Studies*, 10, 373–384.

Eskridge, W.N., Jr. (1993). A history of same-sex marriages. *Virginia Law Review*, 79(October), 1419–1513.

Esterberg, K.G. (1997). *Lesbian* and *bisexual identities: Constructing communities, constructing selves.* Philadelphia: Temple University Press.

Felluga, D. (2003). Modules on Butler: On performativity, introductory guide to critical theory (June 25). Accessed October 11, 2003, at http://www.cla.purdue.edu/academic/engl/theory/genderandsex/modules/.

Felski, R. (1997). The doxa of difference. *Signs*, 23, 1–22.

Ferree, M.M., Lorber, J., and Hess, B.B. (Eds.) (1998). *Revisioning gender*. Lanham, MD: Alta Mira.

Firestein, B.A. (Ed.). (1996). *Bisexuality: The psychology and politics of an invisible minority.* Thousand Oaks, CA: Sage.

Flannigan-Saint-Aubin, A. (1993). "Black Gay Male" discourse: Reading race and sexuality between the lines. In C. Fout and M.S. Tantillo (Eds.), *American sexual politics: Sex, gender, and race since the Civil War* (pp. 381–403). Chicago: University of Chicago Press.

Foucault, M. (1972). The *archaeology of knowledge and the discourse on language*. Trans. A. M. Sheridan Smith. New York: Pantheon.

Foucault, M. (1978). The *history of sexuality* (Vol. 1): *An introduction*. Trans. R. Hurley. New York: Vintage.

Fox, R.C. (2003). Bisexual identities. In L.D. Garnets and D. C. Kimmel (Eds.), *Psychological perspectives on lesbian, gay, and bisexual experiences* (pp. 86–129). New York: Columbia University Press.

Frost, J.C. (1998). Countertransference considerations for the gay male when leading psychotherapy groups for gay men. *International Journal of Group Psychotherapy*, 48, 3–24.

Frumkin, H. (2003). Healthy places: Exploring the evidence. *American Journal of Public Health*, 93, 1451–1459.

Fukuyama, M.A., and Ferguson, A. D. (2000). Lesbian, gay, and bisexual people of color: Understanding cultural complexity and managing multiple oppressions. In R.M. Perez, K.A. DeBord, and K.J. Bieschke (Eds.), *Handbook of counseling and psychotherapy with lesbian, gay, and bisexual clients* (pp. 81–105). Washington, DC: American Psychological Association.

Gambs, D. (2003). Bisexuality: Beyond the binary? *Journal of Sex Research*, 40, 317–320.

Garnets, L. (2002). Sexual orientations in perspective. *Cultural Diversity and Ethnic Minority Psychology*, 8, 115–129.

Gonzalez, M. (2000). The Moor's Last Sigh (Salman Rushdie): Marginal alternatives, the reconstruction of identity through the Carnival of Indetermination. In R. West and F. Lay, *Subverting masculinity: Hegemonic and alternative versions of masculinity in contemporary culture* (pp. 128–143). Atlanta: Rodopi.

Gramsci, A. (1977). *Selections from political writings (1910–1920)*. Trans. John Mathews. London: Lawrence and Wishart.

Gramsci, A., Forgacs, D., and Nowell-Smith, G. (1985). *Selections from cultural writings*. Trans. W. Boelhower. Cambridge: Harvard University Press.

Greene, B. (1994). Ethnic-minority lesbians and gay men: Mental health and treatment issues. *Journal of Consulting and Clinical Psychology, 62*, 243–251.

Greene, B., and Croom, G. L. (Eds.) (2000). *Education, research, and practice in lesbian, gay, bisexual, and transgendered psychology: A resource manual* (pp. 1–45). Thousand Oaks, CA: Sage.

Guterman, J. T., and Rudes, J. (2005). A Narrative Approach to Strategic Eclecticism. *Journal of Mental Health Counseling, 27*(1), 1–13.

Halberstam, J. (1998). *Female masculinity*. Durham, NC: Duke University Press.

Hall, S. (1990). Cultural identity and diaspora. In J. Rutherford (Ed.), *Identity: Community, culture, difference* (pp. 222–237). London: Lawrence and Wishart.

Harris, L. A. (2002). Black feminism and queer families: A conversation with Thomas Allen Harris. *African American Review; 36*, 273–282.

Harrison, L., and Harrison, C. K. (2002). African American racial identity: Theory and application to education, race, and sport in America. *African American Research Perspectives, 8*, 35–46.

Henderson, S., and Whiteford, H. (2003). Social capital and mental health. *Lancet, 362*, 505–508.

Herdt, G. (1998). *Same sex, different cultures: Exploring gay and lesbian lives*. Boulder: Westview.

Hise, G. (2004). Border city: Race and social distance in Los Angeles. *American Quarterly, 56*, 545–559.

hooks, b. (1989). *Talking back: Thinking feminist, thinking black*. Boston: South End.

Hunter, J., and Alexander, P. (1996). Women who sleep with women. In L. D. Long and E. M. Ankrah (Eds.), *Women's experiences with HIV/AIDS: An international perspective* (pp. 42–55). New York: Columbia University Press.

Icard, L. (1985). Black gay men and conflicting social identities: Sexual orientation versus racial identity. *Journal of Social Work and Human Sexuality, 4*, 83–93.

Jackson, G. (1970). *Soledad brother: The prison letters of George Jackson*. New York: Bantam.

Jackson, G. (1990). *Blood in my eye*. Baltimore: Black Classic.

Kellner, D. (1988). Postmodernism as social theory: Some challenges and problems. *Theory, Culture, and Society, 5*, 239–269.

Kimmel, M. S., and Messner, M. A. (1992). *Men's lives*. New York: MacMillan.

King, J. (2003). Remixing the closet. *Village Voice, 48*, 38–46.

Kraft, J. M., Beeker, C., Stokes, J. P., and Peterson, J. L. (2000). *Health Education and Behavior, 27*, 430–441.

Labriola, K. (2003). What is bisexuality? Who is bisexual? Accessed October 13, 2003 at http://www.cat-and-dragon.com/stef/Poly/Labriola/bisexual.html.

Lin, N. (2000). Inequality in social capital. *Contemporary Sociology, 29*, 785–795.

Lipkin, A. (2000). *Understanding homosexuality, changing schools*. Boulder: Westview.

Loiacano, D. K. (1989). Gay identity issues among black Americans: Racism, homophobia, and the need for validation. *Journal of Counseling and Development, 68*, 21–25.

Lubiano, W. (1998a). Black nationalism and black common sense: Policing ourselves and others. In W. Lubiano (Ed.), The house that race built: Black Americans, U.S. terrain (pp. 232–252). New York: Pantheon.

Lubiano, W. (Ed.) (1998b). The *house that race built*. New York: Pantheon.

Luke, C., and Luke, A. (1999). Theorizing interracial families and hybrid identity: An Australian perspective. *Educational Theory, 49*, 223–250.

Lyotard, J. F. (1984). The postmodern condition. Minneapolis: University of Minnesota Press.

McClain, C. S. (2004). Black by choice: Preferences of Americans of black/white parentage. *Black Scholar, 34*, 43–55.

McKirnan, D. J., Stokes, J. P., Doll, L., and Burzette, R. G. (1995). Bisexually active men: Social characteristics and sexual behavior. *Journal of Sex Research, 32*, 65–76.

McPherson, L. K., and Shelby, T. (2004). Blackness and blood: Interpreting African American identity. *Philosophy and Public Affairs, 32*, 171–193.

MacQueen, K. M., McLellan, E., Metzger, D. S., Kegeles, S. (2001). What is community? An evidence-based definition for participatory public health. *American Journal of Public Health, 91*, 1929–1938.

Maroda, K. J. (2000). On homoeroticism, erotic countertransference, and the postmodern view of life: A commentary on papers by Rosiello, Tholfsen, and Meyers. *Journal of Gay and Lesbian Psychotherapy, 4*, 61–70.

May, L. and Strikwerda, R. (Eds.) (1992). Rethinking *masculinity: Philosophical explorations in light of feminism*. Lanham, MD: Rowman and Littlefield.

Mellstrom, U. (2002). Patriarchal machines and masculine embodiment. *Science, Technology, and Human Values, 27*, 460–479.

Mezey, N. (2003). Erasure and recognition: The census, race and the national imagination. *Northwestern University Law Review, 97*, 1701–1736.

Milton, M., and Coyle, A. (1999). Lesbian and gay affirmative psychotherapy: Issues in theory and practice, *Sexual and Marital Therapy, 14*, 43–60.

Mkhize, V. (2001). A gay Zulu language: Behind the mask. Accessed October 24, 2003, at http://www.mask.org.

Moraga, C. L., and Anzaldúa, G. E. (Eds.) (2002). *This bridge called my back: Writings by radical women of color*. Berkeley: Third Women.

Morton, D. (1996). *The material queer: A lesbigay cultural studies reader*. Boulder: Westview.

Munoz, J. E. (1999). *Disidentifications: Queers of color and the performance of politics*. Minneapolis: University of Minnesota Press.

Murray, S. O., and Roscoe, W. (Eds.) (1998). *Boy-wives and female husbands: Studies of African homosexualities*. New York: St. Martin's.

Myrdal, G. (1996). An American dilemma: The Negro problem and modern democracy (Vol. 1). New Brunswick, NJ: Transaction.

Nero, C. I. (2004). Black queer identity, imaginative rationality, and the language of home. In A. Gonzalez, M. Houston, and V. Chen (Eds.), *Our voices: Essays in culture, ethnicity, and communication* (pp. 74–79). Los Angeles: Roxbury.

Nobles, W. W. (1985). Africanity and the Black family: The development of a theoretical model (2d ed.). Oakland: Institute of the Advanced Study of Black Family Life and Culture.

Nobles, W. W. (1986). African psychology: Toward its reclamation, reascension, and revitalization. Oakland: Institute of the Advanced Study of Black Family Life and Culture.

Norton, R. (2002). A critique of social constructionism and postmodern queer theory: Essentialism. Accessed October 11, 2003, at http://www.infopt.demon.co.uk/social03 .htm.

Ongiri, A. A. (1997). We are family: Black nationalism, black masculinity, and the black gay cultural imagination. *College Literature*, 24, 280–294.

Palma, T. V., and Stanley, J. L. (2002). Effective counseling with lesbian, gay, and bisexual clients. *Journal of College Counseling*, 5, 76–90.

Patton, C. (1992). From nation to family: Containing "African AIDS." In A. Parker, M. Russo, D. Sommer, and P. Yaeger (Eds.), *Nationalisms and sexualities* (pp. 218–234). New York: Routledge.

Peplau, L. A., and Spalding, L. R. (2003). The close relationships of lesbians, gay men, and bisexuals. In L. D. Garnets and D. C. Kimmel (Eds.), *Psychological perspectives on lesbian, gay, and bisexual experiences* (pp. 449–475). New York: Columbia University Press.

Perez, R. M., DeBord, K. A., and Bieschke, K. J. (Eds.) (2000). *Handbook of counseling and psychotherapy with lesbian, gay, and bisexual clients*. Washington, DC: American Psychological Association.

Peterson, J. L. (1991). Black men and their same sex desires and behaviors. In G. Herdt (Ed.), *Gay culture in America: Essays from the field* (pp. 147–164). Boston: Beacon.

Pfeiffer, K. (1996). Individualism, success, and American identity in *The Autobiography of an Ex-Colored Man*. *African American Review*, 30, 403–420.

Pilkington, P. (2002). Social capital and health: Measuring and understanding social capital at a local level could help to tackle health inequalities more effectively. *Journal of Public Health Medicine*, 24, 156–159.

Prilleltensky, I., and Nelson, G. (2002). Doing *psychology critically: Making a difference in diverse settings*. New York: Palgrave Macmillan.

Reid-Pharr, R. F. (2001). *Black gay man: Essays*. New York: New York University Press.

Reid-Pharr, R. F. (2002). Extending queer theory to race and ethnicity. *Chronicle of Higher Education*, 48, B7-B9.

Renn, K. A. (2003). Understanding the identities of mixed-race college students through a developmental ecology lens. *Journal of College Student Development*, 44, 383–397.

Reynolds, A. L., and Hanjorgiris, W. F. (2000). Coming out: Lesbian, gay, and bisexual identity development. In R. M. Perez, K. A. DeBord, and K. J. Bieschke (Eds.), *Handbook of counseling and psychotherapy with lesbian, gay, and bisexual clients* (pp. 35–55). Washington, DC: American Psychological Association.

Richardson, B. B. (1981). Racism and child-rearing: A study of Black mothers. *Dissertation Abstracts International*, 42, 125A.

Ritter, K. Y., and Terndrup, A. I. (2002). *Handbook of affirmative psychotherapy with lesbians and gay men*. New York: Guilford.

Rockquemore, K. A., and Laszloffy, T. A. (2003). Multiple realities: A relational narrative approach in therapy with black-white mixed-race clients. *Family Relations*, 52, 119–129.

Rosiello, F. (2000). On lust and loathing: Erotic transference/countertransference between a female analyst and female patients. *Journal of Gay and Lesbian Psychotherapy*, 4, 5–26.

Root, M. P. P. (2001). *Love's revolution: Interracial marriage*. Philadelphia: Temple University Press.

Rubinstein, G. (2003). Does psychoanalysis really mean oppression? Harnessing psychodynamic approaches to affirmative therapy with gay men. *American Journal of Psychotherapy*, 57, 206.

Sabo, D. Men's health studies: Origins and trends. *Journal of American College Health*, 49, 133–143.

Said, E.W. (1993). *Culture and imperialism*. New York: Knopf.

Schueller, M.J. (1999). Performing whiteness, performing blackness: Dorr's cultural capital and the critique of slavery. *Criticism*, 41, 233–256.

Shofield, T., Connell, R.W., Walker, L., Wood, J.F., and Butland, D.L. (2000). Understanding men's health and illness: A gender-relations approach to policy, research, and practice. *Journal of American College Health*, 48, 247–257.

Smith, J.D. (2002). The campaign for racial purity and the erosion of paternalism in Virginia, 1922–1930:"Nominally white, biologically mixed, and legally negro." *Journal of Southern History*, 68, 65–107.

Smith, N. (2003). Adorno: Disenchantment and ethics: Adorno: A critical reader. *Social Theory and Practice*, 29, 487.

Somerville, S.B. (2000). *Queering the color line: Race and the invention of homosexuality in American culture*. Durham, NC: Duke University Press.

Sondik, E.J., Lucas, J.W., Madans, J.H., and Smith, S.S. (2000). Race/ethnicity and the 2000 census: Implications for public health. *American Journal of Public Health*, 90, 1714–1719.

Spickard, P. (1999). Neither black nor white yet both: Thematic explorations of interracial literature/the new colored people, the mixed-race movement in America. *Journal of American Ethnic History*, 18, 153–157.

Stokes, J.P., McKirnan, D.J., and Burzette, R.G. (1993). Sexual behavior, condom use, disclosure of sexuality, and stability of sexual orientation in bisexual men. *Journal of Sex Research*, 30, 203–213.

Stokes, J.P., McKirnan, D.J., Doll, L., and Burzette, R.G. (1996). Female partners of bisexual men: What they don't know might hurt them. *Psychology of Women Quarterly*, 20, 267–284.

Stokes, J.P., and Peterson, J.L. (1998). Homophobia, self-esteem, and risk for HIV among African American men who have sex with men. *AIDS Education and Prevention*, 10, 278–292.

Stokes, J.P., Vanable, P.A., and McKirnan, D.J. (1996). Ethnic differences in sexual behavior, condom use, and psychosocial variables among black and white men who have sex with men. *Journal of Sex Research*, 33, 373–381.

Summers, M. (2002). "This immoral practice": The prehistory of homophobia in black nationalist thought. In T. Lester (Ed.), *Gender nonconformity, race, and sexuality* (pp. 21–43). Madison: University of Wisconsin Press.

Sundstrom, R.R. (2001). Being and being mixed race. *Social Theory and Practice*, 27, 285–308.

Swann, C. (2002). Public health and the gendered body. *Psychologist*, 15, 195–199.

Tashiro, C.J. (2002). Considering the significance of ancestry through the prism of mixed-race identity. *ANS*, 25, 1–22.

Tate, G.T. (1988). Black Nationalism: An angle of vision. *Western Journal of Black Studies*, 12, 41–47.

Thomas, K. (1997). "Ain't nothing like the real thing": Black masculinity, gay sexuality, and the jargon of authenticity. In W. Lubiano (Ed.), *The house that race built* (pp.116–135). New York: Pantheon.

Tierney, W.G. (1993). Building *communities of difference: Higher education in the twenty-first century*. Westport, CT: Bergin and Garvey.

Tolman, D.L., and Diamond, L.M. (2001). Desegregating sexuality research: Cultural and biological perspectives on gender and desire. *Annual Review of Sex Research*, 12, 33–74.

Trebay, G. (2000). Homo thugz blow up the spot. *Village Voice*, 45, 44–48.

Weinberg, M.S., Williams, C.J., and Pryor, D.W. (2004). Becoming bisexual. In M. Stombler, D.M. Baunach, E.O. Burgess, D. Donnelly, and W. Simonds (Eds.), *Sex matters: The sexuality and society reader* (pp. 23–30). Boston: Pearson.

West, C. (2001). *Race matters*. Boston: Beacon.

Westover, J. (2002). Langston Hughes, 1902–1967: African/American *Callaloo*, 25, 1206–1225.

White, J.L., and Cones, J.H. (1999). *Black man emerging: Facing the past and seizing a future in America*. New York: Freeman.

Williams, D., and Williams-Morris, R. (2000). Racism and mental health: The African American experience. *Ethnicity and Health*, 5, 243–268.

Williams, R.M. (1997). Living at the crossroads: Explorations in race, nationality, sexuality, and gender. In W. Lubiano (Ed.), *The house that race built: Black Americans, U.S. terrain* (pp.136–156). New York: Pantheon.

Wilson, K.H. (1999). Towards a discursive theory of racial identity: *The Souls of Black Folk* as a response to nineteenth-century biological determinism. *Western Journal of Communication*, 63, 193–216/

Wood, S.W. (2000). Prison masculinities. *Library Journal*, 125, 167.

Wright, K. (2001). The great down-low debate. *Village Voice*, 46, 23–25.

Wyatt, G.E. (1997). *Stolen women: Reclaiming our sexuality, taking back our lives*. New York: Wiley.

Zack, N. (1995). Mixed black and white race and public policy. *Hypatia*, 10, 120–129.

12

COUNSELING AT THE INTERSECTION OF IDENTITIES

ASIAN/PACIFIC AMERICAN BISEXUALS

James Fuji Collins

AS WE enter the new millennium, ethnic minority psychologists continue to emphasize the need to be culturally aware and culturally competent (Sue et al. 1999). Hall (1997) stressed that it was time for the American Psychological Association to take action to improve the profession in this area before psychology becomes obsolete and irrelevant to diverse populations in the United States. The demographic changes in the United States (U.S.) will demand changes in psychology.

By the year 2050 it is expected that the U.S. population will be 50 percent people of color. Many cities and states are currently at or near this percentage (U.S. Bureau of the Census 1995, 2001); Asian/Pacific Americans will grow from approximately 4 percent of the U.S. population now to nearly 9 percent by the year 2050 (Hong and Ham 2001). Current estimates of gay men and lesbians in the U.S. tend to hover around 10 percent and 12 percent (Crooks and Baur 1990; Gagnon 1977). Gebhart (1972) suggested approximately 25 million Americans may be bisexual, and the rising acceptance of bisexuality among the youth of America (Leland 1995) will require the psychology profession to consider this phenomenon. These expansive changes in population demographics will affect the field of psychology. Psychologists must be proactive in preparing for these shifts.

What about the complex interaction between sexual orientation and ethnicity? Although there are a small number of publications focusing on the important intersection of sexual orientation and ethnicity (Chan 1989; Greene 1997; Morales 1990), this research obscures many issues relevant to ethnic minorities who are bisexual (Collins 2004). According to Dube and Savin-Williams (1999), the lack of empirical research may be due to the inherent difficulties in studying ethnic minorities. Soto (1997) conducted a ten-year review of gay, lesbian, and bisexual publications, finding that less than 5 percent of the journal articles focused primarily on the area of race or ethnicity. This statistic clearly shows how bisexual people of color are often hidden within their communities. Yet, mental health professionals will have to deal with individuals who are both an ethnic and a sexual minority. Despite the limitations in terms of quality and paucity of research on diverse populations, practitioners should become familiar with the current literature to increase their effectiveness in working with bisexuals and people of color (Lam and Sue 2001; Murphy, Rawlings, and Howe 2002). This chapter explores the research on bisexuality and how it intersects with Asian/Pacific Americans (A/PA). It will discuss the cultural, sexual, and racial context in which bisexual A/PA's communication styles, values, and family structure collide and/or integrate with their bisexuality.

THE BORDERLANDS: WHERE ASIAN PACIFIC AMERICANS AND BISEXUALITY INTERSECT

Greene (1997) discusses the ways in which research on ethnic minority groups rarely acknowledges differences in sexual orientation among group members, with few exploring the complex interaction between sexual orientation and ethnic identity development. She presents a framework from which to begin examining clinical work with ethnic minority gay men and lesbians, but not with bisexuals.

Research on homosexuality in Asian Americans has rarely been touched (Chan 1989, 1992, 1995; Horn 1994; Leong 1996). Other research includes the comparative analysis of Latino, black, and Asian men who have sex with men, examining how the intersection of cultural background, race, and ethnicity influence comportment and identity formation over time (Manalansan 1996) as well as how young gay people of color negotiate disclosure of their homosexuality to family members (Merighi and Grimes 2000; Savin-Williams and Dube 1998).

So how about bisexuals? An exhaustive review of the literature on lesbian, gay, and bisexual identities was presented by D'Augelli and Patterson (1995) in a collection of fifteen chapters (Strader 1996). The reviews were comprehensive. Most notable were Chan's (1995) chapter on sexual identity among Chinese Americans and Fox's chapter on bisexual identities. Practitioners should review Fox's (1995) chapter because he presents an overview of bisexuality that provides the practitioner with a theoretical perspective on bisexuality and bisexual identities, bisexuality in research on homosexuality, and research on bisexuality and bisexual identities. He combines the research from several disciplines into a comprehensive overview not heretofore seen in the literature (Strader 1996). Chan (1995) presents a chapter that concerns sexual identity formation in the context of a bicultural background in which one of the cultures is Asian. She indicates that theoretical models of sexual identity development have come from a Western approach and have not accounted for cultural differences. Clearly, our understanding of the borderland of bisexuality and A/PAs is on the horizon.

Current literature has discussed the integration of sexual orientation and eth-nic minority group membership as a process of dealing with multiple oppressed-group memberships (Bohan 1995; Fukuyama and Ferguson 2000; Rothblum 1994). Bohan (1995) suggested that bisexuals of color are caught in the margin between identities, living in crisis, and that many experience a sense of invisibili-ty and marginality. If someone identifies with a minority culture (e.g., Asian American), that individual must confront and cope with one or more forms of oppression (e.g., sexism, racism). Compounded with the experience of being a sexual minority (i.e., bisexual) and belonging to a culture that fosters a collective sense of identity rather than an individualistic identity (which is more likely with a person of color), that someone is truly in the borderlands. The borderlands are a place where one is marginalized because of ethnic background and then addi-tionally marginalized by heterosexuals and homosexuals alike. The literature does not acknowledge concurrent multiple identities, which obscures the com-plexity of integrating multiple social identities and coping with multiple forms of identity (Collins 2000; Fukuyama and Ferguson 2000).

In order for practitioners to become culturally competent, they must incorpo-rate understanding of both the bisexual and A/PA literatures. Although grouping this literature appears unusual, the two share several important elements. Lam and Sue (2001) suggested that both are considered oppressed groups, subject to detrimental stereotypes, have not been targeted for much psychological research, and are often underserved or inappropriately served. Further, the use of a contex-tually anchored approach would ensure that evidence-based interventions respect the values and traditions of those individuals who live in the borderlands. This will require the understanding of race/ethnicity, culture of origin, religion, language, socioeconomic status, age, immigration status, acculturation level, sexual orientation, and how these factors affect beliefs and behaviors.

In 1975 the American Psychological Association (APA) adopted a resolution after the American Psychiatric Association removed homosexuality from its list of mental disorders (American Psychologist 2000). It took over twenty-five years before the APA adopted guidelines for providers of psychological services to cul-turally diverse populations and for psychotherapy with lesbian, gay, and bisexual clients (American Psychological Association 2000, 2003). These guidelines are intended to assist psychologists with a frame of reference for the treatment of les-bian, gay, and bisexual clients and basic information and further references in the areas of assessment, intervention, identity, relationships, and the education and training of psychologists (American Psychological Association 2000:1440).

Since the early 1990s, only a small number of articles have been published on the importance of the intersections of multiple identities, such as ethnicity and sexual orientation (Chan 1989; Greene 1997; Morales 1990). Current litera-ture has discussed the integration of sexual orientation and ethnic minority group membership as dealing with multiple oppressed-group memberships

232 JAMES FUJI COLLINS

(Bohan 1995; Fukuyama and Ferguson 2000). As noted above, Bohan (1995) suggested that bisexual individuals of color are caught on the margins between identities, living in crisis; and many experience a sense of invisibility. For example, according to Collins (2004), if someone identifies with a minority culture (e.g., Asian American), they must confront and cope with one or more forms of oppression (e.g., sexism, racism) each day. Asian American bisexuals must cope with a blend of subcultures based on race, ethnicity, gender, and sexual orientation. There has been research showing that visible racial and ethnic minorities who are lesbian, gay, or bisexual feel pressure to choose one of their marginalized identities over another (Lowe and Mascher 2001). This has been confirmed for many Asians and Asian Americans (Chan 1989).

As society becomes more multiracial and multiethnic, bisexual Asian Americans are gradually finding a reference group with which to compare and identify themselves. However, until there is growth in the literature that explores bisexual orientation within the context of Asian American ethnicity, it is important that practitioners be aware of the borderlands of bisexuality and ethnicity within which their clients exist and the importance of how that combination may affect their clients. The next section will present an understanding of Asian American communication styles, values, and family structure and how these may collide or integrate with bisexuality.

UNDERSTANDING ASIAN AMERICANS

Asian Pacific Americans are one of the fastest growing racial groups in the United States (U.S. Bureau of the Census 2001). As of 2000, there were over 10.2 million Asian Americans; since 1990, this represents a 46 percent increase, making Asian Americans the second fastest growing ethnic group in the U.S. (after Hispanic Americans). This minority group actually is comprised of at least twenty-nine distinct ethnic groups, the rubrick often overshadowing differences in language, religion, values, and immigration history (Atkinson, Morten, and Sue 1998). However, researchers have noted that the degree of adherence to Asian cultural values may well characterize the within-group differences between Asian Americans and has a significant relationship with the quality of the therapeutic process (Kim and Atkinson 2002). Kim, Atkinson, and Yang (1999) found that collectivism, conformity to norms, emotional self-control, family recognition through achievement, filial piety, and humility were cultural values that distinguish this ethnic group. There are subtle but distinct differences among the groups at both the level of beliefs and values and the level of practices. In other words, while the general belief system is similar, the specific ways in which a group practices its belief system will vary. Thus a practitioner will need to understand the client's larger cultural belief system and determine if these beliefs are normative for that particular client's cultural group.

IMPORTANT ASIAN AMERICAN CULTURAL VALUES

Psychotherapy with Asian Americans poses a complex challenge for Western-trained practitioners because of numerous differences in the ethnocultural traditions and practices. According to Marsella (1993) these differences influence the entire therapeutic experience because they intersect with virtually all critical counseling dimensions, including communication patterns and styles, person perception, therapeutic assumptions and processes, and nature of the person. To further compound this issue, Asian Americans are comprised of individuals whose ancestors immigrated to the United States in the 1850s, those who immigrated to the United States after the Immigration Act of 1965 was passed, and those who have immigrated even more recently (Kim and Atkinson 2002).

Kim, Atkinson, and Yang (1999) found that cultural values that distinguish Asian Americans from European Americans include collectivism, conformity to norms, filial piety, humility, emotional self-control, and family recognition through achievement. Further, Atkinson and Matshusita (1991) and Sue and Sue (1990) stressed that Western psychotherapeutic services are often antagonistic, inappropriate, discriminative, insensitive, and oppressive to the experiences of Asian American clients. Due to the broad array of A/PA clients, internal distinctions between groups, assessment and treatment issues, it is not possible to discuss Asian American psychotherapy in depth in this chapter. The intent of this chapter is to introduce the reader to general values and cultural traditions that appear relevant across the Asian American community. It is recommended therapists review the works of Paniagua (1994) and Sue and Sue (1990) for an overview of guidelines in the assessment and treatment of Asian Americans.

POTENTIAL BARRIERS TO TREATMENT

The section focuses on potential barriers therapists may face when working with Asian American clients: family/community, gender roles, and sexuality. Each barrier will also be discussed with respect to bisexuality as well as the way an individual's bisexuality may impact these components.

FAMILY/COMMUNITY

The relational system places the family at the center of life and is highly valued. Family is hierarchical in structure, with roles clearly defined by gender, class, and age. This collectivist orientation conflicts with the individualistic notion found in the U.S. that values autonomy and independence from the family. The Asian American worldview is reflected in the value placed on harmony and the submergence of the self for the collective good through feelings of obligation and shame that dictate and control social behaviors.

The family exerts a great deal of control over its members and parents stress to their children that the children have obligations to the family (Sue and Sue 1990). Communication within the family is unidirectional, flowing from the parent to the children. The behavior of individual members of a family is believed to reflect on the family as a whole. Therapists need to keep in mind the level of the client's acculturation into American cultural norms and behaviors. The client's level of acculturation may influence the degree of openness about bisexual identity since the process of coming out is individualistic in nature and a personal expression (Fukuyama and Ferguson 2000).

GENDER ROLE

Asian American families generally place a higher value on sons than daughters and the culture tends to be patriarchal, patrilocal, and patrilineal, resulting in entitlement for being male (Atkinson, Morten, and Sue 1998). Sons carry on the family line and are the ones responsible for the parents when they become old. The eldest son is considered to be the most important child. Men are expected to marry and have children. Women are expected to recognize the males' importance and derive satisfaction in the roles of dutiful daughter, wife, and mother (Ho 1990). Men and women must marry, procreate, and continue the family name, and these roles are more important and salient to identity than sexuality (Fukuyama and Ferguson 2000).

The most important purpose of marriage is to continue the family line. Historically, unions often have been prearranged, although this is rare in the United States today (Ritter and Terndrup 2002). Men but not women, theoretically, are free to find romantic love or to have affairs with either men or women outside the marriage (Nakajima, Chan, and Lee 1996). According to Chan (1992), many Asian American sexual minorities continue to accommodate their families by entering into heterosexual marriage because they do not want to be seen as rejecting the traditional social roles or rejecting the importance of family or Asian cultural values. The open acknowledgment of being bisexual may be seen as an overt rebellion that brings great shame on the family. Disclosure thus would be viewed as a rejection of the lineage but also as a failure on the part of one's parents (Ritter and Terndrup 2002). It is important to note that gender roles are significantly different in Asian American families and this will impact therapeutic approaches to Asian American clients or families.

Although Chan (1992, 1997) describes gay and lesbian Asian American clients dealing with gender roles, one may assume that bisexual Asian Americans also present therapists with two common themes: the fear of family rejection and the anticipation of complete parental misunderstanding. Further, open disclosure that one is bisexual may be seen as threatening the continuation of the family line and rejection of one's appropriate role within the culture.

SEXUALITY

Sexuality may be a difficult topic to discuss in therapy. This is a topic that is considered private and for intimate and personal expression. Sex is presumed to be unimportant to women, who are deemed to be of lesser importance in Asian American culture (Greene 1994). Since sexuality is associated with emotion, it is expected that public displays of affection and sexuality will be restrained. Thus discussion about sexuality by a therapist may be difficult without understanding cultural rules.

Many Asian Americans see homosexuality as a white Western phenomenon or as an outcome of too much assimilation and losing touch with Asian traditions (Greene 1997); nor do they have a conceptual construct for bisexual identity This places sexual minority Asian Americans between two conflicting cultures.

In the author's experience, bisexual Asian Americans generally report that they feel pressured to choose between their sexual or racial identity. They do not feel acknowledged and accepted in the gay and lesbian community nor do they feel there is a bisexual community available to them. Without an available bisexual community and given the developmental history of appropriate gender roles within their culture, it is clear why sexual minority Asian Americans tend to be invisible. It is known from the research (Ponterotto et al. 2001) and through popular literature (Garber 1995; Rose, Stevens, and the Off-Pink Collective 1996) that people of color who are bisexual feel pressured to choose one of their marginalized identities over another. As such, there is a tremendous lack of overlap between sexual and racial/ethnic identities. In order for bisexual Asian Americans to attempt to bridge their identities, they must cross borders.

NEW BORDERS/NEW IDENTITIES

In a recent issue of *Cultural Diversity and Ethnic Minority Psychology*, Harper, Jernewall, and Zea (2004) state that bisexual individuals may share experiences of oppression related to their sexual orientation or gender nonconformity and that their membership in other groups with varying levels of social power and privilege (e.g., persons of color) may compound these experiences. Further, they state that "it is important to not make generalizations about LGBT people of color from research based solely or primarily on European American/White LGBT people" (p. 190). While this may be true, clinicians will need to understand the potential dynamics when working with bisexual Asian Americans. For example, it is important to acknowledge that these individuals struggle to form multiple and potentially overlapping identities as they attempt to integrate gender, sexuality and ethnicity/race. The literature shows there is potential for internal conflict between sexual and ethnic identity, yet there should also be acknowledgment that the integration of multiple identities is also a possible source of strength (Patterson 1995). To understand more about the complexity of identity development, it is suggested that therapists review the research focusing on the process of gay and lesbian identity development (i.e., Cass 1979, 1983/1984; Coleman 1981/1982; Grace 1992). These researchers represent current mainstream thinking about gay and lesbian identity formation without incorporating bisexual identity formation. In their work it is generally assumed that sexual orientation is a stable core trait. They present models outlining a sequence of stages that culminate in some sort of integration of, and commitment to, a gay or lesbian identity (Ritter and Terndrup 2002). This base knowledge will further enable understanding of bisexual identity development and how the literature has come to describe it.

Poston (1990) developed a five-stage biracial identity model that may have some relevance to the experiences of bisexual persons. Although it was not originally formulated based on sexual identity development, there are parallel processes that may describe the coming out process for bisexuals. Weinberg, Williams, and Pryor (1994) produced what may be considered the first model of bisexual identity formation. They presented a four-stage model that captured their respondents' most common experiences related to the identity development. A more recent model that should be considered is Collins's (2000, 2004) model of development of a biracial/bisexual identity. He states that bisexual individuals may experience a process of developing identity similar to that of biracial individuals. Collins proposed a theory of development that is more fluid and comprehensive in that it proposes an interrelatedness of various aspects of a person's identity and the role of sociohistorical context in which biracial and bisexual individuals negotiate their identities. His model is the first attempt to combine the understanding of sexual and racial/ethnic identity development. Though Weinberg, Williams, and Pryor (1994) and Collins (2000, 2004) have proposed these models. they are descriptive in nature and presently lack empirical support. Nonetheless, they do provide a framework for describing and understanding bisexual identity development.

GENERAL GUIDELINES

Counseling and psychotherapy are foreign concepts to many Asian Americans (Nishio and Bilmes 1987; Lee 1994, personal communication; Chandras 1997). As a result, Asian Americans either underuse such services or terminate prematurely. In an extensive review of the literature, Leong (1986) concluded that Asian Americans' underutilization of mental health services is well documented, despite some evidence of higher than normal need for services. There have been many suggested hypotheses to explain this underutilization of services, most of which assume a conflict between the psychotherapy process and the values of traditional Asian American culture. For example, at the National Asian American Psychology Training Center (NAAPTC) in San Francisco, therapists are instructed that many Asian Americans avoid mental health services because seeking outside help will bring shame upon the families (Root 1985), that Asian Americans are socialized to internalize stress and repress feelings, and that psychological problems are the result of bad thoughts, a lack of willpower or karma, and that they must resolve such problems on their own (Lee 1994, personal communication). Asian Americans generally use mental health services only after using all other sources of help, such as the family and friends, and have not found solutions to their problems. A mismatch between the cultural values held by Asian American clients and their culturally unaware therapists could cause poor responses to psychological services and failure of therapeutic relationships. If a client sees a therapist who understands, respects, and/or even espouses Asian cultural values, this increases the likelihood the client will experience a positive therapeutic relationship.

Over thirty years ago, it became clear there was a need to train psychologists who were culturally competent in working with Asian Americans. As a result, under the leadership of Dr. Stanley Sue, the National Asian American Psychology Training Center (NAAPTC) was established in San Francisco at the Richmond Area Multi-Services agency (Lee 1994, personal communication). Since then, the NAAPTC has trained the largest number of culturally competent therapists and psychologists in the United States with a focus on Asian American cultures. According to the clinical training practices taught at the NAAPTC, the following are some expectations and suggestions for practitioners who work with Asian American clients.

It is important that therapists have an awareness of the historical and cultural background of their Asian American clients. You should review family histories to determine whether they are refugees, immigrants, or American born. If they are a refugee or immigrant, determine the reasons for leaving the country they came from, methods of sponsorship, and expectations of life in the United States. A thorough examination of past histories is important. Therapists must appreciate and understand some basic cultural differences before conducting psychotherapy. Asian Americans tend to value interdependence and collectivity; the welfare of the family or community often has priority over individual needs; and they are more comfortable conforming to society than being individuals. Asian Americans are required to honor the obligations of their roles in society and the family; following norms is a core cultural goal that fosters group harmony. The attempt to assert one's individuality is often considered a disruption of group solidarity.

To be effective, therapists must understand the values found in Asian cultures: authoritarian orientation, conformity, importance of collective goals and responsibilities, extended family structure, interdependence, filial piety, traditional role structures, acculturation, and a sharp delineation in gender roles. Remember that clients are also conditioned by religious traditions, beliefs, rituals, indigenous medicine, and mysticism. Filial piety is required throughout life. One of the most important goals of parenting and education is to make children obedient to elders, tradition, and social norms. Following group norms is a duty and a moral obligation of the responsible and mature person and following norms validates the self as a good person. These are sometimes incongruent with Western views on these same things. The most salient feature is the expectation of unquestioning obedience to one's parents and parental demands for conformity. Moreover, understanding and discussing the development of sexual identity may be difficult because sex is a taboo topic, to be avoided, and it is shameful to openly discuss one's sexuality.

Asian Americans perceive mental health practitioners as experts. Remember that psychotherapy may be a foreign concept. As therapists, you will need to educate your Asian American client about psychotherapy; the purpose and stages of therapy, and why it may be beneficial. Remember, as an expert, they expect you to dress professionally, provide wise and concrete guidance and advice rather than suggestions to seek insight into their own behavior. Therapy should be directive, time limited, and focused on concrete resolution of problems. To indicate that it may be a long-term process will indicate to the client you are not an expert. Finally, it is important to note that it is traditional to follow the guidance of those in authority. Your credibility is enhanced by explaining relevant educational background and experience.

Therapists should consider the first visit by an Asian American as a crisis intervention. Asian Americans will seek mental health help only as a last resort, and many still tend to have little faith in the process. Families all too often wait until the client becomes so severely mentally ill that the family is unable to cope; thus clients are gravely impaired. The major reason is that fear of shaming the family may discourage Asian Americans from seeking therapy. Mental illness carries a strong stigma and produces a deep sense of shame. Repression and denial have long been coping strategies. Generally, they will not want to discuss family relationships, nor will they criticize their parents or make any comments that may reflect poorly on themselves.

As you are conducting therapy you will need to understand that Asian Americans may present their problem in the form of physical illness. This is a culturally sanctioned expression of mental illness. Further, they often regard therapy as a businesslike transaction that should be devoid of emotion and revelation of private matters; because they are taught respect for and deference to authority figures, they may avoid extended eye contact with a person of higher authority. You should show concern—learn the different characteristics of each Asian group along with the client's unique cultural values, understanding their history and plight, and you will be able to connect with your client. The above material was presented by Drs. Evelyn Lee and May Tung during the 1994–1995 NAAPTC training year for pre- and postdoctoral students at Richmond Area Multi-Services, Inc., an American Psychological Association accredited internship site.

Prior to understanding Asian Americans, therapists must understand their Asian American clients from a cross-cultural perspective. Lee (1995, personal communication) suggested conducting self-awareness check by reviewing the following three cultural competence criteria:

1. *Knowledge*
   a. Clinician's self understanding of race, ethnicity, and power.
   b. Understanding the historical factors that impact the mental health of Asian American populations, such as racism and immigration patterns.
   c. Understand the particular psychosocial stressors relevant to Asian American clients. These include war trauma, migration, acculturation stress, and socioeconomic status and racism.
   d. Understand the cultural differences within the Asian American population.
   e. Understand the Asian American client within a family life cycle and intergenerational conceptual framework in addition to a personal developmental network.
   f. Understand the differences between culturally acceptable behavior of Asian American groups and psychopathological behavior.
   g. Understand indigenous healing practices and the role of religion in the treatment of Asian American clients.
   h. Understand the cultural beliefs about mental illness and the help-seeking behavior of Asian American clients.
   i. Understand a community mental health service continuum of care for minority clients.

2. *Skills*

  a. Ability to interview and assess Asian American clients and families based on a psychological/social/biological/cultural/political/spiritual model.

  b. Ability to communicate effectively—cross-cultural use of interpreters.

  c. Ability to diagnose Asian American clients with an understanding of cultural differences in psychopathology. Ability to avoid underdiagnosis or overdiagnosis.

  d. Ability to formulate treatment plans that are culturally sensitive to the client and family's concept of mental illness.

  e. Ability to utilize community resources.

  f. Ability to provide psychotherapeutic and psychopharmacological interventions with an understanding of the cultural differences in treatment expectations and biological responses to medication.

  g. Ability to conduct culturally sensitive psychological testing with Asian American clients.

3. *Attitudes*

 a. Respect the survival merits of immigrants and refugees.

  b. Respect the importance of cultural forces.

  c. Respect the holistic view of health and illness.

  d. Respect the importance of spiritual beliefs.

  e. Respect and appreciate the skills and contributions of other professional and paraprofessional disciplines.

  f. Be aware of transference and countertransference issues.

BORDER CROSSINGS

Page (1997) provided suggestions for therapists who work with bisexuals that are important to note: you must increase your knowledge base regarding bisexuality and related developmental issues; communicate a sense of acceptance, respect, and support for the fluid nature of sexuality; develop specialized proficiency in working with sexual diversity that will encourage the depathologization of bisexuality; confront your own erotophobia, homophobia, and biphobia; and actively validate the existence of bisexuality.

To support that end, therapists should consider reviewing two important publications: 1. Firestein (1996) provides clinicians with an outstanding resource that addresses the essential psychosocial issues surrounding bisexuality and 2. Fox (2004) provides a crucial guide to current theory, research, and practice on bisexuality. Despite the existence of these resources, there remains a paucity of literature regarding bisexual people of color and more specifically bisexual Asian Americans.

Where does that leave the clinician? I recommend consideration of a cultural competency model wherein clinicians examine their own worldview, cultural values, and biases, as well as learn about the developmental and psychosocial experiences of people of color and sexual minorities.

Hays (2001) has suggested ways to become a culturally responsive therapist. She presents a practitioner-oriented approach that outlines specific principles and guidelines for working with people of minority, dominant, and mixed cultural groups. She asserts it is impossible for any clinician to hold insider-level expertise with all the cultural influences for every client. As a result, she has designed a framework that offers a system for organizing and addressing these cultural influences in the form of an acronym: Age and generational influences, Developmental and acquired Disabilities, Religion and spiritual orientation, Ethnicity, Socioeconomic status, Sexual orientation, Indigenous heritage, National origin, and Gender (ADDRESSING) (Hays 1996: 37). Hays moves beyond one-dimensional concepts of identity to an understanding of the multiplicity of cultural influences that form us all.

According to Fox (1996) research on bisexuality has focused on the similarities and differences between bisexual and gay/lesbian identities as well as sexual attractions and relationships of bisexual men and bisexual women. Research then broadened in focus to include studies on bisexuality in communities of color, bisexuality from a cross-cultural perspective, and, most recently, counseling and psychotherapy with bisexual women and bisexual men (Fox 2004). As noted above, it is unfortunate that the research on bisexual Asian Americans is extremely limited. Collins (2004) explored the research on bisexual identity development and the way it intersects with research on people of color, noting the limited availability of literature on understanding bisexual people of color.

This chapter provides an overview of understanding Asian Americans and how their cultural, sexual, and ethnic beliefs may impact psychotherapy. As clinicians, we assess, diagnose, and treat clients with the clinical tools provided us through training, education, the literature, empirical research, and our own experiences. We further understand that it is important to be well versed in the current literature about treatment strategies. Our clients are becoming more diverse and may hold multiple identities simultaneously. As a clinician whose training was focused on working with a diverse range of clients that included many Asian American subgroups as well as sexual minorities, at times crossing the borderlands, it became vitally important to me to realize that one must consider a personal self-exploration in attempts to understand the influence of culture on one's worldview and belief system as well as conducting a self-education about a client's cultures. Gender, ethnicity, culture, sexuality, environment, and identity will all affect a client's journey through life and the dynamics of therapy.

Finally, the reader is cautioned about making generalizations. However, it is my hope that this introduction will expand abilities to understand the complex dynamics that underlie multiple identities (i.e., Asian American and bisexual) and the oppressions those with such identities face. Clinicians need to understand that Asian American sexual minorities have worldviews different than those of non-Asian and sexual majority clinicians (this allows for the fact that some of our readers are Asian A/PA and/or sexual minority clinicians). Our openness to understanding their worldview and the dynamics of their multiple identities and multiple oppressions may assist both client and clinician in working through the psychological, interpersonal, and emotional issues that brought the two of you together.

REFERENCES

American Psychological Association (2000). Guidelines for psychotherapy with lesbian, gay, and bisexual clients. *American Psychologist, 55,* 1440–1451.

American Psychological Association (2003). Guidelines for providers of psychological services to ethnic, linguistic, and culturally diverse populations. Retrieved May 7, 2003, from http://www.apa.org/pi/oema/guide.html.

Atkinson, D. R., and Matsushita, Y. (1991). Japanese-American acculturation, counseling style, counselor ethnicity, and perceived counselor credibility. *Journal of Counseling Psychology, 38,* 473–478.

Atkinson, D. R., Morten, G., and Sue, D. W. (1998). *Counseling American minorities: A cross-cultural perspective* (5th ed.). Dubuque: Brown.

Bohan, J. S. (1995). *Psychology and sexual orientation: Coming to terms.* New York: Routledge.

Cass, V. C. (1979). Homosexual identity formation: A theoretical model. *Journal of Homosexuality, 4,* 219–235.

Cass, V. C. (1983–1984). Homosexual identity: A concept in need of definition. *Journal of Homosexuality, 9,* 105–126.

Chan, C. S. (1989). Issues of identity development among Asian-American lesbians and gay men. *Journal of Counseling and Development, 68,* 16–20.

Chan, C. S. (1992). Cultural considerations in counseling Asian American lesbians and gay men. In S. H. Dworkin and F. J. Gutierrez (Eds.), *Counseling gay men and lesbians: Journey to the end of the rainbow* (pp. 115–124). Alexandria, VA: American Association for Counseling and Development.

Chan, C. S. (1995). Issues of sexual identity in an ethnic minority: The case of Chinese American lesbians, gay men, and bisexual people. In A. R. D'Augelli and C. J. Patterson (Eds.), *Lesbian, gay and bisexual identities over the lifespan.* New York: Oxford University Press.

Chan, C. S. (1997). Don't ask, don't tell, don't know: The formation of a homosexual identity and sexual expression among Asian American lesbians. In B. Greene (Ed.), *Ethnic and cultural diversity among lesbians and gay men* (pp. 240–248). Thousand Oaks, CA: Sage.

Chandras, K. V. (1997). Training multiculturally competent counselors to work with Asian Indian Americans. *Counselor Education and Supervision*, 37, 50–59.

Coleman, E. (1981–1982). Developmental stages of the coming out process. *Journal of Homosexuality*, 7, 31–43.

Collins, F. (2000). Biracial-bisexual individuals: Identity coming of age. *International Journal of Sexuality and Gender Studies*, 5, 221–253.

Collins, F. (2004). The intersection of race and bisexuality: A critical overview of the literature and past, present, and future directions of the "borderlands." *Journal of Bisexuality*, 4, 99–116.

Crooks, R., and Baur, K. (1990). *Our sexuality*. Redwood City, CA: Benjamin/ Cummings.

D'Augelli, A. R., and Patterson, C. J. (Eds.) (1995). *Lesbian, gay, and bisexual identities over the lifespan*. New York: Oxford University Press.

Dube, E. M., and Savin-Williams, R. C. (1999). Sexual identity development among ethnic sexual-minority male youths. *Developmental Psychology*, 35, 1389–1398.

Firestein, B. A. (1996). *Bisexuality: The psychology and politics of an invisible minority*. Thousand Oaks, CA: Sage.

Fox, R. C. (1995). Bisexual identities. In A. R. D'Augelli and C. J. Patterson (Eds.), *Lesbian, gay, and bisexual identities over the lifespan* (pp. 48–86). New York: Oxford University Press.

Fox, R. C. (1996). Bisexuality in perspective: A review of theory and research. In B. A. Firestein (Ed.), *Bisexuality: The psychology and politics of an invisible minority* (pp. 3–50). Thousand Oaks, CA: Sage.

Fox, R. C. (2004). *Current research on bisexuality*. Binghamton, NY: Harrington Park.

Fukuyama, M. A., and Ferguson, A. D. (2000). Lesbian, gay, and bisexual people of color: Understanding cultural complexity and managing multiple oppressions. In R. M. Perez, K. A. DeBord, and K. J. Bieschke (Eds.), *Handbook of Counseling and Psychotherapy with Lesbian, Gay, and Bisexual Clients*. Washington, DC: American Psychological Association.

Gagnon, J. (1977). *Human sexualities*. Glenview, IL: Foresman.

Garber, M. B. (1995). *Vice versa: Bisexuality and the eroticism of everyday life*. New York: Simon and Schuster.

Gebhart, P. H. (1972). Incidence of overt homosexuality in the U.S. and Western Europe. In J. M. Livingod (Ed.), *NIMH Task Force on Homosexuality: Final Report and Papers* (DHEW Publications No. HSM 72–9116, pp. 22–30). Rockville, MD: National Institute of Mental Health.

Grace, J. (1992). Affirming gay and lesbian adulthood. In N. J. Woodman (Ed.), *Lesbian and gay lifestyles: A guide for counseling and education* (pp. 33–47). New York: Irvington.

Greene, B. (1994). Ethnic-minority lesbian and gay mental health and treatment issues. *Journal of Consulting and Clinical Psychology*, 62, 243–251.

Greene, B. (1997). Ethnic minority lesbians and gay men. In B. Greene (Ed.), *Ethnic and cultural diversity among lesbian and gay men*. Thousand Oaks, CA: Sage.

Hall, C. C. I. (1997). Cultural malpractice: The growing obsolescence of psychology with the changing U.S. population. *American Psychologist*, 52, 642–651.

Harper, G. W., Jernewall, N., and Zea, M. C. (2004). Giving voice to emerging science and theory for lesbian, gay, and bisexual people of color. *Cultural Diversity and Ethnic Minority Psychology*, 10, 187–199.

Hays, P. A. (1996). Addressing the complexities of culture and gender in counseling. *Journal of Counseling and Development*, 74, 332–338.

Hays, P. A. (2001). Addressing cultural complexities in practice: A framework for clinicians and counselors. Washington, DC: American Psychological Association.

Ho, C. K. (1990). An analysis of domestic violence in Asian American communities: A multicultural approach to counseling. Women and Therapy, 9, 129–150.

Hong, G. K., and Ham, D. (2001). Psychotherapy and counseling with Asian American clients: A practical guide. Thousand Oaks, CA: Sage.

Horn, A. Y. (1994). Stories from the homefront: Perspectives of Asian American parents with lesbian daughters and gay sons. Amerasia Journal, 20, 19–32.

Kim, B. S. K., and Atkinson, D. R. (2002). Asian American client adherence to Asian cultural values, expression of cultural values, counselor ethnicity, and career counseling process. Journal of Counseling Psychology, 49, 3–13.

Kim, B. S. K., Atkinson, D. R., and Yang, P. H. (1999). The Asian values scale: Development, factor analysis, validation, and reliability. Journal of Counseling Psychology, 46, 342–352.

Lam, A. G., and Sue, S. (2001). Client diversity. Psychotherapy, 38, 479–486.

Leland, J. (1995). Not gay, not straight: A new sexuality emerges. Newsweek (July 17), 126, 44–50.

Leong, F. T. L. (1986). Counseling and psychotherapy with Asian-Americans: Review of the literature. Journal of Counseling Psychology, 33, 196–206.

Leong, R. (1996). Asian American sexualities: Dimensions of the gay and lesbian experience. New York: Routledge.

Lowe, S. M., and Mascher, J. (2001). The role of sexual orientation in multicultural counseling: Integrating bodies of knowledge. In J. G. Ponterotto, J. M. Casas, L. A. Suzuki, and C. M. Alexander (Eds.), Handbook of Multicultural Counseling (pp. 755–778). Thousand Oaks, CA: Sage.

Manalansan, M. R. (1996). Double minorities: Latino, Black, and Asian men who have sex with men. In R. C. Savin-Williams and K. M. Cohen (Eds.), The lives of lesbians, gays, and bisexuals: Children to adults (pp. 393–415). Fort Worth: Harcourt Brace College.

Marsella, A. J. (1993). Counseling and psychotherapy with Japanese Americans: Cross-cultural considerations. American Journal of Orthopsychiatry, 63, 200–208.

Merighi, J. R., and Grimes, M .D. (2000). Coming out to families in a multicultural context. Families in Society, 81, 32–41.

Morales, E. S. (1990). Ethnic minority families and minority gays and lesbians. Marriage and Family Review, 14, 217–239.

Murphy, J. A., Rawlings, E. I., and Howe, S. R. (2002). A survey of clinical psychologists on treating lesbian, gay, and bisexual clients. Professional Psychology: Research and Practice, 33, 183–189.

Nakajima, G. A., Chan, Y. H., and Lee, K. (1996). Mental health issues for gay and lesbian Asian Americans. In R. P. Cabaj and T. S. Stein (Eds.), Textbook of homosexuality and mental health (pp. 563–581). Washington, DC: American Psychiatric.

Nishio, K., and Bilmes, M. (1987). Psychotherapy with Southeast Asian American clients. Professional Psychology: Research and Practice, 18, 342–346.

Page, E. (1997). Psychotherapy experiences and needs of bisexual women and men. Paper presented at the 105th Annual Convention of the American Psychological Association, August, Chicago.

Paniagua, F. A. (1994). Assessing and treating culturally diverse clients. Thousand Oaks, CA: Sage.

Patterson, C. J. (1995). Sexual orientation and human development: An overview. *Developmental Psychology*, 31, 3–11.

Ponterotto, J. G., Casas, J. M., Suzuki, L. A., and Alexander, C. M. (Eds.) (2001). *Handbook of multicultural counseling* (2d ed.). Thousand Oaks, CA: Sage.

Poston, W. S. C. (1990). The biracial identity development model. *Journal of Counseling and Development*, 69, 152–155.

Ritter, K.Y., and Terndrup, A. I. (2002). *Handbook of affirmative psychotherapy with lesbians and gay men*. New York: Guilford.

Root, M. P. P. (1985). Guidelines for facilitating therapy with Asian American clients. *Psychotherapy*, 22, 349–356.

Rose, S., Stevens, C., and the Off-Pink Collective (Eds.) (1996). *Bisexual horizons: Politics, histories, lives*. London: Lawrence and Wishart.

Rothblum, E. D. (1994). Introduction to the special section: Mental health of lesbians and gay men. *Journal of Consulting and Clinical Psychology*, 62, 211–212.

Savin-Williams, R. C., and Dube, E. M. (1998). Parental reactions to their child's disclosure of a gay/lesbian identity. *Family Relations*, 47, 7–13.

Soto, T. A. (1997). Ethnic minority gay, lesbian, and bisexual publications: A ten-year review. *Division 44 Newsletter*, 13, 13–14.

Strader, S. C. (1996). *Lesbian, gay, and bisexual identities over the lifespan* (book review). *Journal of Sex Research*, 33, 82–84.

Sue, D. W., Bingham, R. P., Porche-Burke, L., and Vasquez, M. (1999). The diversification of psychology: A multicultural revolution. *American Psychologist*, 54, 1061–1069.

Sue, D. W., and Sue, D. (1990). *Counseling the culturally different: Theory and practice* (2d ed.). New York: Wiley.

U.S. Bureau of the Census. (1995). *Statistical abstracts of the U.S.* (115th ed.). Washington, DC: U.S. Bureau of the Census.

U.S. Bureau of the Census. (2001). Profiles of general demographic characteristics. Retrieved July 30, 2002, from http://www.census.gov/prod/cen2000/dpl/2khoo.psd.

Weinberg, M. S., Williams, C. J., and Pryor, D. W. (1994). *Dual attraction: Understanding bisexuality*. New York: Oxford University Press.

13

COUNSELING BISEXUAL LATINOS

A MINORITY WITHIN A MINORITY

Luigi Ferrer and L. Angelo Jürgen Gómez

Hispanic is what they call us; Latino is what we call ourselves. Hispanics have been assimilated into mainstream (American) culture; they are part of, and all about preserving the existing power structure, because they think they have a leg up on the rest of us. Latinos are all about our culture and preserving our language and traditions. We are outsiders struggling to change the existing power structure so that we might have a place at the table.

—MAURICIO, LOS ANGELES

THIS IS how my friend Mauricio, a gay Chicano, explained the differences between Hispanics and Latinos to me on my first trip to Los Angeles many years ago. Is this just semantics? I don't think so, because, as Mauricio so eloquently explained, the differences between Hispanic or Latino identity are very real and have to do with how people of Hispanic descent view themselves, how they think about and conceptualize themselves (Santiago-Rivera, Arredondo, Gallardo-Cooper 2002). To a large extent these differences are related to an individual's culture and level of acculturation (the degree of comfort with American culture or how much a part of mainstream American culture ze feels).[1] These differences, in turn, will play an important role in how bisexual Latinos come to terms with and manifest their bisexuality.

The Latino bisexual experience is a veritable crucible of passion and painful struggle. Bisexual Latino men and women are outsiders to more than one culture—not fitting into traditional Latino culture and without a home in either the gay or straight communities. They live a multiple minority identity, experiencing great discrimination and a profound lack of understanding and support from their Latino community, the mainstream U.S. (heterosexual) culture, or the predominantly white LGBT community. Living in this cultural hyphen causes additional stress and isolation, and this heavily colors the bisexual Latino experience. Little has been written or researched to specifically address the experience of the Latino bisexual person.

In this chapter we explore the Latino bisexual experience addressing acculturation, Latino family influences, the coming out process, and risk and resiliency factors relevant to bisexual Latino mental health. We provide a cultural context for this work and conclude with several suggestions for counselors who work, or would like to work, with bisexual Latinos, especially if they are not themselves Latinos. To this purpose, we review some of the common themes, beliefs, and counseling issues that Ferrer encountered in more than twelve years of peer counseling with participants of two bisexual support groups as well as a group of Latino men who have sex with men and their sex and drug-using partners in Miami, Florida.

LATINOS IN THE UNITED STATES

Hispanics[2] are the largest and fastest growing minority group in the U.S. Currently representing about 13 percent of the U.S. population, the population of Hispanics grew by 58 percent from 1990 to 2000 compared to a 13 percent growth rate for the U.S. population as a whole. Hispanics are a diverse group of people of Mexican (58 percent), Puerto Rican (10 percent), Cuban (4 percent), Dominican (2 percent), or Central and South American (25 percent) ancestry. As a group, Hispanics are characterized by their use of the Spanish language, although often second, third, and/or subsequent generations lose Spanish language proficiency. Each subgroup is defined by a different set of historical and sociopolitical factors and cultural and demographic variables (Alcoff 2000; García 2001). Many Latinos do not identify with the term *Hispanic* and label themselves *Latino* or refer to themselves by their country of origin, calling themselves Cuban, Mexican, Puerto Rican, Colombian, Venezuelan, Salvadoran, or Costa Rican instead. Marotta and García (2003) provide a review of the 2000 U.S. Census data, the geographic distribution of Latino groups in the U.S., and several of the sociodemographic variables that characterize each of them. Santiago-Rivera, Arredondo, Gallardo-Cooper (2002) discuss the political and historical factors that have driven Latino immigration to the U.S. and the attributes of the major Latino subpopulations in the United States.

Latinos are a diverse group not only in their origins but also in their racial makeup, socioeconomic backgrounds, educational achievements, and levels of acculturation to U.S. culture. Falicov, one of the pioneers in writing on counseling Latinos, says that "Latinos in the United States are a varied, heterogeneous population of immigrants from many different countries, settings, and cultures. The forces that spurred them toward migration vary widely, from escape from political change to search for better economic or educational opportunities" (1998:33).

Latinos are widely distributed throughout the entire U.S. territory. Not all Latinos are immigrants. Some groups, like Mexicans, have been here for many generations, while other groups are more recent arrivals; the U.S. Latino population continues to be renewed and enriched by subsequent waves of new immigrants of many nationalities. There are many enclaves of national groups, each of which creates a distinct sense of community and fosters the maintenance of cultural links with their countries of origin (Nieto 2004). Examples of these ethnic subcultures include Mexicans in Los Angeles, Cubans in Miami, Dominicans in New York, and Salvadorians in Washington, DC. Therefore, it is important to consider these sociogeographic and historical aspects when counseling or delivering services to Latinos in order to provide culturally competent and effective interventions.

Many queer[3] Latinos immigrate to the U.S. because of homophobia and heterosexism and the intolerance, oppression, and outright violence these cultural forces engender in their countries of origin. Many come seeking the freedom to live their lives as they choose as well as better educational and economic opportunities. The American dream is experienced and viewed in different ways by different people, and sexual minorities are not immune to the inspiring message of hope of the "land of opportunity." Similar to most ethnic minority groups, Latinos tend to arrive and settle primarily in cities and large metropolitan areas, where they are more likely to come into contact with large LGBT communities that facilitate exploration and the opportunity to live out sexual variations that their cultures and countries of origin do not offer them. Ninety-one percent of the U.S. Latino population is concentrated in urban centers (Marotta and García 2003). We turn now to a discussion of the influences of culture and acculturation on bisexual Latino development

CULTURE AND ACCULTURATION

Culture is the lens through which all social interactions are perceived; it is the context in which all human interactions are considered and evaluated (Ibrahim 1994, as cited in Greger and Ponterotto 1995, 2001). It is the accumulation of dos and don'ts and all the stories we tell ourselves about who we are, how we should act, and what is or isn't appropriate (Casas and Pytluk 1995; Robinson 2005). As with American culture, Latino cultures are also diverse, regional, and at times unforgiving of deviation. There is, however, a common sense of what it means to be *Latino, latinoamericano,* or *Hispano.* Some of these commonalities include history or immigration condition, minority status, and often an unprivileged socioeconomic condition, plus a set of cultural values such as religion, family-centered values, and clearly defined gender roles. In some ways, and to differing degrees, this set of variables makes up a Latino identity. And, with the exception of some regionalisms and alternative regional word meanings and the occasional embarrassment they cause, Latinos understand each other through a common language (for those Latinos who continue to speak Spanish) and overlapping cultural assumptions. However, many Latinos are not new immigrants and may have adopted values and ways of looking at life that are not part of their original culture but closer to the mainstream U.S. culture. To one degree or another, they have acculturated, and this brings with it a negotiation of identity and the acceptance of new standard (Ortega et al. 1995). This may cause internal conflicts and conflicts with others, including the potential for conflict with their families.

Acculturation is the process by which members of one cultural group adopt the beliefs and behaviors of another group. It is the process by which we acquire the knowledge, values, and social norms of a culture. Acculturation impacts many aspects of a person's life including attitudes toward sex, sexual behavior, and an individual's level of comfort with hir sexual orientation and self-identity, among others. Acculturation frequently facilitates the integration (Ramos 2005) and acceptance of alternative lifestyles and options, such as bisexuality. Acculturation to American values, such as independence and individuality, may facilitate an immigrant or U.S.-born Latino's ability to embrace bisexuality as a valid and viable sexual identity.

If culture is the lens though which humans experience life, then an individual's level of acculturation can be thought of as eyeglasses or "corrective lenses." Stronger for some than for others, they focus in on the new culture and bring new and different concepts, assumptions, and expectations into view. But while acculturation may measure an individual's level of comfort with the new culture, it does not necessarily reflect an abandonment of all previously held beliefs, prejudices, or values (Schuttle 2000). Even for highly acculturated bisexual Latino men and women, the impact of Latino culture and its widely held beliefs and expectations can be the source of a great deal of social distress, inner conflict, and guilt. Oetting and Beauvais (1991) remind us that acculturation is an orthogonal process, that is, identification with one culture and its values can be essentially independent of identification with any other culture and values. In this light, it is interesting to note that, when compared to the Euro-American majority, Latinos in the United States hold more conservative socials values and ascribe to more traditional gender roles than their Caucasian counterparts (Gómez and Marín 1996; Marín et al. 1997; Marín, Gómez, and Tschann 1998). The story of Alex and Pedro illustrates how differences in the degree of acculturation may influence an individual's comfort with and acceptance of their bisexuality.

ALEX AND PEDRO

Alex and Pedro were both in their mid to late twenties. Alex was born in the U.S. His father was Peruvian, his mother Cuban. He grew up in Miami Beach, where he attended a multiethnic public school. His family had infrequent contact with family members in Cuba or Peru. Pedro came to the United States as young boy. His Cuban parents settled in Little Havana, where he also attended public school, but lived in a predominantly Cuban Spanish-speaking enclave neighborhood. Several members of Pedro's extended family—aunts, uncle, and cousins—lived in the Miami area, and, although difficult, his family kept in touch with family members in Cuba. Alex was a voracious (English) reader, spoke fluent English and Spanish with a slight American accent, and preferred American music. Pedro didn't enjoy reading in either language, spoke English and Spanish well, and listened to both American and Latin music. Alex went on to a career in computer science, while Pedro became a master electrician and worked primarily in a blue-collar environment. Clearly varying somewhat in their level of acculturation, Alex was considerably more accepting of his bisexuality than Pedro, although both men self-identified as bisexual. Alex was a founding member of an LGBT youth group, bartended at a gay bar, and was much more comfortable and open about his sexuality. Although it caused some controversy, Alex was out as bisexual to all of his family. He dated primarily American men and women and disclosed his bisexuality to all his partners. Pedro was not out to his family and lived in fear of what might happen if they found out. He dated only women, primarily Latinas, had sex with men "on the side," and only rarely disclosed his bisexuality to his sex partners.

LATINO CULTURAL VALUES

Widely held values in Latino culture include: *machismo, marianismo, familismo*, and *simpatía* (Santiago-Rivera, Arredondo, Gallardo-Cooper 2002, Trueba 1999).

Machismo, an extreme form of heterosexism, is pervasive in Latino culture. To be *macho* is to be male in an animal sort of way.[4] It implies virility; *machismo* reinforces rigid social, gender, and sexual roles in which females are subjugated to the dominant male, and, by extension, anything submissive is female and anything dominant is *macho*.

Marianismo refers to the ideal woman, cast in the image of the Virgin Mary, who, in accordance with Catholic tradition, is pious and pure, heterosexual, has children, cares for the home, and is validated by her husband.

Familismo is a family-centered value. It refers to the preference for maintaining close connections to family and stresses interdependence and cooperation among family members.

Simpatía refers to the importance placed on being liked, or being likable, to being friendly, charming, sociable, easygoing, and fun to be with.

These traditional social values reinforce and regulate sex roles and behaviors. Family for Latinos includes more than parents and siblings (Moore and Pachon 1985); it refers to members of the extended family, such as aunts, uncles, cousins, grandparents, and sometimes even neighbors and close friends. So the Latino family and those to whom respect is owed and whose respect is valued encompasses a much wider audience of inclusion. As a consequence, it is more challenging for bisexual Latinos to achieve acceptance because they have more people to be attentive to and from whom they fear rejection. This outlook on life has both benefits and drawbacks. On one hand, these factors lead to a more community-oriented vision and behaviors that are responsive to others, a sort of deep social conditioning from an early age. On the other hand, traditional views are guarded more strictly by more community members, limiting an individual's options for individuation in directions that run counter to community values.

Gómez's experience concurs with Ferrer's in that Latinos who are more acculturated are better able to deal with and understand their sexual orientation in a more positive way and more quickly than those who are less acculturated.

MARICARMEN

Maricarmen is the oldest of four siblings. Her father was a Mexican neurosurgeon; her mother had a college degree, helped with some of the office paperwork and billing, and was primarily a housewife. The family lived in the United States for seven years while Maricarmen's father completed his medical training. Maricarmen did most of her elementary education in the U.S., and, when the family returned to Mexico, she understood Spanish but could not read or write it. Her parents, wanting to preserve their children's English language skills, enrolled them in an international school. Maricarmen naturally gravitated toward other English-speaking students at her school. Although she completed high school and college in Mexico, she returned to the U.S. for her graduate degree. In Mexico she had discovered her love for women; knowing that her family would not approve, she decided to return to the United States to put some distance between herself and her family. While in the U.S. she met a young bisexual man. Together they attended a bisexual support group and soon became bisexual activists. Maricarmen's family found out about her bisexuality when Maricarmen, serving as a spokesperson for her local bisexual network, granted an interview for a *Telemundo* (NBC's Spanish-language network) affiliate and the program was seen in Veracruz. Her mother called in tears over the news and expressed outrage over Maricarmen's choice of such a public disclosure. They spoke little over the next couple of years, then, with the help of a bi-friendly therapist, began to rebuild their relationship. Her siblings spoke little of the matter. She and her brother became estranged as he, a Charismatic Catholic, insisted on trying to convert her to his beliefs. When Maricarmen wrote the family expressing her sadness and desire to reestablish closer family ties (while simultaneously reaffirming her sexuality), she received a vitriolic letter from one of her sisters, asking, "why do you insist in rubbing this ugliness in our faces?" and stating that "you reap what you sow." If she felt lonely, it was her fault; she had everything she deserved. Maricamen's youngest sister, who lives with her husband in the U.S. and has many gay friends, has embraced her, and, although they live at a distance, they remain close, speak on the phone often, and visit each other several times a year. In speaking with Maricarmen, it was clear the she and her youngest sister had achieved higher levels of acculturation than other members of their family.

This, nevertheless, does not change the overriding fact that most Latinos will be influenced by values and principles that are not accepting of bisexuality as a viable option. The level of acculturation of family members will also determine the level of inclusion and acceptance that bisexual individuals may or may not enjoy within their families of origin. Santiago-Rivera, Arredondo, and Gallardo-Cooper (2002) also discuss how differing levels of acculturation can be a source of misunderstandings and family conflict. Maricarmen's experience illustrates this well.

BISEXUAL LATINO COUNSELING ISSUES

Many of the counseling issues encountered when counseling Latinos are directly related to how well individuals feel they measure up to a theoretical socially and culturally constructed view of themselves we will call the ideal self. Falling short of the expectations of the ideal self, and fearing what family and friends might think, or how they might act if they knew "the truth," was one of the most common sources of discomfort—even grief—encountered among Latino bisexuals. For Latino men, this ideal self is often measured in terms of athletic ability, sexual conquest, and financial success, qualities reinforced by *machismo*. For women it is the image of the perfect mother or *marianismo* that torments them.

Most of the issues addressed in this section of the chapter were common topics of discussion during support group meetings that Ferrer cofacilitated. The population Ferrer worked with from 1990 through 2004 included three groups: a mixed-ethnicity group (Anglo, Latino, and African American) of bisexual and bi-curious young adults in their twenties and early thirties, a second group of bisexual adults of similar racial makeup but slightly older (mid twenties to fifty), and a third group of Latino gay and bisexual men (twenties to fifty-five) who were participants in an HIV-prevention support group. As it turns out, Miami is a particularly good place to observe and work with Latino clients because its large Latino population reflects much of the ethnic, cultural, and socioeconomic diversity of the U.S. Latino population. In addition to Cubans, support groups often included significant numbers of Colombians, Venezuelans, Mexicans, Puerto Ricans, Dominicans, and other Central and South Americans of various educational and income levels.

COMING OUT

Many people coming to our support groups arrived in agony, looking for "a cure to this curse"[5] and with a very poor understanding of modern views of human sexuality and human sexual identity development. Latinos ascribe to more conservative social norms and gender roles and because of this they often hold strong negative beliefs regarding homosexuality and therefore about lesbians, gay men, and bisexuals. For Latino men and women, coming out often represents a significant loss of standing within their family and community. Work and opportunities for advancement and education can vanish upon disclosure of one's sexual orientation. This is especially true in today's competitive economic environment. These potential losses and their consequences are very tangible and frightening to Latinos coming to grips with same-gender attraction, sexual experimentation, and their sexual orientation. Feelings of shame, guilt, and hopelessness are common. No Latino male wants to be thought of as a sissy—or its Spanish derogatory counterparts, *marica*, *pato*, *mariposa*, or *maricón*; no Latina wants to be thought of as a dyke—or its Spanish derogatory counterparts, *marimacha*, *pata*, *tortillera*, or the less derogative term *lesbiana*. The lack of successful healthy queer role models contributes to these feelings and to feelings of isolation.

As with their American counterparts, the first step in coming out for Latinos is a journey of personal discovery and self-awareness, of coming to grips with new feelings and attractions and beginning to develop a new self-image. Sensitive and multiculturally competent counselors can be of great help and serve as guides in this process. While coming out begins with self-awareness, it often then becomes an issue of when and how we break this news to others. Telling others and dealing with their reactions is the second step in the coming out process. Counselors can help clients get the information they need to better understand their sexual orientation and help prepare and perhaps assist clients in disclosing their sexuality to coworkers, friends, and family. The next step in this progression is socializing with other bisexuals, lesbian, gay, and transgender people and learning about queer history and culture. The final step in the coming out process is the adoption of a positive self-image and the integration and acceptance of one's bisexual sexual orientation as a real and valid identity.

However, for bisexual Latinos, it may be easier to initially escape or avoid directly confronting homophobia and the "heterosexism on steroids" that is *machismo*. Many may feel comfortable, at least for a time, conforming to their prescribed social role, and many bisexual Latinos marry and build families, only to find that, in the end, all they have done is delayed dealing with their sexuality.

FAMILY AND RELATIONSHIPS

For Latinos, our relationship with our family of origin is one of the most fundamental relationships of all (Santiago-Rivera, Arredondo, Gallardo-Cooper 2002). Many of us grew up with the love and support found in the bosom of our large extended families (Zambrana 1995). Our *familias* are not just a source of pride but also of economic security in uncertain times. In this sense our extended families function more like a clan or tribe: no matter what your want or need, there is almost always someone in the family to whom you can turn for help. Whether it was *Tío* Fernando,[6] the police chief, *Tío* Marcos the mechanic, or *Tía* Rosaura, executive secretary to the dean at the local university, there was always someone to count on. This is one of the reasons why it is so difficult when Latinos are shunned by their families because of their sexual orientation or gender identity. For Latinos, when one member of the family succeeds, it reflects positively on the entire family. Many Latinos also believe the opposite is true and struggle with coming out because they do not want to bring shame or discredit to their family. Coming out to a sympathetic sibling, mother, or father is often the first step in negotiating this delicate process.

For bisexual Latinos who have married or are in a long-term relationship, coming out to a spouse or life partner and/or to children is another difficult process many of them face. Bisexual Latinos naturally fear the loss of the relationship, divorce, and the potential loss of custody of their children, and these fears often have a paralyzing effect. Many bisexuals experience a great deal of guilt and shame about their feelings and their actions, especially if they have not always been truthful in their words or actions or have failed to live up to their commitments. For the heterosexual spouse of a bisexual partner, years of silence, secrets, or half-truths can generate strong feelings of betrayal and weaken the bonds of trust in the relationship (Buxton 2001; Buxton, chapter 21). Children often feel confused, do not understand what is going on or fear the breakup of the family, and frequently feel conflicting parental loyalties. Bisexual parents often feel a great deal of guilt and conflict when the ideal self–view of their parental role is at odds with the reality of their behavior. Feeling lost and trapped, bisexual Latinos often suffer from depression and many turn to alcohol or drugs or attempt suicide to escape the painful feelings of having let down spouses, children, and *familia*.

For bisexual Latinos who are dating or starting a new relationship, a common issue is when and how much to disclose about their sexual orientation. My advice to support group participants is that the sooner they can establish open and honest communication with a potential partner of whichever gender, the better. But I also warn that the first thing out of their mouths should not be that they are bisexual, unless that is truly the most important aspect of them they need to share. Relationships are built on a myriad of things and sex or sexuality need not be the defining force in a relationship. Bisexuals commonly enter into relationships with monosexuals (individuals attracted to a single gender), and, whether the new potential partner is straight or gay, there is the potential for controversy, misunderstandings, and hurt feelings. Many bisexual women and men feel that they have to be a combination of sex educator and counselor in their relationships, and many find this to be a difficult and tiring set of roles. Working with a knowledgeable counselor early in the relationship can help clients establish good communication, define "rules of engagement," and identify and clarify issues troubling the relationship.

Honest and open communication becomes even more important when clients are involved, or considering becoming involved, with multiple partners. Negotiating a nonmonogamous relationship (also known as polyamory) can be one of the trickiest issues in a relationship (McLean 2004; Weitzman, chapter 17). Reassuring a monosexual mate that, although there may be others with whom you may wish to establish intimate emotional or sexual relationships, he or she is still important to you and that you are not going to run off with someone else is difficult but essential work. But for some people sharing a mate is simply impossible. Counselors can assist clients to identify and understand their needs, wants, and expectations in relationships and how to communicate them clearly. This can make a positive impact in clients' lives and help them choose partners who have compatible needs and wants. For many bisexual Latinos, the potential sense of discordance with a monosexual partner is accentuated by Latino culture, machismo, and conservative social norms. Counselors can help established couples negotiate a new understanding of their relationship that will allow greater fulfillment of both partners' hopes and dreams.

The stress of having to educate a partner and discordance with a monosexual worldview (either/or versus both/and thinking) are reasons why many bisexuals prefer to date other bisexual partners. There is an ease, a sometimes unspoken understanding of the fluidity of sexual attraction and desire, and often a greater identification with a partner's needs and wants (Firestein, chapter 7).

SEXUAL BEHAVIOR

Latino bisexual behavior has not been well studied. Muñoz-Laboy (2004) says, "Latino male bisexuality has been studied for the most part with a focus on 'men who have sex with other men' (MSM) and with little attention to sexual desire." Much of the writing on this subject to date stereotypes the bisexual Latino man as the active member of the sexual act and, for this reason, fails to account for the complexity of Latino male bisexuality. Even less is know about Latina bisexual behavior. Muñoz-Laboy says, "We have extremely limited understanding of Latino male and female bisexuality" and echoes the call of this chapter when he asserts that "we have limited understanding of the interconnection between identity, desire, and sexual practices, particularly among ethnic minorities in the United States."

In our experience, attitudes, beliefs, and cultural values regarding sex vary widely among bisexual and bi-curious Latinos. As noted earlier, acculturation influences attitudes toward sex, one's knowledge of sex and HIV- and STD-prevention comfort in sexual situations, the number of sexual partners one has, alcohol and drug use, and the use of condoms and other safer sex practices. While conservative social and religious values such as abstinence until marriage and monogamy, when practiced, tend to protect women from sexually transmitted infections, they also reinforce patriarchal views that socially sanction gender inequality and put men in control of sexual matters.

Cultural norms such as "sexual silence" (taboos around talking openly about sex), *machismo*, *marianismo*, and the power imbalance between genders often lead to sexual coercion and prevent women from negotiating for condom use with their male partners, and this may put them at risk for contracting HIV and other STDs (Sabogal et al. 1995). These same cultural factors also appear to be operating in relationships among Latino gay and bisexual men. In our HIV-prevention support group, men assuming a passive role during sexual intercourse expressed the same feelings of powerlessness, low self-esteem, and inability to negotiate safer sex practices as those often expressed by Latinas. In this situation the active partner, the dominant *macho* male, is again in control.

Although contrary to church teachings, it is not out of the norm for Latino men to have more than one sex partner. Marriage is part of the natural developmental process predetermined by Latino cultural values, so many bisexual Latinos marry and may appear to lead traditional lives, but there is a general permissiveness regarding marital infidelity in Latino culture. Falicov (1998) refers to the *casa grande* and the *casa chica* (the big house and the small house), where by the former is meant the wife and by the latter is meant the lover. This is not uncommon and is relatively accepted. It is a *macho* man's prerogative to have an *amante* or lover on the side, and this improves his standing as a true *macho*. However, when "the other woman" is a man, the status quo is challenged, as is the man's sense of masculinity, especially if the man has not always been the top[7] or has admitted any emotional attachment for the other man. When this happens, the sense of shame and disgrace for the woman and her family is much greater—not only is there marital infidelity, but homosexuality calls into question the very foundation of the relationship. The double life, although seemingly acceptable for heterosexual men, is denied to gay or bisexual men. Homophobia produces not only social scorn but may also generate outright violence. Taboos around homosexuality prevent many men who have sex with men (MSM) from openly identifying as such. The result of this combination of social and internal forces is that very often Latino MSM marry women and lead a double life. They do not carry condoms with them because to do so would be an admission to their wives that they are cheating, so they do not protect themselves with casual sex partners and don't use condoms with their wives for the same reason. Montgomery et al. (2003) contends that lack of disclosure of bisexual behavior places many Latinas at risk for acquiring HIV and other STDs. A term currently in vogue for this double life—men living a public heterosexual life while denying their secret affairs with other men—is the *down low* or *DL* (Sternberg 2001). Although "keeping it on the DL" (meaning keeping it hidden) is more commonly associated with African American communities, the term has recently been incorporated into the lingo of Latino youth in LA and other urban centers where Latino youth participate in hip hop culture.

Latinas tend to be more deliberate in their liaisons, particularly sexual liaisons, while men are more likely to engage in anonymous sexual encounters (Sabogal, Faigeles, and Catania 1993). This is facilitated by environmental factors, such as the existence of public sex venues, gay bar back rooms, adult bookstores with video booths and bathhouses for men, and the fact that no such venues exist for women. Conversely, the existence of these venues probably reflects different social and sexual expectations associated with each gender.

Sex without condoms (e.g., unprotected vaginal or anal intercourse) is the behavior that most frequently puts Latino men and women at risk for HIV infection and other STDs. Poor condom use is the common thread and the common threat that affect all Latino subpopulations. As a whole, Latinos have lower rates of condom use and higher STD rates than non-Hispanic whites (Sabogal et al. 1995). Reviews of contraceptive use by teens have found that Hispanic teens have lower condom use rates than non-Hispanic white or African American youth (Centers for Disease Control and Prevention 2002). A University of California, San Francisco/Center for AIDS Prevention Studies examination of sexual behavior and gender roles found that Hispanic men "are more likely to initiate sexual intercourse at an earlier age and have lower condom use rates than non-Hispanic Whites" and that "less acculturated Hispanic men report a younger age of first sexual intercourse and lower condom use rates than did more acculturated Hispanic men" (Sabogal et al. 1995).

As mentioned previously, one of the results of the stigma of homosexuality and *machismo* is that in Latino culture many Latino MSM do not self-identify as gay or bisexual, despite having sex with men. A recent study of HIV+ men and women in the U.S. found that only 56 percent of HIV+ Latino men who have sex with men and women self-identified as bisexual and that 10 percent of them identified as heterosexual, while only 6 percent of HIV+ Latinas reported having a bisexual partner (Montgomery et al. 2003). This phenomenon is also well documented in Mexico (Liguori, González Block, and Aggleton 1996), Costa Rica (Schifter, Madrigal, and Aggleton 1996), the Dominican Republic (DeMoya and García 1996), Peru (Cáceres 1996), and Brazil (Parker 1996), where there are many groups of men who, despite having sex with both men and women, don't feel they belong to any group other than the heterosexual majority, nor do they perceive themselves as having a different sexual orientation from the heterosexual majority. Thus prevention efforts geared toward gay and bisexual men may not reach Latino MSM who do not identify as such.

Each of these studies speaks to the complexities of bisexual sexual behavior, the difference between identity and behavior, and how culture affects and molds both identity and behavior.

ALCOHOL AND DRUG USE AMONG LATINOS

Alcohol is the drug of choice for many Latinos. There is a strong tradition of "drowning one's pain" with alcohol in Latino culture, and the culture has a high tolerance for the consumption of large quantities of alcohol and for drunkenness, especially among men. This use of alcohol carries little or no social stigma, since alcohol consumption is not considered problematic or addictive in many Latino communities.

Latino subpopulations vary in their prevalence of alcohol use and dependency as well as substance abuse and need for alcohol and drug treatment (SAMHSA 1998). Women consistently show lower rates of alcohol and drug use. Latinos of Mexican descent report higher rates of heavy alcohol use and alcohol dependency. And, although most Latino subpopulations report drinking habits less than or equal to that of non-Hispanic whites and the U.S. population as a whole (SAMHSA 1998; Caetano and Clark 1998a), Latinos report a higher incidence of alcohol-related problems than non-Hispanic whites and the U.S. population in aggregate (Caetano and Clark 1998b). Unemployment and poverty were found to be related to both frequent drinking and alcohol-related problems, and Puerto Ricans and Mexicans showed higher rates of illicit drug use, marijuana, and cocaine consumption than Latinos of Caribbean, Central American, Cuban, or South American descent, non-Hispanic whites, and the U.S. population as a whole (SAMHSA 1998).

Substance abuse and alcoholism tend to correlate with depression and emotional instability. Since many Latinos are immigrants or children of immigrants, the physical and cultural displacement and economic hardships they endure may predispose them to substance abuse as a way to ameliorate the sense of hopelessness and abandonment that many Latinos suffer. Racial segregation and cultural isolation, in combination with sexual behaviors that are not commonly understood or accepted, may predispose bisexual Latinos to abuse alcohol and other substances at a higher rate than other populations.

RESILIENCY

Although many factors come together to negatively impact the lives of bisexual Latinos, there are also several aspects of Latino life and queer identity that can act as protective factors and help bisexual Latinos become well-adjusted individuals operating across a multicultural framework. Greene (1994) reminds us that the combined effects of racism, homophobia, and heterosexism (what we previously referred to as multiple minority status) may create intense stress for members of racial or ethnic sexual minorities. Sexual minority youth may be particularly vulnerable because many first experience questions about their sexual orientation during their struggles with adolescence. Garnets and Kimmel (1993), Diaz et al. (1999), and others have related coping with stress to high-risk behaviors and have identified several protective or resiliency factors. Resilience is defined as hardiness, inner strength, the ability to thrive in the face of adversity, or the ability to face new situations with a feeling of challenge, control, and commitment. Garnets and Kimmel (1993) emphasize the importance of social networks in buffering against the negative impact of stress created by racism and heterosexism. Strong social support from family members, relationship partners and from others in the LGBT community as well as high self-esteem help fend off the negative consequences of stress resulting from stigmatization and homophobia. Diaz and Ayala (2001) and Diaz and colleagues (2001) have identified the following important resiliency factors: 1. family acceptance—experiencing acceptance from a mother or father or being able to speak openly about one's sexuality with at least one family member, 2. social and sexual satisfaction—satisfaction with friendships and lover relationships and satisfaction with one's sex life, 3. social/political networking and activism—feeling part of a social network of similar people and being involved in the promotion of LGBT and/or Latino rights, and 4. gay role models in childhood—having older gay friends or relatives to look up to as a child.

Many LGBT Latinos deal well with the many stressors they experience and live happy, productive, and fulfilled lives. For them the challenge of living in a hostile environment leads to personal growth and empowerment. There are real health and psychological benefits to coming out (Garnets and Kimmel 1993). Internalized homophobia (or internalized biphobia) contributes to stress. Self-concealment and the keeping of secrets lead to increased physical and psychological symptoms and reduce resistance to disease. Being resilient and feeling challenged but in control despite minority status can help individuals cope and even thrive under difficult circumstances and lead to better emotional and physical health.

RECOMMENDATIONS FOR COUNSELORS

Counselors need to be aware of the cultural differences among Latino subgroups, including language, gender, age, acculturation level, immigration status, family composition (both nuclear and extended), socioeconomic background, personal history, and time in the country, and take these differences into account when counseling all Latinos (Gloria and Davis-Pope 1997), including bisexual Latino clients.

In Latino culture, seeking help from a mental health professional is generally viewed as a weakness, a personal failing, and still carries a certain degree of stigma. Therefore, as is true for many ethnic minority populations, Latinos have underutilized mental services due to this stigma as well as the lack of culturally competent services for Latinos. A commonly held belief in Latino culture is that this type of "problem" is better handled within the family, under the spiritual guidance of the parish priest, or simply best left unspoken. Bisexuality (or homosexuality) is considered a moral problem, a deviant perversion, or a lack of control over an overactive sex drive. Therefore it is critically important to help clients understand their sexuality as something normal.

Counselors can serve as "information brokers," validating gay and bisexual orientations as legitimate identities and assisting clients with disclosure. Counselors can also play a valuable role by serving as "cultural translators," helping immigrant Latinos adjust to their new surroundings and begin to see themselves in a new light. It can be very helpful to explain human sexuality research to clients, validating bisexuality as a legitimate sexual orientation and helping clients understand that sexuality and sexual orientation are fluid and may change with time. These are some of the most valuable interventions a counselor can provide for bisexual Latino clients. Validation of the client's bisexual identity is the first step toward helping bisexual Latino clients move in the direction of self-acceptance.

It is also helpful to have a list of suggested readings, copies of magazine articles, and handouts available to offer clients to help them understand themselves and the issues with which they are struggling. Unfortunately, it is still difficult to find good educational materials on bisexuality in Spanish and many clients may not have sufficient language skills to absorb the information in English. A couple of good online resources include "¿Por qué mi hijo/a es gay?" www .indiana.edu/~arenal.pflagbro.html, "Hablemos de Nuestros Hijos/as" www .indiana.edu/~arenal/hablemos.html, and the "Guía de Recursos para Salir del Clóset," which can be found on the HRC Web site: www.hrc.org, along with several other useful resources; click on Coming Out, then Communities of Color, then Latinos and "En Español."

Although understanding the nuances of any language and culture is a process that may take many years and, indeed, is never complete, since language, customs, and cultural norms are constantly evolving, counselors who do not speak Spanish or who are not Latinos should not be dissuaded from working with Latino clients because of this. Nor should Latino counselors be overconfident that they share the same worldview as their Latino clients, who may come from different countries or cultures or who may embody differing degrees of acculturation. Nonetheless, in order to effectively communicate with clients, counselor and client must use a common language and counselors must keep in mind the impact of culture and acculturation on a client's command of the English language and a client's view of hirself within a cultural context. Slang, buzzwords, jargon, and colloquialisms pertaining to sexual orientation and gay culture should be avoided whenever possible (unless the client is completely fluent in English) and new words or concepts should be carefully explained. The counselor needs to solicit the client's feedback to ensure that ze has understood the new phrase or concept. No one but the client hirself can describe how the client perceives hir situation. The role of the counselor is to listen to the client and try to understand hir. The variation that the client's culture adds to their bisexual identity needs to be viewed and understood, and the perspective cultivated based on the values the client holds as true and valid.

Some acculturated bisexual Latino clients may find it easier to talk about their sexual desires to non-Latino counselors. They may potentially feel a closer connection and may perceive that they will be better understood (or less judged) by a counselor from the mainstream American culture. Therefore Latinos should not be dismissed by non-Latino counselors just because they are not from the same ethnic group. However, it is the role of counselors to become familiar with some basic values and cultural norms of Latino culture in order to be culturally competent, and, while they should not assume that all Latino clients will have those exact values, an understanding of this value matrix does provide a useful frame of reference.

Religion and spirituality are also important aspects of many Latino clients' culture and individual lives (Burke, Chauvin, and Miranti 2005; Baruth and Manning 2003; Sue and Sue 2003). Counselors should be aware that clients may regard faith and spiritual traditions, maybe even superstition, as important and relevant in their lives (Miller and House 2005; Ponterotto et al. 1995, 2001; Arredondo 1999). Counselors should be aware that there is also a great diversity of beliefs among Latinos of faith. Mendieta (2000) notes, "There are Catholic Hispanic as well as Protestants, Jewish, Muslim, syncretist, and post-Christian Hispanic" (p. 49) and varying degrees in the practice of these and many other faiths. Santiago-Rivera, Arredondo, and Gallardo-Cooper (2002) remind us that including a spiritual framework as part of the counseling intervention may enhance the family's ability to cope with adversity. This may also hold true for some bisexual Latino clients. By the same token, the counselor should be careful not to impose prejudices and views on this matter onto bisexual Latino clients, but be aware of its possible importance and influence and integrate religious and spiritual considerations into counseling when appropriate.

More information on acculturation, a central variable when counseling Latinos (Padilla 1980), and measures of acculturation can be easily found through a quick Web search. Most Internet search engines will produce good results using keywords such as "Hispanic" or "Latino" and "acculturation." Some recent reviews of the literature on this subject in peer-reviewed journals and scholarly publications include articles by Rogler, Cortes, and Malgady (1991), Marín and Marín (1991), Zambrana (1995), Moya (2000), Sanderson (2004), Lara et al. (2005). Journals, such as the *Journal of Hispanic Behavioral Sciences*, are beginning to explore topics of sexuality in ethnic minorities, and counselors should be aware of current publications so as to build their practice on empirical, theoretical, scientific, and emerging philosophical perspectives.

For counselors wishing to expand their understanding of Latinos and multicultural counseling issues, we recommend *Counseling Latinos and la familia: A Practical Guide* by Azara Santiago-Rivera, Patricia Arredondo, and Maritza Gallardo-Cooper (2002). This book provides a good review of the different Latino subpopulations found in the U.S. and the historical, sociopolitical, and economic factors that brought them here. It discusses cultural and socioeconomic differences among groups, acculturation, commonly held Latino cultural concepts and values and includes a useful glossary of Spanish words counselors working with Latino clients are likely to encounter. The book also provides an in-depth discussion of the effects of social and cultural norms and oppression on family and family dynamics and makes the point that counseling for Latinos must include their families as an essential part of any intervention. Interestingly, however, the book fails to even mention sexual orientation as a possible source of conflict. We also recommend *Latino Families in Therapy: A Guide to Multicultural Practice* by Celia Jaes Falicov (1998). A groundbreaking text that provides a good understanding of Latinos as a multicultural group, Falicov's book discusses Latino values that contrast with mainstream American cultural values in a manner relevant for all mental health professionals.

As noted, the immigration experience, time in the country, level of acculturation, socioeconomic background, physical appearance, and command of English play pivotal roles in the understanding of bisexuality and the bisexual identity of Latinos. It is important to take into consideration the client's family, those present with hir in the country, and those in their home countries. Latino families are an extended source of support for Latino immigrants and may be crucial if clients are to develop a healthy bisexual identity. Thus the needs of the sexual minority client's family members should also be taken into consideration when providing counseling services to Latino bisexual clients.

Very little has been written about bisexual Latinos, so counselors may feel frustrated by the lack of information available at this time. Counselors should keep in mind that Latinos are themselves a multicultural group; although they share many values and similar backgrounds, their individual experiences are unique, and even within Latino subgroups significant differences may exist (Falicov

1998; Gloria 2000; Ponterotto et al. (1995, 2001); Santiago-Rivera, Arrendondo, and Gallardo-Cooper 2002; Zapata 1995). It is the bisexual client as a Latino hirself who can best inform the counselor who ze is emotionally and psychologically, and how ze as a Latino is experiencing hir present condition. We invite more qualitative and quantitative research to better understand and serve Latino clients who are bisexual or who are experiencing attraction for, or having relationships with, individuals of more than one gender.

Researchers must keep in mind that Latinos' gender, race, socioeconomic background, countries of origin, time in the country, and reasons for immigrating impact and shape the Latino experience. Where Latinos are living, how many other Latinos of similar cultures live in close proximity, and the ease of travel to and from other Latino cultures all result in the building of different communities that will also shape Latinidades[8] (Oboler 1995, 2000; Aparicio and Chavéz-Silverman 1997) and how accepting of bisexual identity these communities will be. All these factors need to be considered and taken into account when doing research with bisexual Latinos in order to build a reliable and holistic understanding of the bisexual Latino experience within each Latino subgroup (Arredondo and Arciniega 2001; Arredondo 1999; Arredondo et al. 1996; Arredondo and Glauner 1992).

When it comes to counseling bisexual Latinos, one size does not fit all—not all Latinos will be at the same level of acceptance or will experience their bisexual identity in the same fashion. In order to work effectively with bisexual Latinos and their families, counselors will have to cultivate the *art of counseling*; because it is in their differences that Latino clients find validation, their personal identities and the internal resources to make sense of their multicultural and sexual identities.

NOTES

1. Throughout this text the authors will use the gender-neutral pronouns *ze* and *hir* rather than the more awkward *he/she, him/her,* or *his/her.* This gender-neutral construction has gained popularity among transgender activists and is rapidly being adopted by other queer activists and health advocates throughout the U.S.
2. A term created by the Office of Management and Budget in 1978 to denote "a person of Mexican, Puerto Rican, Cuban, Central or South American, or other Spanish culture" (Marín and Marín 1991). Although *Hispanic* and *Latino* are used interchangeably in much of social science literature in this text we will use *Latino* unless we are specifically referring to the census bureau category.
3. Used throughout the text to mean lesbian, gay, bisexual, and/or transgender.
4. In Spanish *varón* is the term usually used for human males, while *macho* is generally reserved for livestock. This distinction, however, does not exist for females where both human and animal are referred to as *hembra.*
5. Referring to their personal struggle in coming to terms with their sexual orientation.

6. *Tío*: uncle; *Tía*: aunt.
7. Active sexual partner, as opposed to the "bottom," the receiving or passive sexual partner.
8. A postmodern term that refers to a hybridized or multiethnic Latino identity that does not exist in practical terms. It expresses the transnational amalgamations and cultural formations that result in multiethnic Latino groups having contact with each other due to immigration and settlement patterns.

REFERENCES

Alcoff, L. M. (2000). Is Latina/o a racial identity? In J. E. Gracia and P. de Greiff (Eds.), *Hispanics/Latinos in the United States: Ethnicity, race, and rights* (pp. 23–44). New York: Routledge.

Aparicio, F., and Chávez-Silverman, S. (Eds.) (1997). *Tropicalizations: Transcultural representations of Latinidad.* Lebanon, NH: University Press of New England.

Arredondo, P. (1999). Multicultural Counseling Competencies as tools to address oppression and racism. *Journal of Counseling and Development*, 77(1), 102–108.

Arredondo, P., and Arciniega, G. M. (2001). Strategies and techniques for counselor training based on the Multicultural Counseling Competencies. *Journal of Multicultural Counseling and Development*, 29 (4), 263–273.

Arredondo, P., and Glauner, T. (1992). *Personal dimensions of identity model.* Boston: Empowerment Workshops.

Arredondo, P., Toporek, R., Brown, Sanchez, J., Locke, D. C., Sanchez, J., and Stadler, H. (1996). Operationalization of the Multicultural Counseling Competencies. *Journal of Multicultural Counseling and Development*, 24(1), 42–78.

Baruth, L. G., and Manning. M. L. (2003). *Multicultural counseling and psychotherapy. A lifespan perspective* (3d ed.). Upper Saddle River, NJ: Pearson.

Burke, M. T., Chauvin, J. C., and Miranti, J. (2005). *Religious spiritual issues in counseling applications across diverse populations.* New York: Brunner-Routledge.

Buxton, A. P. (2001). Writing our own script: How bisexual men and their heterosexual wives maintain their marriages after disclosure. In B. Beemyn and E. Steinman (Eds.), *Bisexuality in the life of men: Facts and fiction* (pp. 157–189). Binghamton, NY: Harrington.

Cáceres, C. F. (1996). Male bisexuality in Peru and the prevention of AIDS. In P. Aggleton (Ed.), *Bisexualities and AIDS: International perspectives* (pp. 136–147). Bristol: Taylor and Francis.

Caetano, R., and Clark, C. L. (1998a) Trends in alcohol consumption patterns among whites, blacks, and Hispanics: 1984 and 1995. *Journal of Studies on Alcohol*, 59, 659–668.

Caetano, R., and Clark, C. L. (1998b) Trends in alcohol-related problems among whites, blacks, and Hispanics, 1984–1995. *Alcoholism: Clinical and Experimental Research*, 22, 534–538.

Casas, J. M., and Pytluk (1995). Hispanic Identity Development: implications for research and practice. In J. G. Ponterotto, J. M. Casas, L. A. Suzuki, and C. M. Alexander (Eds.), *Handbook of Multicultural Counseling* (pp. 155–180). Thousand Oaks, CA: Sage.

Centers for Disease Control and Prevention (2002). Youth risk behavior surveillance: United States, 2001. *Morbidity and Mortality Weekly Report, 51* (SS-4).

DeMoya, E. A., and García, R. (1996). AIDS and the enigma of bisexuality in the Dominican Republic. In P. Aggleton (Ed.), *Bisexualities and AIDS: International perspectives* (pp. 121–135). Bristol: Taylor and Francis.

Diaz, R. M., and Ayala, G. (2001). *Social discrimination and health: the case of Latino gay men and HIV risk.* Policy Institute of the National Gay and Lesbian Task Force.

Diaz, R. M., Ayala, G., Bein, E., Henne, J., and Marín, B. V. (2001). The impact of homophobia, poverty, and racism on the mental health of gay and bisexual men: Findings from three U.S. cities. *American Journal of Public Health, 91,* 927–932.

Diaz, R. M., Morales, E. S., Bein, E., Dilán, E., and Rodriguez, R. A. (1999). Predictors of sexual risk in Latino gay/bisexual men: The role of demographic, developmental, social cognitive, and behavioral variables. *Hispanic Journal of Behavioral Sciences, 21*(4), 480–501.

Falicov, C. J. (1998). *Latino families in therapy.* New York: Guilford.

García, E. (2001). *Hispanic education in the United States: Raices y Alas.* Lanham, MD: Rowman and Littlefield.

Garnets, L. D., and Kimmel, D. L. (1993). Introduction: Lesbian and gay male dimensions in psychological study of human diversity. In L. D. Garnets and D. L. Kimmel (Eds.), *Psychological perspectives on lesbian and gay male experiences* (pp. 1–51). New York: Columbia University Press.

Gloria, A. M. (2000). Counseling Latino university students: Psychosociocultural issues for consideration. *Journal of Counseling and Development, 78,* 145–154.

Gloria, A. M., and Pope-Davis, D. B. (1997). Cultural ambience: The importance of a culturally aware environment in the training and education of counselors. In D. B. Pope-Davis and H. L. K. Coleman (Eds.), *Multicultural counseling competencies: Assessment, education and training, and supervision* (pp. 242–259). Thousand Oaks, CA: Sage.

Gómez, C. A., and Marín, B. V. (1996). Gender, culture and power: Barriers to HIV prevention strategies for women. *Journal of Sex Research, 33*(4), 355–362.

Greene, B. (1994). Ethnic-minority lesbian and gay men: Mental health treatment issues. *Journal of Consulting and Clinical Psychology, 62,* 243–251.

Greger, I., and Ponterotto, J. G. (1995). A framework for assessment in multicultural counseling. In J. G. Ponterotto, J. M. Casas, L. A. Suzuki, and C. M. Alexander (Eds.), *Handbook of Multicultural Counseling* (pp. 357–374). Thousand Oaks, CA: Sage.

Ibrahim, F. A., Oshnishi, H., and Wilson, R. P. (1994). Career assessment in a culturally diverse society. *Journal of Career Assessment, 2,* 276–288.

Lara, M., Gamboa, K., Morales, L. S., and Hayes Bautista, D. E. (2005). Acculturation and Latino health in the United States: A review of the literature and its sociopolitical context. *Annual Reviews of Public Health, 26,* 367–397.

Liguori, A. L., González Block, M., and Aggleton, P. (1996). Bisexuality and AIDS in Mexico. In P. Aggleton (Ed.), *Bisexualities and AIDS: International Perspectives* (pp. 76–98). Bristol: Taylor and Francis.

McLean, K. (2004). Negotiating (non)monogamy: Bisexuality and intimate relationships. *Journal of Bisexuality, 4*(1/2), 83–97.

Marín, B. V., Gómez, C. A., and Tschann, J. (1998). Self-efficacy to condom use in unmarried Latino adults. *Journal of Community Psychology, 26* (1), 53–71.

Marín, B. V ., Gómez, C. A., Tschann, J., and Gregorich, S. (1997). Condom use in unmarried Latino adults: Test of a cultural theory. *Health Psychology*, 16 (5), 458–467.

Marín, G., and Marín, B. V. (1991). *Research with Hispanic populations*. Newbury Park, CA: Sage.

Marotta, S. A., and García, J. G. (2003). Latinos in the United States in 2000. *Hispanic Journal of Behavioral Sciences*, 25(1), 13–34.

Mendieta, E. (2000). The making of new peoples: Hispanizing race. In J. E. Gracia and P. De Greiff (Eds.), *Hispanics/Latinos in the United States: Ethnicity, race, and rights* (pp. 45–59). New York: Routledge.

Miller, J. L., and House, R. M. (2005). Counseling gay, lesbian, and bisexual clients. In D. Capuzzi and D. R. Gross (Eds.), *Introduction to the Counseling Profession* (4th ed., pp. 480–464). Boston: Allyn and Bacon.

Montgomery, J. P., Mokotoff, E. D., Gentry, A. C., and Blair, J. M. (2003). The extent of bisexual behavior in HIV-infected men and implications for transmission to their female sex partners. *AIDS Care*, 15(6) 829–837.

Moore, J., and Pachon, H. (1985). *Hispanics in the United States*. Englewood Cliffs, NJ: Prentice-Hall.

Moya, P. M. (2000). Cultural particularity versus universal humanity: The value of being asimilao. In J. E. Gracia and P. de Greiff (Eds.), *Hispanics/Latinos in the United States: Ethnicity, race, and rights* (pp. 78–97). New York: Routledge.

Muñoz-Laboy, M. (2004). Beyond MSM: Sexual desire among bisexually active Latino men in New York City. *Sexualities*, 7(1), 55–80.

Nieto, S. (2004). *Affirming diversity: The sociopolitical context of multicultural education* (4th ed.). Boston: Allyn and Bacon.

Oboler, S. (1995). *Ethnic labels, Latino lives: Identity and the politics of (re)presentation in the United States*. Minneapolis: University of Minnesota Press.

Oboler, S. (2000). "IT MUST BE FAKE": Racial ideologies, identities, and the question of rights. In J. E. Gracia and P. de Greiff (Eds.), *Hispanics/Latinos in the United States. Ethnicity, race, and rights* (pp. 125–144). New York: Routledge.

Oetting, E. R., and Beauvais, F. (1991). Orthogonal cultural identification theory: The cultural identification of minority adolescents. *International Journal of the Addictions* 25, 655–685.

Ortega, R. M., José, C., Zuñiga, X., and Gutiérrez, L. (1995). Latinos in the United States: A framework for teaching. In D. Schoem, L. Frankel, Zuñiga, X., and Lewis, E. A. (Eds.), *Multicultural teaching in the university* (pp. 51–60). Westport, CT: Greenwood.

Padilla, A. M. (1980). *Acculturation: Theory, models, and some new findings*. Boulder: Westview.

Parker, R. G. (1996). Bisexuality and HIV/AIDS in Brazil. In P. Aggleton (Ed.), *Bisexualities and AIDS: International perspectives* (pp. 148–160). Bristol: Taylor and Francis.

Ponterotto, J., Casas, J. M. Suzuki, L. A., and Alexander, C. M. (1995). *Handbook of multicultural counseling*. Thousand Oaks, CA: Sage.

Ponterotto, J. G., Casas, J. M., Suzuki, L. A., and Alexander, C. M. (Eds.) (2001). *Handbook of multicultural counseling* (2d ed.). Thousand Oaks, CA: Sage.

Ramos, B. (2005). Acculturation and depression among Puerto Ricans in the mainland. *Social Work Research*(2)29, 95–105.

Robinson, L. T. (2005). The convergence of race, ethnicity, and gender: Multiple identities in counseling (2d ed.). Upper Saddle River, NJ: Pearson.

Rogler, L. H., Cortes, D. E., and Malgady, R. G. (1991). Acculturation and mental health status among Hispanics: Convergence and new directions for research. *American Psychologist*, 46, 585–597.

Sabogal, F., Faigeles, B., and Catania, J. A. (1993). Multiple sexual partners among Hispanics in high-risk cities. *Family Planning Perspectives*, 25(6) 257–262.

Sabogal, F., Pérez-Stable, E. J., Otero-Sabogal, R., and Hiatt, R. A. (1995). Ethnic, gender, and acculturative differences in sexual behaviors: Hispanic and non-Hispanic white adults. *Hispanic Journal of Behavioral Sciences*, 17, 139–59.

Sanderson, M. (2004). Acculturation, ethnic identity, and dating violence among Latino ninth-grade students. *Preventive Medicine*, 39 (2), 373–383.

Santiago-Rivera, A. L., Arredondo, P., and Gallardo-Cooper, M. (2002). *Counseling Latinos and la familia: a practical guide*. Thousand Oaks, CA: Sage.

Schifter, J., Madrigal, J., and Aggleton, P. (1996). Bisexual communities and culture in Costa Rica. In P. Aggleton (Ed.), *Bisexualities and AIDS: International perspectives* (pp. 99–120). Bristol: Taylor and Francis.

Schuttle, O. (2000). Negotiating Latina identities. In J. E. Gracia and P. de Greiff (Eds.), *Hispanics/Latinos in the United States: Ethnicity, race, and rights* (pp. 61–75). New York: Routledge.

SAMHSA (Substance Abuse and Mental Health Services Administration). (1998). Prevalence of substance use among racial and ethnic subgroups in the United States, 1991–1993. Office of Applied Studies, Analytic Series H–6, DHHS Publication No. 1994. SMA 98–3204. Rockville, MD.

Sue, W. D., and Sue, D. (2003). *Counseling the culturally diverse. Theory and practice* (4th ed.). New York: Wiley.

Sternberg, S. (2001). The danger of living "down low": Black men who hide their bisexuality can put women at risk. *USA Today* (March 15), D1-D2.

Trueba, E. T. (1999). *Latinos Unidos, from cultural diversity to the politics of solidarity*. Lanham, MD: Rowman and Littlefield.

Zambrana, R. E. (1995). *Understanding Latino families: Scholarship, policy and practice*. Thousand Oaks, CA: Sage.

Zapata, J. T. (1995). Counseling Hispanic children and youth. In C. Lee (Ed.), *Counseling for diversity: A guide for school counselors and related professionals* (pp. 85–108). Needham Heights, MA: Allyn and Bacon.

14

TRANSGENDER IDENTITIES AND BISEXUAL EXPRESSION

IMPLICATIONS FOR COUNSELORS

Dallas Denny

TRANSGENDERED PEOPLE have long suffered from popular and scientific misunderstandings and reductionistic assumptions about their sexuality. Much of this confusion has centered around their perceived sexual orientation.

Because access to medical treatment has often been limited to those having a "correct" (i.e., heterosexual) sexual orientation after sex reassignment, transsexuals have been most directly affected. In 1974 an article in *Archives of Sexual Behavior* reported on the "apparent" heterosexuality of two male individuals seeking sex reassignment (Barr, Raphael, and Hennessey 1974). The authors were skeptical about the purported sexual orientation of the individuals involved, but found their sensibilities challenged—so much so, in fact, that they generated the journal article to raise the consciousness of their peers: "This case . . . makes it clear that a request for SRS is not invariably associated with a homosexual orientation" (p. 330).

Female-to-male transsexuals endured similar misconceptions. There was considered to be but one "type" of FTM—a masculine female with an exclusive sexual interest in women: "All transsexual biological females are homosexual in erotic object choice, and all of them wish to have a penis" (Steiner 1985:353). Pauly (1992) has described the difficulties of FTM Lou Sullivan, who, because he identified as a gay man, had difficulty obtaining needed medical procedures in the 1980s (see also Sullivan 1989). Sullivan died of AIDS in 1991.

The assumption of the day was, of course, that all male-to-female transsexuals were sexually attracted to males; likewise, all female-to-male transsexuals were believed and expected to be sexually attracted to females. This conviction was so strong among professionals that heterosexually identified individuals who sought sex reassignment were often diagnosed as nontranssexual and denied treatment (Abel 1979; Denny 1992; Dixen et al. 1984; Newman and Stoller 1974). This was still happening in some treatment settings in the 1990s (Petersen and Dickey 1995) and is no doubt still occurring. Some clinicians still cling to the naive and outdated notion that transsexualism is a form of repressed homosexuality and transsexuals are gay men or lesbians who cannot accept their sexual orientation (cf. Fagan, Schmidt, and Wise 1994). Similar simplistic presumptions color the autogyne-philia theory of Ray Blanchard and his proponents (Bailey 2002; Blanchard 1989a; Lawrence 1998) and are codified in the *Diagnostic and Statistical Manual of Mental Disorders* of the American Psychiatric Association (APA 2000).

Belief in the universal homosexuality of transsexuals and other transgen-dered persons dates to the work of the early sexologists, who conflated sexual orientation and gender variance, in particular Krafft-Ebing (1894) and Ulrichs. Ulrichs, writing at the close of the nineteenth century (his work was not trans-lated into English until 1994), believed homosexuality was caused by a "con-trary sexual feeling," a feminine or masculine spirit that did not match the body. Ellis (1906) believed this sexual inversion was a sign of latent bisexuality:

> The "invert" was part male, part female, or rather part "masculine" and part "femi-nine." The male invert's "feminine" side desired men; the female invert's "mascu-line" side desired women. Thus human sexuality could still be imagined accord-ing to a heterosexual model. It was "bisexuality" that produced homosexuality. Indeed, the two terms were often used as virtual equivalents. (Garber 1995:239)

It was not until around the time of the Stonewall riots (in 1969; see Duberman 1993), that gay identities and gender variance began to be differentiated in the public consciousness. Before that time, male homosexuals were typically characterized and popularly depicted as effeminate men and lesbians as mascu-line women. Masculine men and feminine women who had sex with gender-nonconforming homosexuals were generally not considered homosexual. In some parts of the world even today—particularly in the Middle East and Latin America—masculine, male-identified men who have sex with feminine, often crossdressing males are not considered gay, although their partners are (cf. Kulick 1998). In contrast, in contemporary Western culture the typical gay male couple is comprised of two masculine, male-identified men. The lesbian community has once again begun to embrace butch identities (cf. Burana, Roxxie, and Due 1994), but most lesbians identify unambiguously as women and female.

In 1952 intense media coverage of Christine Jorgensen's sex reassignment catapulted the as-yet unnamed phenomenon of transsexualism into public con-sciousness (cf. Ex-GI becomes blonde beauty). An immediate result of the pub-licity surrounding Jorgensen was a deluge of frantic requests from men and women wanting sex reassignment procedures (Hamburger 1953). It was in response to this demand, and to the intense anguish that characterized the phe-nomenon that would soon be named transsexualism (Benjamin 1966), that the treatment system typified by Barr and colleagues evolved.

The first real challenge to the orthodoxy of universal homosexual orientation in gender-variant individuals came from an unlikely source—a forming community of male crossdressers with heterosexual identities. Charles (later Virginia) Prince published widely on the heterosexuality of crossdressers, both in her own journal, *Transvestia*, and with P. M. Bentler in a variety of professional journals (cf. Bentler and Prince 1969; Prince 1957; Prince and Bentler 1972). Bentler and Prince convincingly demonstrated the heterosexuality of the majority of their sample of male crossdressers. Their data were the first to challenge the popular notion that gender-variant persons were invariably homosexual.[1]

By the 1970s clinicians had begun to recognize not only that some male-to-female transsexuals were attracted to the opposite biological sex but also to identify two clinically distinct subsets of male-to-female transsexuals. One group tended to be younger, more feminine in appearance and behavior, and sexually attracted to men (Person and Ovesey 1974a). Those in the second group tended to present for treatment later in life, had more difficulty in passing as female, and were attracted to women (Person and Ovesey 1974b). Other authors made similar distinctions (cf. Freund et al. 1974). These clinical subtypes came to be called, respectively, primary and secondary transsexuals. The primary differentiating characteristic was considered to be sexual orientation.

Unfortunately, clinicians continued to regard all female-to-male transsexuals as all "of a type," despite a flourishing and highly visible culture of gay- and bisexual-identified FTMs. This did not begin to change until Devor (1993a) introduced a taxonomy of gender variance in natal females. Researchers began to take note of the sexual orientation of their transsexual clients and sometimes kept demographic information (cf. Dixen et al. 1984; Pauly 1992; Sörensen and Hertoft 1980), but although these workers sometimes demonstrated sexual attractions of transsexuals to both males and females, they did not explore bisexual identities.[2] The literature has been and continues to be largely silent on the issue of bisexual identities in gender-variant people.

BISEXUALITY IN TRANSSEXUAL AND OTHER TRANSGENDERED PERSONS: WHAT DOES THE LITERATURE SAY?

Denny and Green (1996) have reviewed the existing literature on bisexuality in gender-variant persons. Here, I extend their review.

Any number of transsexuals and other transgendered persons have publicly identified themselves as bisexual and explored just what that signifies. In 1973 the late cartoonist Vaughn Bodé appeared on the front and back covers of the comic *Schizophrenia/Cheech Wizard* in photographs, crossdressed; inside, the character that represents Bodé declares himself/herself "auto-sexual, heterosexual, homosexual, masso-sexual, sado-sexual, trans-sexual, uni-sexual, omnisexual" and cries, "Mama, you made me a transvestite!" Transgendered and transsexual people who identify as bisexual have contributed significantly to the now-out-of-publication bisexual magazine *Anything That Moves* (cf. Franek 1998; Lano 1998; and Valerio 1998) and have elsewhere written chapters and articles illustrating their bisexual identities and experiences. In an edited volume Alexander and Yescavage (2004a) have summarized and provided quotations from some of these works, most notably essays by Hemmings (2002) and Martin-Damon (1995). Alexander and Yescavage's book includes additional essays and explorations on what they term "the interSEXion of bisexuality and transgenderism" (cf. Alexander 2004; Chase 2004). At last the convergence of sexual orientation and gender identity is producing discourse.

Although some clinicians have long recognized the complexities of sexual orientation in gender-variant persons (cf. Bockting 1987; Coleman, Bockting, and Gooren1993; Pauly 1989, 1992), the psychomedical literature has for the most part viewed transgender sexuality in simplistic ways—sometimes to the point of deliberate obtuseness. As late as 1997 one prominent clinician with whom I was collaborating refused to acknowledge the existence of female cross-dressers, even though I referred him to articles *by* self-identified female cross-dressers. I find it ironic but in retrospect hardly surprising that the seeds that would lead to a transgender paradigm shift in the 1990s were sowed not by clinicians but by anthropologists and sociologists (Kessler and McKenna 1978; Bolin 1988; and Devor 1989). Clinicians were for the most part too bound up in their work to gain perspective (Denny 1993).

In the psychomedical literature there are two early case reports of bisexual identity in gender-variant persons (Stoller and Newman 1971; W. L. 1956). The former is in a professional journal and concerns transsexuals, the latter is a chapter in a pseudo-scientific popular press book by D. O. Cauldwell and concerns a transvestite. The first real data on bisexuality in transsexuals, however, came not from a clinician but from an anthropologist. Bolin (1988) studied a group of male-to-female transsexuals in the Midwest:

> Of [Bolin's] seventeen subjects who provided data on sexual orientation, one reported being exclusively heterosexual, one reported being heterosexual by preference but open to bisexuality, one was bisexual but preferred males, six were bisexual, six were exclusively lesbian, one reported a lesbian preference but was open to bisexuality, and one did not know her preference. Sexual preferences were reported according to the subjects' roles as women; thus a heterosexual relationship was a relationship with a man. (Denny and Green 1996:93)

Bolin (1988) noted the challenge this diversity of sexual orientation placed on clinicians:

> The assumption behind the conception of transsexual heterosexuality is that if one wants to be a woman then the only appropriate sexual object choice is male.

One vignette of a caretaker-client interaction is illuminating in this respect. Tanya, a preoperative transsexual, saw a psychiatrist as part of an agency employment requirement. Because in this situation the psychiatrist was not going to conduct her psychological evaluation, Tanya, a bisexual, discussed a recent lesbian encounter and her openness to a lesbian relationship postoperatively. The psychiatrist was incredulous. He asked, "Why do you want to go through all the pain of surgery if you are going to be with a female lover?" (p. 62)

Weinberg, Williams, and Pryor (1994) described eleven male-to-female transsexuals, eight of whom identified as bisexual:

Most of the transsexuals . . . still defined themselves as "bisexual" (eight of the eleven). They did not necessarily *behave* "bisexually" though, as only three of these eight reported having had sex with both male and female partners in the last year. And all of these three worked as prostitutes. Of the remaining eight transsexuals, five had *only* male partners in the last twelve months and three had *only* female partners. Overall, more of the transsexuals reported a decrease in the number of sexual partners they had compared to five years ago. Seven of the eleven reported fewer male partners than five years ago, one more, and three the same. Six of the eleven reported fewer female partners than five years ago, three more, and two the same. About half of them had had no partners at all in the last year. (p. 235)

Devor (1993b) published data on the sexual orientation and identities of forty-five FTM transsexuals: "While all but one of the participants in Devor's study reported having been attracted to women, more than half of them were also attracted to men at various times in their lives. Devor reported a 275 percent increase in the number of post-transition participants who began to find themselves sexually attracted to men" (Denny and Green 1996:94). Devor found that the sexual attractions of FTMs to other men often did not develop until years after their transitions (see also Devor 1997).

Blanchard (1989b) believed bisexual individuals with gender dysphoria to be basically heterosexual. Blanchard has written:

The comments of previous clinical observers suggest that markedly bisexual gender dysphorics are basically heterosexual; that their "homosexual" interests are qualitatively different from, and discontinuous with those of preferential homosexuals, and that this homosexual behavior is in fact much more closely related to fetishistic cross-dressing (Benjamin 1967; Freund 1985; Person and Ovesey 1975b, 1986). Benjamin (1967), for example, found gender-dysphoric transvestites to be "bisexual but generally on a low psychosexual level—they are heterosexual in their male role, but can temporarily respond homosexually when they are [cross-] dressed" (p. 109). (p. 321)

Person and Ovesey (1978), who, like Benjamin, regarded the basic sexual orientation of transvestites as heterosexual, also remarked that some of their transvestic patients on occasion enjoyed homosexual practices, but only when dressed as women. They pointed out that such interactions . . . are regarded by the transvestite as heterosexual acts in which he is the "woman." Person and Ovesey concluded that "although the sexual practices may occasionally be ana-tomically homosexual, neither the conscious or unconscious memory appears to be homosexual" (p. 318). Blanchard's theory of autogynephilia extends this same unproven assumption of basic heterosexuality to male-to-female transsex-ualism; according to the theory, sexual arousal at the image of themselves as being female or having female body parts fuels the gender dysphoria of MTF transsexuals who are primarily attracted to women (Blanchard 1989a).

TRANSGENDER SEXUAL ORIENTATION TODAY

In the 1990s a richer and more complex view of transgender sexuality began to emerge. As the transgender community came to embrace its diversity and move beyond the stigmatizing terms and identities bestowed by medical professionals, gender-variant people gave new interpretations to their experiences and coined new terms to describe themselves. One such term was *transgender*, a word that evolved from *transgenderist*, which was coined by Prince in the 1970s to refer to someone who, like herself, lived full-time in the non-natal gender role without surgical modification of the genitals. By 1991, *transgender* was being used as an umbrella term to refer to all gender-variant people (Boswell 1991); by 1993 or 1994, it could be found in mainstream publications. It has now largely replaced the terms *crossdresser, transvestite,* and *transsexual.*

Of course those identities still exist (and some transsexuals don't consider themselves in any sense transgendered), but gender-variant persons now find themselves free to move beyond labels and take on individual or even idiosyn-cratic gendered presentations and identities (Bolin 1994). In 1994 Jan Roberts and I surveyed 340 transgendered men and women about the Standards of Care of the Harry Benjamin International Gender Dysphoria Association, Inc. (Denny and Roberts 1997). By including an "other" category in the demo-graphic question about self-identity, we obtained a total of 44 different self-identities, ranging from the traditional *transsexual* and *crossdresser* to identities such as *metamorph, man wanting to live with breasts, crossdresser/sissy,* and *con-firmed correct gender.*

With the freedom to choose among manifold gender identities, create new identities, or eschew labels altogether, transgendered and transsexual people have begun to view their sexual orientation in more complex ways. Some heterosexual crossdressers, for example, consider themselves *male lesbians* — a term fraught with political implications for feminists. Levels of homophobia and denial of sexual attraction to the non-natal sex, once endemic in the crossdressing community, have decreased greatly, but still exist in some support organizations in the form of exclusionary membership policies (no gays, no transsexuals), even while many of the members engage in same-sex sexual play with one another. Similarly, some individuals who might have earlier identified as transsexual now consider themselves a third sex or as a member of both sexes or as having an essential transgender nature: "Applied to sexuality, one transgendered individual stated to me: 'My sexuality is a transgender sexuality, different from both male and female sexuality.' . . . This illustrates the contribution of social construction to one's identity and sexuality" (Bockting 1997:51).

It is commonly said in the transgender community that one must figure out who one is before one can figure out one's sexual orientation. This is certainly true, but this aphorism refers to the label rather than the individual's sexual attractions. Most transgendered and transsexual persons are not, as some have claimed, "gender confused" (Smith 2002). We know *exactly* who we are, and many of us are well aware of and comfortable with our sexual attractions. From our vantage point, it seems that the confusion lies in a society that cannot deal with gender variance — not us.

Still, transgendered people have much to sort out with regard to sexuality. This is especially true for transsexuals, as transitioning one's gender role calls sexual orientation into question in the most fundamental ways:

> Any discussion of transsexual sexuality is bound to be very confusing and, we would argue, ultimately very instructive about the nature of sexuality in general, and especially of bisexuality. Should homosexuality be considered in relation to the individual's natal sex, or their new role? Is a transsexual woman who is still fulfilling the role of husband in a marriage in a lesbian relationship? Certainly, it does not seem so to the world, which sees a heterosexual relationship. And yet five years later, when the individual has transitioned into the woman's role, the same couple, if publicly affectionate, will be perceived as lesbian. What of a post-transition nonoperative transsexual woman in a sexual relationship with a male? The public sees a heterosexual couple, and yet, in the bedroom, their genitals match. Should their sexual act be considered heterosexual or homosexual? Does it matter if the feminized partner does or does not take the active role in intercourse? And what if the same individual then has surgery and finds a female partner? Is this relationship homosexual or heterosexual? Finally, what if a nonoperative transsexual man has as a partner a post-operative transsexual man? Is this a

gay relationship? A straight one? Are any of these people bisexual? And most significantly, can the term bisexuality have any meaning at all when gender is deconstructed? (Denny and Green 1996:88–89)

Martin-Damon (1995) makes this poignantly personal:

If asked, I say I am bisexual. If I were to say I am gay or straight, it would in
some sense be a lie, even if I choose to identity either way for the rest of my life.
Similarly, I am both genders and neither. As one FTM said. . . . , "I never knew
what it was like to be a woman, even though I gave birth to six children. But I
also don't know what it's like to be a man." (Quoted in Alexander and Yescavage
2004:247–248)

Today, at the midpoint of the first decade of the twenty-first century, transgender sexuality is complex and fluid—and understudied. Gender-variant people are free to choose from a variety of gender identities and many are exploring
not only their sexual attractions, but other aspects of their sexuality, including
fetishism, BDSM, and other varieties of eroticism.

ISSUES FOR THE THERAPIST

Transgendered and transsexual persons seek therapy for any number of reasons
that might also bring nontransgendered individuals to the therapist—grief, loss
of job, substance abuse, depression, problems with their relationships, or any of
the hundreds of psychiatric disorders listed in the DSM—but common reasons
for entering therapy are to sort out and find help for their feelings of gender
dysphoria, or to deal with problems caused by acting on those feelings, or to get
help with relationship problems caused by their transgender feelings or behavior. They may be natal males or natal females, young or old, black, white, or
Asian, married or single, rich or impoverished, fat or thin, transitioned or non-
transitioned, passable or nonpassable, attracted to males or to females or to both
or to neither. Moreover, they will vary in the ways in which they define themselves and in just what they wish to accomplish. Some will embrace their transgender feelings and some will fight them. Some will come into therapy with
clear ideas about what they want to do with their bodies and their lives and some
will be undecided or ambivalent. Some will be well-informed about their life
options, others uninformed. Some may want help with transition, some may
want support for their decision to remain in their natal gender. Some may be
racked with religious or other guilt, some will be free from shame.
    There is a particularly practical reason for transsexuals to consult a therapist:
access to medical treatment, particularly to hormonal therapy and genital sex
reassignment surgery, requires letters of authorization from one (in the case of

hormones) or two (in the case of genital surgery) mental health professionals. These requirements are built into the Standards of Care of the Harry Benjamin International Gender Dysphoria Association, Inc.

While I am convinced the HBIGDA standards safeguard transsexuals by preventing them from making hasty decisions they might later regret (there is, sadly, after twenty-five years of the Standards still no data to substantiate this), they present a considerable obstacle for the therapy process. The required and often desperately desired authorization letters are the proverbial elephant in the living room. The power imbalance set up by the standards can and has led to game playing by both therapists and transsexuals (cf. Stone 1991). In those instances in which authorization letters are at issue, it's critical that both the client and the therapist have clear expectations and are in agreement on any requirements for obtaining them. This agreement should be in writing and should be negotiated early in the therapy process.

There is considerable literature by clinicians directed at other clinicians who work with transgendered persons. Much of the earlier literature is colored by assumptions about transgender lifestyles and personality characteristics that history has shown to be unverified—and, occasionally, by what seems to be the personal distaste of the authors (for instance Laub and Fisk 1974, who began their paper with the statement "To change a person's God-given anatomic sex is a repugnant concept"). More recently, new literature has emerged that focuses on helping the individual explore his or her life options rather than on gatekeeping (cf. Anderson 1998; Brown and Rounsley 1996; Cole et al. 2000; Israel and Tarver 1998; and Lev 2004; all are, in my opinion, excellent resources for therapists with transgendered and transsexual clients).

Even the most mentally healthy and well-adjusted transgendered and transsexual persons will be challenged by their condition. In the past the literature has tended to view their psychological reactions to their guilt and fear, their responses to discrimination, persecution, violence, or various losses they endure as the result of coming out or of being discovered as symptoms of their gender dysphoria (cf. Levine and Lothstein 1981). Current thinking is that these stressors, and not the inherent nature of gender dysphoria, is responsible for much and probably most of the psychopathology that has been ascribed to transsexual and other transgendered persons (Califia 1997; Wilchins 1997).

Transsexuals who decide to transition are faced with great personal loss as well as social and economic obstacles. They risk rejection by family members, friends, acquaintances, churches, schools, and governmental agencies; they may lose their jobs and be unable, because of discrimination or the poor job market, to find another; they may be ridiculed, harassed, or persecuted in public; they are at risk for violence; and they will have substantial bills related to transition (therapy, electrolysis, hormones, surgery, and new wardrobe). They may have expenses due to life changes like divorce, loss of minor children with a resulting requirement to pay child support, loss of residence, retraining after loss of employment, or relocation to a new geographic area.

On top of all this, it is necessary for transsexuals in transition to examine their sexual attractions in light of their new gender role. It's only human nature to seek to put a name to things, and many clients will want to do just that in regard to their sexuality. In the new role, will they be homosexual, bisexual, heterosexual, or asexual? The therapist can help them explore and put a name to their sexual attractions.

It should be noted that transgendered clients will be inclined to name their sexual attractions based on their gender identity (and, in the case of transsexuals, new physical characteristics) rather than on their natal sex. There is a history in psychological and medical literature of using natal sex as an anchor, but most transgendered persons consider this offensive and insulting (Cromwell, Green, and Denny 2001). Therapists should be careful to consider the wishes of their clients and use respectful language in their interactions with them. This means using pronouns that are geared to their gender of presentation and identity rather than their biology and the terms *homosexual* and *heterosexual* in relation to their gender identity rather than their sex at birth. Thus a relationship of a female-to-male transsexual and a natal male is homosexual in nature, and a relationship between a male-to-female transsexual and a natal male is heterosexual.

Many transsexuals will find they are developing new attractions. For instance, formerly heterosexual males, after transition, often find themselves increasingly attracted to males (and thus once again heterosexual). Samons (2001) found that sixteen of ninety-seven of her male-to-female clients changed their sexual orientation in this direction in the course of therapy. Conversely, many post-transition FTM transsexuals find themselves attracted to men for the first time (Devor 1993b). Clearly, the social dynamics, physical interactions, public reaction to, and change in self-image inherent in such a newly arisen (or, in some cases, newly self-permitted) sexual attraction are issues that can be explored in therapy.

Even when sexual attractions don't change, there will be new stressors. For example, a natal male with a lifelong attraction to females may find herself, after transition, in a relationship that is, to the public eye, lesbian. The rules for public displays of affection, the reactions of strangers, even the language used in reference to the relationship will be new and challenging—and not only to the transsexual; the partner may find herself equally challenged. A relationship that is suddenly publicly lesbian may lead to the loss of acquaintances and alliances and the formation of new friendships and social activities. Moreover, even in lesbian circles the relationship and the individuals in that relationship may be suspect and the couple may find themselves shunned or excluded as not "real" lesbians. A formerly heterosexual relationship that is socially redefined because of one partner's decision to transition from female to male faces similar hurdles; so also do relationships in which the male partner is a crossdresser. Cole (1998) has described some of the challenges faced by female partners in such relationships.

Minor children will also be affected, especially when the transsexual is the custodial parent. Children may, for the first time, find themselves with parents who are in a socially homosexual relationship—or vice versa; children who have been in a gay male or lesbian household may find themselves with parents who are seemingly heterosexual. Children may be additionally stressed by the non-transsexual parent, who may be rejecting and scornful of the transsexual parent.

When the transgendered person chooses not to transition, there will be other issues. Many transsexuals, and even many crossdressers who choose to remain in the natal gender role, don't do so because it's their heart's desire. Often there is great stress and distress in fighting their wish to transition, and they require ongoing support to remain in their original gender role. Just as with transsexuals who transition, the therapist can be of great value in helping the nontransitioning individual live with the consequences of his or her decision not to transition. Some may attempt to deny their gender dysphoria; this can lead them to substance abuse, depression, sexual acting out, or risk-taking behaviors. It goes without saying that while the therapist can help the transgender client work through these issues, he or she should not try to direct or force a specific outcome.

Many nontranssexual transgendered persons find that their transgender identity or crossdressing opens the door to new sexual attractions and behaviors. Perhaps, as Kinsey and colleagues (Kinsey, Pomeroy, and Martin 1948; Kinsey et al. 1953) as well as others have argued, all human beings have a bisexual potential and crossdressing lowers inhibitions that are ordinarily firmly in place. Perhaps, as Blanchard (1989b) believes, this bisexual behavior is a manifestation of a paraphilia in male heterosexuals. Or perhaps, as Pauly (1974) has suggested, some people prefer or are attracted to relationships that can be described as heterogenderal (one of each), feeling equally comfortable as either the male or female in such relationships. This is an intriguing question, one with practical consequences for both those who do and don't transition.

Whatever their reasons, many natal male transgendered persons give themselves license, when crossdressed, to engage in sexual behavior they otherwise would not and do not engage in. This includes not only male-to-female transsexuals who are exploring their femininity, but transgenderists and crossdressers. Often, this behavior includes flirtation with and sexual experimentation with other males. For instance, it's common in the transgender community for crossdressers to play the role of the male in escorting crossdressers who are attired as female. This sometimes culminates in oral or anal sex which is rationalized as heterosexual or (if both participants are crossdressed) lesbian.

Paradoxically, many natal male transgendered and transsexual persons don't view their sexual behavior with other males as homosexual. This is because they view themselves as a woman in the context of that relationship. Often, this rationalization leads to unsafe sex practices and risk of venereal disease and HIV.

How common is this? A mid-nineties survey by the Ohio open transgender support group CrossPort of its members resulted in the selection of the sexual orientation "heterosexual except when crossdressed" over heterosexual, homosexual, and bisexual options.

In the context of a life that is otherwise heterosexual and monogamous, the danger posed to marriage and the health of the female partner by such sexual experimentation is apparent. Indeed, crossdressing organizations that stress the heterosexuality of their members do the wives of those members a disservice by disguising and denying the deep-seated feelings of gender dysphoria and sexual experimentation of a significant number of their members (Denny 1996). Not surprisingly, wives are rarely fooled by this posturing (see Boyd 2003 for a cogent analysis by a female partner of a crossdresser).

Certainly, when transgendered or transsexual clients are in denial about the essential male-to-male nature of such sexual encounters, and particularly when they place themselves and their spouses at risk of HIV or other sexually transmitted diseases, the therapist should help them to understand that the risks they face are the same as those faced by gay men. Analogously, FTM transsexuals who, after a lifetime of partnering exclusively with women, find themselves increasingly attracted to men may be in denial about the health risks they face in sexual experimentation with men.

Even when transsexuals are settled into and comfortable with their posttransition sexual orientation, their transsexualism continues to play a role in defining their relationship. Even when the individual in question passes well and has anatomy that is consistent with their gender role, there is a tension around both their homosexual and heterosexual relationships. This tension stems from the problems with defining their attractions and behavior using the usual terms of sexual orientation. Can their relationships accurately be defined as heterosexual or homosexual, or are they something else entirely? I don't presume to know the answer to this; I only know that the tension exists.

When a transsexual is in "stealth mode" there is a constant risk of exposure—and exposure can result in reinterpretation of their relationship by both partner and society. This can lead not only to rejection by their partners and others, but to violence and even murder. The "transsexual panic" defense is frequently used as an argument to justify violence toward transgendered persons (see Wilchins et al. 1997 and the "Remembering our Dead" Web site: http://www.gender.org/remember for statistics on violence toward gender-variant persons.)

Many transsexuals consider themselves heterosexual after transition. Others identify as gay men or lesbians, a phenomenon called transhomosexuality by

Clare and Tully (1989). A considerable number identify as bisexual; of the terms of sexual orientation, this poses less of a conceptual dilemma than do homosexuality or heterosexuality. Thus a social identity as bisexual can be a healthy one for both crossdressers and transsexuals. If an individual identifies as bisexual, that removes the tension as to whether their relationships are gay or straight. This is the case also with asexuality—indeed, a significant percentage of transgendered and transsexuals are, whether by choice or chance, asexual.

Increasingly, transgendered and transsexual people are partnering with one another. Such relationships place extreme challenges on the language of sexual orientation (and sometimes on therapists). Newman and Stoller (1974) cynically wrote of one such relationship, in which a candidate for male-to-female sex reassignment married a post-op MTF, "One hesitates to predict the next act" (p. 439).

Scholars and transgendered persons themselves are only beginning to talk about the complexities of sexual orientation when gender variance is factored in. It is clear at this early stage, however, that unless they are moored to sex or gender, the terms of sexual orientation—*heterosexuality, homosexuality,* and *bisexuality*—lose their meaning (Denny and Green 1996). For this reason, we need to create new terms or expand the existing terms to adequately describe the relationships and attractions to be inclusive of individuals with nontraditional gender identities, gendered presentations, or bodies that do not conform to the male/female dichotomy.

More than that, we must ask ourselves if the challenge raised by transgendered and transsexual people renders the entire vocabulary of sexual orientation moot.

NOTES

1. The focus of Prince's outreach was to proclaim her own heterosexuality (again, basing the notion of "opposite" on her sex of male assignment at birth) and the heterosexuality of male crossdressers in general. The organizations she founded continue to belabor this point and have met with some success, as demonstrated by the fact that today few people are dumbfounded or disbelieving when a man in a dress tells them he is attracted to women. This was assuredly not the case in the 1950s when Prince started her work.

2. In some instances I have used the term *sexual attraction;* I would ordinarily write *sexual orientation.* This is because the terms of sexual orientation become muddy when applied to transgendered persons and especially to those who transition gender roles.

3. HBIGDA is the principle organization for professionals who work with transsexual and other transgendered people. Their Standards of Care (see http://www.hbigda .org) are consensual minimal guidelines for the provision of hormonal and surgical treatment.

REFERENCES

Abel, G. G. (1979). What to do when nontranssexuals seek sex reassignment surgery. *Journal of Sex and Marital Therapy*, 5(4), 374–376.

Alexander, J. (2004). "There are different points in your life where you can go either way": Discussing transsexuality and bisexuality with the ladies of CrossPort. In J. Alexander and J. Yescavage (Eds.), *InterSEXions of the others: Bisexuality and transgenderism*. Binghamton, NY: Haworth.

Alexander, J., and Yescavage, J. (2004a). *InterSEXions of the others: Bisexuality and transgenderism*. Binghamton, NY: Haworth.

Alexander, J., and Yescavage, J. (2004b). Introduction. In J. Alexander and J. Yescavage (Eds.), *InterSEXions of the others: Bisexuality and transgenderism*. Binghamton, NY: Haworth.

American Psychiatric Association. (2000). *Diagnostic and statistical manual of mental disorders* (4th. ed.). Washington, DC: American Psychiatric Association.

Anderson, B. (1998). Therapeutic issues in working with transgendered clients. In D. Denny (Ed.), *Current concepts in transgender identity* (pp. 215–226). New York: Garland.

Bailey, J. M. (2002). *The man who would be queen: The science and psychology of gender-bending and transsexualism*. Henry.

Barr, R. F., Raphael, B., and Hennessey, N. (1974). Apparent heterosexuality in two male patients requesting change of sex operation. *Archives of Sexual Behavior*, 3(4), 325–330.

Benjamin, H. (1966). *The transsexual phenomenon: A scientific report on transsexualism and sex conversion in the human male and female*. New York: Julian.

Bentler, P.M., & Prince, C. (1969). Personality characteristics of male transvestites: III. *Journal of Abnormal Psychology*, 74(2), 140-143.

Bentler, P. M., and Prince, C. (1969b). Personality characteristics of male transvestites: 3. *Journal of Abnormal Psychology*, 74(2), 140–143.

Blanchard, R. (1989a). The concept of autogynephilia and the typology of male gender dysphoria. *Journal of Nervous and Mental Disease*, 177(10), 616–623.

Blanchard, R. (1989b). The classification and labeling of nonhomosexual gender dysphorias. *Archives of Sexual Behavior*, 18(4), 315–334.

Bockting, W. O. (1987). Homosexual and bisexual identity development in female-to-male transsexuals. Paper presented at the International Scientific Conference Homosexuality Beyond Disease, December 10–12, Amsterdam.

Bockting, W. O. (1997). Transgender coming out: Implications for the clinical management of gender dysphoria. In B. Bullough, V. Bullough, and J. Elias (Eds.), *Gender blending*, pp. 48–52. Amherst, NY: Prometheus.

Bodé, V. (1973). *Schizophrenia/Cheech wizard*. Berkeley: Last Gasp Eco Funnies.

Bolin, A. E. (1988). *In search of Eve: Transsexual rites of passage*. South Hadley, MA: Bergin and Garvey.

Bolin, A. E. (1994). Transcending and transgendering: Male-to-female transsexuals, dichotomy, and diversity. In G. Herdt (Ed.), *Third sex, third gender: Essays from anthropology and social history*, pp. 447–485. New York: Zone.

Boswell, H. (1991). The transgender alternative. *Chrysalis Quarterly*, 1(2), 29–31.

Boyd, H. (2003). *My husband Betty: Everything you always wanted to know about cross-dressing but were afraid to ask*. New York: Thunder's Mouth.

Brown, M., and Rounsley, C. A. (1996). *True selves: Understanding transsexualism for family, friends, coworkers, and helping professionals.* San Francisco: Jossey-Bass.

Burana, L., Roxxie, and Due, L. (Eds.) (1994). *Dagger: On butch women.* San Francisco: Cleis.

Califia, P. (1997). *Sex changes: The politics of transgenderism.* San Francisco: Cleis.

Chase, T. (2004). The story so far. In J. Alexander and J. Yescavage (Eds.), *InterSEXions of the others: Bisexuality and Transgenderism.* Binghamton, NY: Haworth.

Clare, D., and Tully, B. (1989). Transhomosexuality, or the dissociation of sexual orientation and sex object choice. *Archives of Sexual Behavior, 18*(6), 531–536.

Cole, S. S. (1998). The female experience of the femme: A transgender challenge. In D. Denny (Ed.), *Current concepts in transgender identity,* pp. 373–390. New York: Garland.

Cole, S. S., Denny, D., Eyler, A. E., and Samons, S. (2000). Diversity in gender identity: Issues of transgender. In L. Szuchman and F. Muscarella (Eds.), *The psychological science of sexuality,* pp. 149–195. New York: Wiley.

Coleman, E., Bockting, W., and Gooren, L. (1993). Homosexual and bisexual identity in sex-reassigned female-to-male transsexuals. *Archives of Sexual Behavior, 22*(1), 37–50.

Cromwell, J., Green, J., and Denny, D. (2001). The language of gender variance. Paper presented at Seventh HBIGDA International Symposium on Gender Dysphoria, October 31–November 4, Galveston.

Denny, D. (1992). The politics of diagnosis and a diagnosis of politics: The university-affiliated gender clinics and how they failed to meet the needs of transsexual people. *Chrysalis Quarterly, 1*(3), 9–20.

Denny, D. (1993). Letter to the editor: Response to Charles Mate-Kole's review of *In search of Eve: Transsexual rites of passage* by Anne Bolin. (South Hadley, MA: Bergin and Garvey). *Archives of Sexual Behavior, 22*(2), 167–169.

Denny, D. (1996). Heteropocrisy: The myth of the heterosexual crossdresser. *Chrysalis: The Journal of Transgressive Gender Issues* (May), 2(3), pp. 23–30. Reprinted in the *Flip Side* (July 1996), 3(7), 7–12, and *The conncecticuTView* (September 1996), 3–8.

Denny, D., and Green, J. (1996). Gender identity and bisexuality. In Firestein, B. (Ed.), *Bisexuality: The psychology and politics of an invisible minority,* pp. 84–102. Thousand Oaks, CA: Sage.

Denny, D., and Roberts, J. (1997). Results of a survey of consumer attitudes about the HBIGDA Standards of Care. In B. Bullough, V. Bullough, and J. Elias (Eds.), *Gender blending,* 320–336. Amherst, NY: Prometheus.

Devor, H. (1989). *Gender blending: Confronting the limits of duality.* Bloomington: Indiana University Press.

Devor, H. (1993a). Toward a taxonomy of gendered sexuality. *Journal of Psychology and Human Sexuality, 6,* 23–55.

Devor, H. (1993b). Sexual orientation, identities, attractions, and practices of female-to-male transsexuals. *Journal of Sex Research, 30*(4), 303–315.

Devor, H. (1997). *FTM: Female-to-male transsexuals in society.* Bloomington: Indiana University Press.

Dixen, J., Maddever, H., Van Maasdam, J., and Edwards, P. W. (1984). Psychosocial characteristics of applicants evaluated for surgical gender reassignment. *Archives of Sexual Behavior, 13*(3), 269–276.

Duberman, M. B. (1993). *Stonewall*. New York: Dutton.

Ellis, H. H. (1906). *Studies in the psychology of sex: Erotic symbolism, mechanism of detumescence, the psychic state in pregnancy.* Philadelphia: Davis.

Ex-GI becomes blonde beauty: Operations transform Bronx youth. (1952). *New York Daily News* (December 1), 1(3), 28.

Fagan, P. J., Schmidt, C. W., and Wise, T. N. (1994). Letter to the editor. *New Yorker,* August 22 and 29.

Franek, H. (1998). Talking about the issues no one's expressing: Telling it like it is in the world of bi-trans romance. *Anything That Moves*, 1(17), 28–31. Available online: http://www.anythingthatmoves.com/ish17/issues-no-ones-expressing.html.

Freund, K., Langevin, R., Zajac, Y., Steiner, B., and Zajac, A. (1974). The trans-sexual syndrome in homosexual males. *Journal of Nervous and Mental Disease*, 158(2), 145–153.

Garber, M. (1995). *Vice versa: Bisexuality and the eroticism of everyday life.* New York: Simon and Schuster.

Hamburger, C. (1953). The desire for change of sex as shown by personal letters from 465 men and women. *Acta Endocrinologica*, 14, 361–375.

Hemmings, C. (2002). *Bisexual spaces: A geography of sexuality and gender.* New York: Routledge.

Israel, G., and Tarver, D. (1998). *Transgender care: Recommended guidelines, practical information, and personal accounts.* Philadelphia: Temple University Press.

Kessler, S. J., and McKenna, W. (1978). *Gender: An ethnomethodological approach.* New York: Wiley. Reprint 1985, Chicago: University of Chicago Press.

Kinsey, A. C., Pomeroy, W. B., and Martin, C. E. (1948). *Sexual behavior in the human male.* Philadelphia: Saunders.

Kinsey, A. C., Pomeroy, W., Martin, C., and Gebhard, P. (1953). *Sexual behavior in the human female.* Philadelphia: Saunders.

Krafft-Ebing, R. von. (1894). *Psychopathia sexualis* (trans. C. G. Chaddock). Philadelphia: Davis. Reprint 1931, Brooklyn: Physicians and Surgeons.

Kulick, D. (1998). *Travesti: Sex, gender and culture among Brazilian transgendered prostitutes.* Chicago: University of Illinois Press.

Lano, K. (1998). Report from the United Kingdom: Bisexuality and transgenderism. *Anything That Moves*, 1(17), 28–31. Available online: http://www.anythingthatmoves.com.ish17/report-from-uk.html.

Laub, D. R., and Fisk, N. (1974). A rehabilitation program for gender dysphoria syndrome by surgical sex change. *Plastic and Reconstructive Surgery*, 53(4), 388–403.

Lawrence, A. (1998). "Men trapped in men's bodies": An introduction to the concept of autogynephilia. *Transgender Tapestry*, 1(85), 65–68.

Lev, A. I. (2004). *Transgender emergence: Therapeutic guidelines for working with gender-variant people and their families.* Binghamton, NY: Haworth.

Levine, S. B., and Lothstein, L. (1981). Transsexualism or the gender dysphoria syndromes. *Journal of Sex and Marital Therapy*, 7(2), 85–114.

Martin-Damon, K. (1995). Essay for the inclusion of transsexuals. In N. Tucker (Ed.), *Bisexual politics: Theories, Queries, and Visions.* Binghamton, NY: Harrington Park.

Newman, L. E., and Stoller, R. J. (1974). Nontranssexual men who seek sex reassignment. *American Journal of Psychiatry*, 131(4), 437–441.

Pauly, I. B. (1974). Female transsexualism: Parts 1 and 2. *Archives of Sexual Behavior*, 3(6), 487–507, 509–525.

Pauly, I. B. (1989). *Sexual preference of female-to-male transsexuals.* Paper presented at the eleventh Harry Benjamin International Gender Dysphoria Association Symposium, September 20–23, Cleveland.

Pauly, I. B. (1992). Review of L. Sullivan, *From female to male: The life of Jack Bee Garland. Archives of Sexual Behavior,* 21(2), 201–204.

Person, E., and Ovesey, L. (1974a). The transsexual syndrome in males: 1. Primary transsexualism. *American Journal of Psychotherapy,* 28, 4–20.

Person, E., and Ovesey, L. (1974b). The transsexual syndrome in males: 2. Secondary transsexualism. *American Journal of Psychotherapy,* 28, 174–193.

Person, E., and Ovesey, L. (1978). Transvestism: New perspectives. *Journal of the American Academy of Psychoanalysis,* 6(3), 301–323.

Petersen, M. A., and Dickey, R. (1995). Surgical sex reassignment: A comparative survey of international centers. *Archives of Sexual Behavior,* 24(2), 135–156.

Prince, C. V. (1957). Homosexuality, transvestism and transsexualism: Reflections on their etiology and differentiation. *American Journal of Psychotherapy,* 11, 80–85.

Prince, C. V., and Bentler, P. M. (1972). Survey of 504 cases of transvestism. *Psychological Reports,* 31(3), 903–917.

Samons, S. (2001). Sexual orientation in high-functioning male-to-female transgendered persons. Dissertation (draft). University of Michigan, Ann Arbor.

Smith, A. (2002). IBM leads way in supporting gender confused: Transsexuals are latest to jump on the "diversity" bandwagon. *Culture and family report* (May 29). Concerned Women for America, http://www.cwfa.org/main.asp.

Sörensen, T., and Hertoft, P. (1980). Transsexualism as a nosological unity in men and women. *Acta Psychiatrica Scandinavica,* 61(2), 135–151.

Steiner, B. W. (1985). Transsexuals, transvestites, and their partners. In B.M. Steiner (Ed.), *Gender dysphoria: Development, research, management,* pp. 351-364. New York: Plenum.

Stoller, R. J., and Newman, L. E. (1971). The bisexual identity of transsexuals: Two case examples. *Archives of Sexual Behavior,* 1(1), 17–28.

Stone, A. R. (Sandy Stone) (1991). The empire strikes back: A posttranssexual manifesto. In J. Epstein and K. Straub (Eds.), *Body guards: The cultural politics of gender ambiguity* (pp. 280–304). New York: Routledge.

Sullivan, L. (1989). Sullivan's travels. *Advocate,* no. 526, 68–71.

Ulrichs, K. H. (1994). *The riddle of "man-manly" love: The pioneering work on male homosexuality* (trans. Michael A. Lombardi-Nash). Vols. 1 and 2. Buffalo, NY: Prometheus.

Valerio, M. W. (1998). The joker is wild: Changing sex + other crimes of passion. *Anything That Moves,* 1(17), 32–36. Available online: http://www.anythingthatmoves.com/ish17/jokers-wild.html.

Weinberg, M. S., Williams, C. J., and Pryor, D. W. (1994). *Dual attraction: Understanding bisexuality.* New York: Oxford University Press.

Wilchins, R. A. (1997). *Read my lips: Sexual subversion and the end of gender.* Ithaca: Firebrand.

Wilchins, R. A., Lombardi, L., Priesing, D., and Malouf, D. (1997). *Genderpac First National Survey of Transgender Violence* (April 13). New York: Gender Political Advocacy Coalition.

W. L. (1956). A bisexual transvestite. In D. O. Cauldwell (Ed.), *Transvestism: Men in female dress* (pp. 119–124). New York: Sexology.

Maricarmen

PART 4

IDENTITY AND LIFESTYLE DIVERSITY
AMONG BISEXUAL WOMEN AND MEN

15

QUEER IDENTITIES AND BISEXUAL IDENTITIES

WHAT'S THE DIFFERENCE?

Evalie Horner

AS THE term *queer* infiltrates popular representations of bisexuals, lesbians, gay, and transgender individuals, and also increasingly defines the politics of activist groups on college campuses, the word is more and more frequently claimed as a sexual identity label by today's youth. However, many counselors seeking to aid transgender, bisexual, lesbian, and gay youth are not particularly familiar with the term, its various contexts, and its history.

HISTORICAL AND POLITICAL DIMENSIONS OF RECLAMATION

"QUEER" AS A POSITIVE DESCRIPTOR

The thrust of the gay liberation movement and gay and lesbian identity political movements had been to achieve cultural tolerance by demonstrating lesbian and gay men's similarities to their heterosexual counterparts (Angelides 2001). The first reclamation of *queer* as a positive rather than negative term occurred in 1990, with the founding of the activist group Queer Nation. Queer Nation rebelled against the predominantly assimilationist gay and lesbian activism of the 1980s. Mainstream gay and lesbian activists had been publicly proclaiming that gay and lesbian individuals were no different from the heterosexual mainstream and could therefore effectively function within it without posing a challenge. Queer Nation embraced the idea that sexual minorities *are* in fact different and sought not to assimilate but to radically transform society, including the heterosexual mainstream.

Queer Nation embraced the word *queer* in order to celebrate this positive understanding of difference, of "strange"ness. Queer Nation's reclamation of the word removed its sting for many sexual minorities, including (or perhaps especially) bisexuals, by effectively agreeing with what had formerly functioned as a hateful insult, but embracing the slur's implications of uniqueness, individuality, and distinctiveness.

Bisexual identified men and women, stigmatized within the predominantly conservative, assimilationist gay and lesbian politics of the 1980s, were embraced beneath the banner of Queer Nation. The acceptance that bisexuals found within Queer Nation paralleled the historically situated attitudes of acceptance of bisexuals that occurred in the 1970s within activist organizations such as the Gay and Lesbian Liberation Front. Like Queer Nation, TGLLF was not invested in a model of homosexuality exclusively based in biology, though they did not necessarily refute such a model. Without this investment, there was no reason to ostracize bisexuals, whose identities clearly announce that sexual attraction to one type of sex does not preclude sexual attraction to another. In other words, homosexuality may or may not be a choice. The question of etiology was and is generally irrelevant to Queer Nation and TGLLF and this nonapologetic stance is central to many contemporary uses of the term *queer*.

Queer Nation turned the tables of the 1980s and asked not why homosexuality exists but, instead, why *homophobia* exists. This shift in perspective provided nonheterosexual individuals with the freedom to fight for the rights of sexual minorities without feeling the need to justify one's sexual orientation as an imprisoning and unavoidable fate. The fact that this ideological shift made room for the acceptance of bisexual-identified people within Queer Nation cannot be emphasized enough. In this particular context, the new approach positively linked and blurred the distinction between the terms *queer* and *bisexual* and between both of these terms and other terms of sexual and gender identification, such as *trans, gay*, and *lesbian*.

"QUEER" AND CULTURAL CONTEXT

Throughout the 1990s, gay and lesbian resource centers were erected on college campuses throughout the country, and, more recently, some of these have moved to embrace the terms *bisexual* and eventually *transgender* in their titles. Although not all of these resource centers embraced the radical and antiassimilationist politics of Queer Nation, many began to embrace the word *queer* as an umbrella term, inclusive of all four major identity categories: gay, lesbian, bisexual, and transgendered. For the most part, the politics of these resource centers were a hybrid of mainstream 1980s gay and lesbian activism and the politics of Queer Nation. Most of these centers embraced bisexual and transgender identified students and community while also fighting to maintain a "respectable" image for the heterosexual mainstream. In this context, *queer* once again indicated a greater chance of safety and acceptance for bisexuals seeking to be included in a "gay and lesbian" community and a commitment to fight for the rights of all those under the queer umbrella these organizations embraced.

Many bisexuals in these contexts began to identify as queer. Some bisexuals identify as both bisexual and queer, while others trade in the label *bisexual* to identify exclusively as queer, allying themselves with the larger group of sexual minorities that fall beneath *queer* as an umbrella term. Also, some individuals who had previously identified as solely gay or lesbian began to identify as solely queer within this context in an attempt to counter the past gay and lesbian exclusion and ostracism of bisexuals and to acknowledge that there is more to sexuality than categorization and labeling.

ACADEMICALLY QUEER

Another reclaiming of the word *queer* occurred during the 1990s within the institution of the Western academy. This reclamation occurred in the context of universities, academic conferences, journals, and academic literature. Professor Teresa de Lauretis first coined the term *queer theory* for a 1991 conference that addressed what were seen as the intellectual limitations of "gay and lesbian studies." The name change was intended to counter white gay male dominance within lesbian and gay theory. Queer theory proposes the goal of untangling the limiting way sexuality has been constructed along a heterosexual/homosexual binary, professing an understanding of sexuality that is far more fluid, or *queer*, than the mere categories of lesbian and gay suggest.

At first glance, queer theory appears to be the ideal context in which to theorize both bisexual and transgender identity. After all, long before the reclamation of "queer," bisexual identity offered a category within which to represent fluid sexuality. However, bi- and trans-identified academics alike have expressed feelings of alienation from queer theory. Writers such as Steven Angelides (2001) and Jay Prosser (1998) criticize prominent queer theorist Judith Butler for dismissing bisexual and transgendered identities. They argue that Butler's famous theories of "gender transgression" and "gender crossing" in her book *Gender Trouble* (1990) focused on the practices of drag queens (gay men) and butch and femme lesbians rather than on transgender individuals themselves. These theorists level the same sort of criticism at Butler's follow-up work, *Bodies That Matter* (1993), in which Butler discusses transgenderism only insofar as it serves her argument about gay and lesbian identity while disavowing the complexity of transgendered experience. She mentions bisexuals only to simplistically and inaccurately conflate bisexuals with "straights" on the opposing side of what is ultimately a solidified, rather than queerly fluid, representation of the homo/hetero divide (p. 230).

Butler's method of compromising bisexuality's queer potential is intellectually contested by the important historical work of bisexual academic Clare Hemmings. Her work *Bisexual Spaces* (2002) documents that many bisexually identified women are and have historically been committed to decades-long monogamous relationships with other women, while many lesbian-identified women have habitually engaged in sex with men. Michael Du Plessis (1996), writing in the excellent anthology, *Re-Presenting Bisexualities* (Hall and Pramaggiore 1996), suggests similar identity overlaps within gay male communities that have historically ostracized bisexual male "outsiders." As with transgender and transsexual identity, Butler shies away from an opportunity to confront the homo/hetero binary head-on, instead oversimplifying bisexual identity into a single unexamined construction. This ignores the remarkably fluid range of sexual behavior that has openly existed beneath the heading of *bisexual*, a term that existed long before the term *queer* was reclaimed in order to, theoretically, perform this same function. While the bisexual-identified person may find acceptance and inclusion in the sociopolitical community of Queer Nation, current academic thinking about queerness often obstructs bisexual participation in the redefinition of sexuality.

Unfortunately, within much academic writing the term *queer* has frequently been collapsed into simply meaning "lesbian and gay." Though there have certainly been exceptions to this rule, it is my estimation, as someone who has spent the last seven years engaged in intense study of Queer Theory within the academy, that most academic work that is often placed under the heading of Queer Theory would not be helpful to an individual struggling with or considering a bisexual identification. Some of these texts might very well cause greater confusion and turmoil—even damage. This is less likely to be the case, however, when academic writing is organized beneath the label of queer studies rather than queer theory. Often, the label queer studies employs the umbrella meaning of the term *queer*, as it does within many college resource centers.

QUEER EYE FOR WHOM?

Today the term *queer* has been adopted by popular culture to describe television shows that include, almost exclusively, white, gay, nonbi, nontrans men. Neither the breakthrough Showtime series *Queer as Folk* (2000) nor the wildly popular *Queer Eye for the Straight Guy* (2003) include any primary bisexual or transgendered characters. In the spirit of some architects of queer theory, popular culture seems to be operating as though queer were simply a synonym for gay, not necessarily inclusive of bisexuality or transgender identity. The implications of this trend are that, while gay and lesbian groups may be experiencing increasing acceptance within the heterosexual majority, the truly queer—those representing fluid and unstable sites of sexuality and identity—remain on the outside fringe relative to their gay and lesbian "queer" neighbors. The most positive aspect of *queer*'s incorporation into the mainstream is the increased comfort level with the word among gay, lesbian, bisexual, and transgender people. This comfort has extended to many heterosexuals who were previously only familiar with *queer* as a derogatory slur. The cry "We're here, we're queer!" has evolved from a sometimes campy declaration to a politically meaningful affirmation. The reclamation of the term involves a slow progression at times, but in some instances the reclamation has been dramatic and effective. Today, it is acceptable to refer to *queer* friends and relatives, and the term is considered freeing and confirmatory.

However, if the mainstream's increasing comfort with *queer* remains unhinged both from the term's former derogatory meaning as well as from the more inclusive reclamations of the term, this current cultural phenomenon will do nothing to further demands for bisexual rights, respect, or inclusion, either within the gay and lesbian community or the mainstream heterosexual community.

CALLING ALL QUEERS

With the religious right continuing to preach an ability to "change" homosexual tendencies and the heavy residue of a medical model that first defined homosexuality as a disease, it is easy to see why gay and lesbian communities might irrationally fear bisexuality, despite the counterproductive and conservative nature of this fear. On a political level, bisexuality is sometimes seen as a threat both to the visibility of the gay and lesbian community and to the common pro-gay political argument that homosexuality represents a fixed identity category (that can't be "cured" as the religious right would wish to argue). Thus, it is also easy to see why many individuals who experience strong same-sex attractions might attempt to disown any opposite-sex attraction. Ironically, these opposite-sex attractions become associated with shame, denial, and identity foreclosure (because these attractions appear to reinforce the "normal"ization of heterosexuality that gay and lesbian activist groups so carefully resist).

For these reasons, it can be extremely helpful for those struggling with bisexual tendencies or behavior to visit a queer or LGBT resource center within their community or on a college campus. Such centers generally reach out to the entire community, including bisexuals, transgender individuals, and supportive heterosexuals of all ages and education levels. Under the umbrella term *queer*, those who previously identified as straight will potentially be exposed to positive and inclusive messages about bisexuals as well as gay, lesbian, and transgender individuals. Those previously identifying as gay or lesbian will be exposed to a different and supportive form of same-sex loving community under the banner of *queer*, a community in which they will have the chance to explore other identifications that might reflect their experience more accurately.

Most colloquial (nonacademic) uses of the word *queer* reference an understanding of the word similar to that forged by Queer Nation, though this may change as the word continues to permeate popular culture. In my experience, queer theory academics tend to harbor negative feelings and ignorant stereotypes about bisexual people and do not use the term *queer*, except when referring to *theory*. Some people argue that the academic, deconstructed understanding of queer is too broad, diffuse, and fluidly boundless to have any useful political or practical use, although this hasn't necessarily proven true.

BISEXUAL AND QUEER YOUTH SELF-IDENTIFICATION

Many of today's youth identify as queer for both political and practical reasons. Specifically, youth may identify as queer in order to make a statement of resistance against what they see as narrow, limiting, dominantly structured, stagnant, and overly constricted categories. *Queer* is viewed as a useful alternative identification to the term *bisexual* for those whose attraction transcends gender lines, though the two forms of identity are certainly not mutually exclusive. Some youth feel most comfortable identifying as both bisexual and queer, although others prefer one over the other. Others may predominantly identify as gay or lesbian but additionally embrace the identity of queer, often to indicate their potential sexual fluidity across gender lines despite their general erotic tendencies. The same is true of some progressively minded, predominantly heterosexual individuals. Additionally, *gender-queer* is a popular contemporary term for identifying one's gender fluidity if one is not necessarily satisfied by the term *transgender* by itself or in combination with other terms of self-identification. The term *gender-queer* functions as a more inclusive term embracing both gender and sexual orientation diversity.

It is very common for today's youth to combine a variety of identifications, for instance "queer, bisexual, and lesbian," or "queer and bisexual," or "queer, gender-queer, and trans," all within the context of understanding their own sexuality and gender as fluid. This practice fits with the ideological description of queer within the texts of queer theory. Though similar language may not be used within youth culture to describe this process of identification, the concept is often similar, if not the same. Conversely, when queer is positioned as merely theory and nothing else, adherents tend to fall back on the gay and lesbian activist ideology that dominated the 1980s for practical and political purposes. Perhaps this helps to explain queer theory's apparently hypocritical exclusion of bisexual identity and its tendency to collapse queer into the socially constructed categories of gay and lesbian.

As noted above, while some young people continue to identify as bisexual, there is an emerging trend for youth to adopt a queer identity instead. A variety of cultural, personal, and political pressures determine patterns of self-identification, and this is not limited to "young people"—though these trends are more prevalent among fifteen to thirty-five year olds. Political pressures, biphobia, and the desire to create a sense of belonging within the larger GLBT community are a few of the factors that may motivate an individual to adopt a primary queer identity, but these same pressures may lead another bisexual youth to adopt a primary bisexual identity. The desire for a category to "belong to" can be as strong as the desire not to be bounded by an identity category.

IMPLICATIONS FOR COUNSELORS

Given the complicated nature of the *queer* identity—participation in a meaningful but evolving community, (mis)representation in the media and society, and the repercussions of such a multivalent term for bisexual-identified people—it is important to speak to the implications for counseling and working therapeutically with queer and bisexual issues. The following questions and answers will give counselors some guidance—*from* the queer community *for* the queer community.

1. *How can I be sensitive to my client's choice of identity? How do I resist labeling him/her?*
Sensitivity develops out of acceptance and understanding. The more you know about the possible labels that your client may choose to apply to herself, the more sensitive you'll be about the choice she has made. Be sure to confirm how your client identifies herself, and be ready to discuss how that identity choice may change as she continues considering this term and other possible terms to represent her sexual and gender identities.

2. *How should I approach understanding my client's chosen sexual identity? Should I help them explore assumptions about what* bisexual, queer, lesbian, gender-queer, *and* gay *mean to this particular client?*
Understanding a client's choice of identity (queer, bisexual, gay, gender-queer, and the like) can represent an opportunity for greater understanding and communication. Simply asking a client how she chooses to identify, and involving her in a conversation aimed at confirming and understanding that choice, will reinforce her power to make that choice.

Above all, validate the choice your client has made. Language use to describe identity is more than simply a *term*—these choices represent issues of personality and psychology. Understanding this will allow you to be sensitive to your client's sexual identification. Every term—even terms as common as *gay* and *lesbian*—have individualized meanings and implications for the individual that are subtle and sometimes far-reaching. Find out from your client what her own identity means to her.

3. *There seem to be a lot of tensions between the various sexual minority communities—queer, lesbian, gay, bisexual, and transgender. Will this be an issue when working with a bisexual or queer client? How should I help them (or should I help them) navigate these tensions?*

It is true that different communities under the umbrella of *queer*—the bisexual, lesbian, gay, trans, and other identifications—can come into conflict based on assumptions, discrimination, prejudice, or prior negative experience with members of a particular group. This is very likely to come up in counseling sessions with your client. For instance, your client may be involved with a group of friends, some of whom identify in different ways than he does (i.e., a queer client may have gay or lesbian friends). Situations like this may bring up conflicts similar to other relationships/friendships in a nonqueer client's life, but with the additional texture of sociopolitical alliance, acceptance, and the simple fact that these categories are always evolving.

Helping your client navigate these difficulties will take a special understanding of the political and social pressures playing on even the most superficial friendships. As a therapist or counselor, you should be prepared to help your client with such issues when asked, primarily by remaining open to the unique ways these conflicts might act on him and by validating these conflicts between identities in his community as important.

4. *What about relationships? How can I help my client with issues about structuring relationships? It's certainly no longer simply a matter of challenging assumptions about male and female behavior and desire.*

Exactly. Bisexual and queer relationships are not a case of Mars and Venus. In a queer relationship, dominant and passive, nurturing and aggressive roles can be as fluid as the sexuality itself. Even butch and femme roles and identities can fluctuate within the relationships of queer-identified youth. It is best to inquire of your client what role(s) she has and/or wishes to play in a relationship before making any assumptions about that role.

In addition, however, keep in mind that queer relationships involve exactly the same issues of self-esteem, integrity, honesty, trust, and communication that are present in nonqueer relationships. Your client's past, future, or current relationships will be colored with issues related to fluid sexuality and issues of identity, but she will still be concerned with how the relationship affects who she is, what she wants, and where she is going in her life. The issues are common, though the context for these issues is unique.

5. *What about other counseling issues that overlap with queer issues—anxiety, depression, OCD, etc.? Are there special considerations concerning the way that these issues overlap?*

Queer individuals may actually be at higher risk for anxiety, depression, and other mood disorders simply because they are operating within a culture that does not understand and, in some cases, does not accept them. Be aware that queer clients are less likely to discuss their identity-related issues with friends, family, and colleagues for fear that such exposure may result in being ostracized from important groups of belonging. Queer- and bisexual-identified individuals are often unaware of resources available to them within their own community, and, even if aware of counseling resources within the community, may have a particularly difficult time finding members of that community who are willing or effectively able to listen to the stressors of living as queer in a nonqueer world.

There are no known psychiatric considerations for treating mood disorders in queer individuals. But it is important to recognize that the nonchemical catalysts for mood/behavior issues may be much more common than in the nonqueer community.

6. *Clearly, my client will be handling social difficulties related to her or his choice of identity. What are some suggestions for working with the social stigma and its psychological and emotional repercussions that a queer-identified person faces in a heterosexually dominant culture?*

Once again, be aware that everyday activities—from talking about your weekend with coworkers to holding hands with a loved one—can cause great distress for the queer individual/couple. The level of acceptance a queer person faces can change literally from location to location during a single day; for example, a queer person may be able to discuss his partner with one friend, but he may not feel comfortable or safe discussing the same relationship with another friend. Issues of trust, safety, and emotional security are in constant fluctuation for the queer individual.

Never downplay the emotional significance of the discrimination a queer client experiences. If you are heterosexual, try to understand that there are things in your daily life that you take for granted—rights that nonqueer people have—that the queer client cannot overlook. (As a side note, be aware that even if you are knowledgeable about queer issues, and express sensitivity to your queer client, he may have unexpected obstacles that interfere with trust and disclosure.)

The queer client will almost always need help finding other members of her community (those who identify the same way she does). If you make it a priority to stay aware of groups, GLBT centers, literature, and other resources that you can recommend to your client, she will benefit greatly.

This chapter raises reader awareness about the history and emergence of the term *queer* and its relationships to bisexual identity. The philosophy of biological determinism and the political strategies implied by this framework of analysis are being replaced by a new analysis—a more radical theory that centralizes nonheterosexual experience and theorizes from this new center. This chapter supplies counselors with useful information regarding contemporary uses of the term *queer* and its similarities to and differences from bisexuality. The word *queer* is being widely adopted by youth-centered social and activist groups. A map is offered to counselors who do not know about these issues so that they might understand how bisexuality does or does not fit into these various queer contexts. This understanding has direct implications for working directly with youth of the next generation who are struggling with issues of sexual and gender identity.

REFERENCES

Angelides, S. (2001). *A history of bisexuality*. Chicago: University of Chicago Press.

Butler, J. (1990). *Gender trouble* (10th ed.). New York: Routledge.

Butler, J. (1993). *Bodies that matter: On the discursive limits of "sex."* New York: Routledge.

Du Plessis, M. (1996). Blatantly bisexual: Or unthinking queer theory. In D. E. Hall and M. Pramaggiore (Eds.), *Re-presenting bisexualities: Subjects and cultures of fluid desire* (pp. 19–54). New York: New York University Press.

Hall, D. E., and Pramaggiore, M. (Eds.) (1996). *Re-presenting bisexualities: Subjects and cultures of fluid desire*. New York: New York University Press.

Hemmings, C. (2002). *Bisexual spaces: Geography of sexuality and gender*. New York: Routledge.

Prosser, J. (1998). *Second skins: The body narratives of transsexuality*. New York: Columbia University Press.

16

GENDER EXPRESSION IN BISEXUAL WOMEN

THERAPEUTIC ISSUES AND CONSIDERATIONS

Heidi M. Levitt and Sara K. Bridges

GENDER IDENTITIES, such as butch and femme, can be used to describe preferences in gender expression for lesbian and bisexual women. This chapter will help the clinician develop sensitivity to the different meanings that gender expressions might hold for bisexual clients. These gender identities and their associated appearances can be misunderstood not only by professionals but by others within both heterosexual and GLBT communities. Clinicians are encouraged to identify and overcome stereotypes associated with gender expressions so that they can assist their clients to accept whatever gender identity or expression feels authentic to them and develop strategies to cope with the prejudices of others.

UNDERSTANDING GENDER EXPRESSION FOR BISEXUAL WOMEN

As we begin this chapter, we would like to provide some information about our own identities so readers will understand the experiences we are bringing to this writing process. There are many different components to sexual identities that we could discuss (Klein, Sepekoff, and Wolf 1987) and it became clear to us that coming out would involve descriptions using multiple elements. It also became clear how complex the process of identification can be. As we wrote our descriptions of ourselves for this chapter, we talked to each other about how vulnerable this disclosure can feel.

HEIDI I identify as bisexual in terms of my attractions and my history, but I also describe myself as being lesbian to reflect my committed relationship. I view the process of identification as one that is political. By claiming an identity, I convey to others my degree of being "like" or "unlike" them. I think that it is useful to make differences known; I will identify either as a lesbian or as bisexual depending on what I feel will push the edge within a given context. When I am in lesbian community, I typically identify as a bisexual woman because I feel this term recognizes my desire and gives voice to my past. When I am in heterosexual community, I identify most often as lesbian when I want to convey my relationship status and signal difference. Although I tend to feel comfortable with my context-bound process of personal identification, it is awkward when I am unsure whether it would be most politically useful in a given context for my identity to communicate my desires, my history, or information about my current relationship. In addition, I identify as femme across settings. After living in a butch-femme community and developing an understanding of these gender identities, this term became a meaningful descriptor of my gender expression.

Also, although I am out to my graduate students and colleagues, I teach undergraduate *Psychology of Gender* classes in which I do not come out and I am sure many of those students assume I am heterosexual because of my femme gender expression. In fact, two students asked me last week if I was married. I prefer that my sexual orientation remain veiled to students in the classroom setting, so that those students are then able to freely express homophobic sentiments and their beliefs can be brought into the classroom more easily. In that context I feel I can best challenge prejudices when perceived as heterosexual. Although many of my closer friends know of my fluid identification process, many people probably would know me as *either* lesbian or bisexual (or may assume I am heterosexual). Writing this passage feels threatening to me because any of these people can interpret my identification strategy as misleading due to its inconsistency. And, ironically, it would not be politically useful (or personally comfortable!) to be perceived as deceptive nor would it recognize my intent.

Writing this passage makes me aware, once again, of how personal the process of identification is and how it tends to force layers of irreconcilable experiences under one ill-fitting rubric. At the same time, there are aspects of my identity that are more comfortable for me. For instance, I can easily identify as Jewish or as femme because these qualities signal my heritage and my gender expression and, for me, do not contain multiple conflicting components. And writing with Sara reminds me that these identities, which are more straightforward for me, may not feel the same for others.

SARA The decision to write about bisexuality and come out as a half-Jewish, half-Quaker, heterosexually married, monogamous, bisexual, vegetarian mom was not an easy one. In the past, when I have written on topics related to gay and lesbian issues, I have been able to remove myself sufficiently to make the topics "comfortable." I was writing about my friends, colleagues, and clients and as a loving supportive "outsider" I could be as open about their struggles and triumphs as I wanted. However, today, as I write about bisexuality, I am writing about me and as I contemplate defining myself for this chapter I am confronted with old anxieties and insecurities. For example, what if my grandmother (currently in her late eighties) suddenly takes a keen interest in my work and decides to read this chapter? She knows that I was her "little hippy" when I was in my twenties, but, as I am now approaching forty, I think she believes I have "straightened" up. I am out to my friends and most colleagues, but what about my students and other people that I haven't had the "chance" to tell? And, finally and most disturbingly, what if my reticence about coming out in printed form means that I am, in fact, doing the same thing that critics of bisexuality in general and myself, in particular, have used as accusations about bisexual women and men: passing as heterosexual because it is easier than facing the difficulties associated with having a nonstraight sexual orientation?

I know that on the one hand I have no desire to simply pass and, on the other, I also don't feel a burning need to talk about my private attractions, behaviors, and identities to those whom I believe do not have a need to know. I am clear about who I am on the inside, and, in general, my process of identification, unlike Heidi's process, has never truly been a political one. I have often found myself on the edge of identities and I rarely open my own identity up for discussion unless necessary. Whereas the process of identification has not been political, the revelation of my identity tends to be, if not political, then at least based on need. Like now. If there was a current need for me to write about being Jewish or Quaker or vegetarian or a mother who is also in academia, I would have done so. Here I have chosen to write about bisexuality and open this discussion because there is a need to explore the unique experiences of bisexual women. Moreover, there is a need to talk about the way gender is expressed in a nonmonosexual (i.e., bisexual) world.

Not everyone expresses their attractions, behaviors, fantasies, or identities based on either their own sex or the sex of their partner (Rust 2000); therefore the importance of sex can vary for individuals when considering their attractions. If I am attracted to someone based on their intelligence, sense of humor, and ability to express empathy, rather than based on their sex, could it be that I am attracted to an expression of gender and not sex? And if the predominant way I describe my love partner or my ideal mate is without the use of a pronoun, what does this then mean about my own expression of gender and its importance in my life? Heidi and I write this chapter to identify clinical issues that might arise from the particular forms of oppression facing bisexual women who have a butch or femme gender expression or identity. I, myself, do not claim either a butch or femme identity; however, if I had lived in a community where these terms were particularly salient, I might have done so.

ASPECTS OF SEXUALITY AND GENDER EXPRESSION

In the following discussion we utilize the division made by many feminists (e.g., Unger and Crawford 1993) between *sex*, a construct relating to biological characteristics, and *gender*, a social construct resulting from the assignment of traits and qualities. For instance, a bisexual femme would have a bisexual sexual orientation, a female sex, and a femme gender. For the purposes of this chapter, we are identifying this distinction and will refer to femme and butch as genders that either men or women can hold, while *sex* will refer to one's biological status as male or female.

SEXUALITY

Kinsey (Kinsey, Pomeroy, and Martin 1948) described sexuality as having three components: sexual attraction, sexual behavior, and sexual identity. *Sexual attraction* is defined as who one feels drawn toward sexually, *sexual behavior* is defined as who one is physically involved with sexually, and *sexual identity* is how one expresses or defines their orientation to others. Although Kinsey is most often associated with sexual behavior as the aspect of sexuality that defines the continuum of sexual orientation (heterosexual at one end and homosexual at the other), it is clear he also appreciated the important role that attraction and identity play in the expression of sexuality. Yet, for many researchers and certainly for the majority of Western society, sexuality and sexual orientation are inexorably linked to behavior. For this reason, the concept of bisexuality is particularly troubling in our culture. If sexuality is synonymous with behavior, then bisexuality by its very name implies sexual behavior with both women and men, thus appearing to rule out the possibility of monogamy, a form of relationship that is highly valued in Western society (Rust 2000). However, Kinsey also considered attraction and identity as components of sexuality, and most sex researchers, therapists, and educators include these factors in their definitions of sexuality.

Furthering the idea that sexuality is multifaceted, Klein, Sepekoff, and Wolf (1987) created a measure of sexual orientation (Klein Sexual Orientation Grid) that included other aspects of sexuality such as fantasy, lifestyle, and an individual's social and emotional preferences for male or female partners. Additionally, Klein, Sepekoff, and Wolf (1987) suggested that these aspects of sexuality can change over time and, as such, the scale inquires about past, present, and ideal ratings of these aspects of sexuality on a continuum that ranges from exclusively heterosexual at one end of the scale to exclusively homosexual at the other, once again placing bisexuality in the middle of the continuum. Although the Klein Sexual Orientation Grid offers a more comprehensive assessment of sexual orientation than simply looking at sexual behavior, it still relegates bisexual individuals to a place of in-between-ness where there is little understanding of the ways in which bisexual people understand their sexuality. This midpoint position may be seen as defining bisexuality by what it is *not* rather than by what it *is* and how it is experienced by people who self-identify as bisexual.

Rust (2000) contended that using a continuum that places *same sex* or *other sex* at opposite ends does little to help define bisexuality and thus she suggested using *monosexual* (meaning attraction, behavior toward only one sex) at one end of the continuum and *bisexual* at the other. She reasoned that this kind of continuum would be more accurate because the traditional continuum is based upon a monosexual model of sexuality and does not speak to the experiences of bisexual people. In fact, historically, the existence of bisexual people has been debated because men and women have been culturally constructed as being *opposites* of each other, thus making attraction to both unfeasible (Angelides 2000). Yet, as will be shown in the following section, it is quite possible that men and women are not opposed but rather share certain aspects of gender expression that could be attractive to people of all sexes. Thus conceptualized, if bisexuality is not defined by an individual's sex (a construct relating to biological characteristics) but by gender (a social construct resulting from the assignation of traits and qualities), then the existence of bisexuality is not only feasible but perhaps more common than is currently realized.

HISTORY OF GENDER EXPRESSION

Within the bisexual community, terms describing gender expression have been adopted from lesbian culture—most notable are *butch* and *femme*. These terms were derived from 1940s–1950s American lesbian communities after World War II when women joined the work force and began wearing pants, creating the possibility for the development of a butch aesthetic and gender expression within gay women's communities (Faderman 1991). The butch-femme culture made lesbians visible for the first time. Butch women adopted a style of appearance that resembled popular male media figures and femme women exaggerated cues of femininity. During this era it was primarily working-class women who joined this community, in part because they had less to lose economically than women from other socioeconomic classes. In addition to the harassment that lesbians suffered, the frequent raids on gay bars often resulted in the disclosure of identities in newspapers and consequently resulted in the loss of employment or social status for some of these women. Lesbians in these communities were expected to adopt either a butch or femme identity to engage in dating and socializing, in much the same way as people are expected to adopt either a male or female identity in heterosexual bars and clubs today. These lesbians also adopted many of the gender expressions that were fashionable for heterosexual couples in the popular media of that time (Faderman 1991), with femme women keeping house and butch women being expected to engage in more typically masculine activities, such as fixing cars or opening doors for femmes.

In the 1960s and 1970s feminists asserted that these gender expressions both resulted from and led to sexist practices, and, as this understanding of gender became popular, butch and femme culture receded. During this time butch women were thought to be assuming male privilege and femme women were accused of objectifying themselves. Instead, a new androgynous ideal and aesthetic pervaded the lesbian community, and women that remained butch- and femme-identified went underground. A shift began in the mid-1980s as women in some lesbian communities began to reclaim these lesbian gender identities and butch-femme cultures reemerged, although this time within a feminist cultural context. These new femme and butch genders were more fluid and women identifying in these ways tended to ascribe to an equal division of labor within relationships and a more flexible assignation of gender traits. In addition, these gender identities were not compulsory but were claimed only by those women for whom they seemed to meaningfully reflect gender experiences.

The terms *femme* and *butch* began infiltrating bisexual communities, and women began writing about their experiences as bisexual femmes (e.g., Albrecht-Samarasinha 1997; Lanzerotti 1998). Although essayists have begun to explore this identity, very little empirical research has been conducted looking at the expression and experience of gender expression and gender identity within bisexual women.

RESEARCH ON BISEXUAL CLIENTS AND GENDER IDENTITIES AND EXPRESSIONS

Preliminary research conducted by Levitt and Bridges (2005) has shown that lesbian and bisexual women have differing patterns of attraction not only in terms of their partners' sex but also in terms of their gender expression. They surveyed 716 lesbians and 279 bisexual women about their attractions using a web-based questionnaire.

The research questionnaire asked women whether they identified as butch or femme and also asked women, regardless of their gender identification, to rate their gender expression on a butch-femme scale and also to indicate the gender expression they most desired in partners. Lesbians were found to be more likely to identify as butch and to evidence more masculine gender expressions than bisexual women. Indeed only 4.5 percent of bisexual women identified as butch as opposed to 30.1 percent of lesbian women. Lesbian women tended to be more attracted to partners whose expressions of gender differed from their own (e.g., a butch lesbian attracted to femme women), while bisexual women tended to be more attracted to partners whose gender expressions were more similar to their own expression (e.g., a femme bisexual attracted to femme women). This finding may be in part due to the different aesthetics that are available and popular within lesbian and bisexual communities.

The women also were asked questions to assess their attractions, identity, and behavior based upon the Kinsey scale (Kinsey, Pomeroy, and Martin 1947) ranging from "exclusively heterosexual" to "exclusively homosexual." As expected, lesbian women indicated more homosexual attractions, identifications, and behaviors than bisexual women who, on average, indicated a nearly equal orientation toward male and female partners. Lesbian or bisexual women who endorsed greater levels of femme expression (either in terms of self-reported identity or gender expression on the butch-femme scale) appeared to rate themselves more bisexually oriented in their attractions, identity, and behavior than women who did not identify as butch or femme. In turn, those women who were neither butch nor femme rated themselves as more bisexually oriented on these questions than butch-identified women.

CLINICAL ISSUES FOR BISEXUAL CLIENTS RELATED TO GENDER IDENTITIES AND EXPRESSIONS

BUTCH BISEXUAL CLIENTS

For clinicians working with bisexual women who have butch identities or gender expressions, it can be important to understand both the personal meaning of their gender expression as well as the reactions a butch presentation may stimulate in communities where diverse gender expression may be less tolerated. Therapists need to recognize that these gender expressions do not necessarily indicate gender dysphoria and do not indicate that these women should undergo gender transition or Sex Reassignment Surgery (SRS), even though these women sometimes present with confusion based on their experience of being "different" than other women.

Butch women have an aesthetic that may be challenging for people because it does not fit with people's expectations. For instance, one butch woman interviewed in a prior study described (Levitt and Hiestand 2004):

Whereas me, people have to look at me and disregard the shell—guys have to get past it. I have some good male friends and I even have some guys that flirt with me . . . but a lot of men find this look distasteful, it's a challenge for them, they don't like it. . . . Whereas they would never, I know they would never feel like that about [femme women]. . . . I, on the other hand, present myself as I am . . . and in fact [am] more vulnerable because of it. Because of the presentation, I could be hurt . . . I could be singled out; I could be shot—for—whatever—because of this. That's just the physical thing, you know there's also the emotional—vulnerability too. (B-08)

Differentiating butch women from female-to-male transsexual individuals can sometimes be challenging, even for the person her- or himself. For butch women, this confusion often fades when she finds communities in which she is valued as the person that she is and her sex and gender are not being repeatedly challenged by members of that community (see Hiestand and Levitt 2004). It is important for therapists to remain open to the needs of their individual clients and help them become aware of the many different ways in which they can deal with gender atypicality.

Butch women routinely experience rejection and harassment and frequently feel the need to defend themselves against these possibilities; these difficulties cause extra stress in butch women's lives that then needs to be managed. There are a variety of ways in which these women cope with threats and experiences of discrimination or violence. Some view their gender expression as a political expression and a form of resistance to heteronormative mandates; others use humor, and those who are able to do so frequently seek support from other butch women (see Levitt and Bigler 2003; Levitt and Hiestand 2004).

Research suggests that within the bisexual community there may be few butch-identified women, however, and it may be more difficult to develop a support group to help ameliorate these pressures. For lesbian butch women, butch friends are important in normalizing these experiences and providing emotional support. One participant comments, "Probably because I can identify with them a little bit better. . . . We all . . . know what each other [is] going through" (B-12). This lack of support can leave butch bisexual women less able to identify and cope with discrimination based upon gender expression differences. Therapy may be the only place where these women can develop strategies to cope with their oppression.

Within heterosexual contexts, butch gender expressions are frequently misread and women may be mistaken as male and forced to clarify their sex regularly. Butch women also tend to be read as "lesbian," and their bisexuality may be invisible or minimized across lesbian, bisexual, and heterosexual groups. They may encounter others' reactions of surprise when in heterosexual relationships, and the genuineness of a butch-identified bisexual woman's relationships with men may be questioned more often than for femme and feminine bisexual women. It may be important in therapy to help women realize that gender expression does not mandate sexual orientation; these terms are often confounded in our culture and therefore in many individual's minds as well.

Butch bisexual women also may face difficulties finding dating partners. They may be considered attractive within bisexual or lesbian community because of their butchness, but the butch aesthetic is often not appreciated or developed within heterosexual contexts. Before developing a sense of their own "butch aesthetic," butch lesbians often report difficulty valuing their own gender presentation and realizing how attractive their butchness can be to others.

One woman who was just beginning to identify as butch described her process of building her sexual self-confidence:

> [It's] helping me to know who I am attracted to and who I'm not attracted to . . . and maybe why they wouldn't be attracted to me. . . . It would help me to accept that more. I always knew why I was more attracted to feminine women, 'cause it's obvious. . . . But, then I don't understand why the feminine lesbians [are attracted to butch women]. I guess I am confused about that. . . . They like a woman that looks like a man, why wouldn't they like a man instead? . . . [But] I'm not complaining. (B-07)

Although she took for granted that feminine women are attractive, she struggled to recognize her own allure as a butch woman. The process of appreciating a butch aesthetic may be even more complex for bisexual butch women. In contrast to lesbian butches who may date only within a butch-femme community, bisexual butch women may be more likely to move between dating circles that endorse radically different aesthetics. Maintaining a positive sexual self-image can therefore be more challenging for some of these women, and therapists may wish to help butch bisexual women locate resources supportive to them.

By validating the fact that butch-identified women or bisexual women with butch gender expressions experience discrimination, therapists can assist these women to name their experiences of oppression and resist them. It may be difficult for bisexual women to recognize the additional prejudices associated with differences in gender expression and how these can add to the psychological and emotional burden of already occurring biphobic experiences due to the difficulties these women face in finding similar others with whom to compare their experiences. An open dialogue with a therapist may allow a woman to contemplate strategies for coping with oppression and seeking support. In order to fully empower their butch clients, therapists first may have to confront their own prejudices and learn to value nontraditional or transgendered gender expressions.

FEMME BISEXUAL CLIENTS

In comparison to butch bisexual women, it may be easier for femme bisexual women to locate male and female dating partners because heterosexual communities and butch-femme communities frequently maintain similar aesthetics for feminine women. At the same time, these clients may find it difficult to find acceptance in heterosexual or lesbian communities because of their bisexuality. Their bisexuality may mark them as suspect in both communities; negative stereotypes may impair interpersonal acceptance (Rust 1995, 2000).

In addition, femme bisexual women may face barriers within bisexual or lesbian communities that do not prize butch-femme relationships or within communities that value a more androgynous aesthetic. One femme participant in a study by Levitt, Gerrish, and Hiestand (2003) described her experience in one such lesbian community:

> There were women that were very butch, and there were women that were androgynous. But there was no—I didn't see any femmes barely at all. . . . I was even like afraid to utter the word. . . . And I would wear pants or I'd be in . . . flat shoes and, and try to sorta kinda fit in. And I was so like miserable. . . . Because . . . that's not me! . . . I mean, you know, I wear pants, but I am talking about when I go out. I want to dress up to go out! I want to put on this short black skirt. It was hard. (F-09)

If these women are in communities that disapprove of femme gender expressions, they may feel pressure to conform to butch and androgynous ideals, creating feelings of artifice or marginality.

Femme women describe how their gender expression would sometimes undermine the credibility of their relationships with women in others' eyes:

> And it was just like I always felt [that] nobody *really* wanted to hear what I had to say or really . . . took me seriously. . . . Like maybe I was just an experiment—you know, maybe it was just a fling for me. . . . Makeup has always been something—at least—traditionally—again has been something that women did for men in order to appear more attractive. . . . I think sometimes women resent that—maybe cause you're still, you know, you're not necessarily standing out and making a statement and fighting . . . the male society . . . so maybe in a way——it lessens your value. (F-02)

This stereotype may be exacerbated when a woman is out as bisexual due to the heightened suspicions that she is insincere in her relationships (Rust 2000). Although this participant did enact a femme gender expression, she described hiding her attractions to men for fear that it would reduce her sense of value even further.

Bisexual femme clients may need to develop a sense of pride in themselves that is congruent with their sense of politics. One femme woman described her understanding of "femme-phobia" within the lesbian community,

> I think its some [what] related to homophobia . . . and I think it's some[what] related to . . . not acceptance of femaleness. . . . I don't really feel like it's right for me to define other people's reality either and say why they would be afraid, but that's what I smell when I hear that stuff [femmephobic remarks] is fear. . . . I think of it as a shame thing. . . . [Instead] I just—get more outrageous— usually. . . . I don't think I've ever allowed anybody to tone down my femme-ness

really. I mean in the beginning when I first came out—I did try and . . . blend in a little bit. . . . I don't know, it saddens me some but it, it doesn't stop me from being who I am. (P-07)

Therapists may have to understand, in spite of being more readily accepted in the heterosexual community for their femininity, that these women may face real hardships within feminist and lesbian communities. Bisexual femme women may need to wrestle in therapy with political questions about maintaining authenticity with respect to their own sense of internal gender while simultaneously working with their desire for social acceptance. In addition to the Web resources listed in a later section of this chapter, therapists may recommend readings to women to provide them with a sense of connection to other queer femme women (e.g., Harris and Crocker 1997; Newman 1995; Levitt, Gerrish, and Hiestand 2003). To work successfully with femme bisexual women, therapists may need to come to terms with their own sexism by recognizing the independence of sexual orientation and gender expression and accepting that some bisexual women may have a strong sense of femininity that feels essential to them. They may then assist these women in reconciling their gender expression with their bisexual identity, even in the face of others' prejudices.

GENERAL CLINICAL ISSUES

For both femme and butch bisexual clients, it is necessary for therapists to help create a safe place for discussing and exploring issues related to their experiences of being multiply marginalized. The distrust and apprehension that accompanies expressions of difference in mainstream society often exist just as strongly within queer communities. There is an assumption that people who have been marginalized will themselves be accepting and open to others who also are marginalized, but unfortunately this does not always hold when tested (Bridges, Selvidge, and Matthews 2003). Bisexuals are difficult to categorize clearly and are often perceived as threatening in the lesbian community because of the apparent fluidity of their sexual identity. Moreover, women who identify as either butch or femme are often seen as moving toward a patriarchal mandate controlling expressions of gender, thus betraying the feminist ideals and efforts of a generation of women who have struggled against sexist oppression. Thus biphobia and butch/femmephobia can exist within the queer community and create yet another avenue for oppression.

In general, people are comfortable with that which they understand and can predict—heterosexual people act one way, gay or lesbian people act in other ways, and this should be clear, regardless of one's particular orientation. However, bisexual women are "unpredictable" in terms of their behaviors and attractions, while butch/femme women defy comprehension for those invested in a clearly delineated world of gender typicality or feminist-generated standards of androgynous gender expression. Therefore identifying as bisexual *and* either butch or femme can place women in a multiply marginalized position within both heterosexual society and queer communities in ways that may require special attention and consideration from therapists.

Similar to the experiences of lesbian-identified women of color, bisexual-identified butch and femme women often have to choose how to identify based on the community in which they live or with which they prefer to affiliate. Identities such as butch and femme and butch/femme expressions of gender are as core to an individual's sense of self as bisexual identification; having to silence one aspect of the self (e.g., bisexual) in order to choose the other (e.g., butch or femme) is an unacceptable compromise of the self. This silencing can lead to feelings of being disingenuous and inauthentic, exactly the experiences many butch/femme bisexual women ardently seek to avoid, and this self-silencing can lead these women to experience anxiety, depression, and feelings of rejection (Hiestand and Levitt 2005; Levitt, Gerrish, and Hiestand 2003; Levitt and Hiestand 2004). For many of these women, being true to their inner feelings and attractions and being comfortable in how they present themselves to others are the keystones of their psychological health (Garnets et al. 1991). Therapists can help these clients explore the impact of living in multiple communities that are sometimes at odds with one another, assisting women to understand the threats these conditions pose to their psychological health and sense of well-being.

Therapists need to become aware of the specific lesbian/bisexual and gendered cultures in the geographic locales in which they work. For example, there are some communities where identifying as either butch or femme is, if not expected, than as least accepted and fully supported. However, in these same communities, identifying as bisexual may be unacceptable to the local lesbian community. On the other hand, a therapist may work with clients in a community where being out as lesbian or bisexual is the norm, but the butch/femme community is mostly invisible. In either situation (or countless other possible combinations) it is necessary for therapists to understand both the communities that exist and the terminologies members of these communities use to describe themselves. Knowing that a community does not overtly support expressions of butch/femme gender will help a therapist to understand the oppression experienced by clients who express their gender in butch/femme terms. Further, knowing that a community does not support the presence of bisexuality will help therapists to heighten their sensitivity when helping clients to explore their attractions, behaviors, and potentially their identity in nonmonosexual ways.

Webpages such as www.butch-femme.com or www.butch-femme.net may offer support for butch or femme women who do not have local butch-femme communities. Often these online communities can provide clients with an anonymous way of exploring these themes and initiating dialogues. Clients who are interested in exploring gender expression also may be referred to the literature described in the introduction or to fictional works, research, and essays on butch gender (e.g., Feinberg 1993; Halberstam 1998; Levitt and Hiestand 2004).

Finally, it is recommended that therapists avoid categorizing any client as butch, femme, or bisexual if she does not self-identify using these terms. Neither gender identity nor sexual identity is something that can be externally dictated. Regardless of attraction, behavior, appearance, or the typicality or atypicality of a given individual's gender expression, the categories (or lack of categories) in which women place themselves must be respected by therapists. For instance, counselors need to understand that it is politically important to some women to identify as lesbian regardless of their choice of behavior. For other women, refusing to identify as butch or femme may be vital to their sense of full allegiance to strongly embraced feminist ideologies. Knowing the client's individual perspective will help therapists build rapport with their clients without inadvertently offending them. Ask your client how, when, and whether she claims any particular gender or sexual orientation identities.

Several therapeutic exercises have been developed to facilitate the discussion of gender. Levitt and Bigler (2003) have developed a worksheet identifying both negative and positive experiences that butch and femme women have reported in relation to their gender expression. This exercise can be given to bisexual or lesbian clients who are interested in exploring themes of gender expression and identity. The constructivist model of sex therapy is another approach to help clients and therapists explore sexual meaning making (Bridges and Neimeyer 2003, 2005). The constructivist model of sex therapy is based on the concept of *holons*, which are defined as parts of a larger system that have sufficient internal complexity to be considered whole in and by themselves. The holons in this model (i.e., gender, eroticism, interpersonal bonding, and reproduction) are all part of a larger system of sexuality. By breaking sexuality down into its component parts and then exploring how these parts combine and interact with each other, personal meanings can be illuminated and processed both intra- and interpersonally. This process of exploration allows space within a therapeutic setting for clients to express how they understand their sexuality (in this case, their bisexuality) and how, in turn, their sexuality relates to their expressions of gender.

As we wrote this chapter together, we constantly had to keep in mind that identification itself has many different meanings. For some, refusing to be classified by definitions created by other people is a political act, while others believe it is important to claim an identity, either because the labels fit or to further political change. For example, we frequently had to stop during our own writing and process together our different understandings of the purpose and meanings of gender and sexual orientation identifiers. While we hold different personal beliefs about whether identification should be primarily based upon political or personal agendas, we agree that neither of these positions should be forced upon anyone from an external source. We feel that identities should be adopted by the people who inhabit them and that we would never assume to know what was best for our friends, colleagues, or clients. In this chapter we endeavor to bring to light some of the challenges that butch/femme bisexual women might face so that therapists can enter their sessions with greater sensitivity to these women's issues. An awareness of the political and personal underpinnings of these issues can help therapists enter into exploration with these clients and help them discover the personal meanings relating to both their sexuality and their expression of gender.

REFERENCES

Albrecht-Samarasinha, L. (1997). On being a bisexual femme. In L. Harris and E. Crocker (Eds.), *Femme: Feminists, lesbians, and bad girls.* New York: Routledge.

Angelides, S. (2000). *A history of bisexuality.* Chicago: University of Chicago Press.

Bridges, S. K., and Neimeyer, R. A. (2003). Exploring and negotiating sexual meanings. In J. S. Whitman, and C. J. Boyd (Eds.), *The therapist's notebook for lesbian, gay and bisexual clients: Homework, handouts, and activities for use in psychotherapy.* New York: Hawthorn.

Bridges, S. K., and Neimeyer, R. A. (2005). The relationship between eroticism, relationship, and interpersonal bonding: A clinical illustration of sexual holonic mapping. *Journal of Constructivist Psychology, 18,* 15–24.

Bridges, S. K., Selvidge, M. M. D., and Matthews, C. H. (2003). Lesbian women of color: Therapeutic issues and challenges. *Journal of Multicultural Counseling and Development, 31,* 113–130.

Faderman, L. (1991). *Odd girls and twilight lovers.* New York: Penguin.

Feinberg, L. (1993). *Stone butch blues: A novel.* Ithaca: Firebrand.

Garnets, L., Hancock, K. A., Cochran, S. D., Goodchilds, J., and Peplau, L. A. (1991). Issues in psychotherapy with lesbians and gay men. *American Psychologist, 46*(9), 964–972.

Halberstam, J. (1998). *Female masculinity.* Durham: Duke University Press.

Harris, L., and Crocker, E. (1997). *Femme: Feminists, lesbians, and bad girls.* New York Routledge.

Hiestand, K., and Levitt, H. M. (2005). Butch Identity Development: The formation of an authentic gender. *Feminism and Psychology, 15,* 61–85.

Kinsey, A., Pomeroy, W. B. and Martin, C. E. (1948). *Sexual behavior in the human male.* Oxford: Saunders.

Klein, F., Sepekoff, B., and Wolf, T. (1987). Sexual orientation: A multi-variable dynamic process. *Journal of Homosexuality, 11,* 35–49.

Lanzerotti, R. (1998). Engendering femme. *Anything That Moves: The Magazine for the Uncompromising Bisexual, 16.* Online journal: http://www.anythingthatmoves.com.

Levitt, H. M., and Bigler, M. (2003). Facilitating lesbian gender exploration. In J. S. Whitman and C. J. Boyd (Eds.), *The therapist's notebook for lesbian, gay, and bisexual clients* (pp. 183–196). Binghamton, NY: Haworth.

Levitt, H. M., and Bridges, S. K. (2005). Examining the connection between gender and sexual orientation: Gender expression for butch and lesbian women. Manuscript.

Levitt, H. M., Gerrish, E., and Hiestand, K. (2003). The misunderstood gender. *Sex Roles: A Journal of Research, 48,* 99–113.

Levitt, H. M., and Hiestand, K. R. (2004). A quest for authenticity: Contemporary butch gender. *Sex Roles: A Journal of Research, 50,* 605–621.

Newman, L. (1995). *The femme mystique.* Boston: Alyson.

Rust, P. C. (1995). *Bisexuality and the challenge to lesbian politics: Sex, loyalty, and revolution.* New York: New York University Press.

Rust, P. C. (2000). Bisexuality: A contemporary paradox for women. *Journal of Social Issues, 56,* 204–211.

Unger, R. K., and Crawford, M. (1993). Sex and gender: The troubled relationship between terms and concepts. *Psychological Science, 4,* 122–124.

17

COUNSELING BISEXUALS IN POLYAMOROUS RELATIONSHIPS

Geri Weitzman

COUNSELORS OFTEN make the assumption that their therapy clients are monogamous in their sexual/romantic relationships. Psychologists and other therapists tend to buy into unquestioned mainstream cultural values that privilege monogamy and pathologize any other relationship structure. Today, however, many heterosexuals, lesbians, gay men, and bisexual people are exploring ethical, honest options to expand the boundaries of intimate primary relationships. Polyamory is a lifestyle in which a person may have more than one romantic relationship, with consent and enthusiasm expressed for this choice by each of the people concerned. Many bisexual people negotiate polyamorous relationship arrangements with their partners.

This chapter describes different types of polyamory, outlines the benefits and challenges of polyamorous lifestyles, and offers therapists insight into how they can provide effective service to their polyamorous clientele. This chapter also reviews the current research on polyamory and mental health and presents results from a recent study that sheds new light on some of the commonly held myths regarding bisexuality and polyamory: 2,169 polyamorous bisexual adults were surveyed, and the results of the survey showed that 1. the majority of polyamorous bisexual people do *not* feel the need to simultaneously date people from more than one gender group, instead prioritizing factors other than gender balance when choosing their intimate partners and 2. the frequency of self-reported STD diagnoses among this population is not any higher than the STD rate among the general population.

BACKGROUND AND DEFINITION OF POLYAMORY

In our culture we tend to assume that people are monogamous. People generally have sexual relationships with only one person at a time. Those who have relationships with more than one person are often assumed to be "unattached and dating," or else "cheating," but there exists a third alternative. Polyamory is a lifestyle in which a person may have more than one romantic relationship, with consent and enthusiasm expressed for this choice by each of the people concerned. Polyamory is distinguished from infidelity by the presence of honest communication between partners and lovers about the existence of each of these relationships in their lives (Hymer and Rubin 1982).

Mental health practitioners typically do not receive any training on how to work with polyamorous clients. Textbooks on family functioning don't typically mention it, and the diversity literature doesn't usually incorporate it. Many members of the polyamory community have reported encounters with therapists who are uninformed about, or even biased against, this lifestyle (Knapp 1976; Roman, Charles, and Karasu 1978; Weber 2002).

This chapter provides psychology professionals with a general understanding of the lifestyles and concerns of people who identify as polyamorous. Professionals can learn how to assist polyamorous clients with challenges such as negotiating the terms of their polyamory and coping with prejudice in a monogamy-centric culture. It should of course be noted that polyamorous individuals may seek therapy for reasons that have nothing to do with their lifestyle; however, the knowledge that their therapist is supportive of their lifestyle as a whole will facilitate a more successful therapeutic rapport.

A third aim of this chapter is to discuss recent research findings that pertain specifically to bisexual people who are in polyamorous relationships. These findings will help to dispel two commonly held myths regarding bisexuality and polyamory—specifically the myth that bisexual people need to be in simultaneous relationships with people from more than one gender group (Rust 1996) and the myth that people who are bisexual and polyamorous are particularly prone to contracting STDs (Munson 1999; Sumpter 1991). It is hoped that the evidence presented will help to reduce some of the stereotyping and prejudice that is often directed at the polyamorous and bisexual communities.

TYPES OF POLYAMORY

There are three main variations of polyamory. In the first variation, known either as the primary/secondary model (Labriola 1999) or as hierarchical polyamory (alt.polyamory FAQ Usenet Newsgroup 1997), a couple considers their relationship to be their "primary" bond, and theirs is the relationship that receives the most time, energy, loyalty, and devotion (Kassoff 1989). Ties with additional lovers are seen as a source of added joy and enrichment in the partners' lives (Peabody 1982). The emotional bonds with these other lovers may be close or they may be casual, but they are not as strong as the bond between the original partners. One subtype of hierarchical polyamory is the "swinging" relationship, in which two or more couples "swap" partners for a limited time under strictly defined circumstances. This subtype is not common among bisexual-identified people (Rust 1996). Another subtype of hierarchical polyamory is the "open relationship," in which one partner's involvement with a secondary lover does not need to occur simultaneously with the other partner being involved with a lover of their own. This subtype of polyamory is more common among bisexual-identified individuals.

The next type of polyamorous relationship, nonhierarchical polyamory (alt. polyamory FAQUsenet Newsgroup 1997), is one in which one relationship is not given priority over another. Each of these relationships is considered to be of importance in the person's life, and significant time and energy is devoted to each. This type of relationship is also known as the multiple nonprimary relationships model (Labriola 1999).

The third type of polyamorous relationship is the poly-family: "an inter-relationship of 3 or more people, in which there is a strong relational commitment between all members (which may or may not include sex)" (D. Corbett, personal communication, March 17, 1999, cited in Weitzman 1999). The members spend significant amounts of time together as a group, and the well-being of each person is a significant priority to each of the others. Some poly-families are polyfidelitous (Labriola 1999), which means that romantic relationships are formed only between members of the poly-family (Rust 1996); others are open to the partners having additional romantic relationships outside the poly-family.

This is not an exhaustive list of potential polyamory configurations, but these are the main patterns upon which specific relationships are typically negotiated. What these relationships have in common is a rejection of the expectation that one partner can meet all of the other's relationship needs—emotional, social, sexual, economic, and intellectual (Peabody 1982:428). Polyamory is seen as enhancing both personal and interpersonal growth, as closer associations are formed with people who have among them a wide variety of personality traits and personal strengths.

BENEFITS OF POLYAMORY

There are many benefits that polyamorous people report gaining from this lifestyle. Many find joy in having close relationships on both sexual and emotional planes with multiple partners and/or lovers (Blasband and Peplau 1985). The opportunity to express and receive affection from more sources is considered a definite plus. Ramey (1975) notes the following positive elements of polyamory: increased personal freedom, greater depth to social relationships, the potential for sexual exploration in a nonjudgmental setting, a strengthening of spousal bonds, a sense of being desired, a feeling of belonging, added companionship, increased self-awareness, intellectual variety, and the chance for new aspects of personality to emerge through relating to more people. The couple that decides to open their relationship to include others is often highly secure in the strength of their partnership bond and welcoming of the opportunities for personal growth that come from close associations with new and diverse people.

Polyamorous individuals tend to gain a lot of practice at communicating their needs and negotiating arrangements that are satisfactory to all (Knapp 1976). The ability to process what is happening between the members of a group is one that the psychology profession can well appreciate. Kassoff (1989) noted that polyamory "can serve as a vehicle to de-merge the merged individual or couple" (p. 169) and can make boundary setting a more explicit process within a relationship, leading to a sense of heightened self-actualization, individuation, and differentiation. Her sample of lesbian participants noted that polyamory was a framework that encouraged them to prioritize their own emotional and sexual needs, whereas in their prior monogamous relationships they had felt more of a pull to accommodate their partners' needs before meeting their own. Moreover, they felt a greater sense of equality in decision making in their poly-amorous relationships. Partners in polyamorous relationships do not feel as much pressure to be all things to one another (Rust 1996) or to be the only ones who can satisfy their partners' needs (Knapp 1976).

Polyamorous people work hard to find ways of coping with jealousy that don't involve restricting their partners' behaviors, and this involves a lot of trust and attention to the primary bond. Dixon (1985) found that the swinging women in her study reported feeling less possessive of their primary partners, and less threatened by (and less competitive with) other women. Keener (2004) found that his study participants felt a deepened trust in their partners and a freedom from worrying about whether their partners were faithful.

In addition, polyamorous people often report feeling an expanded sense of altruism, referred to as *compersion*, with respect to their partner's other partners (Keener 2004). *Compersion* is the opposite of jealousy. It means feeling glad that someone who you love loves another person deeply. One definition is "the feeling of taking joy in the joy that others you love share among themselves—especially taking joy in the knowledge that your beloveds are expressing their love for one another" (Polyamory Society 1997).

Keener's (2004) study participants noted that they benefited from belonging to an extensive network of interwoven relationships in which a greater number of emotional, physical, and financial resources were available—much in the same way that large extended biological families help one another out. Second-ary partners often provide tangible support to a primary couple, pitching in with chores such as babysitting, pet care, or providing rides to and from the train sta-tion. Polyamorous families in which the partners all live together derive the many benefits of household cooperation, which include more people to share chores, watch the children, and pay the rent (Makanjuola 1987). The cost of living per person decreases when there are a greater number of people to pool incomes and energies and share resources.

DISCRIMINATION AGAINST POLYAMOROUS PEOPLE

Despite the polyamorous community's perception of this lifestyle as one from which many benefits may be derived, this view is often contested by others. People who are in polyamorous relationships face social disapproval similar to that experienced by members of the lesbian, gay, and bisexual community (Browning, Reynolds, and Dworkin 1991; Peabody 1982). Often, polyamorous individuals choose not to reveal their multiple relationships to outsiders, as they perceive nonacceptance for their lifestyle from the wider society. Even close family members may be excluded from this knowledge (Ziskin and Ziskin 1975). Weber (2002) found that 93 percent of one thousand plus respondents in the *Loving More* sample were concerned about being treated with prejudice upon coming out and 43 percent of the sample had experienced such prejudice. West (1996) found that 71 percent of lesbian women in her sample of five hundred chose not to reveal to their community that they were polyamorous.

Polyamorous people face institutional discrimination as well. Polyamorous unions are not typically recognized by church or state and spousal health benefits are not available for one's nonmarried partner. A number of employers who offer family health plans to domestic partners do so only under the condition that the partners formally attest that they are monogamous (Barillas 1997; Bricker 2003).

Many polyamorous people fear that their custody of their children would be challenged if their lifestyle were known to conservative family members or school officials (Keener 2004). In 1998 a legal case was heard in which a young child was removed from a polyamorous household of three parents after her grandparents petitioned for custody on the grounds that the home environment was immoral according to the Bible. No evidence of child abuse or neglect was found, and mental health professionals found that the child was well-adjusted, but the child's family still had to fight a court battle in order to have her returned, and, even then, the child was only returned on the grounds that one of the three parents move out (Cloud 1999).

Even when there is not a threat to the polyamorous family's custody of their children, other legal challenges exist. One example is provided by a woman who noted that as her child's third guardian, she does not have authority over his medical care or even the legal right to visit him in the hospital should he fall ill (Keener 2004). It is interesting that a society that deplores single-parent families does not value households in which children have three or more parents to provide them with extra attention, resources, and loving care.

DEMOGRAPHIC DATA ON POLYAMORY

While openly polyamorous relationships are relatively rare (Rubin 1982), there are indications that private polyamorous arrangements within relationships are actually quite common. Blumstein and Schwartz (1983, cited in Rubin and Adams 1986) noted that of 3,574 married couples in their sample 15–28 percent had "an understanding that allows nonmonogamy under some circumstances. The percentages are higher among cohabitating couples (28 percent), lesbian couples (29 percent) and gay male couples (65 percent)" (p. 312). West (1996) found that 20 percent of her five hundred lesbian and bisexual survey respondents stated that polyamory was their usual relationship modality, and 33 percent stated that they preferred a polyamorous lifestyle. She notes that these findings are similar to those revealed in a survey of lesbian and bisexual women conducted by the *Advocate* (1995) in which 20 percent of 8,000 respondents indicated that they were not monogamous. West also found that 92 percent of her respondents had at some point fantasized about being in relationships with more than one woman at a time. Page (2004) found that, among her sample of 217 bisexual adults, 54 percent stated their ideal relationship style would be polyamorous, and 33 percent were currently involved in a polyamorous relationship.

Weber (2002) summarized the results of a readership survey conducted by *Loving More*, a magazine about polyamory: 51 percent of their sample of over one thousand respondents was bisexual, 44 percent were heterosexual, and 4 percent were gay/lesbian. The sample was highly educated (70 percent had bachelor's degrees and 40 percent had a graduate degree, compared with 23 percent and 8 percent respectively in the general population). Forty-two percent of the sample was a parent or guardian of minor children.

POLYAMORY AND MENTAL HEALTH

THERAPISTS' VIEWS OF POLYAMORY

Clearly, such a widespread phenomenon is an important one for mental health professionals to understand. There is a perception within the polyamorous community, however, that therapists are not well-informed about their lifestyles and needs (Knapp 1976). This limits the extent to which polyamorous individuals feel that they have access to quality mental health services (Roman, Charles, and Karasu 1978). Some polyamorous individuals report a reluctance to seek therapy due to fear of bias. Some simply don't come out to their therapists. Weber (2002) found that among those respondents who had participated in therapy from the *Loving More* sample, 38 percent had not come out to their therapists. Among those who told their therapists, 10 percent reported a negative response. Many of those who come out to their therapists find it necessary to use expensive therapy sessions to educate their therapists about what polyamory is and to convince them that a polyamorous lifestyle in itself is no more pathological than, say, a gay lifestyle. Textbooks about "normal family functioning" do not include references to polyamorous lifestyles, and this contributes further to ignorance about polyamory on the part of mainstream therapists.

Hymer and Rubin (1982) conducted a study in which therapists were asked to imagine the psychological profile of a typical polyamorous person. Twenty-four percent of these therapists imagined that polyamorous individuals feared commitment or intimacy, 15 percent imagined that they were in marriages that were not fulfilling, and 7 percent hypothesized that they might have identity problems. In another study Knapp (1975) found that 33 percent of her sample of therapists believed that people who pursued a polyamorous lifestyle had personality disorders and neurotic tendencies, and 20 percent suggested that such people might have antisocial personalities. Between 9 percent and 17 percent of the therapists "stated they would use their professional skills to try to influence clients to abandon sexually open marriages" (p. 509).

As these studies demonstrate, polyamorous clients who seek out therapy "are often stigmatized and penalized by the very system of human services originally set up to help them in such crises" (Sussman 1974, cited in Roman, Charles, and Karasu 1978:409). It is noteworthy that Knapp (1975) found that therapists considered people who were involved in secret extramarital affairs to be more "normal" than those who communicated honestly with their partners about their participation in other relationships. These therapists' views are not concealed from their polyamorous clients. Rubin and Adams (1978, cited in Hymer and Rubin 1982) "found that among those clients who had a sexually open marriage and sought therapy, 27 percent indicated that their therapists were nonsupportive of their nonmonogamous relationship" (p.533).

Sometimes this disapproval was expressed in overt ways and at other times it was more covert. While not all therapists evidenced such biases, enough did that many clients became wary of seeking mental health services. Knapp (1975, cited in Hymer and Rubin 1982) noted that the "three greatest fears facing prospective alternative lifestyle clients were: therapists' condemnation of their lifestyle, pressure to return to a 'healthier' form of marriage, and being diagnosed in terms of psychopathology" (p. 533). Page (2004) noted that some of the bisexual participants in her study experienced difficulty when trying to locate a therapist who would not pathologize their polyamory or their bisexuality.

The clinical portrait that some therapists have painted of polyamorous clients is a rather negative one. Is it in fact a realistic one? The next section of this presentation examines whether the negative view of polyamorous individuals that some therapists have expressed is borne out by empirical data.

WHAT IS KNOWN ABOUT THE PSYCHOLOGICAL AND SOCIAL FUNCTIONING OF POLYAMOROUS INDIVIDUALS?

In 1976 Knapp administered a battery of standardized psychological assessment measures to a sample of polyamorous couples (Peabody 1982). No significant differences were found between the couples in her sample and the general population norms.

> That is, neither group was particularly neurotic, immature, promiscuous, malad-justed, pathological, or sexually inadequate. . . . The response patterns suggested a modal type of individual in a sexually open marriage who was individualistic, an academic achiever, creative, nonconforming, stimulated by complexity and chaos, inventive, relatively unconventional and indifferent to what others said, concerned about his/her own personal values and ethical systems, and willing to take risks to explore possibilities. (Peabody 1982:429)

Watson (1981, cited in Rubin 1982) gave the California Psychological Inventory (Gough 1957) to thirty-eight sexually open individuals, and these subjects also scored within normal bounds. Kurdek and Schmitt (1986) administered the Symptom Checklist 90 (SCL-90) to ninety-eight gay men in open relationships and thirty-four gay men in monogamous relationships and found no differences in psychological adjustment between the two groups.

Additional work has been done in the area of marital adjustment. Buunk (1980, cited in Rubin 1982) found that couples with open marriages in the Netherlands were normal in terms of marriage satisfaction, self-esteem, and neuroticism. Knapp (1976) additionally found that twenty-two out of thirty-four respondents in her study reported increased satisfaction within their primary relationship after becoming involved in polyamory. Another study (Peabody 1982) found that most respondents reported feeling satisfied with their primary relationship and felt positively about their partner having sexual relations with others. Peabody also noted that the respondents valued social activities, warmth, and open communication even more than sex. "The continuing emphasis was a focus on warmth, acceptance, communication and friendship with the freedom to touch, caress, and have the potential for sexual activity if chosen" (p. 429). Keener (2004) also found that his participants valued intimacy with their partners and lovers even more than they valued sex.

Spanier's Dyadic Adjustment Scale (1976) was used to compare sexually open couples with sexually exclusive ones (Rubin 1982), and no differences were found in adjustment or happiness between the two groups. "Nothing in this data argues for the view that sexual openness or exclusivity, in and of themselves, make a difference in the overall adjustment of a married couple" (p. 107). A follow-up study (Rubin and Adams 1986) found that, after several years, there was no significant difference in marital stability (i.e., breaking up versus staying together) between those couples who had been polyamorous and those whose marriages had been exclusive. Similar proportions of each group reported happiness versus unhappiness, compared to the earlier sample. Additionally, "the reasons given for breakup were almost never related to extramarital sex" (p. 318). When polyamorous relationships ended, common reasons given included growing apart in general interests, feeling unequal levels of attraction to one another, and dealing with the stresses of long distance (Ramey 1975).

Findings were similar among polyamorous lesbian, gay and bisexual couples. Peplau (1981) found that gay couples in open relationships did not differ from gay men in monogamous relationships in terms of relationship satisfaction, security, intimacy, and level of commitment. Blasband and Peplau (1985) compared gay men in open relationships with gay men in monogamous relationships, and found no difference between the two groups in terms of the levels of love, respect, and marital satisfaction between the primary partners. Likewise, the two groups did not differ in terms of frequency of sex between the primary partners. Kurdek and Schmitt (1986) similarly reported that the polyamorous gay couples in their sample were similar to the monogamous couples along the dimensions of "Favorable Attitude towards Relationship, Sexual Satisfaction, and Low Tension." West (1996) found that 80 percent of her respondents who had ever been in a polyamorous relationship would be willing to be in a polyamorous relationship again and that 88 percent of her polyamorous respondents found that having multiple honest relationships brought them "much happiness" (p. 323). Dixon (1985) examined a community of bisexual female swingers, and found that 76 percent of her respondents rated their sexual satisfaction within their marriages as good or excellent, with the remainder mostly ranking it as fair.

In terms of relationship longevity, Kurdek and Schmitt (1986) found that the gay men in open relationships in their sample lived together significantly longer than the gay men who were in monogamous relationships. This finding was also borne out by McWhirter and Mattison (1984), who studied 156 gay male couples and found that all those couples whose relationships lasted five years or more were in open relationships. In sum, many polyamorous people "are in relatively stable primary relationships and do not seem to be motivated by neurotic and pathological needs." (Peabody 1982:430).

As these studies show, "the alternative life styles chosen by individuals are not necessarily the cause nor the result of unhealthy personalities; in actuality, the alternative life style behavior may be supportive of the psychological health of the individuals" (Peabody 1982:426, 434). Thus, therapists should not assume that polyamory is maladaptive or that people in polyamorous unions would improve their relationships by shifting to a traditional monogamous style. Therapists who maintain that monogamy is inherently preferable to polyamory may be reflecting their own cultural biases rather than considering what is best for their client's individual needs (Rust 1996).

This perspective is also maintained by the famous psychologist Albert Ellis, who presents support for the viability of polyamorous lifestyles in *The Case for Sexual Liberty* (1965). Ellis advocates that

> sexual morality be made absolutely synonymous with general morality, and that only whatever is deemed wrong in a valid moral sense, *and that alone*, be deemed sexually wrong. That is to say: if a given human deed is wrong, meaning that it gratuitously, unfairly, and needlessly impinges on the rights of other human beings and specifically harms them thereby, then, if it is a sexual deed, it may be termed morally wrong, or immoral; but if any sexual desire, expression, thought, or activity is not morally wrong in itself, then it can never justifiably be termed sexually "wrong" or "sinful," merely because it is a sexual act, and as such reprehensible to some theological and superstitious set of beliefs. (p. 7)

In many cultures multiple partnerships are the norm, and many benefits of this lifestyle have been reported. For instance, in Nigeria it is said that "the sharing of responsibilities among members may greatly dilute the burden, financial or otherwise, of care for members with problems" (Makanjuola 1987:366). Venezuelan Yanomamo women who choose a polygynous lifestyle may not need to work as long on household and child-care tasks as their monogamous sisters do, due to cooperation between cowives (Hames 1996). Elizabeth Joseph, a Mormon polygamous woman, noted that "polygamy is a feminist lifestyle. I can go off 400 miles to law school and the family keeps running" (West 1996:1).

The information presented thus far supports the position that the polyamorous lifestyle is not a pathological one. It can, however, present some unique challenges (Kassoff 1989). The next section of this chapter will describe some of the lifestyle-specific concerns that polyamorous individuals may present in therapy and how therapists can be of help to these clients. It should be remembered, of course, that polyamorous individuals often seek therapy for reasons that have nothing to do with their lifestyle; rather, like so many other individuals, they may seek therapeutic support for grief, depression, anxiety, panic attacks, PTSD, and other problems in living.

SPECIFIC CONCERNS OF POLYAMOROUS INDIVIDUALS

One challenge that polyamorous individuals contend with is the label of deviance (Knapp 1975; Mann 1975). In his analysis of the *Loving More* survey results, Weber (2002) found, out of approximately one thousand people surveyed, the majority had not revealed that they were polyamorous to one or more people in the following categories: their parents, children, extended family members, neighbors, coworkers, or bosses. In general, this was because they feared rejection and discrimination.

There are many strains that accompany keeping so large a secret from such important people in one's life (Browning, Reynolds, and Dworkin 1991). There is the fear of being discovered and shunned by people who might disapprove. There is the stress that comes along with the lack of recognition of one's partners: for example, the partner who is not invited to family gatherings and office parties may feel excluded and devalued. If the polyamorous individual has children who are not aware of the arrangement, there is the need to arrange a time and place to meet in private rather than in the comfort of one's home (Knapp 1976). Coming out is often a relief insofar as the decision to come out allows one to live one's chosen lifestyle openly.

A poly-aware therapist can assist polyamorous people in weighing the pros and cons of coming out to friends, family members, clergy, and coworkers (Rust 1996). They can help the poly client learn how to cope with the above stresses if they choose not to come out and they can support them in deciding how they will cope with prejudice if they do come out.

When one partner in a couple wishes to introduce polyamory into the relationship, the therapist can help them to decide how to bring up the topic and can assist them in preparing for the responses that the partner might have. The therapist can also assist a couple who is first considering a polyamorous lifestyle to determine whether this is a viable choice for them (Peabody 1982) and to decide which type of polyamory suits them best. They can also help the couple determine whether their own bond is strong enough to handle the introduction of other lovers at the present time or whether there are issues of communication and intimacy that need to be resolved in the primary relationship before it can be opened up (Keener 2004).

When a couple makes the decision to open up their relationship, the therapist can assist them in negotiating their ground rules (Rust 1996). There are several issues upon which polyamorous partners commonly negotiate (Ramey 1975). One is the introduction of new lovers and partners. Are new relationships subject to the approval of the existing partner/s? Are any restrictions placed upon the new relationship, such as limits on the amount of time that may be spent together or specific sexual acts that are reserved for the original couple alone (Blasband and Peplau 1985; Knapp 1976; Rust 1996)? What methods will be used to prevent sexually transmitted diseases and unwanted pregnancies (Ziskin and Ziskin 1975)? Can the bedroom that is shared by the longstanding couple be used for time spent together with new partners? Will the new relationship ever become equal in status to the existing one or is the existing one expected to remain primary (Rust 1996)?

Another area is communication (Ramey 1975; Ziskin and Ziskin 1975). Does an individual let their partner know when they are seeing their other partner or is discretion preferred? Are one's newer partners expected to socialize with the existing ones or are the relationships kept separate? And should the disclosure be made before or after the visit occurs (Rust 1996)? Are outsiders to be informed of the existence of the additional relationship (Knapp 1975)?

The needs of the secondary partner are also important to address (Keener 2004). When a third partner begins to date both members of an existing couple, they need to navigate the existing couple's traditions, rituals, and communication patterns. They also need to cope with the fact that they do not have as much shared history with either member of the original couple as those two members do with one another. A secondary partner who is dating only one member of an existing couple may experience a wish to have more time with that partner than the couple can afford to spare. A therapist can help the secondary partner to address these feelings and negotiate for their needs to be met.

There are also some areas of negotiation that are specific to polyamorous families in which three or more adults set up a household together (Ramey 1975). Are money and possessions pooled for group use or maintained individually? How are child-care duties and housework divided? Do all members of the family talk over disputes together as a group or are conflicts settled in pairs? How does the family cope with the fact that there will be stronger pair-bonds between some members of the family than among others (Keener 2004)?

Polyamorous partners often find themselves charting new territories as they look for ways to meet the needs of all who are involved. It is an even more complicated matter to balance the needs of multiple individuals than it is to make compromises between the members of a pair, so the assistance of an experienced mediator can often ease the communication process.

The therapist can also help the couple to foresee any future issues that might come up (Rust 1996). How would each member of the couple feel if their partner found a second lover before they did? Would it be OK for one of the partners to become lovers with someone who is a mutual friend of the couple? How shall the couple proceed if one partner disapproves of the other partner's new lover? Under what circumstances might each partner feel jealousy, and how might they cope with the jealousy if it arises (Labriola 2004)? Might the currently agreed-upon rules ever be subject to renegotiation as the partners' needs change over time? Kassoff (1989) proposes that the newly polyamorous couple set up a regular schedule of check-in conversations so that they may consciously reassess how their agreements are working.

Polyamorous individuals often feel that they need to prove to others that their lifestyle is viable (Falco 1995). When polyamorous relationships end, it is often assumed by outsiders that the relationship structure was to blame, when in fact any number of other factors might have been behind the breakup. Few people would think to ask whether a breakup of a monogamous couple was due to the couple's choice of monogamy as a lifestyle. A polyamory-aware therapist can assist in the aftermath of a breakup by affirming that the client is not letting the polyamorous community down in ending their relationship and by assisting them in regaining the courage to pursue this type of bond again if that is what they choose to do. They can help the client to learn from their mistakes and apply these lessons to future relationships. A therapist can also help people who are in a troubled polyamorous relationship decide whether to continue in this lifestyle and cope with their feelings of regret and loss if they decide not to continue in the lifestyle.

Therapists can point their clients toward the local or online polyamorous community and this can be a tremendous source of support to those who come out as poly. The polyamorous community is geographically scattered (Weber 2002), and it does not have the same visibility that other subcultures, like the gay community, do (Keener 2004). In large cities there may be regular social gatherings, and from time to time there are regional conferences, but one needs to know where to look in order to find these (Rubin 1982). With the advent of the World Wide Web, the polyamorous community has been linked primarily via the Internet. Web pages provide pointers to local social gatherings, listservs, and chat rooms that are devoted to polyamory concerns. A poly-friendly therapist can offer polyamorous clients information about polyamory support groups and resources in their area, and they can recommend books and websites about polyamory (Rust 1996). Some of these resources are listed in the appendix.

Mental health professionals can also help the polyamorous community by raising social awareness about polyamory. Some ways to do this are including polyamory in discussions of multicultural awareness, mentioning polyamory as a viable lifestyle in family therapy books and courses, inviting polyamorous speakers to give lectures at one's university or counseling center, giving case presentations about polyamorous triads/quads, changing the language on intake forms (i.e., "name of partner/s," not "name of spouse"), noting in counseling center brochures that polyamory is understood/accepted, and learning more on their own about polyamory issues via the resources listed. An ethical therapist will examine their own feelings about polyamory and will seek to address any biases or countertransference that may arise (Keener 2004).

RESEARCH ON POLYAMOROUS BISEXUALS

So far this article has given some basic information on polyamory as well as a beginning sense of how counselors can be of assistance to polyamorous people when they come for therapy. Previous research has examined polyamory in the lesbian, gay, and heterosexual communities, but there has been little focus to date on the experiences of polyamorous people who are bisexual. We turn now to some new research findings that are specific to people who are bisexual and polyamorous.

These research findings are part of a larger, Web-based exploratory study on the identity development of bisexual and polyamorous people (Weitzman 2004). In this chapter we will focus on a subset of the data that addresses some stereotypes about bisexuality and polyamory. We will also present some demographic data concerning the household living situations and coming out experiences of the polyamorous bisexuals in this study.

HYPOTHESES

One stereotype about bisexual people is that they need to date people from more than one gender group simultaneously in order to feel fulfilled (Sumpter 1991). Bisexual individuals work hard to dispel this stereotype, as there are many bisexual people who do not feel the need to have multiple genders represented among their lovers at any given moment. For many bisexual people, gender is not a relevant factor in their choice of lovers—they see their bisexuality as a capacity for falling in love with people of any gender, not as a need to be lovers with each gender.

In this effort to dispel stereotypes, however, it is possible that the experiences of that subset of bisexual people for whom it is important to have lovers from more than one gender group may be being overlooked (Rust 1996). My hypothesis, therefore, was that there would be a sizable proportion of people in each of these categories. In order to assess this, one of the study questions asked, "Does it matter to you whether you have lovers from more than one gender group at the same time?" A second question asked, "Some bisexual people choose a polyamorous relationship style because it allows them to simultaneously date people from more than one gender group. To what extent was a desire to simultaneously date people from more than one gender group a motivating factor in your own choice of polyamory?"

Another stereotype about bisexual and polyamorous people is that they are at high risk for catching (and spreading) sexually transmitted diseases (Munson 1999; Sumpter 1991; West 1996). As the bisexual and polyamorous communities tend to be highly aware of the need to practice safer sex (Moore 1998; National Coalition for Sexual Freedom 2003), it was hypothesized that our respondents would not report any greater lifetime incidence of STD-diagnosis than the general population did. Toward that end, participants in this survey were asked to state whether they had ever been diagnosed with a sexually transmitted disease and, if so, whether these STDs were acquired prior or subsequent to their entering their first polyamorous relationship.

METHODOLOGY

A fifty-four-question survey was put up on the World Wide Web, which investigated various aspects of bisexual and polyamorous experience. Some questions were multiple-choice, while others invited open-ended narratives. Announcements were sent to a variety of U.S., Canadian, and international online polyamorous- and bisexual-themed forums, requesting participation from anyone who identified as bisexual and polyamorous and who was at least eighteen years of age. The age restriction was put into place because the researcher did not have the means to verify parental consent for potential minor-age participants. The announcement encouraged participants to disseminate news of the study to other people who might meet the study criteria (snowball method). The survey did not ask for participants' names, and participants were asked to email the author separately if they wished to be informed later about the results of the study. These methods helped to ensure the anonymity of the survey responses.

DEMOGRAPHICS

A total of 2,169 respondents completed the survey between August of 2003 and February of 2004. The average age of the participants was thirty-four, and their ages ranged from eighteen to seventy-nine. Two-thirds of the participants were between twenty-five and forty-five years of age. Of the total number of participants, 1,424 (66 percent) of the participants were female and 684 (32 percent) were male, 44 (2 percent) were male-to-female transgender, and 21 (1 percent) were female-to-male transgender. With respect to other self-identifications, 107 (5 percent) identified as genderqueer, 21 (1 percent) identified as intersex, and 3 (0.1 percent) identified as "two-spirit." Readers were allowed to choose from multiple gender categories, so there is some overlap between the groups.

Of the total respondents, 1,964 (86 percent) of the participants were Caucasian, 94 (4 percent) were Native American, 58 (3 percent) were of African descent, 55 (2 percent) were Latino, 39 (2 percent) were of Asian or Pacific Island descent, and 9 (0.3 percent) were of Arab descent. Some respondents fell into more than one of these categories and an additional 29 (1 percent) noted that they were of mixed racial descent without specifying which races.

With respect to country of residence, 1,780 (83 percent) of the respondents stated that they lived in the USA at the time of the study, 195 (9 percent) lived in Canada, and 176 (8 percent) lived in other countries. Many religions were represented. The most common religions named by participants were Pagan/Wiccan (27 percent), Christian/Catholic (11 percent), Jewish (4 percent), Unitarian (4 percent), and Buddhist (2 percent). A substantial minority of respondents (39 percent) stated that they were agnostic, atheist, or held no religion.

With respect to parenting, 38 percent of the respondents stated that they were actively playing a part in raising children or step-children.

Kinsey, Pomeroy, and Martin (1948) described sexual orientation along a continuum in which o represents heterosexuality, 6 represents homosexuality, and 1 through 5 represent varying degrees of bisexuality. Of the respondents in this study, 1,049 (49 percent) stated that they were attracted more to members of another gender than to members of their own gender (Kinsey 1 and 2), 638 (30 percent) said that they were attracted equally to members of their own gender and members of another gender (Kinsey 3), and 344 (16 percent) said that they were attracted more to members of their own gender than to members of another gender (Kinsey 4 and 5). A smaller number of respondents, 150 (7 percent), said that the Kinsey Scale did not adequately represent their situations, giving reasons such as "I'm attracted to personality, not gender," "I'm attracted to one gender physically and another intellectually or emotionally," and "I'm attracted most to people who are transgender or androgynous."

Within the total number of participants, 1,758 (81 percent) noted that they had identified as heterosexual at some point in the past and 476 (22 percent) said that they had identified as homosexual prior to coming out as bisexual. With respect to preferred style of relationship involvement, 1,376 (64 percent) of participants said that they had preferred monogamy during an earlier time in their lives, but a substantial 779 (36 percent) said that they had never preferred monogamy at any point in their lives. This is quite a significant finding given the power and pervasiveness of the cultural expectation of monogamy.

Participants were asked, "How many of the people who you are presently romantically involved with live in your household at present?" Of the 2,031 who replied, 710 (35 percent) did not live with anyone with whom they were romantically involved, 1,153 (57 percent) lived with one person with whom they were romantically involved, 127 (6 percent) lived together with two people with whom they were romantically involved, 30 (1 percent) lived with three people with whom they were romantically involved, 8 (0.4 percent) lived with four people with whom they were romantically involved, and 3 (0.1 percent) lived with five or more people with whom they were romantically involved.

As noted earlier, Weber (2002) found that out of approximately 1,000 polyamorous people surveyed, the majority had not revealed that they were polyamorous to one or more people in the following categories: their parents, children, extended family members, neighbors, coworkers, or bosses. In general, this was because they feared being shunned or discriminated against. Similarly, we found that 1,051 (52 percent) of the respondents in our sample were not out to their parents as being bisexual, while 1,177 (59 percent) were not out to their parents as being polyamorous. Likewise, 1,433 (71 percent) were not out to their extended families as being bisexual, while 1,560 (79 percent) were not out to their extended families as being poly. This shows that people who are bisexual and polyamorous are often isolated from the types of mainstream family and community support that heterosexual and monogamous people enjoy.

The decision to be selective about who to come out to appears to pay off, however: 1,777 (84 percent) of the people in our sample found that all or most of the people who they came out to were supportive of their bisexuality, and 1,338 (64 percent) found that all or most of the people who they came out to were supportive of their polyamory. It is sobering to note, however, that 756 (36 percent) respondents found that only half or fewer of the people they came out to were supportive of their polyamory. This represents a considerable amount of prejudice that polyamorous people have to contend with in their daily lives. Therapists can be of help to bi-poly people as they go through the process of deciding whether to come out (Rust 1996) and as they cope with discrimination.

RESULTS AND DISCUSSION

DISPELLING THE "ONE OF EACH" MYTH

As noted earlier, one stereotype about bisexual people is that they need to date people from more than one gender group simultaneously in order to feel fulfilled (Sumpter 1991). Many bisexual people state that they have no such need. My hypothesis was that there would be a sizable proportion of participants in each of these groups: many bisexual people would not feel a need for simultaneous partners from multiple gender groups, but there would be some bisexuals who would hold such a preference. To answer this hypothesis, one of the study questions asked, "Does it matter to you whether you have lovers from more than one gender group at the same time?" A second question asked, "Some bisexual people choose a polyamorous relationship style because it allows them to simultaneously date people from more than one gender group. To what extent was a desire to simultaneously date people from more than one gender group a motivating factor in your own choice of polyamory?"

Addressing the first question, 1,515 (70 percent) said that it *did not matter* to them whether their lovers were of the same or different gender from one another at any given time. Ninety-two (4 percent) stated a preference to date lovers *from only one* gender group at a time, and 476 (22 percent) said that they *do prefer* that more than one gender be represented among their lovers at any given time. This is roughly comparable to Rust's (1996) finding that 16.7 percent of the bi women in her sample had partners of two genders. Seventy-eight respondents (4 percent) said that none of these three options applied to them, for reasons such as "I prefer to date people whose gender is very fluid," "my preferences in this regard change over time," "I haven't yet had enough experience to tell," and "my polyamory agreement only allows me to date people who are from a different gender group than my partner is."

In response to the second question, 1,062 respondents, or 50 percent, said that their choice of polyamory *was not* motivated by a desire to simultaneously date members of more than one gender group, although 237 respondents, or 12 percent, said that the *main* motivating factor in their choice of polyamory was the desire to simultaneously date people from more than one gender group. A total of 724 respondents, or 34 percent, said that a desire to date people from more than one gender group was *one of several factors* in their choice of polyamory.

In short, the majority of polyamorous bisexual people do not feel a particular need to date people from more than one gender group simultaneously. Rather, the majority of polyamorous bisexuals would appear to simply not regard gender as an important factor when choosing their intimate partners. There *are* some, however, for whom it *is* important to be intimate with people from more than one gender group. The needs of this latter minority deserve recognition. They should not, however, be taken as representative of the whole population of people who are bisexual, and this has occurred in the past. These results dispel the stereotype that bisexual people need to date people from more than one gender group simultaneously, while affirming the diversity of needs that do exist among bisexuals. Bisexuals are not a homogenous population, and the needs of each subgroup deserve recognition and validation.

DISPELLING THE "STD RISK" MYTH

Bisexual and polyamorous people have been stereotyped as being at high risk for catching (and spreading) sexually transmitted diseases (Munson 1999; Sumpter 1991; West 1996). The polyamorous and bisexual communities are quite conscientious about safer sex practices, however (Moore 1998; National Coalition for Sexual Freedom 2003), and so it was hypothesized that there would be no greater prevalence of STDs in the bi-poly population than in the general population.

Participants were asked to divulge whether they had at any point in their lives been diagnosed with a sexually transmitted disease. If the answer was yes, then they were also asked to specify whether they were diagnosed with the STD before or after they entered their first polyamorous relationship. Of those who responded to the question (n = 1,944), 1,446 (75 percent) stated that they had never been diagnosed with HIV, herpes, trichomoniasis, chlamydia, genital warts, HPV, gonorrhea, or syphilis. (Candidiasis and pubic lice were not included in this analysis, as these conditions can be acquired via nonsexual means). Likewise, the Alan Guttmacher Institute (1993) reports that one in four Americans will contract a sexually transmitted disease in their lifetime, which is exactly equivalent to the number of participants in our study that reported having been diagnosed with an STD.

Looking more closely at some of the specific STDs: out of 1,944 respondents, only 3 (0.16 percent) had been diagnosed with HIV. The national adult prevalence rate of HIV is 0.6 percent (Joint United Nations Programme on HIV/AIDS 2002) so the rate of occurrence in our sample is in fact somewhat lower than that of the general population. With respect to genital herpes, 128 (6.62 percent) of 1,944 respondents in this study stated that they had been diagnosed with the disorder. This is significantly below the lifetime risk national average of 20 percent (American Social Health Association 2001). For genital warts, 99 (5.12 percent) of 1,944 respondents stated that they had been diagnosed with the disorder, which is almost exactly equivalent to the lifetime risk national average of 5 percent (Koutsky 2003). For trichomoniasis, 65 (3.36 percent) out of 1,944 of our respondents had been diagnosed with the disorder compared to a 20 percent lifetime risk national average (Child and Youth Health 2003).

Of the 488 (25 percent) respondents who *had* been diagnosed with one of the aforementioned STDs, 355 responded to the question whether their diagnosis had occurred prior or subsequent to their adoption of a polyamorous lifestyle. A full two-thirds (234) of these 355 respondents noted that their diagnoses had in fact ensued prior to their beginning a polyamorous lifestyle, when their sexual activities were occurring within the context of monogamous relationships. This lends further support to the notion that it is not the number of partners so much as the level of adherence to safer sex practices that determines whether or not STDs are transmitted.

LIMITATIONS OF THE PRESENT STUDY

This study has a number of limitations. First, the 2,169 participants mostly heard about the study in online forums related to polyamory and bisexuality, implying that these aspects of their lives are particularly salient areas of focus for them at present. This also implies that these respondents have successfully located community forums devoted to bisexuality and polyamory, whereas not all bisexual and polyamorous people have yet discovered these discussion venues. It is not possible to know the extent to which these results would be different if people who were in open relationships had been recruited from more mainstream forums.

Participants were also self-selected, therefore, we don't know if those who chose not to participate might have differed from the present sample in some meaningful ways. Furthermore, while news of the survey did find its way to a number of different countries, it was only printed in the English language, and thus it is not clear whether results would have differed had the study been more accessible to people whose primarily spoken language was other than English. In addition, two thirds of the participants in this study identified as female, and it is not certain whether a more balanced male-female gender ratio would have yielded differing results.

An attempt was made to word the survey in such a way that the answer choices would be as transgender-inclusive as possible, but the very concept of bisexuality is frequently not perceived as one that affirms the existence of more than two genders. Hence some transgender respondents reported that they found it difficult to answer certain questions accurately, and this may in turn have affected the accuracy of the results.

With respect to the STD data, there are always dangers inherent in comparing current participants' results to previously collected national sample data. The methodology used to assess the frequency of STDs among participants in the present study (self-report) is not the same as the methodology that was used by the various sexual health agencies to assess the STD frequency within the general population. In addition, not all respondents in this survey were from the United States; nor were the gender ratios even. Results in the STD section should therefore be considered preliminary until corroborated by more precise means of study.

Research has shown that polyamory is a viable lifestyle and that a significant portion of the population participates in this lifestyle. The present study offers some evidence toward debunking some of the stereotypes about people who are bisexual and polyamorous. It is hoped that this chapter as a whole has provided some broader insight into the lifestyles and mental health concerns of the polyamorous community. Clearly, the field of polyamory research is a fertile one and there is a great deal of opportunity—and great need—for continued research into the actual characteristics and concerns of this population.

NOTE

The author would like to thank Emmett Pickerel for his work in creating and maintaining the database that was used to collect the data for the study.

REFERENCES

Alan Guttmacher Institute. (1993). *Testing Positive: Sexually transmitted disease and the public health response.* New York: Alan Guttmacher Institute.

alt.polyamory Usenet Newsgroup. (1997). alt.polyamory frequently asked questions (FAQ). Retrieved April 8, 2004, from http://www.faqs.org/faqs/polyamory/faq.

American Social Health Association (2001). *Herpes: Get the facts.* Retrieved April 8, 2004, from http://www.ashastd.org/hrc/educate.html.

Barillas, C. (1997). Tucson passes benefits law for gay city workers. *Data Lounge* (April 29). Retrieved April 8, 2004, from http://www.datalounge.com/datalounge/news/record.html?record = 1994.

Blasband, D. and Peplau, L.A. (1985). Sexual exclusivity versus openness in gay male couples. *Journal of Sexual Behavior*, 14(5) 395–412.

Bricker, L. (2003). Town insurance plans to cover domestic partners. *Rockingham News* (March 21). Retrieved April 8, 2004, from www.seacoastonline.com/2003news/rock/03212003/news/19004.htm.

Browning, C., Reynolds, A.L., and Dworkin, S.H. (1991). Affirmative psychotherapy for lesbian women. *Counseling Psychologist*, 19(2), 177–196.

Child and Youth Health (2003). *Trichomoniasis.* Retrieved April 8, 2004, from Child and Youth Health Web site: http://www.cyh.com/cyh/youthtopics/usr_srch2.stm?topic_id = 1347andprecis = null.

Cloud, J. (1999). Henry and Mary and Janet and . . . *Time*, 154(20), 90–91.

Dixon, J. K. (1985). Sexuality and relationship changes in married females following the commencement of bisexual activity. In F. Klein and T.J. Wolf (Eds.), *Two lives to lead: Bisexuality in men and women* (pp. 115–133). Binghamton, NY: Harrington Park.

Ellis, A. (1965). *The Case for Sexual Liberty* (vol. 1). Aurora, NY: Seymour.

Falco, K.L. (1995). Therapy with lesbians: The essentials. *Psychotherapy in Private Practice*, 13(4), 69–83.

Hames, R. (1996). Costs and benefits of monogamy and polygyny for Yanomamo women. *Ethnology and Sociobiology*, 17, 181–199.

Hymer, S.M., and Rubin, A.M. (1982). Alternative lifestyle clients: Therapists' attitudes and clinical experiences. *Small Group Behavior*, 13(4), 532–541.

Joint United Nations Programme on HIV/AIDS (2002). *Report on the Global HIV/AIDS Epidemic.* Geneva, Switzerland: UNAIDS.

Kassoff, E. (1989). Nonmonogamy in the lesbian community. *Women and Therapy*, 8(1–2), 167–182.

Keener, M. C. (2004). A Phenomenology of Polyamorous Persons. Unpublished masters thesis submitted to the University of Utah, Salt Lake City. Retrieved April 8, 2004, from http://www.xmission.com/~mkeener/thesis.pdf.

Kinsey, A.C., Pomeroy, W., and Martin, C. (1948). *Sexual Behavior in the Human Male.* Philadelphia: Saunders.

Knapp, J.J. (1975). Some nonmonogamous marriage styles and related attitudes and practices of marriage counselors. *Family Coordinator*, 24(4), 505–514.

Knapp, J. J. (1976). An exploratory study of seventeen sexually open marriages. *Journal of Sex Research*, 12(3), 206–219.

Koutsky, L. (2003). Epidemiology of HPV and prospects for prevention through vaccination. Paper presented at the Fortieth Annual Conference of the Association of Reproductive Health Professionals, September, La Jolla, CA. Retrieved April 8, 2004, from the Association of Reproductive Health Professionals Web site: http://www.arhp.org/files/Koutsky.pdf.

Kurdek, L. A., and Schmitt, J.P. (1986). Relationship quality of gay men in closed or open relationships. *Journal of Homosexuality*, 12(2), 85–99.

Labriola, K. (1996). *Unmasking the green-eyed monster: Managing jealousy in open relationships.* Retrieved April 8, 2004, from http://www.cat-and-dragon.com/stef/Poly/Labriola/jealousy.html.

Labriola, K. (1999). Models of open relationships. In M. Munson and J. Stelboum (Eds.), *The lesbian polyamory reader: Open relationships, non-monogamy, and casual sex* (pp. 217–225). Binghamton, NY: Harrington Park.

McWhirter, D. P., and Mattison, A. M. (1984). *The male couple: How relationships develop.* Englewood Cliffs, NJ: Prentice-Hall.

Makanjuola, R. O. A. (1987). The Nigerian psychiatric patient and his family. *International Journal of Family Psychiatry, 8*(4), 363–373.

Mann, J (1975). Is sex counseling here to stay? *Counseling Psychologist, 5*(1), 60–63.

Moore, J. (1998). *A few key political issues for bi people compared and contrasted to those of lesbian and gay people.* Retrieved April 8, 2004, from http://bitheway.org/Bi/Pol.htm.

Munson, M. (1999). Safer sex and the polyamorous lesbian. In M. Munson and J. Stelboum (Eds.), *The lesbian polyamory reader: Open relationships, non-monogamy, and casual sex* (pp. 209–216). Binghamton, NY: Harrington Park.

National Coalition for Sexual Freedom (2003). *Polyamory sound bites.* Retrieved April 8, 2004 from http://www.ncsfreedom.org/library/polysoundbites.htm.

Page, E. H. (2004). Mental health services experiences of bisexual women and bisexual men: An empirical study. *Journal of Bisexuality 3*(3/4), 137–160.

Peabody, S. A. (1982). Alternative life styles to monogamous marriage: Variants of normal behavior in psychotherapy clients. *Family Relations, 31,* 425–434.

Peplau, L. A. (1981) Research on homosexual couples: An overview. *Journal of Homosexuality, 8*(2), 3–8.

Polyamory Society. (1997). Polyamory society compersion index. Retrieved April 8, 2004, from http://www.polyamorysociety.org/compersion.html.

Ramey, J. W. (1975). Intimate groups and networks: Frequent consequence of sexually open marriage. *Family Coordinator, 24*(4), 515–530.

Roman, M., Charles, E., and Karasu, T. B. (1978). The value system of psychotherapists and changing mores. *Psychotherapy Theory, Research, and Practice, 15*(4), 409–415.

Rubin, A. M. (1982). Sexually open versus sexually exclusive marriage: A comparison of dyadic adjustment. *Alternative Lifestyles, 5*(2), 101–106.

Rubin, A. M., and Adams, J. R. (1986). Outcomes of sexually open marriages. *Journal of Sex Research, 22*(3), 311–319.

Rust, P. C. (1996). Monogamy and polyamory: Relationship issues for bisexuals. In B. A. Firestein (Ed.), *Bisexuality: The psychology and politics of an invisible minority* (pp. 127–148). Thousand Oaks, CA: Sage.

Sumpter, S. F. (1991). Myths/realities of bisexuality. In Hutchins, L. and Ka'ahumanu, L. (Eds.), *Bi any other name: Bisexual people speak out* (pp. 12–13). Boston: Alyson.

Watson, J., and Watson, M. A. (1982). Children of open marriages: Parental disclosure and perspectives. *Alternative Lifestyles, 5*(1), 54–62.

Weber, A. (2002). Who are we? And other interesting impressions. *Loving More, 30,* 4–6.

Weitzman, G. (1999). What psychology professionals should know about polyamory: The lifestyles and mental health concerns of polyamorous individuals. Paper presented at the Eighth Annual Diversity Conference, March, Albany. Retrieved April 8, 2004, from http://www.polyamory.org/~joe/polypaper.htm.

Weitzman, G. (2004). The identity development of bisexual and polyamorous individuals. Manuscript.

West, C. (1996). *Lesbian polyfidelity*. San Francisco: Bootlegger.

Ziskin, J., and Ziskin, M. (1975). Co-marital sex agreements: An emerging issue in sexual counseling. *Counseling Psychologist*, 6(1), 81–83.

APPENDIX: POLYAMORY RESOURCES

POLYAMORY AND THERAPY

What Psychology Professionals Should Know About Polyamory: The Lifestyles and Mental Health Concerns of Polyamorous Individuals, http://www.polyamory.org/~joe/poly-paper.htm, by Geri D. Weitzman, Ph.D., gdw@numenor.org

The Poly-friendly Professionals Directory, http://www.polychromatic.com/pfp

BOOKS ON POLYAMORY

Deborah M. Anapol, *Polyamory: The New Love Without Limits: Secrets of Sustainable Intimate Relationships* (Intinet Resource Center, 1997)

Dossie Easton and Catherine A. Liszt, *The Ethical Slut: A Guide to Infinite Sexual Possibilities* (Greenery, 1998)

Ryam Nearing, *Loving More: The Polyfidelity Primer*, 3d ed. (PEP, 1992)

Marcia Munson and Judith P. Stelboum, eds. *The Lesbian Polyamory Reader: Open Relationships, Nonmonogamy, and Casual Sex* (Haworth, 1999)

Celeste West, *Lesbian Polyfidelity: A Pleasure Guide for the Woman Whose Heart Is Open to Multiple Concurrent Sexualoves, or How to Keep Non-monogamy Safe, Sane, Honest, and Laughing, You Rogue!* (Bootlegger, 1996)

WEBSITES ON POLYAMORY

http://www.polyamory.org
   A Web site of useful Poly 101 info, affiliated with the Usenet newsgroup alt.polyamory

http://www.lovemore.com
   Another Web site of useful Poly 101 info, affiliated with *Loving More*

http://www.google.com/Top/Society/Relationships/Alternative_Lifestyles/Polyamory
   Provides access to a variety of polyamory-related resources and links to organizations

http://www.polyarmorysociety.org
   Educational Web site of the Polyamory Society

http://www.lovethatworks.org Web site for the Institute for 21st Century Relationships

http://www.faqs.org/faqs/polyamory/faq
   Frequently asked questions on polyamory

http://www.faqs.org/faqs/polyamory/faq-supplement
   What not to do in a poly relationship!

http://www.cat-and-dragon.com/stef/Poly/Labriola/jealousy.html
   Coping with jealousy

POLYAMORY MAILING LISTS

poly@polyamory.org
  A national poly list: http://poly.polyamory.org/mailman/listinfo/poly
Usenet Newsgroup alt.polyamory
  See http://www.polyamory.org above
Yahoo group PolyMono
  For poly people who are in a relationship with monogamous people; there is also a MonoPoly group. Sign up with Yahoo groups and then go to http://groups.yahoo.com/group/polymono to subscribe

18

PLAYING WITH SACRED FIRE

BUILDING EROTIC COMMUNITIES

Loraine Hutchins

When we hold the erotic as sacred, we say that our capacity for pleasure has a value in and of itself, that in fact it is one of the ways in which we connect with the deepest purposes of the universe.

—STARHAWK (1995)

EROTIC COMMUNITIES are social or friendship networks that include the sharing of sexual experiences between network members in various combinations. Erotic communities are groups where such behaviors are normalized and supported and the participants, or at least the leaders, put conscious effort into managing the sexual energy of the group in a positive and creative way. Bisexual individuals and those having other sexual orientations that have interests in group sex and/or sacred sexuality rituals are the focus of this chapter. In discussing the beliefs and practices associated with these behaviors I pay particular attention to groups that are most inclusive of the participation of sexual minorities and welcome their leadership.

As counselors it behooves us to understand a wide range of sexual practices so that we can better help clients discern when participation in an activity or group might contribute to their personal health and growth and when it might not. This chapter describes a few of the most interesting new erotic communities developing around the U.S. today, presented within a historic context and analysis of the roots upon which such customs are based. It closes with suggestions for counselors on how to help clients evaluate group sexual practices and sacred sex traditions, especially relative to whether and when such activities are healthy for them.

A WIDER, MORE VARIED, AND BALANCED SENSE OF "SEX"

Many people want to enhance their sex life. They may not consider expanding their definition of sex itself as part of this endeavor. They just want better orgasms and more pleasure in whatever erotic experience they pursue. What those who have not seriously studied such traditions as Tantra don't realize is that it is not so much about finding Ms. Right or Mr. Right and creating that promised "harmony of opposites," as it is about getting *beyond* binaries and polarities entirely and discovering the presence of all sexual aspects within one's *self* and the unity of oneself with all beings and creation.

Sacred sex practitioners are often enticed by concretized visions of the Divine Marriage, sometimes called *Hieros Gamos* by the ancient Greeks. We are taught to focus on a differently gendered partner as representative of all that we lack, but we may find as we study more that loving others is a necessary step, not an end point. It is part of realizing that wondrous enigma that we each contain all of divinity within us and that it is also everywhere around us. Bisexual individuals, especially those who embrace their sexual orientation consciously and publicly, are particularly well-suited to opening themselves up to a wider range of erotic experiences and helping others do the same (Hutchins 2002).

Tantra and other forms of sacred sexuality can be profoundly revolutionary disciplines: paths wherein men discover their female side, women their masculinity, and everyone, if they plunge far enough, realizes how key self-love is and how illusory sex and gender differences really are. Tantra and other sacred sex teachers don't usually emphasize the polymorphous omnisexuality of the discipline publicly, but once the student reaches the higher levels of study it is readily acknowledged.

This more expansive experience of the power of Eros in all of life also explains why a diversity of sexual expression underlies any thorough study of sacred sexuality and why an examination of the roles of women and other sexually marginalized groups must ultimately be addressed by those who practice sacred sex and other erotic forms of group intimacy. However, the immensity and implications of such erotic/spirit transformation can initially be very threatening for some participants to absorb. Most people proceed slowly into exploring sacred sexuality's mysteries and many drop out before getting very far.

The large majority of people doing sacred and group sex identify as heterosexual. However, a number of those most actively engaged in alternative group sexual practices are bisexual, bi-curious, or bi-friendly, and some identify as lesbian and gay. In many arenas the categories themselves are under debate, especially as bisexuals, intersexed individuals, and transgendered people openly join the ranks of those resisting a bifurcated sex and gender system (see chapters by Denny, chapter 14, and Horner, chapter 15). Some call themselves gender-queer to express discomfort with current binary label choices or because they experience sex and gender as fluid, as spectrum, particularly as it relates to their sense of themselves as a spirit within a body (Bornstein 1998; Kaldera 2001). All these people are increasingly coming out into the open and educating society about their true experiences and concerns.

The so-called female aspects of sex—receptivity, nurturance, and full-bodied, multiple orgasmic capacity—are now emphasized in pursuit of a deeper balance for people of all gender expressions, particularly in the groups I have been studying. Participants also report that the attempt to rebalance spirituality and sexuality is a needed, welcome antidote to what is usually called the war between the sexes and the meat market, a social and public environment fraught with the competition and conflict prevalent when sexual desire is openly expressed in heterosexual and male-dominated mixed gender group space.

Erotic energy exchanges with spiritual themes also take place at BDSM or Leather/Fetish community rituals (Califia and Campbell 1997) and other initiatory, ecstatic Sex Magic events based in the traditions of various cultures (Kaldera 2001). In fact, in some contemporary sacred sex circles the crossover between sacred sex and BDSM is so intense that the term *SM* has ceased meaning sado-masochism. *SM* now stands for Sex Magic instead.

As counselors, when we notice these interests and/or activities in the lives of our clients, it is best to be knowledgeable about the range of possibilities available to them and to obtain accurate information on exactly what is involved in specific alternatives. I offer the following descriptions and prescriptions as a partial guide for those who would, or already do embrace this multileveled path of self-education: whether as counselors, clients, celebrants, participants, and teachers, and also in tribute to the aspects of those roles within us all.

TODAY'S SACRED SEX SCENE

Contemporary sacred sex traditions and practices are no longer confined to the educated, esoteric elite (Hutchins 2001a,b). Couples who may never participate in any kind of sacred sex group or ritual still enjoy bedtime fantasies evoked by reading the *Kama Sutra*, the ancient Eastern tome on the art of lovemaking that is now widely available. Group sex does not automatically imply sacred sex and sacred sex does not universally imply group sex. While the two classes of sexual expression do overlap, there are many ways they do not. Group sex can be approached in a solely recreational manner, without any spiritual intent. Sacred sex can be experienced by oneself or with only one other partner. Yet humanity's longing for connection, group intimacy, and community makes sacred sex at least potentially a communal experience. The glossary below provides an explanation of some of the key terms used in this chapter.

GLOSSARY

BDSM The abbreviation for bondage and discipline, dominance and submission, and sado-masochism. This acronym denotes a variety of erotic practices, roles, and relationships based on intensifying sensations, increasing endorphin highs, and exploring the pleasure-pain intersection. The BDSM community overlaps with the Leather/Fetish community but is also somewhat distinct from it as people into leather or fetish may not be into intense sensation, role-playing, or pain. This community was one of the first communities to develop safer sex guidelines during the early part of the HIV/AIDS crisis. Because their practices are often misunderstood and pathologized, they coined the phrase, "safe, sane, and consensual" to distinguish what they do from situations of sexual abuse, assault, or other coerced behaviors.

GENDER QUEER A way of characterizing one's gender without reference to binary oppositions of male or female, masculine or feminine. People who use this self-identifier feel that they are neither or both, that their gender expression cannot be confined or defined by the traditional roles as the culture currently defines them and that they define themselves. Ask them what pronouns they want you to use in referring to them and learn about how they experience gender. You will learn a lot.

INTERSEX A condition distinct from transgender, though sometimes confused with it. Intersexed people used to be called hermaphrodites. They are people born with genitalia that have some aspects of both maleness and femaleness, a condition as common as one in every thousand births. See http://www.isna.org, the Intersex Society of North America, for information.

LEATHER/FETISH COMMUNITY Similar to the BDSM community but distinguished from it in the sense that some people eroticize leather and/or specific fetishes but not necessarily bondage and discipline or dominance and submission.

LGBT (LESBIAN, GAY, BISEXUAL, AND TRANSGENDER) This acronym is used variously, sometimes written as *GLBT*, sometimes used interchangeably with *queer* or *gay community*, sometimes with the addition of *QQI* (Queer, Questioning, and Intersex) as an extension of the term, as in *LGBTQQI*.

POLYAMORY The philosophy and practice of loving more than one person at a time, openly and honestly, and/or having multiple adult relationships in a variety of sexual and intimate forms.

QUEER I use this term interchangeably with *LGBT*; however, I realize not everyone does and that it is a sensitive term that some elder LGBT people, in particular, may find offensive or hurtful, not a term of pride. However, it's an easy shorthand word referring to all sexualities outside the sexual mainstream. When used in this sense, it encompasses the BDSM and Leather/Fetish communities and even other sexually "deviant" groups, such as swingers, the polyamorous, and/or heterosexuals who are a part of such groups.

SACRED INTIMATE This term was developed as an alternative to the term *sacred prostitute* so that the sex-for-money connotations are removed. Sacred intimates are erotic priestesses or priests who minister with their bodies as well as their consciousness, in service to their spiritual guides. Like the Masters and Johnson sex surrogates of old, they are erotic mentors. Unlike those surrogates, they do not usually work with licensed psychologists or within a psychology model per se.

SM A shorthand way of referring to BDSM and DS, as defined above. Sometimes also used to mean *Sex Magic*, i.e., ritualized ways of working with erotic arousal, intention, and communion in sacred space.

SWINGERS A term coined in the 1960s to mean sharing spouses in consensual recreational sex parties that couples participate in together, sometimes also called wife swapping.

TRANSGENDER This is an umbrella term that includes people who were assigned one sex or gender at birth but feel they are truly another, as well as people like transvestites and cross-dressers who feel at home in their birth sex or gender but like to play with dressing up as the other. The term used to differentiate between transsexual people, who had, or were planning to have SRS (Sex Reassignment Surgery), and others, i.e., the rest of the transgender category, who weren't. But that has changed in recent years since, for example, some people who identify as masculine and have biologically female bodies have decided not to pursue a full surgical sex change, blurring the boundaries between transsexual and transgender identities.

The sacred sex scene in contemporary U.S. culture is primarily white and middle class. Although most white people of European descent are completely ignorant of cultures other than their own, many communities of color have esoteric erotic customs and concepts rooted in indigenous traditions that have been handed down from generation to generation despite centuries of suppression. With the legacies of slavery and genocide, and the high levels of institutionalized racism still active today, elders of color who teach such erotic knowledge are understandably wary about sharing their wisdom publicly. They are aware that ethnic and racial minority people are still more at risk of being criminalized and victimized for openly sexual behaviors than the average white person.

Americans, in general, also have a tendency to romanticize the culture of the East and are often more interested in embracing Hindu and Buddhist sacred sex practices that they consider exotic, rather than in discovering the lost roots of their own religious heritage. For example, many Westerners fail to discover that Christianity, Judaism, and Islam all have mystical traditions, albeit minority and hidden ones, that contain rich erotic symbolism.

HISTORY OF U.S. SACRED SEX TRADITIONS

Historically in the U.S., ceremonies focused on sacred sexuality were confined to isolated religious retreat houses in rural settings or within the inner circles of urban high society. Secrecy about the existence of these esoteric practices was paramount. Now information about sacred sex is readily available via New Age newspapers at health food stores, in advertisements inside gift catalogs, on cable television shows, and on the Internet. I have even seen sacred sex workshops listed within the event calendars of some of the more progressive religious communities. Training in sacred sex traditions and practices, albeit considerably watered down, is available at "neo-pagan" summer festivals and more expensive New Age retreat workshops in every region of the United States today. There are also regular Friday-night drop-in erotic massage groups in cities such as Houston, New York, Seattle, Minneapolis, Washington, DC, and in the San Francisco Bay Area, as well as occasionally in other places throughout the southeast and midwest. Tantra is currently the most popular and well-known sacred sex tradition in the United States, in part because it is the most well-documented sacred sex tradition, West or East.

THE TRADITIONS OF WESTERN TANTRA

Tantra has become a catchword to describe any interest in sacred sex. While this is inaccurate, it is important to understand. Technically, Tantra is a specific set of ancient traditions and only one form of sacred sexuality or erotic spirituality practice in use today. But Tantra principles and influence are so widespread that it is often regarded as equivalent to "sacred sex." Thousands of English-language books have been written about the ancient Eastern traditions of Tantra. For purposes of this discussion, it is important to understand that Tantra involves this sequential process: 1. deliberately exploring one's sexuality, 2. learning to prolong arousal, and 3. eventually working with the energy of arousal and spreading it through one's entire system—mind, body and spirit.[1]

American forms of Tantra have developed extensively during the last several decades, as can be seen by any cursory search of Web sites such as http://www.tantra.com. Many of those offering sacred sexuality instruction today learned their skills and philosophies from Tantra teachers such as Baghwan Shree Rajneesh (Osho), Margo Anand, Charles and Caroline Muir, the Ramsdales, Jwala, John Mumford, and Bodhi Avinasha and Sunyata Saraswati. Mantak Chia's Taoist trainings, Stan and Helen Dale's Human Awareness Institute (HAI),[2] Deborah Taj Anapol's Sacred Space Institute, Betty Dodson's bodysex and self-loving workshops for women, and Harley Swift Deer's Quodoshka workshops are also popular formats (Hutchins 2001a,b).

To summarize, in the United States erotic communities encompass a wide behavioral and philosophic spectrum, ranging from a single circle of individuals to several overlapping circles of friends and acquaintances that share occasional partners sequentially and may or may not socialize, work, or live together. Erotic communities can also be more intimate, formalized, and intentional teaching networks that include regular rituals where erotic energy is exchanged in a variety of forms between more than two people at a time.

Within this latter case there is also a wide range of activity, since I purposely use the phrase *erotic energy exchange*, rather than such narrower descriptions as *having oral, anal, and/or vaginal sex*. Erotic energy exchange encompasses a wide variety of behaviors: from hugs, meditation, chanting, deep and rhythmic breathing, to dancing and eye gazing with clothes on in structured Tantra classes. Erotic energy exchange may also include full-on group lovemaking, utilizing safer sex or otherwise, for ceremonial and/or recreational purposes.

It is important to remember that the vast majority of people drawn to exploring sacred sexuality and erotic communities do so as a support to already existing relationships and do the bulk of their exploration through books, videos, and other resources. Those who actually end up engaging in group and or sacred sex ceremonies are in the minority, albeit a minority often fantasized about and somewhat romanticized by other segments of the population.

INTRODUCING EROTIC CELEBRATIONS INTO COMMUNAL SPACE

As a long-time observer of erotic subcultures and the sexual behavior of the human animal, I noticed a significant shift in attitudes toward sexual encounters that occurred following the onset of the HIV/AIDS crisis in the 1980s. The change was this: a dwindling number of people assigned sexuality and spirituality to two separate realms; more sought to unite them, privately and publicly. Perhaps awakened by grief and longing, many now fervently seek to integrate Eros and Spirit as one.

This urge to reclaim a united spirituality and sexuality has led to a reevaluation of both spiritual practices and ideas about sexuality. It has also led to examining all aspects of sexual behavior, from long-term relationships to casual encounters, and even one's erotic connection with oneself, in terms of making each aspect more congruent with our most deeply held values. One prime example of this change is the use of sex-positive group erotic events to explicitly model, teach, and normalize safer sex practices. Sex-positive group erotic events teach safer sex in a much more effective way than any public health poster or brochure-based entreaty could achieve. This sex-positive communal culture includes organizations that range from sex education groups such as the Safer Sex Sluts of the San Francisco Bay Area and Minneapolis/St. Paul, which use simulated sex skits to make safer sex appealing and accessible to a variety of sexually active adults, to groups like the Queen of Heaven, discussed later in this chapter, which invite people into actual, full-on, safer sex erotic experiences in group space. The current movement for sexual liberation and spiritual renewal discussed in this chapter already spans more than one generation of age cohorts and is probably best characterized as a living process. Even the basic terminology for describing these activities is in great flux.

It will come as no surprise to many professionals who have been involved in sexuality-related research and clinical practice that most of the programs described above were started by professional sex educators who are bisexual. Bisexual women and men act anthropologically as society's lubricants, troubadours, and yentas. Such roles are not limited to bisexual individuals of course, but bisexuals frequently assume the role of interpreting same-sex erotic customs for heterosexuals and other-sex sexual customs for same-sex oriented participants.

Despite conservative backlash, bisexual people continue to come out of the closet and share their capacity to enjoy erotic intimacy. Not all people currently involved in building erotic communities are bisexual, bi-aware, or bi-friendly and certainly not all bisexuals are interested in such activities. However, I believe it is this ambassadorial, shape-shifting talent that partly accounts for why so many bisexual women and men are leaders in teaching people how to have healthier sexual expression, including how to create the kinds of erotic communities described in this chapter.

In these circles of explicit sexuality I have observed a slight lessening of focus on penile/vaginal intercourse (supposedly the sine qua non of all human sexual behavior) and, correspondingly, more focus on full-body orgasm, or what some call nongendered orgasm, however it is achieved. This certainly changes the definitions of what orgasm is and what the erotic may encompass. Betty Dodson, the "dean" of contemporary sex educators, has focused her life's work on helping people reclaim masturbation, or solo-sex, as a form of self-love, regardless of whether or not the individual chooses to also have what she calls partner-sex. Dodson is also bisexual and writes extensively about her own sexual life as a vehicle for teaching others to affirm their sex lives (Dodson 1987).

Speakers at one sacred sex conference I attended described humanity's progression in the development of terminology, concepts, and experiences of sexuality as a "paradigm shift," part of our evolutionary process. This progression begins with 1. sex having reproductive intent and focus, moving to 2. the countercultural era in which sex was viewed as more recreational in focus, and now entering a new era of 3. experiencing sexuality's regenerative and spiritual possibilities, related to, but not necessarily linked to penile/vaginal (reproductive) intercourse.

This third stage is focused on intimacy, connection, healing and celebration, more than it is on procreation, and reclaims *recreation*'s truer meaning: "re-creation." As Buddhist scholar and social activist/trainer Joanna Macy has said, in *World as Lover, World as Self* (1991), "to view the world as lover is to look at the world as a most intimate and gratifying partner." But most modern spiritual traditions in the West look at the world "as battlefield or as trap" (Macy 1991), which is quite different from seeing the world as a part of oneself and one's lover.

Some of the richest expressions of our erotic relationship to the world are found, Macy says, in Hinduism and the ancient Goddess religions now being reexplored. Of course, there are hidden spiritual erotic traditions in the West as well, but that's just the point, they *are* hidden and rare. It is much more common for Western organized religion to split sexuality and spirituality, to make the body lesser than the mind.

Centuries of repression have compressed sexuality into strictly proscribed forms. Open, exuberant, joyous exploration of eros is still controversial. And while sensual exploration can give private sexual expression a powerful community and spiritual dimension, you wouldn't know it from a review of mainstream media representations of the connection between religion and sexuality in U.S. culture today. A core part of the current "culture war" concerns major disagreements over how to handle women's birth-giving capacity and erotic energy in general, particularly the many forms of sexuality that exist outside male/female heterosexual marriage. Rather than concerning itself with the many aspects of this culture war, the focus of this chapter will be on better understanding people who *do* personally experience the world as lover and do so with such passion as to create communities where their endeavor is taken seriously.

MOTIVATIONS FOR PARTICIPATION IN EROTIC CELEBRATIONS

Individuals drawn to group erotic celebrations speak of the desire for sexual intimacy with a diverse group of people and how that relates to their sense of oneness with life. Group sexual experiences can foster a sensual, familiar fellowship beyond the dyad, while being simultaneously inclusive of couples and singles. These events can also be high-risk, even unhealthy, experiences for those emotionally unprepared for the intense stimulus and choices inherent in such situations. This is particularly true for those who make impulsive decisions without regard to sometimes complex consequences or those who are not sufficiently prepared to know how to handle others who behave this way.

This chapter covers only a select portion of the vast range of contemporary forms of group sex and alternative sexualities. The more recreational and relatively anonymous group sex forms popularized in writings about heterosexual swinger culture and gay male bathhouse customs, for example, are not the focus of this chapter. Still, historic links exist between swinger/bathhouse influences and the more intimate and ritualized modalities presented in this chapter, as is evident in some of the shared rules of conduct common to virtually all such experiences.

I focus instead on the newer forms of erotic ritual and sharing that developed during the first, panicked years of the HIV/AIDS epidemic. These new forms tended to regard the Other in the sexual encounter not only as source of sexual gratification but also as fellow sacred being.

Some of these events grew out of the Jack-and-Jill-Off parties prevalent in many urban areas after the beginning of the AIDS epidemic. These events began as group masturbation and self-pleasuring circles for men. They emphasized safer sex practices during a time of panic about AIDS. Often called JO or Jack-Off parties, the name was expanded to include women (Jills) after women in the queer community lobbied to be a part of such events as well. These events took direction, in part, from the Leather/Fetish and BDSM communities where safer sex parties were often called *play parties*. These events became arenas where "safe, sane, and consensual" sex play was supported in a clean and sober atmosphere that eschewed drugs, alcohol, and the higher risk-taking behaviors use of such substances fosters.

As these social activities developed more during the 1990s, they served social and recreational functions. Even more significantly, these social activities served as loci for introducing, teaching, modeling, and monitoring safer sex behaviors and relationship-negotiation skills for communities under siege by AIDS. The events also served as group vehicles for grieving and memorializing those already lost to the plague. Out of the three different groups discussed intensively in this chapter, two have their origins in gay and bisexual communities and the third has had some bisexual and gay leadership since its inception.

RESEARCH SOURCES

This chapter is grounded in over thirty years of my experience as participant-observer and leader of erotic rituals in my own and others' communities, as well as from what I have learned as a sexuality coach working with individual clients. I have studied a broad range of local groups, including drop-in erotic massage circles, masturbation workshops, and classes primarily focused on sex education and safer sex tips that utilize simulated sex, nudity, drama, and humor. I have attended many intentional erotic rituals, ranging from a mixed gender Aphrodite ritual based on occult *Sex Magic*, to an all-women's *drawing-down-the goddess* ritual in a forest, to a queer BDSM dungeon ceremony inside a townhouse basement on a busy city street.

During the past ten years I have interviewed sacred sexuality teachers in the United States, many of them bisexual and/or queer-identified or bi-friendly. My doctoral dissertation on this topic, "Erotic Rites: A Cultural Analysis of Contemporary U.S. Sacred Sexuality Traditions and Trends," was completed in 2001. My forthcoming book, *Harlots and Healers*, concerns the erotic teachers and mentors who lead these groups—many of whom hold psychology degrees or training certificates in the health professions and the challenges they face in developing such work in the current reactionary, sex-negative milieu.

THERAPEUTIC APPROACHES TO WORKING WITH CLIENTS INTERESTED IN SACRED SEX

EVALUATING A CLIENT'S READINESS FOR PARTICIPATION

Within the therapeutic relationship it is important to nonjudgmentally address motives for participation in group sex and/or sacred sex activities. Further, counselors may help clients understand their options with new or deeper insight and a sense of personal empowerment. The counselor needs to be aware of all the potential motivations and emotional "starting points" that may motivate a client to become involved in erotic communities and rituals. This can help the client be aware and sort through their complex motivations. It is especially important that the counselor be careful not to oversimplify or automatically pathologize an individual's motivations, instead helping them develop their own criteria for the kinds of experiences they seek and an understanding of their motivations for seeking those experiences.

MANAGING COUNTERTRANSFERENCE

If we, as counselors, find the stories we are hearing about clients' experiences or fantasies to be distracting or upsetting, then we need to take the time to privately explore this, ideally in supervision. Supervision sessions and additional training from teachers skilled in sexuality and sacred sexuality areas can help counselors examine their own attitudes, skills, and values around sexual self-responsibility, consideration of others, negotiating, and communicating sexual needs. When we do this kind of work on ourselves, we can also more easily help others examine how their desires and fantasies sometimes get in the way of their own relationships and personal goals and how our clients can have deeper connections in community with others who are supportive and who advocate for one other.

EVALUATING THE IMPACT OF CLIENTS' PARTICIPATION

One can judge very little by a client's behavior, or by the specific activity alone; i.e., interest in or participation in group sex or erotic rituals. Rather, one needs to help the client discern whether or not this activity is helpful for them at this point in time and why. Clinicians and counselors need to help clients explore where they are in their coming out process and their own personal sexual development (recovery issues, addiction, maturity, coping, and communication skills) and how this relates to what you as a clinician know of resources available in the community that may be appropriate to their needs.

CONTEMPORARY BI-FRIENDLY EROTIC COMMUNITIES, WEST TO EAST

What follows are descriptions of three different kinds of erotic communities. I chose them out of the many traditions I have studied during my doctoral and post-doctoral research as communities most inclusive of sexual minorities, encouraging of women's leadership, and supportive of a variety of relationship styles and spiritual beliefs. These brief descriptions of Queen of Heaven, Body Sacred, and Body Electric are followed by a checklist of strengths and weaknesses often found in these kinds of environments. I offer them as touchstones for counselors to use in helping clients evaluate their own participation in such programs.

QUEEN OF HEAVEN

I wanted to make a space where people are sexual right next to each other . . . where gay, straight, bi, trans, sm/non-sm, everyone comes together . . . present in one another's eroticism. —CAROL QUEEN[3]

Queen of Heaven is an erotic community founded in the San Francisco Bay Area in 1990. Celebrants come together on the pagan high holy days (Samhein or Halloween, Beltane or Mayday, Lupercalia or Valentines, etc.) to create sex parties with the themes of ritual pleasuring, earth honoring, and Goddess worship. Created by bisexual sex educators, Carol Queen and Robert Lawrence, Queen of Heaven is also descendant and inheritor of the many different kinds of traditions developed from safer sex parties, swinger's events, and the SM community play parties that make San Francisco famous. Queen of Heaven is pansexual—all orientations, sexes, genders, proclivities welcome. At any given Queen of Heaven event safer sex practices are demonstrated and modeled; eroticizing safer sex is enthusiastically encouraged and using safer sex practices is constantly validated. In order to attend an event, members agree to abide by safer sex guidelines (regardless of what their own rules are at home) and to be responsible for the behavior of any guests they bring. As at swinger events, single men are discouraged and a rough gender balance is maintained.

Safer sex guidelines are spelled out to mean using lubrication, along with condoms, latex, or polyurethane gloves and other barriers that prevent transmission of bodily fluids. The ground rules include always asking before touching someone and understanding that "no means no," a slogan adopted from the feminist antirape movement. There is a general ban on using drugs and alcohol in ritual space and participants agree to maintain confidentiality about exactly what goes on at the event. In other words, participants can talk about their own experience, but the identities of others who were there or what happened for them or to them is not to be discussed outside of the event. Each event is discretely monitored by designated responsible observers, and those who violate the guidelines are asked to leave. Guests all agree to arrive by a certain time; no one is allowed to enter once the evening's ritual has begun.

Queen of Heaven events are often held at dance studio spaces and in lofts and warehouses where there is a minimum of furniture and decorating is easily accomplished using movable props. The events always start with socializing time during which participants create a communal walk-in closet through the act of changing out of street clothes into loose-fitting, revealing ritual garb or fetish wear. Leather bustiers, chaps, fishnet stockings, sarongs, see-through veils, and other sexy costumes prevail. People—some naked, some playfully garbed— mill about meeting and greeting, eating fresh fruits and chocolate, drinking juice and sodas, and slowly sort themselves into little "nests" of pillows and mats, with couples and small groups of friends arranging themselves around the room.

At a certain time the priestess and priest du jour call everyone formally into ritual space by casting the circle and calling in the elements—earth, air, fire, and water. Seasonal goddesses and gods of pleasure are invoked. Perhaps a song is sung, a chant taught, a dance performed or led, or a short thematic story of revelry, journeying, and triumph told. Often, the dead are remembered and honored by silent prayer or calling out of names. Once celebrants and space are blessed, the festivities begin.

The event itself consists of negotiated sensual and/or erotic exchanges or "scenes" in which what occurs is clearly discussed and agreeable to all participants in the subgroup. A lot of people plan their scenes (sensual, erotic encounters) beforehand. It is considered acceptable to watch someone else's scene from a respectful distance. No one is obligated to "play," but there is usually opportunity for the majority of those attending to participate in some activity if they wish to do so. For those who stay the whole time, there is a formal closing at the end of the evening when people gather back into a circle, hold hands, hug, express appreciation for the good times enjoyed together, and say good-bye.

THE BODY SACRED

I was wounded around my sexuality and spirituality and I had come to the aware-ness that those wounds struck at the core of my being and affected every aspect of my life . . . I came for healing and for tools and for community. I left fulfilled.

—H.T., BODY SACRED PARTICIPANT[4]

The Body Sacred is a yearly weekend gathering that originated in the Pocono Mountains of Pennsylvania in the early 1990s. It has since moved to a retreat center in upstate New York. It started as an interfaith effort between Christians, Pagans and Jews (and representatives of a few other traditions as well). The impetus came from within the larger polyamory community (see Weitzman, chapter 17), yet it has always been inclusive and accepting of a variety of honest and caring relationship styles—from monogamy to multiple partner relation-ships. Body Sacred gatherings only occur once or twice a year, usually in the summer. Similar in composition to the Queen of Heaven events, the group of participants includes both old-timers who have woven themselves into long-term friendship groups as well as newcomers. Newcomers hear about the event from friends or may discover it from the low-key advertising done on the Web and through the retreat center's newsletter calendar of annual events.

Unlike Queen of Heaven, Body Sacred is not an event focused primarily on the celebration of any one culminating explicit group sex ceremony. It is a series of events focused on psychologically and emotionally "clearing out" what comes up for people as they begin acting on their desires for intimacy and contact. Body Sacred events help people feel more erotically empowered and provide a clothing-optional space where individuals are encouraged to attend to their bodily feelings and experience. Each individual's limits and boundaries are honored and their desires are validated. Optional group sex activities and mas-sage exchanges (sometimes erotic) are sanctioned, and space for these activities is set aside near the main group activities.

Whereas Queen of Heaven takes place in the space of one evening, on occa-sions spaced periodically around the calendar year, Body Sacred takes place over an extended, intensive residential weekend. During these three or four days, there is time for get-to-know-you sharing circles and a number of different kinds of communication/awareness exercises such as psychodrama and mat work. *Mat work* is a term used by a number of different Gestalt and body psy-chotherapists. Participants are coached through these exercises in dyads and switch roles halfway through the session. The goal of these sessions is to free blocked emotional and physical energy so that this energy is available for more pleasure, intimacy, and personal growth. Playful activities like body painting and mud bathing are a centerpiece of the Body Sacred weekend, as well as lots of sexy, hot, clothing-optional dancing to world music, rock, jazz, rap, and new age drumming. Overt sexual play is only one facet of expression and participants are encouraged to explore sensual, erotic, and body-centered play in a variety of ways during the course of the weekend.

The philosophy of Body Sacred emphasizes that people need as much permission to feel good and to say *yes* to their sexuality as they do to say *no* to something they don't want to do. Both of these skills are related to being emotionally intelligent and sexually competent adults, yet neither the skills involved in saying yes nor those involved in saying no get enough attention in traditional community institutions where we supposedly learn courtship, flirting, interaction, and mating skills. Groups like Body Sacred provide a safe forum to practice communicating exactly what one wants and how to get it.

THE BODY ELECTRIC SCHOOL

He had made it his ministry to help men reconnect their hearts with their genitals. It was an ambitious undertaking, especially in a time when men aren't comfortable exploring their feelings . . . and sex is commonly a matter of getting rid of energy. . . . It worked. Men wept and had visions. They rediscovered their feelings and their connections with other human beings. —RUDOLPH BALLENTINE (1999)

A gay, Jesuit-trained massage therapist and bodyworker named Joseph Kramer founded Body Electric School during the onset of the HIV/AIDS epidemic in San Francisco in the 1980s. Moved to find a safe way to help men reclaim their life force and sense of wonder in a city devastated by loss and grief, Kramer developed a method he eventually called Taoist Erotic Massage, or TEM. TEM helped men learn how to have full-body energetic-orgasms without ejaculation. This enabled these men to learn how to connect sensations in their pelvis with feeling in their heart and to do so safely by *not* sharing bodily fluids (now more threatening in an age of HIV/AIDS and other STDs).

The whole process encouraged participants to trust their genital awareness of "aliveness" and to spread it throughout their bodies energetically. The first ten years of Body Electric's development are documented in Kramer's doctoral dissertation (Kramer 2002). Since the mid-nineties he and his students have fully incorporated women as well as men and included people of all sexualities into the school's trainings. These trainings have now become popular around the country, particularly in the areas around Seattle, New York, and Atlanta, in the San Francisco Bay Area, and around southern California. Body Electric techniques are usually taught in a weekend or week-long retreat format. The program culminates in an experience called the Big Draw.

The Big Draw is introduced after teaching a number of preliminary sex education, communication-enhancing, meditative, and breathwork-focused exercises. Classes are taught in a room full of massage tables. Each participant has a chance to be the recipient of a full-body erotic massage. At the end of the massage the participant enters an erotic trance where they are guided to focus on their breathing and sensations of heightened arousal and oneness with the universe. They are coached to an intense physical tensing point, followed by an energetic, emotional, and muscular all-over release (the Big Draw).

Kramer sold the school to two friends a number of years ago. He now produces erotic teaching videos based on his work. He has recently developed another more intensive format, which he calls Sexological Bodywork, and has won certification for this method through the state of California's Vocational Education Department in affiliation with the Institute for the Advanced Study of Human Sexuality.

ADVANTAGES AND PROBLEMATICS OF BUILDING HEALTHY EROTIC COMMUNITIES

There are both great advantages and significant risks associated with participation in sacred sex trainings and events. In this section I provide an overview of some of the benefits and problematic aspects of such involvements. The clinician is encouraged to familiarize her- or himself with source materials listed at the end of this chapter for a more thorough understanding of these risks and benefits.

- *Teaching/modeling safer sex techniques in a group setting.* The most critically important short-term positive effect of sacred and/or group sex forms is the life-saving effect of teaching and modeling safer sex techniques[5] in this time of widespread sexually transmitted diseases and a deadly epidemic. Peer encouragement works much better than shaming or punitive measures. Normalizing safer sex practices in a sex-positive and body-affirming group environment also makes it quite clear that safer sex is "hot," not just "right."
- *The additional value of accurately demonstrating sexual activities.* At these events individuals are able to observe without participating and still learn a lot about human sexual diversity and orgasmic response. Being present at group erotic rituals often dispels ignorance and improves people's knowledge of how to pleasure another and how to experience pleasure. Attendance at such events can also dispel unrealistic expectations and build confidence based on real experience and observation rather than fantasy.

- *Permission to experience self-loving, comfort with nudity, sexual confidence, asking for what you want, becoming more aware of the subtleties of your own body's responses, etc.* One of the most excellent and popular ways I've seen people's comfort level with their own bodies improve is with exercises like Genital Show and Tell. In a small group each person has time to talk about their feelings about her or his own body and is supported nonjudgmentally and appreciatively to show her or his genitals to the others. Self-exams were pioneered by the feminist health movement of the 1970s and adapted by Betty Dodson in her excellent teaching videos (http://www.bettydodson.com).

- *Decreasing the likelihood of abuse or vulnerability to sexual manipulation.* In the context of peer observation and encouragement for individuals to get their needs met and connect with others, some sexual abuse survivors report that group erotic experiences feel "safer" for them than most one-on-one encounters. Conscious planning and some amount of prior consensus go into such events and guidelines are clearly stated for all involved. Participants are rewarded for expressing needs, desires, and *limits* and in most erotic rituals there are witnesses and facilitators who "hold the space" and keep the focus on the group's stated goals of being welcoming and beneficial for those involved.

- *Teaching beginning and deeper level communication skills in relation to sexuality.* Communication skills are taught, with ready opportunities for concrete applications and practice in the group setting. It is a lot easier to say what you want or to share a shy or bold fantasy when others are setting examples all around you. Many of the groups I studied set aside time specifically for teaching and practicing communication skill exercises.

- *An opportunity to experience healing, transcendence, belonging, ecstasy, release, and embodiment.* These are the experiences that participants report that creates bonds and keeps people coming back for more. The feeling of being acutely alive and celebrating and connected to all of life is at the core of every good group erotic experience. Some earth-based spiritual traditions call this "raising the energy," or creating a state of erotic trance, and then "grounding it" at the point when the celebration peaks and begins to wind down.

PROBLEMATICS AND RISKS ASSOCIATED WITH EROTIC COMMUNITIES

- *A highly charged sexual scene can be intimidating.* The intensity of direct exposure to explicit sexuality in a group setting may cause some individuals to shut down and mentally or physically "run away" without figuring out how to communicate what they need. This is true for anyone regardless whether or not they have a history of sexual abuse. For people with a history of emotional, spiritual, physical, and/or sexual abuse, such intense experiences may trigger flashbacks. Even if an individual is already dealing well with their recovery process, they may not, for instance, know how to work *with* the trigger rather than run from it and may not have prepared adequate support systems for themselves ahead of time (Haines 1999).

■ *Predatory behaviors.* People are not necessarily attracted to erotic communities for the right reasons. Similar to the context affecting shared activities in the rest of society, dangerous or merely annoying predators are sometimes attracted to groups where erotic communication is being taught and shared. Each group needs to examine how it admits new people and monitors current members to minimize possibility of abuse and confront exploitation promptly when it occurs. Uncomfortable and/or unequal sexual situations resulting from exploitation and unequal power relationships also have their roots in the larger institutionalized oppressions inherent in the culture, such as racial prejudice, sexism, and age discrimination. Of course, the worst possible situation is when the founder or leader of a sacred sex group, often male (but not always), is himself a sexual predator and has an agenda of finding partners for himself through the operation of the group. Fortunately, word gets around about these individuals fairly quickly, and a few well-placed queries to those who know the person in question can usually identify whether or not this is likely to be a problem in a specific group.

■ *The art of conscious touch is not taught in this touch-averse culture.* Most people get little or no training in how to touch someone in a nurturing or helpful way, much less in an intimate way. If people suddenly feel permission to be erotic, they can easily forget the guidelines such as "ask before you touch," "no means no," etc. Therefore, when people move directly into sexual experience, as is the case when signing up to participate in an erotic ritual, there can be miscommunication, and sometimes minor or major hurt may occur. Careful attention must be given to creating opportunities for participant feedback. Group participants need opportunities for simply learning how to touch as well as how to use specifically erotic touch with another person and/or with more than one person at the same time.

■ *There is a tendency, sometimes called premature merging, to skip over useful and usual courtship and communication steps and go immediately for the high-intensity charge of the aroused preorgasmic state.* This is common among couples and especially intensified in a group setting of aroused people who all amplify each other's energetic experience of arousal. However, when there is a group emphasis on first taking the time for slowly unfolding awareness and teaching the communication skills necessary to build true intimacy and satisfaction, the results are much more satisfying. *Premature merging* behavior often cloaks anxiety and unmet needs that tend to go unexpressed when erotic sharing is rushed. (Note: this behavior can be "read" as predatory behavior even when the person is merely misguided and not really a predator.)

■ *Intentional groups can "de-volve" into disorganized recreational sex fests, especially when leadership is weak or faulty.* It takes more than just the presence of desire and the ability to perform sexually to create authentic erotic trust and communion between two people, much less among a larger group. The complications multiply exponentially as more people are added. Permission to unpack the sexual wounds and conditioning of the past is just a beginning. Before anyone is invited to participate in an intimate erotic activity, care must be taken to screen and provide participants with an appropriate orientation. Training exercises, developed by groups like the Human Awareness Institute (HAI), Body Electric, and Body Sacred, teach communication and self-awareness skills that assist people to remain authentic with others and in touch with themselves in such situations. Cleaning up the emotional wreckage *after* feelings have already been hurt is much more difficult than avoiding a situation in the moment because it feels awkward to intervene.

MAKING REFERRALS TO OTHER PROVIDERS WHEN APPROPRIATE

It is also important to remember that while a good knowledge of sexual diversities is critical, it does not replace a wider clinical judgment. Clinical judgment needs to be situational and may need to be adapted to the changing forms of group intimacy that are developing, but counselors need to trust their own judgment and recognize when a situation is emotionally, psychologically, or physically dangerous for a client. In some situations it is useful for the counselor to disclose information about her or his own value structure and perspective and refer the client to other human service professionals who can better meet the client's needs or provide complementary services as an adjunct to the therapy the client is currently receiving.

For example, it is often helpful to refer clients to holistic healers, such as certified massage therapists (CMTs) and acupuncturists, who can be partners in the client's healing process, particularly when the client needs more attention to body awareness than it is possible to provide in a conventional counseling setting. A growing number of CMTs, for instance, are obtaining supplemental training in understanding the psychological issues that come up for clients in the bodywork environment and how to appropriately support clients in such experiences (see Greene and Goodrich-Dunn 2004).

It is also sometimes helpful to refer clients to specialists who are developing new areas of expertise such as sexological bodyworkers, sex surrogates, and that subset of body workers (some trigger point therapists, deep tissue massage therapists, chiropractors, and others) who are specializing in developing and documenting their skills in sexual healing methodologies. Some physical therapists in pain clinics, for example, are working with chronic pelvic pain treatment and beginning to develop criteria for good practice in this area (Wise and Anderson 2003). While it is clear that sexually explicit touch has been used in abusive and exploitive ways by many kinds of professionals, it is also not helpful to exclude or suppress discussion of ways in which it might be a useful methodology or approach. We could benefit greatly, especially in the professions where these abuses have most egregiously occurred (psychotherapy, the clergy, etc.) in encouraging more research and evaluation on what causes such situations as well as what can be learned from them and implications for future practice.

I do not advocate making referrals to strangers or to professionals that one doesn't personally know or trust (or who, at a minimum, have been recommended by someone whom you trust). I am merely suggesting that we must familiarize ourselves with what is happening in new fields of human growth, particularly in our own local areas, so that we can evaluate who is doing reputable work and what resources are available to our clients on local, regional, and national resources levels.

Dismantling the pervasive sex-shaming beliefs woven into our society, the sexual objectification of groups of people, and the deep alienation of body from mind and sexuality from spirituality upon which such shame is based, is profoundly important work. Creating and encouraging the availability of training in basic communication and self-awareness skills is one good way to begin, but we need to let go of the illusion that we can create any kind of charmed utopia without patiently changing the material conditions of the culture as a whole, step by step, over many years. Although glimmers of healing and healthy erotic communities are developing in our lifetimes, I doubt that any of us will see their fully realized efforts—but we can be a part of asserting and teaching the principles that will make them possible.

I am heartened by the beginning transitions toward healthier sexuality that I see in the healing circles and safer sex parties that have developed out of the HIV/AIDS movement, the ways that women and queer people's political empowerment relates to freeing them sexually, and how this is also happening in some ways with other sexual, social, and racial minorities. I also see the beginning of discussions about the rights of people with disabilities to have happy, safe, spiritually fulfilling, and independent sex lives (Tepper 2000; Coffman, chapter 10) as another hopeful example. The current changes in gender roles brought on by the women's, transgender, bisexual, intersex, and lesbian/ gay movements, and the ways in which we are reconceiving our very definitions of sex, are nothing short of revolutionary.

Suffice it to say, for now, that people—both our clients and others we may never know—are beginning to understand radically different ways of experiencing intimacy and orgasm, one small step at a time. Their understanding of the relationship between sex and spirit is a key part of this paradigm shift. While the next steps in the development of these erotic communities remains to be seen, it is definitely important to shed light on the existence of such beliefs and practices and to ask more informed questions about these practices. I hope this chapter provides useful tools to assist you in that process and in your own next steps.

NOTES

1. This definition comes from Dr. John Mumford's tradition, Swami Umeshanand Saraswati (Mark Michaels) and Veenanand (Patricia Johnson), the Kailash Center for Personal Development (www.JonnMumfordconsult.com).
2. HAI (www.hai.org) has trained over fifty thousand people in a series of introductory to advanced workshops dealing with intimate relationships and sexuality since 1968.
3. Interview with the author, October 1997.
4. From a Body Sacred mailing for the 1996 gathering.
5. If you aren't up-to-date on safer sex information, please educate yourself. http://www.sexuality.org/concise.html is a good place to start.

REFERENCES

Ballentine, R. (1999). *Radical healing: Integrating the world's great therapeutic traditions to create a new transformative medicine*. New York. Doubleday.

Bornstein, K. (1998). *My gender workbook: How to become a real man, a real woman, the real you, or something else entirely*. New York: Routledge.

Califia, P., and Campbell, D. (1997). *Bitch goddess: The spiritual path of the dominant woman*. San Francisco: Greenery.

Dodson, B. (1987). *Sex for One*. New York: Harmony.

Greene, E., and Goodrich-Dunn, B. (2004). *The psychology of the body*. Baltimore: Lippincott Williams and Wilkins.

Haines, S. (1999). *The survivor's guide to sex: How to have an empowered sex life after child sexual abuse*. San Francisco: Cleis.

Hutchins, L. (2001a). *Erotic rites: A cultural analysis of contemporary U.S. sacred sexuality traditions and trends*. Takoma Park: self-published at http://www.lorainehutchins.com.

Hutchins, L. (2001b). Erotic spiritualities. In D. Kolodny (Ed.), *Blessed bi spirit: Bisexual people of faith* (pp. 203–217). New York: Continuum.

Hutchins, L. (2002). Bisexual women as sexual healers and the problematics of the embodied sacred whore. *Journal of Bisexuality* 2(2/3), 205–226.

Kaldera, R. (2001). *Hermaphrodeities: The transgender spirituality workbook*. Xlibris.com.

Kramer, J. (2002). A social history of the first ten years of Taoist erotic massage, 1982–1992. Oakland: self-published at http://www.eroticmassage.com.

Macy, J. (1991). *World as lover, world as self.* Berkeley: Parallax.

Starhawk (1995). The sacredness of pleasure. In N. Tucker (Ed.), *Bisexual politics: Theories, queries, and visions.* Seattle: Seal.

Tepper, M. (2000). Tantra and sex: beyond the medical model, *New Mobility Magazine.* Retrieved from the February 2000 issue at http://www.newmobility.com.

Wise, D., and Anderson, R. (2003). *A headache in the pelvis: A new understanding and treatment for prostatitis and chronic pelvic pain syndromes.* Occidental, CA: National Center for Pelvic Pain Research.

19

COUNSELING BISEXUALS ON BDSM LIFESTYLE ISSUES

William A. Henkin

To me, sex is not about sticking a penis into a vagina (unless it's sex for pro-creation). Sex is about tapping into, building, sharing, and utilizing sexual energy. The genitals are simply an exquisitely perfect generator for that sexual energy. Whether the genitals are male or female, or whether there are no genitals at all, does not matter to me. It's about the energy. Since I have learned this I'm reaching whole new levels of sexual intensity, adventure, enjoyment, and satisfaction and have come to use sex for more than recreation and satisfying physical needs. I use sex as a healing tool, as a meditation, as a way of life, and as a path to enlightenment.

—ANNIE SPRINKLE, "BEYOND BISEXUAL" (SPRINKLE 1991)

TASTE OF LEATHER: SERPENT MOUNTAIN SCENES

In the 1980s, when I came out fully and publicly into San Francisco's leathersex subculture, the major SM social event was the Serpent Mountain Scenes party, cohosted every two months by my new lover, partner, and Mistress, Sybil Holiday. Sybil was a luminary in the San Francisco SM community of the time: a highly regarded professional dominant and madam/proprietor of a small house where many of the other best pro-dommes of that time and place—the most experienced, most sophisticated, most creative, and most adept—hung their shingles.

Like those women, as well as the men who also worked out of her house occasionally, Sybil had a preferred orientation, which, in her case, was pansexual. Within that context, also like her associates, she had a wide and sometimes deep personal experience with more specific orientations. Despite having primarily male partners, she was readily accepted in San Francisco's leatherdyke (lesbian SM) community: she was a founding member of The Outcasts, one of the earliest organized woman-to-woman SM educational and support groups, and twice in its first half-dozen years she was invited to be a judge at the International Ms Leather contest. As she often said, what engaged her was the erotic energy that could be exchanged between or among people. Where channels of physical, emotional, psychological, and spiritual communication were open, her erotic desire flourished regardless of her partner's genitalia, sexual orientation, or gender identity; where the channels were closed or obstructed her erotic desire withered. She emphatically preferred wet.

Sybil did not originate the Serpent Mountain Scenes parties but took over their direction from friends and colleagues. Invitations were derived from a closed list of highly experienced SM players Sybil vetted herself, orchestrating the guests so that in combination the party play would make a symphonic tone poem of erotic energies. Almost all the players at those parties were themselves eminently competent to teach the activities they most preferred, and many did so, in fact, both in San Francisco and in the wider network of SM communities then developing across the land, in person and through books, magazines, and instructional videos. But because Sybil was looking for "wet" music, she wanted more than just a group of technically proficient individuals who were skilled at SM activities.

In addition to and perhaps more important than knowledge of specific SM skills, Sybil was looking for people who played with energy consciously, knew how to exchange it with others, and how to move it to achieve results. As a consequence, the energy at her parties tended to begin with a casual warm intimacy and then to build over the course of an evening through a series of crescendos and diminuendos that grew in waves to feel like an upwardly mobile vortex, which people who attended spoke about as a "cone of power." Sometimes abetted by the actual sound system music that helped to score the party, that movement frequently arrived at a climax so furiously passionate no one at a Serpent Mountain party could miss it. I was not surprised, at my first Serpent Mountain parties, to find a fairly even mix of heterosexual, lesbian, and gay male people, nor that some members of every group were transgendered; I was not surprised to see a wide array of fetish interests on exhibit, from flagellation and bondage to age and gender play, from body modifications to extreme and sometimes theatrical edge play, from courtly service to overt slavery; nor was I surprised that many people present were more or less bisexual.

What did surprise me was to see women who asserted that they were absolutely lesbian whipping men who asserted they were absolutely gay, absolutely gay men throwing intricate rope harnesses onto absolutely gay women, and people of both sexes with impeccable heterosexual credentials doing scenes with gay same-sex play partners. What surprised me was discovering how little the exchange of erotic energy really had to do with genitals or gender identity. And what surprised me perhaps most of all was discovering how little erotic energy necessarily had to do with what most people probably regard as sex: it did not have to involve genital orgasm and it did not even have to involve the genitals.

LANGUAGE

There is a basic vocabulary in the BDSM subculture, a set of terms and concepts that educators and therapists need to understand in order to meaningfully assist clients interested in or involved with these activities. In the previous section I used the terms *SM* and *leathersex* where the current procedural terminology would properly be *BDSM*. As Sybil and I wrote in the introduction to the revised, second edition of our book, *Consensual Sadomasochism,*

> All the activities now called BDSM were [in the 1970s and 1980s] generally known by the umbrella term of "SM" (or S/M, or S&M) or "leathersex." Like some other people at the time, we made a conspicuous distinction in our teaching and writing between the physicality of sadism and masochism (SM) and the psychology of dominance and submission (DS); other people especially enjoyed activities they believed were more accurately seen as bondage and discipline (BD). Over time, as the SM community expanded into multiple communities, the single, more encompassing, overlapping letter-conglomerate BDSM emerged as a way to combine all three under a single alphabetic umbrella: BD, DS, SM. (Henkin and Holiday 2004 [1996]:14)

Top and *bottom* are terms that make no reference to sex, gender, class, wealth, education, intelligence, professional status, social standing, or any other conventional distinctions. They simply identify the two most usual roles or poles that otherwise equal human beings agree between or among themselves to occupy in DS relationships or play. In somewhat simplistic terms the *Top*—capitalized in print by long convention—is the person who commands or directs the scene or relationship, who performs the most assertive actions, or who is at least nominally in charge; the bottom is the one who obeys, is acted upon, or toward whom the activity is directed. Long-term, full-time relationships are likely to be founded in DS even though they include SM or BD activities.

When I refer to SM *play*, I mean the activities generally regarded as BDSM, and by *players* I mean the people who engage in those activities. A *scene* is a specific BDSM encounter, although *the scene* refers to all the people, activities, organizations, and events that make up the wide BDSM communities. *Age play* refers to scenes or activities in which one or more persons is treated as if s/he were a considerably different age—usually much younger—than s/he actually is, as *gender play* refers to scenes or activities in which one or more persons is treated as if s/he were a different sex than s/he usually claims or appears to be. *Gender play* occasionally may have to do with genuine transgender *identity* issues but more often has to do with role play or, in some circumstances, with a deliberate attempt to embarrass or "humiliate" the cross-dressed or otherwise cross-gendered player for erotic pleasure. *Edge play* usually refers to those activities that push a person's boundaries but can also refer to activities that are substantially enough outside the usual realms of even BDSM play to be regarded as extreme within the community itself. Edge play might include the use of knives and other instruments designed to penetrate the body envelope or the "consensual nonconsent" of terror and interrogation games: some people positively *like* to be frightened under safe circumstances, as American movies of the past fifty years have shown.

PAIN, PLEASURE, AND THE THEATER OF THE SUBLIME

So much of what takes place under the aegis of BDSM partakes of role play and other aspects of sexual theater that it is a natural sort of home for people who self-identify as bisexual. Certainly there are people both in and out of the communities who live by their labels as Tops or bottoms or something else, but the more people participate in the deeper realms of BDSM, the less weight most labels carry.

As anyone knows who has had a tattoo, worn a corset, or even gotten an ear pierced for an earring, "body modification" is an experience all on its own, without necessary reference to BDSM. But like bondage, which many people also enjoy without reference to BDSM, body modification may be approached as a BDSM activity as when, for example, a Top restricts a bottom's freedom of movement by binding her hands, blindfolding her, and dressing her in a high, stiff collar, a very tight corset, and extremely high heeled shoes chained closely together or when one person who consensually "owns" another marks her property with a piercing, cutting, tattoo, or brand.

Body modification finds expression in the context of BDSM and the larger community has lionized Fakir Musafar. Musafar is the acknowledged father of the Modern Primitive movement and the man who coined the term *body play*. His esteem within the BDSM community further indicates how compatible these activities and communities are with crossover orientations. When he first appeared at San Francisco's pansexual BDSM support club, the Society of Janus, Musafar—a man who famously plays with men though married to a woman who herself plays with women—was challenged because people did not understand how his activities fit into their world. But over time people came to understand the relationship between his activities and theirs. Consequently, his 1985 film, *Dances Sacred and Profane*, became an instant fetish classic, and in

1989 ReSearch employed as a title a term Musafar had coined for its book *Modern Primitives* and built its text largely around an interview with him (ReSearch 1989). In 1993 the National Leather Association honored him with its Man of the Year award.

As with gender play, where people assume roles of the complementary sex, so in body modification men frequently wear jewelry and women tattoos. The very fact that some readers of the preceding sentence might not understand why this is remarkable shows how far the movement has penetrated popular American culture. While tattooed women and bejeweled men have long been customary in other societies and in some relatively underground American subcultures, they would have been unimaginable examples of role-reversal for middle-class men or women in this country in 1960; they would have been revolutionary in 1970, radical in 1980, and commonplace in 1990. Without ascribing cause or effect, it is worth noting that the emergence of a visible and "out" bisexual middle-class culture also reflects this boundary-blurring temporal pattern.

BISEXUALITY, ROLE FLUIDITY, AND BDSM

Language can be tricky in the world of BDSM because we socialized humans are accustomed to speaking in shorthand for convenience, and among our most convenient forms of shorthand are labels. The confusions that follow upon our use of labels are well-known to bisexual people, whose relative attraction to same-sex or complementary-sex pairings may change with available partners, body chemistry, or any number of other variables. These confusions around labeling are among the dilemmas Fritz Klein sought to address by expanding the possibilities inherent, and inherently limiting, in the Kinsey scale.

Bisexuals have a counterpart in the world of BDSM, generally known as "switches." A switch is someone who enjoys both Topping and bottoming. Some switches, like some bisexuals, happily go in either direction pretty much any time, even with the same partner or in a single scene; others are much more specific, and prefer to Top in circumstances that differ from those in which they like to bottom. For many people in the BDSM communities who are clear about their unitary orientations as Top or bottom, sadist or masochist, dominant or submissive, switches are confusing and even challenging in the same way bisexuals are confusing or challenging for some hetero- and homosexual people.

Labels are misleading in other ways as well, of course. For example, based on simple labeling it is easy to believe that the Top runs the scene, administers sensation, and gives orders, as by tying, whipping, or commanding the bottom. The very fact that some people do switch suggests the fallacy in this sort of belief, because it indicates that individuals and not labels engage in BDSM activities. For many years this kind of assumption led to confusions in the communities themselves, when the terms *Top*, *sadist*, and *dominant* were used interchangeably or were conflated with each other. But I keenly recall a class cotaught by a dominant who enjoyed the feelings of intense sensation and required that her teaching partner, a submissive who enjoyed administering such sensations, beg for permission to pierce the dominant. Since the nominal masochist was in command, she was certainly the dominant and hence the Top, while the nominal sadist was clearly the submissive and therefore the bottom. Among other agendas the scene demonstrated the need for clear communication and negotiation in setting up a BDSM scene, whether that scene is intended to provide pleasure for an hour or is an agreement between a Master or Mistress and slave intended, like a marriage, to last a lifetime. In just this sort of way it is easy to imagine that someone who identifies as heterosexual plays only with people of the complementary sex or that someone who identifies as homosexual plays only with people of the same sex. It does not always occur, of course, and is not universally accepted; but at least in the more sophisticated communities where BDSM is practiced it is well established that people may play or love on bases other than genital matches, even when they have a genuine orientation preference. Insofar as it concerns something other than genital satisfaction, BDSM is inherently bisexual.

UNDERSTANDING BDSM

In order to work effectively with bisexual clients or clients of other identities and orientations, therapists and educators need to have an accurate understanding of the phenomena that draw their clients' interest and attention. In the next section of this chapter I will discuss three major concepts with which the professional psychotherapist or counselor should be familiar in order to be able to educate clients and respond appropriately to their questions and concerns about BDSM. These concepts are 1. erotic energy exchange, 2. the BDSM community motto, "safe, sane, and consensual," including the concept of informed consent in the negotiation of BDSM scenes, and 3. the use of safewords in BDSM play.

EROTIC ENERGY EXCHANGE

As I mentioned earlier, BDSM activities are not always directed toward genital orgasm or even, necessarily, toward genital sexuality. By this claim I do not wish to imply that sex is always or even usually excluded from BDSM or that the activities that fall under the BDSM aegis are not erotic. Rather, I wish to underscore a different unifying aspect that frequently takes precedence over the genital, oral, anal, or manual versions of genital stimulation and satisfaction that are conventionally called sex. That unifying aspect, which may pertain to any and all BDSM behaviors, from flagellation to bondage to piercing to slavery, has often been called *erotic energy exchange*.

You do not have to have experience with BDSM or even sex to recognize *energy* as I am using the term. All you have to do is attend a circus, a funeral, a professional sporting event held in a stadium, or a major political party's nominating convention. At any such event you can feel a spirit of the time and place generated by many, most, or all the people present and directed toward an identifiable end.

You can feel energy of this sort erotically, as when your eyes meet the eyes of someone who is a sexual match for you, though erotic energy is about something more than just the visuals: you may have the same kind of response to a voice or tone of voice or to a pheromone or other, more obvious, smells. In any case, we don't all get turned on by someone pretty, even if we recognize the person's good looks, and lovers' choices frequently and famously baffle their friends.

Like the more common definition of energy in physics, erotic energy may either be about something that *is* happening or about something that has the *potential* to happen. Once recognized, therefore, potential erotic energy can be made kinetic: for example, it can be elevated deliberately, which is often the intent of people who take advantage of their charisma, good looks, or powerful positions by seducing acolytes. It can also be elevated by music, from plaintive love ballads and driving rock 'n' roll to sultry jazz and a wide range of classical pieces from the progressively compelling force of Ravel's *Bolero* to the sensuous pas de deux from Prokofiev's *Romeo and Juliet*. It can also be lowered deliberately, as anyone knows who has dressed down or played dumb in order to discourage an unwanted lover or suitor. In "Music from a Bygone Era" Gayle Rubin briefly described this process by considering the selection of music used as a sort of sound track or score to accompany the activities at the Catacombs, San Francisco's legendary 1970s fisting palace.

SAFE, SANE, AND CONSENSUAL

Since at least the mid-1970s the unofficial motto of the organized BDSM communities has been "safe, sane, and consensual," and groups, clubs, events, conferences, and play parties have generally affirmed this credo, sometimes to a fault. The identifiable procedures of safety, consent, and the negotiation they entail tacitly embrace the culturally more ambiguous definitions of sanity and are hallmarks of BDSM activities within those communities, which now are legion. Their practices are among the concerns that distinguish the BDSM of players in these communities from the abuse those activities may resemble and may even be designed to mimic, and whose appearance may, therefore, distress uninformed outsiders. Because I cannot cast my net so wide as to include every-one who does everything, my discussion about safety, negotiation, and consent concerns the common attitudes and approaches of the organized BDSM com-munities. Certainly many people who do not participate in the communities engage in the same and similar behaviors, some with attention to the sorts of issues that concern the communities and some without such attention to these issues.

By definition, abuse concerns harmful misuse. It is about deliberately treat-ing someone or something badly, unjustly, or corruptly, or even treating the person well against his wishes or will, and it is inherently nonconsensual. If you want to kiss me, caress me, spank me, hit me, whip me, tie me up, call me names, or have any variety sex with me and I say *No*, your continued attempt to satisfy your desires against my wishes is prima facie evidence of at least attempt-ed abuse. But if you and I have discussed our desires and discovered that I, too, want you to kiss me, caress me, spank me, hit me, whip me, tie me up, call me names, or have any variety sex with me, our encounter is—at least to this point—consensual.

Moreover, if I am aroused by a fantasy of resisting my assailant and finally being overpowered, I might like to scream *No! No! No!* while you are using me, without for a moment wanting you to stop. In this case we can agree that you will ignore my protests. Before beginning to play we can discuss our desires together and formulate a scene that allows us both to explore, exploit, and fulfill some of our fantasies—whether they are of abduction, seduction, or ego reduc-tion—in order to bring pleasure to us both and harm to no one.

CONSENT AND NEGOTIATION IN BDSM SCENES

Players come to agreements such as these through negotiation. In many politi-cal and business settings, traditional negotiation is the art of getting as much as you can while giving up as little as possible. But in BDSM, as, ideally, in other forms of lovemaking or noncompetitive mutual play, negotiation is the much more difficult and rewarding art of giving all you can so that you may receive all you can. This sort of negotiation is enabled by at least a modicum of self-awareness, as well as an ability to trust, and implies the possibility of intimacy—which is just what many experienced players claim they seek and can achieve through BDSM activities, sometimes to extraordinary measure.

Most of the participant literature regarding the BDSM lifestyle has to do with teaching technical skills associated with the physical aspects of play: how to whip, how to bind, how to execute a scene. But some notable exceptions explore or examine the emotional, spiritual, and other psychological dimen-sions of these activities. Among the best such views are Guy Baldwin's *Slave-*

Craft: Roadmaps for Erotic Servitude, Masochism: A Jungian View by Lyn Cowan, *The Topping Book* and *The Bottoming Book*, both by Dossie Easton and Catherine Liszt, *To Love, to Obey, to Serve: Diary of an Old Guard Slave* by Viola Johnson, *Urban Aboriginals* by Geoff Mains, *Partners in Power* by Jack Rinella, and the essays "The Spiritual Dimensions of Bondage" by Joseph Bean and "One Among Many: The Seduction and Training of a Leatherman" by Tom Magister in *Leatherfolk*, edited by Mark Thompson (Baldwin with "a grateful slave" 2003; Cowan 1982; Easton and Liszt 1994, 1995; Johnson 1999; Mains 2002 [1984]; Rinella 2003; Bean 1991; Magister 1991; Thompson 1991). Some of Michael Rosen's images in *Sexual Magic: The SM Photographs* similarly show intimacy through BDSM practices (1986). For an in-depth perspective on the history of SM in the San Francisco area, Gayle Rubin has documented a considerable amount of colorful cultural SM history in her body of publications (Rubin 1991, 1994, 1997a, 1997b, 1998).

In a BDSM negotiation I tell you everything I can think of that I like, want, or need to make the scene or relationship successful for me, as well as what I cannot or will not do: my limits. I also let you know what skills, talents, experiences, and other resources I can bring to our play so that they can be available to us. You, of course, tell me the same things about you. Then we both know enough to decide together how best to play so we both get what we need and as much as possible of what we want while not doing any of the things either of us would find problematic. As in any other setting, we can distinguish between what we *need* and what we *want* by what we find negotiable. Anything without which we will not be able to find satisfaction in our scene or other undertaking—any experience, item, or expression we must have—is not negotiable and hence a need. Everything else, which we can negotiate, is what we want. It is to be hoped that we also know enough about ourselves and each other that we can agree *not* to play if for any reason we anticipate that one or both of us will end up having a bad time.

In order to negotiate in this manner I must be *able* to consent, and to consent to anything I must have both the information on which to base my consent as well as the capacity to consent. Real information about BDSM practices used to be extremely hard to come by because they were just behaviors people engaged in privately or on the margins of society. Without intending to make rules about their sex lives, those same people evolved through their own experiences some guidelines that later became codified and that I can describe in this chapter.

Until the 1980s nearly all the available literature on the subject was produced by pornographers who earned their livings by appealing to fantasies; psychologists with little or no training in human sexuality who were looking for varieties of human experience outside some abstract norm, which they described as deviant and defined as psychopathology; and journalists looking for sensational stories within the context of their own cultural biases. Beginning with Larry Townsend's *The Leatherman's Handbook* (1972), Gerald and Carolyn Greene's *SM: The Last Taboo* (2003 [1974]), Samois's *Coming to Power* (1987 [1981]), and Geoff Mains's *Urban Aboriginals* (2002 [1984]), however, the shelf of knowledgeable participant literature has burgeoned; by now it includes dozens of well-written and expertly informed volumes on which curious novices or outsiders can rely quite satisfactorily.

Consent is a topic in every one of the relevant participant contributions to the field. Yet the nature of informed consent is frequently open to question. We assume at least the probability that an ordinary adult has the capacity to become informed—hence the notion of *caveat emptor*—and so we allow an adult to take responsibility for her own behavior. But we neither can nor do make the same assumption about children, which is one of several obvious reasons children are excluded from BDSM activities. Children are not generally competent to consent psychologically, and even when they mature as late teens so that they might be competent to consent psychologically, minors are never competent to consent in the eyes of the law. The same holds true, as it does elsewhere in our society, for people who are asleep, under the influence of medications, alcohol, or other drugs, or are mentally incapacitated. Consent is only consent when it is *informed* consent; uninformed consent may very well be or lead to circumstances of abuse.

USE OF SAFEWORDS IN BDSM

Most people in the BDSM communities are greatly concerned to distinguish between their preferred erotic behaviors and abuse. To that end one long-standing strategy is the use of *safe words* to provide readily communicable guidelines for individuals who unexpectedly feel out of their depth in the midst of an otherwise unremarkable scene as well as to accommodate players who enjoy resistance, interrogation, or other consensual nonconsensual play such as cop/prisoner scenarios. Back in 1972, in the original *Joy of Sex*, Alex Comfort recommended neutral safe words such as *pickle* and *radish*, but real players in real scenes either forgot those words in the heat of passion because they were meaningless or found them too silly to adopt. Although variations still abound, the safe words most frequently in use have turned out to be the common colors of traffic signals: *green* for "go," *yellow* for "caution" or "slow down," and *red* for "stop immediately." In a party and other public situations, many communities have adopted the articulated word *safeword* as a sign that nonviolent outside intervention is required for a scene that has gotten out of control. No knowledgeable or experienced player would ignore another player's safe word, and, because the communities tend to be self-policing, players who fail to honor safe words are usually identified quickly.

The danger that some innocent outside observer might well misinterpret behavior that *looks like* abuse is one reason most BDSM takes place indoors or in outdoor settings so secluded or protected as to be considered outdoor "rooms." Containing play also ensures that "civilians" or "vanilla" folk—people who do not participate in BDSM activities—will not be exposed to BDSM play non-consensually. All the attention players give to negotiation and consent makes it more likely that their play will be safe, but safety can no more be guaranteed in BDSM's theatrical erotics than it can be guaranteed in skiing, eating, or driving to work. My informal conversations with physicians suggest that any one of those conventional activities result in more injuries, fatalities, and emergency room admissions every year than all negotiated, consensual BDSM activities combined.

MENTAL HEALTH ISSUES AND BDSM

There is enormous value to the normalization of alternate sexualities because, when seen by the light of reason, almost all turn out to be harmless both to those individuals who practice them and to the society in which they live. Whether the activities are expressions of unusual creativity, symptoms of deep-seated emotional disturbance, or simply ways of being sexual has never been shown; what little has been shown indicates that the profiles of people who engage in BDSM activities differ in no significant way from the profiles of people who do not, just as individuals cannot be distinguished on the basis of sexual orientation (Moser 1979; Baumeister 1989).

At the same time, while the increasing normalization of BDSM has made its practices and practitioners appear less threatening than they used to seem to the general population, it has also lowered the bar for people who want to enter its communities or lifestyles. As BDSM has appeared in more and more "vanilla"[1] households, not only has the most visible BDSM become tamer, but BDSM players as a group have become less knowledgeable. Where the wider acceptance of BDSM seems to be a good thing overall, it is not without concern, simply because BDSM is an unusually sophisticated form of sexuality: for a BDSM encounter some communication is necessary, lest a Top who likes to whip be paired with a bottom who likes to serve tea and because some BDSM activities can be dangerous when practiced by people who do not know the ropes.

The Internet is both part of the blessing and part of the curse. People who are curious can learn a great deal on the net if they know where to go and how to read the Web sites they find. At the same time, many self-proclaimed Masters who say they have huge stables of devoted slaves have never actually played, exercised erotic command with a live consensual partner, or even held a whip:

they can talk the talk, but have no idea how to walk the walk. Similarly, many self-proclaimed slaves have not yet distinguished between the extreme scenes of possession they use as masturbatory fantasy material and the genuine pain that can accompany even a simple spanking or the discomfort they may feel relinquishing control over important facets of their lives. Outside a small, tight-knit community such as the one that used to attend Serpent Mountain parties, there can be no reliable oversight. Consequently, genuinely dangerous people may sometimes find their ways into the confidences of people who trust too readily, and harmful activity can ensue. Surely, too, even where the ideal prevails in the real world of BDSM, it fails occasionally, as ideals also fail from time to time in political parties, academic institutions, or psychotherapeutic guilds. Even experienced players are sometimes swept away by passion and neglect or overstep some bounds; even the most careful player misunderstands a communication now and then. Whether through a failure of ideals or a failure of the system, unintended consequences sometimes befall players, and some of them show up at the doors of psychotherapists.

DIFFERENTIATING PSYCHOPATHOLOGY FROM CONSENSUAL EROTIC POWER EXCHANGE

For some people, under some circumstances, the suffering of the victim is certainly arousing, and in the absence of consent or in the presence of identifiable harm that arousal indicates a concern to be addressed. But when the Top's arousal derives from the bottom's suffering in consensual erotic power exchange, it may have a deeper meaning. The arousal may be associated, for instance, with the trust the bottom offers the Top by making himself extraordinarily vulnerable; the willingness of the Top not to abuse that trust by exercising skill, restraint, and compassion to contain the scene and assure the safety of the bottom; and the intimacy the players can share by venturing into areas that are highly charged erotically in part because they *could* be dangerous or at least unpleasant in other, unsafe hands. In similar conditions of trust with much more palpable possibilities of harm we would not offer up diagnoses for trapeze artists or tandem skydivers who literally place their lives in one another's hands, however much we viewed their acts with trepidation, nor would we diagnose a pathology in devotées of tantric yoga who work for years to achieve the energy movements people sometimes learn to accomplish in a few hours of expertly choreographed flagellation.

The justification for diagnosing consensual sexual acts, urges, and even fantasies as mental disorders closely resembles the justification by which moral judgments used to be rendered in psychiatric terms that marked homosexuality—and, by extension, bisexuality—as a psychiatric disorder. And as it was with that now liberated trait, which may yet turn out to be genetic or biochemical rather than a purely psychological predisposition, the psychiatric judgment itself creates a social justification for intolerance and prejudice that may provoke, among people who engage in erotic power exchange, guilt, shame, anxiety, depression, and other iatrogenic disturbances that are not otherwise significantly inherent in their personalities.

In other words, by pathologizing consensual erotic power exchange as if its activities were nonconsensual and uninformed, the *Diagnostic and Statistical Manual of Mental Disorder* (*DSM*) published by the American Psychiatric Association (APA 2000) has created a class of disorders out of traits that do not otherwise meet clinical criteria for any disorder, that do not impinge upon the rights of others, and that neither impair people's functioning nor cause them distress. Apart from the *DSM*'s historical encounter with homosexuality, the closest parallels our society offers to this sort of confusing evaluation exist in the imposition of morality onto law, which has created whole categories of victimless crime, and of those religions that have invented harmless sin.

Far and away the largest number of useful studies of real BDSM practices has been conducted by Charles Moser, Ph.D., M.D., whose curriculum vita, listing his publications, can be found online. Moser's work includes a couple of papers eloquently proposing that consensual erotic sadism, consensual erotic masochism, and other paraphilias be removed altogether from future editions of the *DSM* (e.g., Moser 2002; Moser and Kleinplatz 2005). For an educated, deeply thoughtful view of the practices of the gay male SM subculture from the vantage of cultural anthropology, see Gayle Rubin's unpublished doctoral dissertation, "The Valley of the Kings: Leathermen in San Francisco, 1960–1990" (Rubin 1994).[2]

Paraphilic activities, like personality traits, are psychologically meaningless by themselves; it is individuals who imbue them with significance. Given the historical and current diagnostic criteria, it is little wonder that many psychotherapists confuse the clinical disorders of sexual sadism and sexual masochism with the give-and-take of intense mental focus or physical sensation that marks much erotic power exchange. But this confusion can be ameliorated by redefining as disorders only those paraphilic behaviors that cause either significant functional impairment or subjective distress and recognizing as traits or preferences those that are victimless, harmless erotic expressions.

Such a redefinition is important beyond the specialized world of psychological or sexological diagnosis because lay people may readily accept professional assertions that a nonstandard behavior is pathologically deviant without considering why or to what extent the definition of deviance itself is created by a committee of psychiatrists or to what extent deviance is simply socially defined. In a society where sex education is as famously lax as it is in the United States, for example, erotic behaviors may be regarded as deviant simply because they are socially or culturally misunderstood rather than because they are signs of psychological disorder.

There is a real difference between pathological behavior that is physically dangerous, psychologically debilitating, and interpersonally nonconsensual, on the one hand, and nonpathological behavior that is physically safe, psychologically uplifting, and interpersonally consensual on the other. Absent distress, harm, or functional impairment, to define such activity as a mental disorder is to place chains on the human spirit and to produce a chilling effect on the very processes we as psychotherapists are trained and charged to abet: the healing and liberation of damaged and imprisoned personalities and their integration in the full creative expression of human beings.

SUGGESTIONS FOR COUNSELORS AND THERAPISTS

For counselors and therapists seeking to serve bisexual clients, familiarity with the BDSM subculture is important if for no other reason than that once a person begins to examine the nature of her own sexuality—as actively bisexual people virtually must have done in order to recognize the ways their desires differ from those of heterosexual people—she is likely at least to consider the nature of erotic power dynamics. To a large extent contemporary BDSM communities are just part of the wider world and not the special places on the margins of society that they were a couple of decades ago. In many BDSM communities, heterosexuals, gay men, and lesbians do not treat bisexual people any differently than bisexual people are treated anywhere else: with ambivalence, uncertainty, apprehension, and derision. In other regards, however, the present-day BDSM communities evolved from a rich base of acceptance and enthusiastic experimentation with sex and erotic energy that can still allow for something more than tolerance in interpersonal relationships. Some communities even pride themselves on celebrating diversity, including diversity of both sexual orientation and gender identity.

Therapists who already understand bisexuality have a great advantage relative to most other professionals in the field when dealing with BDSM because they are familiar with the impact of an inappropriately pathologizing label on otherwise ordinary people. Yet that awareness carries with it a kind of moral imperative to broaden the base of education. For the time being, given that the DSM continues to misrepresent BDSM behaviors as disorders, therapists can serve their clients, bisexual and otherwise, who have an interest in consensual erotic power exchange by getting some education of their own about human sexuality in general and the paraphilias such as sadomasochism in particular.

The following are some key recommendations for counselors seeking to serve this population.

First, it is important that we seek education on alternative sexual practices from people who have hands-on experience with and knowledge of BDSM practices and communities as well as from researchers whose hands may be too clean to be informed. We may learn that things are not as we have been led to believe they seem. This is what happened for Stoller, who regarded consensual sadomasochism as a sexual psychopathology in his early writings, and changed his mind when he took the trouble to educate himself (Stoller 1991). Certainly, too, there is nothing different in educating ourselves about BDSM than there is in educating ourselves about bisexuality. And just as certainly, bisexual people may experience the same sorts of misunderstandings in the current BDSM communities that they experience in the more strictly vanilla world.

Second, as we did or would do concerning bisexuality, we can spend enough time in our own therapies and consultations to become conversant with our countertransference issues concerning sex and power dynamics. In that way we will reduce the chances that we will make hasty, rash, ill-informed judgments about what other people like to do.

Third, if someone consults with us to work on feelings of anxiety or depression, or because of a communication difficulty at home or at work, and he turns out to be involved with BDSM, we can proceed without assuming that the person's sexual lifestyle is the "real" problem any more than we would assume her bisexuality to be a problem in the same situation. That way we can avoid trying to fix what isn't broken and seek instead to address the problems that distress our clients.

Fourth, we can proceed without expecting our clients to pay for the privilege of educating us about what they like to do in bed or in the playroom or dungeon. If we need to know about BDSM in order to interact fruitfully with a client, we can do what we would do if the client was involved with anything else we didn't understand: we can read, take classes, or get consultations or we can refer our client out. If we want to work with people living sexually alternative lifestyles but have difficulty talking with them, whether they are bi, BDSM players, or anything else, we can learn. Charles Moser's easy-to-read reference book *Health Care Without Shame* (1999) should be on the shelf of every health care professional anyway.

Fifth, in the realm of paraphilias and elsewhere, we can become more proactive in educating others, including those authorities charged with formulating our diagnostic criteria for future editions of the DSM (Moser and Kleinplatz 2005).

Sixth, we can proceed with harm reduction in mind. To that end I will next introduce the PLISSIT Model. I have found this model useful when working with clients around issues of alternative sexuality.

APPLYING THE PLISSIT MODEL TO ASSISTING CLIENTS WITH BDSM INTERESTS

In the event that a client really does want to address her concerns about BDSM or some other form of erotic power play, we can proceed with a harm reduction intervention such as the PLISSIT model developed by Jack Annon (1974, 1975).[3] In its very structure, PLISSIT recognizes that not every person coming through my door wants the same thing and asserts that most people want less rather than more—and few want all—of what is available through the psychotherapeutic process.

The first thing nearly every client wants from me is *Permission* to be him- or herself. I don't mean he has not wrestled with and even resolved this matter— maybe he has and maybe he hasn't—but that he needs permission to be himself in *my* life, in *my* space, and in any process we are going to share. In this regard permission is similar to Rogerian *unconditional positive regard* or something related to *empathy*. Permission does not mean *encouragement* any more than it means *discouragement*; it neither applauds nor condemns; it simply *accepts*: permission is acceptance without anything added or taken away.

Most clients who feel accepted—who have permission to be themselves with me—next want some forms of *Limited Information*. One person may want information about her process, another may want information about resources, a third may want information about my training and background. But at this point the underlying quest is more likely for information about where we two might meet, where we might go together as client and therapist, and how we might go there. Often the information is requested and provided implicitly, underneath the conversation that might be transcribed from a tape recording of what we seem to say; frequently the client does not articulate what she is trying to find out. Yet if I fail to read the underlying questions our alliance will likely be short-lived. The client who asks me for resources can surely find them elsewhere, and may chiefly want only to know, for instance, if I have the relevant depth of knowledge that knowing about those resources attests. The client who asks about my training may be confirming or questioning feelings of permission or testing my boundaries. The client who asks about my process may want a model she might adapt personally.

When my client is satisfied that we can build an alliance—and when I am similarly satisfied—he may want *Specific Suggestions* about what to do next. Asking for such suggestions, whether overtly or tacitly, does not imply he doesn't know already. It may mean he is asking me to demonstrate the way I work: to show how we can work together.

Whether she and I will ever do *Intensive Therapy* together, which may or may not be what she came to see me for, we will certainly not do it unless we reach this point. For many clients this is the point at which I become something different than a good parent, a source of referral information, a counselor, a fount of knowledge or advice, an ear, or a paid friend. This is the point at which I become—if I am going to become one at all with a particular client—a psychotherapist.

RETURN TO SERPENT MOUNTAIN

Organizing erotic energy is what Sybil Holiday sought to do at the Serpent Mountain parties, and she made a kind of music with it. It was essential to such delicate orchestration of human interactions that everyone present have at least some general idea what she was about so they would feel consulted rather than manipulated and they could direct their attentions to the parties' common ends as well as to their individual goals. It was equally important that people who attended these parties be able to negotiate their general needs and desires with Sybil and their specific needs and desires with their play partners so they could give or withhold consent concerning activities in which they might be asked to participate. And, while it was never important that an individual play across ori-entation lines, it was certainly taken for granted that no one at a Serpent Moun-tain party was so rigid in his gender roles that he would be upset or even sur-prised to find such play taking place. In the same way that players understood that men or women could equally well be Tops or bottoms, this sort of assump-tion could not have obtained unless the communities were functionally bisexu-al and often led to individuals and groups self-identifying their tastes even more globally, as Sybil did, as *pansexual*.

Although bisexuality was just one area of knowledge people at the Serpent Mountain parties could assume, Serpent Mountain is gone, and the era of elite SM, when anyone who wanted to play almost had to know the ropes in order to find a willing partner, prevails no longer. When Sybil, her colleagues, and their predecessors were running the Serpent Mountain parties in the 1980s, only three or four leather community activities were available in any given month in San Francisco. By 2004, again quoting the introduction to the revised edition of Sybil's and my book,

> Combining the list of SM activities posted under "Directory" at the primarily gay *Leather Journal* http://www.theleatherjournal.com with the list of the het/pansex-ual *BDSM—find the local scene near YOU!* www.darkheart.com/sceneusa.html yields more than 800 active BDSM groups in the United States, ranging from small local meetings to major conventions like Black Rose and Thunder in the Mountains to the annual Leather Leadership Conference. There is no major, sec-ondary, or tertiary urban area in the country where you can't whip, get whipped,

learn to whip, analyze whips and whipping, buy a whip, make a whip, or watch a whipping at a public forum almost any night you want.

It is never my job to decide how my client should live his or her life, of course, but it is always my job to help a person come to his or her own choices. In doing so, it sometimes helps to remember that the paraphilias are not necessarily or exclusively psychological or even sociological expressions. Just as recent research suggests that sexual orientation and gender identities may be consequences of genetics or other biological factors, so also may there be natural predispositions for other sexual tastes. And even if such questions *always and only* arise because of biological factors, there is a great deal of understanding and healing people need in order to live in satisfactory, satisfying, and fulfilling ways. This begins with simple acceptance. In the course of this work it is usually helpful and often essential to have a knowledgeable and compassionate witness who can facilitate the process. And that, I think, is exactly what I am there for.

NOTES

1. *Vanilla* is the term used by players to identify nonplayers. Its use probably began as derisory, but along with other teachers in the communities, Sybil Holiday pointed out often that vanilla was a perfectly good representative in the rainbow of flavors.
2. Rubin has also published several essays derived from her dissertation considered germinal by academics interested in feminist thought and queer studies, as well as anthropology, e.g., "The Miracle Mile: South of Market and Gay Male Leather in San Francisco, 1962–1996" and "Elegy for the Valley of the Kings: AIDS and the Leather Community in San Francisco, 1981–1996." If this subject is of interest to you, one good place to begin your research is Datenschlag's bibliography of publications on sadomasochism, fetishism, and related subjects, available online in English and German. The English version may be accessed at http://www.daten-schlag.org/english/bisam.
3. I have adapted the following remarks about PLISSIT from my own paper, "Coming Out Trans: Questions of Identity for Therapists Working with Transgendered Individuals (Trans Identity from the Queer Perspective)," which I presented originally at the "In the Family" conference in San Francisco in June 2001. An online version of this paper may be accessed at http://www.sexuality.org/l/wh/cot.html.

REFERENCES

American Psychiatric Association (2000). *Diagnostic and statistical manual of mental disorders* (4th ed.). Washington, DC: American Psychiatric Association.

Annon, J. (1974). *The behavioral treatment of sexual problems* (Vol. 1): *Brief therapy*. Honolulu: Enabling Systems.

Annon, J. (1975). *The behavioral treatment of sexual problems* (Vol. 2): *Intensive Therapy*. Honolulu: Enabling Systems.

Baldwin, G., with "a grateful slave." (2003). *SlaveCraft: Roadmaps for erotic servitude — Principles, skills, and tools*. Los Angeles: Daedalus.

Baumeister, R. F. (1989). *Masochism and the self*. Hillsdale, NJ: Erlbaum.

Bean, J. (1991). The spiritual dimensions of bondage. In M. Thompson (Ed.), *Leatherfolk* (pp. 257–266). Boston: Alyson.

Cowan, L. (1982). *Masochism: A Jungian view*. Dallas: Spring.

Easton, D., and Liszt, C. (1994). *The bottoming book*. San Francisco: Greenery.

Easton, D., and Liszt, C. (1995). *The topping book*. San Francisco: Greenery.

Greene, G., and Greene, C. (2003 [1974]). *SM: The last taboo*. New York: Blue Moon.

Henkin, W. A., and Holiday, S. (2004 [1996]). *Consensual sadomasochism: How to talk about it and how to do it safely*. Los Angeles: Daedalus.

Johnson, V. (1999). *To love, to obey, to serve: Diary of an Old Guard slave*. Fairfield, CT: Mystic Rose.

Leather Journal: http://www.theleatherjournal.com.

Magister, T. (1991). One among many: The seduction and training of a Leatherman. In M. Thompson, (Ed.), *Leatherfolk* (pp. 91–105). Boston: Alyson.

Mains, G. (2002 [1984]). *Urban aboriginals: A celebration of Leathersexuality*. Los Angeles: Daedalus.

Moser, C. (1979). An exploratory-descriptive study of a self-defined S/M (Sadomasochistic) sample. Unpublished doctoral dissertation. Institute for Advanced Study of Human Sexuality, San Francisco.

Moser, C. (1999). *Health care without shame: A handbook for the sexually diverse and their caregivers*. San Francisco: Greenery.

Moser, C. (2002). Are any of the paraphilias in the *DSM* mental disorders? *Archives of Sexual Behavior*, 31(6), 490–491.

Moser, C., and Kleinplatz, P. J. (2005). DSM-IV-TR and the paraphilias: An argument for removal. *Journal of Psychology and Human Sexuality*, 17(3/4), 91–109. http://home.netcom.com/~docx2/mk.html.

ReSearch (1989). *Modern primitives: An investigation of contemporary adornment and ritual*. San Francisco: Re/Search no. 12.

Rinella, J. (2003). *Partners in power*. San Francisco: Greenery.

Rosen, M. (1986). *Sexual Magic: The SM photographs*. San Francisco: Shaynew (P.O. Box 425221, San Francisco, CA 94142).

Rubin, G. (1991). The Catacombs: A temple of the butthole. In M. Thompson (Ed.), *Leatherfolk* (pp. 119–141). Boston: Alyson.

Rubin, G. (1994). The Valley of the Kings: Leathermen in San Francisco, 1960–1990. Unpublished Ph.D. Dissertation in Anthropology. Ann Arbor: University of Michigan.

Rubin, G. (1997a). Elegy for the Valley of the Kings: AIDS and the leather community in San Francisco, 1981–1996. In M. P. Levine, P. M. Nardi, and J. H. Gagnon (Eds.), *In changing times: Gay men and lesbians encounter HIV/AIDS* (pp. 101–144). Chicago: University of Chicago Press.

Rubin, G. (1997b). "Music from a bygone era." *Cuir Underground*, Issue 3.4.

Rubin, G. (1998). The Miracle Mile: South of Market and gay male leather in San Francisco, 1962–1996. In J. Brook, C. Carlsson, and N. Peters (Eds.), *Reclaiming San Francisco: History, politics, culture* (pp. 247–272). San Francisco: City Lights.

Samois (Ed.) (1987 [1981]). *Coming to power*. Boston: Alyson.

Sprinkle, A. (1991). Beyond bisexual. In L. Hutchins and L. Ka'ahumanu (Eds.), *Bi any other name: Bisexual people speak out* (pp. 103–107). Boston: Alyson.

Stoller, R. J. (1991). Pain and passion: A psychoanalyst explores the world of S & M. New York/London: Plenum.

Thompson, M. (1991). *Leatherfolk*. Boston: Alyson.

Townsend, L. (1972). *The leatherman's handbook*. New York: Modernismo.

PART 5

FUTURE TRENDS

20

TRAINING COUNSELORS TO WORK ETHICALLY AND EFFECTIVELY
WITH BISEXUAL CLIENTS

Tania Israel

THE NEED FOR COUNSELOR TRAINING
REGARDING BISEXUALITY

The necessity of training counselors to work with bisexual clients has become increasingly apparent. Studies have found that counselor trainees receive less preparation to work with bisexual clients compared to lesbian and gay male clients (Phillips and Fischer 1998), express confusion about bisexuality (Israel et al. 2004), and draw on stereotypes in their assessment of bisexual clients' presenting concerns (Mohr, Israel, and Sedlacek 2001). Thus counselors are likely to be confused about bisexuality, receive little training addressing bisexuality, and treat their clients based on biased views and in the absence of accurate information.

Although bisexuality is not specifically addressed in the ethical or accreditation standards for psychologists and counselors, it is subsumed in the term *sexual orientation*. APA has emphasized respect for differences based on sexual orientation, has encouraged psychologists to eliminate biases related to sexual orientation, and has supported training to ensure competent services regarding sexual orientation issues (American Psychological Association 2002). Furthermore, programs accredited by the APA are charged with providing students with knowledge and experiences about sexual orientation as it relates to the science and practice of professional psychology (American Psychological Association 2000). The ACA ethical code has emphasized nondiscrimination due to sexual orientation and recognition of the effects of sexual orientation on test administration and interpretation (American Counseling Association 1997). The CACREP Standards have specified that training programs should provide students with experiences and knowledge that enable them to develop an understanding of cultural contexts and individual characteristics related to sexual orientation as well as the role of sexual orientation within each specialty area and in terms of assessment (Council for Accreditation of Counseling and Related

Educational Programs 2001). Thus, the expectation exists that counselors should receive training and demonstrate competence in working with clients with a variety of sexual orientations, including bisexuality.

Early literature that addressed counseling bisexual clients (e.g., Blair 1974) reflected monosexist biases by describing bisexual clients as irresponsible, confused, and duplicitous. Although accurate and unbiased information about bisexual women and men is increasingly available in the psychological literature (e.g., Firestein 1996), counselor trainees continue to exhibit biases in their attitudes and assessment of client concerns (Israel et al. 2004; Mohr, Israel, and Sedlacek 2001).

Most studies of counselor trainees' heterosexist biases have not assessed attitudes regarding bisexuality specifically (Pilkington and Cantor 1996). Since there exists some overlap between attitudes regarding lesbians and gay men and attitudes regarding bisexuality (Mohr and Rochlen 1999), it seems safe to assume that biases against bisexual women and men exist where general heterosexist biases have been detected. Although likely present to some extent in all graduate counselor training, such biases may be particularly strong in clinical psychology doctoral programs and in behaviorally oriented programs (Hart 2001).

Although some aspects of attitudes toward bisexuality are similar to attitudes toward lesbians and gay men, there are some unique aspects of attitudes regarding bisexuality (Mohr and Rochlen 1999). Similarly, there are unique facets of information and skills related to counseling bisexual clients. Accordingly, counselor training about lesbian and gay male issues will presumably help counselors with some aspects of working with bisexual clients but will likely fail to increase their competence in other areas. According to Phillips and Fischer (1998), "it appears that increased sensitivity to and training in bisexual issues is warranted. Programs cannot simply assume that training in gay and lesbian issues will be enough" (p. 729). Thus it is imperative that counselors receive training specific to working with bisexual clients.

Some writings on counselor education about sexual minority issues explicitly focus on training therapists to work with lesbians and gay men (e.g., Whitman 1995). Other writings use terms inclusive of bisexual women and men (e.g., LGB), but do not include any material about working with bisexual clients that is distinct from the material presented on working with lesbians and gay men (e.g., Hart 2001; Pearson 2003; Pett 2000; Safren 1999; Tyler et al. 1997). The implicit or explicit absence of bisexual issues in these works leave counselor educators with little guidance regarding training counselors to work with bisexual clients, despite the attention to the topic of training counselors to work with lesbian and gay male clients in research and professional literature (Phillips 2000).

In this chapter I will address this gap by providing guidance regarding training counselors to work with bisexual clients. I will identify areas of knowledge, attitude, and skill training that are specific to counselor education regarding bisexual clients, and I will discuss challenges to training counselors to work with bisexual clients and offer strategies for overcoming these barriers. Overall, I will extend recommendations from the broader literature on training counselors to work with LGB clients to counselor education regarding bisexuality, and I will draw on general literature on bisexuality to identify implications for counselor training.

KNOWLEDGE, ATTITUDES, AND SKILLS

Counselor competence in working with marginalized clients is typically framed in terms of knowledge, attitudes, and skills (Israel and Selvidge 2003). What follows is a description of the ways in which knowledge, attitude, and skill training can be adapted to issues of bisexuality.

KNOWLEDGE

Information about bisexuality is lacking in counselor preparation. As inadequately as lesbian and gay male issues are covered in counselor training, issues of bisexuality receive even less attention (Phillips and Fischer 1998).

Not only is bisexuality explicitly absent from discussions of counseling lesbians and gay men, but it is not adequately integrated into materials that claim to focus on LGB issues. Due to the relative dearth of research on bisexuality compared to research on lesbians and gay men, texts that strive to be inclusive of bisexuality are frequently limited to acknowledging the lack of empirical attention to bisexuality.

Not only is there less information available about bisexuality compared to the knowledge base on lesbians and gay men, counselor trainees may have a greater need for such information due to limited exposure to bisexuality. As sexual orientation is often presumed based on the sex of the partner, people who identify as bisexual may be inappropriately identified by others as lesbian/gay or heterosexual (Ochs 1996). Not only do bisexual individuals lack visibility, but they are commonly members of larger lesbian and gay communities, making it difficult for bisexual groups to be identified by outsiders (Hutchins 1996). Due to the lack of visibility of bisexuals and bisexual communities, counselors may have even less contact (or less awareness of contact) with bisexual individuals and communities than they do with lesbian/gay individuals and communities.

In order to address the dearth of information on bisexuality, several strategies can be implemented. First, counselor educators who recognize that their teaching materials are not inclusive of bisexuality can supplement those materials with resources that can inform counselors about the experiences of bisexual individuals. Counselor educators can provide specific information on bisexuality for topics on which such information is available. Although information on bisexuality may not exist in comparable depth to the information available about lesbians and gay men, there is a growing body of empirical research in this area. The books *Bisexuality in the United States: A Social Science Reader* (Rust 2000) and *Bisexuality: The Psychology and Politics of an Invisible Minority* (Firestein 1996) are excellent compilations of research on bisexuality, and the *Journal of Bisexuality* serves as a repository for much of the emerging research pertaining to this population.

Furthermore, counselor educators can help trainees to distinguish between information that reflects the experiences of bisexual individuals (or LGB individuals as a whole) and information that is true only for lesbians and gay men. By recognizing such within group differences, counselors may be less likely to inappropriately apply information pertaining to lesbians and gay men to bisexual clients.

In addition to drawing on traditional sources of empirically based information, counselor educators may need to consider alternative sources of knowledge about bisexuality. Although there is a growing body of research on bisexuality, empirical investigation in this area is lagging behind research on lesbians and gay men. This is reflected in the fact that the *Journal of Homosexuality* had been in existence since 1974, whereas the *Journal of Bisexuality* has been available only since 2000. Nonetheless, other types of information can help counselor trainees to develop a fuller and more accurate view of bisexuality. Personal histories and conceptual writings on bisexuality provide a wealth of information. Anthologies of such writings include *Bi Any Other Name* (Hutchins and Ka'ahumanu 1991), *Closer to Home: Bisexuality and Feminism* (Weise 1992), *Bisexual Theories, Queries, and Visions* (Tucker 1995), *Plural Desires* (Bisexual Anthology Collective 1995), and a compilation of interviews with bisexual women entitled *Bi Lives: Bisexual Women Tell Their Stories* (Orndorff 1999). These resources illustrate the lived experiences and perspectives of bisexual women and men in a manner that counselor trainees will likely find accessible.

Furthermore, counselor educators can counteract the lack of visibility of bisexuality by providing their students with opportunities to connect with bisexual individuals and communities through guest speakers, videos, community service activities, conference attendance, and Internet resources. Such experiences can increase counselors' knowledge of the experiences of bisexual individuals, as well as community resources, political concerns, and sources for additional professional development.

ATTITUDES

Although some attitudes regarding bisexuality are similar to attitudes toward lesbians and gay men, certain attitudes can be identified that represent unique beliefs about individuals who are bisexual (Israel and Mohr 2004; Mohr and Rochlen 1999). For example, counselor trainees may adhere to attitudes that bisexuality is not a legitimate sexual orientation and that bisexual individuals lack stability and trustworthiness in relationships. Lesbian and gay male counselors may be particularly susceptible to these beliefs as evidenced by the types of bi-negative attitudes expressed by lesbian and gay individuals (Mohr and Rochlen 1999; Rust 1993). Thus, encouraging counselor trainees to explore attitudes regarding lesbian women and gay men may not tap into certain attitudes regarding bisexuality.

In order to address this deficit in attitude exploration, counselor educators can provide opportunities to explore attitudes that are specific to bisexuality. Such exploration may be accomplished through a variety of means. Journal assignments can provide a forum in which trainees can identify and elaborate on their beliefs. Stimulus material for journal assignments could include television or movie clips that show individuals expressing views about bisexuality or questions such as "what do you believe about bisexual women and men that is different from what you believe about lesbian women and gay men?"

Structured values clarification activities may be useful for eliciting attitudes specific to bisexuality. For example, a moving survey can be created in which one area of the room is labeled *strongly agree* and another area of the room is labeled *strongly disagree*. Students can be asked to position themselves along an imaginary continuum between these two points in response to statements such as "bisexuals are confused about their sexuality" or "I would have difficulty trusting a romantic partner who was bisexual."

SKILLS

Counselor trainees can develop skills for working with bisexual clients through experiential activities in a classroom setting. In the context of training counselors to work with LGB clients, counselor educators can provide role play scenarios that include bisexual clients to assure that trainees have exposure to skill development in working with this population (Kocarek and Pelling 2003).

In addition to classroom-based skills training, counselor trainees can benefit from supervised experience working with bisexual clients. As bisexual women and men constitute a particularly hidden population, focused efforts to recruit such clients may be warranted. Although individual counseling may be appealing to some bisexual clients, alternative modes of therapy may create additional opportunities for contact with bisexual clients. Specifically, due to the lack of community experienced by many bisexual individuals, such clients may be receptive to support groups that would put them into contact with other people who have similar identities and experiences. Appropriately supervised facilitation of such groups can provide counselor trainees with much needed experience.

STRATEGIC USE OF KNOWLEDGE, ATTITUDE, AND SKILL TRAINING

In order for training on bisexuality to be optimally effective, it may be helpful to evaluate and target educational interventions based on trainees' stages of readiness for change (Tyler et al. 1997). During the *precontemplation* stage, individuals are unaware of the need for change. Although, counselor trainees who participate in elective instruction on counseling LGB clients may be cognizant of the need to develop competence in working with lesbian and gay clients, their readiness may be more consistent with the precontemplation stage in terms of bisexuality (Israel et al. 2004). Trainees at this stage may benefit from exposure to the perspectives of bisexual individuals through class speakers, role plays, guided imagery, and positive media images (Tyler et al. 1997).

Trainees who have gained an awareness of bisexual perspectives have entered the *contemplation* stage, in which they are ready to consider their own beliefs, behaviors, and identity. Interventions that will promote this shift to a more internal focus include clarification of values related to bisexuality and opportunities to react to vignettes depicting experiences that bisexual individuals may encounter (Tyler et al. 1997). Counselor educators can provide trainees in the subsequent *action* stage with opportunities to identify new behaviors, actions, and coping strategies that will help them develop as competent counselors for bisexual clients. Finally, trainees in the *maintenance* stage will benefit from opportunities to identify their growth and the support they need to maintain change (Tyler et al. 1997). By accurately identifying trainees' stages of readiness for change and by tailoring interventions to these stages, counselor educators can minimize resistance and maximize trainees' learning potential.

CHALLENGES AND STRATEGIES FOR TRAINING COUNSELORS TO WORK EFFECTIVELY WITH BISEXUAL CLIENTS

Although it will be beneficial to include bisexuality in all aspects of counselor training, there are some topics for which counselor training regarding bisexuality is especially needed. In particular, areas where knowledge, attitudes, and skills may differ significantly from counselor training regarding lesbian and gay issues require additional attention. These areas include identity, relationships, and community.

BISEXUALITY AND IDENTITY

Models of sexual orientation identity development have typically reflected the experiences of lesbians and gay men (Cass 1984; McCarn and Fassinger 1996). Thus counselor trainees may have difficulty conceptualizing bisexual identity development or understanding what it means for people to identify as bisexual.

In order for counselor trainees to understand bisexual identity development, they must gain a sense of the various meanings that bisexuality represents for individuals who self-label as such. Counselor educators can lay the groundwork for understanding bisexuality by presenting multidimensional, nondichotomous models of sexual orientation (Klein, Sepekoff, and Wolf 1985). Furthermore, use of language, such as *ambierotic*, may help to clarify the distinction between bisexual identity and erotic attraction to both sexes (Hawkins 1998).

A second key concept regarding bisexuality and identity is related to the stability of a bisexual identity. Similar to attitudes held by the general public, counselor trainees may view bisexuality as only a transitional identity that will ultimately transform into a lesbian or gay identity. In reality, there is considerable variation how people develop a bisexual identity and whether or not that is a lasting identity (Fox 1996). There are people for whom bisexuality is their initial and consistent sexual orientation. Some people may, however, identify initially as bisexual and later embrace a lesbian or gay identity. Alternatively, some individuals who initially identified as lesbian or gay later find that a bisexual identity more appropriately reflects their experiences and attractions.

In addition to the possibilities of individuals changing outward identities in order to come into congruence with their attractions, some people may move in or out of a bisexual (or other) identity due to shifting internal experiences of their sexual orientation. Such fluidity may create discomfort for counselor trainees who believe that sexual orientation is unchanging and unchangeable. The notion of fluidity of sexual orientation may be particularly difficult for lesbian and gay male counselor trainees as lesbian and gay male identities, communities, and politics have been grounded in and promoted the assumption that sexual orientation is an unchanging attribute, much like ethnicity (Rust 1995). Furthermore, lesbians and gay men who formerly identified as bisexual may discount the experiences of people who identify as bisexual by reflecting on their own experience of a bisexual identity as a transitional identity in the process of coming out as lesbian or gay. Counselor educators can provide trainees with opportunities to explore feelings about the fluidity of sexual orientation

Given the variety of paths to developing a bisexual identity, counselor trainees may benefit from gaining an understanding of the range of experiences that may bring their clients to identify as bisexual. Rather than emphasize that bisexuality *is* a stable identity, it may be more useful to acknowledge that bisexuality *can be* a stable identity and to help counselor trainees learn to assess the complexity of their clients' inner experiences and outward identity label.

Not only can inclusion of information be useful for training counselors to work with bisexual clients, focusing material about sexual identity development and management on models of bisexual identity development can help counselor trainees to comprehend the variability and complexity of sexual orientation for lesbian and gay male clients, as well (Lidderdale 2002).

BISEXUALITY AND ROMANTIC/SEXUAL RELATIONSHIPS

As bisexuality is often associated with sexuality (Israel and Mohr 2004), counselor trainees may have strong reactions regarding bisexuality in romantic and sexual relationships. Three aspects of bisexuality and relationships may be particularly important to address in counselor training: sexual excess, polyamory, and loyalty.

Bisexual individuals may be viewed as sexually obsessed and sexually overactive. The sexualizing of bisexual individuals may result in a range of stereotypes. More positive stereotypes frame bisexual individuals, especially women, as sexually adventurous. More negative stereotypes include the view of bisexual individuals—especially men—as vectors of transmission for sexually transmitted diseases. In order to address these stereotypes, counselor educators can provide accurate information about transmission of sexually transmitted diseases and alert trainees to the objectification underlying attraction to bisexual women. As some feelings about bisexual individuals may be related more generally to sexuality than specifically to bisexuality, it can be helpful to encourage trainees to explore socialization messages and resulting feelings and values about sexuality and sexual expression.

Partially related to oversexualized views of bisexual individuals is the assumption that bisexual individuals cannot be monogamous. Not all people who are bisexual engage in nonmonogamous relationships, nor is nonmonogamy practiced only by bisexual people. However, because some people hold the limited view of bisexuality as a requirement for both male and female sexual partners rather than as a possibility of attraction to either women or men, nonmonogamy may be seen as the natural result of bisexuality. Consequently, counselor trainees may be uncomfortable with the idea of bisexuality due to its connection with nonmonogamy.

The first step in helping counselors to address the issue of bisexuality and polyamory is to provide accurate information about the ideal and lived relationships of bisexual individuals. Bisexual people can be monogamous, and for some bisexual women and men, monogamy is the ideal (Edser and Shea 2002; Rust 1996). On the other hand, some bisexual people are not monogamous, and a greater percentage of bisexual people hold nonmonogamy as an ideal compared to lesbian, gay male, and heterosexual individuals (McLean 2004; Rust 1996). It is important that counselors gain an accurate understanding of the relationships between bisexuality and polyamory (see Weitzman, chapter 17).

The disparity between the societal ideal of monogamy and the high rates of marital infidelity reflect and contribute to conflicted feelings about this issue. While acknowledging that polyamory is either real or ideal for some bisexual individuals, it may also be useful to disentangle bisexuality and polyamory by discussing alternatives to monogamy for heterosexual and lesbian/gay individuals. Feminists have articulated the political and economic disadvantages that monogamy poses for heterosexual and lesbian women (Jackson and Scott 2004; Robinson 1997; Rosa 1994), and these arguments hold true for bisexual women, as well. Readings from books such as *Lesbian Polyfidelity* (West 1996), *The Lesbian Polyamory Reader* (Munson and Stelboum 1999), *Polyamory: The New Love Without Limits* (Anapol 1997), or *The Ethical Slut* (Easton and Liszt 1997) may provide counselor trainees with an alternative framework to the traditional negative views of nonmonogamy presented by society.

In addition to negative attitudes about bisexual individuals related to polyamory, counselors may exhibit concerns that bisexual women and men will be disloyal to their romantic partners, in general (Israel and Mohr 2004). Such views have been expressed by college students, who viewed bisexual individuals as untrustworthy and not dependable as romantic partners (Eliason 2001; Spaulding and Peplau 1997). Just as lesbians and gay men may fear that a bisexual partner would leave them for a person of the other sex (Ochs 1996), counselors may doubt the commitment of a bisexual individual to a partner of the same sex.

Counselor educators can provide opportunities for trainees to explore attitudes about bisexual individuals and relationships. One way to do this is to ask counselor trainees to imagine that their romantic partner comes out as bisexual and identify feelings and concerns that arise. More generally, counselor trainees may benefit from identifying the sources, content, and underlying assumptions of their socialization regarding relationships. This could be a helpful means of exploring personal and cultural values about monogamy, polyamory, loyalty, and commitment.

BISEXUALITY AND COMMUNITY

Relationship with lesbian and gay communities is a distinct aspect of lesbian and gay identity development (McCarn and Fassinger 1996). Similarly, understanding bisexual individuals in the context of communities can help counselor trainees to develop a fuller understanding of the population.

Bisexual women and men report alienation from heterosexual as well as lesbian and gay communities (Dworkin 2000). Such isolation may affect aspects of identity development, internalized binegativity, and access to social and psychological resources. Accurate understanding of this lack of community, as well as the consequences of isolation can prepare a counselor to evaluate this aspect of a bisexual client's support network.

Another aspect of community is the relationship of bisexual individuals to lesbian and gay communities. Although some lesbian and gay communities welcome bisexual individuals, others view bisexuals with disbelief and suspicion (Rust 1995). A therapist who is not aware of these dynamics within lesbian and gay male communities may be ill-equipped to help a bisexual client identify welcoming communities as well as anticipate potentially negative reactions that lesbian and gay male individuals might have to the client disclosing a bisexual identity.

Counselor trainees may assume that all lesbian and gay individuals would be accepting of people who are bisexual. Since lesbians and gay men have been marginalized based on their sexual orientation, counselor trainees may not expect them to do the same to another group. Thus, it may be particularly challenging to address biphobic attitudes if they are voiced by lesbian and gay male trainees as other students are likely to view their lesbian and gay male peers as accurate sources of information when it comes to LGB issues.

Counselors may benefit from learning about the history of bisexuality within lesbian communities and the negative attitudes that have ensued (Rust 1995). Lesbian communities and discourse that arose in the wake of second wave feminism reflected a number of views about lesbianism that were challenged by the existence of bisexual women in their midst. For example, as lesbianism was viewed as a form of political protest that was defined by the absence of heterosexual relationships, bisexual women were seen as complying with a system of male domination (Rust 1995). Furthermore, within lesbian feminist communities, relationships between women were idealized and viewed as an expression of valuing women, thus bisexual women's attractions to or relationships with men implicitly diminished women and lesbian relationships (Rust 1995). Some women who affiliated with lesbian communities and later came out as bisexual or developed relationships with men were ostracized from lesbian communities and accused of betrayal and deception (Young 1992). Although these dynamics originated in the context of 1970s lesbian feminism, some of these negative attitudes toward bisexual women continue to be expressed (Rust 1993).

It may also be helpful for counselor educators to point out some of the emotional issues that may contribute to biphobia among lesbian women and gay men. For example, the existence of bisexuality may threaten the binary categories of sexual orientation on which lesbians and gay men have based their identities (Ochs 1996; Udis-Kessler 1990). Such information may help them understand why bisexual individuals might have a difficult time connecting with lesbian or gay people, might encounter mistrust within lesbian and gay communities, and, if they've previously had a lesbian or gay identity, they may struggle with internalized biphobia due to the negative messages they've received from lesbian/gay individuals as well as heterosexuals.

Despite these barriers to the development of communities for bisexual individuals, more recently bisexual communities are emerging, both as part of, and separate from lesbian and gay communities. An excellent source for locating such resources is *The Bisexual Resource Guide* (Ochs 2001), currently in its fourth edition.

The primary goals of counselor training regarding bisexuality are to present sufficient and accurate information about bisexuality, provide opportunities for trainees to explore their attitudes regarding bisexuality, provide alternative perspectives to the monosexist values of society, and engage in activities that will help counselors to develop skills in working with bisexual clients. Although training in working with lesbian and gay male clients will help counselors to develop some aspects of competence with bisexual clients, unique aspects of bisexuality must be addressed in order that counselors receive adequate preparation to address issues of identity, relationships, and community for bisexual individuals.

As bisexual individuals gain visibility within U.S. culture, it becomes increasingly important to integrate bisexual concerns into counselor training. The aspiration to do so is commonly expressed by the inclusion of the word *bisexual* in articles, books, and course titles. For this aspiration of inclusion to be fully realized, substantive content about bisexuality must be integrated into counselor training. Only then will counselors truly be equipped to work ethically and effectively with bisexual clients.

REFERENCES

American Counseling Association. (1997). *ACA Code of Ethics and Standards of Practice*. Alexandria, VA: American Counseling Association.

American Psychological Association. (2000). *Guidelines and principles for accreditation of programs in professional psychology*. Washington, DC: American Psychological Association.

American Psychological Association. (2002). Ethical Principles of Psychologists and Code of Conduct. *American Psychologist, 57,* 1060–1073.

Anapol, D. M. (1997). *Polyamory, the new love without limits: Secrets of sustainable intimate relationships*. San Rafael, CA: IntiNet Resource Center.

Association for Gay Lesbian and Bisexual Issues in Counseling (AGLBIC). (n.d.). *Competencies for counseling gay, lesbian, bisexual and transgendered (GLBT) clients*. Retrieved April 22, 2002, from http://www.aglbic.org/resources/competencies.html.

Bisexual Anthology Collective. (1995). *Plural desires: Writing bisexual women's realities*. Toronto: Sister Vision.

Brown, A. D., Israel, T., Uhm, S. Y., Selvidge, M. M. D., Keeton, M. D. (2004). Development and self-report of counselors' attitudes toward LGB clients. Poster presented at the American Psychological Association Annual Convention, Honolulu, Hawaii.

Cass, V. C. (1984). Homosexual identity formation: Testing a theoretical model. *Journal of Sex Research, 20*(2), 143–167.

Council for Accreditation of Counseling and Related Educational Programs (CACREP). (2001). *The 2001 Standards*. Retrieved April 24, 2002, from http://www.counseling.org/CACREP.

Division 44/Committee on Lesbian Gay and Bisexual Concerns Joint Task Force. (2000). Guidelines for psychotherapy with lesbian, gay, and bisexual clients. *American Psychologist, 55*(12), 1440–1451.

Dworkin, S. H. (2000). Individual therapy with lesbian, gay, and bisexual clients. In R. M. Perez, K. A. DeBord, and K. J. Bieschke (Eds.), *Handbook of counseling and psychotherapy with lesbian, gay, and bisexual clients* (pp. 157–181). Washington, DC: American Psychological Association.

Easton, D., and Liszt, C. A. (1997). *The ethical slut: A guide to infinite sexual possibilities*. San Francisco: Greenery.

Edser, S. J., and Shea, J. D. (2002). An exploratory investigation of bisexual men in monogamous, heterosexual marriages. *Journal of Bisexuality, 2*(4), 7–43.

Eliason, M. J. (2001). Bi-negativity: The stigma facing bisexual men. *Journal of Bisexuality, 1*(2/3), 137–154.

Firestein, B. A. (Ed.) (1996). *Bisexuality: The psychology and politics of an invisible minority*. Thousand Oaks, CA: Sage.

Fox, R. C. (1996). Bisexuality in perspective: A review of theory and research. In Beth A. Firestein (Ed.), *Bisexuality: The psychology and politics of an invisible minority.* (pp. 3–50). Thousand Oaks, CA: Sage.

Haldeman, D. C. (2001). Psychotherapy with gay and bisexual men. In G. R. Brooks, and G. E. Good (Eds.), *The new handbook of psychotherapy and counseling with men* (pp. 796–815). San Francisco: Jossey-Bass.

Hart, T. (2001). Lack of training in behavior therapy and research regarding lesbian, gay, bisexual, and transgendered individuals. *Behavior Therapist, 24,* 217–218.

Hawkins, R. O. (1998). Educating sexuality professionals to work with homoerotic and ambierotic people in counseling and therapy: A voice from the trenches. *Journal of Sex Education and Therapy, 23,* 48–54.

Hutchins, L. (1996). Bisexuality: Politics and community. In B.A. Firestein (Ed.), *Bisexuality: The psychology and politics of an invisible minority* (pp. 240–259). Thousand Oaks, CA: Sage.

Hutchins, L., and Ka'ahumanu, L. (Eds.) (1991). *Bi any other name: Bisexual people speak out*. Boston: Alyson.

Israel, T., and Mohr, J. J. (2004). Attitudes toward bisexual women and men—current research, future directions. *Journal of Bisexuality, 4,* 117–134.

Israel, T., and Selvidge, M. M. D. (2003). Contributions of multicultural counseling to counselor competence with lesbian, gay, and bisexual clients. *Journal of Multicultural Counseling and Development, 31,* 84–98.

Jackson, S., and Scott, S. (2004).The personal *is* still political: Heterosexuality, feminism, and monogamy. *Feminism and Psychology, 14,* 151–157.

Klein, F., Sepekoff, B., and Wolf, T. J. (1985). Sexual orientation: A multi-variable dynamic process. *Journal of Homosexuality, 11*(1–2), 35–49.

Kocarek, C. E., and Pelling, N. J. (2003). Beyond knowledge and awareness: Enhancing counselor skills for work with gay, lesbian, and bisexual clients. *Journal of Multicultural Counseling and Development, 31,* 99–112.

Lidderdale, M. A. (2002). Practitioner training for counseling lesbian, gay, and bisexual clients. *Journal of Lesbian Studies, 6,* 111–120.

McCarn, S. R., and Fassinger, R. E. (1996). Revisioning sexual minority identity formation: A new model of lesbian identity and its implications. *Counseling Psychologist,* 24(3), 508–534.

McLean, K. (2004). Negotiating (non)monogamy: Bisexuality and intimate relationships. *Journal of Bisexuality, 4*(1/2), 83–97.

Mohr, J. J., Israel, T., and Sedlacek, W. (2001). Counselors' attitudes regarding bisexuality as predictors of counselors' clinical responses: An analogue study of a female bisexual client. *Journal of Counseling Psychology, 48,* 212–222.

Mohr, J. J., and Rochlen, A. B. (1999). Measuring attitudes regarding bisexuality in lesbian, gay male, and heterosexual populations. *Journal of Counseling Psychology, 46,* 353–369.

Munson, M., and Stelboum, J. P. (1999). *The lesbian polyamory reader: Open relationships, non-monogamy, and casual sex.* Binghamton, NY: Haworth.

Ochs, R. (1996). Biphobia: It goes more than two ways. In B.A. Firestein (Ed.), *Bisexuality: The psychology and politics of an invisible minority* (pp. 217–239). Thousand Oaks, CA: Sage.

Ochs, R. (2001). *The bisexual resource guide.* Boston: Bisexual Resource Center.

Orndorff, K. (1999). *Bi lives: Bisexual women tell their stories.* Tuscon: See Sharp.

Pearson, Q. M. (2003). Breaking the silence in the counselor education classroom: A training seminar on counseling sexual minority clients. *Journal of Counseling and Development, 81,* 292–300.

Pett, J. (2000). Gay, lesbian and bisexual therapy and its supervision. In D. Davies and C. Neil (Eds.), *Therapeutic perspectives on working with lesbian, gay, and bisexual clients* (pp. 54–72). Philadelphia: Open University Press.

Phillips, J. C. (2000). Training issues and considerations. In R. M. Perez, K. A. DeBord, and K. J. Bieschke (Eds.), *Handbook of counseling and psychotherapy with lesbian, gay, and bisexual clients* (pp. 337–358). Washington, DC: American Psychological Association.

Phillips, J.C., and Fischer, A.R. (1998). Graduate students' training experiences with lesbian, gay, and bisexual issues. *Counseling Psychologist*, 26(5), 712–734.

Pilkington, N.W., and Cantor, J.M. (1996). Perceptions of heterosexual bias in psychology programs: A survey of graduate students. *Professional Psychology: Research and Practice*, 27, 604–612.

Robinson, V. (1997). My baby just cares for me: Feminism, heterosexuality, and non-monogamy. *Journal of Gender Studies*, 6, 143–157.

Rosa, B. (1994). Anti-monogamy: A radical challenge to compulsory heterosexuality. In G. Griffin, M. Hester, S. Rai, and S. Roseneil (Eds.), *Stirring it: Challenges for feminism* (pp. 107–120). London: Taylor and Francis.

Rust, P.C. (1993). Neutralizing the political threat of the marginal woman: Lesbians' beliefs about bisexual women. *Journal of Sex Research*, 30 (3), 214–228.

Rust, P.C. (1995). *Bisexuality and the challenge to lesbian politics: Sex, loyalty, and revolution*. New York: New York University Press.

Rust, P.C. (1996). Monogamy and polyamory: Relationship issues for bisexuals. In B.A. Firestein (Ed.), *Bisexuality: The psychology and politics of an invisible minority* (pp. 127–148). Thousand Oaks, CA: Sage.

Safren, S.A. (1999). Selected issues: Facing gay, lesbian, and bisexual graduate students in clinical psychology training. *Behavior Therapist*, 22, 189–192.

Spaulding, L.R., and Peplau, L.A. (1997). The unfaithful lover: Heterosexuals' perceptions of bisexuals and their relationships. *Psychology of Women Quarterly*, 21 (4), 611–625.

Tucker, N. (Ed.) (1995). *Bisexual politics: Theories, queries, and visions*. Binghamton, NY: Harrington Park.

Tyler, J.M., Jackman-Wheitner, L., Strader, S., and Lenox, R. (1997). A change-model approach to raising awareness of gay, lesbian, and bisexual issues among graduate students in counseling. *Journal of Sex Education and Therapy*, 22, 37–43.

Udis-Kessler, A. (1990). Bisexuality in an essentialist world: Toward an understanding of biphobia. In T. Geller (Ed.), *Bisexuality: A reader and sourcebook* (pp. 51–63). Ojai, CA: Times Change.

Weise, E.R. (1992). *Closer to home: Bisexuality and feminism*. Seattle: Seal.

West, C. (1996). *Lesbian polyfidelity*. San Francisco: Booklegger.

Whitman, J.S. (1995). Providing training about sexual orientation in counselor education. *Counselor Education and Supervision*, 35, 168–176.

Wiederman, M.W., and Sansone, R.A. (1999). Sexuality training for professional psychologists: A national survey of training directors of doctoral programs and predoctoral internships. *Professional Psychology: Research and Practice*, 30, 312–317.

Young, S. (1992). Breaking silence about the "B-word": Bisexual identity and lesbian-feminist discourse. In E.R. Weise (Ed.), *Closer to home: Bisexuality and feminism* (pp. 75–87). Seattle: Seal.

21

COUNSELING HETEROSEXUAL SPOUSES OF BISEXUAL OR TRANSGENDER PARTNERS

Amity Pierce Buxton

August 12, 2004, Trenton, New Jersey Governor James McGreevey, father of two children from two marriages, calls a press conference to announce on national television, "I am a gay American." His wife stands beside him. For the first time, Americans on TV monitors across the nation see an "out," mixed-orientation couple: a heterosexual wife and her gay husband. This scene, reshown for days on newscasts and talk shows, has become an indelible image in the public imagination, making crystal clear that when a spouse comes out, it is no longer an individual event but a family matter.

Within hours of the pronouncement, calls from reporters and producers flooded my phone line as executive director of the Straight Spouse Network, "What about marriages like this? What happens to heterosexual spouses when their partners come out? What are their needs, feelings, concerns? Is this different from any marriage that has secrets, betrayal, or infidelity?" My answers were based on self-reports of more than ten thousand spouses (mostly, but not all, heterosexual) with whom I had communicated since 1986—some over several years—and data from the few studies of straight spouses and mixed-orientation couples who stayed married after the husbands or wives disclosed

My standard reply was that this phenomenon is not uncommon. In up to two million marriages in the United States, current or former, one spouse is gay, lesbian, bisexual, or transgender (GLBT). When GLBT spouses reveal their sexual orientation or a transgender identity, their heterosexual partners face unique issues and experience devastating emotions as their view of the world and their lives is turned upside down by the unexpected changes in their partner and relationship. Spouses of bisexual and transgender partners also need to break through dichotomous ways of thinking in order to understand their partners' bisexuality and transgenderism. Few outsiders understand spouses' concerns, so most cope alone. Some find other spouses who are experiencing this crisis. Peers become their major source of support and help to resolve their concerns constructively.

. What I did not tell reporters is that many spouses cannot find therapists with knowledge or experience with clients of diverse sexual orientations or transgenderism, mixed-orientation couples, or heterosexual spouses in these kinds of relationships. In my study of couples that stayed together after the husbands came out gay or bisexual (Buxton 2001), two fifths of the wives of bisexuals found counseling helpful (slightly more than wives of gay men). Instead, communication between the spouses helped more of them deal with the disclosure effectively. In the companion study (Buxton 2004a) only about one fifth of the husbands of bisexual women said therapy helped, a smaller proportion than that of husbands of lesbians whom therapy helped. As one wrote, "Take what he or she [therapist] says with a grain of salt because there are few experts in this field and even fewer that most insurance companies will pay for. But you may have to do this to start a dialogue." Couple communication helped three times as many husbands cope than did therapy of any kind. The lack of professional help for spouses dealing with profound emotions and couples trying to make their marriages work after disclosure is disheartening.

This lack of knowledge in the counseling profession is explained in part by the fact that spouses in this situation are fewer in number than those who seek therapy for other relationship issues. Most therapists, therefore, have no experience working with heterosexual spouses whose mates have come out and no pressing reason to research factors related to success or failure in postdisclosure mixed-orientation relationships.

With the exponential increase in awareness of the existence of spouses and couples in mixed-orientation relationships following the governor's disclosure as a married gay man, the need for more knowledgeable therapists clearly becomes imperative. Until that time, the documented number of spouses coming out had increased only gradually since such cases were first reported in the early eighties, as measured by calls to the Straight Spouse Network office and accounts in the literature. Meanwhile, more spouses of transgender partners are also now becoming visible and seeking help from the Straight Spouse Network. This combined increase of spouses in need makes it even more urgent to increase counselors' knowledge base of heterosexual spouses whose mates come out as bisexual, lesbian, gay, or transgendered.

To that end, this chapter pinpoints the most striking issues and emotions of heterosexual spouses and the stages through which they progress in resolving them, with particular attention to those with bisexual or transgender mates, in view of the added complexity of these factors. The information in this chapter is drawn from the data mentioned above and responses to a questionnaire developed for this chapter sent to confidential Internet subscription lists. Based on this data, the present chapter provides an overview of basic information by which therapists can better gauge heterosexual spouses' basic concerns and help them sort out their needs, wants, and values. It is, in a sense, a "crash course" for therapists who are meeting a "straight spouse" for the first time or those seeking new ways to tap the self-healing resources of spouses already in their practice. More detailed information and illustrations of these issues and emotions can be found in *The Other Side of the Closet: The Coming-Out Crisis for Straight Spouses and Families* (Buxton 1994) and *Paths and Pitfalls: How Heterosexual Spouses Cope When Their Husbands or Wives Come Out* (Buxton 2004b). Further information about straight spouses and their bisexual, gay, lesbian, or transgender partners as well as about mixed-orientation couples can be found in the research literature cited in this chapter and elsewhere in this volume.

The remaining sections of the chapter describe therapy approaches that spouses of bisexual or transgender partners and mixed-orientation couples have found effective or ineffective, the "ideal" therapist in their eyes, and effective strategies for helping them cope constructively. When heterosexual spouses receive knowledgeable, even-handed counseling as well as peer support, they are better able to reconfigure their identity, integrity, and belief systems to communicate more candidly with their partners and, together with their partners, to forge a couple bond that sustains their friendship and coparenting roles (if they have children) whether or not they stay together. Therapists who have knowledge of the common problems and feelings of heterosexual spouses of GLBT partners are better prepared to anticipate and tease out what concerns lie below the surface and the potential for growth that lies ahead.

RESEARCH BACKGROUND

Comparatively little research has been done on spouses in mixed-orientation or trans/nontransgender marriages since the earliest published study by Imielinsky in 1969 (Buxton 2001, 2004a). Among these, few studies focus on bisexual husbands, even fewer on bisexual wives or transgender spouses, and many of the early reports blur distinctions between bisexual and gay husbands (Buxton 2001). Only a handful of researchers or spouses report on the experiences of both spouses within bisexual-heterosexual couples (Buxton 2001, 2004a; Gochros 1989; Wolfe 1985) or investigates heterosexual spouses of bisexual partners (Auerback and Moser 1987; Buxton 1994, 2004a, b; Hays and Samuels 1988). While a number of studies and books have been written about and by partners of transvestites or cross-dressers, most recently, M. P. Allen's *Transformations* (1989) and *An Autobiography of a Cross Dresser's wife* (Boyd 2003); not many look at spouses of transsexual partners, that is, those partners who change their presenting gender.

Together, these diverse samples present a mosaic of common issues and emotions of heterosexual spouses. Though each individual works through the disclosure aftermath in his or her own way and experience different circumstances that trigger his or her reactions, most spouses share the same array of concerns irrespective of their partners' orientation or gender identity. Their issues are unique and their emotions are profound. Spouses of transgender partners diverge at the point of their singular concern: their partners' visible changes, both physical and psychological. As the spouse of a female-to-male (F2M) partner writes, "Testosterone is one mighty powerful drug and it changes our partners' FACES as well as bodies. I mean, Steve looks sort of the same—sort of like he's now his own brother. And Susan is gone. Gone. I think that's been part of my grief."

ISSUES AND EMOTIONS OF HETEROSEXUAL SPOUSES

Heterosexual spouses face six major issues when their mates disclose. Some issues resemble the relationship problems of any troubled couple, but also involve factors unique to disclosure and postdisclosure changes. Three concerns become evident soon after the husband or wife comes out: sexual rejection as a man or woman, challenge to the marriage, and potential impact on the children. In the sexuality area, spouses feel rejected as a man or a woman when their partners say they are attracted to the same gender or want to change their gender identification to their true gender. Some spouses feel shortchanged sexually or blame themselves for sexual inadequacy. Spouses of bisexual partners feel less loss, because their partners still desire and enjoy lovemaking with them.

Regarding the marriage, the disclosure raises questions about its continuation: If the partner is attracted to the same gender, does that mean the end of the marriage? If the transsexual partner is going to transition completely to his or her true gender, what is the possibility that the marriage can continue? What adjustments would have to be made for the marriage to endure? While spouses ponder the question of the marriage, as parents, they worry about effects of the disclosure on the children. Their parental desire to protect their children from antigay attitudes in the school, neighborhood, or faith community and their desire to affirm the child's bond with the other parent conflicts with their feelings as a spouse. In reality, children are more concerned about their parents' separation and divorce, if that is the outcome, than about their parent's orientation or gender identity. Peer teasing and antigay attitudes will trouble them, of course, and many go into their own closets to process the information. Both parents help them cope, and the straight parent becomes the model for their children's reaction to the disclosure.

Issues of sexual rejection, the marriage, and the children absorb the attention of straight spouses as they go about daily activities. Three other issues emerge slowly, as shock wears off and they sense the impact of the disclosure within themselves. It is a triple crisis of identity, integrity, and faith or belief system. Initially, spouses tend to be primarily concerned about their partners and their disclosure, concerns that send them reeling. Gradually, they ask themselves, "What about me?" Many discover they have lost a sense of who they are. They feel worthless or blameworthy.

Spouses' integrity is in crisis, too. Once their partners disclose their secrets, the straight spouses feel deceived, kept in the dark about something central to their partner's being that they thought they knew intimately. They feel their trust has been betrayed, their moral compass shattered. For those in a conservative or orthodox faith community, their partners are now in an unfavorable moral status. Often having to keep the partners' secret, spouses feel stigmatized. Many feel powerless, still living someone else's lie. The disclosure also sometimes destroys their view of gender, marriage, their future, and life itself. Without a belief system that gives meaning or purpose, many feel hopeless.

Alongside these concerns, heterosexual spouses experience a roller-coaster of emotions. Pain and hurt are initial reactions, causing agony. Some lie in bed in a fetal position, cry for days, or lose weight precipitously. As the wives or husbands of gay, lesbian, or bisexual partners become more aware of the reality of the situation over time, anger erupts over the revealed sexual or gender mismatch between them and their partners. The sexual orientation difference frequently makes them feel shortchanged and/or rendered sexually inadequate. Wives of active gay or bisexual husbands are irate that they may have been put at risk for sexually transmitted diseases, including AIDS. Most spouses are angry that their marriages are now threatened and their children will face teasing and discomfort, enraged that they were lied to or duped, and furious that their belief system is shattered. As they wonder what will happen to the marriage and children and how to cope without a belief system, fear surfaces. Spouses become anxious about being able to cope or survive. Once they look at their situation candidly and realize it will never change back to what had been, grief predominates as they let go of past assumptions and expectations.

Each emotion is a normal reaction to the devastation of disclosure. Yet the power of such feelings when spouses feel bereft of the security of prior assumptions can be terrifying. Many have never felt this depth of anger or pain, fear or grief. In some cases emotions become so extreme that the reality that triggered them is lost in the chaos. A wife writes,

Last night he asked if I was able to find some medicine I was looking for. My reaction was totally unreasonable, totally rude. "That's none of your goddamed business." Whoa. This anger thing is NOT something I'm enjoying. Especially directed at him, since he's been honest and up front with me. I'm having a problem with anxiety, too. It's just heart palpitations and shortness of breath. Like I can't get enough oxygen.

Some spouses become stuck in anger, pain, fear, or grief when they do not find support, especially therapeutic support. These feelings overwhelm a number of spouses, preventing them from facing or coming to terms with reality, coping with it constructively, and taking care of themselves so that they can heal and grow.

STAGES OF RESOLVING ISSUES AND MANAGING EMOTIONS

Because of complexity and depth of their concerns and emotions, spouses need a long time to resolve them. The stages through which they progress to do so are not clear-cut. Rather, stages overlap, and spouses regress from time to time. Even so, there is a forward momentum as long as spouses feel supported and validated along the way. Briefly, the first stage begins with the heterosexual spouse's shock, disbelief, denial, and often relief at their spouse's disclosure: "stunned, lost, unable to cope," a spouse describes it. The second stage, which occurs sometime in the first year after disclosure, is facing, identifying, and acknowledging the reality that prompted their feelings: their partner's revealed orientation or gender identity, postdisclosure changes in their married life, and the spouse's own pain. The third stage, most often taking place during the second or third year, is accepting the present reality. Healing marks the fourth stage, as spouses feel free to tend to their own hurt, healing their mind, body, and spirit so that they can form an authentic self-image of worth (identity) and clarify their values (integrity). Letting go of past assumptions about their partner, the marriage, and themselves forms the fifth stage, usually in the third or fourth year. The sixth stage is reconfiguring their belief system and discovering meaning in life by which to refocus themselves. The seventh and last stage is transforming their lives by acting on their reconfigured belief system, self-image, and value system. This may occur as long as six years after the coming out.

While all heterosexual spouses express these concerns and feel these emotions, straight spouses of bisexual or transgender wives and husbands face an additional layer of complexity. In these cases the sexual orientation or gender identity of the partner breaks down the dichotomous paradigm of "either/or" held by most of us in the Western world. Neither bisexuality nor transgenderism can be categorized in an either/or fashion. Spouses of bisexual partners find it difficult to break through that duality of thinking to conceptualize their partners' orientation within a both/and paradigm, instead of one that separates people as either straight or gay.

Bisexuality may be very difficult to grasp because bisexual persons' orientation is often labeled by outsiders in terms of the gender of their partners, whether they are in a same-gender or opposite-gender relationship. Bisexuality and bisexual persons are, in effect, invisible in a heterosexual relationship (Buxton 2001, 2004a). Thus spouses find it hard to comprehend the fact that their partners may have same-gender desires and possibly behavior while simultaneously feeling and expressing their opposite-gender attraction in the marriage.

While transvestites change their external gender expression periodically and transsexual partners change their expressed gender physically and psychologically partially or totally to the opposite gender, those changes may or may not involve a change in their attraction to their marital partner. Spouses of transsexual mates find it hard to think about their partners' change in gender without extending the shift to that of sexual orientation. At the same time, visible changes denoting their partners' new gender cause many spouses to wonder about their own sexual orientation. "Am I lesbian now that my husband is a woman?" or "Now that my wife is a man, does that make me gay?" If trans/nontrans couples stay married, they are often seen as lesbian or gay couples by outsiders, a challenge to the straight partner's self-image and integrity. Many spouses of transgender individuals talk about a double loss. "It can be continuous and different," one writes. "One gives up the role of wife or husband. I placed a lot of value in my marriage, and the status and acceptance that it brought me from other married couples and people in general."

Despite differences related to their partners' revealed sexual orientation or gender change, heterosexual spouses share common concerns and emotions. Any spouse could have written the following statement by the wife of a male-to-female (M2F) partner: "The main issues are relearning trust, learning to recognize your spouse again, and grieving the loss of the person you thought you knew." A husband of a bisexual woman describes common emotions when he writes, "I'm scared that ultimately she may be gay, and I'm sad that we stand a chance of losing all we have" (Buxton 2004a).

Another spouse of a transsexual mate pinpoints feelings and stages experienced by most spouses:

The most difficult times were trying to deal with the reality and my emotions about my husband's being a repressed female inside and then slowly watching this woman emerge within our family structure. I felt I was losing my husband and did not know how to get him back. I finally realized he was more content and emotionally stable as a female. To this day I feel anger and rage that the man I married wouldn't be the same man I spoke my vows to. I am still adjusting to the changes, but I've accepted that the person I married is actually still there but as a female.

For many spouses, lack of understanding shown by friends, family members, clergy, and therapists leads to isolation, which in turn exacerbates the intensity of these issues and emotions and prolongs their resolving them. The wife of an M2F writes,

> I didn't know of anyone else that I could discuss my feelings with except her. I was a boat without an anchor having to cope with all the emotions each couple faces when their significant other comes out male-to-female or female-to-male. The most difficult was being extremely lonely. It's going to be difficult telling friends and family who don't know. A lot of people don't know and it's driving me crazy.

When any spouse finds the Straight Spouse Network and its support groups, online groups, and state contacts, one of the first comments is always, "Oh what a relief. I thought I was all alone."

Both spouses in a mixed-orientation marriage deal with issues and feelings that mirror each other. The husbands or wives who come out, although further along in resolving their disclosure concerns, still cope with the same issues as their heterosexual spouses: sexuality, marriage, children/family, identity, integrity, and belief system. Not only are they further along, but also their struggle has a different locus. They are trying to integrate their emerging same-sex attractions or a different gender identity from that which they have presented to the world into their self-identity and behavior as married partners and possibly parents. Their coping focuses on something within themselves, internal realities, unlike their heterosexual spouses who are dealing with an external set of factors. Their spouses' task is to integrate their partner's revealed orientation or gender identity into their lives and their concepts of their marriage, family, and future. Cross-dressing and transsexual partners deal with an array of visible, physical, behavioral, and psychological shifts made to match their internal reality, adding yet another set of changes for their spouses to incorporate into their lives. Moreover, outsiders' perceptions of the changed appearance of the trans partner intensifies the impact of the changes on both spouses.

As the two spouses cope at different stages, the one changing and the other trying to understand and adapt to the changes, the family context can be tense and confused. That complicated family environment, the complexity of issues and depth of the heterosexual spouses' feelings, and their partner's parallel internal struggle pose huge challenges to both of them. For heterosexual spouses, new to the disclosed information, resolving their issues is rarely completed in fewer than three years and, as noted, may take six or more years. Peers, if they find them, provide powerful support, validation, and reality checks to help them work through these stages constructively. Therapists feature less often in spouses' self-reports, though many spouses yearn for counselors who "get" their issues and can help them navigate the postdisclosure challenges.

What do spouses need and want from therapists? The following section summarizes what spouses report as helpful and not so helpful about the counseling they received and the kind of therapy they would find ideal. Quoted comments spell out what they think therapists need to know, effective and ineffective approaches, and which strategies heterosexual spouses perceive as "ideal." While spouses of gay or lesbian partners echo the main thrust of the points made, only responses of spouses of bisexual or transgender partners are cited here, in view of the singular complexities they face.

THE "IDEAL" THERAPIST'S KNOWLEDGE, APPROACH, AND GUIDANCE

The spouses' picture of the ideal therapist can be summed up in "know, listen, guide, and challenge." First, spouses of bisexual or transsexual partners want counselors to know about sexual orientations, gender identity, and mixed-orientation marriages so they can better understand the spouses' issues, their partners, and their marriage. The wife of a bisexual man writes,

> My therapist said some psychiatrists don't believe there is true bisexuality. I countered, "I know, they think it's a transition stage to being gay. In some cases this is true. But in our case, my husband is defiantly bi. Maybe straight down the middle bisexual. He is a terrible flirt of both men and women. I think if we were not together, he would pursue both." I told her of many studies that say this, like the Klein report. (Klein 1993)

In contrast, the spouse of an M2F partner writes, "My therapist helped me understand what my husband was going through with his transition and what I could expect for myself and for our relationship."

Key facts that spouses want therapists to know are that men and women with same-gender attractions do marry and have children and that sexual orientation or gender identity is not something someone can change. They also want counselors to understand stigmatization, discrimination, and what it is like to be in the closet, factors that impact the heterosexual spouses as well as their bisexual or transsexual partners.

Spouses of bisexual partners want therapists to give the same-gender attraction within a marriage its proper weight: "The extent of the damage it does to a marriage and the straight spouse is greatly underestimated," one says. "Know how the disclosure permeates the spouse's perceptions or reactions to everything." Another writes, "I told my grief counselor about tgt (the gay thing) and while we talked about my failing marriage, she never referred to tgt in connection with that. I wondered if she had any clue what an effect it had on our relationship and me."

Of most importance, "Therapists need to know that the disclosure is as difficult for the heterosexual spouse as for the disclosing spouse, be they bisexual or transsexual. It is a new challenge to them, while their partners have already struggled for a time with it." As a clinical social worker who is the former partner of a bisexual man comments, "Therapists need to know that straight spouses have no intact coping mechanisms for this type of situation. In my opinion, this is totally unique to the straight spouse and the coming out process" (Voorhees 2004).

Therapists need to know that, after disclosure, couples more often separate than stay together. Roughly a third end rather quickly, another third of the couples stay together to sort things out and then separate, and the last third commit to staying married. Of these, half are still together after three years; the other half divorce (Buxton 1994, 2001, 2004a). Regardless of the final outcome, many spouses want to work on their relationship so that they create a bond that helps them stay together or that carries over into coparenting or friendship should they divorce. Rather than say disclosure automatically means divorce, therapists need to know and share information about lasting mixed-orientation marriages and what it takes to make them work. They need to let couples know that marriages can endure, but that it takes hard work, honest communication, peer support, lots of time, acceptance and resilience, flexibility and mutual respect, and compromise (Buxton 2001, 2004a). A spouse stated that it was helpful, too, "to know how others coping with the same thing tend to react."

Spouses want counselors to know that, like all relationships, theirs is also about compromise, understanding, listening, caring, and daily work. It is not only about the partner's disclosed sexual orientation or gender identity. The wife of a M2F partner writes, "It is not just about the transition. The focus cannot always be on one spouse. What's best for that person may not always be best for the other. There will be times when one has to wait for the other to catch up." Both the couple and each of the individuals that comprise the couple go through the transition or coming out.

Above all, spouses want therapists to know their singular issues, the depth and source of their feelings, and the stages of their coping. They also want them to realize that it takes a long time to progress from their initial trauma to eventual transformation. A spouse states, "Therapists need to know that the disclosure is as difficult for the heterosexual spouse as for the disclosing spouse, be they bisexual or transsexual."

Beyond this knowledge and understanding, heterosexual spouses want therapists to be accepting of both spouses and not to be biased or judgmental about their partner's revealed sexual orientation or true gender, or about mixed-orientation marriages. Armed with this knowledge and acceptance, therapists can discern underlying issues and anticipate typical trajectories for spouses as well as share information to validate their experience and help them figure out for themselves what path to take.

LISTENING TO, GUIDING, AND CHALLENGING SPOUSES

Counselors most valued are those who validate spouses' concerns, help them discern their issues, identify their feelings, and clarify their needs, wants, and values so that they can forge a strong identity, integrity, and belief system from which to move forward. In order to feel validated, spouses want to feel they are listened to, that their issues are no less important than their partners' issues. They want to feel that the therapist's office is a safe place "to vent, explore feelings, [and] express fears without a patronizing attitude." They want therapists "who can get below what they say or help them identify what pains them." They do not want a therapist to take sides. "The first therapist I went to kept trying to get me to be angry with my husband," states the wife of a bisexual man.

Spouses want help to restore their sense of self worth and heal their damaged self-esteem. "I had been pegged into the role of the good wife, always trying to keep others happy, the strong person, [and] the angel for standing by my husband's side through all this," writes the wife of a M2F:

> I sacrificed my own happiness and self for my family to have some stability. When I couldn't take living in my self-imposed closet any more, I became depressed. I finally broke and started seeing a counselor. I'm still in counseling a year and a half after the transition started, trying to find a way to work out this relationship without sacrificing myself any further.

Spouses therefore want therapists to "keep at them" to refocus on themselves rather than on their partners or the situation. The husband of a bisexual wife describes telling his therapist about being low on his wife's priority list, making him feel lonely. "When the therapist said, 'You deserve better,' I started to defend her as a really good person. 'No,' the therapist replied, 'you don't understand. This isn't about her. You deserve to be loved, to have a fulfilled sex life, to receive attention. You deserve better.'" A bisexual man's wife man reports,

> My therapist was always having to bring me back to address my needs and how I felt or reacted when I, the caretaker, enabler, was more concerned with figuring out what my husband was thinking or feeling or how he might react to things. The first few times I was frustrated. I didn't think she was trying to help me with what

I needed to know. Finally, she made me realize I could only change one person, me, and that was what we needed to work on.

Spouses want validation of their sentiments, not what happened to the partners. A wife of a bisexual man states,

My counselor made me believe I was a prude for being repulsed by the idea he was attracted to men. She said his fantasies were none of my business. When I had suspicions he may be involved with a man, she said I was showing elements of paranoia and should be medicated.

Another declares, "Never should the patient hear, 'Well, don't you think it's difficult for your spouse to have admitted this to you?' or 'How do you think your spouse feels?' Had my therapist said something like that, I may have punched her in the mouth."

"Don't negate my anger at deception and betrayal and mourning," pleads the spouse of a transsexual husband. "The transitioner doesn't want any of the old person and the wife wants the old person. I am angry at my spouse and myself, afraid of losing family and friends, the changes, the costs, and fighting for marriage rights."

One spouse, amazed at the diversity of experiences on an Internet mailing list, cautions, "Don't assume you know anything about what type of experience the spouse is having. Let them tell you." Another says, "Let clients come to terms with their own problem and define what they see as success. Don't tell them what the outcome should be." Letting spouses speak for themselves and make their own decisions empowers them. In addition, many spouses want therapists to challenge them and "not necessarily make this process easy," writes the wife of a bisexual man. "No pain, no gain."

At the same time, as a spouse of a transsexual mate writes, "Spouses don't want therapists to predict how the other spouse will react, as in one case, warning the spouse of a trans mate to expect the worst after he transitions."

KNOWING, LISTENING, GUIDING, AND CHALLENGING COUPLES

In couples counseling, heterosexual spouses want equal treatment and respect. They also want neutrality toward both spouses and no bias toward a particular outcome. They want therapists to let each spouse speak without fear of repercussion.

Most important, spouses want therapists to help them discern the facts of their situation and deal with them together. They want to learn about mixed-orientation relationships, to be helped to understand and accept each other and themselves, and to be supported and validated as they forge whatever path they choose. One spouse writes, "I think our therapist could have helped each of us understand our needs, why intimacy was such a huge problem and explain the pros and cons of marriage/separation/divorce. When you deal honestly with the facts and the truth, your decisions are far better." Another wife of a bisexual man found such a therapist, "the only therapist who validated and helped both of us, and we have come to a new level of honesty about the issues."

Facing the truth includes advising couples after a husband has come out as bisexual that he be tested for HIV and other STDs and helping both spouses understand the risks of unprotected sex if the husband has been or is sexually active outside the marriage. A challenge to truth seeking is their partner's denial of outside liaisons, reported by a growing number of spouses who have cause to suspect their husbands or wives experience same-sex attractions. Many call it the "elephant in the living room." It is important therapists admit the possibility or acknowledge evidence that the partner is gay, lesbian, or bisexual, despite his or her protests. A wife says, "The husband finds it comforting if the therapist accepts him as someone who isn't sure he's gay. To me, this is just leaving you in limbo." Uncovering this core truth is key to a couple's working through their issues. Rather than supporting the partners' denial or ignoring issues brought up by the heterosexual spouses, counselors need to help partners face and acknowledge their sexual orientation. Spouses want therapists to question the integrity and truthfulness of a partner who continues to deny. Some say, "push him or her," if need be.

A bisexual man's wife describes what happened when therapists ignored her plea to deal with sexual issues she felt were the underlying problem in the marriage. "I lobbied for a sex therapist, but my husband's therapists saw no need. They concentrated on communication, sharing household duties, encouraged us to touch each other more, have 'date' nights. They just didn't know what to do with SSA (same-sex attraction) issues."

This spouse's complete story illustrates what can happen when a heterosexual spouse's hunches and her husband's denial are not addressed.

The first therapist said my insecurity and depression were the fault of our relationship problems. My husband obviously loved me. [I] went on antidepressants. [The] second therapist was after my husband's public park arrest. She said this happens more regularly than I could imagine and it didn't mean my husband was gay or that he'd eventually leave the marriage. When same-sex attractions returned in midlife, I went to a third psychologist. She said the problems were too much stress, not enough together time, and I was too dependent and needed a life on my own. "You don't do anything," she said and wanted me to come back with a list of activities in which to get involved. At the time, I had a preschooler at home and one on the way. Finally, a fourth psychologist prescribed antidepressants. As I recited all the reasons why our marriage was unhappy (too much work, small children at home, depressed husband, too dependent wife) she said, "All this is a lot easier to discuss than your husbands' sexual identity, isn't it?" Though I didn't feel sympathized with, that comment jolted me into reality. I began to confront my husband and the professionals he was seeing about why the same-sex urges weren't about sexual identity.

Finally we have a couples therapist, our lesbian minister, who validates each of us and asks the hard questions. She was not afraid to confront us, especially him about his bisexuality. She confronts him about his same-sex urges, while the others let him set the agenda, bought his reasons, and allowed him to stay in the comfort zone of denial. She doesn't take the easier course.

As important as seeking the truth is, spouses also want therapists to be sensitive to the bisexual or trans spouses. "Understand that fear of discovery and [the] consequences of infidelity is [*sic*] about 15 on a 1–10 scale," writes the spouse of a bisexual man:

The fallout can not only destroy their comfort and life as they know it, but they will be face to face with their darkest secret and so will other people. Both spouses will need immense comforting at the outset, but they will be so angry and afraid that it is hard [for a therapist] to give comfort to them or for them to comfort each other.

Sometimes it helps for a therapist to encourage a bisexual spouse to face and learn about his or her same-sex attractions. The wife of such a man explains that this is important "so the buried part doesn't grow more powerful in the closet." She continues,

Investigating makes it less threatening. She urged that I learn a little about the bi spouse's sexual fantasies and same-gender sex. It was that or repeat the cycle. I found I could accommodate much of what he thought of as gay sex in our sex life. Also, as we both liked to look at male body parts and found them sexy, we could share (only photos.). Our sex life is actually better than it has ever been. There is nothing to lose and everything to lose—our marriage and family.

Spouses want relational behaviors to be addressed, too. A man formerly married to a wife who came out writes, "Therapists treat these as 'str8s' affairs, pander to gay issues, or say she's evil cuz gay. They didn't evaluate my wife's behavior that was deceitful, manipulative and untrustworthy. Sexuality had nothing to do with that."

Spouses want attention and support equal to that of their partners.

I did not feel compassion or support from most of the six counselors. It was as if his problem was more interesting, but mine was more textbook, not as scintillating. When it came time to change things in the marriage, I was relied upon to make the changes. They weren't even the right changes because they were based on traditional couples therapy. Maybe the therapist intuited he could not change his nature, so they tried to get me to change my behavior. I was always angry because I felt we were missing something important, but neither the therapist nor my bi husband would acknowledge it. Because of that, my husband did not feel support-ed either, because he was asked to do the impossible: shut off part of who he was and go back into the closet for the sake of the marriage, where we would pretend and create a new, false existence based on lies about our reality. I asked that of him, and the therapists, not one said, "Hold on, that is not a viable option."

"Look below the articulate spouse and the wife in tears," another suggests:

The counselor was snowed by my husband and never dealt with the sexual issues I brought up. She thought that if we worked out my "control issues," the relation-ship would improve so he would want to be sexual with me. I selected this coun-selor after some violent incidents. Her answer to me was "stop provoking him." When another violent episode happened, he was sent to a hospital and diagnosed with adjustive reactive disorder. When I attended domestic violence counseling for that, I finally figured out that I was not to blame for what had transpired.

Therapists need to explain to the bisexual or transgender partner that their spouses need time to process. Just because the partners have come out or started to transition does not mean that the heterosexual spouse is anywhere near inte-grating the new information into their self-concept, their part of the relation-ship, or family life. It also helps to explain that the spouses' anger is not a sign of homo- or transphobia but a reaction to having their lives so totally uprooted by sexual rejection, prior deception, and the partner's revealed change.

Spouses also want therapists to focus on problems they present and not let the couple drift into blaming games that exacerbate tension and divert them from addressing core issues. A bisexual man's former wife writes, "Keep focused on the partner's being bi, rather than go off on a tangent and haggle about how annoying it was to my husband when I happened to scrape my cereal bowl with my spoon or my dinner plate with my fork."

It is critical that counselors listen to both spouses to help each see the other's perspective and help them to focus on the reality so they can deal with the truth. Ideal counseling occurs when therapists support both spouses. The spouse of a transsexual partner describes it this way: "Respect the choices of spouses, the one to transition and the other to stay with that person. Offer whatever hope, reassurance, reality checks, and coping mechanisms the therapist has at his/her disposal."

Taking sides hurts both spouses. The story of one wife whose husband is transgendered illustrates what can happen if that occurs. The wife is bisexual, but the story illustrates the danger of taking sides, the importance of letting spouses think for themselves, and the effectiveness of a later counselor. She writes,

> The first therapist saw her job as the defender of my daughter and me and took it upon herself to convince my spouse not to transition but to find other ways to express his feminine side that wouldn't alter the way any of us was perceived by the outside world. "It will ruin your life," she said. "It will ruin your marriage and rob your daughter of her childhood." She also said it would inevitably ruin my spouse's career, because even if her company has a nondiscrimination policy to protect trans people, she will be perceived as a woman and experience discrimination and a glass ceiling and probably lose her job within five years.
>
> My spouse was devastated. Sunk into acute depression. Saw herself as bad. Saw obstacles to transition as insurmountable. I was alarmed that I'd been told my relationship would be ruined and my children's life irreparably altered in negative ways. But I decided it was ruining our relationship for her not to feel free to transition and said we needed to find a therapist who would be supportive, who would help us confront, understand, and deal with the difficulties of this new reality and not try to dissuade us from doing so due to her prejudice or values or negative perceptions.
>
> This new therapist respects our ability to be aware and analytical of our feelings and objectives. Doesn't let us off the hook when we are struggling with things he thinks are up to us to solve. He's gracious and warm and gives us insight and tools for dealing with the question and hardships we confront on this journey.
>
> Yesterday I told him I feel frozen and confused how to respond to my spouse at any given moment. I feel guilty when my spouse is in girl mode and does something that makes me more in love with her. I feel as if I'm tempted to influence her to choose being female so I can have that in my life. But I'll love her whether she fully transitions or not. The therapist said that being the spouse of a trans person is very confusing, and that's part of what I'll have to face, but it's not bad or unreasonable to have things I want out of the relationship. He said I might be happier if I reinforced behaviors I like, regardless of what my spouse looks like or sounds like genderwise, by saying, "When you did/said that, it made me so happy and in love with you," or "When you do that it really turns me on." That made me feel lighter and hopeful. It gave me more freedom to express affection and appreciation without thinking much about her gender.

Looking back, it would have more helpful if the first therapist had said. "Do you have the skills to use to help support your family in the unfortunate event that through whatever means your spouse loses her job?" If I'd said, "No," then it would have been great if she'd said, "I know your spouse has been a great provider and you're happy being a homemaker, but the reality is that the world isn't yet evolved so that transpeople are immune to losing their jobs due to discrimination. You really should think of a plan by which you could help support your family should the need arise." She could have recommended some resources, perhaps one to evaluate costs of living and social diversity in parts of the country that might be more livable than where we are.

Spouses suggest that therapists look a little deeper into both sides of the relationship. "If one spouse feels major rejection," one advises," then that needs to be investigated. If there is violence, it needs to be prosecuted, not treated in a psych ward and have the spouse blamed for the violence." Another spouse suggests therapists assist bisexual partners who engage in dangerous sex to explore underlying reasons such as shame and a self-imposed need for punishment. Yet another advises counselors to warn spouses to think carefully about questions they ask their partners about their same-sex activities, because "they'll never get rid of pictures in their heads created by the replies."

At the same time, spouses want therapists to respect their limits of accepting or exploring alternative behaviors. A wife of a bisexual mate says, "Don't encourage either spouse or couple to do things that make them uncomfortable or they don't want to do."

At the core of effective counseling is the key challenge described by the wife of a bisexual man:

> Help couples get rid of the dissonance they experience, since they don't fit the traditional sense of marriage. Therapists need to encourage spouses to realize that a decision doesn't have to made right away and to help couples explore options, figure out what each spouse can tolerate, find compromises and help each other step by step.

HELPFUL STRATEGIES FOR COUNSELING

Therapists have many strategies at their fingertips to help heterosexual spouses face reality and cope constructively. However, to underscore what spouses need most to heal and transform themselves into authentic, strong individuals, whether or not they stay married, I have selected strategies that are most often cited by spouses as most helpful.

Help spouses talk about the intimate, private subject of sexuality. Broaching such a sensitive topic may be difficult for some counselors because of its sensitive nature. Anne Voorhees, quoted earlier, suggests asking couples whether their "intimate sexual relationship is impacted by (whatever the presenting problem is)." This puts the emphasis on the presenting problem rather than the sexuality. However, a spouse advises, "Once the same-sex attraction is out of the closet, don't try to stuff it back into the closet and think the couple will do just fine."

Tell the spouse of a bisexual partner that it is not his or her fault, over and over. "He/she needs to know there is nothing she/he can do to change the mates' same-gender attraction. Say, 'This is not about you,' right away. Help them understand this." Help the spouse understand that the priorities of the bisexual or trans spouse are not about their heterosexual spouse. Irrespective of their mate's sexual orientation or gender identity shift, the straight spouse is worthy of attention, love, and fulfilled sexuality. Let the spouse define what she/he sees as a successful outcome. "You, the client should [define the goal]. Don't be afraid to make that known."

Advise spouses to take care of their own health: mental, physical, and spiritual. This includes getting tested for sexually transmitted diseases, including AIDS. Encourage spouses to become involved with other people: friends and straight spouses, whether in a support group, online, by phone, or a one-on-one meeting. A spouse states,

> Make sure you give them information about the Straight Spouse Network so they can find some of the Internet mailing lists. I went eight years without it. If I had had them from the outset, it would have been a very different eight years. We were reinventing the wheel, and doing it all alone with no concept of 'round.' It was a long journey.

Stick with how the client feels and is doing, possibly helping him/her explore reasons behind self-esteem issues.

> Whatever I presented, she quickly zeroed in on the fact that my self-esteem and belief in myself were extremely low. Her therapy focused on getting me to believe in myself and trust my own judgment. Thus, when my spouse finally outed himself to me, I felt mentally healthy and trusted myself.

Help spouses put feelings and concerns into words. Teach them how to clarify and communicate how they feel, what they need, and what they value. Help them formulate questions of their partners so that they do not get defensive. Teach them how to respond or not respond to their mates' blaming/accusing or enthusiasm about their new lives. Assist the spouse in self-exploration. A bisexual man's wife writes,

> There were things [I'd done to] other people that I'd held in my mind and about which I kicked myself. My therapist had me write them down and we talked about each one. At some point, she said, "You know, they've likely long forgotten this." I forgave myself. As a result, I no longer held grudges against my husband for things that had made me angry.

Look for another side of a situation unrelated to the marriage problem or sexual orientation that might ignite positive couple interaction. That same wife writes about them thinking of remodeling their kitchen when their relationship was still shaky after his disclosure. "I thought this was disastrous. The counselor said he'd love to have a partner who was so creative and capable. So we did it. Three and a half years later we're enjoying a wonderful kitchen where we entertain friends and ourselves."

For spouses who have divorced, "Ask the spouse to refocus on the reason for the divorce, not just the gay side, but the relationship stuff so she/he doesn't let history repeat itself with a straight partner." This spouse has a masters degree in counseling but blinded herself to the problems in the marriage partly out of love, partly out of insecurity, partly out of a desire to keep the family intact, and partly for financial reasons.

"Meds are not the answer," writes a woman formerly married to a bisexual man. She explains her experience with one therapist who prescribed and the other who guided:

> I haven't found a therapist that understands the aversion I have to anything that will turn me back into the Stepford wife I was for so long with my ex. I know I contributed to the mess of the marriage by being too tolerant of his deceptive, angry, manipulative, abusive behavior. A helpful technique to deal with this is my current therapist's reiterating my sentiments with an added level of anger. If I say, "H. isn't being very nice about this," she'll paraphrase, "H. is being a fucking asshole about this." This was very therapeutic.

In couples counseling, help couples learn ways to incorporate bisexuality or gender transition into their relationship, to set boundaries, and to work out changeable guidelines of acceptable or nonacceptable behavior for both spouses. A spouse adds, "Our therapist helped us find what our absolutes 'really' were, not just demands made out of frustration or fear of the unknown." Another suggests helping bisexual partners to consider "ongoing responsibilities and consequences of 'freedom to explore sexuality.'"

Guide the couple in developing skills of honest communication and mutual respect and support. Help them realize that redefining their relationship takes time, whether or not they stay together. Encourage flexibility. Provide examples from research of other couples working on their marriages, like the words of the husband of a bisexual woman: "I compare my wife and me to a glove with fingers that fit absolutely perfect. It's the thumb that's just wrong. The more we struggle to make the thumb fit, the worse we make the fingers. If we free ourselves to adjust the gloves for our thumbs, then the fingers return to their old wonderful fit" (Buxton 2004a).

Ultimately, effective counseling for heterosexual spouses of bisexual and transgender spouses depends upon the degree of the therapist's information and understanding about sexual orientation, gender identity and transgenderism, and mixed-orientation relationships as well as the amount of attention given to spouses who seek help.

DISCUSSION

The therapist's key role in helping heterosexual spouses of bisexual and transsexual partners is to support and guide them to cope constructively with their issues, emotions, and obstacles. Knowing underlying issues that heterosexual spouses face makes it easier for therapists to ask them questions that will help them identify their concerns and deal with them. Spouses' concerns relate to sexual rejection, challenges to the marriage, worries about the children, and the more profound personal challenges of shattered identity, integrity, and belief system. Knowing which emotions most often appear at which stages of the spouses' coping helps therapists figure out more quickly at what stage a spouse might be struggling. Pain and confusion characterize early stages. Denial decreases as spouses slowly face reality. Fear increases once they face reality and again as they begin to transform their lives. Grief is strongest as spouses accept postdisclosure changes and turns into sadness as they let go of the past. Anger erupts as each issue is faced, most often in reaction to those related to their sexuality, identity, and integrity.

While many spouses find counseling ineffective, some report successful counseling experiences. Effective therapists were crucial to spouses who found themselves drowning in thoughts of low self-esteem or stuck in an emotional morass that kept them from dealing with issues like sexual inadequacy, loss of purpose, despair, or concern for their children. Counseling helped them work through their feelings and problems so that they developed a sense of self-worth, authenticity, power, and a hopeful worldview.

Bisexual/heterosexual or trans/nontransgender couples can more easily create a positive bond, whether or not they stay married, if their therapists are knowledgeable about bisexuality and transgenderism, sensitive to their concerns, and skilled in helping each spouse clarify needs, wants, values, and goals and negotiate ways to achieve them that are mutually acceptable. Helping each of them learn how to practice honest communication with their partner buoys self-confidence and realistic optimism as well as making more effective parenting possible. Knowing that they are doing the best they can, trying anything feasible to continue the marriage, expressing their feelings honestly, and listening to their partners without being defensive affirms each spouse's identity and integrity. The resultant understanding and support reinforces the couple's bond so that it can support them as they navigate the shifting sands of postdisclosure life, with or without each other.

The number of spouses coming out continues to increase, and this trend may persist for years despite the growing acceptance of gay and lesbian persons. It may take even longer for bisexual and transgender persons to be understood and embraced. When heterosexual spouses of these men and women are better understood and supported by peers and counselors, they can add their voices to the call for social justice and raise awareness of the fallout from discrimination and prejudice on them as well as their partners. As the heterosexual wife of a bisexual man writes, "It's not easy in today's society to be gay, but the awareness is there. It's never going to be easy, however, no matter how much awareness there is, no matter how accepting society becomes and no matter how far in the future we go, for a spouse to become 'straight' by default from a spouse's coming out."

REFERENCES

Allen, M. P. (1989). *Transformations: Crossdressers and those who love them.* New York: Dutton.

Auerback, S., and Moser, C. (1987). Groups for the wives of gays and bisexual men. *Social Work*, 32(4) , 321–325.

Boyd, B. (2003). *My husband, Betty: Love, sex, and life with a crossdresser.* New York: Thunder's Mouth.

Boylan, J. L. (2003). *She's not there: A life in two genders.* Broadway.

Buxton, A. P. (1994). *The other side of the closet: The coming-out crisis for straight spouses and families.* New York: Wiley.

Buxton, A. P. (2000). The best interest of children of lesbian and gay parents. In R. Galatzer-Levy and L. Kraus (Eds.), *The scientific basis for custody decisions* (pp. 319–346). New York: Wiley.

Buxton, A. P. (2001). Writing our own scripts: How bisexual men and their heterosexual wives maintain their marriages after disclosure. In B. Beemyn and E. Steinman (Eds.), *Bisexuality in the lives of men: Facts and fiction* (pp. 157–189). Binghamton, NY: Harrington Park.

Buxton, A. P. (2004a). Works in progress: How mixed-orientation couples maintain their marriages after the wives come out. In R.C. Fox (Ed.), *Current research on bisexuality* (pp.57–82). Binghamton, NY: Harrington Park.

Buxton, A. P. (2004b). Paths and pitfalls: How heterosexual spouses cope when their husbands or wives come out. In J. J. Bigner and J. L. Wetchler (Eds.), *Relationship therapy with same-sex couples* (pp. 95–109). Binghamton, NY: Haworth.

Gochros, J. S. (1989). When *husbands come out of the closet*. Binghamton, NY: Harrington Park.

Hays, D., and Samuels, A. (1988). Heterosexual women's perceptions of their marriages to homosexual or bisexual men. *Journal of Homosexuality, 17*(3/4), 81–100.

Imielinsky, K. (1969). Homosexuality in males with particular attention to marriage. *Psychotherapy and Psychosomatics, 17*, 126–132

Klein, F. (1993). *The bisexual option* (2d ed.). Binghamton, NY: Harrington Park.

Voorhees, A. Personal communication, November 2, 2004.

Wolfe, T. J. (1985). Marriages of bisexual men. *Journal of Homosexuality, 11*(1/2), 135–148.

INDEX

Abandonment, 112–13

Ableism, at intersection of gender and queer desire, 186–201

Acceptance, xiii–xiv; disclosure, clinicians and, 56, 57, 64; by elders, 178; empathy and, 120, 373

Acculturation: by Asian Americans, 234; Latinos and, 246–52, 255–56, 261–62

Adam, B. D., 5

Adams, J. R., 318

ADDRESSING (cultural influence acronym), 241

Adolescents, lesbian, gay and bisexual, developmental issues of, 89–91; *see also* Youths

Adoption, xxii, 124

Adulthood, developmental theories of, 166–67

Affirmative Psychotherapy with Bisexual Women and Bisexual Men (Fox), xxi–xxii

African Americans, xxiv–xxv; acceptable terms for, 189; bisexuality population percentages of, 29; recruitment of, for mental health research, 34; sexual risk and substance abuse among, 39

African Americans, multiracial bisexual: as bi-/multiracial, xxv, 77; coming out by, 218–19; countering hegemonic gender/identity/sex systems and, 216; countering hegemonic representations of bisexual as "other" and, 214–15; DL and, 118, 257; hegemony and, 207–8,

213, 214–15, 216, 219; heteronormative-hegemonic structures and, 208, 213, 219; identity and, 207–8, 210–15, 217–20; identity, critical race theory and, 210–11; invalidation of, xxiv–xxv, 207–28; jargon of authenticity and, 212–13, 220; positionality and, 207, 214; self and, 208–9, 210, 218, 220; well-being, social capital and, 209–10, 211, 214–16, 217, 220

African self-consciousness, 208, 212

African's psychological blackness, 208, 212

Africentric patriarchal psychologies, 208, 213, 216

Age play, in BDSM, 360

Ageism, 168, 178

Aging, GLBT, xxiv, 164–85; *see also* Elders, bisexual

AIDS, *see* HIV/AIDS

Alan Guttmacher Institute, 329–30

Alcohol, 254, 256, 258

Alexander, J., 271

Alexander the Great, 196

Allen, M. P., 397

Allport, G., 73, 74–75

Ambierotic, 387

Ambisexuality, xx, 9, 89, 92, 96

American dream, 196, 248

American Psychiatric Association: on homosexuality, 30–31, 52, 91–92, 109, 172, 231, 370; on reparative/conversion therapies, 117